A Beginner's Guide to Designing Embedded System Applications on Arm® Cortex®-M Microcontrollers

A Beginner's Guide to Designing Embedded System Applications on Arm® Cortex®-M Microcontrollers

ARIEL LUTENBERG,
PABLO GOMEZ,
ERIC PERNIA

arm Education Media

Contents

9   File Storage on SD Cards and Usage of Software Repositories   387

Preface

In 2009, a small group of professors, teaching assistants, and students gathered together in order to create the Embedded Systems Laboratory at the School of Engineering of Universidad de Buenos Aires. The aim was to study and teach embedded system technologies, a topic that was not very developed at the university at that time. Pablo Gomez and Ariel Lutenberg were among this group.

During the following years, many undergraduate and graduate courses on embedded systems, as well as related courses, were organized by the group. Events on embedded systems were also held, and, in this way, a network of embedded systems professors was organized in Argentina.

In this context, an open hardware and software project named "Proyecto CIAA" (Computadora Industrial Abierta Argentina, Argentine Open Industrial Computer) was developed. Eric Pernia arrived as an expert on embedded systems programming.

Since then, many courses have been organized, including for people who had never programmed an embedded system before. After this experience, the idea of writing this book arose as a way to disseminate our 'learn-by-doing' teaching approach applied to embedded system more broadly.

This book follows our "learn-by-doing" approach, supported by hands-on activities. Basic ideas are explained and then demonstrated by means of examples that progressively introduce the fundamental concepts, techniques, and tools. In this way, a range of knowledge of electronics, informatics, and computers is introduced.

Theoretical concepts are kept to a minimum while still allowing students to properly understand the proposed solutions. Thus, the target audience of this book is beginners who have never before programmed embedded systems, or even had any prior knowledge of electronics.

Arm technology and C/C++ technology was chosen for this book because of the remarkable results we got during all our years of using them and the prevalence of Arm-based microcontrollers in embedded system design. The NUCLEO-F429ZI board was selected because of its ubiquity and low cost, and because it provides a broad set of interfaces that allows us to connect a wide variety of devices, as will be shown in the examples.

Through the examples, a smart home system that is shown in Figure 1 is gradually built. It is provided with an over temperature detector and a gas detector in order to implement a fire alarm. It also has a motion sensor that is used to detect intruders. If a fire or an intruder is detected, an alarm that is provided with a siren and a strobe light is turned on. To turn off the alarm, a code should be entered using the alarm control panel. If the code is incorrect, then the Incorrect code LED is turned on. Up to five codes can be entered before the system is blocked, which is indicated by means of the System blocked LED.

The alarm control panel has an LCD display, which is used to indicate the readings of the sensors and the status of the alarm (see Figure 1). It has also a slot for an SD memory card, where the events are stored, and the capability to play back a welcome audio message.

There is also a gate control panel, which allows the opening and closing of a gate, as shown in Figure 1. This panel is also provided with a light intensity control that is used to regulate the intensity of a decorative light. The intensity of this light is monitored using a light sensor, in order to control its brightness. The color of this light can also be changed using the alarm control panel.

The whole system can be monitored and configured using a PC by means of serial communication over a USB connection. Also, the most relevant information on the system can be accessed using an application on a smartphone, which is connected to the smart home system over a Bluetooth Low Energy connection. The application can also be used to open and close the gate.

It is also possible to monitor the smart home system using a smartphone or a PC by means of a web page that is served by the smart home system. In this case, the connection is made using the Wi-Fi protocol, as shown in Figure 1.

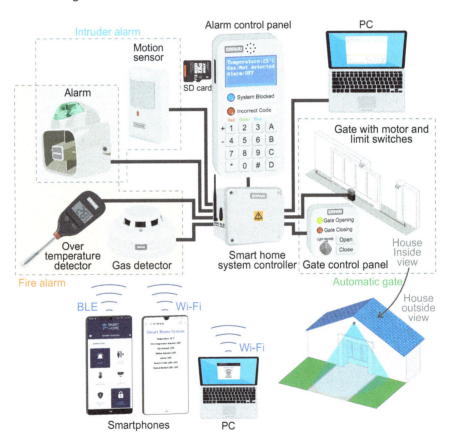

Figure 1 Smart home system that is built in this book.

Figure 2 shows how the NUCLEO board and a set of modules are used to implement the smart home system. Figure 3 shows how the pins in the ST Zio connectors of the NUCLEO board are occupied as the elements are gradually connected through the chapters. In this way, it is possible to present the reader with the difficulties that arise when a project starts to become bigger and bigger, and show how these can be addressed by means of appropriate techniques. The proposed solutions are used to discuss how to implement efficient software design for embedded systems and how to make appropriate pin assignments for the elements.

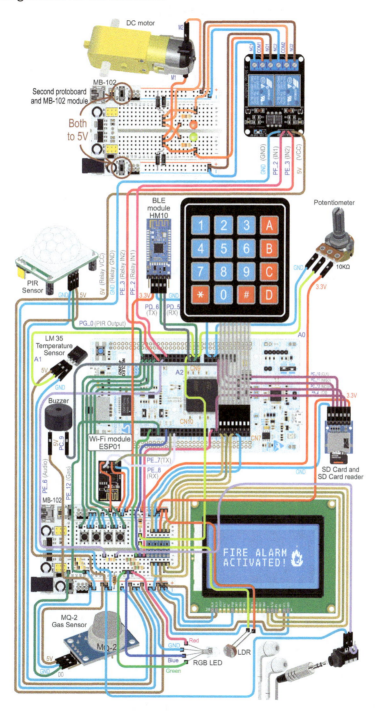

Figure 2 Diagram of the elements that are connected through the chapters.

In this way, Arm processor architecture and, in particular, the main peripherals of the Cortex-M4 processor are introduced, with the different elements (UARTs, timers, interrupts, etc.) that are required to efficiently implement the features of the smart home system. As the examples incorporate more and more functionality, the fundamentals of time management and multitasking operation in embedded systems are explained.

In addition, different methods for how an embedded system gets, receives, sends, manages, and stores data are shown, as well as many interfaces between the development board and the external devices being described and implemented. During this process, different embedded system designs for a given application are reviewed, and their features are compared.

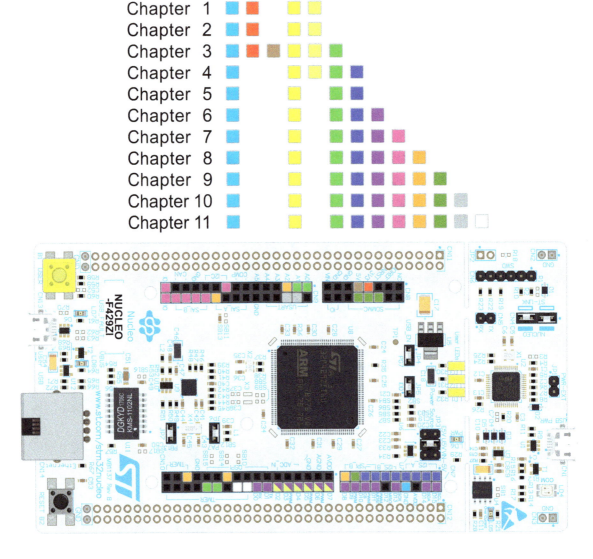

Figure 3 Diagram showing how the elements are gradually connected through each chapter.

In Figures 4 to 7, some of the user interfaces that are developed and used in the book are shown, which include a serial terminal on a PC, a character LCD display, an application for a smartphone, and a website that is accessed using a Wi-Fi connection and a web browser.

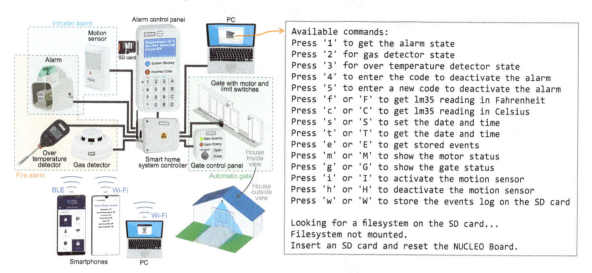

```
Available commands:
Press '1' to get the alarm state
Press '2' for gas detector state
Press '3' for over temperature detector state
Press '4' to enter the code to deactivate the alarm
Press '5' to enter a new code to deactivate the alarm
Press 'f' or 'F' to get lm35 reading in Fahrenheit
Press 'c' or 'C' to get lm35 reading in Celsius
Press 's' or 'S' to set the date and time
Press 't' or 'T' to get the date and time
Press 'e' or 'E' to get stored events
Press 'm' or 'M' to show the motor status
Press 'g' or 'G' to show the gate status
Press 'i' or 'I' to activate the motion sensor
Press 'h' or 'H' to deactivate the motion sensor
Press 'w' or 'W' to store the events log on the SD card

Looking for a filesystem on the SD card...
Filesystem not mounted.
Insert an SD card and reset the NUCLEO Board.
```

Figure 4 User interface implemented using a UART connection and a serial terminal running on a PC.

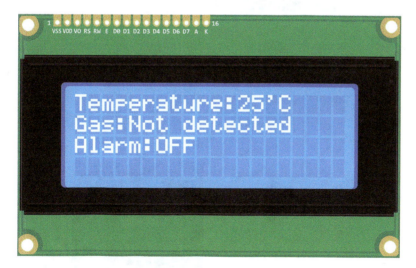

Figure 5 User interface implemented using I2C bus connection and a character LCD display.

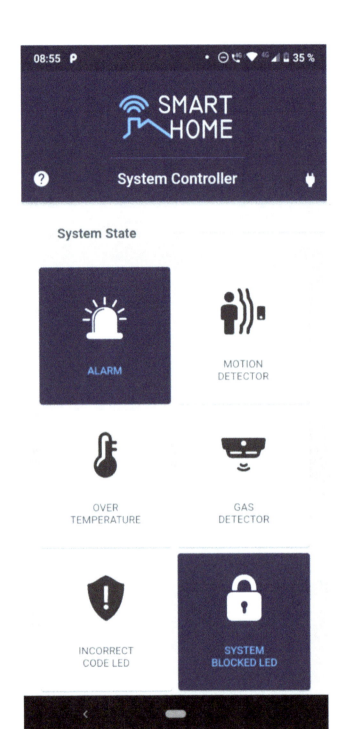

Figure 6 User interface implemented using a Bluetooth connection and a smartphone application.

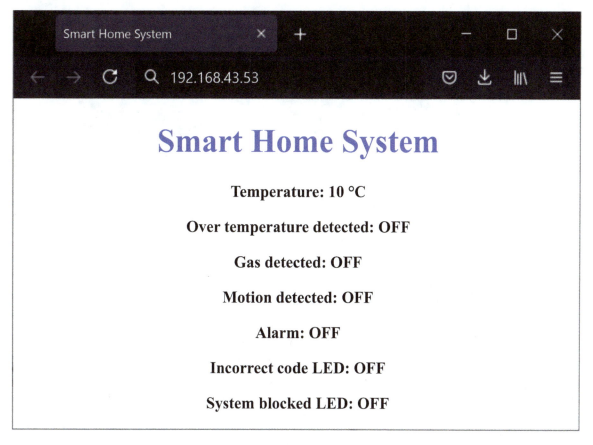

Figure 7 User interface implemented using a Wi-Fi connection and a web browser.

In this process, the Mbed™ OS 6 platform core generic software components, plus the HAL (Hardware Abstraction Layer) ports that allow Mbed to transparently run on microcontrollers from different manufacturers, are introduced.

In the final chapter, the main ideas are summarized by means of an irrigation system, shown in Figure 8, that is developed from scratch. In this way, a guide to designing and implementing an embedded system project is provided for the reader.

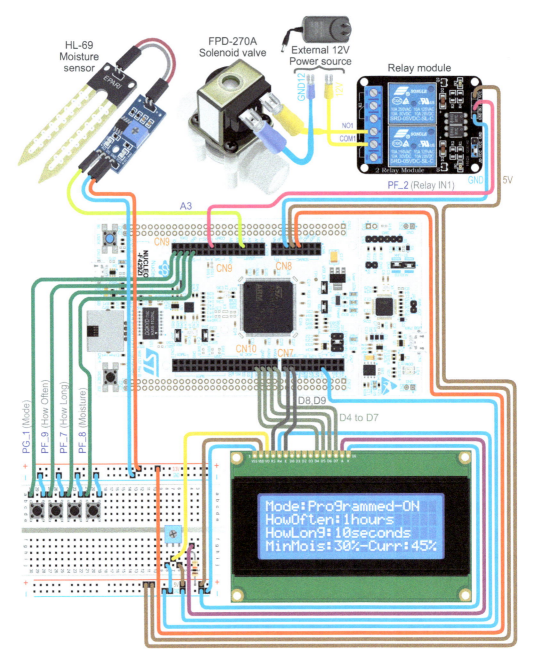

Figure 8 Home irrigation system that is implemented in Chapter 12.

To the best of our knowledge, there is no other book regarding Arm technology that follows the approach used in this book. We believe that the reader can benefit from it and combine learning skills with having fun.

We hope you enjoy the book!

Acknowledgments

We particularly thank our partners for supporting us during this year. Without their understanding, it wouldn't have been possible to write this book.

We would like to thank Arm Ltd for trusting us, especially Liz Warman, Director of Educational Content & Technology, for her support and guidance during the long year that it took us to write this book. The follow-up meetings with Liz, as well as her reviews, helped us to enhance the book and its narrative. We appreciate her candor and organization, being firm and kind in her suggestions.

We also thank our professors, colleagues, and students for teaching us so much. During recent years, the *Facultad de Ingeniería* (School of Engineering) of the *Universidad de Buenos Aires* (UBA) allowed us to develop a set of master's programs on embedded systems, the Internet of Things, and Artificial Intelligence that enriched our vision of how to teach using the learn-by-doing approach. Also, our research activities in the field of railway systems design, with the support of CONICET (the *National Scientific and Technical Research Council of Argentina*), prompted us to be up to date in a broad set of technologies, many of them included in this book. Colleagues of the *Departamento de Ciencia y Tecnología* (Science and Technology Department) of the *Universidad Nacional de Quilmes* (UNQ) shared their knowledge and advice.

The assistance of ACSE (*Civil Association for Research, Promotion and Development of Embedded Electronic Systems*) was extremely important for this publication. The immense number of activities organized by ACSE (symposiums, training for teachers and professors, calls for papers, courses for beginners, the *Argentine Open Industrial Computer*, etc.) allowed us to meet many people who enlightened us in different ways. ACSE also supported this book by providing most of the hardware used to implement and test the examples.

CADIEEL, the *Argentine Chamber of Electronic, Electromechanical and Lighting Industries*, promoted all the aforementioned activities. Especially noteworthy is the commitment to education and technological development of the small- and medium-sized companies that make up the chamber. CADIEEL has collaborated for years with the postgraduate programs and outreach activities mentioned above, as well as with this book in particular.

This book has significantly improved from the suggestions and comments of Carlos Pantelides. He is the one who has undoubtedly done the most detailed review of the book, and also gave us valuable ideas on how to address his suggestions on the book. We are very grateful to María Eloísa Tourret and Camila Belén Silva Sabarots, from UTN-FRBB, for developing the "Smart Home System App" that is used in this book, as well for their very useful comments about the chapter where Bluetooth Low Energy is explained. We are also thankful to Enrique Sergio Burgos, from UTN-FRP, for his very valuable help regarding the use of Doxygen for documentation and developing the corresponding example that is included in this book and setting up the continuous integration environment in GitLab. Juan Manuel Reta and Eduardo Filomena, from UNER, provided us with very enriching conversations, which we greatly appreciate, regarding how to use this book for teaching. The contribution of Martin Alejandro Ribelotta was very important in order to improve the *Brief Introduction to the Cortex-M*

Processor Family and the NUCLEO Board section. Finally, the reading by Alejandro Salvatierra helped us to correct details, and the conversations with Juan Manuel Cruz (UBA, UTN-FRBA, ACSE) about how the examples in this book can be adapted to other boards and the revisions of the circuits used in this book by Adrián Laiuppa (UTN-FRBB) were very enlightening.

Dedications

Ariel dedicates this book to Sebastián, his first child who will be born in March 2022.

Pablo dedicates this book to Germán, his child who was born in October 2020.

Eric dedicates this book to the memory of his father, Jorge Sergio Pernia, who passed away in October 2021.

Authors' Biographies

Ariel Lutenberg is currently a full-time Professor at the School of Engineering of the University of Buenos Aires (UBA), Researcher at the National Council of Scientific and Technical Research (CONICET), and Director of the master's degree on the Internet of Things and the master's degree on Embedded Artificial Intelligence at the same University. He has supervised dozens of graduate, postgraduate, and doctoral students. He has published almost a hundred papers in international journals and conferences and done work for important Argentine and international companies and institutions. He started and led for many years Proyecto CIAA (Argentine Open Industrial Computer), where dozens of Argentinean universities, companies, and institutions together developed embedded computers, including their hardware and software.

He received an Electronic Engineering degree from the University of Buenos Aires in 2006, obtaining the prize "To the Best Graduates of Engineering Careers of Argentine Universities" from the National Academy of Engineering as the best graduate. In 2009, he obtained his diploma of Doctor of Engineering from the UBA, with honorable mention "Summa Cum Laude." In 2018, he won the INNOVAR Award of the Argentine Ministry of Science, Technology and Productive Innovation in the Researchers category and the INNOVAR Grand Prize of the Jury for the development of a remote monitoring system for automatic rail barriers.

Pablo Martín Gomez is full-time researcher at the School of Engineering of the University of Buenos Aires (UBA). He directs the master's program on Embedded Systems, coordinates the master's programs on the Internet of Things and Embedded Artificial Intelligence, and is teaching assistant of Acoustics at the same university. He received his diploma in Electronic Engineering in 2007 and finished his doctoral studies in 2015 with honorable mention "Summa Cum Laude." Pablo also studied at the National University of Lanús (UNLa), where he received a "University Technician on Sound and Recording" degree in 2008. He is editor of the "Acoustics and Audio" section of the Elektron journal published by the School of Engineering of UBA.

He has been working on embedded systems projects since 2003, designing products for companies and institutions in Argentina and the USA. In 2018, he won the INNOVAR Award of the Argentine Ministry of Science, Technology, and Productive Innovation in the Researchers category and the INNOVAR Grand Prize of the Jury for the development of a remote monitoring system for automatic rail barriers. He is author of several papers in the fields of embedded systems and acoustics in journals and for conferences. Teaching has a central role in his life. For almost 15 years he has been giving courses on acoustics, embedded system programming, protocols, real-time operating systems, and rapid prototyping for a wide audience, from novices to graduate students.

 **Eric Nicolás Pernia** is currently a research Professor at the Science and Technology department (CyT) of the National University of Quilmes (UNQ) and a Field Application Engineer on Quectel wireless solutions. He has supervised several graduate and postgraduate students. He has published many papers in conferences, led the Proyecto CIAA (Argentine Open Industrial Computer) program for two years, and has broad experience in hardware, software, and firmware development for Argentine and international companies. He has a large portfolio of contributions in open-source hardware, firmware, and software, which is available on GitHub.

He received an Industrial Automation and Control Engineer degree from the National University of Quilmes (UNQ) in 2013, where he developed as a graduation project a free software application for PLC Ladder Diagram programming (IEC 61131-3 compliant), named IDE4PLC. In 2015, he obtained his diploma of Specialist on Embedded Systems from the University of Buenos Aires (UBA), where he created a Java SCJ implementation for CIAA Project boards as his graduation project. In 2018, he obtained his master's in Embedded Systems from the University of Buenos Aires (UBA), where he created an open-source, abstract, and highly portable embedded system programming library named sAPI as his graduation project.

Authors' Contributions

Ariel Lutenberg wrote most of the explanations in this book. This includes the preface, the introductory section of each chapter, the indications on how to connect the elements, the explanations of the program code examples, and the Under the Hood and Case Study sections. In particular, he selected which content to include in the introductory section of each chapter, as well as in the Under the Hood and Case Study sections. He also wrote the final versions of the program code of Chapter 6 and wrote all of Chapter 12 including the corresponding program code. In the other chapters, he revised the program code and made suggestions in order to simplify the implementation, to make it easier for the reader to understand the concepts introduced in each chapter. He also made important suggestions about how to rename the functions and variables in order to use more meaningful names. He contributed with many figures and in the revision of all the figures. He also started the relationship with Arm and was responsible for communicating with the editor and addressing the comments of all the reviewers. Perhaps his most important contributions were to propose the learn-by-doing approach followed in this book and to use the smart home system project as the common thread of the book, and the inclusion of a different project following a structured approach in the last chapter.

Pablo Martín Gomez proposed most of the examples that gradually built the smart home system and wrote most of the final versions of the program code of this book. This includes all the changes in the program code related to the reordering of the book chapters after concluding the first draft and the migration from Mbed OS 5 to Mbed OS 6, which was a very relevant contribution in order to update the preliminary versions of the program code. He also wrote many explanations of the examples (in particular in Chapters 7, 8, and 10, where he wrote all the code) and also contributed to and reviewed all the other explanations. He also tested all the examples on the NUCLEO board and kept the program code updated in the repositories using continuous integration and various automated tools that he set up. These tools also eased the process of maintaining, repairing, enhancing, and updating the program code, which grows in complexity from Chapters 1 to 11 as the smart home system increases its functionality. In this way, he identified many aspects to improve on the preliminary versions of the program code, making it easier to explain the fundamental concepts to the reader, as he made implementations clearer and more straightforward. He also carried out the migration to Mbed Online and Keil Studio Cloud when Arm suggested using those programs.

Eric Nicolás Pernía produced most of the figures in this book. He had a central role in writing the first versions of the program code of Chapters 1 to 5 and Chapter 9 and wrote the preliminary version of the program code in Chapters 6 and 11. He also reviewed many of the code samples and explanations. He suggested which hardware modules to use and made relevant contributions to include in the book the topics of modularization of a program into functions and files, finite-state machines, and different non-blocking delay techniques. He also contributed with a proposal about how to reorder the book chapters, which improved the reader experience.

Book Organization

This book is organized into five parts that take the reader, who has never before programmed embedded systems, from an introduction to embedded systems to the implementation of wireless communications and a set of proposed steps to develop embedded systems:

Part 1 – Introduction and Primary Tools

- Chapter 1: Introduction to Embedded Systems

- Chapter 2: Fundamentals of Serial Communication

- Chapter 3: Time Management and Analog Signals

Part 2 – Advanced Concepts in Embedded Systems

- Chapter 4: Finite-State Machines and the Real-Time Clock

- Chapter 5: Modularization Applied to Embedded Systems Programming

- Chapter 6: LCD Displays and Communication between Integrated Circuits

Part 3 – Solutions Based on the Processor Peripherals and Filesystems

- Chapter 7: DC Motor Driving using Relays and Interrupts

- Chapter 8: Advanced Time Management, Pulse-Width Modulation, Negative Feedback Control, and Audio Message Playback

- Chapter 9: File Storage on SD Cards and Usage of Software Repositories

Part 4 – Wireless Communications in Embedded Systems

- Chapter 10: Bluetooth Low Energy Communication with a Smartphone

- Chapter 11: Embedded Web Server over a Wi-Fi Connection

Part 5 – Proposed Steps to Develop Embedded Systems

- Chapter 12: Guide to Designing and Implementing an Embedded System Project

Chapter 1 addresses a general introduction to embedded systems and the smart home system project using LEDs and buttons. The basic concepts of embedded systems communications are tackled in Chapter 2, by means of connecting the NUCLEO board with a PC using serial communication.

Chapter 3 explains how to manage time intervals and analog signals, and some sensors and connectors are connected to the board.

Chapter 4 explains how to organize complex programs using finite-state machines. Modularization in files, which allows organization of large and complex programs, is introduced in Chapter 5. In Chapter 6, a character-based display and a graphical LCD display are connected and controlled using the same code for four different interfaces: 4/8-bit parallel interface, I2C bus, and SPI bus. In this way, the concept of a hardware abstraction layer is introduced.

In Part 3, more advanced concepts are explained, such as the use of interrupts in Chapter 7; microcontroller timers, pulse-width modulation, negative feedback control, and audio message playback in Chapter 8; and filesystems and software repositories in Chapter 9.

In Chapter 10, the smart home system is communicated with via a smartphone using a Bluetooth Low Energy connection, and an embedded web server is developed in Chapter 11 in order to provide web pages to a computer by means of a Wi-Fi network.

Lastly, in Chapter 12, a complete example of a different embedded system development is presented in order to show the reader in detail how a project can be addressed from beginning to end.

In this way, a multitude of useful concepts, techniques, and tools are presented in just twelve chapters, starting from the level of a complete beginner and building up to relatively complex and advanced topics.

More advanced concepts, such as integration of RTOS (Real-Time Operating Systems) with an embedded system, learning of the lower-level details, USB protocol, and applications related to the Internet of Things and Artificial Intelligence, are not included in this book.

Each chapter starts with a Roadmap section, where the corresponding learning objectives are described in "What You Will Learn," followed by "Review of Previous Chapters," and then "Contents of This Chapter."

Usually, this is followed by a section that explains how to connect the devices that are incorporated into the smart home system setup, as well as the fundamentals of their operation.

This is followed by Examples that are used to explain the practical use of the elements. The Examples are tackled in seven steps:

■ Objective of the Example

■ Summary of the Expected Behavior

■ Test the Proposed Solution on the Board

- Discussion of the Proposed Solution

- Implementation of the Proposed Solution

- Proposed Exercises

- Answers to the Exercises.

At the end of each chapter, there is an Under the Hood section, where more advanced concepts are introduced, to motivate the reader to explore beyond the limits of this book.

Most of the chapters conclude with a Case Study section, whose aim is to illustrate to the target audience of this book (beginners who have never programmed embedded systems before and have little or no prior knowledge of electronics) how the learned technologies are used in real-world applications.

How This Book Can Be Used for Teaching in Engineering Schools

This book was planned considering that in many countries, educational institutions hold classes for about twelve weeks. Given that this book is organized into twelve chapters, one chapter can be addressed to the students every week by means of the organization shown in Table 1 (in the case of two 90-minute or 120-minute lessons per week) or in Table 2 (if there is one 180-minute lesson per week).

In both cases, students are requested to connect and test a given setup every week, prior to the lessons, following the steps indicated in the first column of Table 1 and Table 2. This homework is estimated to take the students about one or two hours every week and is aimed at developing curiosity and enthusiasm for learning about how those systems work.

Table 1 and Table 2 show how the lessons can be organized. It is important to note that the setups that are connected and tested prior to the lessons every week are used in the examples in that week without the need for any change in the setup. This increases productivity during the lessons, because in this way all the lesson time is used to introduce new ideas and to test and discuss the examples in each chapter.

The activities each week are closed by the discussion of the Under the Hood and Case Study sections of each chapter, which can lead to different types of activities, for example asking the students to:

- look on the internet for more information about the topics discussed in the Under the Hood section;

- look on the internet for more case studies where the topics introduced in the chapter are applied.

For several reasons, Chapters 5, 6, and 12 are organized in a slightly different way than the other chapters. In these particular cases, Table 1 and Table 2 can be considered one option among many other possibilities.

Lastly, it is suggested to ask the students to implement a short project every two or three weeks, applying the concepts introduced in the lessons. Also, it is recommended to ask the students to implement a final project at the end of the course, following the process and techniques that are introduced in Chapter 12.

Table 1 Organization in the case of two 90-minute or 120-minute lessons per week.

Week	Pre-lesson activities	First lesson	Second lesson
1	1.2.3	1.1.1, 1.1.2, 1.2.1, 1.2.2 Examples 1.1, 1.2 and 1.3	Examples 1.4 and 1.5, 1.3.1, 1.4.1
2	2.2.1	2.1.1, 2.1.2, 2.1.3, 2.2.2, Examples 2.1, 2.2 and 2.3	Examples 2.4 and 2.5, 2.3.1, 2.4.1
3	3.2.1, 3.2.2	3.1.1, 3.1.2, 3.1.3, Examples 3.1, 3.2 and 3.3	Examples 3.4 and 3.5, 3.3.1, 3.4.1

Week	Pre-lesson activities	First lesson	Second lesson
4	4.2.1, 4.2.2	4.1.1, 4.1.2, 4.1.3 Examples 4.1 and 4.2	Examples 4.3 and 4.4 4.3.1, 4.4.1
5	-	5.1.1, 5.1.2, 5.1.3, 5.2.1	5.3.1, 5.3.2, 5.4.1, 5.4.2
6	6.2.1, 6.2.3, 6.2.4	6.1.1, 6.1.2, 6.1.3, 6.2.2 Examples 6.1 and 6.2	Examples 6.3, 6.4, and 6.5 6.3.1, 6.4.1
7	7.2.1	7.1.1, 7.1.2, 7.1.3, 7.2.2 Examples 7.1 and 7.2	Examples 7.3 and 7.4 7.3.1, 7.4.1
8	8.2.1	8.1.1, 8.1.2, 8.1.3, 8.2.2 Examples 8.1, 8.2, 8.3, and 8.4	Examples 8.5 and 8.6 8.3.1, 8.4.1
9	9.2.1	9.1.1, 9.1.2, 9.1.3, 9.2.2 Examples 9.1 and 9.2	Examples 9.3 and 9.4 9.3.1, 9.4.1
10	10.2.1	10.1.1, 10.1.2, 10.1.3, 10.2.2 Examples 10.1 and 10.2	Examples 10.3 and 10.4 10.3.1, 10.4.1
11	11.2.1	11.1.1, 11.1.2, 11.1.3, 11.2.2 Examples 11.1 and 11.2	Examples 11.3 and 11.4 11.3.1, 11.4.1
12	-	12.1.1, 12.1.2, 12.1.3, 12.2.1 Examples 12.1 to 12.4	Examples 12.5 to 12.10, 12.3.1

Table 2 Organization in the case of one 180-minute lesson per week.

Week	Pre-lesson activities	First part of the lesson	Second part of the lesson	Third part of the lesson
1	1.2.3	1.1.1, 1.1.2, 1.2.1, 1.2.2 Examples 1.1, 1.2, and 1.3	Examples 1.4 and 1.5	1.3.1, 1.4.1
2	2.2.1	2.1.1, 2.1.2, 2.1.3, 2.2.2 Examples 2.1, 2.2 and 2.3	Examples 2.4 and 2.5	2.3.1, 2.4.1
3	3.2.1, 3.2.2	3.1.1, 3.1.2, 3.1.3 Examples 3.1, 3.2 and 3.3	Examples 3.4 and 3.5	3.3.1, 3.4.1
4	4.2.1, 4.2.2	4.1.1, 4.1.2, 4.1.3 Examples 4.1 and 4.2	Examples 4.3 and 4.4	4.3.1, 4.4.1
5	-	5.1.1, 5.1.2, 5.1.3, 5.2.1	5.3.1, 5.3.2	5.4.1, 5.4.2
6	6.2.1, 6.2.3, 6.2.4	6.1.1, 6.1.2, 6.1.3, 6.2.2 Examples 6.1 and 6.2	Examples 6.3, 6.4 and 6.5	6.3.1, 6.4.1
7	7.2.1	7.1.1, 7.1.2, 7.1.3, 7.2.2 Examples 7.1 and 7.2	Examples 7.3 and 7.4	7.3.1, 7.4.1
8	8.2.1	8.1.1, 8.1.2, 8.1.3, 8.2.2 Examples 8.1, 8.2, 8.3, and 8.4	Examples 8.5 and 8.6	8.3.1, 8.4.1
9	9.2.1	9.1.1, 9.1.2, 9.1.3, 9.2.2 Examples 9.1 and 9.2	Examples 9.3 and 9.4	9.3.1, 9.4.1
10	10.2.1	10.1.1, 10.1.2, 10.1.3, 10.2.2 Examples 10.1 and 10.2	Examples 10.3 and 10.4	10.3.1, 10.4.1
11	11.2.1	11.1.1, 11.1.2, 11.1.3, 11.2.2 Examples 11.1 and 11.2	Examples 11.3 and 11.4	11.3.1, 11.4.1
12	-	12.1.1, 12.1.2, 12.1.3, 12.2.1 Examples 12.1 to 12.4	Examples 12.5 to 12.8	Examples 12.9 and 12.10, 12.3.1

Bill of Materials

The materials that are used in this book from Chapter 1 to Chapter 11 are summarized in Table 3. The aim is to help the reader to get all the components needed to implement the setups used in each chapter.

There is an additional bill of materials in Table 4, which lists the materials used in Chapter 12. These are not essential because the concepts that are introduced in this chapter can be learned without connecting all of the elements. For example, if the solenoid valve is not connected, the reader will still be able to see the relay module switching on and off, and the moisture sensor can be mocked using a potentiometer.

In addition, many tools are included in the listing shown in Table 5 because they may be useful.

Table 3 Bill of materials (BOM) used in Chapters 1 to 11.

Chapter	Component/Module	Quantity
	NUCLEO-F429ZI	1
	Jumper wires (male–male)	80
	USB–micro USB cable	1
	Breadboard	2
1	Tactile switches	10
2	(The same elements are used as in Chapter 1.)	–
	LM35 temperature sensor	1
	10 kΩ potentiometer	2
	MQ-2 gas sensor	1
	5V buzzer	1
	Resistors: 100 Ω, 150 Ω, 330 Ω, 1 kΩ, 10 kΩ, 47 kΩ, 100 kΩ (100 kΩ are used in this chapter and the other resistors in different chapters. See note below.)	10 of each value
3	Jumper wires (male–female)	80
	Matrix keypad (4 × 4)	1
	90-degrees 2.54 mm (.1") pitch pin header	40
	MB102 breadboard power supply (One is used in this chapter and the other in Chapter 7.)	2
4	USB–mini-USB cable	2
5	BC548C NPN transistor (One is used in this chapter and the other in Chapter 8.)	2
	Character-based LCD display 20 × 4, based on HD44780	1
	I2C PCF8574 expander	1
	10 kΩ trimpot	1
	Bidirectional logic level converter	1
	Jumper wires (female–female)	40
6	Graphic LCD display, based on ST7920	1

Chapter	Component/Module	Quantity
	3 mm red LED	1
	3 mm green LED	1
	5 V DC motor	1
	HC-SR501 PIR sensor module	1
	Relay module	1
7	1N5819 diodes	4
	LED RGB	1
	LDR	1
	10 nF ceramic capacitor	1
8	Female audio jack 3.5 mm (for PCB)	1
	SD card module	1
9	Micro SD memory card	1
10	Bluetooth HM-10 module	1
11	Wi-Fi ESP8266 ESP-01 module	1

 NOTE: The resistors are used as follows: Chapter 3: 3 × 100 kΩ; Chapter 5: 1 × 1 kΩ; Chapter 6: 1 × 1 kΩ; Chapter 7: 2 × 330 Ω; Chapter 8: 3 × 150 Ω, 1 × 10 kΩ, 1 × 47 kΩ, 1 × 1k Ω, and 1 × 100 Ω.

Table 4 Bill of materials (BOM) used in Chapter 12.

Chapter	Component/Module	Quantity
12	Moisture sensor	1
	12 V solenoid valve	1
	12 V × 1 A power supply	1

Table 5 Tools for soldering, measuring, and setting the modules.

Chapter	Quantity
Soldering iron	1
Wire solder	100 grams
Plier	1
Multimeter	1
Small screwdriver	1

List of Figures

List of Tables

Chapter 1

Introduction to
Embedded Systems

1.1 Roadmap

1.1.1 What You Will Learn

After you have studied the material in this chapter, you will be able to:

- Implement basic programs on the NUCLEO board using flow control, logical operators, and variables.

- Explain the basic concepts about how microcontrollers operate.

1.1.2 Contents of This Chapter

In every embedded system there is an element that reads the inputs, drives the outputs, and controls the communications and interfaces. This element is usually a microcontroller. To perform its tasks, the microcontroller runs a program. In this chapter, the process of writing a program is explained as well as how to upload it to the NUCLEO-F429ZI board (hereinafter called the NUCLEO board) that is used in this book. Detailed information about this board can be found in [1].

The chapter also explains how to control the LEDs of the NUCLEO board and the connected buttons. These buttons are used in example problems related to a smart home system project.

The examples in this chapter make use of some elements of the Arm Mbed OS 6, which is a free, open-source, rapid development platform designed to help developers get started building *Internet of Things (IoT)* applications quickly. An introduction to Mbed OS 6 can be found in [2].

In this way, some of the main concepts about embedded programming using the C and C++ languages are introduced, such as *nested if* statements, OR and AND logical operators, and *Boolean* and *non-Boolean* variables.

Throughout the chapter, the reader is guided on how to *compile* the examples and load them onto the NUCLEO board using Keil Studio Cloud, which allows the developer to write code from scratch or import an existing project and modify it to suit the developer's requirements. An introduction to Keil Studio Cloud is available in [3].

To use Keil Studio Cloud, the only thing the reader needs is an Arm Mbed account. [4] explains how to create an Arm Mbed account or log in if an account is already created. Keil Studio Cloud is available from [5] and a quick-start guide is available from [6].

 NOTE: Those readers who prefer to use a dedicated desktop setup can use the Mbed Studio IDE (*Integrated Development Environment*), which is available from [7], or any other IDE, for example the STM32CubeIDE, which is introduced in [8].

In the Under the Hood section, the basic principles of microcontrollers are introduced. Finally, in the Case Study section, a smart door lock based in Mbed OS is analyzed in order to show that many of the concepts introduced in this chapter are used in commercial products.

1.2 Fundamentals of Embedded Systems

1.2.1 Main Components of Embedded Systems

Throughout the chapters in this book, a smart home system project will be implemented. In this section, different smart home system implementations are analyzed in order to highlight the fundamentals of embedded systems.

Figure 1.1 shows four different implementations of a smart home system, adapted from different sources. The inputs are indicated in yellow, the microcontroller in light blue, the outputs in light red, the communication links in light gray, the human interfaces in blue, and the power supply in green. The elements contained in the block diagrams illustrated in Figure 1.1 are summarized in Table 1.1.

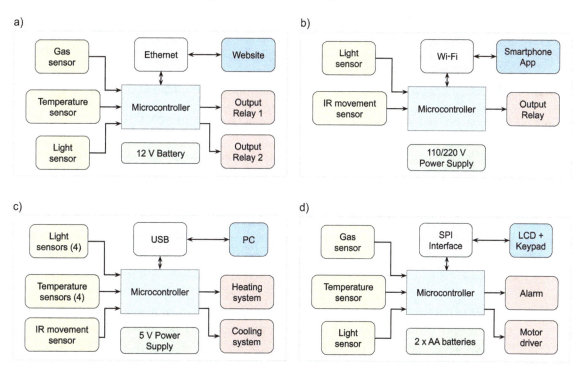

Figure 1.1 Four different block diagram representations of a smart home system.

Table 1.1 Elements contained in the smart home system block diagrams illustrated in Figure 1.1.

Smart Home	Inputs (yellow)	Microcontroller (light blue)	Outputs (light red)	Communication (light gray)	Interface (blue)	Power supply (green)
(a)	Gas, light, and temperature sensors	Yes	Two relays	Ethernet	Website	12 V battery
(b)	IR movement and light sensors	Yes	One relay	Wi-Fi	Smartphone App	110/220 V
(c)	Light, IR movement, and temperature sensors	Yes	Heating/ cooling system	USB	PC	5 V
(d)	Gas, light, and temperature sensors	Yes	Alarm/ motor driver	SPI	Keypad + LCD display	2 × AA batteries

From Table 1.1, the following conclusions can be made:

- All the implementations have a *microcontroller*.

- The type and number of sensors depends on the implementation.

- All the implementations have outputs, a relay being the most frequent one.

- Communications are implemented by different technologies (Ethernet, Wi-Fi, USB).

- Different interfaces are used: a website, a smartphone app, a keypad plus an LCD display.

- The power supply is indicated in the four diagrams (12 V battery, 110/220 V, etc.).

The microcontroller is the heart of the system: all the inputs are connected to the microcontroller and all the outputs are driven by the microcontroller, while the communications and the interfaces are controlled by the microcontroller. For this reason, every embedded system has one microcontroller (at least), or a similar element that plays the same role.

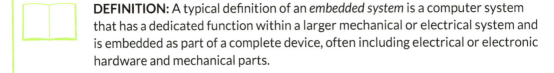

DEFINITION: A typical definition of an *embedded system* is a computer system that has a dedicated function within a larger mechanical or electrical system and is embedded as part of a complete device, often including electrical or electronic hardware and mechanical parts.

DEFINITION: A typical definition of a *microcontroller* is a small computer on a single integrated circuit (IC) chip which typically contains one or more processor cores along with memory and programmable peripherals.

NOTE: The Under the Hood section, at the end of this chapter, discusses in detail what is inside a microcontroller. The aim is to make the reader use a microcontroller before explaining how they work.

The microcontroller runs a program made up of instructions by means of which the programmer instructs the microcontroller what to do. This book aims to enable the reader to write this type of program and to connect the appropriate sensors, actuators, and interfaces to the inputs and outputs of the microcontroller. The sensors will provide measurements of the environment, while the actuators will allow the microcontroller to have control over elements and devices within the environment.

Proposed Exercises

1. Using Table 1.1 as a reference, propose a smart home system having a maximum of two types of sensors (inputs), one type of actuator (output), one communication link, and two human interfaces.

2. Make the block diagram of the proposed smart home system.

Answers to the Exercises

1. The smart home system may include a gas sensor, a temperature sensor, an alarm, a keypad, and a communication link with a PC.

2. The diagram of the proposed smart home system is shown in Figure 1.2.

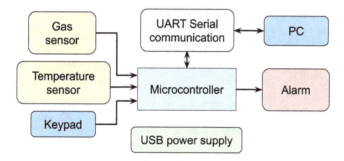

Figure 1.2 Diagram of the proposed smart home system.

 NOTE: In Figure 1.2, the link with the PC is implemented by means of a UART serial communication (*Universal Asynchronous Receiver-Transmitter*). The UART peripheral is introduced later in Chapter 2.

1.2.2 First Implementation of the Smart Home System

This section will begin the implementation of the smart home system, following the diagram shown in Figure 1.3. This first implementation will detect fire using an over temperature detector and a gas detector and, if it detects fire, it will activate the alarm until a given code is entered. For this purpose, the NUCLEO board [1] provided with the STM32F429ZIT6U microcontroller [9] (referred to as the *STM32 microcontroller*) is used.

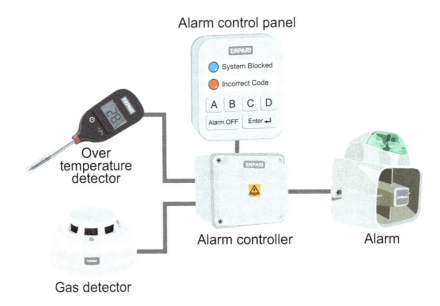

Figure 1.3 The smart home system that is implemented in this chapter.

The reader might notice that there are not as many buttons in the NUCLEO board as in the alarm control panel shown in Figure 1.3. Instead, the NUCLEO board is provided with only one user button and three LEDs, as shown in Figure 1.4. It can be concluded that a way to connect more buttons to the NUCLEO board is needed. For this purpose, the ST Zio connectors of the NUCLEO board shown in Figure 1.4 are used.

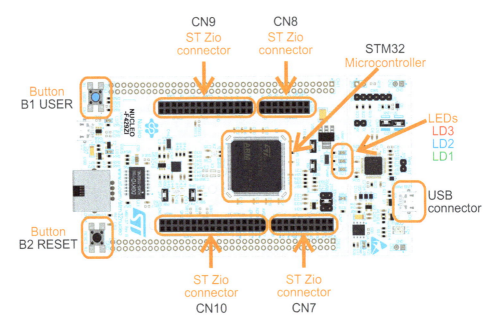

Figure 1.4 The NUCLEO-F429ZI board used in this book.

The overall diagram of the embedded system that will be connected in this chapter is shown in Figure 1.5. It can be seen that a breadboard is used, together with the most common buttons used in electronics, technically known as *tactile switches*. For breadboarding, any appropriate wire can be used, but it is recommended to use *jumper wires*.

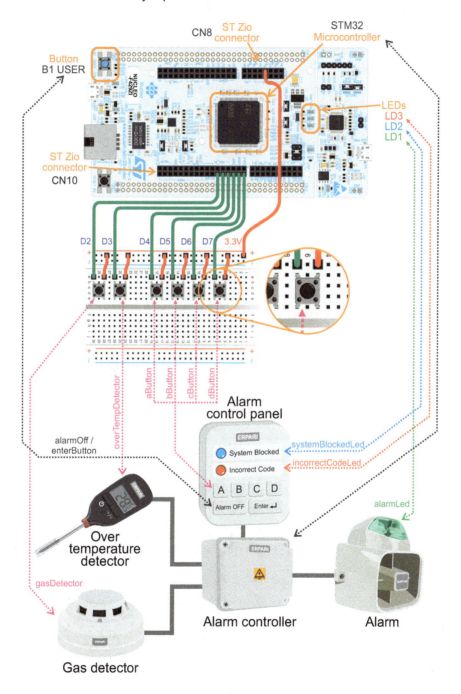

Figure 1.5 The elements of the smart home system introduced in Figure 1.3 with their corresponding components.

Figure 1.5 shows the elements of the smart home system introduced in Figure 1.3 and their proposed representation by means of the components connected. The names that will be used in the code to refer to each element are indicated in Figure 1.5 (i.e., gasDetector, alarmLed, etc.). It can be seen that the activation of the gas detector and the over temperature detector are simulated by buttons D2 and D3 placed over the breadboard. All these connections are summarized in Table 1.2.

TIP: It may be useful to indicate the function of each button and LED using a card next to each one.

NOTE: In Chapters 1 and 2, the alarm will be represented by an LED. In Chapter 3, a buzzer will be incorporated into the alarm in order to represent a siren. In later chapters it will be explained how to incorporate a strobe light into the alarm. In this way the alarm will have light and sound, as in Figure 1.5.

Table 1.2. Elements of the smart home system and the corresponding representation implemented.

Smart home system	Representation used
Alarm	LD1 LED (green)
System blocked LED	LD2 LED (blue)
Incorrect code LED	LD3 LED (red)
Alarm Off / Enter button	B1 USER button
Gas detector	Button connected to D2 pin
Over temperature detector	Button connected to D3 pin
A button	Button connected to D4 pin
B button	Button connected to D5 pin
C button	Button connected to D6 pin
D button	Button connected to D7 pin

In Table 1.2 it should be noticed that the B1 USER button is used for the Alarm Off and also for the Enter button. The specific use will vary during the examples and will be clearly indicated as it becomes necessary.

In Figure 1.6 and Figure 1.7 the details of the connections that should be made on the CN8 and CN10 ST Zio Connectors are shown.

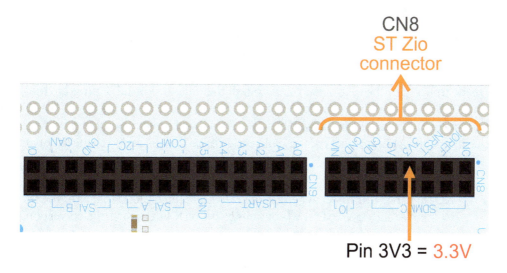

Figure 1.6 Detail of the connection made in the CN8 ST Zio connector of the NUCLEO board.

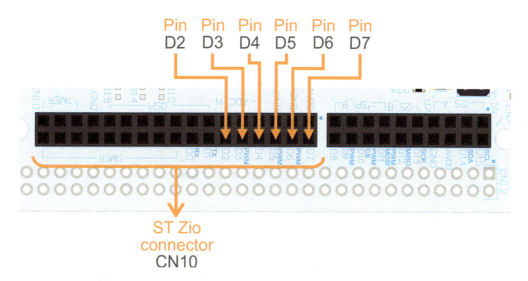

Figure 1.7 Detail of the connections made in the CN10 ST Zio connector of the NUCLEO board.

 WARNING: It is crucial to connect the jumper wires and buttons exactly as indicated in Figure 1.5, Figure 1.6, and Figure 1.7. Otherwise, the programs presented in this chapter will not work.

To make all the connections, unplug the USB power supply from the NUCLEO board. Prior to reconnecting the USB power supply, check that there are no short circuits.

1.2.3 Getting Ready to Program the First Implementation of the Smart Home System

This subsection explains how to load a program onto the STM32 microcontroller of the NUCLEO board using Keil Studio Cloud in order to test if the buttons that were connected are working properly.

First, the reader must copy the URL of the repository of the "Subsection 1.2.3" program that is available in [10]. Then, in the "File" menu of Keil Studio Cloud, select "Import project". The "Import project" window will be displayed in the web browser. Press "Add project" without modifying any of the configurations, and a new project named "Subsection 1.2.3" will be added to the list of available projects as the active project.

 NOTE: If in the future changes are made in Keil Studio Cloud that alter the steps to compile and download the programs to the NUCLEO board, the corresponding instructions will be published in [10].

The program that was imported has the behaviors detailed in Table 1.3. When the B1 USER button of the NUCLEO board is pressed, LEDs LD1, LD2, and LD3 of the board are turned on. This is to ensure that the three LEDs and the program are working correctly. If the external buttons connected to D2 or D3 are pressed, LD1 is turned on. In this way it can be tested whether the buttons connected to D2 and D3 are properly connected and working. The same applies to the buttons connected to D4 and D5 by means of LD2, and the buttons connected to D6 and D7 by means of LD3.

Table 1.3 Behaviors of the program that is used in this subsection to test the buttons.

LED	Turns on if any of the following is pressed
LD1 (green)	B1 USER button, button connected to D2, button connected to D3
LD2 (blue)	B1 USER button, button connected to D4, button connected to D5
LD3 (red)	B1 USER button, button connected to D6, button connected to D7

 NOTE: The code of the program that has been loaded onto the NUCLEO board to test if the six external buttons are working correctly will not be analyzed in this subsection. This is due to the fact that the behavior of this code is based on some elements that will be introduced and explained in the following subsections. For now, it is enough to be able to check if the six buttons are working.

In order to load the program onto the NUCLEO board, connect it to the computer as shown in Figure 1.8. If "NUCLEO-F429ZI" is not shown in the "Target hardware" section, press the "Find target" button. If a popup menu is displayed, select the "STM32 STLink" connection and follow the instructions. Once "NUCLEO-F429ZI" is shown in the "Target hardware" section, press the "Build project" button. The progress will be shown in the "Output" tab. Once the program has been compiled, a *.bin* file will be automatically downloaded by the web browser. Drag the downloaded *.bin* file to the drive assigned to the NUCLEO board (for example, D:\, named NODE_F429ZI). A "copying" window will open, LED LD4 of the NUCLEO board will alternate red and green light, and when the window closes the program will already be running on the NUCLEO board.

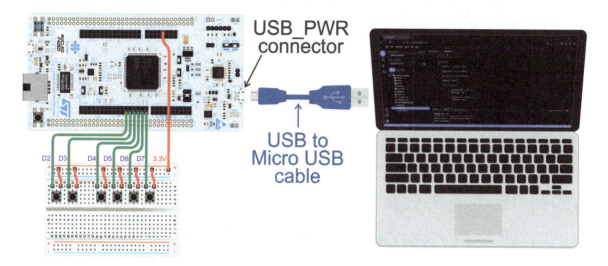

Figure 1.8 How to connect the NUCLEO board to a PC.

Next, press the B1 USER button and the buttons connected to D2, D3, D4, D5, D6, and D7, one after the other. If the behavior of the LEDs is as described in Table 1.3 then the buttons that were connected are working fine and the program has been correctly loaded onto the NUCLEO board.

 TIP: If the B1 USER button is working as described in Table 1.3 but one of the switches D2 to D7 is not working as expected, check the corresponding connections. If the B1 USER button is not working as described in Table 1.3 then the program has not been properly loaded onto the NUCLEO board.

As stated in the preface, in this book selected problems, named Examples, are tackled in seven steps. The first set of examples are presented below.

Example 1.1: Activate the Alarm When Gas is Detected

Objective

Write the first program of the book, load it onto the NUCLEO board, and introduce the *if* statement.

Summary of the Expected Behavior

LD1 must turn on when the button connected to pin D2 of the NUCLEO board is pressed and turn off when this button is released.

Test the Proposed Solution on the Board

Import the project "Example 1.1" using the URL available in [10], build the project, and drag the *.bin* file onto the NUCLEO board. Then press and release the button connected to pin D2 and look at the behavior of LD1. The LED should turn on when the button is pressed and turn off when the button is released.

Discussion of the Proposed Solution

In embedded systems there is a set of *statements* that are executed forever until the power supply is removed. Figure 1.9 illustrates the general structure, which is composed of two main parts:

▦ *Libraries, Definitions and Global Declarations and Initializations*, indicated in blue.

▦ *Implementation of the main() function*, indicated in green.

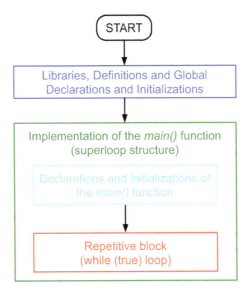

Figure 1.9 Structure of the proposed solution.

Libraries, Definitions and Global Declarations and Initializations includes the *software libraries* that are used. In addition, here some definitions of values can be established, and *global variables* can be declared and initialized, among other elements.

Implementation of the *main()* function consists of two parts, which are illustrated in Figure 1.9:

▦ *Declarations and Initializations of the main() function*, indicated in light blue.

▦ *Repetitive block*, indicated in red.

In Initializations of the *main()* function, the *inputs* and *outputs* of the board that are used are declared, and the initial states and other configurations are established.

The *repetitive block* is made by the statements that are executed repeatedly in the *while (true)* loop. This kind of structure is known as a *superloop*. That is, the code block corresponding to a *while* statement is executed as long as the condition of the *while* loop is true. If this condition is explicitly defined as *true* (i.e., *while (true)*) the code block of the *while* loop is executed forever.

Implementation of the Proposed Solution

The *main.cpp* file is where the main program is written in C or C++ language (the differences and history of C and C++ are discussed in Chapter 10 and in [11]). The *main.cpp* file of Example 1.1 is shown in Code 1.1. The parts corresponding to Figure 1.9 are highlighted in color. An explanation of each part is included over the code. In lines 1 and 2 of Code 1.1, *#include "mbed.h"* and *#include "arm_book_lib.h"* are used to instruct the Mbed Online Compiler to insert pre-written files that describe, among other things, the interfaces to external libraries that will then be included automatically by the tools, where *classes* and *macros* such as *DigitalIn*, *DigitalOut*, *ON*, and *OFF* are defined. The *main()* function is implemented from line 4 to line 23.

```
1  #include "mbed.h"
2  #include "arm_book_lib.h"
3
4  int main()
5  {
6      DigitalIn gasDetector(D2);
7
8      DigitalOut alarmLed(LED1);
9
10     gasDetector.mode(PullDown);
11
12     alarmLed = OFF;
13
14     while ( true ) {
15         if ( gasDetector == ON ) {
16             alarmLed = ON;
17         }
18
19         if ( gasDetector == OFF ) {
20             alarmLed = OFF;
21         }
22     }
23 }
```

Include the libraries "mbed.h" and "arm_book_lib.h"

- A digital input object (DigitalIn) named *gasDetector* is declared and assigned to D2.
- A digital output object (DigitalOut) named *alarmLed* is declared and assigned to LED1.
- *gasDetector* is configured with an internal pull-down resistor.
- *alarmLed* (LED1) is assigned OFF.

Do forever loop:
- If *gasDetector* is active, *alarmLed* is assigned ON.

- If *gasDetector* is not active, *alarmLed* is assigned OFF.

Code 1.1 Implementation of Example 1.1.

NOTE: Double straight quotes (") are used in lines 1 and 2 of Code 1.1. In the program codes that are introduced in this book, double and single straight quotes (') will gradually be introduced and used for different purposes. It is important for the reader to understand that double and single curly quotes (", ", ', ') are different characters that cannot be used for the same purpose in the program codes. Similarly, a double straight quote cannot be replaced in the code by two consecutive straight single quotes.

NOTE: The colors used by different code editors to highlight reserved words and parts of the code may vary (i.e., some use green for *if* and others use blue). However, it has no relevance for the program code itself.

NOTE: C and C++ are free-form programming languages in which the positioning of characters in the program text is insignificant. However, to clarify the code structure in this book the Kernighan and Ritchie (K&R) indentation style [12] is used. The indentation rules of the K&R style are not discussed for the sake of brevity.

The instructions in line 6 and line 8 are to instruct the microcontroller that the button connected to D2 and LD1 (named LED1 in the code) will be used. The button will be used as an input, while LD1 will be used as an output (as indicated in Table 1.2). Line 6 declares a digital input with the name *gasDetector* and assigns it to button D2. Line 8 declares a digital output with the name *alarmLed* and assigns it to LED1. All these configurations are achieved by the *DigitalIn gasDetector(D2)* and *DigitalOut alarmLed(LED1)* declarations, where the corresponding *objects* are created.

NOTE: In this book, objects' names are stylized using *camel case* convention without capitalization of the first letter (known as *lower camel case* or *dromedary case*), as in *gasDetector* and *alarmLed*. In this way, these names can be easily differentiated from names defined by Mbed OS, like *DigitalIn*, *DigitalOut* or *PullDown*, which use the camel case convention with capitalization of the first letter.

In Line 10, *gasDetector.mode(PullDown)* is used to enable an internal pull-down resistor connected to the *DigitalIn* object *gasDetector*. A typical connection between a button and a microcontroller digital input based on a pull-down resistor is as shown on the left side of Figure 1.10. When the button is pressed, the NUCLEO board reads +3.3 V (high state). When the button is not pressed, the NUCLEO board reads 0 V (low state) because of the pull-down resistor ("R_pulldown"). In order to avoid connecting one resistor for each button, the internal pull-down resistors that are provided by the STM32 microcontroller are used in this example.

The right side of Figure 1.10 shows the simplified diagram of a typical connection between a button and a microcontroller digital input based on a pull-up resistor. In this case, when the button is pressed, the NUCLEO board reads a low state (0 V), and it reads a high state (3.3 V) when the button is not pressed. In the latter part of this book, pull-up resistors will be used so that the reader becomes familiar with them.

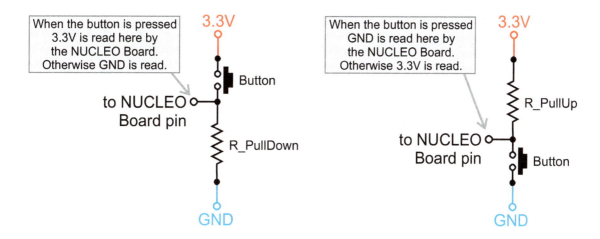

Figure 1.10 Conceptual diagram of how to connect a button to the NUCLEO board using pull-down and pull-up resistors.

In line 12, *alarmLed* is initialized to OFF. This instruction, together with lines 6 to 10, is highlighted in light blue in Code 1.1 and are called *Declarations and Initializations of the main() function.*

In line 14, the *while(true)* statement is used to indicate the beginning of the repetitive block that is repeated forever. In Example 1.3, the concept of a *Boolean variable* will be introduced, and this line will be explained in more detail.

Between lines 16 and 20, the following behavior is implemented: if the *gasDetector* is on (button connected to D2 is pressed) turn on the alarm (turn on LD1). If the *gasDetector* is off (button connected to D2 is not pressed) turn off the alarm (turn off LD1).

 NOTE: To implement the comparison inside the *if* statements (line 15 and line 19) a double equals sign is used (i.e., "=="), while in order to assign values (line 16 and line 20) a single equals sign is used (i.e., "=").

The reader should note that the braces "{" and "}" play a very important role in the code, because they are used to separate the code into parts.

The reader should also note that semicolons ";" are used to separate different statements, and parentheses "(" and ")" are used to indicate the beginning and ending of the arguments of the statements, as in *if()*, *while()*, and *main()*. Parentheses are also used to indicate which elements of the board are referred to with the objects *alarmLed* and *gasDetector*.

Proposed Exercises

1. What happens if one of the semicolons is replaced by a comma?

2. What happens if one of the *gasDetector* occurrences is replaced by *gasdetector*?

3. What can be changed in the code in order to use LD2 instead of LD1?

4. Is it possible to turn on LD1 and LD2 as the button connected to D2 is pressed?

5. What would happen if the *while (true)* statement was removed?

6. What will happen if the code in Table 1.4 is used?

Table 1.4 New proposed implementation for Example 1.1.

Lines in Code 1.1	New code to be used

15 if (gasDetector == ON) {
16   alarmLed = ON;
17 }
18
19 if (gasDetector == OFF) {
20   alarmLed = OFF;
21 }
	16 if (gasDetector == ON) {
	17 alarmLed = ON;
	18 } else {
	19 alarmLed = OFF;
	20 }
	21

Answers to the Exercises

1. The Online Compiler will not be able to compile the code and will indicate an error in the line where the semicolon was replaced by a comma.

2. The C/C++ code is case sensitive, so *gasdetector* will be interpreted as a different element than *gasDetector* and, as a consequence, an error will be indicated.

3. Line 8 should be changed to *DigitalOut alarmLed (LD2);*

4. Yes. The lines indicated in Table 1.5 should be changed.

5. The program will work once and will be over in a few microseconds.

6. The program will work in the same way as Code 1.1. The new code has the advantage of being more compact.

Table 1.5 Proposed modifications of the code in order to achieve the new behavior.

Lines in Code 1.1	New code to be used
8 DigitalOut alarmLed(LED1);	8 DigitalOut alarmLed1(LED1); 9 DigitalOut alarmLed2(LED2);
12 alarmLed = OFF;	13 alarmLed1 = OFF; 14 alarmLed2 = OFF;
17 alarmLed = ON;	19 alarmLed1 = ON; 20 alarmLed2 = ON;
20 alarmLed = OFF;	23 alarmLed1 = OFF; 24 alarmLed2 = OFF;

Example 1.2: Activate the Alarm on Gas Presence or Over Temperature

Objective

Review the *if* statement and introduce the *OR* operator.

Summary of the Expected Behavior

An LED must turn on/off as one or more buttons connected to the NUCLEO board are pressed or released.

Test the Proposed Solution on the Board

Import the project "Example 1.2" using the URL available in [10], build the project, and drag the *.bin* file onto the NUCLEO board. Then press and release the buttons connected to D2 or to D3 and look at the behavior of LD1. LD1 should turn on when any of the buttons connected to D2 and D3 are pressed. LD1 should turn off when both buttons connected to D2 and D3 are released.

Discussion of the Proposed Solution

In Example 1.1, the alarm (LD1) was activated when gas was detected (button connected to D2 was pressed). In this example, the over temperature detector is incorporated into the system and is simulated by the button connected to D3.

In Example 1.1, the *if* statement was used to implement the proposed behavior depending on the state of the button connected to D2. In this case, if the gas detector (D2) *or* the over temperature detector (D3) is active, the alarm should turn on. Otherwise, the alarm should turn off. The logical OR behavior is indicated by means of the || operator in C/C++.

Figure 1.11 shows the proposed parts to implement the solution, following the structure proposed in Figure 1.9. In the *Libraries, Definitions and Global Declarations and Initializations* (Figure 1.11 [a]), the *mbed.h* and *arm_book_lib.h* libraries are included. In the *Declarations and Initializations of the main() function* (Figure 1.11 [b]), the digital inputs *gasDetector* and *overTempDetector* are declared and assigned to D2 and D3, and a digital output named *alarmLed* is declared and assigned to LD1. The repetitive block (Figure 1.11 [c]) turns on *alarmLed* if *gasDetector* or *overTempDetector* is pressed and turns off *alarmLed* if both are not pressed.

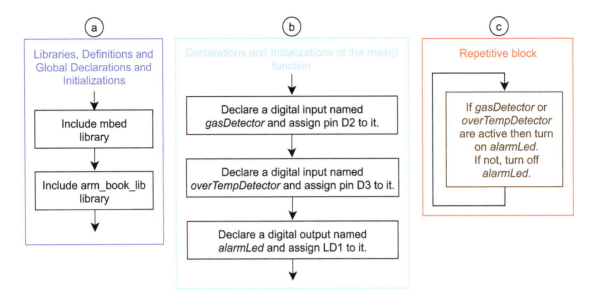

Figure 1.11 Main parts of the program of Example 1.2.

Figure 1.12 shows the details of the repetitive block. This block turns *alarmLed* (LD1) on if *gasDetector* or *overTempDetector* is active (buttons connected to D2 or D3 are pressed).

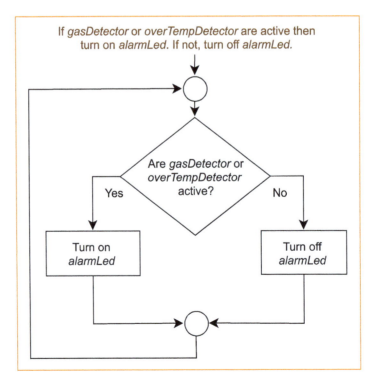

Figure 1.12 Details of the blocks that make up the repetitive block of Example 1.2.

Implementation of the Proposed Solution

In Code 1.2, the implementation of the proposed solution is presented. The parts corresponding to Figure 1.11 and Figure 1.12 are highlighted in color. An explanation of each part is included beside the code.

```
1 #include "mbed.h"
2 #include "arm_book_lib.h"
3
4 int main()
5 {
6     DigitalIn gasDetector(D2);
7     DigitalIn overTempDetector(D3);
8
9     DigitalOut alarmLed(LED1);
10
11     gasDetector.mode(PullDown);
12     overTempDetector.mode(PullDown);
13
14     while ( true ) {
15
16         if ( gasDetector || overTempDetector ) {
17             alarmLed = ON;
18         }
19             alarmLed = OFF;
20         }
21     }
22 }
```

Include the libraries "mbed.h" and "arm_book_lib.h"

- Digital input objects named *gasDetector* and *overTempDetector* are declared and assigned to D2 and D3, respectively.
- Digital output object named *alarmLed* is declared and assigned to LED1.
- *gasDetector* and *overTempDetector* are configured with internal pull-down resistors.

Do forever loop:
- If *gasDetector* or *overTempDetector* are active, *alarmLed* is assigned ON.
- Else, *alarmLed* is assigned OFF.

Code 1.2 Implementation of Example 1.2.

Proposed Exercises

1. What should be modified in order to simulate the alarm by means of LD2?

2. How can it be implemented so that when gas presence is detected or over temperature is detected LD1 and LD2 are both turned on?

3. How can line 16 of Example 1.2 be modified in order to use an explicit formulation of the condition, as in Example 1.1?

4. Is there another way to indicate the OR logical operator beside the || symbols used in Example 1.6?

Answers to the Exercises

1. In line 8, LED1 should be replaced by LED2.

2. It can be achieved by means of the changes in Table 1.6.

Table 1.6 Proposed modifications in the code in order to achieve the new behavior.

Lines in Code 1.2	New code to be used
`9 DigitalOut alarmLed(LED1);`	`9 DigitalOut alarmLed1(LED1);` `10 DigitalOut alarmLed2(LED2);`
`17 alarmLed = ON;`	`18 alarmLed1 = ON;` `19 alarmLed2 = ON;`
`19 alarmLed = OFF;`	`21 alarmLed1 = OFF;` `22 alarmLed2 = OFF;`

3. Line 16 can be rewritten as follows:

```
if ( gasDetector == ON || overTempDetector == ON )
```

4. The logical operator OR can be expressed as follows

```
if ( gasDetector == ON or overTempDetector == ON )
```

 NOTE: In this book, the notation || is used because of historical reasons. However, in Mbed OS, *or* can be used to indicate the logical operator OR; in addition, other reserved words such as *not*, *and*, etc. can be used.

Example 1.3: Keep the Alarm Active After Gas or Over Temperature Were Detected

Objective

Learn how to use a Boolean variable to keep track of the state of a given element.

Summary of the Expected Behavior

The LED is turned on when one or more of the alarm conditions are activated (simulated by buttons connected to the NUCLEO board) and remains on until those alarm conditions are removed and another button is pressed.

Test the Proposed Solution on the Board

Import the project "Example 1.3" using the URL available in [10], build the project, and drag the *.bin* file onto the NUCLEO board. Then press and release the buttons connected to D2 and D3 and look at the behavior of LD1. LD1 should turn on when the buttons connected to D2 and D3 are pressed and turn off when the B1 USER button is pressed.

Discussion of the Proposed Solution

In Example 1.2, the alarm was directly controlled by the buttons connected to D2 and D3 that simulated the gas detector and the over temperature detector, respectively. When any of these buttons were pressed the alarm was turned on, and when both buttons were released the alarm was turned off. To keep the alarm activated until another condition occurs, the alarm state must be stored. This can be done by means of a *Boolean variable*. In this scheme, the activation of the alarm is determined by the state of the variable *alarmState*. This variable is assigned ON when the gas detector or the over temperature detector is activated and is assigned OFF when the B1 USER button is pressed.

NOTE: Strictly speaking, a Boolean variable has only two valid states: *true* or *false*. However, for practical purposes, we will use ON and OFF to refer to the values *true* and *false* of the variable *alarmState*.

It is worth noting that the *while(true)* instruction used to indicate the beginning of the repetitive block is based on the idea that what is inside the braces of the *while* statement should be repeated until the condition inside the parentheses of the *while* becomes false. Given that it is written *while(true)*, it will never be false. Therefore, the instructions inside the braces will be repeated forever.

Figure 1.13 shows the proposed main parts to implement the solution of this example. In the *Libraries, Definitions and Global Declarations and Initializations* (Figure 1.13 [a]), the *mbed.h* and *arm_book_lib.h* libraries are included. In the *Declarations and Initializations of the main()* function (Figure 1.13 [b]), the digital inputs *gasDetector*, *overTempDetector*, and *alarmOffButton* are declared and assigned to buttons D2, D3, and B1 USER, respectively, the digital output *alarmLed* is declared and assigned to LD1, and the variable *alarmState* is declared and initialized to OFF.

The *repetitive block* (Figure 1.13 [c]) is made up of three blocks: a block indicated in brown, which assigns ON to *alarmState* if *gasDetector* or *overTempDetector* is activated; a block indicated in orange, which assigns the value of *alarmState* to *alarmLed*; and a block indicated in violet, which assigns OFF to *alarmState* if the *alarmOffButton* is pressed.

NOTE: In this book names of variables are stylized using the lower camel case format, as in *alarmState*.

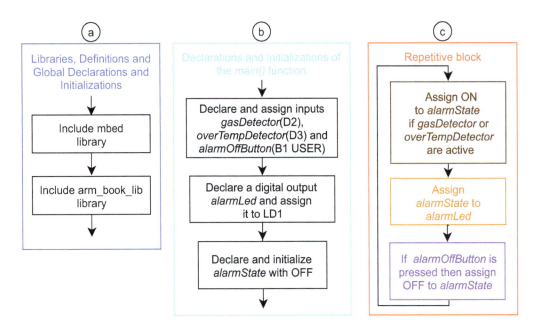

Figure 1.13 Main parts of the program of Example 1.3.

Figure 1.14 shows the details of the blocks that compose the repetitive block. Figure 1.14 (a) shows the block that assigns ON to *alarmState* if *gasDetector* or *overTempDetector* is active. Figure 1.14 (b) shows the details of the block that assigns *alarmState* to *alarmLed*. Figure 1.14 (c) shows the details of the block that assigns OFF to *alarmState* if *alarmOffButton* is pressed.

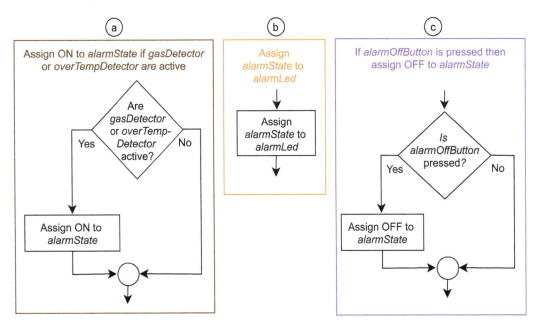

Figure 1.14 Details of the blocks that compose the repetitive block of Example 1.3.

Implementation of the Proposed Solution

In Code 1.3 the implementation of the proposed solution is presented. The parts corresponding to Figure 1.13 and Figure 1.14 are highlighted in color. An explanation of each part is included beside the code.

 NOTE: In the code, "BUTTON1" is used to refer to the "B1 USER button" because it is defined this way in the mbed.h library. For the same reason, "LED1" is used to refer to "LD1", such as in Examples 1.1 and 1.2.

```cpp
1  #include "mbed.h"
2  #include "arm_book_lib.h"
3
4  int main()
5  {
6      DigitalIn gasDetector(D2);
7      DigitalIn overTempDetector(D3);
8      DigitalIn alarmOffButton(BUTTON1);
9
10     DigitalOut alarmLed(LED1);
11
12     gasDetector.mode(PullDown);
13     overTempDetector.mode(PullDown);
14
15     alarmLed = OFF;
16
17     bool alarmState = OFF;
18
19     while ( true ) {
20
21         if ( gasDetector || overTempDetector ) {
22             alarmState = ON;
23         }
24
25         alarmLed = alarmState;
26
27         if ( alarmOffButton ) {
28             alarmState = OFF;
29         }
30     }
31 }
```

Include the libraries "mbed.h" and "arm_book_lib.h"

- Digital input objects named *gasDetector*, *overTempDetector* and *alarmOffButton*, are declared and assigned to D2, D3, and BUTTON1 (B1 USER), respectively.
- Digital output object named *alarmLed* is declared and assigned to LED1.
- *gasDetector* and *overTempDetector* are configured with internal pull-down resistors.
- *alarmLed* is assigned OFF.
- *alarmState* is declared and assigned OFF.

Do forever loop:
- If *gasDetector* or *overTempDetector* are active, assign *alarmState* with ON.
- Assign *alarmLed* with *alarmState*.
- If *alarmOffButton*, assign *alarmState* with OFF.

Code 1.3 Implementation of Example 1.3.

 NOTE: It is not necessary to enable an internal pull-down resistor for the B1 User button. This is because this button is already connected to an external pull-down resistor placed in the NUCLEO board, as well as to other elements that are used to reduce the *electrical noise* of the signal that is supplied to the microcontroller.

Proposed Exercises

1. How can the code be changed in such a way that LD1 is turned on at the beginning, is turned off when gas presence or over temperature is detected, and is turned on when the B1 USER button is pressed?

2. What should be modified in order to turn off the alarm by means of the button connected to D4?

Answers to the Exercises

1. It can be achieved by means of the changes shown in Table 1.7.

2. In line 16, BUTTON1 should be replaced by D4.

Table 1.7 *Proposed modifications in the code in order to achieve the new behavior.*

Lines in Code 1.3	New code to be used
17 bool alarmState = OFF	17 bool alarmState = ON
22 alarmState = ON;	22 alarmState = OFF;
28 alarmState = OFF;	28 alarmState = ON;

Example 1.4: Secure the Alarm Deactivation by Means of a Code

Objective

Introduce the AND and NOT operators.

Summary of the Expected Behavior

An LED must turn on when one or more buttons connected to the NUCLEO board are pressed, and it must be kept on until a combination of certain buttons is entered.

Test the Proposed Solution on the Board

Import the project "Example 1.4" using the URL available in [10], build the project, and drag the .*bin* file onto the NUCLEO board. Then press and release either of the buttons connected to D2 or D3. Look at the behavior of LD1. LD1 should turn on when any of the buttons connected to D2 and D3 are pressed and turn off only when the buttons connected to D4 and D5 are pressed together at the same time.

Discussion of the Proposed Solution

In general, the behavior of this code is similar to the code in Example 1.3, but in this example the way the alarm is turned off is different. In this case, a combination of certain buttons must be pressed simultaneously. To turn off the alarm, the buttons connected to D4 *and* D5 should be pressed while at the same time the buttons connected to D6 and D7 should *not* be pressed. In C/C++, the logical AND is indicated by means of the && operator and the logical operator NOT is indicated by means of the ! operator.

Figure 1.15 shows the proposed main parts to implement the solution of this example. In the *Libraries, Definitions and Global Declarations and Initializations* (Figure 1.15 [a]), the *mbed.h* and *arm_book_lib.h* libraries are included. In the *Declarations and Initializations of the main() function* (Figure 1.15 [b]), the pins connected to D2, D3, D4, D5, D6 and D7 are configured as inputs, the pin connected to LD1 is configured as output, and the variable *alarmState* is declared and initialized to OFF.

The repetitive block (Figure 1.15 [c]) is made up of three blocks: a block indicated in brown, which assigns ON to *alarmState* if *gasDetector* or *overTempDetector* is activated; a block indicated in orange, which assigns the value of *alarmState* to *alarmLed*; and a block indicated in violet, which assigns OFF to *alarmState* if the buttons connected to D4 and D5 are pressed while the buttons connected to D6 and D7 are *not* pressed.

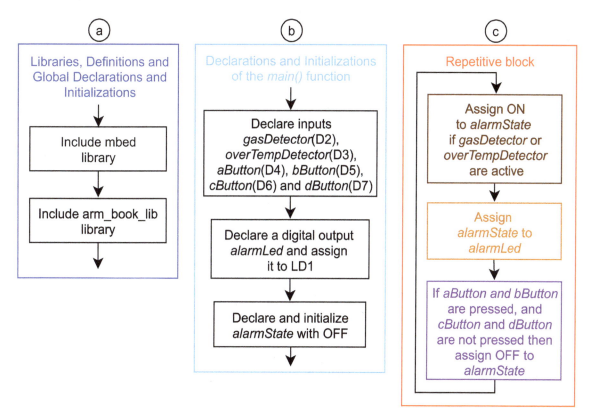

Figure 1.15 Main parts of the program of Example 1.4.

Figure 1.16 shows the details of the blocks that compose the repetitive block. In this case, only the block indicated in violet is included because the brown and orange blocks are the same as in Figure 1.16 (a) and Figure 1.16 (b), respectively. Figure 1.16 (c) shows the block that assigns OFF to *alarmState* if the buttons connected to D4 *and* D5 are pressed and the buttons connected to D6 and D7 are not pressed.

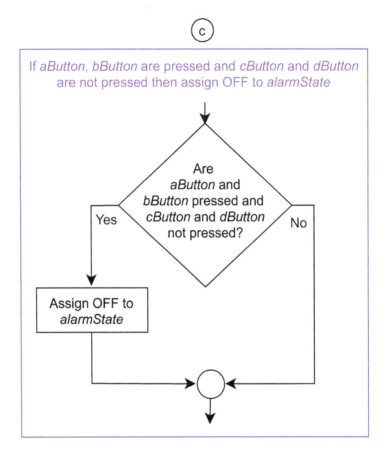

Figure 1.16 Details of the blocks that make up the repetitive block of Example 1.4.

Implementation of the Proposed Solution

In Code 1.4 the implementation of the proposed solution is presented. The parts corresponding to Figure 1.15 and Figure 1.16 are highlighted in different colors. An explanation of each part is also included beside the code.

```
 1 #include "mbed.h"
 2 #include "arm_book_lib.h"
 3
 4 int main()
 5 {
 6     DigitalIn gasDetector(D2);
 7     DigitalIn overTempDetector(D3);
 8     DigitalIn aButton(D4);
 9     DigitalIn bButton(D5);
10     DigitalIn cButton(D6);
11     DigitalIn dButton(D7);
12
13     DigitalOut alarmLed(LED1);
14
15     gasDetector.mode(PullDown);
16     overTempDetector.mode(PullDown);
17     aButton.mode(PullDown);
18     bButton.mode(PullDown);
19     cButton.mode(PullDown);
20     dButton.mode(PullDown);
21
22     alarmLed = OFF;
23
24     bool alarmState = OFF;
25
26     while (true) {
27
28         if ( gasDetector || overTempDetector ) {
29             alarmState = ON;
30         }
31
32         alarmLed = alarmState;
33
34         if ( aButton && bButton && !cButton && !dButton) {
35             alarmState = OFF;
36         }
37     }
38 }
```

Include the libraries "mbed.h" and "arm_book_lib.h"

- Digital input objects named *gasDetector*, *overTempDetector* and *aButton* to *dButton*, are declared and assigned to D2 to D7, respectively.
- Digital output object named *alarmLed* is declared and assigned to LED1.
- *gasDetector*, *overTempDetector* and *aButton* to *dButton* are configured with internal pull-down resistors.
- *alarmLed* is assigned OFF.
- *alarmState* is declared and assigned OFF.

Do forever loop:
- If *gasDetector* or *overTempDetector* is pressed, assign *alarmState* with ON.
- Assign *alarmLed* with *alarmState*.
- If *aButton* and *bButton* are pressed, and neither *cButton* nor *dButton* are pressed, assign *alarmState* with OFF.

Code 1.4 Implementation of Example 1.4.

Proposed Exercises

1. How can the code be changed in such a way that the alarm is turned off by means of pressing the buttons connected to D6 and D7, while the buttons connected to D4 and D5 are not pressed?

2. How can the code be changed in such a way that the alarm is turned off by means of pressing the buttons connected to D4, D5, and D6, while the button connected to D7 is not pressed?

Answers to the Exercises

1. It can be achieved by means of the changes in Table 1.8.

2. It can be achieved by means of the changes in Table 1.9.

Table 1.8 Proposed modifications in the code in order to achieve the new behavior.

Lines in Code 1.4	New code to be used
34 if (aButton && bButton && !cButton && !dButton)	34 if (!aButton && !bButton && cButton && dButton)

Table 1.9 Proposed modifications in the code in order to achieve the new behavior.

Lines in Code 1.4	New code to be used
34 if (aButton && bButton && !cButton && !dButton)	34 if (aButton && bButton && cButton && !dButton)

Example 1.5: Block the System when Five Incorrect Codes are Entered

Objective

Introduce nested *ifs* and the usage of non-Boolean variables to count the number of iterations.

Summary of the Expected Behavior

If five wrong passwords are introduced, the system is blocked.

Test the Proposed Solution on the Board

Import the project "Example 1.5" using the URL available in [10], build the project, and drag the *.bin* file onto the NUCLEO board. Then press and release the buttons connected to D2 or to D3 and look at the behavior of LD1. LD1 should turn on. If buttons A, B, and Enter (D4, D5, and B1 USER Button) are pressed, LD1 will turn off. Again, press and release the buttons connected to D2 or to D3. LD1 should turn on. If another combination of buttons is pressed (for instance A and B1 USER) the LD3 (Incorrect code) will turn on. A new combination of buttons can be tried after all four buttons connected to D4–D7 are pressed simultaneously. The fifth time that an incorrect combination of buttons is entered, LD2 (System blocked) will turn on, indicating that the system has been blocked. Press the reset button to reset the NUCLEO board and turn off the System blocked LED.

A summary of the buttons that have to be pressed in each case is shown in Table 1.10.

Table 1.10 Summary of the smart home system buttons that should be pressed in each case.

Functionality	Buttons that should be pressed	Corresponding DigitalIn
To test if a given code turns off the Alarm LED	Any of A, B, C, and/or D + Enter	(D4, D5, D6, D7) + BUTTON1
The correct code that turns off the Alarm LED	A + B + Enter	D4 + D5 + BUTTON1
To turn off the Incorrect code LED and enable a new attempt to turn off the Alarm LED	A + B + C + D	D4 + D5 + D6 + D7
To turn off the System Blocked LED (that is turned on after entering five incorrect passwords)	No buttons available (power should be removed or B2 RESET button pressed)	

Discussion of the Proposed Solution

In Example 1.4 there was no limit to the number of incorrect combinations of buttons that could be entered. In this example, the system is blocked when five incorrect combinations are entered. In order to count the number of incorrect combinations entered, *non-Boolean* variables are introduced. Non-Boolean variables can be used to store integer or non-integer numbers depending on the specific type used, as discussed below.

Figure 1.17 shows the proposed main parts to implement the solution of this example. In the *Libraries, Definitions and Global Declarations and Initializations* (Figure 1.17 [a]), the *mbed.h* and *arm_book_lib.h* libraries are included. In the *Declarations and Initializations of the main() function* (Figure 1.17 [b]), several inputs are declared and assigned to D2, D3, D4, D5, D6, D7, and BUTTON1; several outputs are declared and assigned to LD1, LD2, and LD3; the variable *alarmState* is declared and initialized to OFF; and the variable *numberOfIncorrectCodes* is declared and initialized to 0.

The repetitive block (Figure 1.17 [c]) is made up of three blocks: a block indicated in brown, which assigns *ON* to *alarmState* if *gasDetector* or *overTempDetector* is active; a block indicated in orange, which assigns the value of *alarmState* to *alarmLed*; and a block indicated in violet. In the violet block, if *numberOfIncorrectCodes* has reached five, the system is blocked. If *numberOfIncorrectCodes* has not reached five, then it checks if the user wants to enter a new code to turn off the alarm. If so, it checks if the entered code is correct in order to turn off the alarm LED. The *incorrectCodeLed* (LD2) is turned on if an incorrect code is entered.

Figure 1.18 shows the details of the blocks that comprise the repetitive block. In this case, only the block indicated in violet is included because the brown and orange blocks are the same as in Figure 1.14 (a) and Figure 1.14 (b), respectively.

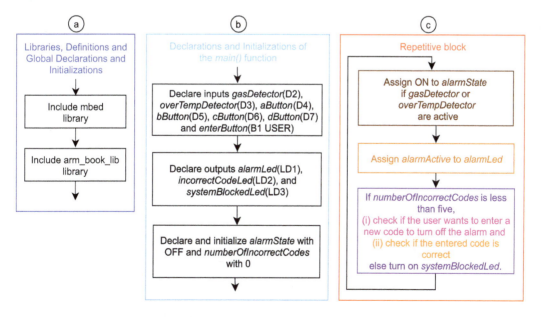

Figure 1.17 Main parts of the program of Example 1.5.

Figure 1.18 shows that the first step is to evaluate if *numberOfIncorrectCodes* is less than five. If five or more incorrect codes have been entered, then the system is blocked, and the System blocked LED is turned on. Buttons are not checked any more, and the only way to unblock the system is to turn off the power supply.

If *numberOfIncorrectCodes* is less than five, a check is made to see if buttons A, B, C, and D are all pressed at the same time, while the Enter button is not pressed, which means that the user wants to enter a code to turn off the alarm. In this case, the Incorrect code LED is turned off.

Next, it is assessed whether the following conditions are all accomplished at the same time: i) the Enter button is being pressed, ii) the Incorrect code LED is OFF, iii) the alarm is ON. In this way, it is determined if the user wants to enter a code (recall Table 1.10), and that a code can be entered (i.e., Incorrect code LED is off) and that a code must be entered (the alarm is ON).

If that is the case, to turn off the Alarm LED, buttons A and B should be pressed, while buttons C and D are not pressed. In this case, OFF is assigned to *alarmState* and *numberOfIncorrectCodes* is set to 0.

If any other combination of buttons A, B, C, and D is entered then the Incorrect code LED is turned on and *numberOfIncorrectCodes* is incremented by one.

NOTE: It is important to mention that this is the first time in this book that an *if* condition is evaluated inside of another *if* condition. This grouping of *if* statements is known as *nested ifs*.

WARNING: Two *if* conditions can also be evaluated one after the other, no matter the result of the first *if* condition. In this case, the structure does not correspond to a nested *if*.

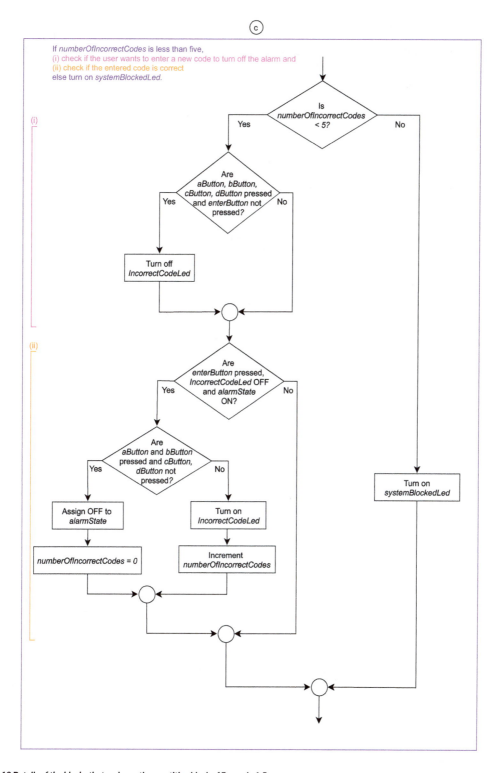

Figure 1.18 Details of the blocks that make up the repetitive block of Example 1.5.

Implementation of the Proposed Solution

In Code 1.5 the implementation of the proposed solution is presented. The parts corresponding to Figure 1.17 and Figure 1.18 are highlighted in different colors. An explanation of each part is also included beside the source code.

It is important to emphasize that all the considerations regarding the nested *if* discussed above correspond to lines 40 to 58 in Code 1.5. These lines are not discussed here because their behavior has already been discussed in detail in the explanation regarding Figure 1.18.

```
1  #include "mbed.h"
2  #include "arm_book_lib.h"
3
4  int main()
5  {
6      DigitalIn enterButton(BUTTON1);
7      DigitalIn gasDetector(D2);
8      DigitalIn overTempDetector(D3);
9      DigitalIn aButton(D4);
10     DigitalIn bButton(D5);
11     DigitalIn cButton(D6);
12     DigitalIn dButton(D7);
13
14     DigitalOut alarmLed(LED1);
15     DigitalOut incorrectCodeLed(LED3);
16     DigitalOut systemBlockedLed(LED2);
17
18     gasDetector.mode(PullDown);
19     overTempDetector.mode(PullDown);
20     aButton.mode(PullDown);
21     bButton.mode(PullDown);
22     cButton.mode(PullDown);
23     dButton.mode(PullDown);
24
25     alarmLed = OFF;
26     incorrectCodeLed = OFF;
27     systemBlockedLed = OFF;
28
29     bool alarmState = OFF;
30     int numberOfIncorrectCodes = 0;
31
32     while (true) {
33
34         if ( gasDetector || overTempDetector ) {
35             alarmState = ON;
36         }
37
38         alarmLed = alarmState;
39
40         if ( numberOfIncorrectCodes < 5 ) {
41
42             if ( aButton && bButton && cButton && dButton && !enterButton ) {
43                 incorrectCodeLed = OFF;
44             }
45
46             if ( enterButton && !incorrectCodeLed && alarmState) {
47                 if ( aButton && bButton && !cButton && !dButton ) {
48                     alarmState = OFF;
49                     numberOfIncorrectCodes = 0;
50                 } else {
51                     incorrectCodeLed = ON;
52                     numberOfIncorrectCodes = numberOfIncorrectCodes + 1;
53                 }
54             }
55         } else {
56             systemBlockedLed = ON;
57         }
58     }
59 }
```

Include the libraries "mbed.h" and "arm_book_lib.h"

- Digital input objects named *gasDetector*, *overTempDetector* and *aButton* to *dButton*, are declared and assigned to D2 to D7, respectively.
- Digital output objects named *alarmLed* *incorrectCodeLed*, and *systemBlockedLed* are declared and assigned to LED1, LED2 and LED3, respectively.
- *gasDetector*, *overTempDetector* and *aButton* to *dButton* are configured with internal pull-down resistors.
- *alarmLed*, *incorrectCodeLed*, and *systemBlockedLed* are assigned OFF.
- *alarmState* is declared and assigned OFF.
- *numberOfIncorrectCodes* is declared and assigned 0 (zero).

Do forever loop:
- If *gasDetector* or *overTempDetector* are active, assign *alarmState* with ON.
- Assign *alarmLed* with *alarmState*.
- If *numberOfIncorrectCodes* is less than five, implement the logic (discussed in the text) in order to determine the state of *incorrectCodeLed* and if *alarmState* must be assigned with OFF, and if *numberOf-IncorrectCodes* must be set to 0 (zero) or increased by 1.
- If *numberOfIncorrectCodes* is greater than or equal to five, assign *systemBlockedLed* with ON.

Code 1.5 Implementation of Example 1.5.

Proposed Exercise

1. How can the code be changed in such a way that the system is blocked after three incorrect codes are entered?

Answer to the Exercise

1. It can be achieved by means of the change in Table 1.11.

Table 1.11 Proposed modification in the code in order to achieve the new behavior.

Line in Code 1.5	New code to be used
`40 if ( numberOfIncorrectCodes < 5 )`	`40 if ( numberOfIncorrectCodes < 3 )`

1.3 Under the Hood

1.3.1 Brief Introduction to the Cortex-M Processor Family and the NUCLEO Board

In this chapter, many programs were developed using the NUCLEO board, provided with the STM32F429ZIT6U microcontroller. This microcontroller is manufactured by STMicroelectronics [13] using a Cortex-M4 processor designed by Arm Ltd. [14]. In order to support some concepts that were introduced through this chapter, as well as concepts that will be presented in the following chapters, in this subsection a brief introduction to Cortex-M processors and some details on the NUCLEO board are provided.

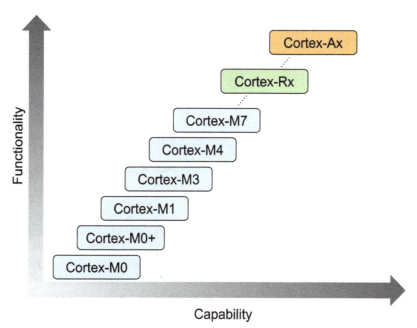

Figure 1.19 Simplified diagram of the Cortex processor family.

In Figure 1.19, a simplified diagram of the Cortex family of processors is shown. The Cortex-M processors are the most energy-efficient embedded devices of the family and have the lowest cost; therefore, they are typically used in microcontrollers and sensors. The Cortex-Rx are robust real-time performance processors, ideal for automotive and safety-critical applications. The Cortex-Ax processors have supreme performance and are used in smartphones, computers, and high-end microprocessors.

NOTE: The Cortex-M family currently has more than ten members (a list is available from [15]), and only six of them are shown in the diagram. In addition, the "Cortex-Rx" and "Cortex-Ax" frames represent whole families, which at the time of writing have half a dozen members and over twenty members, respectively.

In this Under the Hood section, only the Cortex-M0, Cortex-M3, and Cortex-M4 processors are analyzed, because they are more likely to be the processors used in the microcontrollers for elementary embedded systems projects. These processors are primarily focused on delivering highly deterministic behavior in a wide range of power-sensitive applications.

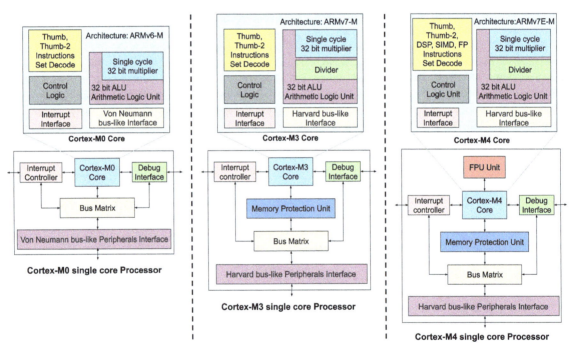

Figure 1.20 Simplified diagram of the Cortex M0, M3, and M4 processors, and details of the corresponding cores.

In Figure 1.20, diagrams of the Cortex-M0, M3, and M4 processors are shown, as well as some details of their corresponding cores. It can be appreciated how there are some similarities among the processors, such as interruption handling (a topic that will be discussed later in this book), and some differences, for example:

- The Cortex-M0 is Von Neumann bus-like (one bus for data/instruction), while the Cortex-M3 and M4 are Harvard bus-like (data and instruction in separate buses), which allows for faster communication.

- The Cortex-M3 and M4 processors have a Memory Protection Unit, which allows safer operation.

- The Cortex-M4 has a larger set of instructions and has a Floating Point Unit (FPU), which speeds up certain calculations because the FPU is used instead of using a multitude of elementary operations.

To indicate the complexity of the different cores, Figure 1.21 shows the set of instructions that each of the cores can process. This is called the *Instruction Set Architecture* (ISA). It can be seen that the Cortex-M0 core implements a reduced number of instructions, while the Cortex-M3 core handles those instructions and incorporates many more instructions, and the Cortex-M4 incorporates even more. Instructions added in the Cortex-M7 are shown in Figure 1.21 to stress that more advanced and powerful cores are available in the Cortex-M family, as shown in [16]. Those cores are not used in this book, hence are not discussed here.

Floating Point (Cortex-M4 FPU) — top band:

VABS	VADD	VCMP	VCMPE	VCVT	VCVTR	VCVTB	VCVTT	VDIV

DSP (SIMD, fast MAC) — Cortex-M4:

PKHBT	PKHTB	QADD	QADD16	QADD8	QASX	QDADD	QDSUB
QSAX	QSUB	QSUB16	QSUB8	SADD16	SADD8	SASX	SEL
SHADD16	SHADD8	SHASX	SHSAX	SHSUB16	SHSUB8	SMLABB	SMLABT
SMLATB	SMLATT	SMLAD	SMLADX	SMLALBB	SMLALBT	SMLALTB	SMLALTT
SMLALD	SMLALDX	SMLAWB	SMLAWT	SMLSD	SMLSDX	SMLSLD	SMLSLDX
SMMLA	SMMLAR						
SMMLS	SMMLSR						
SMMUL	SMMULR						
SMUAD	SMUADX						
SMULBB	SMULBT						
SMULTB	SMULTT						
SMULWB	SMULWT						
SMUSD	SMUSDX						
SSAT16	SSAX						
SSUB16	SSUB8						
SXTAB	SXTAB16						
SXTAH	UADD16						
UADD8	UASX						
UHADD16	UHSUB8						
UMAAL	UQADD16						
UQADD8	UQASX						
UQSAX	UQSUB16						
UQSUB8	USAD8						
USADA8	USAT16						
USAX	USUB16						
USUB8	UXTAB						
UXTAB16	UXTAH						
UXTB16							

Advanced data processing / bit field manipulations — Cortex-M3:

ADC	ADD	ADR	AND	ASR	B
BFC	BFI	BIC	CBNZ CBZ	CDP	CDP2
CLREX	CLZ	CMN	CMP	DBG	EOR
LDC	LDC2	LDMIA	LDMDB	LDR	LDRB
LDRBT	LDRD	LDREX	LDREXB	LDREXH	LDRH
LDRHT	LDRSB	LDRSBT	LDRSH	LDRT	LSL
LSR	MCR	MCR2	MCRR	MCRR2	MLA
MLS	MOV	MOVT	MRC	MRC2	MRRC
MRRC2	MUL	MVN	NOP	ORN	ORR
PLD	PLI	POP	PUSH	RBIT	REV
REV16	REVSH	ROR	RRX	RSB	SBC
SBFX	SDIV	SEV	SMLAL	SMULL	SSAT
STC	STC2	STMIA			
STMDB	STR	STRB			
STRBT	STRD	STREX			
STREXB	STREXH	STRH			
STRHT	STRT	SUB			
SXTB	SXTH	TBB			
TBH	TEQ	TST			
UBFX	UDF	UDIV			
UMLAL	UMULL	USAT			
UXTB	UXTH	WFE			
WFI	YIELD	IT			

General data processing / I/O control tasks — Cortex-M0:

ADC	ADD	ADR	AND	ASR	B
BIC	BKPT	BL	BLX	BX	
CMN	CMP	CPS	DMB	EOR	
DSB	ISB	LDMIA	LDR		
LDRB	LDRH	LDRSB	LDRSH	LSL	LSR
MOV	MRS	MSR	MUL		
MVN	NOP	ORR	POP	PUSH	REV
REV16	REVSH	ROR	RSB	SBC	SEV
STMIA	STR	STRB	STRH	SUB	SVC
SXTB	SXTH	TST	UDF	UXTB	UXTH
WFE	WFI	YIELD			

Floating Point — Cortex-M4 FPU (VDIV column):

VDIV, VFMA, VFMS, VFNMA, VFNMS, VLDM, VLDR, VMLA, VMLS, VMOV, VMRS, VMSR, VMUL, VNEG, VNMLA, VNMLS, VNMUL, VPOP, VPUSH, VSQRT, VSTM, VSTR, VSUB

Floating Point FPv5 — Cortex-M7 FPU:

VCVTA, VCVTN, VCVTP, VCVTM, VMAXNM, VMINNM, VRINTA, VRINTN, VRINTP, VRINTM, VRINTX, VRINTZ, VRINTR, VSEL

Figure legend:

General data processing I/O control tasks	Advanced data processing bit field manipulations	DSP (SIMD, fast MAC)	Floating Point	Floating Point FPv5

Figure 1.21 Arm Cortex M0, M3, and M4 Instruction Set Architecture (ISA).

The instructions shown in Figure 1.21 are in assembly language (also called assembler language), which is not as easy to read and write for programmers as the C/C++ language. Thus, a program called a *compiler* is used to automatically translate C/C++ language code into the corresponding assembly language code. The compiler also verifies that the C/C++ language code complies with the language rules defined in the standards. If there is a syntax issue, the compiler cannot generate the assembly code and an error is indicated to the programmer. Keil Studio Cloud includes all these features.

TIP: Don't worry about needing to learn assembly language, it is not used in most elementary projects.

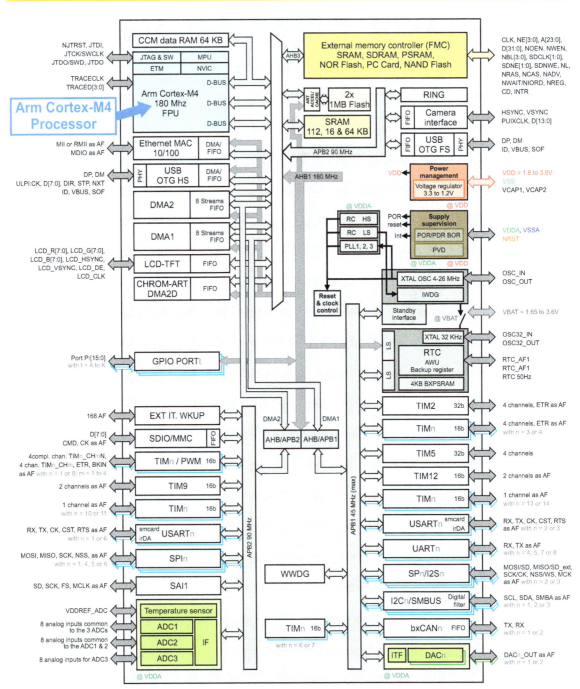

Figure 1.22 STM32F429ZI block diagram made using information available from [9].

The STM32F429ZIT6U microcontroller includes a Cortex-M4 processor, as shown in Figure 1.22. It can be appreciated that, beyond the processor, the microcontroller includes other peripherals such as communication cores (ethernet, USB, UART, etc.), memory, timers, and GPIO (General Purpose Input Output) ports.

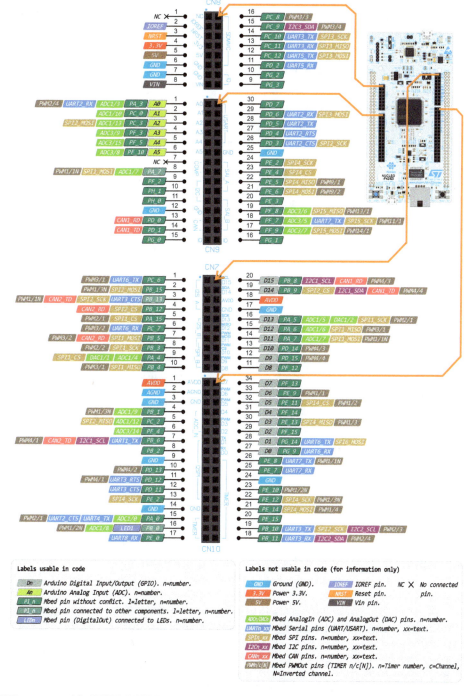

Figure 1.23 ST Zio connectors of the NUCLEO-F429ZI board.

Figure 1.23 shows how different elements of the STM32F429ZIT6U microcontroller are mapped to the Zio and Arduino-compatible headers of the NUCLEO-F429ZI board. Some other elements are mapped to the CN11 and CN12 headers of the NUCLEO-F429ZI board, as will be discussed in upcoming chapters. Further information on these headers is available from [17].

In this chapter, buttons were connected to the NUCLEO board using pins D2 to D7. From Figure 1.23, it can be seen that those digital inputs can also be referred to as PF_15, PE_13, P_14, PE_11, PE_9, and PF_13, respectively. Throughout this book, many pins of the ST Zio connectors will be used, and they will be referred to in the code using the names shown in Figure 1.23.

 WARNING: Keil Studio Cloud translates the C/C++ language code into assembly code while considering the available resources of the target board. For this reason, the reader should be very careful to use only pin names that are shown in Figure 1.23.

From the above discussion, it is possible to derive the hierarchy that is represented in Figure 1.24. It should be noted that a given Arm processor can be used by different microcontroller manufacturers, and a given microcontroller can be used in different development boards or embedded systems.

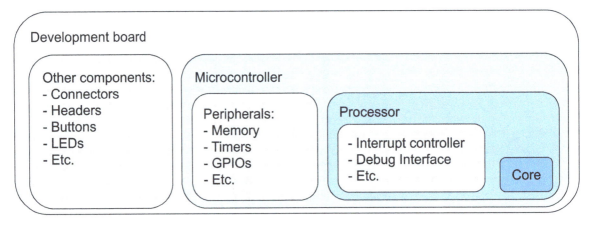

Figure 1.24 Hierarchy of different elements introduced in this chapter.

 NOTE: A microcontroller may have one or many processors, while a processor may have one or many cores. A microprocessor consists of the processor, named in this context as the Central Processing Unit (CPU), and uses an external bus to interface with memory and peripherals.

Proposed Exercise

1. How can the code of Example 1.5 be modified in order to use the alternative names of D2 to D7?

Answer to the Exercise

1. It can be achieved by means of the changes shown in Table 1.12.

Table 1.12 Proposed modifications in the code in order to use the alternative names of D2 to D7.

Lines in Code 1.5	New code to be used
2 DigitalIn gasDetector(D2);	2 DigitalIn gasDetector(PF_15);
3 DigitalIn overTempDetector(D3);	3 DigitalIn overTempDetector(PE_13);
4 DigitalIn aButton(D4);	4 DigitalIn aButton(PF_14);
5 DigitalIn bButton(D5);	5 DigitalIn bButton(PE_11);
6 DigitalIn cButton(D6);	6 DigitalIn cButton(PE_9);
7 DigitalIn dButton(D7);	7 DigitalIn dButton(PF_13);

1.4 Case Study

1.4.1 Smart Door Locks

In this chapter, we implemented the functionality to turn on an alarm based on the activation of sensors that were represented by means of buttons. A code was also implemented. A brief view of a commercial "smart door lock" built with Mbed and containing some of these features can be found in [18]. A representation of the system is shown in Figure 1.25.

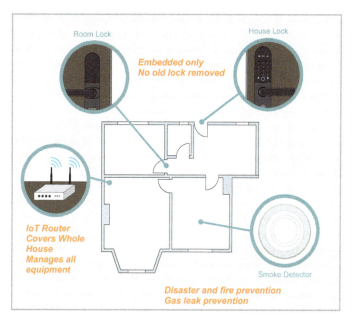

Figure 1.25 "Smart door locks" built with Mbed contains elements introduced in this chapter.

In Figure 1.25 it can be seen that the "smart door lock" has a smoke detector (similar to the gas detector mentioned in this chapter) and a locking system that employs passwords. The system was developed using Mbed OS and is based on a Cortex-M4 core. It is important to highlight that the STM32 microcontroller of the NUCLEO board is also based on a Cortex-M4 core.

Proposed Exercises

1. Are there buttons in Figure 1.25? Where are they located?

2. How is the password entered? Is it like in Example 1.4?

Answers to the Exercises

1. A keypad to enter the password can be seen in Figure 1.25, but there are no switches under the numbers. Instead, ultra-thin capacitive fingerprints are used.

2. The password is entered by pressing the numbers one after the other (not simultaneously like in Example 1.4). Later in this book, it will be explained how to implement a sequential reading of a matrix keypad.

References

[1] "NUCLEO-F429ZI - STMicroelectronics". Accessed July 9, 2021.
https://os.mbed.com/platforms/ST-Nucleo-F429ZI/

[2] "Introduction - Mbed OS 6 | Mbed OS 6 documentation". Accessed July 9, 2021.
https://os.mbed.com/docs/mbed-os/v6.12/introduction/index.html

[3] "Arm Keil | Cloud-based Development Tools for IoT, ML and Embedded". Accessed July 9, 2021.
https://www.keil.arm.com/

[4] "Log In | Mbed". Accessed July 9, 2021.
https://os.mbed.com/account/login/

[5] "Keil Studio". Accessed July 9, 2021.
https://studio.keil.arm.com/

[6] "Documentation - Arm Developer". Accessed July 9, 2021.
https://developer.arm.com/documentation

[7] "Arm Mbed Studio". Accessed July 9, 2021.
https://os.mbed.com/studio/

[8] "STM32CudeIDE - Integrated Development Environment". Accessed July 9, 2021.
https://www.st.com/en/development-tools/stm32cubeide.html

[9] "STM32F429ZI - High-performance advanced line, Arm Cortex-M4". Accessed July 9, 2021.
https://www.st.com/en/microcontrollers-microprocessors/stm32f429zi.html

[10] "GitHub - armBookCodeExamples/Directory". Accessed July 9, 2021.
https://github.com/armBookCodeExamples/Directory/

[11] "cplusplus.com - The C++ Resources Network". Accessed July 9, 2021.
https://www.cplusplus.com/

[12] "Indentation style - Wikipedia". Accessed July 9, 2021.
https://en.wikipedia.org/wiki/Indentation_style

[13] "Home - STMicroelectronics". Accessed July 9, 2021.
https://www.st.com/

[14] "Artificial Intelligence Enhanced Computing - Arm". Accessed July 9, 2021.
https://www.arm.com/

[15] "Microprocessors Cores and Technology - Arm". Accessed July 9, 2021.
https://www.arm.com/products/silicon-ip-cpu

[16] "ARM Cortex-M7: Bringing High Performance to the Cortex-M Processor Series. Accessed July
9, 2021.
http://www.armtechforum.com.cn/2014/bj/B-1_BringingHighPerformancetotheCortex-
MProcessorSeries.pdf

[17] "NUCLEO-F429ZI | Mbed". Accessed July 9, 2021.
https://os.mbed.com/platforms/ST-Nucleo-F429ZI/#zio-and-arduino-compatible-headers

[18] "Smart door locks | Mbed". Accessed July 9, 2021.
https://os.mbed.com/built-with-mbed/smart-door-locks/

Chapter 2

Fundamentals of Serial Communication

2.1 Roadmap

2.1.1 What You Will Learn

After you have studied the material in this chapter, you will be able to:

- Use a serial terminal to communicate between the NUCLEO board and a PC.

- Implement programs to use the UART of the microcontroller to share data between the NUCLEO board and a PC.

- Describe basic concepts about serial communications.

2.1.2 Review of Previous Chapter

In Chapter 1, the basic concepts of embedded systems programming were introduced. The reader was able to load different programs onto the microcontroller of the NUCLEO board, understand how they work, and modify their behavior using the Keil Studio Cloud application.

It was also explained how to expand the functionality of the NUCLEO board using the ST Zio connectors, a breadboard, jumper wires, and buttons. By means of these elements, a representation of a smart home system was implemented and was provided with different features, including a password code to deactivate the alarm once it was activated.

Finally, a brief introduction to the Cortex-M processor family and the NUCLEO board was presented.

2.1.3 Contents of This Chapter

This chapter will explain how to set up the NUCLEO board to communicate with a PC. This will be done by means of the *UART (Universal Asynchronous Receiver Transmitter)* of the STM32 microcontroller of the NUCLEO board, which is accessed via a USB connection with the PC.

The concepts *software maintainability, code modularization, functions, switch statements, for loops, define,* and *arrays,* among others, will be introduced in the examples for this chapter.

This chapter will also show how to use a *serial terminal* to visualize the information exchange between the PC and the NUCLEO board. By means of the serial terminal it will be possible to visualize different parameters and to configure and operate the smart home system being implemented with the NUCLEO board.

2.2 Serial Communication between a PC and the NUCLEO Board

2.2.1 Connect the Smart Home System to a PC

In this chapter, the smart home system will be connected to a PC, as shown in Figure 2.1. This will be done by means of serial communication using a USB cable. The aim of this setup is to monitor and configure the smart home system from the PC.

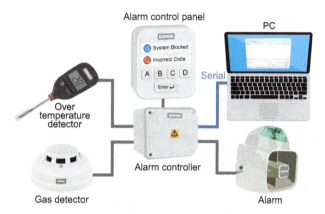

Figure 2.1 The smart home system is now connected to a PC.

It is important to notice that in this chapter nothing new has to be connected to the NUCLEO board in order to implement the smart home system shown in Figure 2.1, because the USB cable has already been connected in the previous chapter to load programs onto the microcontroller of the NUCLEO board, and because buttons are still used in this chapter to simulate the activation of the over temperature detector and the gas detector.

 WARNING: to implement the examples in this chapter, and also to test the serial communication with the PC as explained in the following subsection, it is crucial to be sure that everything is connected just as in Figure 1.5.

In order to test the serial communication between the PC and the NUCLEO board, the *.bin* file of the program "Subsection 2.2.1" should be downloaded from the URL available in [1] and dragged onto the NUCLEO board.

To monitor and manage the serial communication data exchange between the PC and the NUCLEO board, usually a piece of software called a *serial terminal* is used. The reader may choose any serial terminal of their preference from the hundreds of options available on the internet.

 NOTE: At the time of writing this book, the serial terminal embedded in Keil Studio Cloud does not support ST devices. When Keil Studio Cloud includes serial terminal support for ST devices, the corresponding instructions will be published in [1]. In that way the reader will be able to use Keil Studio Cloud to test the programs used in this book and will not have to download and install a separate serial terminal.

TIP: Given that the serial terminal will be used only for very basic operations, it is convenient for the reader to choose a serial terminal that is as simple as possible. In this way, just a few configurations will be needed. Tutorials about how to configure and use each serial terminal are available on the internet.

WARNING: It is crucial to ensure that in the serial terminal, the *baud rate* is configured to "115200", data bits is set to "8", parity to "none", stop bits to "1", handshaking to "none", and to send character <CR> (Carriage Return, '\r') when the Enter key is pressed. In the Under the Hood subsection, the meaning of these parameters is explained. It is also important to select in the serial terminal the "COM port" assigned by the operating system to the NUCLEO board.

To test if the serial terminal is working as expected, press the B2 RESET button of the NUCLEO board. A "Hello" message should appear on the serial terminal. In this way it is confirmed that the NUCLEO board is properly sending data and that this data is being received by the PC.

TIP: If the "Hello" message is not displayed on the serial terminal, then select another COM port and press the B2 RESET button. Repeat this operation with all the available COM ports until the "Hello" message appears on the serial terminal.

NOTE: This chapter does not discuss how each of the characters that are transferred between the PC and the NUCLEO board (for example, 'H', 'e', 'l', 'l', and 'o') are codified using the ASCII standard. This topic is addressed in Chapter 6.

To continue with the test, hold the B1 USER button of the NUCLEO board. The NUCLEO board should send the message "Button pressed" to the PC, and it should be displayed on the serial terminal.

To finish the test, release the B1 USER button of the NUCLEO board. The NUCLEO board sends the message "Button released" to the PC, and this message should be displayed on the serial terminal.

NOTE: It is important to note that the aim of this subsection is to test the serial communication between the NUCLEO board and the PC. For that reason, the details of the program being used in the testing and the technical background about serial communications are not presented in this subsection. These topics are addressed in the examples and in the Under the Hood section of this chapter.

NOTE: The text in the serial terminal is not erased until it is closed. Even if the B2 RESET button is pressed on the NUCLEO board, the previous messages will remain visible on the serial terminal.

2.2.2 Modularization of a Program into Functions

In Example 1.5, Code 2.1, shown below, was presented. If even more functionality is included in the smart home system, then the code will become longer, and its behavior will become difficult to understand.

```
1    #include "mbed.h"
2    #include "arm_book_lib.h"
3
4    int main()
5    {
6        DigitalIn enterButton(BUTTON1);
7        DigitalIn gasDetector(D2);
8        DigitalIn overTempDetector(D3);
9        DigitalIn aButton(D4);
10       DigitalIn bButton(D5);
11       DigitalIn cButton(D6);
12       DigitalIn dButton(D7);
13
14       DigitalOut alarmLed(LED1);
15       DigitalOut incorrectCodeLed(LED3);
16       DigitalOut systemBlockedLed(LED2);
17
18       gasDetector.mode(PullDown);
19       overTempDetector.mode(PullDown);
20       aButton.mode(PullDown);
21       bButton.mode(PullDown);
22       cButton.mode(PullDown);
23       dButton.mode(PullDown);
24
25       alarmLed = OFF;
26       incorrectCodeLed = OFF;
27       systemBlockedLed = OFF;
28
29       bool alarmState = OFF;
30       int numberOfIncorrectCodes = 0;
31
32       while (true) {
33
34           if ( gasDetector || overTempDetector ) {
35               alarmState = ON;
36           }
37
38           alarmLed = alarmState;
39
40           if ( numberOfIncorrectCodes < 5 ) {
41
42               if ( aButton && bButton && cButton && dButton && !enterButton ) {
43                   incorrectCodeLed = OFF;
44               }
45
```

```
46              if ( enterButton && !incorrectCodeLed   && alarmState ) {
47                  if ( aButton && bButton && !cButton && !dButton ) {
48                      alarmState = OFF;
49                      numberOfIncorrectCodes = 0;
50                  } else {
51                      incorrectCodeLed = ON;
52                      numberOfIncorrectCodes = numberOfIncorrectCodes + 1;
53                  }
54              }
55          } else {
56              systemBlockedLed = ON;
57          }
58      }
59  }
```

Code 2.1 Original code used in Example 1.5.

In order to improve the code understandability, the program will be divided and reorganized into *declarations* and *functions*. In this context, the following definitions apply:

DEFINITION: A *declaration* is a section of code where variables or other elements are declared and, sometimes, initialized.

DEFINITION: A *function* is a piece of code that carries out one or more specific tasks and can be used in a given program one or more times.

The use of functions provides two advantages:

- Code modularization: organizing program code into different modules makes it easier to understand a program, which improves its *maintainability*.

- Code reutilization: the usage of functions avoids the need to write the same piece of code many times. In this way, code size is reduced, and the maintainability of the program is increased.

DEFINITION: *Software maintainability* is defined as the degree to which it is feasible for other programmers to understand, repair, and enhance program code over time.

In Code 2.2 and Code 2.3, the declarations and functions that were identified in Code 2.1, according to the definitions of *declaration* and *function* presented above, are shown.

In Code 2.2, the declaration and initialization of variables and objects is indicated in magenta, and the code that can be grouped into functions in order to improve the code maintainability is indicated in orange.

```
1   #include "mbed.h"                              Libraries
2   #include "arm_book_lib.h"
3
4   int main()
5   {
6       DigitalIn enterButton(BUTTON1);            Declaration and
7       DigitalIn gasDetector(D2);                 initialization of
8       DigitalIn overTempDetector(D3);            local objects
9       DigitalIn aButton(D4);
10      DigitalIn bButton(D5);
11      DigitalIn cButton(D6);
12      DigitalIn dButton(D7);
13
14      DigitalOut alarmLed(LED1);
15      DigitalOut incorrectCodeLed(LED3);
16      DigitalOut systemBlockedLed(LED2);
17
18      gasDetector.mode(PullDown);
19      overTempDetector.mode(PullDown);
20      aButton.mode(PullDown);
21      bButton.mode(PullDown);                    → Function: inputsInit()
22      cButton.mode(PullDown);
23      dButton.mode(PullDown);
24
25      alarmLed = OFF;
26      incorrectCodeLed = OFF;                    → Function: outputsInit()
27      systemBlockedLed = OFF;
28
29      bool alarmState = OFF;                      Declaration and
30      int numberOfIncorrectCodes = 0;            initialization of
31                                                 local variables
```

Code 2.2 Analysis of the first part of the code of Example 1.5.

 NOTE: In this book, the names of functions are stylized using the lower camel case format, as in *inputsInit()*.

In Code 2.3, two different groups of code are identified. One is called *alarmActivationUpdate()* and is used to activate the Alarm LED when gas presence or over temperature is detected. The other is identified as *alarmDeactivationUpdate()* and is responsible for the deactivation of the Alarm LED when the correct code is entered, as well as being responsible for blocking the system if more than five incorrect codes are entered.

```
32        while (true) {
33
34            if ( gasDetector || overTempDetector ) {          Function: alarmActivationUpdate()
35                alarmState = ON;
36            }
37
38            alarmLed = alarmState;                             Function: alarmDeactivationUpdate()
39
40            if ( numberOfIncorrectCodes < 5 ) {
41
42                if ( aButton && bButton && cButton && dButton && !enterButton ) {
43                    incorrectCodeLed = OFF;
44                }
45
46                if ( enterButton && !incorrectCodeLed  && alarmState ) {
47                    if ( aButton && bButton && !cButton && !dButton ) {
48                        alarmState = OFF;
49                        numberOfIncorrectCodes = 0;
50                    } else {
51                        incorrectCodeLed = ON;
52                        numberOfIncorrectCodes = numberOfIncorrectCodes + 1;
53                    }
54                }
55            } else {
56                systemBlockedLed = ON;
57            }
58        }
59    }
```

Code 2.3 Analysis of the second part of the code of Example 1.5.

In Code 2.4, the libraries and declarations that had been identified are presented in a more structured way, following the conclusions obtained from the analysis of Code 2.2.

The code identified in Code 2.2 as "declaration and initialization of local objects" was moved outside the *main()* function and is now located, in Code 2.4, in the section "Declaration and initialization of public global objects." The name given to this section is due to the fact that, by the modification of the location of these objects, they change from being local (only available to the *main()* function) to being global (available to every function in the program).

The same rationale applies to the variables identified in Code 2.2 that are located in Code 2.4 in the section "Declaration and initialization of public global variables."

A section called "Declarations (prototypes) of public functions" is also introduced in Code 2.4. This section was not previously identified in Code 2.2 but is necessary because in the C/C++ language functions have to be declared before using them for the first time (i.e., *calling* them from another function). This declaration is named *function prototype.*

The keyword *void* used in Code 2.4 specifies that the function does not return a value. In Example 2.5, it will be shown that functions can return a value that results, for example, from a mathematical operation.

> **NOTE:** In Code 2.4, single-line comments (indicated by "//") are used for the first time in the book. Comments are completely ignored by C/C++ compilers and can be used to increase software maintainability because the purpose of the code can be explained above the code itself. Multiple-line comments can also be used (they begin with "/*" and end with "*/"). Comments will be extensively used throughout this book, mainly to indicate the beginning of code sections. Many programmers also use comments alongside their code.

```
1    //=====[Libraries]===============================================
2
3    #include "mbed.h"                    Libraries
4    #include "arm_book_lib.h"
5
6    //=====[Declaration and initialization of public global objects]==========
7
8    DigitalIn  enterButton(BUTTON1);      Declaration and initialization of
9    DigitalIn  gasDetector(D2);           public global objects
10   DigitalIn  overTempDetector(D3);
11   DigitalIn  aButton(D4);
12   DigitalIn  bButton(D5);
13   DigitalIn  cButton(D6);
14   DigitalIn  dButton(D7);
15
16   DigitalOut alarmLed(LED1);
17   DigitalOut incorrectCodeLed(LED3);
18   DigitalOut systemBlockedLed(LED2);
19
20   //=====[Declaration and initialization of public global variables]==========
21
22   bool alarmState = OFF;                 Declaration and initialization
23   int numberOfIncorrectCodes = 0;       of public global variables
24
25   //=====[Declarations (prototypes) of public functions]==================
26
27   void inputsInit();                    Declarations (prototypes)
28   void outputsInit();                   of public functions
29
30   void alarmActivationUpdate();
31   void alarmDeactivationUpdate();
32
```

Code 2.4 Libraries and declarations of the modularized version of Example 1.5.

Code 2.5 shows the *main()* function and all the other functions of Code 2.1 after applying the proposed modularization indicated in Code 2.2 and Code 2.3.

The code of the examples that will be introduced in this chapter will be organized as shown in Code 2.4 and Code 2.5.

In this way, all the programs in this chapter will have at least the following parts:

▪ Libraries

▪ Declaration and initialization of public global objects

▪ Declaration and initialization of public global variables

▪ Declarations (prototypes) of public functions

▪ Main function

▪ Implementations of public functions

In the following chapters, some other possibilities for declarations and function prototypes will be also explored.

NOTE: In Chapter 5 this topic will be addressed in greater depth, and it will be explained in more detail how to apply modularization to embedded systems programming.

WARNING: Objects and variables must be declared before being used. The order of the other elements in the program code can be given by conventions and good practices.

```
33   //=====[Main function, the program entry point after power on or reset]=========
34        Implementation of the main() function
35   int main()
36   {
37       inputsInit();
38       outputsInit();
39       while (true) {
40           alarmActivationUpdate();
41           alarmDeactivationUpdate();
42       }
43   }
44
45   //=====[Implementations of public functions]==================================
46        Implementation of inputsInit() function
47   void inputsInit()
48   {
49       gasDetector.mode(PullDown);
50       overTempDetector.mode(PullDown);
51       aButton.mode(PullDown);
52       bButton.mode(PullDown);
53       cButton.mode(PullDown);
54       dButton.mode(PullDown);
55   }
56   Implementation of outputsInit() function
57   void outputsInit()
58   {
59       alarmLed = OFF;
60       incorrectCodeLed = OFF;
61       systemBlockedLed = OFF;
62   }
63        Implementation of alarmActivationUpdate() function
64   void alarmActivationUpdate()
65   {
66       if ( gasDetector || overTempDetector ) {
67           alarmState = ON;
68       }
69       alarmLed = alarmState;
70   }
71              Implementation of alarmDeactivationUpdate() function
72   void alarmDeactivationUpdate()
73   {
74       if ( numberOfIncorrectCodes < 5 ) {
75           if ( aButton && bButton && cButton && dButton && !enterButton ) {
76               incorrectCodeLed = OFF;
77           }
78           if ( enterButton && !incorrectCodeLed  && alarmState ) {
79               if ( aButton && bButton && !cButton && !dButton ) {
80                   alarmState = OFF;
81                   numberOfIncorrectCodes = 0;
82               } else {
83                   incorrectCodeLed = ON;
84                   numberOfIncorrectCodes = numberOfIncorrectCodes + 1;
85               }
86           }
87       } else {
88           systemBlockedLed = ON;
89       }
90   }
```

Code 2.5 Functions of the modularized version of Example 1.5.

Proposed Exercise

1. How can comments be inserted in Code 2.4 and Code 2.5 to document the code above the code itself?

Answer to the Exercise

1. Code 2.6 and Code 2.7 show how detailed comments can be included. The comments between lines 1 to 21 and lines 32 to 47 of Code 2.6, and the comments between lines 3 to 5, 10 to 34, and 38 to 44 of Code 2.7, follow the Doxygen standard. This standard is available from [2] and allows the use of a program to generate a website with the documentation, as shown in Figure 2.2.

 NOTE: In this book, comments as shown in Code 2.6 and Code 2.7 are not included above the code because all the programs are explained in detail in the text. However, the reader is encouraged to include this type of comment above the code of their own programs.

```
1   /*! @mainpage Example 1.5 Modularized and with doxygen comments
2    * @date Friday, January 29, 2021
3    * @authors Pablo Gomez, Ariel Lutenberg and Eric Pernia
4    * @section genDesc General Description
5    *
6    * This is a preliminary implementation of the smart home system, where the
7    * code has been modularized using functions and documented using Doxygen.
8    * The entry point to the program documentation can be found at
9    * this \ref Example_1_5_Modularized_withDoxygenComments.cpp "link"
10   *
11   * @section genRem General Remarks
12   * [Write here relevant information about the program]
13   *
14   * @section changelog Changelog
15   *
16   * |   Date     | Description                                              |
17   * |:----------:|:---------------------------------------------------------|
18   * | 29/01/2021 | First version of program                                 |
19   *
20   *
21   */
22
23   /* Example of comment that follows C/C++ format, but not the doxygen standard */
24
25   //=====[Libraries]==============================================================
26
27   #include "mbed.h"
28   #include "arm_book_lib.h"
29
30   //=====[Declaration and initialization of public global objects]===============
31
32   DigitalIn enterButton(BUTTON1); /**< Object associated to
33                                        Enter key (B1 User Button) */
34   DigitalIn gasDetector(D2);      /**< Object associated to gas detector (D2) */
35   DigitalIn overTempDetector(D3); /**< Object associated to over temperature
36                                        detector (D3) */
37   DigitalIn aButton(D4); /**< Object associated to A key (pin D4) */
38   DigitalIn bButton(D5); /**< Object associated to B key (pin D5) */
39   DigitalIn cButton(D6); /**< Object associated to C key (pin D6) */
40   DigitalIn dButton(D7); /**< Object associated to D key (pin D7) */
41
42   DigitalOut alarmLed(LED1); /**< Output associated to alarm
43                                  led indicator (LD1)*/
44   DigitalOut incorrectCodeLed(LED3); /**< Output associated to incorrect
45                                          code indicator (LD3)*/
46   DigitalOut systemBlockedLed(LED2); /**< Output associated to system blocked
47                                          indicator (LD2)*/
```

Code 2.6 Modularized version of Example 1.5 with comments included over the code (Part 1/3).

```
1   //=====[Declaration and initialization of public global variables]==============
2
3   bool alarmState = OFF;  /**< Alarm state flag */
4   int numberOfIncorrectCodes = 0;  /**< Accounts for the number of incorrect codes
5                                        entered */
6
7   //=====[Declarations (prototypes) of public functions]===========================
8
9   void inputsInit();
10  /**<
11   This function configures gasDetector, overTempDetector and aButton to dButton
12   with internal pull-down resistors.
13   @param none
14  */
15
16  void outputsInit();
17  /**<
18  This function initializes the outputs of the system:
19  -# alarmLed = OFF
20  -# incorrectCodeLed = OFF
21  -# systemBlockedLed = OFF
22  */
23
24  void alarmActivationUpdate();
25  /**<
26  This function assigns ON to alarmLed if gasDetector or overTempDetector are
27  active, and assigns alarmLed with alarmState.
28  */
29
30  void alarmDeactivationUpdate();
31  /**<
32  This function assesses the entered code and controls the activation of
33  alarmLed, incorrectCodeLed, and systemBlockedLed.
34  */
35
36  //=====[Main function, the program entry point after power on or reset]=========
37
38  /**
39   * Calls functions to initialize the declared input and output objects, and to
40   * implement the system behavior.
41   * @param none
42   * @return The returned value represents the success
43   * of application.
44   */
45  int main()
46  {
47      inputsInit();
48      outputsInit();
49      while (true) {
50          alarmActivationUpdate();
51          alarmDeactivationUpdate();
52      }
53      return 0;
54  }
```

Code 2.7 Modularized version of Example 1.5 with comments included over the code (Part 2/3).

NOTE: In line 53 of Code 2.7, the return statement has been included because the main function is expected to return an integer value (line 45), as required by most compilers. Line 53 establishes a return value (zero), which is considered to be the return value corresponding to a successful execution of the program. However, notice that the *while* statement in line 49 is executed forever and, therefore, line 53 is never reached. Thus, in most programs of this book, the "return 0" statement is not included at the end of the *main()* function, despite *main()* being declared as *int main()*.

```
1   //=====[Implementations of public functions]========================================
2
3   void inputsInit()
4   {
5       gasDetector.mode(PullDown);
6       overTempDetector.mode(PullDown);
7       aButton.mode(PullDown);
8       bButton.mode(PullDown);
9       cButton.mode(PullDown);
10      dButton.mode(PullDown);
11  }
12
13  void outputsInit()
14  {
15      alarmLed = OFF;
16      incorrectCodeLed = OFF;
17      systemBlockedLed = OFF;
18  }
19
20  void alarmActivationUpdate()
21  {
22      if ( gasDetector || overTempDetector ) {
23          alarmState = ON;
24      }
25      alarmLed = alarmState;
26  }
27
28  void alarmDeactivationUpdate()
29  {
30      if ( numberOfIncorrectCodes < 5 ) {
31          if ( aButton && bButton && cButton && dButton && !enterButton ) {
32              incorrectCodeLed = OFF;
33          }
34          if ( enterButton && !incorrectCodeLed && alarmState ) {
35              if ( aButton && bButton && !cButton && !dButton ) {
36                  alarmState = OFF     ;
37                  numberOfIncorrectCodes = 0;
38              } else {
39                  incorrectCodeLed = ON;
40                  numberOfIncorrectCodes = numberOfIncorrectCodes + 1;
41              }
42          }
43      } else {
44          systemBlockedLed = ON;
45      }
46  }
```

Code 2.8 Modularized version of Example 1.5 with comments included over the code (Part 3/3).

Figure 2.2 shows the website with the documentation of the program that is generated using Doxygen. The website is available as a *.zip* file from [1]. To navigate to the website, the reader must download the *.zip* file, uncompress it, and double click on the *index.html* file. From [1] the source files that were used to generate the website using Doxygen are also available; these comprise the file *Example_1_5_Modularized_ withDoxygenComments.cpp* and a subset of the Mbed OS files, where for the sake of simplicity and brevity only Mbed OS *entities* that are used in the example were included.

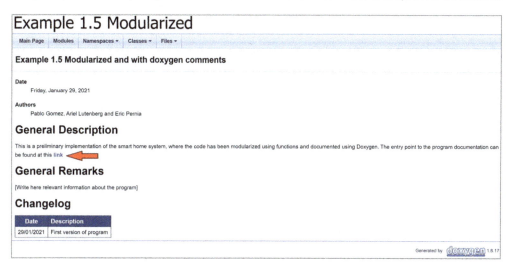

Figure 2.2 Website with the program documentation generated with Doxygen.

By clicking over the link that is highlighted with a red arrow in Figure 2.2, the web page shown in Figure 2.3 is displayed in the web browser. By means of scrolling down this web page, a detailed description of each function and variable based on the Doxygen formatted comments introduced in Code 2.6 and Code 2.7 can be seen, as shown in Figure 2.4 and Figure 2.5.

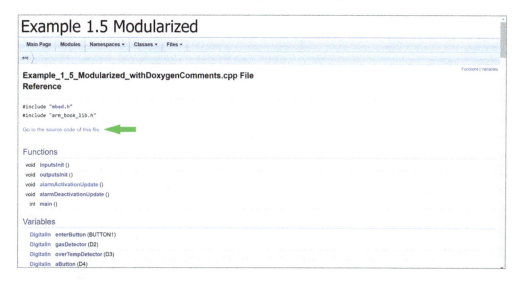

Figure 2.3 Detailed description of functions and variables of the program that is available on the website (Part 1/3).

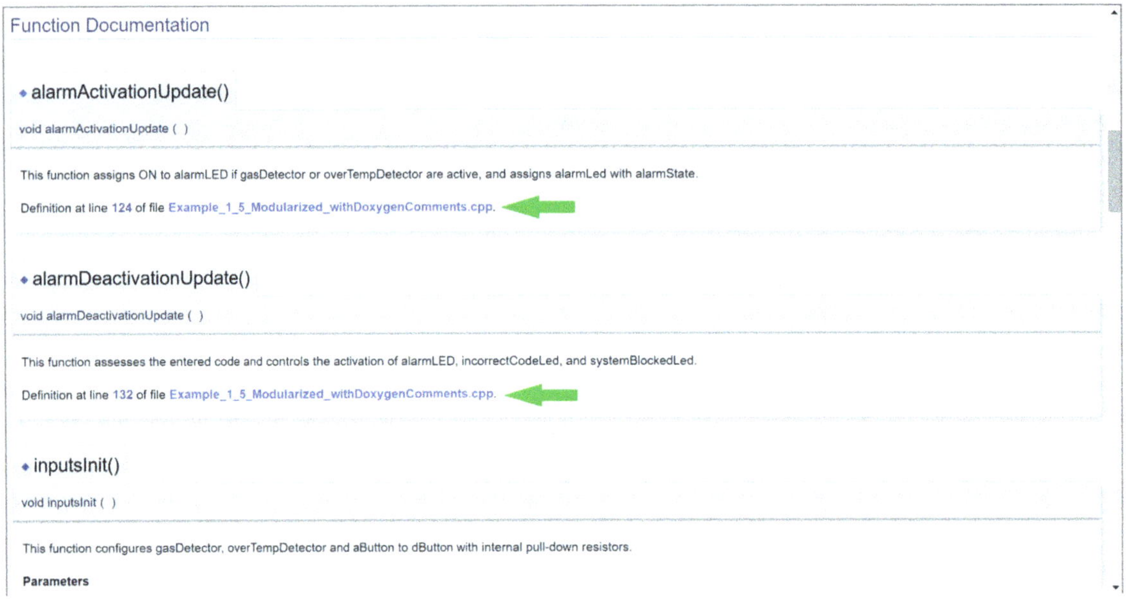

Figure 2.4 Detailed description of functions and variables of the program that is available on the website (Part 2/3).

Figure 2.5 Detailed description of functions and variables of the program that is available on the website (Part 3/3).

By clicking on the green arrows shown in Figure 2.3, Figure 2.4, and Figure 2.5, an interactive view of the code is displayed in the web browser, which grants information about the different elements as well as linking to the corresponding documentation that is available in the website, as shown in Figure 2.6.

Finally, it is worth mentioning that in the "Classes" menu can be found a "Class List" item, where reference information on *DigitalIn* and *DigitalOut* can be accessed, as shown in Figure 2.7. This reference information is a subset of the complete information on Mbed OS elements that can be found in [3], as can be seen in Figure 2.8.

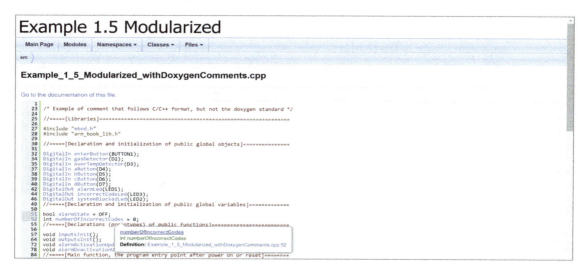

Figure 2.6 Interactive view of the code.

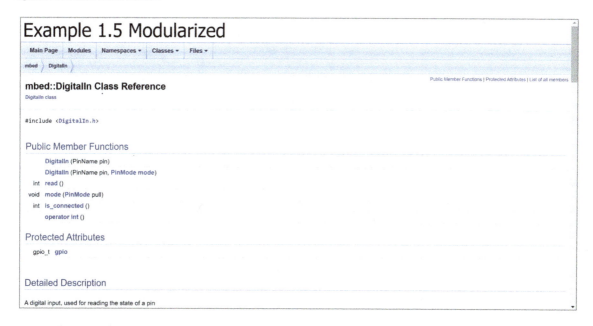

Figure 2.7 DigitalIn class reference.

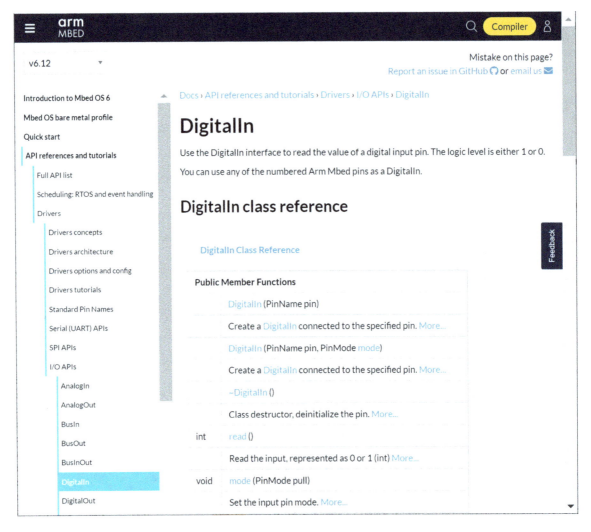

Figure 2.8 Website of Mbed with detailed information about DigitalIn and the whole Application Programming Interface.

Example 2.1: Monitor the Alarm State with a PC

Objective

Introduce functions and methods to exchange data between the NUCLEO board and the PC.

Summary of the Expected Behavior

If key "1" is pressed on the PC, the NUCLEO board sends a message to the PC indicating the alarm state, and the message is printed on the serial terminal.

Test the Proposed Solution on the Board

Import the project "Example 2.1" using the URL available in [1], build the project, and drag the

.bin file onto the NUCLEO board. Open the serial terminal. Read the message that appears on the serial terminal summarizing the list of available commands. Press "1" on the PC keyboard and read the message that appears on the serial terminal regarding the state of the alarm. Press the button connected to D2 that represents gas detection. Press "1" again on the PC and read the message that appears on the serial terminal indicating the new state of the alarm. Press "2" (or any other key) on the PC and read the message that appears on the serial terminal indicating that the only valid command is "1".

Discussion of the Proposed Solution

In this example, the functionality of monitoring the smart home system from a PC using a serial terminal is incorporated. For this purpose, an object that will drive the serial port is declared by means of *UnbufferedSerial uartUsb(USBTX, USBRX, 115200)*, which does not use intermediary buffers to store bytes to transmit to or read from the hardware; thus, the program is responsible for processing each received byte. The parameters USBTX and USBRX indicate that those pins are to be used for transmission and reception of the data of the serial communication, respectively. The parameter 115200 is used to configure the baud rate of the serial communication. In the Under the Hood section of this chapter, the main concepts behind serial communication will be analyzed in more detail.

In the definition of the variables, the data type *char* is used for the variables that are storing characters. This is because Mbed OS uses this data type to store characters. This data type has 8 bits, the same as the data package that is exchanged in each message using the serial communication. This will also be explained in the Under the Hood section of this chapter.

The proposed solution to this example follows the structure that was introduced in Code 2.4 and Code 2.5. Moreover, most of the code used in this proposed solution is the same as the code presented in Code 2.4 and Code 2.5. Therefore, only the differences between those code listings and the code used in this proposed solution will be discussed in the following pages.

A new function called *uartTask()* is used to send and receive information from the PC by means of one of the UARTs of the STM32 microcontroller of the NUCLEO board. The details of the function *uartTask()*, which receives commands from the PC and transmits to the PC the messages that should be displayed on the serial terminal, are presented in Figure 2.9. If there is a new character to be read, it is stored in the variable *receivedChar*. Then, if *receivedChar* is '1', the message reporting the alarm state is sent to the serial terminal. If the received character is not '1', a message containing the list of available commands is sent to the serial terminal. This is shown in Figure 2.9.

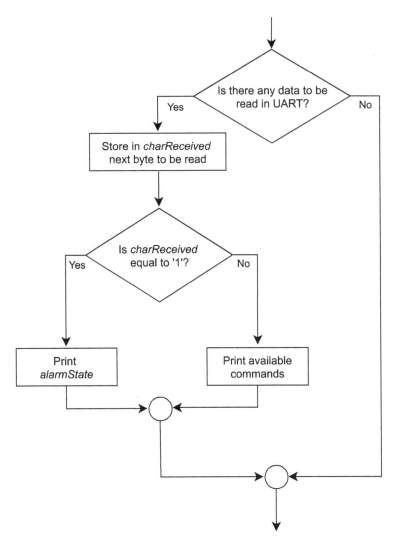

Figure 2.9 Details of the function uartTask() used in this proposed solution to Example 2.1.

Implementation of the Proposed Solution

Lines added in specific sections of the program code presented in Code 2.4 and Code 2.5 are shown in Table 2.1. The three functions that were included are discussed below in this example.

Table 2.1 Sections in which lines were added to Code 2.4 and Code 2.5.

Section	Lines that were added to Code 2.4 and Code 2.5.
Declaration and initialization of public global objects	`UnbufferedSerial uartUsb(USBTX, USBRX, 115200);`
Declarations (prototypes) of public functions	`void uartTask();` `void availableCommands();`

In order to periodically check if there is a new character sent by the PC, a call to the function *uartTask()* is included in the *main()* function, as shown in Code 2.9.

```
1   int main()
2   {
3       inputsInit();
4       outputsInit();
5       while (true) {
6           alarmActivationUpdate();
7           alarmDeactivationUpdate();
8           uartTask();
9       }
10  }
```

Code 2.9 New implementation of main.cpp.

The implementation of *uartTask()* is shown in Code 2.10. On line 3, a variable of type char named *receivedChar* is declared and set to '\0'. The character '\0' is named the null character and represents the zero-element character (i.e., a '\0' written to *uartUsb* is not printed on the serial terminal). The null character has the ASCII code 0, as will be shown on Chapter 6. For that reason, some programmers use 0 instead of '\0'. Confusion should be avoided with character '0', which is used to print '0' on the serial terminal and has the ASCII code 48, as will be shown in Chapter 6. In this book, '\0' is preferred to indicate the null character.

On line 4, *uartUsb.readable()* is used to determine if there is data available to be read in the UART connected to the USB (see Figure 2.1). If so, *uartUsb.read()* is used in line 5 to get the next available character. It uses "&receivedChar" to indicate where to store the character (the meaning of the & will be discussed in chapter 10) and "1" to indicate that one character must be read. In line 6, the read character is compared with '1', which corresponds to the key used in this example to get the alarm state.

If the key pressed is "1", then the state of the alarm is assessed in line 7. If *alarmState* is true, then in line 8 the message "The alarm is activated\r\n" is sent to the PC using *uartUsb.write()*. The "\r\n" at the end of the message is to indicate that the next message should appear on a new line (\n), at the beginning of the line (\r). The number "24" is the number of characters of "The alarm is activated\r\n" that must be sent (in this case, all the characters, considering that each of "\n" and "\r" count as a single character). If *alarmState* is false, then "The alarm is not activated\r\n" is sent on line 10 (note that this message has 28 characters).

If the received character is not '1', then the available commands are printed in line 13 because it is considered that the user has to be informed about the available commands. The implementation of the function *availableCommands()* is shown in Code 2.11. A specific function is used to print the available commands in order to show how a function can call another function, and also because in the following examples more available commands will be incorporated; therefore, it is convenient to have a specific function to print the list of available commands. Notice that "\r\n\r\n" is used on line 4 in order to print a blank line (a line without text).

NOTE: *readable()*, *read()*, and *write()* are part of the "UnbufferedSerial" API. For more functions of the UnbufferedSerial API, refer to [4].

```
1   void uartTask()
2   {
3       char receivedChar = '\0';
4       if( uartUsb.readable() ) {
5           uartUsb.read( &receivedChar, 1 );
6           if ( receivedChar == '1') {
7               if ( alarmState ) {
8                   uartUsb.write( "The alarm is activated\r\n", 24 );
9               } else {
10                  uartUsb.write( "The alarm is not activated\r\n", 28 );
11              }
12          } else {
13              availableCommands();
14          }
15      }
16  }
```

Code 2.10 Details of the function uartTask().

```
1   void availableCommands()
2   {
3       uartUsb.write( "Available command:\r\n", 20 );
4       uartUsb.write( "Press '1' to get the alarm state\r\n\r\n", 36 );
5   }
```

Code 2.11 Details of the function availableCommands().

 NOTE: From this chapter onwards, comments alongside the code (as in Chapter 1) will not be included, because it is considered that the reader does not need them anymore.

Proposed Exercises

1. What would happen if "\r\n" were removed from lines 7 and 9 of Code 2.10?

2. In section 2.2.1, some configurations such as the number of data bits, the parity, and the number of stop bits were mentioned. What function of the UnbufferedSerial API can be used to configure those parameters?

3. How can a report of the state of the gas detector and the over temperature detector be added to the function *uartTask()* using an *if* and *else if* structure?

Answers to the Exercises

1. All the messages would be printed on the same line.

2. The serial communication can be configured using *uartUsb.format()*, as discussed in [4]. In this chapter, there is no need to make this configuration because the default configuration is used, which is 8 bits, no parity, and one stop bit. All the available configurations are summarized in Table 2.2. To make the configuration used in this example, *uartUsb.format(8, SerialBase::None , 1)* should be used.

Table 2.2 Available configurations of the UnbufferedSerial object.

Configuration	Available values	Default value
Number of bits in a word	5, 6, 7, 8	8
Parity used	SerialBase::None, SerialBase::Odd, SerialBase::Even, SerialBase::Forced1, SerialBase::Forced0	SerialBase::None
Number of stop bits	1, 2	1

3. For this purpose, the *if else* structure shown in Code 2.12 could be used.

```
1   void uartTask()
2   {
3       char receivedChar = '\0';
4       if( uartUsb.readable() ) {
5           uartUsb.read( &receivedChar, 1 );
6           if ( receivedChar == '1') {
7               if ( alarmState ) {
8                   uartUsb.write( "The alarm is activated\r\n", 24 );
9               } else {
10                  uartUsb.write( "The alarm is not activated\r\n", 28 );
11              }
12          } else if ( receivedChar == '2') {
13              if ( gasDetector ) {
14                  uartUsb.write( "Gas is being detected\r\n", 23 );
15              } else {
16                  uartUsb.write( "Gas is not being detected\r\n", 27 );
17              }
18          } else if ( receivedChar == '3') {
19              if ( overTempDetector ) {
20                  uartUsb.write( "Temperature is above the maximum level\r\n", 40 );
21              } else {
22                  uartUsb.write( "Temperature is below the maximum level\r\n", 40 );
23              }
24          } else {
25              availableCommands();
26          }
27      }
28  }
```

Code 2.12 Details of the function uartTask() used in the implementation of proposed exercise 3.

Example 2.2: Monitor Over Temperature and Gas Detection with a PC

Objective

Introduce the switch-case statement.

Summary of the Expected Behavior

The expected behavior is similar to Example 2.1, but in this example when key "2" is pressed on the PC, the state of the gas detector is sent to the PC; when key "3" is pressed on the PC, the state of the over temperature detector is sent to the PC. In fact, this is the same behavior as in the second proposed exercise of Example 2.1. The difference is the way in which this behavior will be achieved: not using a group of nested *if*s, but the switch-case statement.

Test the Proposed Solution on the Board

Import the project "Example 2.2" using the URL available in [1], build the project, and drag the *.bin* file onto the NUCLEO board. Open the serial terminal, press "4" on the PC keyboard and read the message that appears on the serial terminal indicating the list of available commands. Press "2" on the PC keyboard and read the message that appears on the serial terminal, indicating that gas is not being detected. Press and hold the button connected to D2 in order to simulate gas detection. Press "2" again on the PC and read the message that appears on the serial terminal, indicating that gas is being detected. Repeat this operation with key "3" and the button connected to D3 to simulate the detection of over temperature.

Discussion of the Proposed Solution

In Example 2.1, the alarm state was reported to the PC by means of serial communication. The aim of this example is to extend the report functionality that was introduced in proposed exercise 3 of Example 2.1. The difference in this proposed solution is the use of the *switch statement*.

In the *switch* statement, a variable is compared in sequence to a list of values. Each value of the list is called a *case*. In this example, the variable being compared is *receivedChar* and there are three cases: '1', '2', and '3'. There is also a *default* case that is executed if none of the cases is equal to the variable being compared.

Even though the behavior is exactly as in proposed exercise 2 of Example 2.1, the reader will be able to see in the code shown below that by using the *switch* statement the code becomes easier to understand.

The flow diagram of the new function *uartTask()* is presented in Figure 2.10. If there is a new character to be read, the corresponding byte is stored in the variable *receivedChar*. Then, *receivedChar* is evaluated by means of the *switch* statement, and the NUCLEO board reports the corresponding value to the PC using the serial communication.

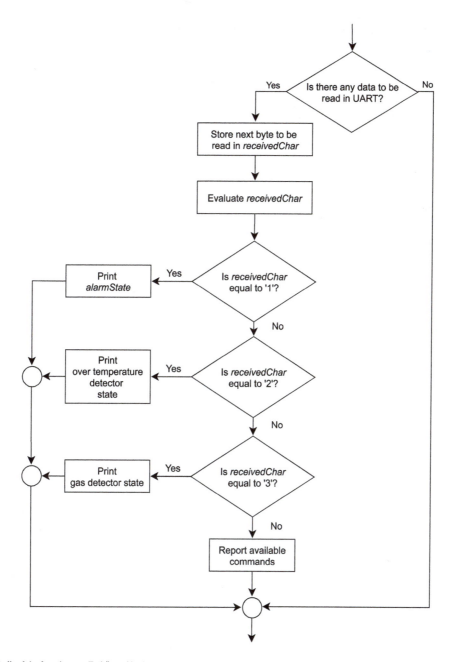

Figure 2.10 Details of the function uartTask() used in the proposed solution to Example 2.2.

Implementation of the Proposed Solution

In Code 2.13, the new implementation of *availableCommands()*, where the new commands are included, is shown. Note that in Code 2.11 there were 36 characters in line 4, while in Code 2.13 there are 34 characters in line 4. This is because only one "\r\n" is used in line 4 of Code 2.13 because the last command listed is now "3" (get the over temperature detector state). In Code 2.14, the new implementation of the function *uartTask()* is presented. The code is very similar to the program code examples discussed earlier, and therefore for the sake of brevity it is not discussed here again.

```
1   void availableCommands()
2   {
3       uartUsb.write( "Available commands:\r\n", 21 );
4       uartUsb.write( "Press '1' to get the alarm state\r\n", 34 );
5       uartUsb.write( "Press '2' to get the gas detector state\r\n", 41 );
6       uartUsb.write( "Press '3' to get the over temperature detector state\r\n\r\n", 56
7   );
    }
```

Code 2.13 New implementation of availableCommands().

```
1   void uartTask()
2   {
3       char receivedChar = '\0';
4       if( uartUsb.readable() ) {
5           uartUsb.read( &receivedChar, 1 );
6           switch (receivedChar) {
7           case '1':
8               if ( alarmState ) {
9                   uartUsb.write( "The alarm is activated\r\n", 24 );
10              } else {
11                  uartUsb.write( "The alarm is not activated\r\n", 28 );
12              }
13              break;
14          case '2':
15              if ( gasDetector ) {
16                  uartUsb.write( "Gas is being detected\r\n", 23 );
17              } else {
18                  uartUsb.write( "Gas is not being detected\r\n", 27 );
19              }
20              break;
21          case '3':
22              if ( overTempDetector ) {
23                  uartUsb.write( "Temperature is above the maximum level\r\n", 40 );
24              } else {
25                  uartUsb.write( "Temperature is below the maximum level\r\n", 40 );
26              }
27              break;
28          default:
29              availableCommands();
30              break;
31
32          }
33      }
34  }
```

Code 2.14 Details of the function uartTask().

Proposed Exercises

1. What would happen if the default case were removed?

2. How can a command be implemented using the switch-case statement such that if the "d" key is pressed on the keyboard of the computer, then the serial terminal indicates the state of the gas and

over temperature detectors?

Answers to the Exercises

1. There will be no response when a character that is not listed in the cases is pressed on the PC keyboard.

2. A new case could be added to the *switch* statement of *uartTask()*, as shown in Code 2.15.

```
1   case 'd':
2       if ( gasDetector ) {
3           uartUsb.write( "Gas is being detected\r\n", 23 );
4       } else {
5           uartUsb.write( "Gas is not being detected\r\n", 27 );
6       }
7
8       if ( overTempDetector ) {
9           uartUsb.write( "Temperature is above the maximum level\r\n", 40 );
10      } else {
11          uartUsb.write( "Temperature is below the maximum level\r\n", 40 );
12      }
13      break;
```

Code 2.15 Details of the new case in function uartTask().

Example 2.3: Deactivate the Alarm Using the PC

Objective

Develop more complex programs that make use of serial communication.

Summary of the Expected Behavior

The behavior is the same as in Example 2.2, but now the alarm can be deactivated from the PC.

Test the Proposed Solution on the Board

Import the project "Example 2.3" using the URL available in [1], build the project, and drag the .*bin* file onto the NUCLEO board. Open the serial terminal and press and release the button connected to D3 to simulate an over temperature situation. Press "4" on the PC keyboard and look at the message that appears on the serial terminal. Press the code sequence, "1", then "1", then "0", and finally "0", and look at the message that appears on the serial terminal indicating that the entered code is correct. Check that the Alarm LED is turned off. Press the button connected to D3. Press "4" on the PC. Enter an incorrect code sequence, for instance, "1", then "0", then "0", and finally "0". Check that the Incorrect code LED is turned on. A new code sequence can be tried without the need for turning off the Incorrect code LED, as in example 1.5. After five incorrect attempts, the System blocked LED will turn on.

NOTE: Even when the system is blocked, because five incorrect codes have been entered and codes cannot be entered at the control panel anymore, the proposed implementation allows a code to be entered from the PC to unblock the smart home system without the need to reset the NUCLEO board or turn off the alarm.

The reader is encouraged to activate the alarm, enter five incorrect codes in a row (either from the control panel or from the PC), see how the System blocked LED turns on, and then press "4" on the PC keyboard to enter the correct code in order to unblock the system.

Discussion of the Proposed Solution

In Example 1.4, a code was introduced that allowed the user to turn off the alarm. The code was entered using the buttons connected to D4, D5, D6, and D7. The alarm was turned off only when the right code was entered: the buttons connected to D4 and D5 were both pressed, and at the same time the buttons connected to D6 and D7 were both released. In this example, the functionality to turn off the alarm by means of the PC is implemented. Due to the fact that in this chapter only one PC keyboard key is read at a time, the code should be entered as a sequence.

Implementation of the Proposed Solution

In this example, some lines were added to the program code of Example 2.2, as shown in Table 2.3. In Code 2.16, only the fragment of the code corresponding to case '4' of the *switch* statement of *uartTask()* is shown because all the rest of the code remains the same as in Example 2.2. An explanation of each part is also included above Code 2.16.

In this example, the NUCLEO board sends messages through the serial port asking for the code (lines 2 to 12 of Code 2.16). The code entered in the PC is called the *code sequence*. In this example, a '1' represents a pressed button and '0' represents a released button. Then, four PC keys are read and stored in four different variables (*receivedAButton* to *receivedDButton*). Finally, this sequence is compared with the code stored in the NUCLEO board (line 14 to line 17) and depending on the result the Alarm LED is turned off or the Incorrect code LED is turned on, in the same way as in Example 1.5, and a message reporting the result is sent through the serial port.

Table 2.3 Lines that were added to the program of Example 2.2.

Section	Lines that were added

Declaration and initialization of public global variables	`char receivedAButton = '\0';`
	`char receivedBButton = '\0';`
	`char receivedCButton = '\0';`
	`char receivedDButton = '\0';`

Function	Lines that were added
availableCommands	`uartUsb.write( "Press '4' to enter the code sequence\r\n\` `r\n", 40 );`

```
1   case '4':
2       uartUsb.write( "Please enter the code.\r\n", 24 );
3       uartUsb.write( "Type 1 for button pressed\r\n", 27 );
4       uartUsb.write( "Type 0 for button not pressed\r\n", 31 );
5       uartUsb.write( "Enter the value for 'A' Button\r\n", 32 );
6       uartUsb.read( &receivedAButton, 1 );
7       uartUsb.write( "Enter the value for 'B' Button\r\n", 32 );
8       uartUsb.read( &receivedBButton, 1 );
9       uartUsb.write( "Enter the value for 'C' Button\r\n", 32 );
10      uartUsb.read( &receivedCButton, 1 );
11      uartUsb.write("Enter the value for 'D' Button\r\n\r\n", 34 );
12      uartUsb.read( &receivedDButton, 1 );
13
14      if ( (receivedAButton == '1') &&
15           (receivedBButton == '1') &&
16           (receivedCButton == '0') &&
17           (receivedDButton == '0') ) {
18          uartUsb.write( "The code is correct\r\n\r\n", 23 );
19          alarmState = OFF;
20          incorrectCodeLed = OFF;
21          numberOfIncorrectCodes = 0;
22      } else {
23          uartUsb.write( "The code is incorrect\r\n\r\n", 25 );
24          incorrectCodeLed = ON;
25          numberOfIncorrectCodes = numberOfIncorrectCodes + 1;
26      }
27      break;
```

Code 2.16 Details of the new lines in the function uartTask().

Proposed Exercises

1. How can the code be changed in such a way that the order in which the keys are asked for is D, C, B, and finally A?

2. How can the code be changed to add a case that shows the state of the Incorrect code LED?

3. How can more buttons be incorporated into the smart home system?

Answers to the Exercises

1. The order of lines 5 to 12 should be modified.

2. In the *switch* statement, a case similar to the one implemented for the key "1" but reporting the Incorrect code LED instead of the alarm state should be incorporated.

3. More variables similar to *receivedAButton* should be declared, and those variables should be incorporated in the *uartTask()* function.

Example 2.4: Improve the Code Maintainability using Arrays

Objective

Introduce the use of a *for* loop, #define and arrays.

Summary of the Expected Behavior

The behavior is the same as in Example 2.3, but the program is implemented using a *for loop* and *arrays* in order to improve the code maintainability.

Test the Proposed Solution on the Board

Import the project "Example 2.4" using the URL available in [1], build the project, and drag the *.bin* file onto the NUCLEO board. Perform the same actions as in Example 2.3.

Discussion of the Proposed Solution

In proposed exercise 3 of Example 2.3, the reader was encouraged to think about how to incorporate more buttons into the smart home system. It was seen that under the implementation used in Example 2.3, the complexity of the program is increased as the number of buttons is incremented. This example will show how to tackle this problem using a *for* loop.

The aim of this example is to show a more convenient implementation, based on a *for* loop and arrays. An array is a variable that stores a set of values. Each of those values can be individually read and modified by using an *index*. For example, if there is an array called *vector*, its first value can be accessed using *vector*[0], its second value can be accessed using *vector*[1], etc.

 NOTE: It is important to remember that the first position of an array is accessed using the index [0].

Figure 2.11 details the flow diagram corresponding to case '4' of the *switch* statement of *uartTask()*. In case '4', the program uses a *for* loop to compare the PC keys pressed against the code sequence.

The *for* loop indicated in Figure 2.11 is used to check the keys being pressed one after the other. As the keys are entered, they are compared with the given code. If one of the keys does not correspond to the code sequence, then the variable *incorrectCode* is set to true.

Once those four keys are pressed on the PC (i.e., *buttonBeingCompared* is equal to NUMBER_OF_KEYS) the *for* loop is concluded. Then, depending on the state of *incorrectCode*, OFF is assigned to *alarmState* and 0 is assigned to *numberOfIncorrectCodes*, or the Incorrect code LED is turned on and the variable *numberOfIncorrectCodes* is incremented by one.

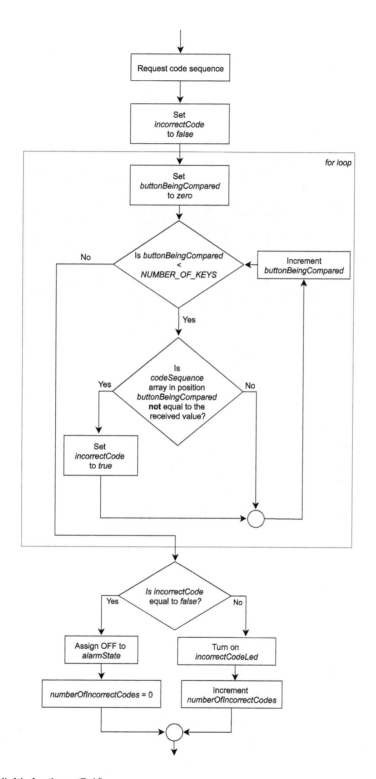

Figure 2.11 Details of the '4' of the function uartTask().

Implementation of the Proposed Solution

In this example, an array called *codeSequence* is declared to store the code sequence of four keys. The size of the array and the type of data that is to be stored in the array need to be declared. A macro called "NUMBER_OF_KEYS" is used to indicate the size of the array. Below the section "Libraries", a new section named "Definitions" is added, where NUMBER_OF_KEYS is defined. The lines that were added to this new section are shown in Table 2.4. Some other changes made to the code are also indicated in Table 2.4.

Table 2.4 Lines that were added and removed from the code used in Example 2.3.

Section	Lines that were added
Definitions	`#define NUMBER_OF_KEYS 4`

Declaration and initialization of public global variables	`bool incorrectCode = false;`
	`int buttonBeingCompared = 0;`
	`char codeSequence[NUMBER_OF_KEYS] = {'1','1','0','0'};`

Section	**Lines that were removed**

Declaration and initialization of public global variables	`char receivedAButton = 0;`
	`char receivedBButton = 0;`
	`char receivedCButton = 0;`
	`char receivedDButton = 0;`

Any time the compiler finds NUMBER_OF_KEYS, it will replace it for the corresponding number 4. In this way, the length of the code can be modified, changing only the definition of NUMBER_OF_KEYS.

 NOTE: In this book, names of defines are stylized using the CONSTANT_CASE (also known as MACRO_CASE or SCREAMING_SNAKE_CASE), as in NUMBER_OF_KEYS.

In the section "Declaration and initialization of public global variables," the array *codeSequence* is declared and initialized with the values '1', '1', '0', and '0'. This means that in the first position of the array the value '1' is stored, in the second position of the array the value '1' is stored, in the third position '0' is stored, and in the last position '0' is stored.

It can be seen in Code 2.17 that in the case corresponding to '4', there is a *for* loop (line 14). The *for* loop allows the programmer to create repetitive blocks that are executed a given number of times. This *for* loop is started with *buttonBeingCompared=0* and is concluded when the condition "*buttonBeingCompared < NUMBER_OF KEYS*" becomes false. In every loop of the *for* loop the variable *buttonBeingCompared* is incremented in order to compare the variable located in the next position of the array *codeSequence*. This is done by means of *buttonBeingCompared++* in the *for* statement.

In this particular example, to assess the code sequence entered by means of the PC keyboard the *for* loop is executed four times. In each of the repetitions, the received character is compared with the corresponding position of the array *codeSequence*. If the key entered is neither "1" or "0", then *incorrectCode* is set to true (line 30).

Finally, depending on the state of *incorrectCode*, OFF is assigned to *alarmState* and 0 is assigned to *numberOfIncorrectCodes*, or the Incorrect code LED is turned on and the variable *numberOfIncorrectCodes* is incremented by one. Note that in line 42, "++" is now used to increment the value of *numberOfIncorrectCodes* by one. This is used to make the code more compact.

```
1    case '4':
2        uartUsb.write( "Please enter the code sequence.\r\n", 33 );
3        uartUsb.write( "First enter 'A', then 'B', then 'C', and ", 41 );
4        uartUsb.write( "finally 'D' button\r\n", 20 );
5        uartUsb.write( "In each case type 1 for pressed or 0 for ", 41 );
6        uartUsb.write( "not pressed\r\n", 13 );
7        uartUsb.write( "For example, for 'A' = pressed, ", 32 );
8        uartUsb.write( "'B' = pressed, 'C' = not pressed, ", 34);
9        uartUsb.write( "'D' = not pressed, enter '1', then '1', ", 40 );
10       uartUsb.write( "then '0', and finally '0'\r\n\r\n", 29 );
11
12       incorrectCode = false;
13
14       for ( buttonBeingCompared = 0;
15             buttonBeingCompared < NUMBER_OF_KEYS;
16             buttonBeingCompared++) {
17
18           uartUsb.read( &receivedChar, 1 );
19           uartUsb.write( "*", 1 );
20
21           if ( receivedChar == '1' ) {
22               if ( codeSequence[buttonBeingCompared] != 1 ) {
23                   incorrectCode = true;
24               }
25           } else if ( receivedChar == '0' ) {
26               if ( codeSequence[buttonBeingCompared] != 0 ) {
27                   incorrectCode = true;
28               }
29           } else {
30               incorrectCode = true;
31           }
32       }
33
34       if ( incorrectCode == false ) {
35           uartUsb.write( "\r\nThe code is correct\r\n\r\n", 25 );
36           alarmState = OFF;
37           incorrectCodeLed = OFF;
38           numberOfIncorrectCodes = 0;
39       } else {
40           uartUsb.write( "\r\nThe code is incorrect\r\n\r\n", 27 );
41           incorrectCodeLed = ON;
42           numberOfIncorrectCodes++;
43       }
44       break;
```

Code 2.17 Details of the new lines in the function uartTask().

Proposed Exercises

1. How can the code sequence be changed?

Answers to the Exercises

1. The array *codeSequence* in the section "Declaration and initialization of public global variables" should be modified.

Example 2.5: Change the Alarm Turn Off Code Using the PC

Objective

Develop more complex programs using *for* loops and arrays.

Summary of the Expected Behavior

The expected behavior is the same as Example 2.4, but now the code can be changed from the PC.

Test the Proposed Solution on the Board

Import the project "Example 2.5" using the URL available in [1], build the project, and drag the *.bin* file onto the NUCLEO board. Open the serial terminal. Press "5" on the PC keyboard and look at the message that appears on the serial terminal, indicating that a new code sequence can be set. Enter a new code, for instance, "0", then "0", then "1", and finally "1", and look at the message that appears on the serial terminal indicating that the new code has been created. Press the button connected to D2 that represents gas detection. Press "4" on the PC keyboard. Enter the new code. Check that the Alarm LED is turned off. Press the button connected to D2. To check that the control panel code has also been changed, enter the new code with those buttons by pressing the buttons connected to D6 and D7 and the B1 USER button at the same time. Check that the Alarm LED is turned off.

Discussion of the Proposed Solution

Following the same logic as in Example 2.4, a new case is added to the *switch*: case '5'. The reader will notice that it is very similar to case '4'. The new code sequence is stored in the array *codeSequence*. The details of the implementation are discussed below.

Implementation of the Proposed Solution

In this example, some lines were added to the program of Example 2.4, as shown in Table 2.5. Note that *areEqual()* is the first function in this book that returns a value (a Boolean), as is discussed below.

Table 2.5 Lines that were added from the code used in Example 2.4.

Section	Lines that were added
Declaration and initialization of public global variables	`char buttonsPressed[NUMBER_OF_KEYS] = {'0','0','0','0'};`
Declarations (prototypes) of public functions	`bool areEqual();`

Function	Lines that were added
availableCommands	`uartUsb.write( "Press '5' to enter a new code\r\n\r\n", 33 );`

In this example, *alarmDeactivationUpdate()* is modified to allow the user to change the code. Code 2.18 shows the fragment of the code corresponding to case '5' of the *switch* statement within *uartTask()* that implements this change. The code sequence is loaded into the array *codeSequence* using the *for* loop.

In Code 2.19, the condition in line 7 is the same as in line 78 of Code 2.5. The difference is that lines 8 to 11 are used to assign the value of each button (*A* to *D*) to the corresponding positions of the array *buttonsPressed*. Then the function *areEqual()*, shown in Code 2.20, is used to compare each position of *buttons Pressed* with the corresponding position of *codeSequence*.

In Code 2.20, it is shown how *areEqual()* is implemented using a *for* loop indexed by the local variable *i*, where one after the other each of the positions of *codeSequence* and *buttonsPressed* are compared. It is important to note that the return value of the function is implemented in line 7 or line 11, depending on the result of the *if* statement of line 6. Lines 18 to 22 are used to store the number 1 or 0 in the corresponding position of *codeSequence* depending on the value of *receivedChar*, in order to be able to use *areEqual()* to compare *codeSequence[i]* and *buttonsPressed[i]*.

> **NOTE:** If the key pressed is not "1" or "0", then the value stored at *codeSequence[buttonBeingCompared]* is not modified, as can be seen between lines 19 and 23 of Code 2.19.

```
1   case '5':
2       uartUsb.write( "Please enter new code sequence\r\n", 32 );
3       uartUsb.write( "First enter 'A', then 'B', then 'C', and ", 41 );
4       uartUsb.write( "finally 'D' button\r\n", 20 );
5       uartUsb.write( "In each case type 1 for pressed or 0 for not ", 45 );
6       uartUsb.write( "pressed\r\n", 9 );
7       uartUsb.write( "For example, for 'A' = pressed, 'B' = pressed,", 46 );
8       uartUsb.write( " 'C' = not pressed,", 19 );
9       uartUsb.write( "'D' = not pressed, enter '1', then '1', ", 40 );
10      uartUsb.write( "then '0', and finally '0'\r\n\r\n", 29 );
11
12      for ( buttonBeingCompared = 0;
13            buttonBeingCompared < NUMBER_OF_KEYS;
14            buttonBeingCompared++) {
15
16          uartUsb.read( &receivedChar, 1 );
17          uartUsb.write( "*", 1 );
18
19          if ( receivedChar == '1' ) {
20              codeSequence[buttonBeingCompared] = 1;
21          } else if ( receivedChar == '0' ) {
22              codeSequence[buttonBeingCompared] = 0;
23          }
24      }
25
26      uartUsb.write( "\r\nNew code generated\r\n\r\n", 24 );
27      break;
```

Code 2.18 Details for case "5" of the switch statement of uartTask().

```
1    void alarmDeactivationUpdate()
2    {
3        if ( numberOfIncorrectCodes < 5 ) {
4            if ( aButton && bButton && cButton && dButton && !enterButton ) {
5                incorrectCodeLed = OFF;
6            }
7            if ( enterButton && !incorrectCodeLed && alarmState ) {
8                buttonsPressed[0] = aButton;
9                buttonsPressed[1] = bButton;
10               buttonsPressed[2] = cButton;
11               buttonsPressed[3] = dButton;
12               if ( areEqual() ) {
13                   alarmState = OFF;
14                   numberOfIncorrectCodes = 0;
15               } else {
16                   incorrectCodeLed = ON;
17                   numberOfIncorrectCodes++;
18               }
19           }
20       } else {
21           systemBlockedLed = ON;
22       }
23   }
```

Code 2.19 Details of the function alarmDeactivationUpdate().

```
1    bool areEqual()
2    {
3        int i;
4
5        for (i = 0; i < NUMBER_OF_KEYS; i++) {
6            if (codeSequence[i] != buttonsPressed[i]) {
7                return false;
8            }
9        }
10
11       return true;
12   }
```

Code 2.20 Details of the function areEqual().

Proposed Exercises

1. What should be modified in order to implement a five-key code?

2. Is it possible to implement a code of any arbitrary length?

Answers to the Exercises

1. NUMBER_OF_KEYS should be changed to 5. The text in the request should be modified. Some other parts of the code should also be modified, for example the reading of the buttons inside the *switch* statement.

2. There are many limitations. For example, the number of buttons that can be connected to the NUCLEO board using the technique explained in Chapter 1.

2.3 Under the Hood

2.3.1 Basic Principles of Serial Communication

In the examples of this chapter, information was exchanged between a PC and the NUCLEO board by means of a USB cable. This section explains how this information exchange is implemented.

 WARNING: In this subsection, the fundamental concepts of serial communication are presented. In the communication between the PC and the NUCLEO board, these concepts are applied, but there are some other details that are not covered in this subsection. USB works very differently than UART.

Most of the wired connections used nowadays, like USB, HDMI, and Ethernet, are based on what is called *serial communication*. The details of how serial communication is implemented in each of those cases is quite complex, but for now it is enough to get the basic idea behind UART serial communication.

UART serial communication between two devices, A and B, in its most common setup requires three wires, as shown in Figure 2.12. One wire is used to establish a 0 volts reference (usually called *Ground* or *GND*) between both devices. A second wire is used to transmit the information from A to B (TxA-RxB, standing for Transmitter A - Receiver B), and a third wire is used to transmit information from B to A (TxB-RxA, standing for Transmitter B - Receiver A).

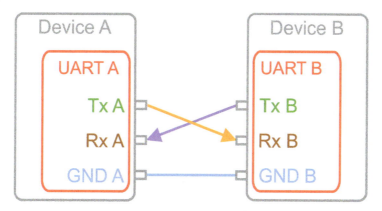

Figure 2.12 Basic setup for a serial communication between two devices.

Initially, the wires that are used to transmit information between the devices are in an *idle state*. This idle state is indicated by means of a previously agreed value, for example 3.3 volts. Then, if, for example, device A wants to start a message transmission to device B, it can indicate this by means of asserting 0 volts in the cable TxA-RxB. This notification is called a *start bit* and is shown in Figure 2.13. In this way, device B realizes that device A will send a message using the cable TxA-RxB.

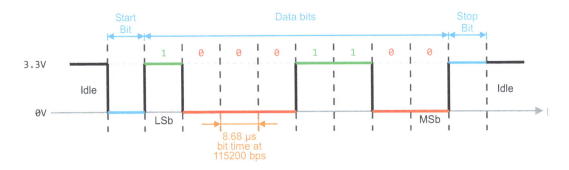

Figure 2.13 Basic sequence of a serial communication between two devices.

After sending the start bit, device A sends the first bit of the character. Frequently, the *little endian* format is used, which implies that the first bit that is sent is the first starting from the right. The first bit starting from the right is called the *Least Significant bit* or LSb.

 WARNING: In this book, "LSb" is used to indicate the Least Significant bit. It should be noted that in some books LSB is used to indicate the Least Significant Bit.

For example, if the bits "00110001" represent a given character to be sent, the first bit that is sent is the 1 on the right (the LSb). Device A holds 3.3 volts in the cable TxA-RxB, as indicated by the LSb in Figure 2.13. The next bit to be sent is the 0 that is in the second position starting from the right. For this purpose, device A holds 0 volts in the cable TxA-RxB, as indicated in Figure 2.13.

In a similar way the remaining five bits are sent one after the other from device A to device B. The last bit to be sent is called the *Most Significant bit* or MSb.

Arrays of eight bits, called *bytes*, are sent in each transmission because most microcontrollers and computers internally organize the information in sets of integer multiples of eight bits (i.e., 8, 16, 32, 64, etc.).

There might be a *parity bit* sent after the eight bits if both devices have been previously configured to use this feature. This is not the case in the configuration used in this chapter, so this topic is not explained now.

Finally, device A sends a *stop bit*, to indicate that the transmission is over. This is achieved by means of setting 3.3 volts in the cable TxA-RxB as shown in Figure 2.13. In this way, for every byte of data transmitted, there are actually ten bits being sent: a start bit, eight data bits, and one stop bit.

In the examples of this chapter there was a parameter called "baud rate" that was configured in the serial terminal to "115200". This means that 115,200 bits are transmitted every second. That is, the time holding each of those bits high (3.3 volts) or low (0 volts) is 1/(115,200 bps) or 8.68 μs per bit.

Given that ten bits for every byte of data sent are transmitted, at 115,200 bps, there are 11,520 bytes being sent per second.

The baud rate is a very important parameter because it allows the device that is receiving the bits to know when to read the Rx digital input to get a new bit.

 WARNING: In some systems the communication can be implemented using 5 volts or +/- 12 volts signals. Those voltage levels may damage the NUCLEO board.

 TIP: Sequences like the one shown in Figure 2.13 can be seen each time the NUCLEO board and the PC exchange messages by means of connecting an oscilloscope or a logic analyzer to the pins Tx and Rx of CN5, as shown in Figure 2.14. It is not explained here how to use oscilloscopes and logic analyzers because that topic is beyond the scope of this book.

Proposed Exercises

1. In the basic sequence of a serial communication between two devices shown in Figure 2.12, how can Device B be sure that the received information has no errors?

2. In the scheme shown in Figure 2.12, how can Device A be sure that Device B received the information with no errors?

3. Assuming 115,200 bps serial communication, how long will it take to send a 1 MB file?

Answers to the Exercises

1. The only way for Device B to be sure that there are no bits with errors is if there is some kind of verification. In the implementation of this verification, both Devices, A and B, must be involved. This will be explained in more advanced chapters of this book.

2. Device B should work with Device A in order to ascertain this. The parity bit can be used for this purpose.

3. 1 MB is equal to 1,000,000 bytes; thus, it will take 86 seconds (1,000,000 bytes / 11,520 bytes/ second).

 NOTE: In the following chapters, other communications protocols will be explored, which will allow higher transfer rates.

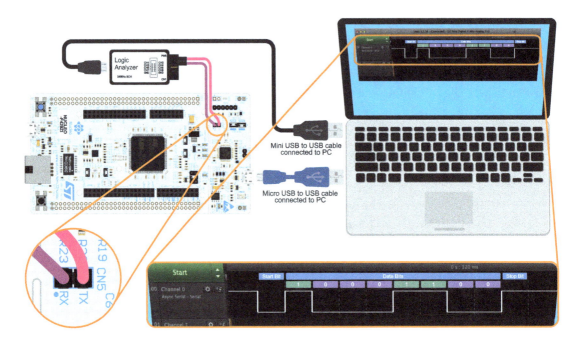

Figure 2.14 The bits transmitted or received by the NUCLEO board UART can be seen by connecting an oscilloscope or a logic analyzer on CN5. These bits do not correspond to the USB protocol.

2.4 Case Study

2.4.1 Industrial Transmitter

In this chapter, the NUCLEO board communicated with a PC by means of the UART of the microcontroller, a USB cable, and a serial terminal, as shown in Figure 2.15. In this way, the state of the gas and over temperature detectors were transmitted to the PC, the alarm could be turned off from the PC, and the password could be changed from the PC.

A brief of a commercial "Industrial transmitter" built with Mbed containing some similar features can be found in [5] and is shown in Figure 2.15. It can be seen that the "Petasense Motes" send the data to a *server* indicated by the "Petasense Cloud." Then, a program running on a PC gets the data from the "Petasense Cloud" and shares it with a software application called "Pi Vision."

By comparing both implementations shown in Figure 2.15, it can be seen that there is a device sending data and a PC used to visualize those data. In the case of the smart home system, the data is transmitted directly from the device to the PC by means of a serial communication based on a UART. In the case of the "Petasense Motes," there is a microcontroller ("MCU") that gets the values of vibration, ultrasound, current, and temperature and transmits this information using serial communication to a Wi-Fi module. The Wi-Fi module sends the information to the Petasense Cloud using the internet. The last chapters of this book will explain how to send information to a PC using a Wi-Fi module.

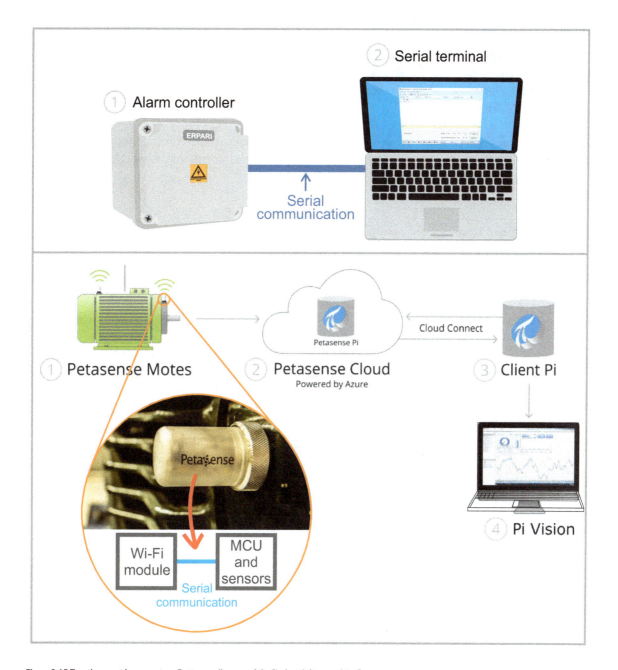

Figure 2.15 Top, the smart home system. Bottom, a diagram of the "Industrial transmitter."

Proposed Exercises

1. How is the information transmitted from the Petasense Motes to the Petasense Cloud?

2. Is a serial terminal being used on the PC?

Answers to the Exercises

1. By carefully looking in Figure 2.15 at the Petasense Motes, it is possible to see the Wi-Fi symbol. This is used to indicate that Wi-Fi is being used to transmit the information from the Petasense Motes to the Petasense Cloud. Moreover, in [5] it can be seen that the connectivity being used is "Ethernet/Wi-Fi."

2. No, there is no serial terminal involved. This is because the microcontroller that gets the values of vibration, ultrasound, current, and temperature transmits this information using UART to a Wi-Fi module.

References

[1] "GitHub - armBookCodeExamples/Directory". Accessed July 9, 2021.
https://github.com/armBookCodeExamples/Directory/

[2] "Doxygen: Doxygen". Accessed July 9, 2021.
https://www.doxygen.nl/index.html

[3] "DigitalIn - API references and tutorials | Mbed OS 6 Documentation". Accessed July 9, 2021.
https://os.mbed.com/docs/mbed-os/v6.12/apis/digitalin.html

[4] "UnbufferedSerial - API references and tutorials | Mbed OS 6 Documentation". Accessed July 9, 2021.
https://os.mbed.com/docs/mbed-os/v6.12/apis/unbufferedserial.html

[5] "Industrial Transmitter | Mbed". Accessed July 9, 2021.
https://os.mbed.com/built-with-mbed/industrial-transmitter/

Chapter 3

Time Management and
Analog Signals

3.1 Roadmap

3.1.1 What You Will Learn

After you have studied the material in this chapter, you will be able to:

▨ Describe how to connect sensors to the NUCLEO board using an analog signal interface.

▨ Develop programs to get and manage analog signals with the NUCLEO board.

▨ Develop programs that use parameter passing in C/C++ functions.

▨ Summarize the fundamentals of analog to digital conversion.

▨ Introduce time management in microcontroller programs.

▨ Implement basic character string management.

3.1.2 Review of Previous Chapters

In previous chapters, the reader learned how to communicate between the NUCLEO board and a PC using UART serial communication. A broad variety of functions were implemented, and much of that functionality relayed the state of the gas detector and the over temperature detector. These were not sensors, but representations by means of buttons.

Also, in the implementation within previous chapters, the Alarm LED was activated because of gas detection, or over temperature detection, or both being detected at the same time. The user had no information from looking at the Alarm LED about why the LED was active.

3.1.3 Contents of This Chapter

This chapter introduces a way to indicate to the user whether an alarm is caused by gas detection, over temperature detection, or simultaneous gas and over temperature detection. This is based on controlling the blinking rate of the Alarm LED. It will be explained how to utilize time with the NUCLEO board, and the usage of delays is introduced. In Example 3.1 and Example 3.2, two different ways of implementing a given delay are shown in order to compare the responsiveness of both techniques.

It will also be explained how to measure analog signals with the NUCLEO board using one of the *analog to digital converters* (ADCs) included in the STM32 microcontroller. By means of a potentiometer, an LM35 temperature sensor, and an MQ-2 gas sensor module, the concepts of analog to digital converters are explored. The over temperature detection is done using a temperature sensor and the gas detection is implemented using a gas sensor. It will also be shown how to activate a 5 V buzzer using one of the 3.3 V digital outputs of the NUCLEO board. Finally, the basic principles of analog to digital conversion are explained and a case study related to temperature measurement is shown in the Under the Hood and Case Study sections, respectively.

3.2 Analog Signals Measurement with the NUCLEO Board

3.2.1 Connect Sensors, a Potentiometer, and a Buzzer to the Smart Home System

In this chapter, an LM35 temperature sensor [1], an MQ-2 gas sensor module [2], a potentiometer, and a buzzer are connected to the smart home system, as shown in Figure 3.1. The aim of this setup is to introduce the reading of analog signals.

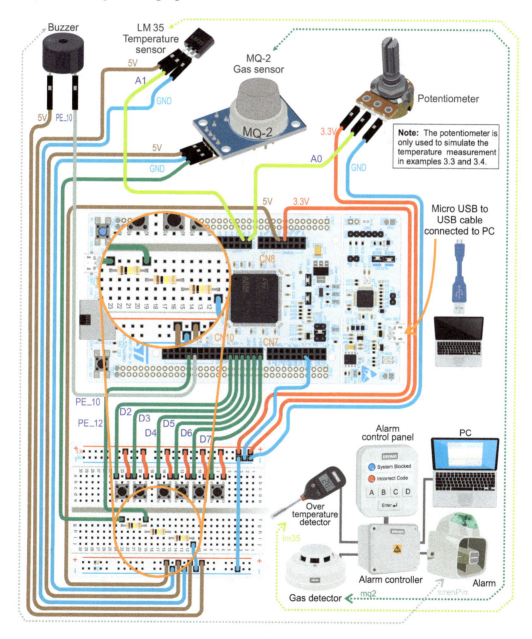

Figure 3.1 The smart home system is now connected to a temperature sensor, a gas detector, a potentiometer, and a buzzer.

NOTE: The LM35 temperature sensor, the MQ-2 gas sensor, and the buzzer must be connected to 5 V, as indicated in Figure 3.1.

WARNING: To connect modules and elements, unplug the USB power supply from the NUCLEO board, and prior to reconnecting the USB power supply check that the connections are made properly and safely.

WARNING: Some MQ-2 modules have a different pinout. Follow the VCC, GND, and DO labels of the module when making the connections to 5 V, GND, and PE_12, respectively.

Figure 3.2 shows a potentiometer. This component allows the user vary the resistance between terminal 2 and terminals 1 and 3, depending on the angular position of its knob. It will be used in this chapter to explore some concepts beyond analog to digital conversion.

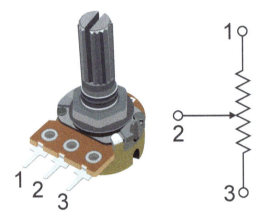

Figure 3.2 A typical potentiometer and its corresponding electrical diagram.

The most common way to connect a potentiometer to a development board is as shown in Figure 3.3. It can be seen that terminal (1) is connected to a 3.3 Volt supply voltage, terminal (3) is connected to GND, and terminal (2) is connected to an analog input pin, which in this case is the A0 pin.

NOTE: It is recommended to use a potentiometer with a full-scale resistance of 10 kΩ. If the resistance is too small, the NUCLEO board could be damaged, and if it is too big, the measurement could be unstable.

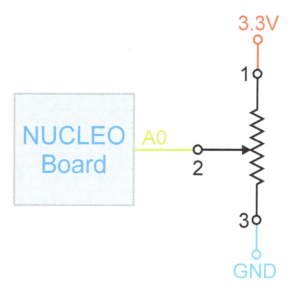

Figure 3.3 Diagram of the connection of the potentiometer to the NUCLEO board.

The LM35 temperature sensor is an integrated circuit that delivers an output voltage linearly proportional to its temperature. It has three terminals, which are identified with the names GND, +VS, and VOUT, as shown in Figure 3.4. These names stand for Ground, Voltage Supply, and Voltage Out, respectively.

Figure 3.4 The LM35 temperature sensor in a TO-92 package.

 TIP: If necessary, the LM35 in the TO-220 package described in [3] can be used. In that case, the code remains the same, but the reader must properly identify the terminals GND, +VS , and VOUT [1]. An LM35 from any brand can be used in any of its different order number options (e.g., LM35CZ, LM35DZ, etc.).

The most basic setup for the LM35 temperature sensor is as shown in Figure 3.5. This setup is the one used in Figure 3.1 and provides an output signal in VOUT that increases at a rate of 10 mV/°C (millivolts per Celsius degree) in the range of 2 to 150°C, as indicated in [1].

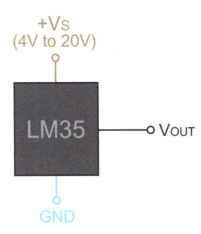

Figure 3.5 Basic setup for the LM35 temperature sensor.

In Table 3.1, some examples of the voltage at VOUT are shown for different temperatures. For the convenience of readers from the United States, temperatures are also expressed in degrees Fahrenheit. To convert a temperature expressed in °C into degrees Fahrenheit, it must be multiplied by 9/5 and 32 must be added.

Table 3.1 Examples of the voltage at V_{OUT} using the connection shown in Figure 3.5.

Temperature		Voltage at V_{OUT}
[°C]	[°F]	[mV]
2	35.6	20
3	37.4	30
10	50.0	100
30	86.0	300
150	302	1500

Figure 3.6 shows a diagram of the connection of the LM35 temperature sensor to the NUCLEO board.

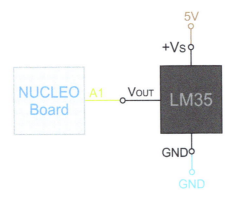

Figure 3.6 Diagram of the connection of the LM35 to the NUCLEO board.

NOTE: In this particular case, the sensor is connected directly to the NUCLEO board to simplify the circuitry. In a real application, conditioning circuits are often used. Those circuits allow the user, for example, to make use of the entire signal range of the analog input (0 to 3.3 V).

In Figure 3.7, the MQ-2 gas sensor is connected to the NUCLEO board. This sensor is supplied with 5 V and detects LPG, i-butane, propane, methane, alcohol, hydrogen, and smoke. Its AOUT (Analog Output) pin is left unconnected, and the DOUT (Digital Output) pin is used. The DOUT pin provides 0 V when gas presence over a certain concentration is detected and 5 V when the concentration is below a certain level.

 WARNING: The maximum voltage that can be applied to most of the NUCLEO board pins without damage is 4 V, while the DOUT pin provides 5 V. Therefore, the NUCLEO board can be damaged if DOUT is connected without a voltage limitation. The resistors R1, R2, and R3 shown in Figure 3.7 are used to attenuate DOUT by a factor of 2/3, which produces 3.3 V when DOUT is 5 V and 0 V when DOUT is 0 V.

 NOTE: In this particular case, pin PE_12 is a 5 V tolerant I/O, so strictly speaking the resistor divider is not needed. However, it is included to show how to proceed when a given input pin is not 5 V tolerant.

NOTE: In Figure 3.7, 100 kΩ resistors are shown, but if they are not available they can be replaced with three resistors of similar resistance values, provided they are in the range of 47 to 150 kΩ.

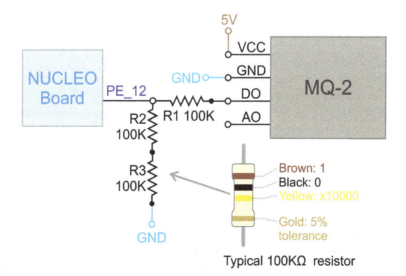

Figure 3.7 Diagram of the connection of the MQ-2 to the NUCLEO board.

NOTE: In the next chapters, different techniques to adapt voltage levels are introduced as they are needed. In this way the reader will be able to compare the techniques in terms of cost, performance, complexity, etc.

In Figure 3.8, the buzzer connection is summarized. The buzzer represents a siren that is activated when there is an alarm situation, such as gas or over temperature detection.

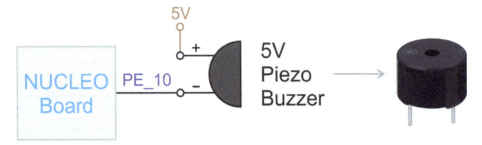

Figure 3.8 Diagram of the connection of the buzzer to the NUCLEO board.

 NOTE: With the connection shown in Figure 3.8, the buzzer is activated when LOW is assigned to the PE_10 pin. In this way, a 5 V device such as the buzzer can be activated using a 3.3 V digital output of the NUCLEO board. To turn off the buzzer, the PE_10 pin is configured as *open drain output*, in order to not assert any voltage to the buzzer "-" pin, causing the buzzer to turn off. Open drain means that the output is the drain terminal of a MOSFET transistor [4] without a pull-up resistor. It can establish 0 V if the MOSFET is activated and behaves like an open circuit otherwise. This is implemented in Example 3.5.

3.2.2 Test the Operation of the Sensors, the Potentiometer, and the Buzzer

This subsection will explain how to load a program onto the STM32 microcontroller in order to test if the components that were connected are working properly. This will be achieved by using the serial terminal to show the reading of the LM35 temperature sensor, the potentiometer, and the status of the DOUT signal of the MQ-2 sensor. The buzzer will be activated or deactivated depending on the readings. For this purpose, the *.bin* file of the program "Subsection 3.2.2" should be downloaded from the URL available in [5] and the *.bin* file dragged onto the NUCLEO board.

In Table 3.2, the available commands for the program that will be used in this subsection are shown. If the key "a" is pressed on the PC keyboard, then the reading of the analog input A0 of the NUCLEO board is continuously displayed on the serial terminal. In this case, because of the Mbed OS function being used, this is a value between 0.0 and 1.0, depending on the angular position of the knob. Rotate the knob of the potentiometer from one side to the other in order to test if the potentiometer is working correctly and is well connected to the NUCLEO board. After verifying that the potentiometer is working correctly, press "q" to quit this verification and continue with the next step.

Table 3.2 Available commands of the program used to test the LM35 temperature sensor and the potentiometer.

Key pressed	Information that is displayed in the serial terminal
a	Reading from the analog input A0 of the NUCLEO board (a value between 0.0 and 1.0)
b	Reading from the analog input A1 of the NUCLEO board (a value between 0.0 and 1.0)
c	Reading of the temperature measured by the LM35 expressed in °C
d	Reading of the temperature measured by the LM35 expressed in °F
e	Reading of the temperature measured by the LM35 expressed in °C and reading of the potentiometer scaled by the same factor
f	Reading of the temperature measured by the LM35 expressed in °F and reading of the potentiometer scaled by the same factor
g	Reading of the DOUT signal of the MQ-2 gas sensor
q	Quit the last entered command

Press the "b" key to get the reading at the analog input A1 of the NUCLEO board. This input is connected to the LM35 temperature sensor and will be a value between 0 and 1. Press "q" to continue with the next step.

When the "c" key is pressed, the reading of the temperature measured by the LM35, which is connected to A1, is displayed on the serial terminal and expressed in °C. The formula used to convert the analog reading to temperature expressed in degrees Celsius is:

$$\text{Temperature [°C]} = \frac{\text{Analog Reading} \times 3.3 \text{ V}}{0.01 \text{ V/°C}} \qquad (1)$$

This formula indicates that the analog reading, which is a non-integer value between 0 and 1, is first multiplied by 3.3 V in order to get the corresponding voltage. This is due to the fact that the analog to digital converter of the NUCLEO board provides approximately 0.0 for a 0 V input and gives its maximum value (in this case 1.0) for a 3.3 V input. The analog to digital conversion used in the NUCLEO board will be explained in detail in the Under the Hood section. The result is then divided by 0.01 V/°C because the output signal VOUT of the LM35 increases by 10 mV/°C in the range of 2 to 150 °C.

The reader is encouraged to hold the LM35 between two fingers and to observe that the temperature displayed on the serial terminal becomes about 32 °C.

If the "d" key is pressed, then the temperature measured by the LM35 that is connected to A1 is displayed on the serial terminal expressed in °F. The conversion formula from Celsius to Fahrenheit is:

$$\text{Temperature [°F]} = \frac{\text{Temperature [°C]} \times 9}{5} + 32 \qquad (2)$$

The commands that are activated by the keys "e" and "f" are provided only to compare the noise in the readings of A0 (connected to the potentiometer) and A1 (connected to the LM35 temperature sensor). In order to make the comparison more straightforward in these two commands, formula (1) is applied to the readings from analog input A0, and the following formula is applied to A1 in order to scale its reading between 2 and 150:

$$\text{Value expressed in [°C] = Analog Reading} \times 148 + 2 \qquad (3)$$

NOTE: It should be clear that formula (1) has a physical meaning only when an LM35 temperature sensor is connected to the analog input. The result of formula (3), applied to the analog signal coming from the potentiometer, is only valid for the purpose of comparing the noise in the readings of A0 and A1 (i.e., there is no variation in temperature when the knob of the potentiometer is rotated).

Press the "e" key to get the readings at the analog inputs A0 and A1 of the NUCLEO board at the same time, as discussed above. Rotate the knob of the potentiometer in order to get a reading for the potentiometer similar to the reading obtained for the LM35.

Press the "f" key to get the readings at the analog inputs A0 and A1 of the NUCLEO board at the same time, as discussed above. This result is obtained by first applying formula (1) or formula (3) and then applying formula (2). The combination of formulas (1) and (2) will be used in some of the proposed exercises in this chapter.

NOTE: The examples in this chapter will explore how to reduce the noise in the measurements by means of averaging a set of consecutive readings.

Finally, press the "g" key to continuously print the reading of the DOUT signal from the MQ-2 gas sensor. The reading should be consistent with the state of the DO-LED shown in Figure 3.9: if gas is not detected, the DO-LED should be off and the message on the serial terminal should be "Gas is not being detected." If gas is detected, the DO-LED should be on and the message on the serial terminal should be "Gas is being detected." When gas is detected, the buzzer should sound.

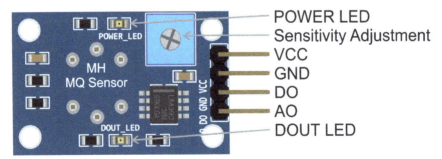

Figure 3.9 Diagram of the connection of the MQ-2 gas sensor module.

Modify the Sensitivity Adjustment of the MQ-2 gas sensor module (Figure 3.7) in one direction and then in the other. The DO-LED should turn on and off, as should the buzzer, and the message on the serial terminal should change between "Gas detected" and "Gas not detected."

To adjust the Sensitivity Adjustment to an appropriate level, use a lighter. Press the button to open the gas valve without rotating the spark wheel. In this way, a small amount of gas will be released without producing a flame on the top of the lighter, and the sensitivity of the MQ-2 gas sensor module can be easily adjusted.

 WARNING: Be careful not to rotate the spark wheel of the lighter in order to avoid lighting the flame.

Example 3.1: Indicate which Sensor has Triggered the Alarm

Objective

Introduce time management by means of delays.

 NOTE: In this example, the sensors are still activated by means of the buttons connected to D2 and D3.

Summary of the Expected Behavior

If the alarm has been triggered by the gas detector, then the Alarm LED (LD1) should blink at a rate of one second (1,000 milliseconds) on and one second off. If the alarm has been triggered by the over temperature detector, the Alarm LED should blink at a rate of 500 ms on and 500 ms off. If gas is being detected and the temperature is above the maximum level, then LD1 should blink at a rate of 100 ms on and 100 ms off.

Test the Proposed Solution on the Board

Import the project "Example 3.1" using the URL available in [5], build the project, and drag the *.bin* file onto the NUCLEO board. Press the button connected to D2 in order to activate the alarm for gas detection. The Alarm LED (LD1) should start blinking, at a rate of one second on and one second off. Deactivate the alarm by simultaneously pressing buttons A + B + Enter on the control panel (i.e., D4 + D5 + B1 USER). Note that there is a slight delay in the response because of the way in which the program is implemented, as discussed below. Press the button connected to D3 in order to activate the alarm for over temperature detection. The Alarm LED should start blinking at a rate of half of a second on and half of a second off. Press the button connected to D2 in order to add a gas detection state. LD1 should blink faster, being one tenth of a second on and one tenth of a second off.

Discussion of the Proposed Solution

The proposed solution is based on the *delay()* function defined in the *arm_book_lib.h* library. This function is based on the Mbed OS *thread_sleep_for()* function and pauses the execution of the program, causing a delay. Depending on the situation, a delay with a different length can be used when turning the Alarm LED on and off. In this way, it can be indicated if the Alarm LED is active because of gas detection, over temperature detection, or the simultaneous detection of gas and over temperature.

Implementation of the Proposed Solution

The definitions and variables that were added to the program of Example 2.5 in order to implement the new functionality are shown in Table 3.3. It can be seen that three constants are defined that will be used in the delays. In the case of BLINKING_TIME_GAS_ALARM, the delay will be one second (1000 ms); in the case of BLINKING_TIME_OVER_TEMP_ALARM, the delay will be half of one second (500 ms); and in the case of BLINKING_TIME_GAS_AND_OVER_TEMP_ALARM, the delay will be one tenth of a second (100 ms). There are also two public Boolean variables, *gasDetectorState* and *overTempDetectorState*. These variables will be used to store the state of the gas detector and the over temperature detector.

In Code 3.1, the new implementation of the function *alarmActivationUpdate()* is shown. On lines 3 to 6, it can be seen that if *gasDetector* is active, then *gasDetectorState* and *alarmState* are both set to ON. A similar piece of code is used from lines 7 to 10 regarding over*TempDetector*, over*TempDetectorState*, and *alarmState*. On line 11, *alarmState* is checked to see if it is ON. If it is ON, the state of the Alarm LED is toggled on line 12. Next, a delay is introduced in lines 13 to 19, whose length depends on the state of *gasDetectorState* and *overTempDetectorState*. If *alarmState* is OFF, then on line 21 the Alarm LED is turned off and the variables *gasDetectorState* and *overTempDetectorState* are set to OFF.

Table 3.3 Sections in which lines were added to Example 2.5.

Section	Lines that were added

Defines	`#define BLINKING_TIME_GAS_ALARM                1000`
	`#define BLINKING_TIME_OVER_TEMP_ALARM_          500`
	`#define BLINKING_TIME_GAS_AND_OVER_TEMP_ALARM  100`

Declaration and initialization of public global variables	`bool gasDetectorState      = OFF;` `bool overTempDetectorState = OFF;`

```
1   void alarmActivationUpdate()
2   {
3       if( gasDetector) {
4           gasDetectorState = ON;
5           alarmState = ON;
6       }
7       if( overTempDetector ) {
8           overTempDetectorState = ON;
9           alarmState = ON;
10      }
11      if( alarmState ) {
12          alarmLed = !alarmLed;
13          if( gasDetectorState && overTempDetectorState ) {
14              delay( BLINKING_TIME_GAS_AND_OVER_TEMP_ALARM );
15          } else if ( gasDetectorState ) {
16              delay( BLINKING_TIME_GAS_ALARM );
17          } else if ( overTempDetectorState ) {
18              delay( BLINKING_TIME_OVER_TEMP_ALARM );
19          }
20      } else{
21          alarmLed = OFF;
22          gasDetectorState = OFF;
23          overTempDetectorState = OFF;
24      }
25  }
```

Code 3.1 Details of the new implementation of the function alarmActivationUpdate().

Proposed Exercise

1. Is there any consequence for the program responsiveness if the delays are increased by a factor of ten?

Answer to the Exercise

1. Table 3.4 shows the values to be used to increase the delays by a factor of ten. The reader should repeat the steps detailed in the subsection "Implement the Proposed Solution on the Board" of Example 3.1 using these new values for BLINKING_TIME_GAS_ALARM, BLINKING_TIME_OVER_TEMP_ALARM, and BLINKING_TIME_GAS_AND_OVER_TEMP_ALARM. It can be seen that the responsiveness of the program is severely affected by these long delays. Example 3.2 will show how to implement a change in the code in order to overcome this problem.

Table 3.4 Lines that were modified from Example 3.1.

Section	Lines that were added
Definitions	``` #define BLINKING_TIME_GAS_ALARM 10000 #define BLINKING_TIME_OVER_TEMP_ALARM 5000 #define BLINKING_TIME_GAS_AND_OVER_TEMP_ALARM 1000 ```

Example 3.2: Increase the Responsiveness of the Program

Objective

Introduce a technique to avoid non-responsive behavior when long times are used in the delays.

> **NOTE:** In this example, the sensors are still activated by means of the buttons connected to D2 and D3.

Summary of the Expected Behavior

The expected behavior is the same as in Example 3.1, but the new method of implementing delays leads to a more responsive behavior, even if long delays are used.

Test the Proposed Solution on the Board

Import the project "Example 3.2" using the URL available in [5], build the project, and drag the *.bin* file onto the NUCLEO board. Repeat the same steps that were described in the subsection "Test the Proposed Solution on the Board" of Example 3.1. The behavior should be exactly the same but exhibit a more responsive behavior.

Discussion of the Proposed Solution

The proposed solution is based on the idea of using a given number of short delays in order to achieve a longer delay. For instance, in this example ten 10 ms delays are consecutively used to achieve a

100 ms delay, or fifty 10 ms delays are consecutively used to achieve a 500 ms delay. In this way, every 10 ms, the buttons can be read in order to see if the user is asking for a given response. The result is that the program becomes much more responsive.

NOTE: This technique of counting small delays is the first approach that is used in this book in order to manage a program with pauses in a "non-blocking" way.

Implementation of the Proposed Solution

The new implementation of the *main()* function is shown in Code 3.2. It can be seen that a delay of TIME_INCREMENT_MS is included on line 9.

```
1   int main()
2   {
3       inputsInit();
4       outputsInit();
5       while (true) {
6           alarmActivationUpdate();
7           alarmDeactivationUpdate();
8           uartTask();
9           delay(TIME_INCREMENT_MS);
10      }
11  }
```

Code 3.2 Details of the new implementation of the main() function.

The lines that were added to Example 3.1 are shown in Table 3.5. It can be seen that TIME_ INCREMENT_MS is defined as 10, and the integer variable *accumulatedTime* is declared and initialized to 0. As was discussed in "Discussion of the Proposed Solution," 10 ms delays are accumulated to implement longer delays.

Table 3.5 Section where a line was added to Example 3.1.

Section	Lines that were added
Definitions	`#define TIME_INCREMENT_MS 10`
Declaration and initialization of public global variables	`int accumulatedTime = 0;`

Code 3.3 shows the new implementation used in *alarmActivationUpdate()*. Lines 1 to 10 are the same as the previous implementation used in Example 3.1. The difference is the way the delays are implemented inside the *if* statement in line 11 when *alarmState* is active (lines 11 to 35). In line 12, *accumulatedTime* is increased by TIME_INCREMENT_MS, accounting for the 10 ms delay introduced in the *main()* function.

Line 14 checks if *alarmState* is active due to the gas detector and the over temperature detector both being active. If so, *accumulatedTime* is checked to see if it has reached the time established by

BLINKING_TIME_GAS_AND_OVER_TEMP_ALARM. If that is the case, *accumulatedTime* is set to 0 for the next iteration and the state of *alarmLed* is toggled.

The same behavior is implemented in lines 19 to 23 for the case in which *alarmState* is active only because of the gas detector. In the case of *alarmState* being active because of the over temperature detector alone, the executed statements are those between lines 24 and 28.

If *alarmState* is not true, then *alarmLed*, *gasDetectorState*, and *overTempDetector State* are set to OFF in lines 31 to 33.

In this way, the delays are always divided into *pieces* of 10 ms. As a consequence, the smart home system is never blocked for a long time waiting for the elapse of a long delay (i.e., 1000 ms or 500 ms).

 NOTE: The 10 ms delay is not perceptible to human beings but is a long time for a microcontroller. More advanced time management techniques will be introduced later on in this book.

```
1   void alarmActivationUpdate()
2   {
3       if( gasDetector) {
4           gasDetectorState = ON;
5           alarmState = ON;
6       }
7       if( overTempDetector ) {
8           overTempDetectorState = ON;
9           alarmState = ON;
10      }
11      if( alarmState ) {
12          accumulatedTimeAlarm = accumulatedTimeAlarm + TIME_INCREMENT_MS;
13
14          if( gasDetectorState && overTempDetectorState ) {
15              if( accumulatedTimeAlarm >= BLINKING_TIME_GAS_AND_OVER_TEMP_ALARM ) {
16                  accumulatedTimeAlarm = 0;
17                  alarmLed = !alarmLed;
18              }
19          } else if( gasDetectorState ) {
20              if( accumulatedTimeAlarm >= BLINKING_TIME_GAS_ALARM ) {
21                  accumulatedTimeAlarm = 0;
22                  alarmLed = !alarmLed;
23              }
24          } else if ( overTempDetectorState ) {
25              if( accumulatedTimeAlarm >= BLINKING_TIME_OVER_TEMP_ALARM  ) {
26                  accumulatedTimeAlarm = 0;
27                  alarmLed = !alarmLed;
28              }
29          }
30      } else{
31          alarmLed = OFF;
32          gasDetectorState = OFF;
33          overTempDetectorState = OFF;
34      }
35  }
```

Code 3.3 Details of the new implementation of the function alarmActivationUpdate().

Proposed Exercise

1. Given the new implementation used in Code 3.3, does the program become non-responsive if the delays are increased by a factor of ten?

Answer to the Exercise

1. Table 3.6 shows the values to be used to result in an increase in the delays by a factor of ten. The reader should repeat the steps detailed in the subsection "Implement the Proposed Solution on the Board" of Example 4.1 using these new values for the delays. It can be seen that the responsiveness of the program is no longer affected by these long delays.

Table 3.6 Lines that were modified from Example 3.2.

Section	Lines that were added
Defines	`#define BLINKING_TIME_GAS_ALARM` 10000 `#define BLINKING_TIME_OVER_TEMP_ALARM` 5000 `#define BLINKING_TIME_GAS_AND_OVER_TEMP_ALARM` 1000

Example 3.3: Activate the Over Temperature Alarm by Means of the Potentiometer

Objective

Introduce the measurement of analog signals, the use of float variables, and the use of strings.

Summary of the Expected Behavior

The alarm should be activated when the knob of the potentiometer is rotated beyond half of its rotational travel. The corresponding reading should be shown on the serial terminal when the "p" key is pressed on the PC keyboard.

Test the Proposed Solution on the Board

Import the project "Example 3.3" using the URL available in [5], build the project, and drag the .*bin* file onto the NUCLEO board. Open the serial terminal. Press "p" on the PC keyboard and read the message that appears on the serial terminal. Rotate the knob in both directions and see how the values displayed on the serial terminal change in the range of 0 to 1. Rotate the knob until a reading of about 0.2 is obtained and deactivate the alarm by simultaneously pressing the A + B + Enter buttons on the control panel (i.e., D4 + D5 + B1 USER). Then, slowly rotate the knob until a reading above 0.5 is obtained. The alarm should turn on.

Discussion of the Proposed Solution

The proposed solution is based on the reading of the analog signal that is provided by the central terminal of the potentiometer. This signal, which is proportional to the rotation of the knob, is connected to the analog input 0 (*A0*) of the NUCLEO board. If the reading is below 0.5, then *overTempDetector* is set to OFF, and if it is above 0.5, *overTempDetector* is set to ON.

Implementation of the Proposed Solution

The object and variables that were added to the program of Example 3.2 in order to implement the new functionality are shown in Table 3.7. It can be seen that POTENTIOMETER_OVER_TEMP_LEVEL has been defined as 0.5. It is declared as an analog input object called *potentiometer* and assigned to the analog input 0 (A0) of the NUCLEO board. Finally, a Boolean global variable *overTempDetector* and a global variable *potentiometerReading* of type float are declared. *overTempDetector* is used to keep track of the current state of the over temperature detector, which is implemented by the potentiometer. In this example, the float variable is used to store the values in the range of 0.0 to 1.0 that are obtained when the analog A0 is read. A float variable can store a value in the range of $\pm1.18 \times 10^{-38}$ to $\pm3.4 \times 10^{38}$.

Table 3.8 and Table 3.9 show some lines that were removed from Example 3.2. Code 3.4 shows the code used to get the potentiometer reading. This code is included in the *alarmActivationUpdate()* function. As can be seen, in line 3 the reading is obtained by *potentiometer.read()*. In line 5, the potentiometer reading is compared with POTENTIOMETER_OVER_TEMP_LEVEL. Depending on the result, the state of *overTempDetector* is set to ON or OFF in lines 6 or 8. The remaining lines (10 to 44) were not changed.

Table 3.7 Sections in which lines were added to Example 3.2.

Section	Lines that were added
Definitions	`#define POTENTIOMETER_OVER_TEMP_LEVEL 0.5`
Declaration and initialization of public global objects	`AnalogIn potentiometer(A0);`
Declaration and initialization of public global variables	`bool overTempDetector = OFF;` `float potentiometerReading = 0.0;`

Table 3.8 Sections in which lines were removed from Example 3.2.

Section	Lines that were removed
Declaration and initialization of public global objects	`DigitalIn overTempDetector(D3);`

Table 3.9 Functions in which lines were removed from Example 3.2.

Function	Lines that were removed
void inputsInit()	`overTempDetector.mode(PullDown);`

```
1   void alarmActivationUpdate()
2   {
3       potentiometerReading = potentiometer.read();
4
5       if ( potentiometerReading > POTENTIOMETER_OVER_TEMP_LEVEL ) {
6           overTempDetector = ON;
7       } else {
8           overTempDetector = OFF;
9       }
10
11      if( gasDetector) {
12          gasDetectorState = ON;
13          alarmState = ON;
14      }
15      if( overTempDetector ) {
16          overTempDetectorState = ON;
17          alarmState = ON;
18      }
19      if( alarmState ) {
20          accumulatedTimeAlarm = accumulatedTimeAlarm + TIME_INCREMENT_MS;
21
22          if( gasDetectorState && overTempDetectorState ) {
23              if( accumulatedTimeAlarm >= BLINKING_TIME_GAS_AND_OVER_TEMP_ALARM ) {
24                  accumulatedTimeAlarm = 0;
25                  alarmLed = !alarmLed;
26              }
27          } else if( gasDetectorState ) {
28              if( accumulatedTimeAlarm >= BLINKING_TIME_GAS_ALARM ) {
29                  accumulatedTimeAlarm = 0;
30                  alarmLed = !alarmLed;
31              }
32          } else if ( overTempDetectorState ) {
33              if( accumulatedTimeAlarm >= BLINKING_TIME_OVER_TEMP_ALARM  ) {
34                  accumulatedTimeAlarm = 0;
35                  alarmLed = !alarmLed;
36              }
37          }
38      } else{
39          alarmLed = OFF;
40          gasDetectorState = OFF;
41          overTempDetectorState = OFF;
42      }
43  }
```

Code 3.4 New implementation of the function alarmActivationUpdate().

Table 3.10 shows the lines that were added to *availableCommands()* to inform how to get the potentiometer reading.

Table 3.10 Lines added to the function availableCommands().

Function	Lines that were added
void availableCommands()	uartUsb.write("Press 'P' or 'p' to get potentiometer reading\r\n\r\n", 49);

Code 3.5 shows the lines that were added to *uartTask()* to inform the user of the reading of the potentiometer. In the event of "p" or "P" being pressed, the potentiometer reading is checked (line 3) and a message is sent to the PC by means of *uartUsb.write* (line 6). In order to prepare the message, a *string* is conformed in line 4, as discussed below.

```
1  case 'p':
2  case 'P':
3      potentiometerReading = potentiometer.read();
4      sprintf ( str, "Potentiometer: %.2f\r\n", potentiometerReading );
5      stringLength = strlen(str);
6      uartUsb.write( str, stringLength );
7      break;
```

Code 3.5 Lines that were added into the function uartTask().

A *string* is an array of char terminated with the null character ('\0') which is usually used to process and store words or sentences in C/C++. As was explained in Chapter 2, in C/C++ the character '\0' represents the zero-element character (i.e., a '\0' written to *uartUsb* is not printed on the serial terminal), which is different from the character '0' which is used to indicate the number zero. In Chapter 6, the ASCII standard that is used in most computers and microcontrollers to encode characters will be introduced, and it will be seen that the character '0' is encoded with the number 48, while the null character '\0' is encoded with the number 0.

The null character is used in C/C++ to indicate the ending of strings because it is usual to deal with messages whose length may vary depending on certain circumstances. For instance, in Example 3.4 it will be seen that the number of characters in a message that will be used to indicate the temperature will vary depending on the temperature value. For example, if the temperature reading is equal to or above ten degrees, then one more character will be included in the message that will be used to report the reading (i.e., "Temperature: 12.2 °C" has one more character than "Temperature: 9.8 °C"). Therefore, the null character is appended at the end of the message to indicate where the message ends (i.e., "Temperature: 12.2 °C\0" and "Temperature: 9.8 °C\0"). In this way, a function can be used in order to print the message characters that are stored in an array until the null character is found.

This idea about *strings* is used in lines 4 and 5 of Code 3.5. The array is declared in the function *uartTask()*, as can be seen in Table 3.11. It is declared having 100 positions in order to stress that only the characters delimited by the null character will be printed in the message sent to the PC. There is also declared an int type variable named *stringLength* that will be used to store the length of the string (which might be different to the length of the array, as was discussed above).

Table 3.11 New variables that are declared in the function uartTask().

Function	Lines that were added
void uartTask()	`char str[100];` `int stringLength;`

NOTE: In order to save memory, it is good practice to use arrays of chars that are as small as possible to store the strings. In this example, 100 positions were used just to stress that not all the array positions are printed.

On line 4 of Code 3.5, the function *sprintf* provided by Mbed OS is used to write formatted data into the string. The string is composed of "Potentiometer: ", followed by the value of *potentiometerReading* displayed with a precision of two decimal digits (*%.2f* format stands for a float variable with two decimal digits; for more information on how to set the format, please refer to [6]). On line 4 it can be seen that "\r\n" is also appended to the *content* of the string. After the content is complete (as indicated by the last " symbol on line 4), a terminating null character is automatically appended to the string by the function *sprintf*.

NOTE: The size of the *buffer* where the string is composed (in this case the array of char named *string*) should be large enough to contain the entire resulting string. Otherwise, problems may occur, as discussed later in this book.

On line 5 of Code 3.5, the function *strlen()* provided by Mbed OS is used to get the length of the string, which is stored in the variable *stringLength* that was introduced in Table 3.11. On line 6, *uartUsb.write()* is used to send the string having a length of *stringLength* to the PC.

NOTE: In order to enable the *%.2f* format that is used in Code 3.5, the file *mbed_app.json* was added to the "Example 3.3" project. For more information, please refer to [7].

NOTE: The C language provides four basic types: *char, int, float,* and *double,* and the modifiers *signed, unsigned, short,* and *long.* Table 3.12 lists the most common data types. The C99 standard (ISO/IEC 9899:1999) added the Boolean type. C99 includes definitions of new integer types to enhance the portability of programs, as the size of previous integer types may vary across different systems. The new types are especially useful in embedded systems, and the most common ones are listed in Table 3.13.

Table 3.12 C language basic arithmetic type specifiers.

Type	Details	Size (bits)	Format specifier
char	Smallest addressable integer type. Can contain the basic character set.	8	%c
signed char	Of the same size as char, but capable of containing the range [−127 to +127].	8	%c
unsigned char	Of the same size as char, but capable of containing the range [0 to 255].	8	%c
int	Basic signed integer type. Capable of containing the range [−32,767 to +32,767].	16	%i or %d
unsigned int	Basic unsigned integer type. Capable of containing the range [0 to 65,535].	16	%u

Type	Details	Size (bits)	Format specifier
long	Long signed integer type. Capable of containing the range [−2,147,483,647 to +2,147,483,647].	32	%li or %ld
float	Real floating-point type. Actual properties unspecified, but typically contains the range [±1.2E-38 to ±3.4E+38].	32	%f
double	Real floating-point type. Actual properties unspecified, but typically contains the range [±2.3E-308 to ±1.7E+308].	64	%lf

 NOTE: The sizes of int, unsigned int, and long types are not specified by C99 and are platform-dependent. For more information on floating-point types, see the IEEE Standard for Floating-Point Arithmetic (IEEE 754) established by the Institute of Electrical and Electronics Engineers (IEEE).

Table 3.13 C99 standard definitions of new integer types.

Type	Details	Size (bits)
uint8_t	Capable of containing the range [0 to 255].	8
uint16_t	Capable of containing the range [0 to 65,535].	16
uint32_t	Capable of containing the range [0 to 4,294,967,295].	32
int8_t	Capable of containing the range [−128 to +127].	8
int16_t	Capable of containing the range [−32,768 to +32,767].	16
int32_t	Capable of containing the range [−2,147,483,648 to +2,147,483,647].	32

Proposed Exercises

1. How can the code be modified in order to implement the over temperature alarm activation when the knob of the potentiometer is at 30% of its rotational travel?

2. Are A0 to A5 the only analog inputs that can be used in the NUCLEO board?

Answers to the Exercises

1. The line "#define POTENTIOMETER_OVER_TEMP_LEVEL 0.5" should be modified to: "#define POTENTIOMETER_OVER_TEMP_LEVEL 0.3".

2. In Figure 1.23, it can be seen that A0 corresponds to PA_3 and ADC1/3 (i.e., Channel 3 of ADC 1). It implies that "AnalogIn potentiometer(A0);" is the same as "AnalogIn potentiometer(PA_3);". In the same way, any of the ADCs that are shown in Figure 1.23 can be used. For example, if it is declared as "AnalogIn analogInput(PF_4)", then pin 7 of CN10 will be used as an analog input.

Example 3.4: Usage of Functions to Compute the Temperature Value

Objective

Introduce parameter passing in C/C++ functions.

Summary of the Expected Behavior

When "c" is pressed on the PC keyboard, formula (1), introduced in section 3.2.2, is applied to the reading of the potentiometer:

$$\text{Temperature [°C]} = \frac{\text{Analog Reading} \times 3.3\text{ V}}{0.01\text{ V/°C}} \qquad (1)$$

The result of this formula is shown on the serial terminal with a legend indicating "Temperature: xx.xx °C".

When "f" is pressed on the PC keyboard, the result of (1) is processed using formula (2), introduced in section 3.2.2:

$$\text{Temperature [°F]} = \frac{\text{Temperature [°C]} \times 9}{5} + 32\text{ °C} \qquad (2)$$

The result of this formula is shown on the serial terminal with a legend indicating "Temperature: xx.xx °F".

 NOTE: In this example, the LM35 temperature sensor is not read, but its reading is simulated by means of the potentiometer reading. The LM35 temperature sensor will be read in Example 3.5, and the formulae introduced in this example will be applied to its reading.

Test the Proposed Solution on the Board

Import the project "Example 3.4" using the URL available in [5], build the project, and drag the *.bin* file onto the NUCLEO board. Open the serial terminal. Press "p" on the PC keyboard and read the message that appears on the serial terminal. Rotate the knob in both directions and see how the values displayed on the serial terminal change in the range of 0 to 1. Press "c" on the PC keyboard and read the message that appears on the serial terminal. Rotate the knob in both directions and see how the values displayed on the serial terminal change. Press "f" on the PC keyboard and read the message that appears on the serial terminal. Rotate the knob in both directions and see how the values displayed on the serial terminal change.

Discussion of the Proposed Solution

The proposed solution is based on two functions, one to implement formula (1), *analogReadingScaledWithTheLM35Formula()*, and another to implement formula (2), *celsiusToFahrenheit()*. Each of these functions receives one value, known in C/C++ as the function *parameter*. These values are, respectively, the value of "Analog Reading" in formula (1) and the value of "Temperature [°C]" in formula (2). After making the corresponding calculation, the function *analogReadingScaledWithTheLM35Formula()* returns the value indicated as "Temperature [°C]" in formula (1), while the function *celsiusToFahrenheit()* implements the calculation shown in formula (2) and returns the value of "Temperature [°F]".

NOTE: In this example, the return value of *analogReadingScaledWithTheLM35Formula()* can be in the range of 0 to 330, given that the reading of the potentiometer is in the range of 0.0 to 1.0. Consequently, in this example the return value of *celsiusToFahrenheit()* can be in the range of 32 to 626. In Example 3.5, the return value of these two functions will correspond to the measurement range of the LM35 sensor.

Implementation of the Proposed Solution

The lines shown in Table 3.14 were modified and added to the code used in Example 3.3. The value of POTENTIOMETER_OVER_TEMP_LEVEL has been changed to 50, because the range of the value is no longer between 0.0 and 1.0, as discussed above. In addition, a new variable named *potentiometerReadingScaled* of type float has been declared, and two new functions have been declared: *analogReadingScaledWithTheLM35Formula()* and *celsiusToFahrenheit()*. In Code 3.6, the implementation of these two functions is shown. The first (lines 1 to 4) corresponds to formula (1) and the second (lines 6 to 9) corresponds to formula 2. Some lines were added as shown in Table 3.15.

Table 3.14 Sections in which lines were modified and added to Example 3.3.

Section	Lines that were modified
Definitions	`#define POTENTIOMETER_OVER_TEMP_LEVEL 50`

Section	Lines that were added
Declaration and initialization of public global variables	`float potentiometerReadingScaled;`
Declarations (prototypes) of public functions	`float analogReadingScaledWithTheLM35Formula( float analogReading )` `float celsiusToFahrenheit( float tempInCelsiusDegrees )`

Table 3.15 Functions in which lines were added to Example 3.3.

Function	Lines that were modified and added

void availableCommands()	`uartUsb.write( "Press 'f' or 'F' to get potentiometer`
	`    reading in Fahrenheit\r\n", 61 );`
	`uartUsb.write( "Press 'c' or 'C' to get potentiometer`
	`    reading in Celsius\r\n\r\n", 60 );`

```
1   float analogReadingScaledWithTheLM35Formula( float analogReading )
2   {
3       return ( analogReading * 3.3 / 0.01 );
4   }
5
6   float celsiusToFahrenheit( float tempInCelsiusDegrees )
7   {
8       return ( tempInCelsiusDegrees * 9.0 / 5.0 + 32.0 );
9   }
```

Code 3.6 Details of the new functions added to the code introduced in Example 3.3.

In Code 3.7, the modifications introduced in the function *alarmActivationUpdate()* are shown. In lines 3 and 4 it can be seen that the reading of the potentiometer is processed by the function *analogReadingScaledWithTheLM35Formula()* and then stored in *potentiometerReadingScaled*. This variable is used in the *if* statement on line 6. The remaining lines of Code 3.7 are the previous existing implementation of *alarmActivationUpdate()*.

The lines added to *uartTask()* to get the temperature in Celsius and Fahrenheit are shown in Code 3.8. On line 4, it can be seen that the function *analogReadingScaledWithTheLM35Formula()* is used to obtain the temperature in °C. \xB0 is used to print the ° symbol in the string. Line 13 of Code 3.8 shows that the function *celsiusToFahrenheit()* is used to convert the result obtained on line 14 into °F.

```
1   void alarmActivationUpdate()
2   {
3       potentiometerReadingScaled =
4           analogReadingScaledWithTheLM35Formula (potentiometer.read() );
5
6       if ( potentiometerReadingScaled > POTENTIOMETER_OVER_TEMP_LEVEL ) {
7           overTempDetector = ON;
8       } else {
9           overTempDetector = OFF;
10      }
11
12      if( gasDetector) {
13          gasDetectorState = ON;
14          alarmState = ON;
15      }
16      if( overTempDetector ) {
17          overTempDetectorState = ON;
18          alarmState = ON;
19      }
20      if( alarmState ) {
21          accumulatedTimeAlarm = accumulatedTimeAlarm + TIME_INCREMENT_MS;
22
23          if( gasDetectorState && overTempDetectorState ) {
24              if( accumulatedTimeAlarm >= BLINKING_TIME_GAS_AND_OVER_TEMP_ALARM ) {
25                  accumulatedTimeAlarm = 0;
26                  alarmLed = !alarmLed;
27              }
28          } else if( gasDetectorState ) {
29              if( accumulatedTimeAlarm >= BLINKING_TIME_GAS_ALARM ) {
30                  accumulatedTimeAlarm = 0;
31                  alarmLed = !alarmLed;
32              }
33          } else if ( overTempDetectorState ) {
34              if( accumulatedTimeAlarm >= BLINKING_TIME_OVER_TEMP_ALARM   ) {
35                  accumulatedTimeAlarm = 0;
36                  alarmLed = !alarmLed;
37              }
38          }
39      } else{
40          alarmLed = OFF;
41          gasDetectorState = OFF;
42          overTempDetectorState = OFF;
43      }
44  }
```

Code 3.7 Modifications introduced to the function alarmActivationUpdate().

```
1    case 'c':
2    case 'C':
3        sprintf ( str, "Temperature: %.2f \xB0 C\r\n",
4            analogReadingScaledWithTheLM35Formula (
5                potentiometer.read() ) );
6        stringLength = strlen(str);
7        uartUsb.write( str, stringLength );
8        break;
9
10   case 'f':
11   case 'F':
12       sprintf ( str, "Temperature: %.2f \xB0 F\r\n",
13           celsiusToFahrenheit(
14               analogReadingScaledWithTheLM35Formula (
15                   potentiometer.read() ) ) );
16       stringLength = strlen(str);
17       uartUsb.write( str, stringLength );
18       break;
```

Code 3.8 Lines that were added to the function uartTask().

Proposed Exercise

1. How can a C/C++ function be implemented to compute a temperature expressed in degrees Celsius from a temperature expressed in degrees Fahrenheit?

Answer to the Exercise

1. A possible implementation is shown in Code 3.9.

```
1    float fahrenheitToCelsius( float tempInFahrenheitDegrees )
2    {
3        return ( (tempInFahrenheitDegrees - 32.0) * 5.0 / 9.0 );
4    }
```

Code 3.9 Implementation of fahrenheitToCelsius().

Example 3.5: Measure Temperature and Detect Gas using the Sensors

Objective

Review the measurement of analog signals and introduce mathematical operations with arrays.

Summary of the Expected Behavior

The temperature measured by the LM35 temperature sensor should be displayed on the serial terminal in degrees Celsius when the "c" key is pressed on the computer keyboard, or in degrees Fahrenheit when the "f" key is pressed. In addition, the alarm should be activated when the temperature measured by the LM35 is above 50 °C (122 °F). When the "g" key is pressed, the serial terminal should indicate if gas is being detected or not by the MQ-2 gas sensor module. The potentiometer is not used in this example.

NOTE: Hereinafter, the buttons connected to D2 and D3 are not used to simulate gas detection and over temperature detection. Gas and temperature are sensed using the corresponding sensors. The button connected to D2 is used as the Alarm test button, in order to test if the alarm system is working without the need for gas or over temperature. When this button is pressed, the siren (implemented by a buzzer) sounds, and the Alarm LED turns on. The button connected to D3 has no functionality in this example.

The buzzer should sound continuously if any of the alarm conditions described in the previous examples occur. The Alarm LED should blink at the same rates described in previous examples. When the Alarm test button is pressed, the condition of simultaneous gas and over temperature detection is simulated.

Test the Proposed Solution on the Board

Import the project "Example 3.5" using the URL available in [5], build the project, and drag the *.bin* file onto the NUCLEO board. Open the serial terminal. Press "c" on the PC keyboard and read the message that appears on the serial terminal, indicating in degrees Celsius the temperature measured by the LM35. Press "f" and read the message indicating the measured temperature in degrees Fahrenheit. By means of a hairdryer or any similar method, increase the temperature of the LM35. When the temperature exceeds 50 °C, the Alarm LED should turn on with a blink period of 1000 ms, and the buzzer should sound.

Once the temperature of the LM35 sensor has reduced, use a lighter as described in section 3.2.2 to trigger the gas sensor. The Alarm LED should turn on with a blink of 500 ms and the buzzer should sound.

Finally, press the Alarm test button (the button connected to D2). The Alarm LED should turn on with a blink period of 100 ms (representing gas and over temperature detection) and the buzzer should sound.

Discussion of the Proposed Solution

The proposed solution is based on the reading of the analog signal that is provided by the LM35 temperature sensor. This signal increases by 10 mV/°C and is connected to the analog input 1 (*A1*) of the NUCLEO board. In subsection 3.2.2, it was shown that the reading of this signal is quite noisy. In order to overcome this problem, consecutive readings are averaged. If this average indicates that the temperature is below 50 °C, *overTempDetector* is set to OFF, and if it indicates that it is above 50 °C, *overTempDetector* is set to ON.

The proposed solution is also based on the DOUT signal of the MQ-2 gas sensor module, which was introduced in subsection 3.2.2. It also makes use of the buzzer, which is activated by means of setting the PE_10 pin of the NUCLEO board to GND. In this example, the button connected to D2 is used as the Alarm test button, as discussed above.

Implementation of the Proposed Solution

The objects and variables that were added to the program of Example 3.4 in order to implement the new functionality are shown in Table 3.16. NUMBER_OF_AVG_SAMPLES has been defined as 10 and OVER_TEMP_LEVEL as 50. The definition of POTENTIOMETER_OVER_TEMP_LEVEL was deleted because it is not used anymore. A DigitalIn object named *alarmTestButton* has been declared and assigned to D2, while a DigitalIn object named *mq2* has been declared and assigned to PE_12.

A DigitalInOut object named *sirenPin* has been declared and assigned to PE_10. This object is used to control the buzzer, as is explained below. An analog input object called *lm35* has also been declared and assigned to the analog input 1 (A1) of the NUCLEO board.

Finally, five public global variables are declared. The variable *lm35SampleIndex* will be used for the index of the array *lm35ReadingsArray*. The variable *lm35ReadingsArray* is an array of floats where 10 (i.e., NUMBER_OF_AVG_SAMPLES) consecutive readings will be stored. The variable *lm35ReadingsSum* will be used to store the sum of the ten positions of *lm35ReadingsArray*. *lm35ReadingsAverage* will be used to store the average of all the positions of *lm35ReadingsArray*, and finally, *lm35TempC* will be used to store the value of *lm35ReadingsAverage*, expressed in degrees Celsius. The variable *potentiometerReadingScaled* was deleted because it is not used anymore.

Table 3.16 Sections in which lines were added or modified in Example 3.4.

Section	Lines that were added
Definitions	`#define NUMBER_OF_AVG_SAMPLES        10` `#define OVER_TEMP_LEVEL            50`

Declaration and initialization of public global objects	`DigitalIn alarmTestButton(D2);`
	`DigitalIn mq2(PE_12);`
	
	`DigitalInOut sirenPin(PE_10);`
	
	`AnalogIn lm35(A1);`

Declaration and initialization of public global variables	`int lm35SampleIndex        = 0;`
	
	`float lm35ReadingsArray [NUMBER_OF_AVG_SAMPLES];`
	`float lm35ReadingsSum = 0.0;`
	`float lm35ReadingsAverage = 0.0;`
	`float lm35TempC = 0.0;`

Code 3.10 shows the new implementation of *inputsInit()*. On line 3, the *alarmTestButton* is configured with a pull-down resistor. Lines 4 to 7 remain just as in the previous examples. On line 8, *sirenPin* is configured as "*OpenDrain*", and on line 9 it is configured as an input. In this way, *sirenPin* is not energized, which turns off the buzzer.

```
1   void inputsInit()
2   {
3       alarmTestButton.mode(PullDown);
4       aButton.mode(PullDown);
5       bButton.mode(PullDown);
6       cButton.mode(PullDown);
7       dButton.mode(PullDown);
8       sirenPin.mode(OpenDrain);
9       sirenPin.input();
10  }
```

Code 3.10 New implementation of inputsInit().

In Code 3.11, the new implementation of *alarmActivationUpdate()* is shown, with the following modified lines:

▨ The lines regarding the potentiometer were all removed (lines 3 to 10 of Code 3.7).

▨ Lines 6 to 17: the calculation of the temperature is implemented. The analog input is read and stored in the current position of the *lm35ReadingsArray* on line 6. The index is incremented (line 7), and it is set to 0 if it is beyond the last position of the array (lines 8 and 9). Then, all the array positions are summed (lines 12 to 15), the average value is computed (line 16), and the value of *lm35TempC* is obtained (line 17).

▨ Line 25: the digital input *mq2* is used to assess gas detection (it is active in low state).

▨ Lines 33 to 37: the Alarm test button functionality is implemented (if it is pressed, then *overTempDetectorState*, *gasDetectorState*, and *alarmState* are set to ON).

▨ Lines 40 and 41: *sirenPin* is configured as output, and its value is set to LOW to activate the buzzer.

▨ Line 63: *sirenPin* is configured as input, which turns off the buzzer.

```
1   void alarmActivationUpdate()
2   {
3       static int lm35SampleIndex = 0;
4       int i = 0;
5
6       lm35ReadingsArray[lm35SampleIndex] = lm35.read();
7       lm35SampleIndex++;
8       if ( lm35SampleIndex >= NUMBER_OF_AVG_SAMPLES) {
9           lm35SampleIndex = 0;
10      }
11
12      lm35ReadingsSum = 0.0;
13      for (i = 0; i < NUMBER_OF_AVG_SAMPLES; i++) {
14          lm35ReadingsSum = lm35ReadingsSum + lm35ReadingsArray[i];
15      }
16      lm35ReadingsAverage = lm35ReadingsSum / NUMBER_OF_AVG_SAMPLES;
17      lm35TempC = analogReadingScaledWithTheLM35Formula ( lm35ReadingsAverage );
18
```

```
19        if ( lm35TempC > OVER_TEMP_LEVEL ) {
20            overTempDetector = ON;
21        } else {
22            overTempDetector = OFF;
23        }
24
25        if( !mq2) {
26            gasDetectorState = ON;
27            alarmState = ON;
28        }
29        if( overTempDetector ) {
30            overTempDetectorState = ON;
31            alarmState = ON;
32        }
33        if( alarmTestButton ) {
34            overTempDetectorState = ON;
35            gasDetectorState = ON;
36            alarmState = ON;
37        }
38        if( alarmState ) {
39            accumulatedTimeAlarm = accumulatedTimeAlarm + TIME_INCREMENT_MS;
40            sirenPin.output();
41            sirenPin = LOW;
42
43            if( gasDetectorState && overTempDetectorState ) {
44                if( accumulatedTimeAlarm >= BLINKING_TIME_GAS_AND_OVER_TEMP_ALARM ) {
45                    accumulatedTimeAlarm = 0;
46                    alarmLed = !alarmLed;
47                }
48            } else if( gasDetectorState ) {
49                if( accumulatedTimeAlarm >= BLINKING_TIME_GAS_ALARM ) {
50                    accumulatedTimeAlarm = 0;
51                    alarmLed = !alarmLed;
52                }
53            } else if ( overTempDetectorState ) {
54                if( accumulatedTimeAlarm >= BLINKING_TIME_OVER_TEMP_ALARM  ) {
55                    accumulatedTimeAlarm = 0;
56                    alarmLed = !alarmLed;
57                }
58            }
59        } else{
60            alarmLed = OFF;
61            gasDetectorState = OFF;
62            overTempDetectorState = OFF;
63            sirenPin.input();
64        }
65    }
```

Code 3.11 New implementation of alarmActivationUpdate().

NOTE: After a reset, the NUMBER_OF_AVG_SAMPLES positions of *lm35ReadingsArray* are not initialized. Therefore, until all of the positions of *m35ReadingsArray* are written at least once, the implementation shown in Code 3.11 may lead to wrong values in *lm35TempC*. This issue lasts for only one second and is addressed in the Proposed Exercise of this example.

The lines that were modified in *uartTask()* are shown in Code 3.12. It can be seen that in case '2', the digital input connected to the DOUT pin of the MQ-2 gas sensor is checked. If it has a low state, then it implies that gas is being detected. In case 'c' or 'C', the temperature expressed in degrees Celsius is shown on the serial terminal, while in case 'f' or 'F', the temperature expressed in degrees Fahrenheit is shown.

```
1   case '2':
2       if ( !mq2 ) {
3           uartUsb.write( "Gas is being detected\r\n", 22);
4       } else {
5           uartUsb.write( "Gas is not being detected\r\n", 27);
6       }
7       break;
8
9   case 'c':
10  case 'C':
11      sprintf ( str, "Temperature: %.2f \xB0 C\r\n", lm35TempC );
12      stringLength = strlen(str);
13      uartUsb.write( str, stringLength );
14      break;
15
16  case 'f':
17  case 'F':
18      sprintf ( str, "Temperature: %.2f \xB0 F\r\n",
19          celsiusToFahrenheit( lm35TempC ) );
20      stringLength = strlen(str);
21      uartUsb.write( str, stringLength );
22      break;
```

Code 3.12 Lines that were modified in the function uartTask().

Proposed Exercise

1. It has been mentioned that until all the positions of *lm35ReadingsArray* are written (i.e., during the first second), the value of *lm35TempC* is not correct because many positions of this array were not initialized. How can this problem be solved?

Answer to the Exercise

1. The function shown in Code 3.13 can be executed once after power on in order to initialize all the positions of *lm35ReadingsArray* to zero. In this way, at the beginning the value of *lm35TempC* will not be correct but will not trigger the over temperature alarm anyway, because the resulting average temperature will be very low (due to the fact that many zero values will be used in the average calculation). After one second, all the positions of *lm35ReadingsArray* will have correct values and, therefore, the value of *lm35TempC* will be correct. Be aware that if an under temperature condition is being checked, then this solution must be adapted.

```
1   void lm35ReadingsArrayInit()
2   {
3       int i;
4       for( i=0; i<NUMBER_OF_AVG_SAMPLES ; i++ ) {
5           lm35ReadingsArray[i] = 0;
6       }
7   }
```

Code 3.13 Implementation of the proposed function lm35ReadingsArrayInit().

3.3 Under the Hood

3.3.1 Basic Principles of Analog to Digital Conversion

In this chapter, the analog signal provided by the LM35 was *digitized* by the NUCLEO board by means of an analog to digital converter (ADC) included in the STM32 microcontroller. The aim of this subsection is to explain how the analog to digital converter works.

The STM32 microcontroller of the NUCLEO board includes a *Successive Approximation Register* (SAR) ADC. A simplified diagram of an SAR ADC is shown in Figure 3.10. The analog input of the ADC is indicated at the top of the figure, and the digital output value that is obtained as a result of the conversion process is indicated at the right side. The SAR ADC consists of three main elements: (1) an *Analog Comparator*, (2) a *Digital to Analog Converter* (DAC), and (3) an *Iterative Conversion Controller* (ICC). The analog signals and elements are indicated in light green, while the digital signals are indicated in dark green. A color gradient is used to indicate that a given element has inputs of one type and outputs of another type (i.e., the DAC has digital inputs and an analog output, while the analog converter has analog inputs and a digital output).

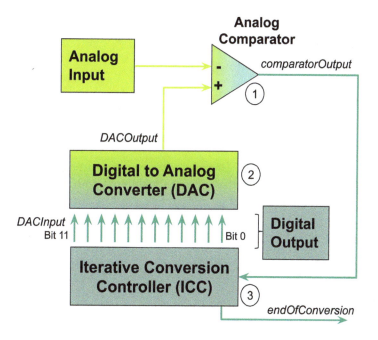

Figure 3.10 *Simplified diagram of a Successive Approximation Register analog to digital converter.*

As its name indicates, the SAR ADC is based on an iterative process. At the beginning of the process, the ICC sets Bit 11 at the *DACInput* to 1 (i.e., *DACInput* = 1000 0000 0000). In this way, a value equal to half of its full range is obtained at *DACOutput*. Then, the ICC analyzes the value of the *comparatorOutput*. If the *comparatorOutput* indicates that the voltage of the Analog Input is bigger than the *DACOutput*, the value at the *DACInput* is increased to 1100 0000 0000. In this way, a value equal to three quarters (75%) of the full range is obtained at the *DACOutput*. Conversely, if the value of the *comparatorOutput* indicates that the Analog Input is smaller than the *DACOutput*, then the ICC decreases the value at the *DACInput* to 0100 0000 0000. As a consequence, a value equal to one quarter (25%) of the *DACOutput* full range is obtained.

This process continues until the values of the twelve bits of *DACInput* are determined. At that point, the *End of Conversion* is reached, the signal *endOfConversion* is set to the active state, and the *DACOutput* value is the best possible digitalization of the analog input voltage. Then, the twelve bits that the ICC has established at *DACInput* are shared by the SAR ADC as the Digital Output result of the conversion. In the particular case of the functionality provided for the AnalogIn objects by the *mbed.h* library used in this chapter, the result of the conversion is scaled in the range of 0 to 1 (i.e., it returns 1.0 if 1111 1111 1111 is obtained, and 0.0 if 0000 0000 0000 is obtained).

TIP: For more information on SAR ADCs, see Maxim's application note 1080, available from [8].

Proposed Exercise

1. How can a successive approximation register (SAR) ADC be implemented on the NUCLEO board?

Answer to the Exercise

1. The proposed solution is available from [5] with the name "Under the Hood Chapter 3." The reader is encouraged to load the proposed solution onto the NUCLEO board and follow the prompts on the serial terminal to see how the implemented SAR ADC works.

In the proposed solution, the libraries *mbed.h* and *arm_book_lib.h* are used, as shown in Code 3.14. There are also two #defines, one to indicate the number of bits, NUMBER_OF_BITS, defined as 12, and another one, MAX_RESOLUTION, that is used to normalize the output into the 0 to 1 range, defined as 4095 (i.e., $2^{12} - 1$).

```
1   //=====[Libraries]==================================================
2
3   #include "mbed.h"
4   #include "arm_book_lib.h"
5
6   //=====[Defines]===================================================
7
8   #define NUMBER_OF_BITS 12
9   #define MAX_RESOLUTION 4095.0
```

Code 3.14 Libraries and defines used in the implementation of the proposed solution.

The public global objects that are used are shown in Code 3.15. The B1 USER button of the NUCLEO board is declared as the *nextStepButton* (line 3) and is used to advance one step in the iterative conversion process. The analog input A0 (line 5) is used earlier to get a reading of the analog signal at terminal (2) of the potentiometer, in the same way as it was used in this chapter. The LD1 of the

NUCLEO board is used to indicate the start of a new conversion (line 7), LD2 is used to indicate a new step in the conversion process (line 8), and LD3 is used to announce the end of the conversion (line 9). Finally, on line 11, the UnbufferedSerial object *uartUsb* is declared and will be used to send messages to the PC to show the current state of the conversion process.

```
1    //=====[Declaration and initialization of public global objects]================
2
3    DigitalIn nextStepButton(BUTTON1);
4
5    AnalogIn potentiometer(A0);
6
7    DigitalOut startOfConversionLed(LED1);
8    DigitalOut stepOfConversionLed(LED2);
9    DigitalOut endOfConversionLed(LED3);
10
11   UnbufferedSerial uartUsb(USBTX, USBRX, 115200);
```

Code 3.15 Public global objects used in the implementation of the proposed solution.

The public global variables that are used are shown in Code 3.16. On line 3, the variable *comparatorOutput* is declared and initialized to 0 and is used to implement the output of the Analog Comparator, as illustrated in Figure 3.10. An array called *DACInput* of type bool, of size NUMBER_OF_BITS, is declared on line 4. This is used to implement the input to the Digital to Analog Converter (see Figure 3.10). On line 5, an array called *digitalOutput* of type bool, of size NUMBER_OF_BITS, is declared. This is used to provide the digital output, as shown in Figure 3.10.

On line 7 of Code 3.16, an integer type variable called *conversionStep* is declared, which is used to keep track of the current conversion step. On line 9, the variable *analogInput* of type float is declared. This variable is used to get a reading of terminal 2 of the potentiometer. On line 10, a float type variable (*digitalOutputScaledIntoRange0to1*) is declared that is used once the conversion is finished to provide an output normalized in the range 0 to 1. Finally, on line 11, a float type variable *DACOutput* is defined that is used to implement the output of the Digital to Analog Converter (see Figure 3.10).

```
1    //=====[Declaration and initialization of public global variables]==============
2
3    bool comparatorOutput = 0;
4    bool DACInput[NUMBER_OF_BITS];
5    bool digitalOutput[NUMBER_OF_BITS];
6
7    int conversionStep = 0;
8
9    float analogInput;
10   float digitalOutputScaledIntoRange0to1 = 0;
11   float DACOutput = 0;
```

Code 3.16 Public global variables used in the implementation of the proposed solution.

In Code 3.17, the public functions used in the implementation of the proposed solution are shown. Line 3 declares the function *inputsInit()* that is used to initialize the inputs, and on line 4, the function *outputsInit()* that is used to initialize the outputs is declared. On line 6, the function *startOfConversion()* is declared and, on line 12, the function *endOfConversion()*. These two functions are used to turn on and off LD1 and LD3, respectively, and to send messages to the user by means of *uartUsb*. On line 7, the function *analogComparator()*, which is used to implement the Analog Comparator, is declared (see Figure 3.10). On line 8, the function that is used to implement one step of the Iterative Conversion Controller, *iterativeConversionControllerStep()*, is declared. The function used to implement the Digital to Analog Converter (DAC) is declared on line 9. On line 10, a function is declared that is used to reset the Iterative Conversion Controller. The function that is used to show the conversion status is declared on line 11. This function will send messages to the PC by means of *uartUsb* and will also turn on and off the LD2 of the NUCLEO board. Finally, the function that will show the result, *endOfConversion()*, is declared on line 12.

```
1   //=====[Declarations (prototypes) of public functions]=============================
2
3   void inputsInit();
4   void outputsInit();
5
6   void startOfConversion();
7   bool analogComparator();
8   bool iterativeConversionControllerStep();
9   float digitalToAnalogConverter();
10  void resetIterativeConversionController();
11  void showConversionStatus();
12  void endOfConversion();
```

Code 3.17 Public functions used in the implementation of the proposed solution.

In Code 3.18, the *main()* function is shown. On line 5, the function used to initialize the inputs is called (i.e., *inputsInit()*), and on line 6 the function used to initialize the outputs is called (*outputsInit()*). On line 8, the function *startOfConversion()* is used to send a message by means of *uartUsb* and to turn on LD1 for one second. On line 9, *resetIterativeConversionController()* is called in order to reset some specific variables.

The *for* loop between lines 10 and 22 is used to implement the SAR ADC following the diagram illustrated in Figure 3.10. From lines 10 to 12, it can be seen that the number of loops that are executed is equal to NUMBER_OF_BITS and that the current conversion step is tracked by *conversionStep*. On line 14, the variable *DACOutput* is assigned the return value of the function *digitalToAnalogConverter()*. On line 16, the variable *comparatorOutput* is assigned the return value of the function *analogComparator()*. The assignment of the Boolean state at the position "NUMBER_OF_BITS - conversionStep" of the array *DACInput* is made on line 18, using the return value of the function *iterativeConversionControllerStep()*. Line 21 is used to send the status of the conversion via *uartUsb* and LD2 by means of the function *showConversionStatus()*. Finally, on line 24, the function *endOfConversion()* is used to send the corresponding message by means of *uartUsb* and to turn on LD3 for one second.

```
1    //=====[Main function, the program entry point after power on or reset]=========
2
3    int main()
4    {
5        inputsInit();
6        outputsInit();
7        while (true) {
8            startOfConversion();
9            resetIterativeConversionController();
10           for ( conversionStep = 1;
11                 conversionStep <= NUMBER_OF_BITS;
12                 conversionStep++) {
13
14               DACOutput = digitalToAnalogConverter( );
15
16               comparatorOutput = analogComparator( );
17
18               DACInput[NUMBER_OF_BITS - conversionStep] =
19                   iterativeConversionControllerStep( );
20
21               showConversionStatus( );
22           }
23
24           endOfConversion( );
25       }
26   }
```

Code 3.18 Public functions used in the implementation of the proposed solution.

The implementation of the first two public functions is shown in Code 3.19. It is important to note that the function *inputsInit()* is empty and that the only reason this function is kept is to follow the organization of the programs established in previous chapters. On line 7, the implementation of *outputsInit()* is shown. It can be seen that the three LEDs are turned off.

```
1    //=====[Implementations of public functions]==================================
2
3    void inputsInit()
4    {
5    }
6
7    void outputsInit()
8    {
9        startOfConversionLed = OFF;
10       stepOfConversionLed = OFF;
11       endOfConversionLed = OFF;
12   }
```

Code 3.19 Implementation of the functions inputsInit() and outputsInit().

The implementation of the function *startOfConversion()* is shown in Code 3.20. In line 3, the message "Please press Next Step Button (B1 USER)" is sent over *uartUsb*. Line 4 is used to wait until the *nextStepButton* is pressed. In line 5, a message is sent to indicate that the conversion has started. On line 6, the reading of terminal 2 of the potentiometer is stored in the variable *analogInput*. Finally, lines 7 to 9 turn on *startofConversionLed* for one second.

```
1   void startOfConversion()
2   {
3       uartUsb.write( "Please press Next Step Button (B1 USER)\r\n\r\n" , 43 );
4       while (!nextStepButton) {};
5       uartUsb.write( "Conversion started\r\n\r\n" , 22 );
6       analogInput = potentiometer.read();
7       startOfConversionLed = ON;
8       delay(1000);
9       startOfConversionLed = OFF;
10  }
```

Code 3.20 Implementation of the function startOfConversion().

In Code 3.21, the implementation of the function *resetIterativeConversionController()* is shown. On line 3, a local integer variable named *I* is declared. This variable is used from line 4 to 6 in order to store a 0 in each of the NUMBER_OF_BITS positions of *DACInput*. Finally, in line 7, a message indicating that *DACinput* has been reset is sent by *uartUsb*.

```
1   void resetIterativeConversionController( )
2   {
3       int i;
4       for ( i = 0; i < NUMBER_OF_BITS; i++) {
5           DACInput[i]=0;
6       }
7       uartUsb.write( "DACinput reseted\r\n\r\n" , 20 );
8   }
```

Code 3.21 Implementation of the function resetIterativeConversionController().

Code 3.22 shows the implementation of the function *iterativeConversionControllerStep()*. It can be seen in line 3 that if *comparatorOutput* is equal to 1, then 1 is returned (line 4), and if *comparatorOutput* is not equal to 1, then 0 is returned (line 6).

```
1   bool iterativeConversionControllerStep( )
2   {
3       if (comparatorOutput == 1) {
4           return 1;
5       } else {
6           return 0;
7       }
8   }
```

Code 3.22 Implementation of the function iterativeConversionControllerStep().

The implementation of the function *digitalToAnalogConverter()* is shown in Code 3.23. Three variables are declared in lines 3 to 5: a float called *output*, which is initialized to 0 and is used to compute the output value; an integer variable called *power*, which is initialized to 1 and is used to implement some mathematical operations; and an integer auxiliary variable called *i*. The *for* loop on line 7 is used to implement the operation between lines 8 and 14 NUMBER_OF_BITS times. The condition inside the *if* statement on line 8 is true only when the variable *i* has the same value as "NUMBER_OF_BITS - *conversionStep*". For example, in the first conversion step the variable *conversionStep* is equal to 1. Then, considering that NUMBER_OF_BITS is defined as 12, "NUMBER_OF_BITS - *conversionStep*" is equal to 11. So the condition "*i* == NUMBER_OF_BITS - *conversionStep*" is only valid for *i* being 11. In this way, considering that at the beginning all the positions of *DACInput* are equal to 0, after 11 executions of line 11 with *i* varying from 0 to 10, *output* will be equal to 0 and *power* will be equal to 2^{11}. Then, with *i* being 11, 2^{11} (2048) will be added to *output* and, therefore, the return value (line 16) will be 0.5001 (2048/4095).

```
1   float digitalToAnalogConverter( )
2   {
3       float output = 0;
4       int power = 1;
5       int i;
6
7       for (i=0; i<NUMBER_OF_BITS; i++) {
8           if (i == ( NUMBER_OF_BITS - conversionStep ) ) {
9               output += 1*power;
10          } else {
11              output += DACInput[i]*power;
12          }
13          power *= 2;
14      }
15
16      return output / MAX_RESOLUTION;
17  }
```

Code 3.23 Implementation of the function digitalToAnalogConverter().

In Code 3.24, the implementation of the *analogComparator()* function is shown. It returns 1 if "*analogInput* >= *DACOutput*" and returns 0 otherwise.

```
1   bool analogComparator( )
2   {
3       if ( analogInput >= DACOutput ) {
4           return 1;
5       } else {
6           return 0;
7       }
8   }
```

Code 3.24 Implementation of the function analogComparator().

The implementation of the function *showConversionStatus()* is shown in Code 3.25. Lines 5 to 10 are used to send the current value of *conversionStep, analogInput,* and *DACOutput* over *uartUsb*. On line 11, the message "DAC Input:" and then one after the other "1" and "0" are sent, depending on the content of each of the positions of the array *DACInput* (lines 13 to 19). Line 20 is used to send a message that contains only a vertical separation. A delay of one second is introduced in line 21, then in line 22 *stepOfConversion* is turned ON and waits until the *nextStepButton* is pressed (line 23) to turn it OFF (line 24).

```
1   void showConversionStatus ( )
2   {
3       int i;
4       char str[30];
5       sprintf ( str, "Conversion step: %i\r\n", conversionStep );
6       uartUsb.write( str, strlen(str) );
7       sprintf ( str, "Analog Input: %.3f\r\n", analogInput );
8       uartUsb.write( str, strlen(str) );
9       sprintf ( str, "DAC Output: %.3f\r\n", DACOutput );
10      uartUsb.write( str, strlen(str) );
11      uartUsb.write( "DAC Input: " , 11);
12
13      for (i=1; i<=NUMBER_OF_BITS; i++) {
14          if (DACInput[NUMBER_OF_BITS-i] == 1) {
15              uartUsb.write( "1" , 1 );
16          } else {
17              uartUsb.write(  "0" , 1 );
18          }
19      }
20      uartUsb.write( "\r\n\r\n" , 4 );
21      delay(1000);
22      stepOfConversionLed = ON;
23      while (!nextStepButton);
24      stepOfConversionLed = OFF;
25  }
```

Code 3.25 Implementation of the function showConversionStatus().

Finally, in Code 3.26, the implementation of the function *endOfConversion()* is shown. It is quite similar to the implementation of the function *showConversionStatus()*. The differences are that there is now an "End of conversion message" on line 4 and *endOfConversionLed* is turned on instead of *stepOfConversionLed*. Additionally, *DACInput* is not shown because it is an internal value that has no meaning once the conversion is finished.

```
1   void endOfConversion ( )
2   {
3       char str[30];
4       sprintf ( str, "End of conversion\r\n\r\n" );
5       uartUsb.write( str, strlen(str) );
6       sprintf ( str, "Analog Input: %.3f\r\n", analogInput );
7       uartUsb.write( str, strlen(str) );
8       sprintf ( str, "DAC Output: %.3f\r\n", DACOutput );
9       uartUsb.write( str, strlen(str) );
10
11      endOfConversionLed = ON;
12      delay(1000);
13      endOfConversionLed = OFF;
14  }
```

Code 3.26 Implementation of the function endOfConversion().

3.4 Case Study

3.4.1 Vineyard Frost Prevention

In this chapter, a temperature sensor was connected to the NUCLEO board and the measured temperature was sent to a PC using serial communication. In this way, the alarm was activated if over temperature was detected, and using a serial terminal, it was possible to read the temperature on the PC. A vineyard frost prevention system, where low temperatures are detected, built with Mbed and containing some similar features, can be found in [9]. Figure 3.11 shows a representation of the system.

Figure 3.11 "Vineyard frost prevention" built with Mbed contains elements introduced in this chapter.

The localized sensors of the vineyard frost prevention system are designed to be mounted over the vines, and their measurements are transmitted via a wireless LoRa network. Therefore, specific vines requiring protection from frost can be detected, which improves the yield of grapes. Better performance is obtained in comparison with centralized sensing systems.

It can be appreciated that the functionality shown in Figure 3.11 is very similar to the functionality implemented in this chapter (i.e., temperature measurement plus results displayed on a PC). The following chapters will explain how to implement a wireless connection to the NUCLEO board and will also introduce the knowledge required to understand the use and utility of some other technologies mentioned in [9], such as LoRa networking.

Proposed Exercises

1. Does the vineyard frost prevention system measure any other variables besides temperature?

2. Is the core of the microcontroller used by the vineyard frost prevention system the same as the core of the STM32 microcontroller of the NUCLEO Board?

Answers to the Exercises

1. The vineyard frost prevention system is also provided with humidity sensors.

2. The vineyard frost prevention system is based on an Arm Cortex-M3 running at 32 MHz, while the NUCLEO board has an Arm Cortex-M4 that can run at 180 MHz. This implies that the NUCLEO board is provided with a more powerful processor that runs up to six times faster.

References

[1] "LM35 data sheet, product information and support | TI.com". Accessed July 9, 2021.
https://www.ti.com/product/LM35

[2] "MQ2 Gas Sensor Pinout, Features, Equivalents & Datasheet". Accessed July 9, 2021.
https://components101.com/sensors/mq2-gas-sensor

[3] "List of integrated circuit packaging types - Wikipedia". Accessed July 9, 2021.
https://en.wikipedia.org/wiki/List_of_integrated_circuit_packaging_types

[4] "What is MOSFET: Symbol, Working, Types & Different Packages". Accessed July 9, 2021.
https://components101.com/articles/mosfet-symbol-working-operation-types-and-applications

[5] "GitHub - armBookCodeExamples/Directory". Accessed July 9, 2021.
https://github.com/armBookCodeExamples/Directory/

[6] "printf - C++ Reference". Accessed July 9, 2021.
https://www.cplusplus.com/reference/cstdio/printf/

[7] "mbed-os/README.md at master · ARMmbed/mbed-os · GitHub". Accessed July 9, 2021.
https://github.com/ARMmbed/mbed-os/blob/master/platform/source/minimal-printf/README.md#usage

[8] "Understanding SAR ADCs: Their Architecture and Comparison with Other ADCs". Accessed July 9, 2021.
https://pdfserv.maximintegrated.com/en/an/AN1080.pdf

[9] "Vineyard frost prevention | Mbed". Accessed July 9, 2021.
https://os.mbed.com/built-with-mbed/vineyard-frost-prevention/

Chapter 4

Finite-State Machines and
the Real-Time Clock

4.1 Roadmap

4.1.1 What You Will Learn

After you have studied the material in this chapter, you will be able to:

▪ Describe how to connect matrix keypads to the NUCLEO board.

▪ Summarize the fundamentals of programs based on finite-state machines (FSMs).

▪ Develop programs that implement FSMs with the NUCLEO board.

▪ Implement programs that make use of the real-time clock (RTC).

▪ Use pointers to manage character strings.

4.1.2 Review of Previous Chapters

In previous chapters, many features were added to the smart home system. Those features were controlled by a set of buttons, which in some cases had to be pressed in a particular order and in other cases had to be pressed at the same time (e.g., A + B + Enter or A + B + C + D). Pressing multiple buttons at the same time can be both difficult and impractical. It is, therefore, desirable to find a more convenient way to control the system.

An alarm was also included in the system and could be activated due to gas detection, over temperature detection, or the simultaneous occurrence of both. In the current implementation, the system has no way to record which alarms have been triggered or which events triggered those alarms.

4.1.3 Contents of This Chapter

As the complexity of the system increases, it becomes necessary to introduce more powerful techniques in order to sustain software maintainability and increase flexibility. In this chapter, the concept of a *finite-state machine* (FSM) is introduced and its support in organizing programs will be described.

FSMs are introduced by means of a new feature that is added to the system: the "double-press" functionality on the Enter button. Using this, the Enter button can be pressed twice consecutively to turn off the Incorrect code LED. This improvement will be accompanied by the use of a matrix keypad instead of buttons connected to the breadboard. This replacement will be completed gradually through the chapter, as new concepts must be developed to fully incorporate the usage of the matrix keypad.

Finally, the *real-time clock* (RTC) of the STM32 microcontroller will be used to incorporate a time stamp into the events that are detected by the smart home system. In this way, it will be possible, for example, to register or log the time and date of the alarm activations and access this information from the PC.

WARNING: The program code of the examples introduced in this chapter gets quite large. For example, the program code in Example 4.4 has almost 600 lines. The reader will see that it is not easy to follow a program with so many lines in a single file. This problem will be tackled in the next chapter, where modularization applied to embedded systems programming is introduced in order to reorganize the program code into smaller files. In this way, the learn-by-doing principle is followed.

4.2 Matrix Keypad Reading with the NUCLEO Board

4.2.1 Connect a Matrix Keypad and a Power Supply to the Smart Home System

In this chapter, more buttons will be added to the alarm control panel of the smart home system, as shown in Figure 4.1. The aim is to improve the functionality and to allow the use of numeric codes as is common in this type of system.

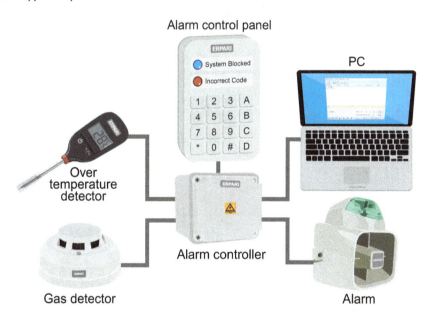

Figure 4.1 The smart home system is now connected to a matrix keypad.

It will also be explained through the examples how an FSM can be used to improve the way in which the numeric code is entered. By using an FSM it will be possible to enter the digits of the code one after the other. This contrasts with the method of pressing multiple buttons at once, as in Chapter 1.

To implement the new functionality, a matrix keypad such as the one described in [1] should be connected to the smart home system, as shown in Figure 4.2. An MB102 module, such as the one presented in [2], should also be connected. Matrix keypads are usually found in calculators, microwaves, door locks, and similar devices. They are available in different sizes, but 4 × 4 and 4 × 3 are the most common. The MB102 module is a breadboard power supply used to avoid overloading power supplied by the NUCLEO board.

In the following examples, new functions will be introduced into the program to gradually replace the buttons connected to D4–D7 by the matrix keypad.

 NOTE: The buttons connected to D2 and D4–D7 are used in Examples 4.1 and 4.2. They can be removed from the setup in Example 4.3, as their functionality will be assigned to the B1 User button and the matrix keypad, respectively.

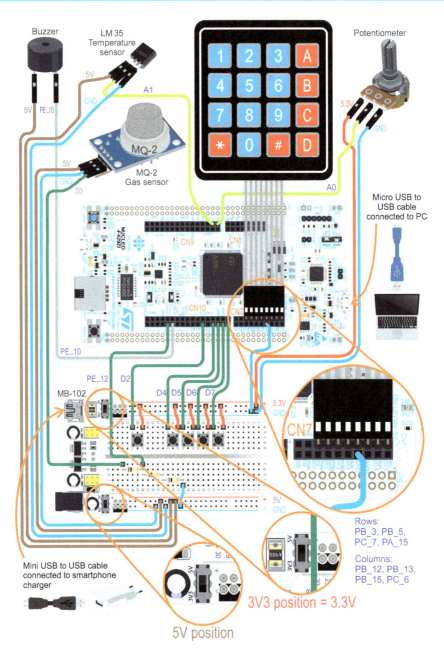

Figure 4.2 The smart home system is now connected to a matrix keypad.

Figure 4.3 shows how to use a 90-degree 2.54 mm (0.1") pitch pin header to prepare the connector of the matrix keypad for the proposed setup.

Figure 4.3 Detail showing how to prepare the matrix keypad connector using a pin header.

A diagram illustrating the connections of the matrix keypad is shown in Figure 4.4. It can be seen that four pins are used for the rows (R1–R4) and four pins are used for the columns (C1–C4).

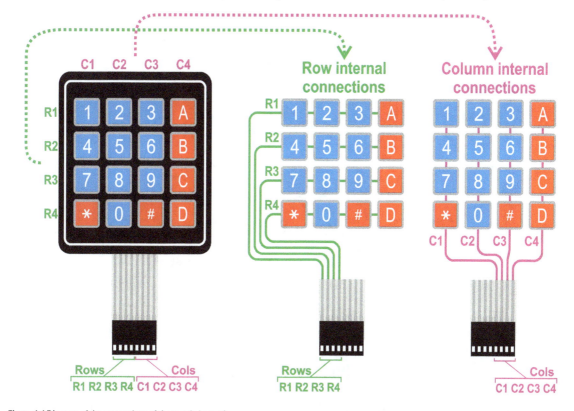

Figure 4.4 Diagram of the connections of the matrix keypad.

The internal connections of the matrix keypad are shown in Figure 4.5. For example, when key "1" is pressed, a connection is established between R1 and C1; when key "2" is pressed, R1 is connected to C2.

In Figure 4.5, the connections of the NUCLEO board and the matrix keypad are also shown. To scan if key "1" is pressed, a 0 V signal is connected to PB_3 (which is connected to R1), and the state of PB_12 (which is connected to C1) is read. If PB_12 is OFF, it means that key "1" is pressed; otherwise it is not pressed. This is because .mode(PullUp) is used to configure the digital inputs that are used (PB_12, PB_13, PB_15, and PC_6). The same procedure is used to determine if key "2" is pressed, but replacing PB_12 by PB_13, since PB_13 is connected to C2, as can be seen in Figure 4.5. To scan other keys, the corresponding rows and columns should be used.

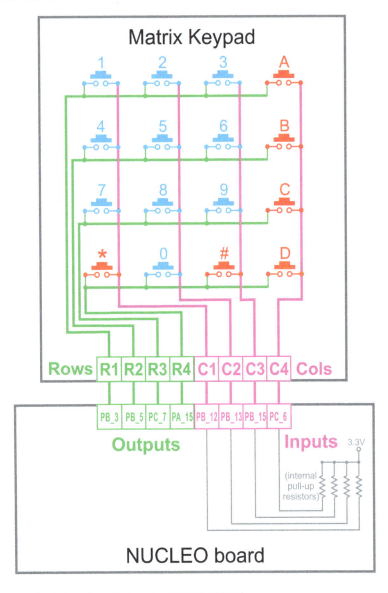

Figure 4.5 Diagram of the connections between the matrix keypad and the NUCLEO board.

NOTE: The use of a matrix for the connection of the keys of the keypad allows a reduction in the number of wires that are used to get the state of the keys. For example, instead of using 17 wires to read 16 keys (one for each key and one for GND), in Figure 4.5, 8 wires are used to read 16 keys.

The following subsection explains how to test if the matrix keypad is working properly. In addition, the examples explain how to tackle glitches and bounces in the signal, which are common in any types of keys or buttons, as shown in Figure 4.6. Glitches are unexpected variations in the signal due to electrical noise, while bounces are a consequence of the spring that is part of the key or button.

Typically, a glitch lasts for less than 1 millisecond, while a bounce can last up to 30 milliseconds. This chapter will explain how the signal can be processed, using an FSM, in order to distinguish between a key or button being pressed and a glitch or a bounce. By filtering glitches and bounces using software, it is possible to avoid, or at least reduce, the usage of electronic components for filtering purposes.

 NOTE: The voltage levels shown in Figure 4.6 correspond to the connections in Figure 4.5. The techniques that are explained in this chapter can also be applied if the voltages are reversed in such a way that the signal is 0 V if the key or button is not pressed and 3.3 V if it is pressed, as in the previous chapters.

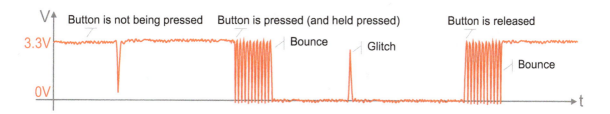

Figure 4.6 Voltage signal over time for a given button, including typical glitches and bounces.

 NOTE: In previous chapters, glitches and bounces caused no problems as the system behavior was specially designed in order to avoid problems regarding unwanted consecutive readings of the buttons. For example, the Enter and A, B, C, and/or D buttons were used to enter a code. Therefore, once the buttons had been read, it didn't matter if those buttons were held down for a long time because before entering a new code, the Enter button should be released and A + B + C + D all pressed together. In this chapter, the keys of the matrix keypad will be pressed one after the other, so glitches and bounces could be interpreted as a key being pressed many times, leading to unexpected behavior of the system.

In Figure 4.7, a diagram of the MB102 module is shown. As mentioned previously, this power supply module is used to avoid overloading the capability of the 3.3 V and 5 V pins of the NUCLEO board. In [3] it is stated: "Caution: In case the maximum current consumption of the STM32 Nucleo-144 board and its shield boards exceeds 300 mA, it is mandatory to power the STM32 Nucleo-144 board with an external power supply connected to E5V, VIN or +3.3 V." As the 300 mA limit will be exceeded in the next chapters, hereafter all the elements connected to the NUCLEO board will be powered by the MB102 module, as shown in Figure 4.2. This can provide up to 700 mA [2].

The MB102 module can be supplied either by a standard USB connector or by a 7 to 12 V power supply, as shown in Figure 4.7. The diagram also shows that this module has many 3.3 V and 5 V outputs, some fixed and some selectable.

> **WARNING:** The selectable outputs should be configured as indicated in Figure 4.7. Otherwise, some modules may be harmed.

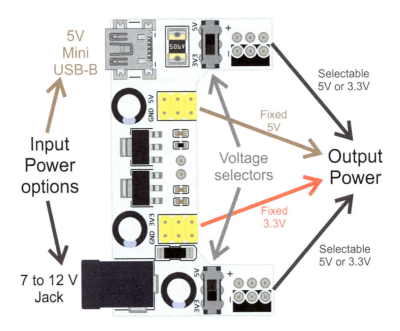

Figure 4.7 Diagram of the MB102 module.

4.2.2 Test the Operation of the Matrix Keypad and the RTC

This subsection explains how to load a program onto the STM32 microcontroller in order to test if the matrix keypad that has been connected is working properly. It will also show how to configure the RTC of the STM32 microcontroller. The serial terminal will display the keys that are pressed on the matrix keypad, and the PC keyboard will be used to configure the date and time of the RTC. The *.bin* file of the program "Subsection 4.2.2" should be downloaded from the URL available in [4] and dragged onto the NUCLEO board.

In Table 4.1, the available commands for the program that is used in this subsection are shown. If the "k" key is pressed on the PC keyboard, then the buttons pressed on the matrix keypad are shown on the serial terminal. This behavior continues until "q" is pressed on the PC keyboard.

Table 4.1 *Available commands for the program used to test the matrix keypad and to configure the RTC.*

Key pressed	Description of the commands
k	Show the keys pressed on the matrix keypad
q	Quit the k command
s	Set the current date and time
t	Get the current date and time

Press the "s" key and follow the instructions to set the current date and time for the RTC. Then press the "t" key to get the current date and time. Wait for a few seconds and press "t" again in order to verify that the RTC is working properly. The new date and time shown in the PC should reflect the time progression.

 WARNING: The NUCLEO board must be powered in order to keep the RTC working. If the power supply is removed, the time and date of the RTC have to be set again.

Example 4.1: Turn Off the Incorrect Code LED by Double-Pressing the Enter Button

Objective

Introduce enumerated data type definitions and the implementation of FSMs.

Summary of the Expected Behavior

To turn off the Incorrect code LED, the Enter button (B1 USER button of the NUCLEO board) must be double-pressed (pressed twice consecutively). This replaces simultaneously pressing the buttons connected to D4–D7 (A + B + C + D) as implemented in Chapter 1.

Test the Proposed Solution on the Board

Import the project "Example 4.1" using the URL available in [4], build the project, and drag the .*bin* file onto the NUCLEO board. Press the Alarm test button (button connected to D2) to activate the alarm. The Alarm LED (LD1) should start blinking, at a rate of 100 ms on and 100 ms off. Enter an incorrect deactivation code for the alarm by means of simultaneously pressing the buttons A + C + Enter on the control panel (i.e., D4 + D6 + B1 USER button). The Incorrect code LED (LD3) will turn on. Double press the Enter button (B1 USER button). The Incorrect code LED (LD3) turns off to indicate that a new attempt to enter the code can be made. Deactivate the alarm by simultaneously pressing the buttons A + B + Enter on the control panel (i.e., D4 + D5 + B1 USER button).

Discussion of the Proposed Solution

The proposed solution is based on identifying the state of the Enter button among its four possible states:

▣ Button released (it is stable "up")

▣ Button being pressed (it has just been pressed and is moving from "up" to "down", i.e., is "falling")

▣ Button pressed (it is stable "down")

▣ Button being released (it has just been released and is moving from "down" to "up", i.e., is "rising")

 NOTE: As shown in section 4.2.1, the transition from being "down" to being "up" (or the other way around) entails multiple fast bounces between the two states. For this reason, a *debounce* sequence is used in order to avoid treating bounces as multiple presses of the button.

Implementation of the Proposed Solution

Table 4.2 shows the DEBOUNCE_BUTTON_TIME_MS #define that is used to implement the debounce of the B1 USER button. A value of 40 is used to give a safety margin above the bounce time of 30 milliseconds discussed in subsection 4.2.1.

A new section that is introduced in this chapter is also shown in Table 4.2. This section is called "Declaration of public data types" and is used to implement the definition of new data types that are specified by the programmer. The data type *buttonState_t* is declared using an enumerated data type and four possible values (known as *enumerators*): BUTTON_UP, BUTTON_FALLING, BUTTON_DOWN, and BUTTON_RISING. The suffix "_t" is used to indicate that *buttonState_t* is a user-defined data type.

The variable *accumulatedDebounceButtonTime*, declared as shown in Table 4.2, will be used to account for the debounce time, while the variable *numberOfEnterButtonReleasedEvents* will be used to implement the double-pressed functionality. In addition, a variable *enterButtonState* of the data type *buttonState_t* is declared.

In the section "Declarations (prototypes) of public functions", three new functions are declared. The function *lm35ReadingsArrayInit()* was introduced and discussed in the proposed exercise of Example 2.5 and therefore is not discussed here again. The functions *debounceButtonInit()* and *debounceButtonUpdate()* will be used to implement the debounce.

Finally, a call to the function *debounceButtonInit()* is included in the function *inputsInit()*.

Table 4.2 Sections and functions in which lines were added to Example 3.5.

Section or function	Lines that were added
Definitions	`#define DEBOUNCE_BUTTON_TIME_MS    40`
Declaration of public data types	```typedef enum {` ` BUTTON_UP` ` BUTTON_FALLING` ` BUTTON_DOWN` ` BUTTON_RISING` `} buttonState_t;```

Declaration and initialization of public global variables	`int accumulatedDebounceButtonTime = 0;`
	`int numberOfEnterButtonReleasedEvents = 0;`
	`buttonState_t enterButtonState;`

Declarations (prototypes) of public functions	`void lm35ReadingsArrayInit();`
	`void debounceButtonInit();`
	`bool debounceButtonUpdate();`

Function inputsInit()	`debounceButtonInit();`

In Code 4.1, the function *debounceButtonInit()* is shown. This function is used to establish the initial state of the Enter button. If the Enter button is pressed (line 3), *enterButtonState* is set to BUTTON_DOWN (line 4). If it is not pressed, *enterButtonState* is set to BUTTON_UP (line 6).

```
1   void debounceButtonInit()
2   {
3       if( enterButton ) {
4           enterButtonState = BUTTON_DOWN;
5       } else {
6           enterButtonState = BUTTON_UP;
7       }
8   }
```

Code 4.1 Details of the function debounceButtonInit().

In Code 4.2, the new implementation of the function *alarmActivationUpdate()* is shown. To allow a new code to be entered after an incorrect code has been entered by pressing the Enter button (B1 USER) twice, lines 4 to 12 are changed from Example 3.5. If the variable *numberOfIncorrectCodes* is less than 5, a Boolean variable called *enterButtonReleasedEvent* is declared (line 4) and is assigned the value returned by the function *debounceButtonUpdate()*. The implementation of *debounceButtonUpdate()* will be discussed in Code 4.3.

On line 5, a check is made as to whether there is a new button released event. If so, line 6 evaluates whether *incorrectCodeLed* is ON, and if so, the variable *numberOfEnterButtonReleasedEvents* is increased by one. Line 8 evaluates whether there were two or more enter button released events, and if so then the Incorrect code LED is turned off and *numberOfEnterButtonReleasedEvents* is set to zero (line 9 and line 10). This implements the double-press functionality for the Enter button.

 NOTE: In the proposed implementation it doesn't matter how much time elapses between two consecutive presses of the Enter button; they will be considered a double-press.

Lines 12 to 25 show the implementation of the Incorrect code LED deactivation by means of the control panel. The statements are very similar to those used in previous chapters. First, the variable *alarmState* is evaluated (line 13) and, if the alarm LED is on, then the states of the buttons A to D are loaded into the corresponding positions of the array *buttonsPressed*. Then, the function *areEqual()* is used to compare the buttons pressed on the control panel with the corresponding code, and if they are equal, then *alarmState* is set to OFF and *numberOfIncorrectCodes* is set to zero. Otherwise, *incorrectCodeLed* is turned on, and the variable *numberOfIncorrectCodes* is incremented.

Finally, on line 28 it can be seen that if *numberOfIncorrectCodes* is greater than or equal to 5, then *systemBlockedLed* is set to ON.

```
1   void alarmDeactivationUpdate()
2   {
3       if ( numberOfIncorrectCodes < 5 ) {
4           bool enterButtonReleasedEvent = debounceButtonUpdate();
5           if( enterButtonReleasedEvent ) {
6               if( incorrectCodeLed ) {
7                   numberOfEnterButtonReleasedEvents++;
8                   if( numberOfEnterButtonReleasedEvents >= 2 ) {
9                       incorrectCodeLed = OFF;
10                      numberOfEnterButtonReleasedEvents = 0;
11                  }
12              } else {
13                  if ( alarmState ) {
14                      buttonsPressed[0] = aButton;
15                      buttonsPressed[1] = bButton;
16                      buttonsPressed[2] = cButton;
17                      buttonsPressed[3] = dButton;
18                      if ( areEqual() ) {
19                          alarmState = OFF;
20                          numberOfIncorrectCodes = 0;
21                      } else {
22                          incorrectCodeLed = ON;
23                          numberOfIncorrectCodes++;
24                      }
25                  }
26              }
27          }
28      } else {
29          systemBlockedLed = ON;
30      }
31  }
```

Code 4.2 Modifications introduced in the function alarmDeactivationUpdate().

The implementation of the function *debounceButtonUpdate()* is shown in Code 4.3. On line 3, the Boolean variable *enterButtonReleasedEvent* is declared and initialized to false. On line 5, there is a *switch* statement over the variable *enterButtonState*. In the case of *enterButtonState* being equal to BUTTON_UP (line 6), the program verifies if the Enter button has been pressed (line 7). If so, the variable *enterButtonState* is set to BUTTON_FALLING (line 8), and *accumulatedDebounceTime* is set to zero.

In the case of *enterButtonState* being equal to BUTTON_FALLING (line 13), the program first verifies whether *accumulatedDebounceTime* is greater than or equal to DEBOUNCE_BUTTON_TIME_MS. If the Enter button is being pressed (*enterButton* is true, assessed in line 15), then *enterButtonState* is set to BUTTON_DOWN; otherwise it is set to BUTTON_UP. On line 21, *accumulatedDebounceTime* is incremented by TIME_INCREMENT_MS.

> **NOTE:** In this proposed solution, 40 is used in the definition of DEBOUNCE_BUTTON_TIME_MS. Depending on the matrix keypad, this time might be too small or too big. The user is encouraged to modify this value if the program behavior is not as expected.

On line 25 it can be seen that the case for BUTTON_DOWN is very similar to the case for BUTTON_UP. The difference is that if *enterButton* is not true (i.e., is false), then *enterButtonState* is set to BUTTON_RISING. The case for BUTTON_RISING on line 32 is also very similar to the case for BUTTON_FALLING. One difference is that !*enterButton* is used in the *if* statement, as well as the variable *enterButtonReleasedEvent* being set to true on line 36.

> **NOTE:** It should be noted that the following statements are all equivalent: if (!enterButton), if (enterButton == 0), if (enterButton == false).

```
1   bool debounceButtonUpdate()
2   {
3       bool enterButtonReleasedEvent = false;
4       switch( enterButtonState ) {
5
6       case BUTTON_UP:
7           if( enterButton ) {
8               enterButtonState = BUTTON_FALLING;
9               accumulatedDebounceButtonTime = 0;
10          }
11          break;
12
13      case BUTTON_FALLING:
14          if( accumulatedDebounceButtonTime >= DEBOUNCE_BUTTON_TIME_MS ) {
15              if( enterButton ) {
16                  enterButtonState = BUTTON_DOWN;
17              } else {
18                  enterButtonState = BUTTON_UP;
19              }
20          }
21          accumulatedDebounceButtonTime = accumulatedDebounceButtonTime +
22                                  TIME_INCREMENT_MS;
23          break;
24
25      case BUTTON_DOWN:
26          if( !enterButton ) {
27              enterButtonState = BUTTON_RISING;
28              accumulatedDebounceButtonTime = 0;
29          }
30          break;
31
32      case BUTTON_RISING:
33          if( accumulatedDebounceButtonTime >= DEBOUNCE_BUTTON_TIME_MS ) {
34              if( !enterButton ) {
```

```
35                    enterButtonState = BUTTON_UP;
36                    enterButtonReleasedEvent = true;
37              } else {
38                    enterButtonState = BUTTON_DOWN;
39              }
40          }
41          accumulatedDebounceButtonTime = accumulatedDebounceButtonTime +
42                              TIME_INCREMENT_MS;
43          break;
44
45      default:
46          debounceButtonInit();
47          break;
48      }
49      return enterButtonReleasedEvent;
50  }
```

Code 4.3 Details of the function debounceButtonUpdate().

 NOTE: In Code 4.3, the four different *states* are indicated by BUTTON_UP, BUTTON_FALLING, BUTTON_DOWN, and BUTTON_RISING. In the Under the Hood section, these four states and their corresponding transitions are shown alongside the signal variations over time, in order to show in more detail how the glitches and bounces are processed.

Proposed Exercise

1. How can the code be modified in order to properly debounce a button with a bouncing time of about 400 ms?

Answer to the Exercise

1. The value of DEBOUNCE_BUTTON_TIME_MS could be increased above 400. It should be noted that if the user presses and releases the Enter button in less than 400 ms with this implemented, then the implemented code will ignore the pressing of the Enter Button. The reader is encouraged to test this behavior.

Example 4.2: Introduce the Usage of the Matrix Keypad

Objective

Get familiar with the usage of FSMs.

Summary of the Expected Behavior

The matrix keypad buttons labeled A, B, C, and D should replace the functionality of the buttons connected to D4, D5, D6, and D7, respectively.

Test the Proposed Solution on the Board

Import the project "Example 4.2" using the URL available in [4], build the project, and drag the *.bin* file onto the NUCLEO board. Press the Alarm test button (button connected to D2) to activate the alarm. The Alarm LED (LD1) should start blinking at a rate of 100 ms on and 100 ms off. Enter an incorrect code to deactivate the alarm by means of pressing first the "A" key, then the "C" key, and finally the "#" key, which is used as the Enter button. The Incorrect code LED (LD3) will turn on. Double click the Enter button (the "#" key). The Incorrect code LED (LD3) turns off to indicate that a new attempt to enter the code can be made. Press the keys "A", "B", then "#" and the alarm should deactivate.

Discussion of the Proposed Solution

The proposed solution is based on an FSM that has three states. One state is used to scan the matrix keypad, another state is used to debounce the key pressed at the matrix keypad, and the last state is used to determine if a key has been held pressed or released.

Implementation of the Proposed Solution

In Table 4.3, the #defines that were added to Example 4.1 are shown. The numbers of rows and columns have been defined as four in both cases. A new enumerated data type has also been defined, named *matrixKeypadState_t*, having the three states that will be used in the FSM (MATRIX_KEYPAD_SCANNING, MATRIX_KEYPAD_DEBOUNCE, and MATRIX_KEYPAD_KEY_HOLD_PRESSED).

In the section "Declaration and initialization of public global objects," two arrays of objects are declared. One, *keypadRowPins*, will be used to introduce signals into the matrix keypad by means of pins PB_3, PB_5, PC_7, and PA_15. This array is declared as an array of DigitalOut. The second array, *keypadColPins*, will be used to read the signals at the pins PB_12, PB_13, PB_15, and PC_6. This is declared as an array of DigitalIn. Note that this is the first time in the book that arrays of DigitalIn and DigitalOut objects are created.

The variables *accumulatedDebounceMatrixKeypadTime* and *matrixKeypadLastKeyPressed* are declared and initialized to zero and the null character ('\0'), respectively. An array of char, *matrixKeypadIndexToCharArray*, is declared and initialized and will be used to identify the keys being pressed on the matrix keypad. Finally, a variable of the user-defined type *matrixKeypadState_t* is declared as *matrixKeypadState*.

In the section "Declarations (prototypes) of public functions," three new functions are declared: *matrixKeypadInit()*, *matrixKeypadScan()*, and *matrixKeypadUpdate()*. These functions are explained in the example.

Finally, Table 4.3 shows that a call to the function *matrixKeypadInit()* is included in the function *inputsInit()*.

Table 4.3 Sections and functions in which lines were added to Example 4.1.

Section or function	Lines that were added
Definitions	`#define KEYPAD_NUMBER_OF_ROWS    4` `#define KEYPAD_NUMBER_OF_COLS    4`

Declaration of public data types	`typedef enum{`
	`        MATRIX_KEYPAD_SCANNING,`
	`        MATRIX_KEYPAD_DEBOUNCE,`
	`        MATRIX_KEYPAD_KEY_HOLD_PRESSED`
	`} matrixKeypadState_t;`

Declaration and initialization of public global objects	`DigitalOut keypadRowPins[KEYPAD_NUMBER_OF_ROWS] =`
	`    {PB_3, PB_5, PC_7, PA_15};`
	`DigitalIn keypadColPins[KEYPAD_NUMBER_OF_COLS]  =`
	`    {PB_12, PB_13, PB_15, PC_6};`

Declaration and initialization of public global variables	`int accumulatedDebounceMatrixKeypadTime = 0;`
	`char matrixKeypadLastKeyPressed = '\0';`
	`char matrixKeypadIndexToCharArray[] = {`
	`    '1', '2', '3', 'A',`
	`    '4', '5', '6', 'B',`
	`    '7', '8', '9', 'C',`
	`    '*', '0', '#', 'D',`
	`};`
	`matrixKeypadState_t matrixKeypadState;`

Declarations (prototypes) of public functions	`void matrixKeypadInit();`
	`char matrixKeypadScan();`
	`char matrixKeypadUpdate();`

Function inputsInit()	`matrixKeypadInit();`

In Code 4.4, the new implementation of the function *alarmDeactivationUpdate()* is shown. The changes begin on line 5, where a variable called *keyReleased* is defined and assigned the returned value of the function *matrixKeypadUpdate()*. On line 6 it can be seen that if *keyReleased* is not equal to the null character or '#', then there is a switch over *keyReleased*; if the key pressed is equal to "A", "B", "C", or "D", then the corresponding position of the array *buttonsPressed* is set to 1.

On line 22 it is determined whether there was an Enter button released event or the "#" key was pressed on the matrix keypad. If so, lines 23 to 27 are executed, having similar behavior to lines 6 to 10 of Code 4.2. The difference is that lines 28 to 31 set all the positions of the array *buttonsPressed* to zero. Note that in the implementations of *alarmDeactivationUpdate()* used in previous chapters, it was not necessary to set all the positions of the array *buttonsPressed* to zero because all the buttons were read simultaneously. In the case of the matrix keypad, the keys are pressed one after the other, and when a given key is pressed, a "1" is stored in the corresponding position of the *buttonsPressed* array. For example, if "A" is pressed, a "1" is stored in *buttonsPressed[0]*, and if "B" is pressed, a "1" is stored in *buttonsPressed[1]*. Because of this, the array must be reset (i.e., all its positions set to zero) in order to allow a new attempt to enter the code.

Note that because this implementation is the same, the order in which the keys are pressed, or even if one of the keys is pressed many times, is irrelevant. For example, if the user presses the keys "A", "B", "#", "#" it will be considered a correct code, but "B", "A", "#", "#" or "A", "A", "B", "#", "#" will also be considered correct.

The remaining lines of Code 4.4 are identical to the corresponding lines of Code 4.2.

```
1   void alarmDeactivationUpdate()
2   {
3       if ( numberOfIncorrectCodes < 5 ) {
4           bool enterButtonReleasedEvent = debounceButtonUpdate();
5           char keyReleased = matrixKeypadUpdate();
6           if( keyReleased != '\0' && keyReleased != '#' ) {
7               switch (keyReleased) {
8               case 'A':
9                   buttonsPressed[0] = 1;
10                  break;
11              case 'B':
12                  buttonsPressed[1] = 1;
13                  break;
14              case 'C':
15                  buttonsPressed[2] = 1;
16                  break;
17              case 'D':
18                  buttonsPressed[3] = 1;
19                  break;
20              }
21          }
22          if( enterButtonReleasedEvent || keyReleased == '#' ) {
23              if( incorrectCodeLed ) {
24                  numberOfEnterButtonReleasedEvents++;
25                  if( numberOfEnterButtonReleasedEvents >= 2 ) {
26                      incorrectCodeLed = OFF;
27                      numberOfEnterButtonReleasedEvents = 0;
28                      buttonsPressed[0] = 0;
29                      buttonsPressed[1] = 0;
30                      buttonsPressed[2] = 0;
31                      buttonsPressed[3] = 0;
32                  }
33              } else {
34                  if ( alarmState ) {
35                      if ( enterButtonReleasedEvent ) {
36                          buttonsPressed[0] = aButton;
37                          buttonsPressed[1] = bButton;
38                          buttonsPressed[2] = cButton;
39                          buttonsPressed[3] = dButton;
40                      }
41                      if ( areEqual() ) {
42                          alarmState = OFF;
43                          numberOfIncorrectCodes = 0;
44                      } else {
45                          incorrectCodeLed = ON;
46                          numberOfIncorrectCodes++;
47                      }
48                  }
49              }
50          }
51      } else {
52          systemBlockedLed = ON;
53      }
54  }
```

Code 4.4 Details of the function alarmDeactivationUpdate().

Code 4.5 shows the implementation of the function *matrixKeypadInit()*. The initial state of
matrixKeypadState is set on line 3 to MATRIX_KEYPAD_SCANNING. On line 4, the variable *pinIndex*
is declared and set to zero. The *for* loop on line 5 is used to properly configure each of the pins of
keypadColPins.

```
1  void matrixKeypadInit()
2  {
3      matrixKeypadState = MATRIX_KEYPAD_SCANNING;
4      int pinIndex = 0;
5      for( pinIndex=0; pinIndex<KEYPAD_NUMBER_OF_COLS; pinIndex++ ) {
6          (keypadColPins[pinIndex]).mode(PullUp);
7      }
8  }
```

Code 4.5 Details of the function matrixKeypadInit().

The implementation of the function *matrixKeypadScan()* is shown in Code 4.6. On lines 3 and 4, the variables *row* and *col* are declared. They will be used as indexes in *for* loops to indicate which row and column is being scanned. The variable *i* is used in another *for* loop, as is explained below.

On line 7, it can be seen that there is a *for* loop that is used to scan all the rows of the matrix keypad. On line 9, the four keypad row pins are first set to ON by means of a *for* loop. On line 13, the pin of the current row being scanned is set to OFF. On line 15, another *for* loop is used to scan all the columns, one after the other. If a given key is being pressed, its value is returned on line 17 by returning the value in the appropriate position of the array *matrixKeypadIndexToCharArray*. Otherwise, if no key is being pressed in the matrix keypad, then the null character ('\0') is returned on line 21.

 NOTE: Once a key press is detected, the scanning is stopped, as can be seen on line 17 of Code 4.6. In this way, if, for example, keys "1" and "2" are pressed simultaneously, only key "1" is reported. In the same way, if keys "A" and "B" are pressed simultaneously, only key "A" is reported.

```
1  char matrixKeypadScan()
2  {
3      int row = 0;
4      int col = 0;
5      int i = 0;
6
7      for( row=0; row<KEYPAD_NUMBER_OF_ROWS; row++ ) {
8
9          for( i=0; i<KEYPAD_NUMBER_OF_ROWS; i++ ) {
10             keypadRowPins[i] = ON;
11         }
12
13         keypadRowPins[row] = OFF;
14
15         for( col=0; col<KEYPAD_NUMBER_OF_COLS; col++ ) {
16             if( keypadColPins[col] == OFF ) {
17                 return matrixKeypadIndexToCharArray[row*KEYPAD_NUMBER_OF_ROWS + col];
18             }
19         }
20     }
21     return '\0';
22 }
```

Code 4.6 Details of the function matrixKeypadScan().

Code 4.7 shows the implementation of the function *matrixKeypadUpdate()*. On lines 3 and 4, the variables *keyDetected* and *keyReleased* are declared and initialized to the null character. On line 6 there is a switch over the variable *matrixKeypadState*. In the case of MATRIX_KEYPAD_SCANNING, the matrix keypad is scanned, and the resulting value is stored in *keyDetected*. If no key was pressed (identified on line 10), then *matrixKeypadLastKeyPressed* is assigned the value of *keyDetected*, *accumulatedDebounceMatrixKeypadTime* is set to zero, and *matrixKeypadState* is set to MATRIX_KEYPAD_DEBOUNCE.

In the case of MATRIX_KEYPAD_DEBOUNCE, if *accumulatedDebounceMatrixKeypadTime* is greater than or equal to DEBOUNCE_BUTTON_TIME_MS, then the matrix keypad is scanned, and the resulting value is stored in *keyDetected* (line 20). If *keyDetected* is equal to *matrixKeypadLastKeyPressed*, then *matrixKeypadState* is set to MATRIX_KEYPAD_HOLD_PRESSED. Otherwise, *matrixKeypadState* is set to MATRIX_KEYPAD_SCANNING. Finally, on line 27, *accumulatedDebounceMatrixKeypadTime* is incremented.

```
1   char matrixKeypadUpdate()
2   {
3       char keyDetected = '\0';
4       char keyReleased = '\0';
5
6       switch( matrixKeypadState ) {
7
8       case MATRIX_KEYPAD_SCANNING:
9           keyDetected = matrixKeypadScan();
10          if( keyDetected != '\0' ) {
11              matrixKeypadLastKeyPressed = keyDetected;
12              accumulatedDebounceMatrixKeypadTime = 0;
13              matrixKeypadState = MATRIX_KEYPAD_DEBOUNCE;
14          }
15          break;
16
17      case MATRIX_KEYPAD_DEBOUNCE:
18          if( accumulatedDebounceMatrixKeypadTime >=
19              DEBOUNCE_BUTTON_TIME_MS ) {
20              keyDetected = matrixKeypadScan();
21              if( keyDetected == matrixKeypadLastKeyPressed ) {
22                  matrixKeypadState = MATRIX_KEYPAD_KEY_HOLD_PRESSED;
23              } else {
24                  matrixKeypadState = MATRIX_KEYPAD_SCANNING;
25              }
26          }
27          accumulatedDebounceMatrixKeypadTime =
28              accumulatedDebounceMatrixKeypadTime + TIME_INCREMENT_MS;
29          break;
30
31      case MATRIX_KEYPAD_KEY_HOLD_PRESSED:
32          keyDetected = matrixKeypadScan();
33          if( keyDetected != matrixKeypadLastKeyPressed ) {
34              if( keyDetected == '\0' ) {
35                  keyReleased = matrixKeypadLastKeyPressed;
36              }
37              matrixKeypadState = MATRIX_KEYPAD_SCANNING;
38          }
39          break;
40
41      default:
42          matrixKeypadInit();
43          break;
44      }
45      return keyReleased;
46  }
```

Code 4.7 Details of the function matrixKeypadUpdate().

The case for MATRIX_KEYPAD_HOLD_PRESSED is shown on line 31. First, the matrix keypad is scanned (line 32). If *keyDetected* is not equal to *matrixKeypadLastKeyPressed* and if *keyDetected* is equal to the null character, then *matrixKeypadLastKeyPressed* is assigned to *keyReleased*. The fact that the state remains in MATRIX_KEYPAD_HOLD_PRESSED avoids the issue of a key being held for a long time and the same value being returned many times. In this way, it exits the state only if the pressed key is released or if a key connected to a row or column with a "higher priority" in the scanning (i.e., a lower number of *row* or *col*) is pressed.

Finally, *matrixKeypadState* is assigned to MATRIX_KEYPAD_SCANNING. This is done to allow the detection of a new key being pressed, as the MATRIX_KEYPAD_SCANNING state is the only one in which the FSM is waiting for a new key to be pressed.

Line 41 implements the "default" statement of the implementation of the FSM. It ensures that the function *matrixKeypadInit()* is executed if for any reason the value of *matrixKeypadState* is neither MATRIX_KEYPAD_SCANNING, MATRIX_KEYPAD_DEBOUNCE, nor MATRIX_KEYPAD_HOLD_PRESSED.

 NOTE: Defining a default case in the implementation of the FSM is a safety measure that is strongly recommended to handle errors.

Finally, on line 45, the value of *keyReleased* is returned. This value was used in Code 4.4 as described previously.

Proposed Exercise

1. What should be adapted in the code if a keypad having five rows and five columns is to be used?

Answer to the Exercise

1. The definitions KEYPAD_NUMBER_OF_ROWS and KEYPAD_NUMBER_OF_COLS should be set to 5, and more elements should be added to *keypadRowPins*, *keypadColPins*, and *matrixKeypadIndexToCharArray*.

Example 4.3: Implementation of Numeric Codes using the Matrix Keypad

Objective

Explore more advanced functionality regarding the usage of the matrix keypad.

Summary of the Expected Behavior

The code implemented in the previous example, based only on the keys A, B, C, and D, is replaced by a numeric code that is entered by means of the matrix keypad.

NOTE: In this example, the buttons connected to D4–D7 (*aButton–dButton*) are not used anymore. Consequently, *buttonBeingPressed* will be replaced by *keyBeingPressed*, as discussed below.

Test the Proposed Solution on the Board

Import the project "Example 4.3" using the URL available in [4], build the project, and drag the *.bin* file onto the NUCLEO board. Press the Alarm test button (implemented hereafter with B1 USER button) to activate the alarm. The Alarm LED (LD1) should start blinking at a rate of 100 ms on and 100 ms off. Press the keys "1", "8", "0", "5", and "#" on the matrix keypad. The Alarm LED (LD1) should be turned off. Press the Alarm test button to activate the alarm. The Alarm LED (LD1) should start blinking. Press the keys "1", "8", "5", "5" (incorrect code), and "#" on the matrix keypad. The Incorrect code LED (LD3) should be turned on. Press "#" twice in the matrix keypad. The incorrect code LED (LD3) should be turned off.

NOTE: The code "1805" is configured by default in this example; the user can change it by pressing "5" on the PC keyboard. The code would be "1805" again after resetting or powering off the NUCLEO board.

Press the Alarm test button again to activate the alarm. Now press the "4" key on the PC keyboard. Type the code "1805" to deactivate the alarm. Now press the "5" key on the PC keyboard. The code can be modified.

Discussion of the Proposed Solution

The proposed solution is based on the program code that was introduced in previous examples. By means of the matrix keypad functionality that was presented in Example 4.1 and Example 4.2, the keys pressed by the user are read and compared with the correct code (1805). The function *uartTask()* is modified in order to adapt the commands related to pressing keys "4" and "5" on the PC keyboard. These are the commands used to enter a code from the PC and to change the correct code from the PC, respectively.

Implementation of the Proposed Solution

Table 4.4 shows the variables *matrixKeypadCodeIndex* and *numberOfHashKeyReleasedEvents* that are declared in this example. The variable *matrixKeypadCodeIndex* will be used to keep track of the buttons that are pressed on the matrix keypad. The variable *numberOfHashKeyReleasedEvents* will be used to keep track of the number of times that the "#" key of the matrix keypad is pressed. In addition, Table 4.4 shows that BUTTON1 is assigned to the *alarmTestButton* object. Therefore, B1 User is now the Alarm test button and the button connected to D2 can be removed from the setup.

In Table 4.5, the definitions, variable names, and variable initializations that were modified are shown. It can be seen that "button" was replaced by "key" and the array of char *codeSequence* is assigned { '1', '8', '0', '5' }. Note that it is not a string because it is not ended by a null character, '\0'. Because the functionality of the Enter button and the buttons connected to D4–D7 is replaced by the matrix keypad, all the data types, variables, and functions related to them are removed. This is shown in Table 4.6 and Table 4.7. Additionally, the implementations of the functions *debounceButtonInit()* and *debounceButtonUpdate()* are removed.

 NOTE: *codeSequence* and *keyPressed* are the only arrays of char in this book initialized using = { 'x', 'y', 'z' }. In upcoming chapters, it will be shown how to assign values to an array of char when it is used as a string.

Table 4.4 Sections in which lines were added to Example 4.2.

Section	Lines that were modified
Declaration and initialization of public global variables	`int matrixKeypadCodeIndex = 0;` `int numberOfHashKeyReleasedEvents = 0;`
Declaration and initialization of public global objects	`DigitalIn alarmTestButton(BUTTON1);`

Table 4.5 Definitions, variable names, and variable initializations that were modified from Example 4.2.

Declaration in Example 4.2	Declaration in Example 4.3
`#define DEBOUNCE_BUTTON_TIME_MS 40`	`#define DEBOUNCE_KEY_TIME_MS 40`
`int buttonBeingCompared = 0;`	`int keyBeingCompared = 0;`
`int codeSequence[NUMBER_OF_KEYS] =` `{ 1, 1, 0, 0 };`	`char codeSequence[NUMBER_OF_KEYS] =` `{ '1', '8', '0', '5' };`
`int buttonsPressed[NUMBER_OF_KEYS] =` `{ 0, 0, 0, 0 };`	`char keyPressed[NUMBER_OF_KEYS] =` `{ '0', '0', '0', '0' }`

Table 4.6 Sections in which lines were removed from Example 4.2.

Section	Lines that were removed

Declaration of public data types	`typedef enum {`
	`    BUTTON_UP,`
	`    BUTTON_DOWN,`
	`    BUTTON_FALLING,`
	`    BUTTON_RISING`
	`} buttonState_t;`

Declaration and initialization of public global objects	`DigitalIn enterButton(BUTTON1);`
	`DigitalIn alarmTestButton(D2);`
	`DigitalIn aButton(D4);`
	`DigitalIn bButton(D5);`
	`DigitalIn cButton(D6);`
	`DigitalIn dButton(D7);`

Declaration and initialization of public global variables	`int accumulatedDebounceButtonTime    = 0;`
	`int numberOfEnterButtonReleasedEvents = 0;`
	`buttonState_t enterButtonState;`

Declarations (prototypes) of public functions	`void debounceButtonInit();` `bool debounceButtonUpdate();`

Table 4.7 Functions in which lines were removed from Example 4.2.

Section	Lines that were removed

void inputsInit()	aButton.mode(PullDown);
	bButton.mode(PullDown);
	cButton.mode(PullDown);
	dButton.mode(PullDown);
	debounceButtonInit();

Code 4.8 shows the new implementation of the function *alarmDeactivationUpdate()*. On line 3, the number of incorrect codes is checked to see if it is less than 5. If so, the matrix keypad is read on line 4. If there was a released key (i.e., *keyReleased* != '\0') and if the released key was not "#", then the *keyReleased* is assigned to the current position of the *buttonsPressed* array (line 6). On line 7, a check is made to see if *matrixKeypadCodeIndex* is greater than or equal to NUMBER_OF_KEYS. If so, *matrixKeypadCodeIndex* is set to zero, and if not, then it is incremented by one.

The remaining lines of Code 4.8 are identical to the corresponding lines of Code 4.2 except for the removal of the lines related to the external buttons and the addition of line 26 that assigns 0 to *matrixKeypadCodeIndex*.

```
1   void alarmDeactivationUpdate()
2   {
3       if ( numberOfIncorrectCodes < 5 ) {
4           char keyReleased = matrixKeypadUpdate();
5           if( keyReleased != '\0' && keyReleased != '#' ) {
6               keyPressed[matrixKeypadCodeIndex] = keyReleased;
7               if( matrixKeypadCodeIndex >= NUMBER_OF_KEYS ) {
8                   matrixKeypadCodeIndex = 0;
9               } else {
10                  matrixKeypadCodeIndex++;
11              }
12          }
13          if( keyReleased == '#' ) {
14              if( incorrectCodeLed ) {
15                  numberOfHashKeyReleasedEvents++;
16                  if( numberOfHashKeyReleasedEvents >= 2 ) {
17                      incorrectCodeLed = OFF;
18                      numberOfHashKeyReleasedEvents = 0;
19                      matrixKeypadCodeIndex = 0;
20                  }
21              } else {
22                  if ( alarmState ) {
23                      if ( areEqual() ) {
24                          alarmState = OFF;
25                          numberOfIncorrectCodes = 0;
26                          matrixKeypadCodeIndex = 0;
27                      } else {
28                          incorrectCodeLed = ON;
29                          numberOfIncorrectCodes++;
30                      }
31                  }
32              }
33          }
34      } else {
35          systemBlockedLed = ON;
36      }
37  }
```

Code 4.8 Details of the function alarmDeactivationUpdate().

In Code 4.9, the lines that were modified in the function *uartTask()* are shown. In the case of '4', the user is asked to enter the four-digit numeric code (lines 2 and 3), and *incorrectCode* is set to false (line 5). On line 7, there is a *for* loop, where the keys pressed on the PC keyboard are read until NUMBER_OF_KEYS keys have been read sequentially. The read keys are stored in *receivedChar* (line 10) and compared with the corresponding position of *codeSequence* on line 11; *incorrectCode* is set to true (line 12) if one of the keys does not match the code sequence. Line 14 is used to print a "*" on the PC in correspondence with each key that is pressed.

If *incorrectCode* is equal to false on line 17, then the user is informed (line 18) and the corresponding values of *alarmState*, *incorrectCodeLed*, and *numberOfIncorrectCodes* are set (lines 19 to 21). Otherwise, if the code is incorrect, the user is informed (line 23), *incorrectCodeLed* is set to ON, and *numberOfIncorrectCodes* is incremented by one.

In the case of '5' (line 29), the user is asked to enter the new four-digit numeric code. The *for* loop from lines 33 to 38 is used to get the keys and store them in *codeSequence*. Line 12 is used to inform the user that the new code has been configured.

```
1   case '4':
2       uartUsb.write( "Please enter the four digits numeric code ", 42 );
3       uartUsb.write( "to deactivate the alarm: ", 25 );
4
5       incorrectCode = false;
6
7       for ( keyBeingCompared = 0;
8             keyBeingCompared < NUMBER_OF_KEYS;
9             keyBeingCompared++) {
10          uartUsb.read( &receivedChar, 1 );
11          uartUsb.write( "*", 1 );
12          if ( codeSequence[keyBeingCompared] != receivedChar ) {
13              incorrectCode = true;
14          }
15      }
16
17      if ( incorrectCode == false ) {
18          uartUsb.write( "\r\nThe code is correct\r\n\r\n", 25 );
19          alarmState = OFF;
20          incorrectCodeLed = OFF;
21          numberOfIncorrectCodes = 0;
22      } else {
23          uartUsb.write( "\r\nThe code is incorrect\r\n\r\n", 27 );
24          incorrectCodeLed = ON;
25          numberOfIncorrectCodes++;
26      }
27      break;
28
29  case '5':
30      uartUsb.write( "Please enter the new four digits numeric code ", 46 );
31      uartUsb.write( "to deactivate the alarm: ", 25 );
32
33      for ( keyBeingCompared = 0;
34            keyBeingCompared < NUMBER_OF_KEYS;
35            keyBeingCompared++) {
36          uartUsb.read( &receivedChar, 1 );
37          uartUsb.write( "*", 1 );
38      }
39
40      uartUsb.write( "\r\nNew code generated\r\n\r\n", 24 );
41      break;
```

Code 4.9 Lines that were modified in the function uartTask().

Proposed Exercise

1. How can the code be modified in order to use a three-digit code?

Answer to the Exercise

1. In the arrays *codeSequence* and *buttonsPressed*, three positions must be assigned, and NUMBER_OF_KEYS must be defined as 3.

Example 4.4: Report Date and Time of Alarms to the PC Based on the RTC

Objective

Introduce the use of data structures and the RTC.

Summary of the Expected Behavior

The smart home system should store up to 20 events, each one with the corresponding date and time of occurrence, and display those events on the serial terminal when they are requested.

Test the Proposed Solution on the Board

Import the project "Example 4.4" using the URL available in [4], build the project, and drag the .*bin* file onto the NUCLEO board. Press "s" on the PC keyboard in order to configure the date and time of the RTC of the NUCLEO board. Press "t" on the PC keyboard to confirm that the RTC is working properly. Press the Alarm test button to activate the alarm. The Alarm LED (LD1) should start blinking at a rate of 100 ms on and 100 ms off. Enter the code to deactivate the alarm (1805#). Press "e" on the PC keyboard to view the date and time that the gas and over temperature detection and alarm activation occurred.

Discussion of the Proposed Solution

The proposed solution is based on the RTC of the STM32 microcontroller of the NUCLEO board. Its date and time are used to tag the events related to the alarm. In order to have a meaningful date and time related to each event, the RTC must be configured.

 NOTE: The registered events and the date and time configuration of the RTC are lost when power is removed from the NUCLEO board.

Implementation of the Proposed Solution

Table 4.8 shows the sections in which lines were added to Example 4.3. First, two #defines were included: EVENT_MAX_STORAGE, to limit the number of stored events to 20, and EVENT_NAME_MAX_LENGTH, to limit the number of characters associated with each event.

In the section "Declaration of public data types," a new public data type is declared. The reserved word *struct* is used to declare special types of variables that have internal members. These members can have different types and different lengths. The type *systemEvents_t* is declared, having two members: *seconds*, of type *time_t*, and an array of char called *typeOfEvent*.

The type *time_t* used to represent times is part of the standard C++ library and is implemented by the Mbed OS [5]. For historical reasons, it is generally implemented as an integer value representing the number of seconds elapsed since 00:00 hours, Jan 1, 1970 UTC, which is usually called Unix timestamp or epoch time. The maximum date that can be represented using this format is 03:14:07 UTC on 19 January 2038.

Many variables are also declared. The variable *eventsIndex* will be used to keep track of the number of events stored.

Table 4.8 shows that an array *arrayOfStoredEvents* is declared, being of type *systemEvents_t* (the *struct* that has been declared in the section "Declaration of public data types"), as well as the variable *timeAux* of type *time_t*.

Finally, two functions are declared: *eventLogUpdate()* and *systemElementStateUpdate()*. These functions will be shown and analyzed in the code below.

Table 4.8 Sections in which lines were added to Example 4.3.

Section	Lines that were added
Definitions	`#define EVENT_MAX_STORAGE      20` `#define EVENT_NAME_MAX_LENGTH  14`

Declaration of public data types	`typedef struct systemEvent {`
	`    time_t seconds;`
	`    char typeOfEvent[EVENT_NAME_MAX_LENGTH];`
	`} systemEvent_t;`

Declaration and initialization of public global variables	`bool alarmLastState      = OFF;`
	`bool gasLastState         = OFF;`
	`bool tempLastState        = OFF;`
	`bool ICLastState          = OFF;`
	`bool SBLastState          = OFF;`
	`int eventsIndex = 0;`
	`systemEvent_t arrayOfStoredEvents[EVENT_MAX_STORAGE];`

Declarations (prototypes) of public functions	`void eventLogUpdate();`
	`void systemElementStateUpdate( bool lastState,`
	`                              bool currentState,`
	`                              const char* elementName );`

In Code 4.10, some of the lines that were included in the function *uartTask()* are shown. Starting at lines 1 and 2, the reader can see that in case of the keys "s" or "S" being pressed, the variable *rtcTime* is declared in line 3, being a struct of the type *tm*. The struct tm is part of the standard C++ library, is implemented by Mbed OS, and has the members detailed in Table 4.9. The member *tm_sec* is generally in the range 0–59, but sometimes 60 is used, or even 61 to accommodate leap seconds in certain systems. The Daylight Saving Time flag (*tm_isdst*) is greater than zero if Daylight Saving Time is in effect, zero if Daylight Saving Time is not in effect, and less than zero if the information is not available. In line 4, *strIndex* is declared to be used as discussed below.

Table 4.9 Details of the struct tm.

Member	Type	Meaning	Range
tm_sec	int	seconds after the minute	0–59
tm_min	int	minutes after the hour	0–59
tm_hour	int	hours since midnight	0–23
tm_mday	int	day of the month	1–31
tm_mon	int	months since January	0–11
tm_year	int	years since 1900	
tm_wday	int	days since Sunday	0–6
tm_yday	int	days since January 1	0–365
tm_isdst	int	Daylight Saving Time flag	

The user is asked to enter, one after the other, the values of most of the members of the variable *rtcTime* (lines 6 to 58). In each case, first a message is displayed using *uartUsb.write()*. Then, a *for* loop is used to read a character, store that character in a given position of the array, and send that character to the serial terminal using *uartUsb.write()*, so the user has an echo of the entered character. After this, the null character is appended to the string, as, for example, on line 11. Then the function *atoi()*, which is provided by Mbed OS, is used to convert the string to an integer, as, for example, on line 12. The resulting value is stored in the corresponding member of *rtcTime*, as can be seen on line 12. Finally, "\r\n" is written to move to a new line.

Note that some minor operations are made on the values entered by the user, such as on line 12, where 1900 is subtracted, and on line 211, where 1 is subtracted. Also note that *str[strIndex]* is preceded by the reference operator (&), as in line 8 or 9. The reference operator is related to the usage of *pointers* and will be discussed in more detail in upcoming chapters. Finally, note that no check is made on the digits entered by the user. If values outside the ranges indicated in Table 4.9 are entered, unexpected behavior may result.

NOTE: The scope of *rtcTime* and *strIndex* is the switch-case where they are declared (i.e., those variables don't exist outside the brackets of the corresponding switch-case).

```
1    case 's':
2    case 'S':
3        struct tm rtcTime;
4        int strIndex;
5
6        uartUsb.write( "\r\nType four digits for the current year (YYYY): ", 48 );
7        for( strIndex=0; strIndex<4; strIndex++ ) {
8            uartUsb.read( &str[strIndex] , 1 );
9            uartUsb.write( &str[strIndex] ,1 );
10       }
11       str[4] = '\0';
12       rtcTime.tm_year = atoi(str) - 1900;
13       uartUsb.write( "\r\n", 2 );
14
15       uartUsb.write( "Type two digits for the current month (01-12): ", 47 );
16       for( strIndex=0; strIndex<2; strIndex++ ) {
17           uartUsb.read( &str[strIndex] , 1 );
18           uartUsb.write( &str[strIndex] ,1 );
19       }
20       str[2] = '\0';
21       rtcTime.tm_mon  = atoi(str) - 1;
22       uartUsb.write( "\r\n", 2 );
23
24       uartUsb.write( "Type two digits for the current day (01-31): ", 45 );
25       for( strIndex=0; strIndex<2; strIndex++ ) {
26           uartUsb.read( &str[strIndex] , 1 );
27           uartUsb.write( &str[strIndex] ,1 );
28       }
29       str[2] = '\0';
30       rtcTime.tm_mday = atoi(str);
31       uartUsb.write( "\r\n", 2 );
32
33       uartUsb.write( "Type two digits for the current hour (00-23): ", 46 );
34       for( strIndex=0; strIndex<2; strIndex++ ) {
35           uartUsb.read( &str[strIndex] , 1 );
36           uartUsb.write( &str[strIndex] ,1 );
37       }
38       str[2] = '\0';
39       rtcTime.tm_hour = atoi(str);
40       uartUsb.write( "\r\n", 2 );
41
42       uartUsb.write( "Type two digits for the current minutes (00-59): ", 49 );
43       for( strIndex=0; strIndex<2; strIndex++ ) {
44           uartUsb.read( &str[strIndex] , 1 );
45           uartUsb.write( &str[strIndex] ,1 );
46       }
47       str[2] = '\0';
48       rtcTime.tm_min  = atoi(str);
49       uartUsb.write( "\r\n", 2 );
50
51       uartUsb.write( "Type two digits for the current seconds (00-59): ", 49 );
52       for( strIndex=0; strIndex<2; strIndex++ ) {
53           uartUsb.read( &str[strIndex] , 1 );
54           uartUsb.write( &str[strIndex] ,1 );
55       }
56       str[2] = '\0';
57       rtcTime.tm_sec  = atoi(str);
58       uartUsb.write( "\r\n", 2 );
59
60       rtcTime.tm_isdst = -1;
61       set_time( mktime( &rtcTime ) );
62       uartUsb.write( "Date and time has been set\r\n", 28 );
63
64       break;
```

Code 4.10 Lines that were included in the function uartTask() (Part 1/2).

On line 60, the value of the member *tm_isdst* is set to "-1" to indicate that the information is not available. On line 61, two operations are carried out. First the function *mktime()*, which is provided by the implementation of the library *time.h* by Mbed OS, is used to convert the variable *rtcTime* from the *tm* structure to the *time_t* structure. Then, the function *set_time()* is called to set the time on the RTC of the STM32 microcontroller. This function is also provided by Mbed OS. Note that the reference operator (&) is used in line 61. Lastly, the message "Date and time has been set" is written in line 62.

The case of the keys "t" or "T" being pressed is shown in Code 4.11. Lines 3 and 4 are used to declare the variable *epochSeconds*, of type *time_t*, and to store the value of the RTC of the STM32 microcontroller in the variable *epochSeconds*. This is done on line 4 by means of the function *time()*, which is also provided by Mbed OS. Then, the function *ctime()* is used on line 5 to convert the *time_t* value of seconds to a string having the format *Www Mmm dd hh:mm:ss yyyy*, where *Www* is the weekday, *Mmm* the month (in letters), *dd* the day of the month, *hh:mm:ss* the time, and *yyyy* the year. The string is written to *uartUsb* on line 6.

In the case of the keys "e" or "E" being pressed, all the events stored in *arrayOfStoredEvents* are transmitted one after the other to the PC, as can be seen on lines 10 to 21 of Code 4.11.

```
1   case 't':
2   case 'T':
3       time_t epochSeconds;
4       epochSeconds = time(NULL);
5       sprintf ( str, "Date and Time = %s", ctime(&epochSeconds));
6       uartUsb.write( str , strlen(str) );
7       uartUsb.write( "\r\n", 2 );
8       break;
9
10  case 'e':
11  case 'E':
12      for (int i = 0; i < eventsIndex; i++) {
13          sprintf ( str, "Event = %s\r\n",
14              arrayOfStoredEvents[i].typeOfEvent);
15          uartUsb.write( str , strlen(str) );
16          sprintf ( str, "Date and Time = %s\r\n",
17              ctime(&arrayOfStoredEvents[i].seconds));
18          uartUsb.write( str , strlen(str) );
19          uartUsb.write( "\r\n", 2 );
20      }
21      break;
```

Code 4.11 Lines that were included in the function uartTask() (part 2/2).

Code 4.12 shows the new implementation of the function *availableCommands()*. The new values "s", "t", and "e" have been included.

```
1   void availableCommands()
2   {
3       uartUsb.write( "Available commands:\r\n", 21 );
4       uartUsb.write( "Press '1' to get the alarm state\r\n", 34 );
5       uartUsb.write( "Press '2' to get the gas detector state\r\n", 41 );
6       uartUsb.write( "Press '3' to get the over temperature detector state\r\n", 54 );
7       uartUsb.write( "Press '4' to enter the code sequence\r\n", 38 );
8       uartUsb.write( "Press '5' to enter a new code\r\n", 31 );
9       uartUsb.write( "Press 'f' or 'F' to get lm35 reading in Fahrenheit\r\n", 52 );
10      uartUsb.write( "Press 'c' or 'C' to get lm35 reading in Celsius\r\n", 49 );
11      uartUsb.write( "Press 's' or 'S' to set the date and time\r\n", 43 );
12      uartUsb.write( "Press 't' or 'T' to get the date and time\r\n", 43 );
13      uartUsb.write( "Press 'e' or 'E' to get the stored events\r\n\r\n", 45 );
14  }
```

Code 4.12 New implementation of the function availableCommands().

In order to periodically check if there is an event to be stored, the *main()* function is modified, as can be seen in Code 4.13. A call to the function *eventLogUpdate()* has been added on line 9.

```
1   int main()
2   {
3       inputsInit();
4       outputsInit();
5       while (true) {
6           alarmActivationUpdate();
7           alarmDeactivationUpdate();
8           uartTask();
9           eventLogUpdate();
10          delay(TIME_INCREMENT_MS);
11      }
12  }
```

Code 4.13 New implementation of the function main().

In Code 4.14, the implementation of the function *eventLogUpdate()* is shown. It calls the function *systemElementStateUpdate()* to determine if there has been a change in the state of any of the elements. For example, on line 3, the function *systemElementStateUpdate()* is called to determine if the state of the alarm has changed. After calling *systemElementStateUpdate()*, the value of *alarmLastState* is updated on line 4. On the following lines (6 to 16), the same procedure is followed for the gas detector, the over temperature, the Incorrect code LED, and the System blocked LED.

```
1   void eventLogUpdate()
2   {
3       systemElementStateUpdate( alarmLastState, alarmState, "ALARM" );
4       alarmLastState = alarmState;
5
6       systemElementStateUpdate( gasLastState, !mq2, "GAS_DET" );
7       gasLastState = !mq2;
8
9       systemElementStateUpdate( tempLastState, overTempDetector, "OVER_TEMP" );
10      tempLastState = overTempDetector;
11
12      systemElementStateUpdate( ICLastState, incorrectCodeLed, "LED_IC" );
13      ICLastState = incorrectCodeLed;
14
15      systemElementStateUpdate( SBLastState, systemBlockedLed, "LED_SB" );
16      SBLastState = systemBlockedLed;
17  }
```

Code 4.14 Implementation of the function eventLogUpdate().

The implementation of the function *systemElementStateUpdate()* is shown in Code 4.15. This function accepts three parameters: the last state, the current state, and the element name. The element names are stored in arrays of char type, so the third parameter of this function is a memory address of an array of char. This is indicated by *char** (line 3), which means "a *pointer* to a char type." In this way, *elementName* is a pointer that points to the first position of an array of char. Note that the third parameter type is declared as *const char** (line 3). In this context, the addition of the reserved word *const* indicates that the content of the memory address pointed by *elementName* cannot be modified by the function *systemElementStateUpdate()*. The usage of pointers is discussed in detail in upcoming chapters.

On line 5, an array of char called *eventAndStateStr* is declared, having EVENT_NAME_MAX_LENGTH positions. It is initialized using "", which assigns the null character to its first position (i.e., *eventAndStateStr[0]* = '\0'), which makes *eventAndStateStr* an *empty string* (a string with no printable characters). On line 7, it is determined if *lastState* is different from *currentState*. If so, on line 9 the content of the array of char pointed by *elementName* is appended to the string *eventAndStateStr* by means of the function *strncat()*, provided by Mbed OS.

NOTE: More functions regarding strings are available in [6]. Some of them are used in the next chapters.

In lines 10 to 14, ON or OFF is appended to *eventAndStateStr*, depending on the value of *currentState*. The members of *arrayOfStoredEvents* (*seconds* and *typeOfEvent*) at the position *eventsIndex* are assigned the time of the RTC of the STM32 microcontroller using the function *time()* (line 16) and the type of event by means of the function *strcpy()*, provided by Mbed OS (line 17). On line 18, a check is made whether *eventsIndex* is smaller than EVENT_MAX_STORAGE - 1. If so, there is still space in the array to store new events, and *eventsIndex* is incremented by one. If not, the array is full, and *eventsIndex* is set to zero in order to start filling the array *arrayOfStoredEvents* again from its first position. Finally, the *eventAndStateStr* is printed on the serial terminal (lines 24 and 25).

```
1   void systemElementStateUpdate( bool lastState,
2                                  bool currentState,
3                                  const char* elementName )
4   {
5       char eventAndStateStr[EVENT_NAME_MAX_LENGTH] = "";
6
7       if ( lastState != currentState ) {
8
9           strcat( eventAndStateStr, elementName );
10          if ( currentState ) {
11              strcat( eventAndStateStr, "_ON" );
12          } else {
13              strcat( eventAndStateStr, "_OFF" );
14          }
15
16          arrayOfStoredEvents[eventsIndex].seconds = time(NULL);
17          strcpy( arrayOfStoredEvents[eventsIndex].typeOfEvent, eventAndStateStr );
18          if ( eventsIndex < EVENT_MAX_STORAGE - 1 ) {
```

```
19              eventsIndex++;
20          } else {
21              eventsIndex = 0;
22          }
23
24      uartUsb.write( eventAndStateStr , strlen(eventAndStateStr) );
25      uartUsb.write( "\r\n", 2 );
26      }
27  }
```

Code 4.15 Implementation of the function systemElementStateUpdate().

WARNING: The improper usage of pointers can lead to software errors. In upcoming chapters it will be shown that the memory address pointed to by the pointer can be modified (i.e., increased or decreased) and that a value can be assigned to the memory address pointed to by the pointer using the reference operator (&), as, for example, in line 8 of Code 4.10. This means that the pointer can be pointed to a memory address that is already in use and an improper modification of the content of that memory address can be made.

A similar problem can take place when string-related functions are used without the proper precautions. For example, in line 9 of Code 4.15, a copy of *elementName* is appended to *eventAndStateStr*. This operation will happen no matter the number of positions that were reserved for *eventAndStateStr* in line 5 of Code 4.15. Therefore, a "buffer overflow" may occur if *elementName* has more characters than EVENT_NAME_MAX_LENGTH. The usage of objects of type string instead of using arrays of char can be a solution in certain situations, but it may lead to memory issues when applied in the context of embedded systems. In upcoming chapters, different solutions for safely managing strings in embedded systems are discussed.

Proposed Exercise

1. How can a change be implemented in the code in order to allow up to 1000 events to be stored?

Answer to the Exercise

1. The value of MAX_NUMBER_OF_EVENTS should be changed to 1000.

4.3 Under the Hood

4.3.1 Graphical Representation of a Finite-State Machine

This section explains how an FSM can be represented by means of a diagram. It is common to start by drawing the diagram of the FSM, then analyze and adjust the behavior of the system using the diagram. Only when the behavior is as expected is the corresponding code implemented.

Before introducing the graphical representation, the behavior of the FSM should be reviewed.

In Figure 4.8, the voltage at a given button over time is shown by a red line, following the diagram that was introduced in section 4.2.1. Initially (at t_0) the button is released, the voltage is 3.3 V, and the FSM is in the BUTTON_UP state (as indicated by the light blue line). Then there is a *glitch* at t_1, after which the signal goes back to 3.3 V. It can be seen that the FSM state changes to BUTTON_FALLING (because of the glitch) and then reverts to BUTTON_UP at t_2 because it is determined that it was not an actual change in the button state.

At t_3, bounce in the voltage signal is shown because the button is pressed. It can be seen that the FSM state changed to BUTTON_FALLING. At t_4, the FSM state changes to BUTTON_DOWN as the voltage signal is stable at 0 V. At t_5 there is a new glitch, after which the FSM state changes to BUTTON_RISING. But, as after the glitch the voltage signal remains at 0 V, the FSM state reverts back to BUTTON_DOWN at t_6.

At t_7, there is a transition from released to pressed, which is accompanied by a bounce in the signal. It can be seen that the FSM state changed to BUTTON_RISING. After the bounce time, the signal stabilizes to 3.3 V and, therefore, at t_8 the FSM state changes to BUTTON_UP.

The behavior shown in Figure 4.8 continues over time as the button is pressed and released. It might be that there are no glitches or there are many glitches. If so, the transitions between the FSM states will be the same as shown in Figure 4.8, with the only difference being the number of BUTTON_FALLING states between two consecutive BUTTON_UP and BUTTON_DOWN states and the number of BUTTON_RISING states between two consecutive BUTTON_DOWN and BUTTON_UP states.

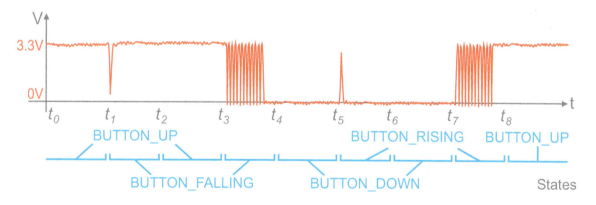

Figure 4.8 Voltage signal over time for a given button as it is pressed or released.

Figure 4.9 shows a state diagram for the FSM discussed above Figure 4.8. This is the FSM that was implemented in Example 4.1 by means of the statements shown in Code 4.3.

NOTE: In Figure 4.9, and in the corresponding discussion that is presented below, "== 1" is used to indicate that a given Boolean variable is in the *true* state, and "== 0" is used to indicate that a given Boolean variable is in the *false* state. Do not confuse this with "= 0", which is used to indicate that the value zero is assigned to the integer variable *accumulatedDebounceTime*. In the case of the Boolean variable *enterButtonReleasedEvent*, "= true" is used to indicate that the logical value *true* is assigned.

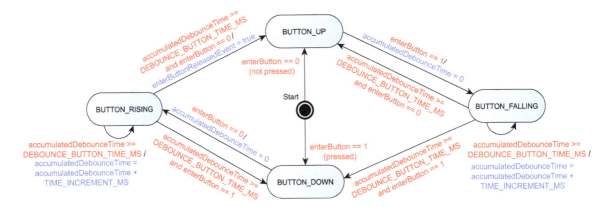

Figure 4.9 Diagram of the FSM implemented in Example 4.1.

The four states of the FSM implemented in Code 4.3 are represented in Figure 4.9 by means of the light blue ovals (i.e., BUTTON_UP, BUTTON_RISING, BUTTON_DOWN, and BUTTON_FALLING). The arrows from one state to another state, or from a given state to itself, or from the start point to a state, represent a *transition*. A transition can be between a given state and another state, to the same state, or could be the initial transition.

The red labels over the arrows indicate the *input* that triggers a given transition, while the blue label over an arrow indicates the *action* that is performed before the transition takes place. Note that every transition is triggered by a given input, but not all the transitions have an action associated with them.

After *power on*, the FSM is at the start point. Depending on the value of *enterButton*, the initial transition from the start point is to BUTTON_UP (if *enterButton* is 0, implying that the button is initially not pressed) or to BUTTON_DOWN (if *enterButton* is 1, implying that the button is initially pressed). This was implemented in the *debounceButtonInit()* function shown in Code 4.1. The FSM will remain in those states (BUTTON_UP or BUTTON_DOWN) while there are no changes in the value of *enterButton*.

Consider, for example, that at the start point *enterButton* is 0 (implying that the button is initially not pressed) and, therefore, the first state is BUTTON_UP. By referring back to Code 4.3, it can be seen that the only way of moving to a different state is if *enterButton* becomes 1 (i.e., the button is pressed). In that condition, BUTTON_FALLING is assigned to *enterButtonState* (line 8 of Code 4.3), and *accumulatedDebounceTime* is set to zero (line 9). This is shown in Figure 4.9 by the arrow from

BUTTON_UP to BUTTON_FALLING, and a red label "enterButton == 1" indicates the condition that triggers the transition, as well as the blue label "accumulatedDebounceTime = 0" indicating the action that is performed during the transition.

Once in the BUTTON_FALLING state, Code 4.3 can be analyzed to determine all the possible transitions. It can be seen on line 14 that in order to have a transition, *accumulatedDebounceTime* has to reach DEBOUNCE_BUTTON_TIME_MS. In that situation, if *enterButton* is 1 (i.e., the button is pressed), the transition is to the BUTTON_DOWN state (line 16), and if *enterButton* is 0 (i.e., the button is not pressed), the transition is to the BUTTON_UP state (line 18). While in BUTTON_FALLING state, *accumulatedDebounceTime* is incremented by TIME_INCREMENT_MS every 10 ms. This is indicated by the re-entering arrow above BUTTON_FALLING and is implemented on line 22 of Code 4.3.

The only possible transition from BUTTON_DOWN is to BUTTON_RISING. This transition takes place if *enterButton* == 0, as is shown in Figure 4.9. This represents the behavior of line 26 in Code 4.3.

Finally, it can be seen in Figure 4.9 that the behavior at the BUTTON_RISING state is very similar to the behavior at the BUTTON_FALLING state, in the same way as lines 13 to 23 of Code 4.3 are very similar to lines 32 to 43 of the same code. The only difference is that in the BUTTON_FALLING state, the variable *enterButtonReleasedEvent()* is set to true on line 36. This call is shown in Figure 4.9 by the arrow that goes from BUTTON_RISING to BUTTON_UP.

> **NOTE:** The states BUTTON_UP and BUTTON_DOWN last until there is a glitch or the button is either pressed or released. The states BUTTON_FALLING and BUTTON_RISING always last the same amount of time (i.e., DEBOUNCE_BUTTON_TIME_MS), as can be seen in Figure 4.8.

> **WARNING:** The diagram used in Figure 4.9 is only one of multiple possible representations of an FSM, known as a "Mealy machine." It is beyond the scope of this book to introduce other representations of FSMs.

Proposed Exercise

1. How can the FSM used in the implementation of Example 4.2 be represented by means of a diagram similar to the one used in Figure 4.9 to illustrate the FSM of Example 4.1?

Answer to the Exercise

1. The diagram is shown in Figure 4.10.

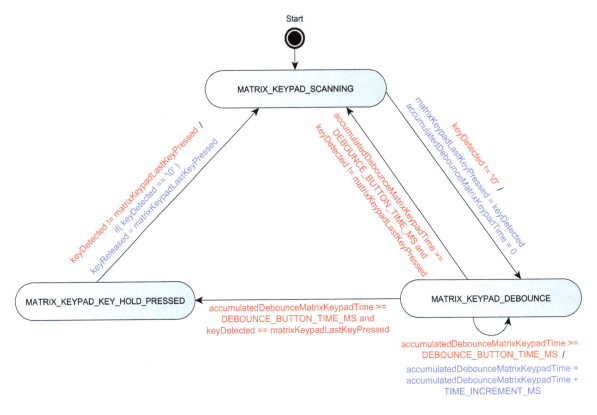

Figure 4.10 Diagram of the FSM implemented in Example 4.2.

4.4 Case Study

4.4.1 Smart Door Locks

In chapter 1, the case study of the smart door lock was introduced [7]. A representation of the keypad that is used by the smart door lock is shown in Figure 4.11. This is very similar to the matrix keypad that was introduced in this chapter.

The smart door lock is not provided with RTC functionality. However, the reader may realize that interesting access control features could be included if information about date and time is available. For example, each user may be provided with a specific time range to open the lock. This idea is explored in the proposed exercise.

Figure 4.11 Smart door lock built with Mbed contains a keypad similar to the one introduced in this chapter.

Proposed Exercise

1. How can a program be implemented in order to achieve the following behavior?

- The lock should open only if the code 1-4-7 is entered, and the current time is within the designated opening hours (8 am to 4 pm).

- To enter the code, the letter "A" should be pressed.

Answer to the Exercise

1. The proposed solution is shown in this section. The aim is to analyze a whole program (from the include files to all the functions used) in order to familiarize the reader with solving real-life problems.

Test the Proposed Solution on the Board

Import the project "Case Study Chapter 4" using the URL available in [4], build the project, and drag the *.bin* file onto the NUCLEO board. The LED LD2 will turn on to indicate that the door is locked. Press the "s" key on the PC keyboard to set a time between 8 am and 4 pm. Press the "t" key on the PC keyboard to get the current time and date. Press the keys "A", "1", "4", "7" on the matrix keypad. The LED LD1 should turn on to indicate that the door is now open. Press the B1 USER button to represent that the door has been closed. The LED LD2 will turn on to indicate that the door is locked.

Press the keys "A", "1", "2", "3" on the matrix keypad. The LED LD3 will turn on to indicate that an incorrect code has been entered. Press the keys "A", "1", "4", "7" on the matrix keypad. The LED LD1 should turn on to indicate that the door is now open. Press the B1 USER button to represent that the door has been closed. The LED LD2 will turn on to indicate that the door is locked.

Press the "s" key on the PC keyboard to set a time not in the range of 8 am to 4 pm. Press the keys "A", "1", "4", "7" on the matrix keypad. The LED LD1 will not turn on because it is not the correct opening hour.

Discussion of the Proposed Solution

The proposed solution is very similar to the solution presented throughout this chapter. However, some variations have been introduced in order to show the reader other ways to implement the code. These variations are discussed below as the proposed implementation is introduced.

Implementation of the Proposed Solution

In Code 4.16, the libraries that are used in the proposed solution are included: *mbed.h* and *arm_book_lib.h*. The definitions are also shown in Code 4.16. The number of digits of the code is defined as 3 (line 8). Then, the number of rows and columns of the keypad is defined (lines 9 and 10). The two definitions that are used in the FSMs to manage time, TIME_INCREMENT_MS and DEBOUNCE_BUTTON_TIME_MS, are defined on lines 11 and 12. Finally, on lines 13 and 14, the opening hours are defined.

In Code 4.17, the declaration of the public data type *doorState_t* is shown. It is used to implement an FSM and has three states: DOOR_CLOSED, DOOR_UNLOCKED, and DOOR_OPEN. In Code 4.17, the data type *matrixKeypadState_t* is also declared, just as in Example 4.2.

```
1    //=====[Libraries]=====================================================
2
3    #include "mbed.h"
4    #include "arm_book_lib.h"
5
6    //=====[Defines]=======================================================
7
8    #define CODE_DIGITS                        3
9    #define KEYPAD_NUMBER_OF_ROWS              4
10   #define KEYPAD_NUMBER_OF_COLS              4
11   #define TIME_INCREMENT_MS                 10
12   #define DEBOUNCE_BUTTON_TIME_MS           40
13   #define START_HOUR                         8
14   #define END_HOUR                          16
```

Code 4.16 Libraries and definitions used in the proposed solution.

```
1    //=====[Declaration of public data types]===================================
2
3    typedef enum {
4        DOOR_CLOSED,
5        DOOR_UNLOCKED,
6        DOOR_OPEN
7    } doorState_t;
8
9    typedef enum {
10       MATRIX_KEYPAD_SCANNING,
11       MATRIX_KEYPAD_DEBOUNCE,
12       MATRIX_KEYPAD_KEY_HOLD_PRESSED
13   } matrixKeypadState_t;
```

Code 4.17 Declaration of the public data types doorState_t and matrixKeypadState_t.

The section "Declaration and initialization of public global objects" is shown in Code 4.18. On line 3, an array of DigitalOut objects, called *keypadRowPins*, is defined. This array is used to indicate the pins used to connect the matrix keypad pins corresponding to the rows, as in Example 4.2. A similar implementation is used on line 4 to indicate the pins used to connect the matrix keypad columns.

On line 6 of Code 4.18, the DigitalIn object *doorHandle* is declared and linked to the B1 User button. This button will be used to indicate whether the door handle is in the opened or locked position. LD1, LD2, and LD3 are assigned on lines 8 to 10 to *doorUnlockedLed*, *doorLockedLed*, and *incorrectCodeLed*, respectively. Finally, on line 12 the UnbufferedSerial object *uartUsb* is created, in the same way as in the smart home system.

```
1    //=====[Declaration and initialization of public global objects]================
2
3    DigitalOut keypadRowPins[KEYPAD_NUMBER_OF_ROWS] = {PB_3, PB_5, PC_7, PA_15};
4    DigitalIn keypadColPins[KEYPAD_NUMBER_OF_COLS]  = {PB_12, PB_13, PB_15, PC_6};
5
6    DigitalIn doorHandle(BUTTON1);
7
8    DigitalOut doorUnlockedLed(LED1);
9    DigitalOut doorLockedLed(LED2);
10   DigitalOut incorrectCodeLed(LED3);
11
12   UnbufferedSerial uartUsb(USBTX, USBRX, 115200);
```

Code 4.18 Declaration of the public global objects.

In Code 4.19, the section "Declaration and initialization of public global variables" is shown. On lines 3 and 5, the variables *accumulatedDebounceMatrixKeypadTime* and *matrixKeypadLastKeyPressed* are declared and initialized to zero and the null character, respectively. On line 6, an array of char that will be used to get the character corresponding to the pressed key is defined. This is based on the column and row that are activated, as in Example 4.2. On line 12, a variable of the user-defined type *matrixKeypadState_t* is declared as *matrixKeypadState*. On line 14, the variable *DoorState*, which is used to implement the FSM, is declared. On lines 16 and 18, the variables *rtcTime* and *seconds* are declared, just as in Example 4.4. Finally, on line 22 the array *codeSequence* is declared and assigned the code 1-4-7.

```
1   //=====[Declaration and initialization of public global variables]==============
2
3   int accumulatedDebounceMatrixKeypadTime = 0;
4
5   char matrixKeypadLastkeyReleased = '\0';
6   char matrixKeypadIndexToCharArray[] = {
7       '1', '2', '3', 'A',
8       '4', '5', '6', 'B',
9       '7', '8', '9', 'C',
10      '*', '0', '#', 'D',
11  };
12  matrixKeypadState_t matrixKeypadState;
13
14  doorState_t doorState;
15
16  struct tm RTCTime;
17
18  time_t seconds;
19
20  char codeSequence[CODE_DIGITS] = {'1','4','7'};
```

Code 4.19 Declaration and initialization of public global variables.

In Code 4.20, the public functions are declared. The functions *uartTask()* and *availableCommands()* have the same role as in the smart home system but will have an implementation that is specific to this proposed exercise. The functions *doorInit()* and *doorUpdate()* are used to initiate and implement the FSM related to the door. The functions *matrixKeypadInit()*, *matrixKeypadScan()*, and *matrixKeypadUpdate()* are used to initiate, scan, and update the state of the matrix keypad, respectively. From lines 10 to 12, three functions that will be used to get and send strings and characters using serial communication with the PC are declared. Note that some of these functions use pointers (lines 10 and 12), a concept that was introduced in Example 3.5.

```
1   //=====[Declarations (prototypes) of public functions]=========================
2
3   void uartTask();
4   void availableCommands();
5   void doorInit();
6   void doorUpdate();
7   void matrixKeypadInit();
8   char matrixKeypadScan();
9   char matrixKeypadUpdate();
10  void pcSerialComStringWrite( const char* str );
11  char pcSerialComCharRead();
12  void pcSerialComStringRead( char* str, int strLength );
```

Code 4.20 Declaration of public functions used in the proposed solution.

The implementation of the *main()* function is shown in Code 4.21. First, the door and the matrix keypad are initialized (lines 5 and 6) and then there is a *while (true)* loop to continuously update the door state (line 8) and communicate with the PC using the uart (line 9).

```
1   //=====[Main function, the program entry point after power on or reset]========
2
3   int main()
4   {
5       doorInit();
6       matrixKeypadInit();
7       while (true) {
8           doorUpdate();
9           uartTask();
10      }
11  }
```

Code 4.21 Declaration of public functions used in the proposed solution.

In Code 4.22, the implementation of the *uartTask()* function is shown. The principal idea is the same as in the *uartTask()* function used in the smart home system implementation. If the key "s" is pressed, then the user is asked to enter the date and time (lines 17 to 52), in quite a similar way to the implementation introduced in Example 4.4. By means of comparing lines 19 to 52 with Code 4.10, the reader can see that the same functionality is now obtained using a more modular program. Finally, in lines 54 to 60, the implementation for the key "t" is shown, as in Example 4.4.

 NOTE: The function *pcSerialComStringRead()* that is called on lines 20, 25, 30, 35, 40, and 45 reads the number of characters indicated by its second parameter (for example, four characters when it is called on line 20), stores the read characters in the array of char indicated by its first parameter (e.g., *year* when it is called on line 20), and writes the null character, '\0', in the next position of the array (e.g., the fifth position of *year* when it is called on line 20). The implementation of *pcSerialComStringRead()* is discussed below.

```
1   void uartTask()
2   {
3       char str[100] = "";
4       char receivedChar = '\0';
5       struct tm rtcTime;
6       char year[5] = "";
7       char month[3] = "";
8       char day[3] = "";
9       char hour[3] = "";
10      char minute[3] = "";
11      char second[3] = "";
12      time_t epochSeconds;
13      receivedChar = pcSerialComCharRead();
14      if( receivedChar != '\0') {
15          switch (receivedChar) {
16
17          case 's':
18          case 'S':
19              pcSerialComStringWrite("\r\nType four digits for the current year (YYYY): ");
20              pcSerialComStringRead( year, 4);
21              pcSerialComStringWrite("\r\n");
22              rtcTime.tm_year = atoi(year) - 1900;
23
```

```
24              pcSerialComStringWrite("Type two digits for the current month (01-12): ");
25              pcSerialComStringRead( month, 2);
26              pcSerialComStringWrite("\r\n");
27              rtcTime.tm_mon  = atoi(month) - 1;
28
29              pcSerialComStringWrite("Type two digits for the current day (01-31): ");
30              pcSerialComStringRead( day, 2);
31              pcSerialComStringWrite("\r\n");
32              rtcTime.tm_hour = atoi(hour);
33
34              pcSerialComStringWrite("Type two digits for the current hour (00-23): ");
35              pcSerialComStringRead( hour, 2);
36              pcSerialComStringWrite("\r\n");
37              rtcTime.tm_hour = atoi(hour);
38
39              pcSerialComStringWrite("Type two digits for the current minutes (00-59): ");
40              pcSerialComStringRead( minute, 2);
41              pcSerialComStringWrite("\r\n");
42              rtcTime.tm_min  = atoi(minute);
43
44              pcSerialComStringWrite("Type two digits for the current seconds (00-59): ");
45              pcSerialComStringRead( second, 2);
46              pcSerialComStringWrite("\r\n");
47              rtcTime.tm_sec  = atoi(second);
48
49              rtcTime.tm_isdst = -1;
50              set_time( mktime( &rtcTime ) );
51              pcSerialComStringWrite("Date and time has been set\r\n");
52              break;
53
54          case 't':
55          case 'T':
56              epochSeconds = time(NULL);
57              sprintf ( str, "Date and Time = %s", ctime(&epochSeconds));
58              pcSerialComStringWrite( str );
59              pcSerialComStringWrite("\r\n");
60              break;
61
62          default:
63              availableCommands();
64              break;
65          }
66      }
67  }
```

Code 4.22 Implementation of the function uartTask().

The implementation of the function *availableCommands()* is shown in Code 4.23. This function is used to list all the available commands. In this particular case there are only two: set the time and get the time.

In Code 4.24, the statements used in the function *doorInit()* are shown. The LEDs used to indicate that the door is unlocked and that an incorrect code has been entered are turned off. The LED used to indicate that the door is locked is turned on, and the door state is set to DOOR_CLOSED.

Code 4.25 shows the implementation of the function *doorUpdate()*. From lines 3 to 7, the variables *incorrectCode, keyPressed, currentTime, prevKeyPressed*, and *i* are declared. The variable *currentTime* is preceded by a "*" symbol. This indicates that this variable is a *pointer* and is used because the function *localtime* (on line 14) needs this type of variable, as discussed in Example 4.4.

On line 9, there is a switch over the *doorState* variable. In the case of DOOR_CLOSED, the matrix keypad is scanned (line 11), and if the "A" key is pressed, the date and time of the RTC of the STM32 microcontroller is assigned to *currentTime* (line 14). On line 16, it is determined whether the current time corresponds to the opening hours. If so, *incorrectCode* is set to false (line 17), and *prevKeyPressed* is set to "A" (line 18). The *for* loop on lines 21 to 31 is used to read a number of digits equal to CODE_DIGITS (line 21). Lines 22 to 26 are used to wait until a new key (different to the previous one) is pressed. On line 27, the new key is stored in *prevKeyReleased*. On line 28, the key pressed is compared with the corresponding digit of the code; if they are not equal, then *incorrectCode* is set to true. On line 33, *incorrectCode* is evaluated and if true then the Incorrect code LED is turned on for one second (lines 34 to 36); otherwise, *doorState* is set to DOOR_UNLOCKED, the *doorLockedLED* is turned off, and the *doorUnlockedLED* is turned on.

In the case of DOOR_UNLOCKED (line 46), if *doorHandle* is true, then *doorUnlockedLED* is set to OFF and *doorState* is set to DOOR_OPEN. Lastly, in the case of DOOR_OPEN (line 53), if *doorHandle* is false, *doorLockedLED* is set to ON and *doorState* is set to DOOR_CLOSED. In the *default* case, the function *doorInit()* is called, as was described in Example 4.2 (it is safest to always define a default case).

In Code 4.26, Code 4.27, and Code 4.28, the implementation of the functions *matrixKeypadInit()*, *matrixKeypadScan()*, and *matrixKeypadUpdate()* are shown. It can be seen that this is the same code as in Code 4.6. Therefore, the explanation is not repeated here.

```
1   void availableCommands()
2   {
3       pcSerialComStringWrite( "Available commands:\r\n" );
4       pcSerialComStringWrite( "Press 's' or 'S' to set the time\r\n\r\n" );
5       pcSerialComStringWrite( "Press 't' or 'T' to get the time\r\n\r\n" );
6   }
```

Code 4.23 Implementation of the function availableCommands().

```
1   void doorInit()
2   {
3       doorUnlockedLed = OFF;
4       doorLockedLed = ON;
5       incorrectCodeLed = OFF;
6       doorState = DOOR_CLOSED;
7   }
```

Code 4.24 Implementation of the function doorInit().

```
1   void doorUpdate()
2   {
3       bool incorrectCode;
4       char keyReleased;
5       struct tm * currentTime;
6       char prevkeyReleased;
7       int i;
8
9       switch( doorState ) {
10      case DOOR_CLOSED:
11          keyReleased = matrixKeypadUpdate();
12          if ( keyReleased == 'A' ) {
13              seconds = time(NULL);
14              currentTime = localtime ( &seconds );
15
16              if ( ( currentTime->tm_hour >= START_HOUR ) &&
17                  ( currentTime->tm_hour <= END_HOUR ) ) {
18                  incorrectCode = false;
19                  prevkeyReleased = 'A';
20
21                  for ( i = 0; i < CODE_DIGITS; i++) {
22                      while ( ( keyReleased == '\0' ) ||
23                              ( keyReleased == prevkeyReleased ) ) {
24
25                          keyReleased = matrixKeypadUpdate();
26                      }
27                      prevkeyReleased = keyReleased;
28                      if ( keyReleased != codeSequence[i] ) {
29                          incorrectCode = true;
30                      }
31                  }
32
33                  if ( incorrectCode ) {
34                      incorrectCodeLed = ON;
35                      delay (1000);
36                      incorrectCodeLed = OFF;
37                  } else {
38                      doorState = DOOR_UNLOCKED;
39                      doorLockedLed = OFF;
40                      doorUnlockedLed = ON;
41                  }
42              }
43          }
44          break;
45
46      case DOOR_UNLOCKED:
47          if ( doorHandle ) {
48              doorUnlockedLed = OFF;
49              doorState = DOOR_OPEN;
50          }
51          break;
52
53      case DOOR_OPEN:
54          if ( !doorHandle ) {
55              doorLockedLed = ON;
56              doorState = DOOR_CLOSED;
57          }
58          break;
59
60      default:
61          doorInit();
62          break;
63      }
64  }
```

Code 4.25 Implementation of the function doorUpdate().

```
1   void matrixKeypadInit()
2   {
3       matrixKeypadState = MATRIX_KEYPAD_SCANNING;
4       int pinIndex = 0;
5       for( pinIndex=0; pinIndex<KEYPAD_NUMBER_OF_COLS; pinIndex++ ) {
6           (keypadColPins[pinIndex]).mode(PullUp);
7       }
8   }
```

Code 4.26 Implementation of the function keypadInit().

```
1   char matrixKeypadScan()
2   {
3       int r = 0;
4       int c = 0;
5       int i = 0;
6
7       for( r=0; r<KEYPAD_NUMBER_OF_ROWS; r++ ) {
8
9           for( i=0; i<KEYPAD_NUMBER_OF_ROWS; i++ ) {
10              keypadRowPins[i] = ON;
11          }
12
13          keypadRowPins[r] = OFF;
14
15          for( c=0; c<KEYPAD_NUMBER_OF_COLS; c++ ) {
16              if( keypadColPins[c] == OFF ) {
17                  return matrixKeypadIndexToCharArray[r*KEYPAD_NUMBER_OF_ROWS + c];
18              }
19          }
20      }
21      return '\0';
22  }
```

Code 4.27 Implementation of the function matrixKeypadScan().

```
1   char matrixKeypadUpdate()
2   {
3       char keyDetected = '\0';
4       char keyReleased = '\0';
5
6       switch( matrixKeypadState ) {
7
8       case MATRIX_KEYPAD_SCANNING:
9           keyDetected = matrixKeypadScan();
10          if( keyDetected != '\0' ) {
11              matrixKeypadLastkeyReleased = keyDetected;
12              accumulatedDebounceMatrixKeypadTime = 0;
13              matrixKeypadState = MATRIX_KEYPAD_DEBOUNCE;
14          }
15          break;
16
17      case MATRIX_KEYPAD_DEBOUNCE:
18          if( accumulatedDebounceMatrixKeypadTime >=
19              DEBOUNCE_BUTTON_TIME_MS ) {
20              keyDetected = matrixKeypadScan();
21              if( keyDetected == matrixKeypadLastkeyReleased ) {
22                  matrixKeypadState = MATRIX_KEYPAD_KEY_HOLD_PRESSED;
23              } else {
24                  matrixKeypadState = MATRIX_KEYPAD_SCANNING;
25              }
26          }
27          accumulatedDebounceMatrixKeypadTime =
28              accumulatedDebounceMatrixKeypadTime + TIME_INCREMENT_MS;
```

```
29              break;
30
31          case MATRIX_KEYPAD_KEY_HOLD_PRESSED:
32              keyDetected = matrixKeypadScan();
33              if( keyDetected != matrixKeypadLastkeyReleased ) {
34                  if( keyDetected == '\0' ) {
35                      keyReleased = matrixKeypadLastkeyReleased;
36                  }
37                  matrixKeypadState = MATRIX_KEYPAD_SCANNING;
38              }
39              break;
40
41          default:
42              matrixKeypadInit();
43              break;
44          }
45          return keyReleased;
46  }
```

Code 4.28 Implementation of the function matrixKeypadUpdate().

Finally, in Code 4.29 the functions related to sending and receiving characters using the serial communication with the PC are shown. On line 1, *pcSerialComStringWrite()* is implemented in order to be able to send a string to the serial terminal. *pcSerialComCharRead()* on line 6 implements the reading of a single character. It returns '\0' if there is not a character to be read, or the received character otherwise. Lastly, *pcSerialComStringRead()* implements the reading of a number of characters specified by its second parameter, *strLength*. The read characters are stored in the array of char pointed to by the first parameter of this function, *str*.

 WARNING: If the value of *strLength* is greater than the number of positions in the array of char pointed by *str*, then a buffer overflow will take place. As discussed in Example 4.4, this can lead to software errors.

```
1   void pcSerialComStringWrite( const char* str )
2   {
3       uartUsb.write( str, strlen(str) );
4   }
5
6   char pcSerialComCharRead()
7   {
8       char receivedChar = '\0';
9       if( uartUsb.readable() ) {
10          uartUsb.read( &receivedChar, 1 );
11      }
12      return receivedChar;
13  }
14
15  void pcSerialComStringRead( char* str, int strLength )
16  {
17      int strIndex;
18      for ( strIndex = 0; strIndex < strLength; strIndex++) {
19          uartUsb.read( &str[strIndex] , 1 );
20          uartUsb.write( &str[strIndex] ,1 );
21      }
22      str[strLength]='\0';
23  }
```

Code 4.29 Implementation of the functions related to the PC serial communication.

References

[1] "4x4 Keypad Module Pinout, Configuration, Features, Circuit & Datasheet". Accessed July 9, 2021.

[2] "Breadboard Power Supply Module". Accessed July 9, 2021.
https://components101.com/modules/5v-mb102-breadboard-power-supply-module

[3] "UM1974 User manual - STM32 Nucleo-144 boards (MB1137)". Accessed July 9, 2021.
https://www.st.com/resource/en/user_manual/dm00244518-stm32-nucleo144-boards-mb1137-stmicroelectronics.pdf

[4] "GitHub - armBookCodeExamples/Directory". Accessed July 9, 2021.
https://github.com/armBookCodeExamples/Directory/

[5] "Time - API references and tutorials | Mbed OS 6 Documentation". Accessed July 9, 2021.
https://os.mbed.com/docs/mbed-os/v6.12/apis/time.html

[6] "<cstring> (string.h) - C++ Reference". Accessed July 9, 2021.
https://www.cplusplus.com/reference/cstring/

[7] "Smart door locks | Mbed". Accessed July 9, 2021.
https://os.mbed.com/built-with-mbed/smart-door-locks/

Chapter 5

Modularization Applied to
Embedded Systems Programming

5.1 Roadmap

5.1.1 What You Will Learn

After you have studied the material in this chapter, you will be able to:

- Describe how the concept of modularity can be applied to embedded systems programming.

- Develop programs that are organized into modules and are separated into different files.

- Summarize the fundamental concepts of public and private variables and functions.

5.1.2 Review of Previous Chapters

In the preceding chapters, the smart home system was incrementally provided with a broad range of functionality. The main goal was to introduce different concepts about embedded systems programming by means of practical examples. The resultant code had hundreds of lines, as can be seen in the final example in Chapter 4. The reader may have noticed that it starts to become hard to remember which part of the program relates to which implemented function of the system. It can be even harder to find specific functionality within the code. It becomes increasingly difficult to introduce new functionality and improvements to the program.

5.1.3 Contents of This Chapter

This chapter will explain how to overcome this issue by means of *modularization*. For this purpose, the code presented in Example 4.4 is revised and the program is reorganized into different *modules*. Each resulting module will contain a piece of code that deals with a particular area of the smart home system functionality. In this way, the resultant code will be easier to understand, maintain, and improve. The original 600 lines of code will be divided into a set of files, each having precise functionality and a correspondingly smaller number of lines.

 NOTE: In this chapter, the reader may notice that there are no Example, Case Study, or Under the Hood sections. In addition, in this chapter there are just a few Proposed Exercises, all located at the end. This is due to the fact that this chapter is not about including new functionality in the program, but rather explaining to the reader how the code that was introduced in the previous chapters can be improved.

5.2 Basic Principles of Modularization

5.2.1 Modularity Principle

Modularity is a basic principle in engineering. The principle states that it is better to build systems from loosely coupled components, called *modules*. These modules should have well-defined functionality and must be easy to understand, reuse, and replace.

The advantages of using modularization in embedded systems programming can be summarized as follows:

- It is easier to understand a program made of independent modules (the *maintainability* is improved).

- It is simple to reuse modules in different programs, which improves the *productivity* of the programmer.

The reader may remember that subsection *2.2.2 Modularization of a Program in Functions* was an initial introduction to the topic of modularization. A program that was previously organized into a single long piece of code was divided into different, shorter pieces of code called functions. These functions complete one or more specific tasks and can be used in a given program one or more times.

The problem arises when a given function has a very specific task, but this task is closely related to the tasks of another function. For example, consider the following two functions:

- *Function 1*: turns the alarm on or off after reading a code the user enters using the matrix keypad

- *Function 2*: turns the alarm on or off after reading a code the user enters using the PC keyboard

Both of these functions have very specific tasks, but they are closely coupled, as both of them modify the state of the alarm. If something should be modified in the way the alarm is turned on or off, then the two functions (*Function 1* and *Function 2*) must both be modified.

The scenario changes if the same functionality is implemented in the following way:

- *Function A*: read a code that the user enters using the matrix keypad

- *Function B*: read a code that the user enters using the PC keyboard

- *Function C*: gets a code that the user enters using either the matrix keypad (*Function A*) or the PC keyboard (*Function B*) and, depending on the code, turns the alarm on or off.

Here it can be seen that *Functions A and B* are loosely coupled to one other, and that only *Function C* deals with turning off the alarm. This increases software maintainability, which means that the code is easier for different programmers to understand, repair, and enhance over time.

In this context, two very important concepts in computer programming arise, namely *cohesion* and *coupling*.

> **DEFINITION:** *Cohesion* refers to the degree to which the elements inside a module belong together, while *Coupling* is a measure of how closely connected two routines or modules are.

This whole chapter is about taking the code from Example 4.4 as the starting point and improving it by means of applying modularization techniques. This is because, for pedagogical reasons, the code used in Example 4.4 was gradually developed through the preceding chapters and is, therefore, not properly modularized.

The process of restructuring existing code – changing the factoring without changing its external behavior – is called *code refactoring*. In the following section, the code used in Example 4.4 will be refactored, as a first step to increase its modularity, by preparing modules with appropriate cohesion and coupling.

5.3 Applying Modularization to the Program Code of the Smart Home System

5.3.1 Refactoring the Program Code of the Smart Home System

As was discussed in the previous section, the code of the proposed solution introduced in Example 4.4 does not follow the principles of modularity. For example, the function *uartTask()* has approximately one hundred and fifty lines and deals with a broad range of functionality:

▪ Gets and processes the keys that are pressed on the PC keyboard

▪ Sends the messages that are displayed to the user on the PC

▪ Turns on/off several LEDs depending on the entered code

▪ Shows the present temperature read by the LM35 sensor

▪ Configures the new code used to deactivate the alarm

▪ Sets the date and time of the real-time clock

▪ Displays the list of events stored in memory.

The function *uartTask()* is only one example; there are many other functions in the code used in Example 4.4 that do not follow the principles of modularity:

▪ *alarmActivationUpdate()*: gets the reading of the sensors and also turns on/off the Alarm LED.

▪ *alarmDeactivationUpdate()*: assesses the entered code and also turns on/off the Incorrect code and System blocked LEDs.

Conversely, *availableCommands()* can be mentioned as an example of a function that does follow the principles of modularity; this function only displays messages to the user on the PC. It has well-defined functionality and is easy to understand, reuse, and replace.

In order to modularize the functionality of the smart home system, the core functionality can initially be grouped into the modules shown in Figure 5.1. The colors and the layout used in Figure 5.1 are intentionally the same as in Figure 1.2 so as to stress that the current smart home system functionality is very similar to the smart home system proposed in Chapter 1. The proposed improvement (i.e., modularize the code) must be done without interfering with the current smart home system functionality.

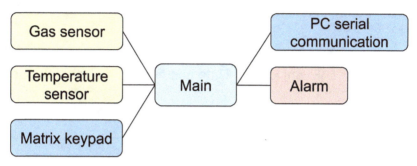

Figure 5.1 Diagram of the first attempt to modularize the smart home system program.

It is important to note that Figure 5.1 represents a first approach to the *software* modules, while Figure 1.2 represents the *hardware* modules. Very often a software module is directly related to a given hardware module, but this is not always the case. A hardware module might not have a software module related to it (because it is not controlled by a microcontroller), or it may have more than one software module related to it.

Another important concept that was mentioned previously is that it is desirable to write the modules in such a way that they can be reused in other projects. Therefore, it is convenient to have a *main()* function as small and simple as possible, its role being to call a few functions that in turn trigger all the functionality of the system.

Finally, the modules should be organized with consideration of future improvements and functionality that could be added to the system. This is a strong reason to group the system functionalities into small modules, with all modules having a well-defined functionality.

Considering all these concepts, the proposed modules for the smart home system implementation are shown in Figure 5.2. The *main.cpp* file is not a module. However, it is included in Figure 5.2 to stress that it only uses functions provided by the smart home system module. In turn, to implement the system functionality, the smart home system module will call functions from other modules. The functionality of each module is briefly described in Table 5.1. In the table, the role of each module is classified as *system*, *subsystem*, or *driver*.

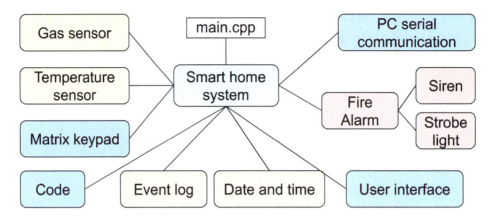

Figure 5.2 Diagram of the modules used in the smart home system program.

Table 5.1 Functionalities and roles of the smart home system modules.

Module	Description of its functionality	Role
Smart home system	Manages the functionality of all the subsystems.	System
Fire alarm	Controls the siren and the strobe light.	Subsystem
Code	Assesses entered codes and manages setting of new codes.	Subsystem
User interface	Manages the user interface (LEDs and matrix keypad).	Subsystem
PC serial com	Manages the communication with the PC (send/receive data).	Subsystem
Event log	Logs the system events.	Subsystem
Siren	Drives the siren (implemented by a buzzer).	Driver
Strobe light	Drives the strobe light (implemented by an LED).	Driver
Gas sensor	Reads the MQ-2 gas sensor.	Driver
Temperature sensor	Reads the LM35 temperature sensor.	Driver
Matrix keypad	Reads the keys pressed on the matrix keypad.	Driver
Date and time	Reads and writes the date and time of the real-time clock.	Driver

In Tables 5.2 to 5.13, the functions provided by each of the proposed modules shown in Table 5.1 are detailed, together with a brief description of their functionality and the modules (or *main.cpp* file) that make use of each function. The tables are presented following the order used in Table 5.1. The code will be shown and discussed in detail in subsection 5.3.2.

It is important to note that in Tables 5.2 to 5.13, there is a bold line to separate functions that are called by other modules from functions that are used only within the module itself. For example, in Table 5.3, the first four functions (from *fireAlarmInit()* to *overTemperatureDetectorStateRead()*) are used by functions that belong to other modules, while the last six functions (from *gasDetectedRead()* to *fireAlarmStrobeTime()*) are used only by functions that belong within the fire alarm module itself. There is no reason to grant other modules access to the functions *gasDetectedRead()*, *overTemperatureDetectedRead()*, *fireAlarmActivationUpdate()*, *fireAlarmDeactivationUpdate()*, *fireAlarmDeactivate()*, and *fireAlarmStrobeTime()*. The terminology and concepts related to this differentiation are discussed in this chapter.

Table 5.2 Functions of the smart home system module.

Name of the function	Description of its functionality	File that uses it
smartHomeSystem Init()	Initializes the subsystems and drivers of the smart home system.	main.cpp
smartHomeSystem Update()	Calls the functions that update the modules Fire alarm, User interface, PC serial com, and Event log. Also manages the system timing.	main.cpp

Table 5.3 Functions of the fire alarm module.

Name of the function	Description of its functionality	Modules that use it
fireAlarmInit()	Initializes the fire alarm subsystem by calling temperatureSensorInit(), gasSensorInit(), sirenInit(), and strobeLightInit().	Smart home system
fireAlarmUpdate()	Updates the fire alarm subsystem by calling fireAlarmActivationUpdate(), fireAlarmDeactivationUpdate(), sirenUpdate(), and strobeLightUpdate().	Smart home system
gasDetectorStateRead()	Returns the current state of the gas detector.	Event log PC serial com
overTemperatureDetectorState Read()	Returns the current state of the over temperature detector.	Event log PC serial com
gasDetectedRead()	Returns true if gas has been detected.	Fire alarm
overTemperatureDetectedRead()	Returns true if over temperature has been detected.	Fire alarm
fireAlarmActivationUpdate()	Controls the activation of the siren and the strobe light.	Fire alarm
fireAlarmDeactivationUpdate()	Controls the deactivation of the siren and the strobe light.	Fire alarm
fireAlarmDeactivate()	Implements the deactivation of the siren and the strobe light.	Fire alarm
fireAlarmStrobeTime()	Controls the siren and strobe light time.	Fire alarm

Table 5.4 Functions of the code module.

Name of the function	Description of its functionality	Modules that use it
codeWrite()	Writes the new code set by the user into CodeSequence[].	PC serial com
codeMatchFrom()	Checks if a new code is entered and assesses the code.	Fire alarm
codeMatch()	Returns a Boolean indicating if the code is correct.	Code
codeDeactivate()	Sets systemBlockedState and incorrectCodeState to OFF.	Code

Table 5.5 Functions of the user interface module.

Name of the function	Description of its functionality	Modules that use it
userInterfaceInit()	Sets systemBlockedState and incorrectCodeState to OFF and calls matrixKeypadInit().	Smart home system
userInterfaceUpdate()	Calls incorrectCodeIndicatorUpdate(), userInterfaceMatrixKeypadUpdate(), and systemBlockedIndicatorUpdate().	Smart home system
userInterfaceCodeCompleteRead()	Returns a Boolean indicating if the read of the code is complete or not.	Code
userInterfaceCodeCompleteWrite()	Sets the state of codeComplete.	Code
incorrectCodeStateRead()	Returns a Boolean indicating if the code is correct or incorrect.	Event log User interface
incorrectCodeStateWrite()	Sets the state of incorrectCodeState.	Code
systemBlockedStateRead()	Returns a Boolean indicating if the system is blocked or not.	Event log User interface
systemBlockedStateWrite()	Sets the state of systemBlockedState.	Code
incorrectCodeIndicatorUpdate()	Controls the object incorrectCodeLed.	User interface
systemBlockedIndicatorUpdate()	Controls the object systemBlockedLed.	User Interface
userInterfaceMatrixKeypadUpdate()	Gets a new code using the matrix keypad and manages incorrectCodeState.	User interface

Table 5.6 Functions of the PC serial communication module.

Name of the function	Description of its functionality	Modules that use it
pcSerialComInit()	Calls the function availableCommands().	Smart home system
pcSerialComStringWrite()	Writes a string to the PC serial port.	Code Event log
pcSerialComUpdate()	Gets the commands and the entered codes.	Smart home system
pcSerialComCodeComplete Read()	Returns a Boolean variable indicating if the code read from the PcSerialCom is complete.	Code
pcSerialComCodeComplete Write()	Writes the state of codeCompleteFromPcSerialCom.	Code
pcSerialComCharRead()	Returns a char corresponding to a read value.	PC serial com
pcSerialComStringRead()	Reads a string from the PC serial port.	PC serial com
pcSerialComSaveCode Update()	Receives a new char of the entered code.	PC serial com
pcSerialComSaveNewCode Update()	Receives a new char of the new code.	PC serial com
pcSerialComCommand Update()	Depending on the entered char, triggers one of the commands of the PC serial com module.	PC serial com
availableCommands()	Displays the available commands on the PC.	PC serial com

Name of the function	Description of its functionality	Modules that use it
commandShowCurrent AlarmState()	Displays whether the alarm is activated or not on the PC.	PC serial com
commandShowCurrent GasDetectorState()	Displays whether the gas is being detected or not on the PC.	PC serial com
commandShowCurrent OverTempDetectorState()	Displays whether the temperature is above the maximum level or not on the PC.	PC serial com
commandEnterCode Sequence()	Configures the UART to receive a code and displays a message on the PC asking for the code.	PC serial com
commandEnterNewCode()	Configures the UART to receive a code and displays a message on the PC asking for the new code.	PC serial com
commandShowCurrent TemperatureInCelsius()	Displays the temperature in Celsius on the PC.	PC serial com
commandShowCurrent TemperatureInFahrenheit()	Displays the temperature in Fahrenheit on the PC.	PC serial com
commandSetDateAndTime()	Gets date and time and writes it to the RTC.	PC serial com
commandShowDateAndTime()	Displays the date and time on the PC.	PC serial com
commandShowStoredEvents()	Displays the stored events on the PC.	PC serial com

Table 5.7 Main functionality of the event log module.

Name of the function	Description of its functionality	Modules that use it
eventLogUpdate()	Updates the log of events.	Smart home system
eventLogNumberOfStoredEvents()	Returns the number of stored events.	PC serial com
eventLogRead()	Reads an event stored in the log.	PC serial com
eventLogWrite()	Stores an event in the log.	Event log
eventLogElementStateUpdate()	Stores the new events in the log.	Event log

Table 5.8 Functions of the siren module.

Name of the function	Description of its functionality	Modules that use it
sirenInit()	Sets the siren to OFF (OpenDrain).	Fire alarm
sirenUpdate()	Updates the state of the siren.	Fire alarm
sirenStateRead()	Returns the Boolean variable sirenState.	Event log Fire alarm PC serial com User interface
sirenStateWrite()	Writes the state of Boolean variable sirenState.	Fire alarm

Table 5.9 Functions of the strobe light module.

Name of the function	Description of its functionality	Modules that use it
strobeLightInit()	Sets alarmLed to OFF.	Fire alarm
strobeLightUpdate()	Updates the state of the strobe light.	Fire alarm
strobeLightStateRead()	Returns the Boolean variable strobeLightState.	Fire alarm User interface
strobeLightStateWrite()	Writes the state of Boolean variable strobeLightState.	Fire alarm

Table 5.10 Functions of the gas sensor module.

Name of the function	Description of its functionality	Modules that use it
gasSensorInit()	Has no functionality. Reserved for future use.	Fire alarm
gasSensorUpdate()	Has no functionality. Reserved for future use.	Fire alarm
gasSensorRead()	Returns the reading of the gas sensor detector.	Fire alarm

Table 5.11 Functions of the temperature sensor module.

Name of the function	Description of its functionality	Modules that use it
temperatureSensorInit()	Has no functionality. Reserved for future use.	Fire alarm
temperatureSensorUpdate()	Updates the temperature reading.	Fire alarm
temperatureSensorReadCelsius()	Returns the temperature in °C.	Fire alarm
temperatureSensorReadFahrenheit()	Returns the temperature in °F.	PC serial com
celsiusToFahrenheit()	Converts a reading in °C to °F.	Temperature sensor
analogReadingScaledWithTheLM35Formula()	Converts an LM35 reading to temp.	Temperature sensor

Table 5.12 Main functionality of the matrix keypad module.

Name of the function	Description of its functionality	Modules that use it
matrixKeypadInit()	Initializes the matrix keypad pins and FSM.	User interface
matrixKeypadUpdate()	Implements the matrix keypad FSM.	User interface
matrixKeypadScan()	Scans the matrix keypad and returns the read char.	Matrix keypad
matrixKeypadReset()	Resets the matrix keypad FSM.	Matrix keypad

Table 5.13 Functions of the date and time module.

Name of the function	Description of its functionality	Modules that use it
dateAndTimeRead()	Returns the RTC date and time.	PC serial com
dateAndTimeWrite()	Writes the RTC date and time.	PC serial com

Looking at Tables 5.2 to 5.13, it can be appreciated how the different modules are related to each other. These relationships are summarized in Figure 5.3.

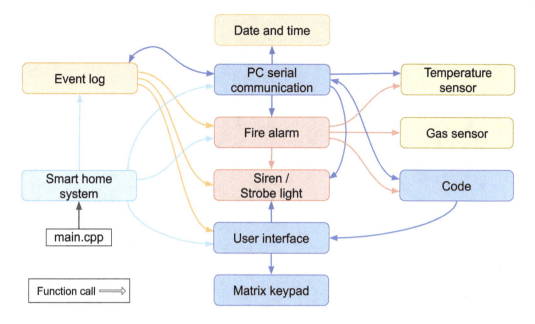

Figure 5.3 Diagram of the relationships between the modules used in the smart home system.

 NOTE: For the sake of simplicity, the Siren and Strobe light modules are drawn together in Figure 5.3 despite being independent modules. In section 5.3.2, it will be shown that they have many similarities.

As was briefly described in Table 5.1, the roles of the modules indicated in Figure 5.3 are:

- The Smart home system is the only module that is called from the *main.cpp* (its role is *system*).

- The Fire alarm, Code, User interface, PC serial communication, and Event log are *subsystem* modules. They are called by other modules and call functions from other modules.

- The Siren, Strobe light, Gas sensor, Temperature sensor, Matrix keypad, and Date and time are *driver* modules. They are called by other modules, but they do not call functions from other modules.

5.3.2 Detailed Implementation of the Refactored Code of the Smart Home System

This subsection shows the program code that is proposed in order to implement the functions introduced in Tables 5.2 to 5.13. The whole program can be imported using the URL available in [1].

The libraries and defines that are used are shown in Code 5.1. It can be seen that the #defines are now organized according to the different modules that were defined. Some names have been changed in comparison with Example 4.4 (for example, OVER_TEMP_LEVEL was changed to TEMPERATURE_C_ LIMIT_ALARM, KEYPAD_NUMBER_OF_ROWS was changed to MATRIX_KEYPAD_NUMBER_OF_ ROWS), and some prefixes have been incorporated, such as "CODE_", "EVENT_LOG_", and "SIREN_".

```
1   //=====[Libraries]===================================================
2
3   #include "mbed.h"
4   #include "arm_book_lib.h"
5
6   //=====[Defines]======================================================
7
8   // Module: code --------------------------------------------
9
10  #define CODE_NUMBER_OF_KEYS      4
11
12  // Module: event_log ---------------------------------------
13
14  #define EVENT_LOG_MAX_STORAGE         20
15  #define EVENT_HEAD_STR_LENGTH          8
16  #define EVENT_LOG_NAME_MAX_LENGTH     13
17  #define DATE_AND_TIME_STR_LENGTH      18
18  #define CTIME_STR_LENGTH              25
19  #define NEW_LINE_STR_LENGTH            3
20  #define EVENT_STR_LENGTH              (EVENT_HEAD_STR_LENGTH + \
21                                         EVENT_LOG_NAME_MAX_LENGTH + \
22                                         DATE_AND_TIME_STR_LENGTH  + \
23                                         CTIME_STR_LENGTH + \
24                                         NEW_LINE_STR_LENGTH)
25
26  // Module: fire_alarm --------------------------------------
27
28  #define TEMPERATURE_C_LIMIT_ALARM     50.0
29  #define STROBE_TIME_GAS               1000
30  #define STROBE_TIME_OVER_TEMP          500
31  #define STROBE_TIME_GAS_AND_OVER_TEMP  100
32
33  // Module: matrix_keypad -----------------------------------
34
35  #define MATRIX_KEYPAD_NUMBER_OF_ROWS    4
36  #define MATRIX_KEYPAD_NUMBER_OF_COLS    4
37  #define DEBOUNCE_BUTTON_TIME_MS        40
38
39  // Module: smart_home_system -------------------------------
40
41  #define SYSTEM_TIME_INCREMENT_MS    10
42
43  // Module: temperature_sensor ------------------------------
44
45  #define LM35_NUMBER_OF_AVG_SAMPLES    100
```

Code 5.1 Libraries and defines used in the refactored version of the smart home system code.

 NOTE: From now on, the names of modules will be written following the snake_case format shown on lines 12, 26, 33, 39, and 43 of Code 5.1. In this format, each space is replaced by an underscore (_) character, and the first letter of each word is written in lowercase.

Many definitions were added to the *event_log* module, as can be seen between lines 14 and 24. Figure 5.4 shows a diagram that illustrates the rationale behind the number of characters assigned to each of these definitions, as it can be obtained after analyzing the implementation of *eventLogRead()*, which is introduced later in this chapter. EVENT_STR_LENGTH, which is obtained as the sum of the other values (line 20 to line 24), will be used in the function *commandShowStoredEvents()*, as discussed below.

EVENT_HEAD_STR_LENGTH 8	EVENT_LOG_NAME_MAX_LENGTH 13	DATE_AND_TIME_STR_LENGTH 18

```
Event = OVER_TEMP_OFF '\r' '\n' ...
Date and Time = Wed Jan 27 17:04:47 2021 '\n'
'\r' '\n' '\0'
```

NEW_LINE_STR_LENGTH 3   CTIME_STR_LENGTH 25

Figure 5.4 Diagram showing how the definitions of the event_log module were made.

NOTE: Remember that the characters '\0' (null), '\r' (carriage return), and '\n' (line feed) are not printed on the serial terminal, but still occupy one position in an array of char. '\0' is stored with the code 0, '\r' with the code 10, and '\n' with the code 13.

In Code 5.2, the declarations of public data types are shown. The first data type that is declared, *codeOrigin_t*, as well as the last data type that is declared, *pcSerialComMode_t*, are introduced in this chapter with the aim of modularizing the program code, as discussed below. All of the remaining data types are the same as in Example 4.4, but they are now grouped with regard to the respective modules where they are used.

```
1   //=====[Declaration of public data types]=======================================
2
3   // Module: code --------------------------------------------
4
5   typedef enum{
6       CODE_KEYPAD,
7       CODE_PC_SERIAL,
8   } codeOrigin_t;
9
10  // Module: event_log --------------------------------------------
11
12  typedef struct systemEvent {
13      time_t seconds;
14      char typeOfEvent[EVENT_LOG_NAME_MAX_LENGTH];
15  } systemEvent_t;
16
17  // Module: matrix_keypad --------------------------------------------
18
19  typedef enum {
20      MATRIX_KEYPAD_SCANNING,
21      MATRIX_KEYPAD_DEBOUNCE,
22      MATRIX_KEYPAD_KEY_HOLD_PRESSED
23  } matrixKeypadState_t;
24
25  // Module: pc_serial_com --------------------------------------------
26
27  typedef enum{
28      PC_SERIAL_COMMANDS,
29      PC_SERIAL_GET_CODE,
30      PC_SERIAL_SAVE_NEW_CODE,
31  } pcSerialComMode_t;
```

Code 5.2 Public data types of the refactored version of the smart home system code.

In Code 5.3, the declarations and initializations of public global objects are shown. Again, the objects are the same as in Example 4.4, although they have been subdivided into modules. The only object that is declared in a different way is *sirenPin* (PE_10). This object was introduced in Example 3.5 and declared in Chapters 3 and 4 as a DigitalInOut object to turn on the buzzer by asserting 0 V in PE_10 and turn off the buzzer by configuring PE_10 as an open drain input.

In Code 5.3, it can be seen that PE_10 is now declared as a *DigitalOut* object. Using this method, the buzzer can be turned on by asserting 0 V to PE_10 and turned off by asserting 3.3 V to PE_10. From now on, when the alarm is activated, the buzzer will be turned off and on intermittently, concurrently with the LD1 *alarmLed*. The code to implement this behavior is simpler if PE_10 is declared as a DigitalOut object. In this way, the buzzer will now generate a "beep beep" sound instead of the continuous sound that was implemented in previous chapters.

```
1   //=====[Declaration and initialization of public global objects]================
2
3   // Module: fire_alarm ------------------------------------
4
5   DigitalIn alarmTestButton(BUTTON1);
6
7   // Module: gas_sensor ------------------------------------
8
9   DigitalIn mq2(PE_12);
10
11  // Module: matrix_keypad ------------------------------------
12
13  DigitalOut keypadRowPins[MATRIX_KEYPAD_NUMBER_OF_ROWS] = {PB_3, PB_5, PC_7, PA_15};
14  DigitalIn keypadColPins[MATRIX_KEYPAD_NUMBER_OF_COLS] = {PB_12, PB_13, PB_15, PC_6};
15
16  // Module: pc_serial_com ------------------------------------
17
18  Serial uartUsb(USBTX, USBRX, 115200);
19
20  // Module: siren ------------------------------------
21
22  DigitalOut sirenPin(PE_10);
23
24  // Module: strobe_light ------------------------------------
25
26  DigitalOut strobeLight(LED1);
27
28  // Module: temperature_sensor ------------------------------------
29
30  AnalogIn lm35(A1);
31
32  // Module: user_interface ------------------------------------
33
34  DigitalOut incorrectCodeLed(LED3);
35  DigitalOut systemBlockedLed(LED2);
```

Code 5.3 Public global objects of the refactored version of the smart home system code.

NOTE: When *sirenPin* is defined as a *DigitalOut* object (line 22 of Code 5.3), the buzzer does not turn off completely when PE_10 is configured in HIGH state but makes a very soft sound. This is due to the fact that when 3.3 V is applied to PE_10, there is 1.7 V between the "+" and "-" buzzer pins, as shown in Figure 5.5. In order to completely turn off the buzzer while using PE_10 as a *DigitalOut* object, the circuit shown in Figure 5.6 can be used. In this circuit, PE_10 activates or deactivates transistor Q1, which allows current to circulate through the buzzer, just like a switch. RB1 is used to limit the base current.

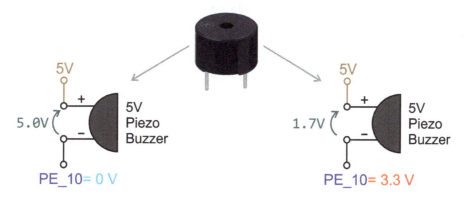

Figure 5.5. Diagram of the voltage through the buzzer pins when PE_10 is set to 0 V and 3.3 V.

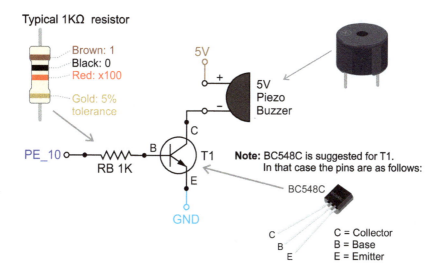

Figure 5.6 Diagram of the circuit that can be used to completely turn on and off the buzzer.

NOTE: In the implementation shown in Figure 5.5, the buzzer is turned on when 0 V is asserted in PE_10 and is turned off when 3.3 V is asserted in PE_10. However, in the circuit shown in Figure 5.6, the buzzer is turned on when 3.3 V is asserted in PE_10 and is turned off when 0 V is asserted in PE_10. As a consequence, the code should be modified if the latter circuit is used. This is discussed below.

In Code 5.4, the declaration and initialization of public global variables is shown. In this new implementation, the variables *gasDetected* and *overTemperatureDetected* are used to indicate that gas and over temperature have been detected, respectively, while *gasDetectorState* and *overTemperatureDetectorState* are used to indicate, respectively, that gas and over temperature are currently being detected.

The reader should note that the new variables *systemBlockedState* and *incorrectCodeState* are used to indicate the state of the LEDs, in order to differentiate them from the LEDs themselves. These are managed by means of the objects *systemBlockedLed* and *incorrectCodeLed*. This is a consequence of the modularization: the state of *systemBlockedState* and *incorrectCodeState* are controlled by the *code* module, while the LEDs are controlled by the *user_interface* module.

The reader should also note that there are many new variables declared, for example in the *pc_serial_com* and *siren* modules. The use of these variables will be explained in the following pages, together with the functions of the modules.

```
1   //=====[Declaration and initialization of public global variables]==============
2
3   // Module: code ------------------------------------------------
4
5   int numberOfIncorrectCodes = 0;
6   char codeSequence[CODE_NUMBER_OF_KEYS] = { '1', '8', '0', '5' };
7
8   // Module: event_log ------------------------------------------
9
10  bool sirenLastState = OFF;
11  bool gasLastState   = OFF;
12  bool tempLastState  = OFF;
13  bool ICLastState    = OFF;
14  bool SBLastState    = OFF;
15  int  eventsIndex    = 0;
16  systemEvent_t arrayOfStoredEvents[EVENT_LOG_MAX_STORAGE];
17
18  // Module: fire_alarm -----------------------------------------
19
20  bool gasDetected                   = OFF;
21  bool overTemperatureDetected       = OFF;
22  bool gasDetectorState              = OFF;
23  bool overTemperatureDetectorState  = OFF;
24
25  // Module: matrix_keypad --------------------------------------
26
27  matrixKeypadState_t matrixKeypadState;
28  int timeIncrement_ms = 0;
29  int accumulatedDebounceMatrixKeypadTime = 0;
30  char matrixKeypadLastKeyPressed = '\0';
31
32  // Module: pc_serial_com --------------------------------------
33
34  char codeSequenceFromPcSerialCom[CODE_NUMBER_OF_KEYS];
35  pcSerialComMode_t pcSerialComMode = PC_SERIAL_COMMANDS;
36  bool codeCompleteFromPcSerialCom = false;
37  int numberOfCodeCharsFromPcSerialCom = 0;
38  char newCodeSequence[CODE_NUMBER_OF_KEYS];
39
```

```
40   // Module: siren -----------------------------------------
41
42   bool sirenState = OFF;
43   int accumulatedTimeAlarm = 0;
44
45   // Module: strobe_light ----------------------------------
46
47   bool strobeLightState = OFF;
48
49   // Module: temperature_sensor ----------------------------
50
51   float lm35TemperatureC = 0.0;
52   float lm35ReadingsArray[LM35_NUMBER_OF_AVG_SAMPLES];
53   int lm35SampleIndex    = 0;
54
55   // Module: user_interface --------------------------------
56
57   char codeSequenceFromUserInterface[CODE_NUMBER_OF_KEYS];
58   bool incorrectCodeState = OFF;
59   bool systemBlockedState = OFF;
60   bool codeComplete = false;
61   int numberOfCodeChars = 0;
62   int numberOfHashKeyReleased = 0;
```

Code 5.4 Public global variables of the refactored version of the smart home system code.

In Code 5.5 and Code 5.6, the declarations of the public functions are shown. All these functions will be discussed one after the other in the following pages.

```
1   //=====[Declarations (prototypes) of public functions]=========================
2
3   // Module: code ------------------------------------------
4
5   void codeWrite( char* newCodeSequence );
6   bool codeMatchFrom( codeOrigin_t codeOrigin );
7   bool codeMatch( char* codeToCompare );
8   void codeDeactivate();
9
10  // Module: date_and_time ---------------------------------
11
12  char* dateAndTimeRead();
13  void dateAndTimeWrite( int year, int month, int day,
14                         int hour, int minute, int second );
15
16  // Module: event_log -------------------------------------
17
18  void eventLogUpdate();
19  int eventLogNumberOfStoredEvents();
20  void eventLogRead( int index, char* str );
21  void eventLogWrite( bool currentState, const char* elementName );
22  void eventLogElementStateUpdate( bool lastState,
23                                   bool currentState,
24                                   const char* elementName );
25
26  // Module: fire_alarm ------------------------------------
27
28  void fireAlarmInit();
29  void fireAlarmUpdate();
```

```
30   bool gasDetectorStateRead();
31   bool overTemperatureDetectorStateRead();
32   bool gasDetectedRead();
33   bool overTemperatureDetectedRead();
34   void fireAlarmActivationUpdate();
35   void fireAlarmDeactivationUpdate();
36   void fireAlarmDeactivate();
37   int fireAlarmStrobeTime();
38
39   // Module: gas_sensor ----------------------------------
40
41   void gasSensorInit();
42   void gasSensorUpdate();
43   bool gasSensorRead();
44
45   // Module: matrix_keypad ------------------------------
46
47   void matrixKeypadInit( int updateTime_ms );
48   char matrixKeypadUpdate();
49   char matrixKeypadScan();
50   void matrixKeypadReset();
```

Code 5.5 Declarations of public functions of the refactored version of the smart home system code (Part 1/2).

```
1    // Module: pc_serial_com ----------------------------
2
3    void pcSerialComInit();
4    char pcSerialComCharRead();
5    void pcSerialComStringWrite( const char* str );
6    void pcSerialComStringRead( char* str, int strLength );
7    void pcSerialComUpdate();
8    bool pcSerialComCodeCompleteRead();
9    void pcSerialComCodeCompleteWrite( bool state );
10   void pcSerialComGetCodeUpdate( char receivedChar );
11   void pcSerialComSaveNewCodeUpdate( char receivedChar );
12   void pcSerialComCommandUpdate( char receivedChar );
13   void availableCommands();
14   void commandShowCurrentAlarmState();
15   void commandShowCurrentGasDetectorState();
16   void commandShowCurrentOverTemperatureDetectorState();
17   void commandEnterCodeSequence();
18   void commandEnterNewCode();
19   void commandShowCurrentTemperatureInCelsius();
20   void commandShowCurrentTemperatureInFahrenheit();
21   void commandSetDateAndTime();
22   void commandShowDateAndTime();
23   void commandShowStoredEvents();
24
25   // Module: siren -------------------------------------
26
27   void sirenInit();
28   bool sirenStateRead();
29   void sirenStateWrite( bool state );
30   void sirenUpdate( int strobeTime );
31
32   // Module: strobe_light ------------------------------
33
34   void strobeLightInit();
35   bool strobeLightStateRead();
```

```
36   void strobeLightStateWrite( bool state );
37   void strobeLightUpdate( int strobeTime );
38
39   // Module: smart_home_system --------------------------
40
41   void smartHomeSystemInit();
42   void smartHomeSystemUpdate();
43
44   // Module: temperature_sensor --------------------------
45
46   void temperatureSensorInit();
47   void temperatureSensorUpdate();
48   float temperatureSensorReadCelsius();
49   float temperatureSensorReadFahrenheit();
50   float celsiusToFahrenheit( float tempInCelsiusDegrees );
51   float analogReadingScaledWithTheLM35Formula( float analogReading );
52
53   // Module: user_interface --------------------------
54
55   void userInterfaceInit();
56   void userInterfaceUpdate();
57   bool userInterfaceCodeCompleteRead();
58   void userInterfaceCodeCompleteWrite( bool state );
59   bool incorrectCodeStateRead();
60   void incorrectCodeStateWrite( bool state );
61   void incorrectCodeIndicatorUpdate();
62   bool systemBlockedStateRead();
63   void systemBlockedStateWrite( bool state );
64   void systemBlockedIndicatorUpdate();
65   void userInterfaceMatrixKeypadUpdate();
```

Code 5.6 Declarations of public functions of the refactored version of the smart home system code (part 2/2).

The main function of the refactored version of the smart home system code is shown in Code 5.7. Just one function is used to initialize the system (*smartHomeSystemInit()*), and only one function is used to update the system (*smartHomeSystemUpdate()*).

```
1   //=====[Main function, the program entry point after power on or reset]=========
2
3   int main()
4   {
5       smartHomeSystemInit();
6       while (true) {
7           smartHomeSystemUpdate();
8       }
9   }
```

Code 5.7 The main function of the refactored version of the smart home system code.

In Code 5.8, the implementations of some of the functions of the *code* module are shown. The function *codeWrite()* receives as a parameter a pointer to the new code set by the user (recall from Chapter 4 that a pointer is a variable that stores a *memory address*, usually corresponding to another variable) and writes the new code into *CodeSequence[]*. The implementation of this functionality was previously in case '5' of the switch of the *uartTask()* function. In this new implementation, the storage of the code is detached from the functionality of sending the code through the UART. This improves the responsiveness of the system (e.g., in the previous implementation the system remained waiting for the four digits, which impacted the blinking of the LEDs).

The function *codeMatch()* receives as a parameter a pointer to the code to compare (i.e., the memory address where *codeToCompare* is stored) and returns a Boolean indicating whether the code is correct. This functionality was previously implemented by the function *areEqual()* for the control panel and directly coded in case '4' of the *uartTask()* function for the serial communication. By means of this new function, the functionality of assessing the code is unified for both the code entered using the PC and the code entered using the matrix keypad.

```
1   //=====[Implementations of public functions]=====================================
2
3   // Module: code -----------------------------------------
4
5   void codeWrite( char* newCodeSequence )
6   {
7       int i;
8       for (i = 0; i < CODE_NUMBER_OF_KEYS; i++) {
9           codeSequence[i] = newCodeSequence[i];
10      }
11  }
12
13  bool codeMatch( char* codeToCompare )
14  {
15      int i;
16      for (i = 0; i < CODE_NUMBER_OF_KEYS; i++) {
17          if ( codeSequence[i] != codeToCompare[i] ) {
18              return false;
19          }
20      }
21      return true;
22  }
```

Code 5.8 Implementation of the functions of the code module (Part 1/2).

In Code 5.9, the implementations of the remaining functions of the *code* module are shown. *codeMatchFrom()* checks if a new code is entered, assesses the code, and, if it is correct, deactivates the alarm. This function receives the parameter *codeOrigin* of type *codeOrigin_t*, as introduced in Code 5.2, to indicate where the code came from. It is called by *fireAlarmDeactivationUpdate()* and compares two codes. By using the functions *pcSerialComCodeCompleteRead()* and *userInterfaceCodeCompleteRead()*, it checks if there is a new code to call *codeMatch()* to assess if the code is correct.

On line 8 of Code 5.9, it can be seen that *userInterfaceCodeCompleteWrite()* is used to set the variable *codeCompleteFromUserInterface* to false, while on line 21 *pcSerialComCodeCompleteWrite()* is used to set *codeCompleteFromPcSerialCom* to false. If the code entered by means of the *user_interface* module or the *pc_serial_com* module is correct, the function *codeDeactivate()* is called (lines 10 and 23) in order to turn off the *systemBlockedState* and the *incorrectCodeState* (lines 46 and 47) as well as setting the variable *numberOfIncorrectCodes* (line 48) to zero. If the entered code is incorrect, then *incorrectCodeState* is set to on, and *numberOfIncorrectCodes* is incremented (lines 12 and 13 and lines 26 and 27).

```
 1  bool codeMatchFrom( codeOrigin_t codeOrigin )
 2  {
 3      bool codeIsCorrect = false;
 4      switch (codeOrigin) {
 5          case CODE_KEYPAD:
 6              if( userInterfaceCodeCompleteRead() ) {
 7                  codeIsCorrect = codeMatch(codeSequenceFromUserInterface);
 8                  userInterfaceCodeCompleteWrite(false);
 9                  if ( codeIsCorrect ) {
10                      codeDeactivate();
11                  } else {
12                      incorrectCodeStateWrite(ON);
13                      numberOfIncorrectCodes++;
14                  }
15              }
16              break;
17
18          case CODE_PC_SERIAL:
19              if( pcSerialComCodeCompleteRead() ) {
20                  codeIsCorrect = codeMatch(codeSequenceFromPcSerialCom);
21                  pcSerialComCodeCompleteWrite(false);
22                  if ( codeIsCorrect ) {
23                      codeDeactivate();
24                      pcSerialComStringWrite( "\r\nThe code is correct\r\n\r\n" );
25                  } else {
26                      incorrectCodeStateWrite(ON);
27                      numberOfIncorrectCodes++;
28                      pcSerialComStringWrite( "\r\nThe code is incorrect\r\n\r\n" );
29                  }
30              }
31              break;
32
33          default:
34              break;
35      }
36
37      if ( numberOfIncorrectCodes >= 5 ) {
38          systemBlockedStateWrite(ON);
39      }
40
41      return codeIsCorrect;
42  }
43
44  void codeDeactivate()
45  {
46      systemBlockedStateWrite(OFF);
47      incorrectCodeStateWrite(OFF);
48      numberOfIncorrectCodes = 0;
49  }
```

Code 5.9 Implementation of the functions of the code module (part 2/2).

In Code 5.10, the implementation of the functions of the module *date_and_time* is shown. The function *dateAndTimeRead()* reads the date and time from the RTC, while the function *dateAndTimeWrite()* configures the RTC using the date and time indicated by the received parameters. This functionality was previously implemented inside cases 's' and 't' of the function *uartTask()*.

```
1   // Module: date_and_time ---------------------------------
2
3   char* dateAndTimeRead()
4   {
5       time_t epochSeconds;
6       epochSeconds = time(NULL);
7       return ctime(&epochSeconds);
8   }
9
10  void dateAndTimeWrite( int year, int month, int day,
11                         int hour, int minute, int second )
12  {
13      struct tm rtcTime;
14
15      rtcTime.tm_year = year - 1900;
16      rtcTime.tm_mon  = month - 1;
17      rtcTime.tm_mday = day;
18      rtcTime.tm_hour = hour;
19      rtcTime.tm_min  = minute;
20      rtcTime.tm_sec  = second;
21
22      rtcTime.tm_isdst = -1;
23
24      set_time( mktime( &rtcTime ) );
25  }
```

Code 5.10 Implementation of the functions of the date_and_time module.

In Code 5.11, the implementation of the function *eventLogUpdate()* of the *event_log* module is shown. This function updates the log of events. The reader should note the usage of the variable *currentState* in each of the five parts of this function, together with calls to functions from different modules (i.e., *sirenStateRead(), gasDetectorStateRead()*, etc.).

```
1   // Module: event_log -----------------------------------
2
3   void eventLogUpdate()
4   {
5       bool currentState = sirenStateRead();
6       eventLogElementStateUpdate( sirenLastState, currentState, "ALARM" );
7       sirenLastState = currentState;
8
9       currentState = gasDetectorStateRead();
10      eventLogElementStateUpdate( gasLastState, currentState, "GAS_DET" );
11      gasLastState = currentState;
12
13      currentState = overTemperatureDetectorStateRead();
14      eventLogElementStateUpdate( tempLastState, currentState, "OVER_TEMP" );
15      tempLastState = currentState;
16
17      currentState = incorrectCodeStateRead();
18      eventLogElementStateUpdate( ICLastState, currentState, "LED_IC" );
19      ICLastState = currentState;
20
21      currentState = systemBlockedStateRead();
22      eventLogElementStateUpdate( SBLastState ,currentState, "LED_SB" );
23      SBLastState = currentState;
24  }
```

Code 5.11 Implementation of the functions of the Event log module (Part 1/2).

In Code 5.12, the new function *eventLogNumberOfStoredEvents()*, which returns the number of stored events, is shown. The function *eventLogRead()*, which reads an event stored in the log, is also shown. In Example 4.4, this functionality was implemented in case 'E' of the *uartTask()* function, and is now called by the function *commandShowStoredEvents()*, as will be seen in Code 5.20. The first parameter of *eventLogRead()* is the event index. Its second parameter, *str*, is a *pointer* to an array of chars. In that array, first "Event = " (line 9) is written, then the content of the corresponding type of event: *arrayOf StoredEvents[index].typeOfEvent* (line 10), then "\r\nDate and Time = " (line 11), then the corresponding time, *ctime(&arrayOfStoredEvents[index].seconds* (line 12), and finally "\r\n" (line 13). Remember that Figure 5.4 showed a diagram about the content that is obtained for the array *str* after executing this function.

```c
1   int eventLogNumberOfStoredEvents()
2   {
3       return eventsIndex;
4   }
5
6   void eventLogRead( int index, char* str )
7   {
8       str[0] = '\0';
9       strcat( str, "Event = " );
10      strcat( str, arrayOfStoredEvents[index].typeOfEvent );
11      strcat( str, "\r\nDate and Time = " );
12      strcat( str, ctime(&arrayOfStoredEvents[index].seconds) );
13      strcat( str, "\r\n" );
14  }
15
16  void eventLogWrite( bool currentState, const char* elementName )
17  {
18      char eventAndStateStr[EVENT_LOG_NAME_MAX_LENGTH] = "";
19
20      strcat( eventAndStateStr, elementName );
21      if ( currentState ) {
22          strcat( eventAndStateStr, "_ON" );
23      } else {
24          strcat( eventAndStateStr, "_OFF" );
25      }
26
27      arrayOfStoredEvents[eventsIndex].seconds = time(NULL);
28      strcpy( arrayOfStoredEvents[eventsIndex].typeOfEvent, eventAndStateStr );
29      if ( eventsIndex < EVENT_LOG_MAX_STORAGE - 1) {
30          eventsIndex++;
31      } else {
32          eventsIndex = 0;
33      }
34
35      pcSerialComStringWrite(eventAndStateStr);
36      pcSerialComStringWrite("\r\n");
37  }
38
39  void eventLogElementStateUpdate( bool lastState,
40                                   bool currentState,
41                                   const char* elementName )
42  {
43      if ( lastState != currentState ) {
44          eventLogWrite( currentState, elementName );
45      }
46  }
```

Code 5.12 Implementation of the functions of the event_log module (Part 2/2).

Finally, the implementation of *systemElementStateUpdate()* is replaced by the functions *eventLogWrite()*, which stores an event in the log, and *eventLogElementStateUpdate()*, which calls the function *eventLogWrite()* if the state being evaluated changes. Note that these functions receive a pointer to a constant string as a parameter (named *elementName* in both cases). Remember that more information about the functions *strcat* and *strcpy*, which were introduced in Chapter 4 and are used in Code 5.12, is available in [2].

Many functions of the *fire_alarm* module are shown in Code 5.13. *fireAlarmInit()* initializes the fire alarm subsystem by calling the functions *gasSensorInit()*, *temperatureSensorInit()*, and *sirenInit()*; *fireAlarmUpdate()* updates the fire alarm subsystem by calling the functions *fireAlarmActivationUpdate()*, *fireAlarmDeactivationUpdate()*, and *sirenUpdate()*; *gasDetectorStateRead()* returns the state of the gas detector; *overTemperatureDetectorStateRead()* returns the state of the over temperature detector; *gasDetectedRead()* returns true if gas is being detected; and *overTemperatureDetectedRead()* returns true if over temperature is being detected.

```
1   // Module: fire_alarm ---------------------------------
2
3   void fireAlarmInit()
4   {
5       temperatureSensorInit();
6       gasSensorInit();
7       sirenInit();
8       strobeLightInit();
9
10      alarmTestButton.mode(PullDown);
11  }
12
13  void fireAlarmUpdate()
14  {
15      fireAlarmActivationUpdate();
16      fireAlarmDeactivationUpdate();
17      sirenUpdate( fireAlarmStrobeTime() );
18      strobeLightUpdate( fireAlarmStrobeTime() );
19  }
20
21  bool gasDetectorStateRead()
22  {
23      return gasDetectorState;
24  }
25
26  bool overTemperatureDetectorStateRead()
27  {
28      return overTemperatureDetectorState;
29  }
30
31  bool gasDetectedRead()
32  {
33      return gasDetected;
34  }
35
36  bool overTemperatureDetectedRead()
37  {
38      return overTemperatureDetected;
39  }
```

Code 5.13 Implementation of the functions of the fire_alarm module (Part 1/2).

In Code 5.14, other functions of the *fire_alarm* module are shown. The function *fireAlarmActivationUpdate()* controls the activation of the siren. In the previous code, this functionality was part of *alarmActivationUpdate()*. On lines 3 and 4, the functions *temperatureSensorUpdate()* and *gasSensorUpdate()* are called in order to update the reading of those sensors, since the functions *temperatureSensorReadCelsius()* on line 6 and *gasSensorRead()* on line 15 return the last readings without updating.

```
1   void fireAlarmActivationUpdate()
2   {
3       temperatureSensorUpdate();
4       gasSensorUpdate();
5
6       overTemperatureDetectorState = temperatureSensorReadCelsius() >
7                           TEMPERATURE_C_LIMIT_ALARM;
8
9       if ( overTemperatureDetectorState ) {
10          overTemperatureDetected = ON;
11          sirenStateWrite(ON);
12          strobeLightStateWrite(ON);
13      }
14
15      gasDetectorState = !gasSensorRead();
16
17      if ( gasDetectorState ) {
18          gasDetected = ON;
19          sirenStateWrite(ON);
20          strobeLightStateWrite(ON);
21      }
22
23      if ( alarmTestButton ) {
24          overTemperatureDetected = ON;
25          gasDetected = ON;
26          sirenStateWrite(ON);
27          strobeLightStateWrite(ON);
28      }
29  }
30
31  void fireAlarmDeactivationUpdate()
32  {
33      if ( sirenStateRead() ) {
34          if ( codeMatchFrom(CODE_KEYPAD) ||
35               codeMatchFrom(CODE_PC_SERIAL) ) {
36              fireAlarmDeactivate();
37          }
38      }
39  }
40
41  void fireAlarmDeactivate()
42  {
43      sirenStateWrite(OFF);
44      strobeLightStateWrite(OFF);
45      overTemperatureDetected = OFF;
46      gasDetected = OFF;
47  }
48
49  int fireAlarmStrobeTime()
50  {
51      if( gasDetectedRead() && overTemperatureDetectedRead() ) {
52          return STROBE_TIME_GAS_AND_OVER_TEMP;
53      } else if ( gasDetectedRead() ) {
54          return STROBE_TIME_GAS;
55      } else if ( overTemperatureDetectedRead() ) {
56          return STROBE_TIME_OVER_TEMP;
57      } else {
58          return 0;
59      }
60  }
```

Code 5.14 Implementation of the functions of the fire_alarm module (Part 2/2).

The function *fireAlarmDeactivationUpdate()* controls the deactivation of the siren. When the alarm is active, the function *codeMatchFrom()* on lines 34 and 35 assesses if there is a new deactivation code to check. If there is a new deactivation code, the *fireAlarmDeactivate()* function is called. This implementation decouples the condition to deactivate the alarm from the actual deactivation of the alarm.

The function *fireAlarmDeactivate()* implements the deactivation of the siren and the strobe light by setting them to the OFF state, as well as setting *overTemperatureDetected* and *gasDetected* to OFF. The function *fireAlarmStrobeTime()* controls the siren and the strobe light on and off time. This function was part of the function *alarmActivationUpdate()* in the former version of the code.

In general, much of the functionality that was included in *alarmActivationUpdate()* in the previous version of the code (Example 4.4) is now organized in the *fire_alarm* and *siren* modules in order to decouple the control of the activation and deactivation of the siren from the activation and deactivation itself. In this way, more actions can be easily included on line 9 and/or line 17, following the modularity principle. For example, water sprinklers could be turned on, or a phone call could be made (which are not included in this example).

In Code 5.15, the implementation of the gas sensor functionality is shown. This module implements the reading of the gas sensor. The first two functions are actually useless but are included in order to keep the same structure as in the other module.

```
1    // Module: gas_sensor -----------------------------------
2
3    void gasSensorInit()
4    {
5    }
6
7    void gasSensorUpdate()
8    {
9    }
10
11   bool gasSensorRead()
12   {
13       return mq2;
14   }
```

Code 5.15 Implementation of the functions of the gas_sensor module.

In Code 5.16, Code 5.17, and Code 5.18 the functions of the *matrix_keypad* module are shown. There are small changes from the previous version of the code:

■ The function *matrixKeypadInit()* receives the parameter *timeIncrement_ms* instead of using the value defined by TIME_INCREMENT_MS.

■ The implementation of the function *matrixKeypadReset()* is used to reset the FSM of the matrix keypad. In the previous version of the code, this was done by *matrixKeypadInit()*.

```
1    // Module: matrix_keypad --------------------------------
2
3    void matrixKeypadInit( int updateTime_ms )
4    {
5        timeIncrement_ms = updateTime_ms;
6        matrixKeypadState = MATRIX_KEYPAD_SCANNING;
7        int pinIndex = 0;
8        for( pinIndex=0; pinIndex<MATRIX_KEYPAD_NUMBER_OF_COLS; pinIndex++ ) {
9            (keypadColPins[pinIndex]).mode(PullUp);
10       }
11   }
```

Code 5.16 Implementation of the functions of the matrix_keypad module (Part 1/3).

```
1    char matrixKeypadUpdate()
2    {
3        char keyDetected = '\0';
4        char keyReleased = '\0';
5
6        switch( matrixKeypadState ) {
7
8        case MATRIX_KEYPAD_SCANNING:
9            keyDetected = matrixKeypadScan();
10           if( keyDetected != '\0' ) {
11               matrixKeypadLastKeyPressed = keyDetected;
12               accumulatedDebounceMatrixKeypadTime = 0;
13               matrixKeypadState = MATRIX_KEYPAD_DEBOUNCE;
14           }
15           break;
16
17       case MATRIX_KEYPAD_DEBOUNCE:
18           if( accumulatedDebounceMatrixKeypadTime >=
19               DEBOUNCE_KEY_TIME_MS ) {
20               keyDetected = matrixKeypadScan();
21               if( keyDetected == matrixKeypadLastKeyPressed ) {
22                   matrixKeypadState = MATRIX_KEYPAD_KEY_HOLD_PRESSED;
23               } else {
24                   matrixKeypadState = MATRIX_KEYPAD_SCANNING;
25               }
26           }
27           accumulatedDebounceMatrixKeypadTime =
28               accumulatedDebounceMatrixKeypadTime + timeIncrement_ms;
29           break;
30
31       case MATRIX_KEYPAD_KEY_HOLD_PRESSED:
32           keyDetected = matrixKeypadScan();
33           if( keyDetected != matrixKeypadLastKeyPressed ) {
34               if( keyDetected == '\0' ) {
35                   keyReleased = matrixKeypadLastKeyPressed;
36               }
37               matrixKeypadState = MATRIX_KEYPAD_SCANNING;
38           }
39           break;
40
41       default:
42           matrixKeypadReset();
43           break;
44       }
45       return keyReleased;
46   }
```

Code 5.17 Implementation of the functions of the matrix_keypad module (Part 2/3).

```
1   char matrixKeypadScan()
2   {
3       int row = 0;
4       int col = 0;
5       int i = 0;
6
7       char matrixKeypadIndexToCharArray[] = {
8           '1', '2', '3', 'A',
9           '4', '5', '6', 'B',
10          '7', '8', '9', 'C',
11          '*', '0', '#', 'D',
12      };
13
14      for( row=0; row<MATRIX_KEYPAD_NUMBER_OF_ROWS; row++ ) {
15
16          for( i=0; i<MATRIX_KEYPAD_NUMBER_OF_ROWS; i++ ) {
17              keypadRowPins[i] = ON;
18          }
19
20          keypadRowPins[row] = OFF;
21
22          for( col=0; col<MATRIX_KEYPAD_NUMBER_OF_COLS; col++ ) {
23              if( keypadColPins[col] == OFF ) {
24                  return matrixKeypadIndexToCharArray[
25                      row*MATRIX_KEYPAD_NUMBER_OF_ROWS + col];
26              }
27          }
28      }
29      return '\0';
30  }
31
32  void matrixKeypadReset()
33  {
34      matrixKeypadState = MATRIX_KEYPAD_SCANNING;
35  }
```

Code 5.18 Implementation of the functions of the matrix_keypad module (Part 3/3).

The communication with the PC is implemented in the *pc_serial_com* module, as shown from Code 5.19 to Code 5.22. The function *uartTask()*, which was implemented in previous chapters, was removed, and its behavior is now implemented in a different way. One of the reasons for this change is that *uartUsb.read()* was used in *uartTask()* in such a way that the responsiveness of the program was affected. In particular, *uartUsb.read()* was used four times in *uartTask()*: first, to assess if there is a readable character in *uartUsb*; second, to get the four digits of the numeric code, one after the other; third, to get the four digits to set a new numeric code, one after the other; and fourth, to flush *uartUsb* once a new date and time had been set. The usage of *uartUsb.read()* in the second and third cases blocked the program execution until four new characters were entered, which reduced the program's responsiveness to other inputs.

In order to solve this problem, the new implementation of the program uses *uartUsb.read()* only twice: first, to assess if there is a readable character in *uartUsb* (in the new function *pcSerialComCharRead()*, line 12 of Code 5.19); second, to read one character in *pcSerialComStringRead()*, in line 5 of Code 5.20. With the new implementation, if the alarm is activated, the Alarm LED does not stop blinking when the program is waiting for the user to enter the alarm deactivation code, as can be concluded from the following explanation.

In this new implementation, *pcSerialComCharRead()* is called only in line 24 of Code 5.19 by the function *pcSerialComUpdate()*. This function implements an FSM, as can be seen from lines 22 to 41 of Code 5.19. There is a switch over *pcSerialComMode* and, depending on its value, the functions *pcSerialComCommandUpdate()*, *pcSerialComGetCodeUpdate()*, or *pcSerialComSaveNewCodeUpdate()* are executed. The implementation of these three functions is shown on Code 5.20 and is discussed below.

It is important to note that prior to the first execution of *pcSerialComUpdate()*, *pcSerialComMode* is initialized as PC_SERIAL_COMMANDS (line 35 of Code 5.4). So, the first time a character is received, the FSM will call *pcSerialComCommandUpdate()* in order to determine what function to call depending on the received command, as can be seen from lines 37 to 52 of Code 5.20.

If the received command is '4', the function *commandEnterCodeSequence()* is called (line 43 of Code 5.20). This function modifies the state of *pcSerialComMode* to PC_SERIAL_GET_CODE, as can be seen on line 31 of Code 5.21. In this way, the next time the FSM is executed, the function *pcSerialComGetCodeUpdate()* is called (line 31 of Code 5.19). This function will be called by the FSM until four characters are received, because once the statement of line 16 of Code 5.20 becomes true, *pcSerialComMode* is set to PC_SERIAL_COMMANDS on line 17. In this way, a new command will be expected by the FSM. A similar behavior is true for *pcSerialComSaveNewCodeUpdate()*, which can be seen from lines 23 to 35 of Code 5.20.

The remaining program code shown in Code 5.19 to Code 5.22 is very similar to the program code discussed in the previous chapters, the only difference being that the code is now refactored into functions in order to increase its modularity, with appropriate cohesion and coupling. Also note that *pcSerialComInit()* calls *availableCommands()*. Thus, the list of available commands is printed during the initialization process.

```
1   // Module: pc_serial_com ---------------------------------
2
3   void pcSerialComInit()
4   {
5       availableCommands();
6   }
7
8   char pcSerialComCharRead()
9   {
10      char receivedChar = '\0';
11      if( uartUsb.readable() ) {
12          uartUsb.read( &receivedChar, 1 );
13      }
14      return receivedChar;
15  }
16
17  void pcSerialComStringWrite( const char* str )
18  {
19      uartUsb.write( str, strlen(str) );
20  }
21
22  void pcSerialComUpdate()
23  {
24      char receivedChar = pcSerialComCharRead();
25      if( receivedChar != '\0' ) {
26          switch ( pcSerialComMode ) {
```

```
27                  case PC_SERIAL_COMMANDS:
28                      pcSerialComCommandUpdate( receivedChar );
29                      break;
30                  case PC_SERIAL_GET_CODE:
31                      pcSerialComGetCodeUpdate( receivedChar );
32                      break;
33                  case PC_SERIAL_SAVE_NEW_CODE:
34                      pcSerialComSaveNewCodeUpdate( receivedChar );
35                      break;
36                  default:
37                      pcSerialComMode = PC_SERIAL_COMMANDS;
38                      break;
39              }
40          }
41  }
42
43  bool pcSerialComCodeCompleteRead()
44  {
45      return codeComplete;
46  }
47
48  void pcSerialComCodeCompleteWrite( bool state )
49  {
50      codeComplete = state;
51  }
```

Code 5.19 Implementation of the functions of the pc_serial_com module (Part 1/4).

```
1   void pcSerialComStringRead( char* str, int strLength )
2   {
3       int strIndex;
4       for ( strIndex = 0; strIndex < strLength; strIndex++) {
5           uartUsb.read( &str[strIndex] , 1 );
6           uartUsb.write( &str[strIndex] ,1 );
7       }
8       str[strLength]='\0';
9   }
10
11  void pcSerialComGetCodeUpdate( char receivedChar )
12  {
13      codeSequenceFromPcSerialCom[numberOfCodeChars] = receivedChar;
14      pcSerialComStringWrite( "*" );
15      numberOfCodeChars++;
16      if ( numberOfCodeChars >= CODE_NUMBER_OF_KEYS ) {
17          pcSerialComMode = PC_SERIAL_COMMANDS;
18          codeComplete = true;
19          numberOfCodeChars = 0;
20      }
21  }
22
23  void pcSerialComSaveNewCodeUpdate( char receivedChar )
24  {
25      char newCodeSequence[CODE_NUMBER_OF_KEYS];
26      newCodeSequence[numberOfCodeChars] = receivedChar;
27      pcSerialComStringWrite( "*" );
28      numberOfCodeChars++;
29      if ( numberOfCodeChars >= CODE_NUMBER_OF_KEYS ) {
30          pcSerialComMode = PC_SERIAL_COMMANDS;
31          numberOfCodeChars = 0;
32          codeWrite( newCodeSequence );
33          pcSerialComStringWrite( "\r\nNew code configured\r\n\r\n" );
34      }
```

```
35  }
36
37  void pcSerialComCommandUpdate( char receivedChar )
38  {
39      switch (receivedChar) {
40          case '1': commandShowCurrentAlarmState(); break;
41          case '2': commandShowCurrentGasDetectorState(); break;
42          case '3': commandShowCurrentOverTemperatureDetectorState(); break;
43          case '4': commandEnterCodeSequence(); break;
44          case '5': commandEnterNewCode(); break;
45          case 'c': case 'C': commandShowCurrentTemperatureInCelsius(); break;
46          case 'f': case 'F': commandShowCurrentTemperatureInFahrenheit(); break;
47          case 's': case 'S': commandSetDateAndTime(); break;
48          case 't': case 'T': commandShowDateAndTime(); break;
49          case 'e': case 'E': commandShowStoredEvents(); break;
50          default: availableCommands(); break;
51      }
52  }
53
54  void availableCommands()
55  {
56      pcSerialComStringWrite( "Available commands:\r\n" );
57      pcSerialComStringWrite( "Press '1' to get the alarm state\r\n" );
58      pcSerialComStringWrite( "Press '2' to get the gas detector state\r\n" );
59      pcSerialComStringWrite( "Press '3' to get the over temperature detector state\r\n" );
60      pcSerialComStringWrite( "Press '4' to enter the code to deactivate the alarm\r\n" );
61      pcSerialComStringWrite( "Press '5' to enter a new code to deactivate the alarm\r\n" );
62      pcSerialComStringWrite( "Press 'f' or 'F' to get lm35 reading in Fahrenheit\r\n" );
63      pcSerialComStringWrite( "Press 'c' or 'C' to get lm35 reading in Celsius\r\n" );
64      pcSerialComStringWrite( "Press 's' or 'S' to set the date and time\r\n" );
65      pcSerialComStringWrite( "Press 't' or 'T' to get the date and time\r\n" );
66      pcSerialComStringWrite( "Press 'e' or 'E' to get the stored events\r\n" );
67      pcSerialComStringWrite( "\r\n" );
68  }
```

Code 5.20 Implementation of the functions of the pc_serial_com module (Part 2/4).

```
1   void commandShowCurrentAlarmState()
2   {
3       if ( sirenStateRead() ) {
4           pcSerialComStringWrite( "The alarm is activated\r\n");
5       } else {
6           pcSerialComStringWrite( "The alarm is not activated\r\n");
7       }
8   }
9
10  void commandShowCurrentGasDetectorState()
11  {
12      if ( gasDetectorStateRead() ) {
13          pcSerialComStringWrite( "Gas is being detected\r\n");
14      } else {
15          pcSerialComStringWrite( "Gas is not being detected\r\n");
16      }
17  }
18
19  void commandShowCurrentOverTemperatureDetectorState()
20  {
21      if ( overTemperatureDetectorStateRead() ) {
22          pcSerialComStringWrite( "Temperature is above the maximum level\r\n");
23      } else {
24          pcSerialComStringWrite( "Temperature is below the maximum level\r\n");
25      }
```

```
26  }
27
28  void commandEnterCodeSequence()
29  {
30      if( sirenStateRead() ) {
31          pcSerialComStringWrite( "Please enter the four digits numeric code " );
32          pcSerialComStringWrite( "to deactivate the alarm: " );
33          pcSerialComMode = PC_SERIAL_GET_CODE;
34          codeComplete = false;
35          numberOfCodeChars = 0;
36      } else {
37          pcSerialComStringWrite( "Alarm is not activated.\r\n" );
38      }
39  }
40
41  void commandEnterNewCode()
42  {
43      pcSerialComStringWrite( "Please enter the new four digits numeric code " );
44      pcSerialComStringWrite( "to deactivate the alarm: " );
45      numberOfCodeChars = 0;
46      pcSerialComMode = PC_SERIAL_SAVE_NEW_CODE;
47
48  }
49
50  void commandShowCurrentTemperatureInCelsius()
51  {
52      char str[100] = "";
53      sprintf ( str, "Temperature: %.2f \xB0 C\r\n",
54                      temperatureSensorReadCelsius() );
55      pcSerialComStringWrite( str );
56  }
57
58  void commandShowCurrentTemperatureInFahrenheit()
59  {
60      char str[100] = "";
61      sprintf ( str, "Temperature: %.2f \xB0 C\r\n",
62                      temperatureSensorReadFahrenheit() );
63      pcSerialComStringWrite( str );
64  }
```

Code 5.21 Implementation of the functions of the pc_serial_com module (Part 3/4).

```
1   void commandSetDateAndTime()
2   {
3       char year[5] = "";
4       char month[3] = "";
5       char day[3] = "";
6       char hour[3] = "";
7       char minute[3] = "";
8       char second[3] = "";
9
10      pcSerialComStringWrite("\r\nType four digits for the current year (YYYY): ");
11      pcSerialComStringRead( year, 4);
12      pcSerialComStringWrite("\r\n");
13
14      pcSerialComStringWrite("Type two digits for the current month (01-12): ");
15      pcSerialComStringRead( month, 2);
16      pcSerialComStringWrite("\r\n");
17
18      pcSerialComStringWrite("Type two digits for the current day (01-31): ");
19      pcSerialComStringRead( day, 2);
```

```
20        pcSerialComStringWrite("\r\n");
21
22        pcSerialComStringWrite("Type two digits for the current hour (00-23): ");
23        pcSerialComStringRead( hour, 2);
24        pcSerialComStringWrite("\r\n");
25
26        pcSerialComStringWrite("Type two digits for the current minutes (00-59): ");
27        pcSerialComStringRead( minute, 2);
28        pcSerialComStringWrite("\r\n");
29
30        pcSerialComStringWrite("Type two digits for the current seconds (00-59): ");
31        pcSerialComStringRead( second, 2);
32        pcSerialComStringWrite("\r\n");
33
34        pcSerialComStringWrite("Date and time has been set\r\n");
35
36        dateAndTimeWrite( atoi(year), atoi(month), atoi(day),
37            atoi(hour), atoi(minute), atoi(second) );
38  }
39
40  void commandShowDateAndTime()
41  {
42        char str[100] = "";
43        sprintf ( str, "Date and Time = %s", dateAndTimeRead() );
44        pcSerialComStringWrite( str );
45        pcSerialComStringWrite("\r\n");
46  }
47
48  void commandShowStoredEvents()
49  {
50        char str[EVENT_STR_LENGTH];
51        int i;
52        for (i = 0; i < eventLogNumberOfStoredEvents(); i++) {
53            eventLogRead( i, str );
54            pcSerialComStringWrite( str );
55            pcSerialComStringWrite( "\r\n" );
56        }
57  }
```

Code 5.22 Implementation of the functions of the pc_serial_com module (Part 4/4).

 NOTE: The implementations of *pcSerialComCharRead()* and *pcSerialComStringWrite()*, which are shown in Code 5.19, and *pcSerialComStringRead()*, which is shown in Code 5.20, were already introduced in the Case Study section of Chapter 4 and, therefore, are not discussed here.

Code 5.23 shows the implementation of the functions of the siren module. The functions of this module are called by the functions *fireAlarmActivationUpdate()* and *fireAlarmDeactivationUpdate()*. They have the duty of turning on and off the siren (implemented by means of the buzzer), as can be seen on line 26, which is used to toggle the state of the buzzer every time *accumulatedTimeAlarm* reaches *strobeTime*. In this way, the buzzer now generates an intermittent sound instead of the continuous sound that was implemented in Chapter 3.

NOTE: On lines 5 and 29 of Code 5.23, the *sirenPin* is set to ON in order to turn off the buzzer. This is because of the assumption that the circuit introduced in Figure 5.5 is being used. If, instead, the circuit introduced in Figure 5.6 is being used, lines 5 and 29 of Code 5.23 should be modified to "sirenPin = OFF" in order to turn off the buzzer.

```
1   // Module: siren ---------------------------------------
2
3   void sirenInit()
4   {
5       sirenPin = ON;
6   }
7
8   bool sirenStateRead()
9   {
10      return sirenState;
11  }
12
13  void sirenStateWrite( bool state )
14  {
15      sirenState = state;
16  }
17
18  void sirenUpdate( int strobeTime )
19  {
20      static int accumulatedTimeAlarm = 0;
21      accumulatedTimeAlarm = accumulatedTimeAlarm + SYSTEM_TIME_INCREMENT_MS;
22
23      if( sirenState ) {
24          if( accumulatedTimeAlarm >= strobeTime ) {
25              accumulatedTimeAlarm = 0;
26              sirenPin= !sirenPin;
27          }
28      } else {
29          sirenPin = ON;
30      }
31  }
```

Code 5.23 Implementation of the functions of the siren module.

The functions of the *smart_home_system* module are shown in Code 5.24. Both functions *smartHomeSystemInit()* and *smartHomeSystemUpdate()* are called by *main()*, as was shown in Code 5.7. By means of these functions, the *user_interface*, *fire_alarm*, and *pc_serial_com* modules are initialized, and those modules, together with the *event_log* module, are updated at a rate given by the delay on line 16.

```
1   // Module: smart_home_system ---------------------------
2
3   void smartHomeSystemInit()
4   {
5       userInterfaceInit();
6       fireAlarmInit();
7       pcSerialComInit();
8   }
9
10  void smartHomeSystemUpdate()
11  {
12      fireAlarmUpdate();
13      userInterfaceUpdate();
14      pcSerialComUpdate();
15      eventLogUpdate();
16      delay(SYSTEM_TIME_INCREMENT_MS);
17  }
```

Code 5.24 Implementation of the functions of the smart_home_system module.

Code 5.25 shows the functions of the *strobe_light* module. Its functionality is very similar to the functionality of the *siren* module and, therefore, is not discussed here.

```
1   // Module: strobe_light ----------------------------
2
3   void strobeLightInit()
4   {
5       strobeLight = OFF;
6   }
7
8   bool strobeLightStateRead()
9   {
10      return strobeLightState;
11  }
12
13  void strobeLightStateWrite( bool state )
14  {
15      strobeLightState = state;
16  }
17
18  void strobeLightUpdate( int strobeTime )
19  {
20      static int accumulatedTimeAlarm = 0;
21      accumulatedTimeAlarm = accumulatedTimeAlarm + SYSTEM_TIME_INCREMENT_MS;
22
23      if( strobeLightState ) {
24          if( accumulatedTimeAlarm >= strobeTime ) {
25              accumulatedTimeAlarm = 0;
26              strobeLight= !strobeLight;
27          }
28      } else {
29          strobeLight = OFF;
30      }
31  }
```

Code 5.25 Implementation of the functions of the strobe light module.

Code 5.26 shows the functions of the *temperature_sensor* module. The functionality implemented by *temperatureSensorUpdate()* was, in the previous code (Example 4.4), implemented by the function *alarmActivationUpdate()*. The other functions of this module are very similar to the functions of Example 4.4, besides the changes in their names (which were in order to indicate that they belong to the *temperature_sensor* module).

```
1   // Module: temperature_sensor --------------------------
2
3   void temperatureSensorInit()
4   {
5       int i;
6
7       for( i = 0; i < LM35_NUMBER_OF_AVG_SAMPLES ; i++ ) {
8           lm35ReadingsArray[i] = 0;
9       }
10  }
11
12  void temperatureSensorUpdate()
13  {
14      static int lm35SampleIndex = 0;
15      float lm35ReadingsSum = 0.0;
16      float lm35ReadingsAverage = 0.0;
17
18      int i = 0;
19
20      lm35ReadingsArray[lm35SampleIndex] = lm35.read();
21      lm35SampleIndex++;
22      if ( lm35SampleIndex >= LM35_NUMBER_OF_AVG_SAMPLES) {
23          lm35SampleIndex = 0;
24      }
25
26      lm35ReadingsSum = 0.0;
27      for (i = 0; i < LM35_NUMBER_OF_AVG_SAMPLES; i++) {
28          lm35ReadingsSum = lm35ReadingsSum + lm35ReadingsArray[i];
29      }
30      lm35ReadingsAverage = lm35ReadingsSum / LM35_NUMBER_OF_AVG_SAMPLES;
31      lm35TemperatureC = analogReadingScaledWithTheLM35Formula ( lm35ReadingsAverage);
32  }
33
34  float temperatureSensorReadCelsius()
35  {
36      return lm35TemperatureC;
37  }
38
39  float temperatureSensorReadFahrenheit()
40  {
41      return celsiusToFahrenheit( lm35TemperatureC );
42  }
43
44  float celsiusToFahrenheit( float tempInCelsiusDegrees )
45  {
46      return ( tempInCelsiusDegrees * 9.0 / 5.0 + 32.0 );
47  }
48
49  float analogReadingScaledWithTheLM35Formula( float analogReading )
50  {
51      return ( analogReading * 3.3 / 0.01 );
52  }
```

Code 5.26 Implementation of the functions of the temperature_sensor module.

Finally, Code 5.27 and Code 5.28 show the implementation of the functions of the user interface. The core of the functionality of this module is the function *userInterfaceMatrixKeypadUpdate()*. Two details must be highlighted about this function:

1. On line 12 it can be seen that *codeComplete* is set to true once four keys have been pressed on the matrix keypad. Hence, the "#" is not used anymore to signal the end of a code being entered.

2. If *sirenStateRead()* returns true and *systemBlockedStateRead()* returns false, then the entered keys are stored. Alternatively, the Incorrect code LED is turned off only if the "#" key is pressed twice (line 18).

```
1   // Module: user_interface -------------------------------
2
3   void userInterfaceInit()
4   {
5       incorrectCodeLed = OFF;
6       systemBlockedLed = OFF;
7       matrixKeypadInit( SYSTEM_TIME_INCREMENT_MS );
8   }
9
10  void userInterfaceUpdate()
11  {
12      userInterfaceMatrixKeypadUpdate();
13      incorrectCodeIndicatorUpdate();
14      systemBlockedIndicatorUpdate();
15  }
16
17  bool incorrectCodeStateRead()
18  {
19      return incorrectCodeState;
20  }
21
22  void incorrectCodeStateWrite( bool state )
23  {
24      incorrectCodeState = state;
25  }
26
27  void incorrectCodeIndicatorUpdate()
28  {
29      incorrectCodeLed = incorrectCodeStateRead();
30  }
31
32  bool systemBlockedStateRead()
33  {
34      return systemBlockedState;
35  }
36
37  void systemBlockedStateWrite( bool state )
38  {
39      systemBlockedState = state;
40  }
41
42  void systemBlockedIndicatorUpdate()
43  {
44      systemBlockedLed = systemBlockedState;
45  }
46
47  bool userInterfaceCodeCompleteRead()
48  {
49      return codeComplete;
50  }
51
52  void userInterfaceCodeCompleteWrite( bool state )
53  {
54      codeComplete = state;
55  }
```

Code 5.27 Implementation of the functions of the user_interface module (Part 1/2).

```
1   void userInterfaceMatrixKeypadUpdate()
2   {
3       char keyReleased = matrixKeypadUpdate();
4
5       if( keyReleased != '\0' ) {
6
7           if( sirenStateRead() && !systemBlockedStateRead() ) {
8               if( !incorrectCodeStateRead() ) {
9                   codeSequenceFromUserInterface[numberOfCodeChars] = keyReleased;
10                  numberOfCodeChars++;
11                  if ( numberOfCodeChars >= CODE_NUMBER_OF_KEYS ) {
12                      codeComplete = true;
13                      numberOfCodeChars = 0;
14                  }
15              } else {
16                  if( keyReleased == '#' ) {
17                      numberOfHashKeyReleased++;
18                      if( numberOfHashKeyReleased >= 2 ) {
19                          numberOfHashKeyReleased = 0;
20                          numberOfCodeChars = 0;
21                          codeComplete = false;
22                          incorrectCodeState = OFF;
23                      }
24                  }
25              }
26          }
27      }
28  }
```

Code 5.28 Implementation of the functions of the user_interface module (Part 2/2).

NOTE: Given the changes introduced by the *userInterfaceMatrixKeypadUpdate()* function, to deactivate the alarm, keys "1", "8", "0", and "5" must be pressed on the matrix keypad (i.e., it is no longer necessary to press key "#" after entering a code). If an incorrect code is entered, the "#" key must be pressed twice on the matrix keypad to enable the entering of a new code, just as in the implementation shown in Chapter 4.

5.4 Organizing the Modules of the Smart Home System into Different Files

5.4.1 Principles Followed to Organize the Modules into Files: Variables and Functions

In order to organize the modules into files, each variable will be declared only in the file of the specific module that makes use of it. Some variables are used only inside a given function, and their value must remain in memory from one execution of that given function to the next one. For example, when the FSM of the matrix keypad is in the MATRIX_KEYPAD_DEBOUNCE state, then the variable *accumulatedDebounceMatrixKeypadTime* is incremented by *timeIncrement_ms* with each execution of the *matrixKeypadUpdate()* function until it reaches the value DEBOUNCE_BUTTON_TIME_MS. For this reason, *accumulatedDebounceMatrixKeypadTime* must remain in memory from one execution of *matrixKeypadUpdate()* to the next one and, therefore, is declared as *static*. This can be seen on line 3 of Code 5.29.

```
1   char matrixKeypadUpdate()
2   {
3       static int accumulatedDebounceMatrixKeypadTime = 0;
4       static char matrixKeypadLastKeyPressed = '\0';
5
6       char keyDetected = '\0';
7       char keyReleased = '\0';
8
9       switch( matrixKeypadState ) {
```

Code 5.29 The first lines of the function matrixKeypadUpdate(), where some variables are declared as static.

On line 4 of Code 5.29, it can be seen that the variable *matrixKeypadLastKeyPressed* is also declared as *static*, as its value must remain in memory from one execution of *matrixKeypadUpdate()* to the next one. In contrast, the values of *keyDetected* and *keyReleased* are not declared as *static*, as the value of *keyDetected* is assigned after a call to the function *matrixKeypadScan()*, while *keyReleased* is assigned the value of *matrixKeypadLastKeyPressed* inside the MATRIX_KEYPAD_KEY_HOLD_PRESSED case.

In Table 5.14, the variables declared as *static* inside different functions are listed. These *static* local variables remain in memory while the program is running, even after the execution of those functions is completed. A variable that is not declared as *static* inside a function is erased when the execution of the function is over.

Table 5.14 Variables that will be declared as static inside given functions.

Module	Function	Variables declaration
matrix_keypad	matrixKeypadUpdate()	static int accumulatedDebounceMatrixKeypadTime = 0; static char matrixKeypadLastKeyPressed = '\0';
pc_serial_com	pcSerialComSaveNew CodeUpdate()	static char newCodeSequence[CODE_NUMBER_OF_KEYS];
temperature_ sensor	temperatureSensor Update()	static int lm35SampleIndex = 0;
user_interface	userInterfaceMatrix KeypadUpdate()	static int numberOfHashKeyReleased = 0;

With the aim of guaranteeing that the *private scope* of each module is not *invaded* by other modules, some variables that are used by multiple functions of a single module (but not outside the module) are declared as private inside that module. This is done by means of declaring those variables as *static*, but outside the functions. In this way, a variable declared as *static* outside of a function can only be used by other functions within the same *.c/cpp* file. The public and private variables that will be declared in each module are listed in Table 5.15. The modules *date_and_time*, *gas_sensor*, and *smart_home_system* have neither private nor public variables.

WARNING: Variables declared as *static* inside a function (as in Code 5.29 and Table 6.14) are local variables that retain their values as explained, while variables declared as *static* outside of a function (as in Table 5.15) are global variables that can only be accessed by functions declared in the same file.

Table 5.15 Public and private variables declared in each module.

Module	Public variables
code	None
	Private variables
	static int numberOfIncorrectCodes = 0; static char codeSequence[CODE_NUMBER_OF_KEYS] = {'1','8','0','5'};

Module	Public variables
event_log	None
	Private variables

	static bool sirenLastState = OFF;
	static bool gasLastState = OFF;
	static bool tempLastState = OFF;
	static bool ICLastState = OFF;
	static bool SBLastState = OFF;
	static int eventsIndex = 0;
	static systemEvent_t arrayOfStoredEvents[EVENT_LOG_MAX_STORAGE];

Module	Public variables
fire_alarm	None
	Private variables

	static bool gasDetected = OFF;
	static bool overTemperatureDetected = OFF;
	static bool gasDetectorState = OFF;
	static bool overTemperatureDetectorState = OFF;

Module	Public variables
matrix_keypad	None
	Private variables
	static matrixKeypadState_t matrixKeypadState; static int timeIncrement_ms = 0;

Module	Public variables
pc_serial_com	char codeSequenceFromPcSerialCom[CODE_NUMBER_OF_KEYS];
	Private variables

	static pcSerialComMode_t pcSerialComMode = PC_SERIAL_COMMANDS;
	static bool codeCompleteFromPcSerialCom = false;
	static int numberOfCodeCharsFromPcSerialCom = 0;

Module	Public variables
siren	None
	Private variables
	static bool sirenState = OFF;

Module	Public variables
strobe_light	None
	Private variables
	static bool strobeLightState = OFF;

Module	Public variables
temperature_ sensor	None
	Private variables
	float lm35TemperatureC = 0.0; float lm35AvgReadingsArray[LM35_NUMBER_OF_AVG_SAMPLES];

Module	Public variables
user_interface	char codeSequenceFromUserInterface[CODE_NUMBER_OF_KEYS];
	Private variables

	static bool incorrectCodeState = OFF;
	static bool systemBlockedState = OFF;
	static bool codeComplete = false;
	static int numberOfCodeChars = 0;

In Table 5.2 to Table 5.13, some functions were shown that are used by different modules, while other functions are used only by functions in the same module. The functions that must be available to other modules are called *public functions*, while the functions that must be available only for functions in the same module are called *private functions*. Table 5.16 shows which public and private functions will be declared in each module. The private functions are identified by the word *static* prior to their declaration.

Table 5.16 Public and private functions.

Module	Public functions
code	void codeWrite(char* newCodeSequence); bool codeMatchFrom(codeOrigin_t codeOrigin);
	Private functions
	static bool codeMatch(char* codeToCompare); static void codeDeactivate();

Module	Public functions
date_and_time	char* dateAndTimeRead(); void dateAndTimeWrite(int year, int month, int day, int hour, int minute, int second);
	Private functions
	None

Module	Public functions

event_log	void eventLogUpdate();
	int eventLogNumberOfStoredEvents();
	void eventLogRead(int index, char* str);
	void eventLogWrite(bool currentState, const char* elementName);

	Private functions
	static void eventLogElementStateUpdate(bool lastState, bool currentState, const char* elementName);

Module	Public functions

fire_alarm	void fireAlarmInit();
	void fireAlarmUpdate();
	bool gasDetectorStateRead();
	bool overTemperatureDetectorStateRead();
	bool gasDetectedRead();
	bool overTemperatureDetectedRead();

	Private functions

	static void fireAlarmActivationUpdate();
	static void fireAlarmDeactivationUpdate();
	static void fireAlarmDeactivate();
	static int fireAlarmStrobeTime();

Module	Public functions

gas_sensor	void gasSensorInit();
	void gasSensorUpdate();
	bool gasSensorRead();

	Private functions
	None

Module	Public functions
matrix_keypad	void matrixKeypadInit(int updateTime_ms); char matrixKeypadUpdate();
	Private functions
	static char matrixKeypadScan(); static void matrixKeypadReset();

Module	Public functions

pc_serial_com	void pcSerialComInit();
	char pcSerialComCharRead();
	void pcSerialComStringWrite(const char* str);
	void pcSerialComUpdate();
	bool pcSerialComCodeCompleteRead();
	void pcSerialComCodeCompleteWrite(bool state);

	Private functions

	static void pcSerialComStringRead(char* str, int strLength);
	static void pcSerialComGetCodeUpdate(char receivedChar);
	static void pcSerialComSaveNewCodeUpdate(char receivedChar);
	static void pcSerialComCommandUpdate(char receivedChar);
	static void availableCommands();
	static void commandShowCurrentSirenStrobeLightState();
	static void commandShowCurrentGasDetectorState();
	static void commandShowCurrentOverTemperatureDetectorState();
	static void commandEnterCodeSequence();
	static void commandEnterNewCode();
	static void commandShowCurrentTemperatureInCelsius();
	static void commandShowCurrentTemperatureInFahrenheit();
	static void commandSetDateAndTime();
	static void commandShowDateAndTime();
	static void commandShowStoredEvents();

Module	**Public functions**

siren	void sirenInit();
	bool sirenStateRead();
	void sirenStateWrite(bool state);
	void sirenUpdate(int strobeTime);

	Private functions
	None
Module	**Public functions**

strobe_light	void strobeLightInit();
	bool strobeLightStateRead();
	void strobeLightStateWrite(bool state);
	void strobeLightUpdate(int strobeTime);

	Private functions
	None
Module	**Public functions**
smart_home_system	void smartHomeSystemInit(); void smartHomeSystemUpdate();
	Private functions
	None

Module	Public functions

Temperature sensor	void temperatureSensorInit();
	void temperatureSensorUpdate();
	float temperatureSensorReadCelsius();
	float temperatureSensorReadFahrenheit();
	float celsiusToFahrenheit(float tempInCelsiusDegrees);

	Private functions
	static float analogReadingScaledWithTheLM35Formula(float analogReading);

Module	Public functions

User interface	void userInterfaceInit();
	void userInterfaceUpdate();
	bool userInterfaceCodeCompleteRead();
	void userInterfaceCodeCompleteWrite(bool state);
	bool incorrectCodeStateRead();
	void incorrectCodeStateWrite(bool state);
	bool systemBlockedStateRead();
	void systemBlockedStateWrite(bool state);

	Private functions

	static void incorrectCodeIndicatorUpdate();
	static void systemBlockedIndicatorUpdate();
	static void userInterfaceMatrixKeypadUpdate();

 NOTE: The function *eventLogWrite()* is public even though no other modules use it. The reason it is declared public instead of private is that it will be used by a module that will be created in Example 10.3.

5.4.2 Detailed Implementation of the Code of the Smart Home System in Different Files

In order to implement modularization in C/C++, every module must have a well-defined *interface*. By means of its interface, each module specifies how its public functions can be requested by other modules. It is very important to understand that the modules that call a public function from another module should not get involved in, or even get access to, the way in which those functions are implemented. This concept is known as *encapsulation*. For this purpose, header (*.h*) files are used. This model is shown in Figure 5.7.

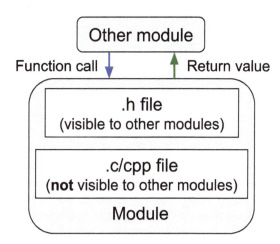

Figure 5.7 Diagram of modularization in C/C++ using header files.

The main goal is to improve the program organization and to guarantee that each module does not get involved in the *responsibilities* of other modules. In order to achieve this goal, it is common to separate the *.h* files and the *.c/cpp* files into different file folders, or even to only grant other programmers access to the *.h* files, and provide the *.c/cpp* files as *object* files, which cannot be read by a programmer.

Another important concept arises here: the *prototypes* of the functions declared in the *.h* file are *public*, while the prototypes of the functions declared as static in the *.c/cpp* file are *private*.

To implement the *.h* and *.cpp* files of each module, some templates that are used are available in subsection 5.4.2 at [1].

The *.h* file template begins with *"#include guards - begin"*, where it uses the preprocessor directive *"#ifndef"* to indicate that the *.h* file must be included only if it was not previously included. This is to ensure that each *.h* file is included only once, because if a *.h* file is included more than once, the compiler will report an error. The line *"#include guards - end"* at the end of the *.h* file template is used to indicate the ending of the preprocessor directive by an *#endif*.

In Table 5.17, the sections of the template that are used to write the *.h* file of each module are shown. The three sections of the *.h* file template (*Declaration of public #defines, Declaration of public data types,* and *Declarations (prototypes) of public functions*) are all public declarations. As explained in subsection *5.2.2 Implementation of Modularization in C/C++ Programs*, these *.h* files are the ones that should be provided to the users of each module.

Table 5.17 Sections of the template that are used to write the .h file of each module.

Name of the section	Purpose of the section
Declaration of public defines	Declaration of #defines that are public.
Declaration of public data types	Declaration of data types that are public.
Declarations (prototypes) of public functions	Declaration functions that are public.

In Table 5.18, the sections of the template used to write the *.cpp* file of each module are shown. The reader should note that this template includes:

- The libraries that are used by the module (i.e., a set of *.h* files).

- The declaration of definitions, data types, variables, and functions.

- The implementation of public and private functions.

Table 5.18 Sections of the template used to write the .cpp file of each module.

Name of the section	Purpose of the section
Libraries	Include .h files used by the module.
Declaration of private defines	Declare the defines used only by the module.
Declaration of private data types	Declare the data types used only by the module.
Declaration and initialization of public global objects	Declare the objects that are used only by other modules and maybe also by the same module.
Declaration of external public global variables	Declare the *extern* public global variables (this concept is explained at the end of this section).
Declaration and initialization of public global variables	Declare the variables that are used by other modules and maybe also by the same module.
Declaration and initialization of private global variables	Declare the variables that are used only by the module.
Declarations (prototypes) of private functions	Declare the private functions that are used only by the module.
Implementations of public functions	Implement the public functions used by other modules.
Implementations of private functions	Implement the private functions.

 NOTE: The #defines and data types declared in sections *Declaration of private definitions* and *Declaration of private data types* of a *.cpp* file can be used only by code in the same *.cpp* file, while #defines and data types in sections *Declaration of public definitions* and *Declaration of public data types* of a *.h* file are public.

Using these *.h* and *.cpp* file templates and the public and private classification of variables and functions discussed in Table 5.15 and Table 5.16, the files and folders shown in Figure 5.8 were prepared. An extra *.cpp* file for the *main* function and an extra *.h* file for the *arm_book_lib* library are included.

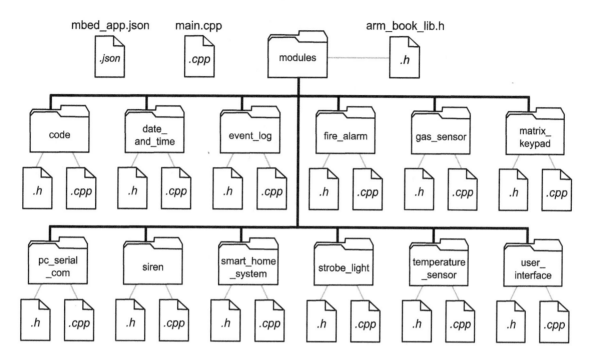

Figure 5.8 File organization proposed for the smart home system code.

It is important to mention that the libraries that are included in each module are just the ones that are needed by that module. For example, the section "Libraries" of the file *siren.cpp* includes the following files: *mbed.h, arm_book_lib.h, siren.h, smart_home_system.h*, and *fire_alarm.h*.

Given that all the functions have already been discussed in subsection 5.3.2, no code will be shown or discussed in this section. The reader is encouraged to download the files and explore the code behavior themselves. All the folders and files shown in Figure 5.8 are available in subsection 5.4.2 at [1]. Even though the project is organized in modules, it is built in the same way as in previous chapters. Drag the *.bin* file onto the NUCLEO board, and test how the program works in order to *verify* that its functionality is similar to Example 4.4. Some differences are that now if the alarm is activated, the Alarm LED does not stop blinking when the program is waiting for the user to enter the alarm deactivation code (because of the changes introduced in the *pc_serial_com* module), and the list of available commands is shown after power on even if the user does not press any key.

Table 5.19 shows the only two variables that are defined using the prefix *extern*. These two variables, *codeSequenceFromUserInterface* and *codeSequenceFromPcSerialCom*, are declared in the *user_interface* module and in the *pc_serial_com* module, respectively, and are used also in the *code* module. In order to make them usable by other modules, they are declared as public variables in the section "Declaration and initialization of public global variables" of the *user_interface* and *pc_serial_com* modules, respectively, and due to the extern prefix, the compiler is notified that these two variables, which are referred to in the section "Declaration of external public global variables" of the *code* module, are actually declared somewhere else.

Table 5.19 Example of extern variables that are used in the implementation of the smart home system.

Module	External public global variables
code	extern char codeSequenceFromUserInterface[CODE_NUMBER_OF_KEYS]; extern char codeSequenceFromPcSerialCom[CODE_NUMBER_OF_KEYS];

This concept of extern variables applies whenever a global variable must be used in different modules. Therefore, in that case it is not valid to declare the global variable only in one of the modules and use it in the other modules, because an error of "use of undeclared identifier" will be obtained. Neither is it valid to declare the global variable in each of the modules, because in that case an error of "multiply defined" will be obtained. As explained above, in that situation, the global variable must be declared in one of the modules as usual, and in the other modules it should be declared using the reserved word *extern*, as shown in Table 5.19.

Lastly, it is very important to note that as a consequence of the modularization process, some libraries were created that can be reused in other systems. For example, the *temperature_sensor* module can be used in any other system provided with an LM35 sensor. The *matrix_keypad* module could also be reused by the reader in future projects.

 NOTE: This book started from a non-modular design for pedagogical reasons. It is always recommended to start with a modularized design from the beginning.

Proposed Exercises

1. What should be modified in order to change the blinking time of the siren?

2. What should be modified in order to change the conversion formula of the temperature sensor?

Answers to the Exercises

1. The values of the #defines STROBE_TIME_GAS, STROBE_TIME_OVER_TEMP, and STROBE_TIME_GAS_AND_OVER_TEMP should be modified in the file *fire_alarm.cpp*.

2. The conversion formula should be modified in the function *analogReadingScaledWithTheLM35Formula()* of the *temperature_sensor* module.

References

[1] "GitHub - armBookCodeExamples/Directory". Accessed July 9, 2021.
https://github.com/armBookCodeExamples/Directory/

[2] "<cstring> (string.h) - C++ Reference". Accessed July 9, 2021.
https://www.cplusplus.com/reference/cstring/

Chapter 6

LCD Displays and Communication between Integrated Circuits

6.1 Roadmap

6.1.1 What You Will Learn

After you have studied the material in this chapter, you will be able to:

- Explain and compare the characteristics of the most commonly used buses for connecting integrated circuits.

- Describe how to connect an LCD display to the NUCLEO board using GPIOs, I2C, and SPI buses.

- Develop programs to show information as characters and graphics on suitable LCD displays.

- Summarize the concept of a hardware abstraction layer (HAL).

 DEFINITION: A typical definition of *bus* in computer architecture is a communication system that transfers data between components inside a computer. The term covers all related hardware components and software, including communication protocols. Buses can have parallel or serial wired connections (i.e., not wireless).

DEFINITION: A communication protocol is a system of rules that allows two or more entities to transmit information via any kind of variation of a physical quantity. The protocol defines the rules, syntax, semantics, and synchronization of communication and possible error recovery methods.

6.1.2 Review of Previous Chapters

In previous chapters, different sensors and elements were connected to the NUCLEO board using GPIOs and analog inputs. The NUCLEO board was connected to a PC using serial communication implemented through a UART. In this way, the information gathered by means of the sensors was shown on the PC screen using the serial terminal.

6.1.3 Contents of This Chapter

It is not always feasible or possible to use a PC to show information, due to room and cost limitations; an LCD display can be more convenient. There are also modules whose interface is neither a set of GPIO pins nor an analog output, but a serial communication protocol based on something other than the UART technology introduced in previous chapters.

In this chapter, two different types of LCD displays will be connected to the NUCLEO board: character displays and graphical displays. The former is able to display only characters, while the latter is able to display graphics as well as characters. The character LCD display will be connected to the NUCLEO board by means of GPIOs (General Purpose Input Output pins) and the I2C (Inter-Integrated Circuit) bus, while the graphical LCD display connection will be made using the SPI (Serial Peripheral Interface) bus.

The aim is to introduce most of the buses used to connect integrated circuits and sensors, and through examples show how software implementation can be made independent from the hardware details. This will be explained by means of a software module that displays information on an LCD display, regardless of whether the LCD is a character or a graphical display, or whether the connection to the display is by means of GPIOs, the I2C bus, or the SPI bus. In this way, the concept of a *hardware abstraction layer* (HAL) will be introduced.

 NOTE: In previous chapters, the details of the connections to be made and the explanation of the technical concepts that were used in the examples were all located at the beginning of the chapter. In this chapter, these sections are interleaved with the examples as the same character display is connected to the NUCLEO board in different ways, using different technologies. In this chapter, the explanations of the technologies involved have a higher level of detail than in the previous chapters. This level of detail is necessary to understand how LCD displays can be controlled using I2C and SPI buses.

6.2 LCD Display Connection using GPIOs, I2C, and SPI Buses

6.2.1 Connect a Character LCD Display to the Smart Home System using GPIOs

In this chapter, an LCD display is connected to the smart home system, as shown in Figure 6.1. In this way, it is possible to show in the Alarm control panel information regarding temperature reading, as well as the state of the gas detector and the activation of the alarm.

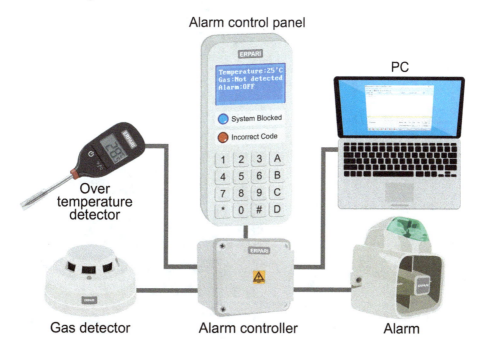

Figure 6.1 The smart home system is now connected to an LCD display.

Figure 6.2 shows how to connect the character LCD display module [1], which is based on the HD44780 dot matrix liquid crystal display (LCD) controller [2]. The reader may notice that standard inputs and outputs of the NUCLEO board, usually called GPIOs (General Purpose Input Output), are used, as summarized in Figure 6.3. The aim of this setup is to introduce the basics of character LCD displays.

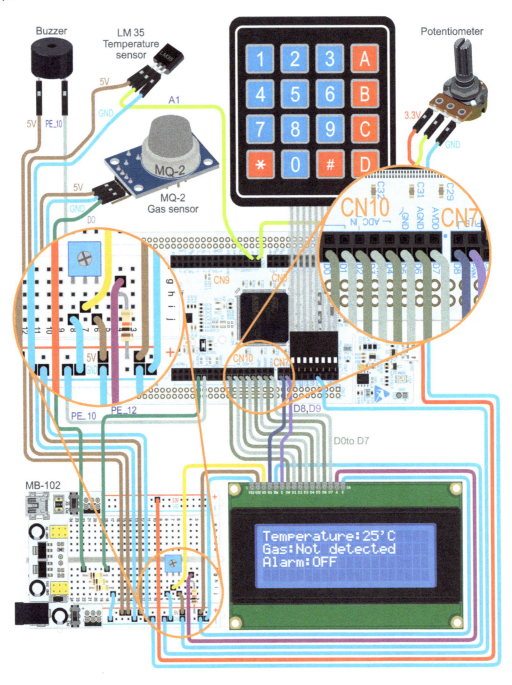

Figure 6.2 The smart home system connected to the character LCD display using GPIOs.

WARNING: Some displays have a different pin layout. In that case make the connections following the pin names indicated in Figure 6.3, even if the pins are arranged in a different way on the display.

In Figure 6.3, the connections that must be made are shown. The GPIOs D0–D9 are used to send commands to the LCD display, as discussed below. The contrast of the character LCD display can be adjusted by means of the trimmer potentiometer or "trimpot." The 1 kΩ resistor connected to the A (anode) pin together with the K (cathode) pin are used to power the backlight of the character LCD display.

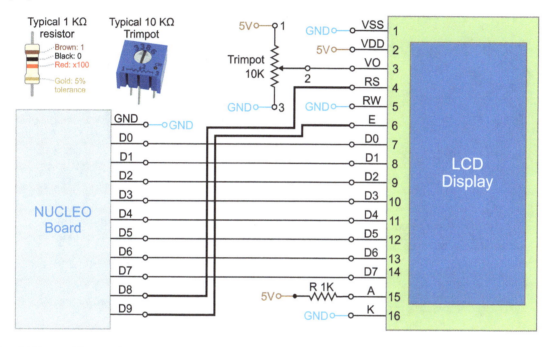

Figure 6.3 Diagram of the connections between the character LCD display and the NUCLEO board using GPIOs.

WARNING: Some displays require different resistor values. Check the datasheet of the display you use.

To test if the character LCD display is working, the *.bin* file of the program "Subsection 6.2.1" should be downloaded from the URL available in [3] and dragged onto the NUCLEO board. After power on, the most pertinent information from the smart home system should be shown on the character LCD display, as in Figure 6.2.

NOTE: As in previous chapters, the code that is provided to test the connections will not be discussed. The code to control the LCD character and graphical displays will be explained in detail in the examples.

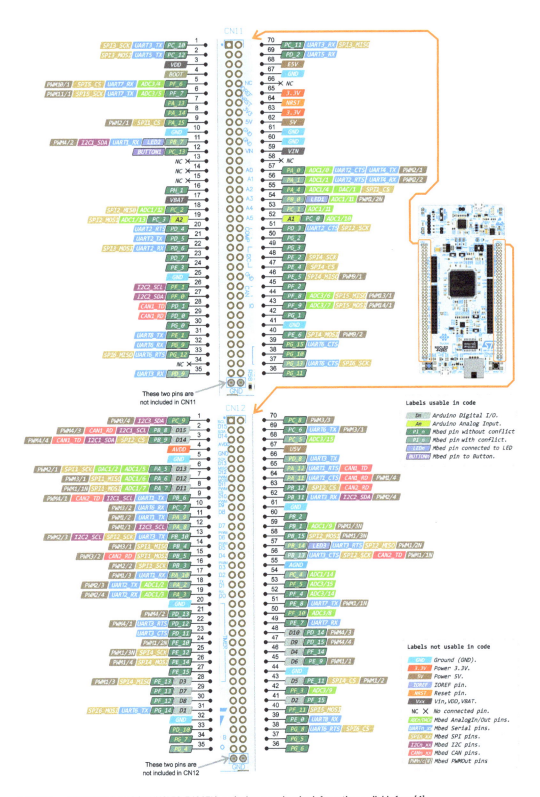

Figure 6.4 CN11 and CN12 headers of the NUCLEO-F429ZI board scheme made using information available from [4].

TIP: If the display is not working as expected, the corresponding connections can be checked using the CN11 and CN12 headers and a multimeter. For example, in Figure 6.3 it can be seen that pin D8 of the NUCLEO board (which corresponds to PF_12, as can be seen in [4]) should be connected by means of a wire to pin RS of the character LCD display. However, once this wire is connected it is not easy to access the D8 pin of the CN7 header to make a continuity test using a multimeter. Nevertheless, PF_12 is also available on the CN12 connector, as can be seen in Figure 6.4 (adapted from [4]). Hence, a continuity test can be made between PF_12 and pin RS of the character LCD display by placing one probe at the pin corresponding to PF_12 in the CN12 header and placing the other probe on pin RS of the character LCD display. If they are continuous, and the multimeter is properly configured, it beeps and displays a value near zero. This procedure can be used to check all the connections shown on Figure 6.3.

WARNING: In strict terms, the display must be controlled by signals that have a high level of at least $0.7 \times 5\ V = 3.5\ V$, as indicated in [2], while the expected high level of the NUCLEO board digital outputs is about 3.3 V. However, in order to avoid the usage of many voltage-level converters, the character display is connected directly because it was proven to work without the voltage converters. Section 6.2.5 shows an example of how voltage converters can be used to adapt voltage levels when it is necessary.

6.2.2 Basic Principles of Character LCD Displays

Character displays, such as the one used in this chapter, are available in a range of different layouts, such as 20 × 4 (4 lines of 20 characters), 16 × 2, 8 × 2, 8 × 1, etc. Each character is displayed on a 5 × 8 pixel matrix (the 8th pixel line is reserved for the cursor) as shown in Table 6.1. The code corresponding to each character is obtained by adding the row and column values. For example, the character "A" is in the intersection of the column labeled 64 and the row labeled 1, so its code is 65. The character "a" is in the intersection of the column labeled 96 with the row labeled 1, so its code is 97. The characters corresponding to the first eight codes (0 to 7) in Table 6.1 correspond to the *Custom Generated Random-Access Memory* (CGRAM) characters that can be defined pixel-by-pixel by the user. The next eight codes (8 to 15) are also mapped to the same eight CGRAM characters and are not shown in Table 6.1. CGRAM characters are not covered in this book. Characters corresponding to codes 16 to 31 and 128 to 159 are not included in Table 6.1 because they may vary between different versions of the HD44780 dot matrix LCD controller, as can be seen in [2].

Table 6.1 A typical character set of an LCD character display.

In Chapter 2, it was mentioned that characters transferred between the PC and the NUCLEO board (for example, 'H', 'e', 'l', 'l', and 'o') are codified using the ASCII standard (*American Standard Code for Information Interchange*), which is described in [5]. ASCII was created in the 1960s, having 128 characters. Of these, 95 are printable (digits 0 to 9, lowercase letters a to z, uppercase letters A to Z, punctuation symbols, etc.). The other 33 are non-printing control codes, most of which are now obsolete, although a few are still commonly used, such as the carriage return (\r), line feed (\n), and tab codes (\t).

While 95 printable ASCII characters are sufficient in English, other languages that use Latin alphabets need additional symbols. ISO/IEC 8859 sought to solve this problem using the eighth bit in an 8-bit byte to allow positions for another 96 printable characters. In Table 6.2, some of the corresponding characters are shown. The reader may notice its similarity to the character set shown in Table 6.1. Therefore, in this chapter, characters to be sent to the display are stated in the program code in a similar way to previous chapters. However this may not be valid in some cases, where Table 6.1 and Table 6.2 may differ.

Table 6.2 Part of the character set defined by ASCII and ISO/IEC 8859.

	0	32	40	48	56	64	72	80	88	96	104	112	120	160	168	176	184	192	200	208	216	224	232	240	248
0	\0	space	(	0	8	@	H	P	X	`	h	p	x		¨	°	,	À	È	Ð	Ø	à	è	ð	ø
1		!	)	1	9	A	I	Q	Y	a	i	q	y	¡	©	±	¹	Á	É	Ñ	Ù	á	é	ñ	ù
2		"	*	2	:	B	J	R	Z	b	j	r	z	¢	ª	²	º	Â	Ê	Ò	Ú	â	ê	ò	ú
3		#	+	3	;	C	K	S	[	c	k	s	{	£	«	³	»	Ã	Ë	Ó	Û	ã	ë	ó	û
4		$	,	4	<	D	L	T	\	d	l	t	|	¤	¬	´	¼	Ä	Ì	Ô	Ü	ä	ì	ô	ü
5		%	-	5	=	E	M	U	]	e	m	u	}	¥		µ	½	Å	Í	Õ	Ý	å	í	õ	ý
6		&	.	6	>	F	N	V	^	f	n	v	~	¦	®	¶	¾	Æ	Î	Ö	Þ	æ	î	ö	þ
7		'	/	7	?	G	O	W	_	g	o	w		§	¯	·	¿	Ç	Ï	×	ß	ç	ï	÷	ÿ

> **NOTE:** For space reasons, other character mappings are not analyzed in this book.

In an LCD character display, there is *Display Data Random Access Memory* (DDRAM), which stores the character to be displayed in each position of the LCD display. In a 20 × 4 character LCD display, the code of the character to be displayed in the first position of the first line is written into address 0 of the DDRAM, the character to be displayed in the second position of the first line is written in address 1, and so on. The address of each position of the 20 × 4 character LCD display is shown in Figure 6.5.

0	1	2	3	4	5	6	7	8	9	10	11	12	13	14	15	16	17	18	19
64	65	66	67	68	69	70	71	72	73	74	75	76	77	78	79	80	81	82	83
20	21	22	23	24	25	26	27	28	29	30	31	32	33	34	35	36	37	38	39
84	85	86	87	88	89	90	91	92	93	94	95	96	97	98	99	100	101	102	103

Figure 6.5 Addresses corresponding to each of the positions of a 20 × 4 LCD character display.

From Figure 6.6 to Figure 6.8, the addresses of each of the positions of some typical LCD character display layouts are shown. The reader will notice that there are more addresses than characters that can be shown on the display. To show the characters that are written in those addresses (for example, 16 and 80 in Figure 6.6), a *shift* instruction is used. This idea is illustrated in Figure 6.9.

Figure 6.6 Addresses corresponding to each of the positions of a 16 × 2 LCD character display.

Figure 6.7 Addresses corresponding to each of the positions of an 8 × 2 LCD character display.

Figure 6.8 Addresses corresponding to each of the positions of an 8 × 1 LCD character display.

Figure 6.9 An 8 × 2 LCD character display where a left shift has been applied once.

NOTE: The number 64 is written in binary notation as 01000000. Therefore, it makes sense to use the number 64 for the position 0 of the second line considering that "01" indicates line 2 and "000000" its first position.

NOTE: Usually DDRAM addresses are expressed in datasheets in hexadecimal notation. Therefore, the number "10" is indicated as "0A", "11" is "0B", ... , "20" is "14", ... , "64" is "40", ... , "84" is "54", etc. In this book, decimal notation is used in order to make addresses easier to understand for the reader.

The instructions that are used in this chapter are summarized in Table 6.3. These instructions are sent to the display following the timing diagram shown in Figure 6.10. First, the states of the pins E (Enable), RS (Register Select), R/W (Read, Write), and DB7 to DB0 (Data Bus) are established. Then, a pulse is set into the E pin (it should last at least 1 µs). During the falling edge of the E pin the code is written: if RS is set to low, the code is written into the *instruction register*, while if RS is set to high, the code is written into the *data register*. These registers are internally used by the HD44780 dot matrix LCD controller to process the codes received from the microcontroller [2].

Table 6.3 Summary of the character LCD display instructions that are used in this chapter.

Instruction	Code										Description	Execution time
	RS	R/W	DB7	DB6	DB5	DB4	DB3	DB2	DB1	DB0		
Clear display	0	0	0	0	0	0	0	0	0	1	Clears entire display and sets DDRAM address 0 in address counter.	1.52 ms
Entry mode set	0	0	0	0	0	0	0	1	I/D	S	Sets cursor move direction and specifies display shift.	1.52 ms
Display control	0	0	0	0	0	0	1	D	C	B	Sets entire display (D) on/off, cursor on/off (C), and blinking of cursor (B).	37 µs
Function set	0	0	0	0	1	DL	N	F	*	*	Sets interface data length (DL), number of display lines (N), and character font (F).	37 µs
Set DDRAM address	0	0	1	A6	A5	A4	A3	A2	A1	A0	Sets DDRAM address.	37 µs

Instruction		Code									Description	Execution time
	RS	R/W	DB7	DB6	DB5	DB4	DB3	DB2	DB1	DB0		
Write data to DDRAM	1	0	D7	D6	D5	D4	D3	D2	D1	D0	Writes data into DDRAM.	37 μs

I/D = 1: Increment,   I/D = 0: Decrement
S = 1: Accompany display shift,
S = 0: Don't accompany display shift,
D = 1: Display on,   D = 0: Display off
C = 1: Cursor on,   C = 0: Cursor off
B = 1: Cursor blink on, B = 0: Cursor blink off

DL = 1: 8 bits,   DL = 0: 4 bits
N = 1: 2 lines,   N = 0: 1 line
F = 1: 5 × 10 dots,   F = 0: 5 × 8 dots
* = don't care
A6 ... A0 = Address,
D7 ... D0 = Data

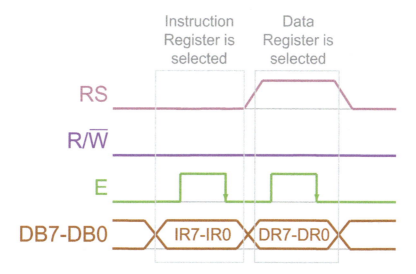

Figure 6.10 Transfer timing sequence of writing instructions when an 8-bit interface is configured.

 NOTE: In the examples in this book, the R/W pin is connected to GND because only write operations are made to the registers. Sometimes it might be necessary to read a register to confirm if the previous instruction sent to the display was successfully executed, but this is not the case in this book.

The procedure to initialize the display when an 8-bit interface is used is described in [2] and is shown in Figure 6.11. First, there should be a waiting period of more than 40 milliseconds after power on. Then, the "Function Set" instruction should be sent four times with different delays in between and with DB4 (corresponding to the DL, Data Length configuration) set to 1. The first three times "Function Set" is sent, the values of DB3 to DB0 do not matter (those bits can be set either to 1 or 0), while the fourth time "Function Set" is sent, the values of N (number of lines in the display) and F (font size) must be set. In the case of the 20 × 4 character display, N must be set to 1 (2 lines) and F must be set to 0 (5 × 8 dots).

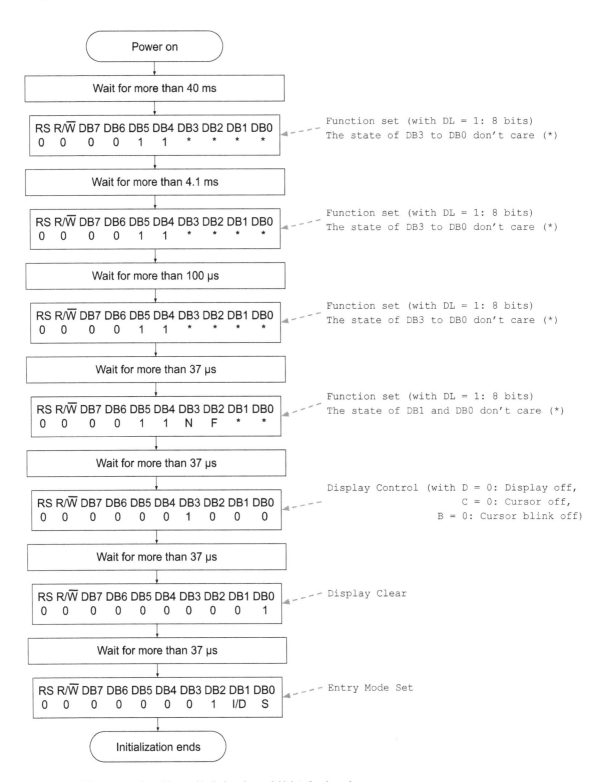

Figure 6.11 Initialization procedure of the graphic display when an 8-bit interface is used.

NOTE: The addresses of a 20 × 2 LCD character display are very similar to those shown in Figure 6.6. In a 20 × 2 character display, the addresses of line 1 range from 0 to 39 and the addresses of line 2 from 64 to 103. Only addresses 0 to 19 and 64 to 83 are visible without a shift instruction. Addresses 20 to 39 and 84 to 103 can be seen only if a shift is made. A 20 × 4 display (Figure 6.5) is considered a special case of a 20 × 2 display, where all the DDRAM content is distributed in four lines and is shown at the same time. For this reason, N is set to two lines in a 20 × 4 character display.

In Figure 6.11, it can be seen that the "Display Control" instruction is followed by D = 0 (Display off), C = 0 (Cursor off), and B = 0 (Cursor blink off). This is followed by the "Display Clear" instruction. Lastly, the "Entry Mode Set" instruction is set, where the value of I/D and S can be configured according to programmer preference. In this book, I/D is configured to 1 (Increment), in order to automatically increment the DDRAM address immediately after a given character is written into the display, and S is set to 0, because it is not necessary to shift the display. In this way, the initialization ends, and messages can be shown on the display.

Typically, to write a message on the display, the "Set DDRAM address" instruction is used to indicate the position of the first letter of the message. Then the "Write data to DDRAM" instruction is used to write the corresponding character according to Table 6.1. Given that I/D is configured to 1, the next character of the message can be sent to the display using the "Write data to DDRAM" instruction, without the need to increment the DDRAM address by means of the "Set DDRAM address" instruction. In this way, the characters of the message can easily be written one after the other, as shown in Example 6.1.

Example 6.1: Indicate Present Temperature, Gas Detection, and Alarm on the Display

Objective

Introduce the usage of a character-based LCD display by means of a GPIO connection.

Summary of the Expected Behavior

The present temperature is shown on the first line of the character LCD display, the state of the gas detector is shown on the second line, and the state of the alarm is shown on the third line. The fourth line is left empty to reserve space so that in the future more information can be shown on the display.

Test the Proposed Solution on the Board

Import the project "Example 6.1" using the URL available in [3], build the project, and drag the .*bin* file onto the NUCLEO board. The present temperature, the gas detection state, and the alarm state should be shown on the display. Hold the temperature sensor between two fingers in order to change its reading. The corresponding value should be displayed on the first line of the display. Activate the alarm by pressing the Alarm test button. This condition should be indicated on the display. When the alarm is turned off (use the same steps as in the previous chapters), its state should be updated on the display.

Discussion of the Proposed Solution

The proposed solution is based on a new software module named *display*. This new module is composed of two files, *display.cpp* and *display.h*, following the modularized structure discussed in the previous chapter. The *main()* function in the *main.cpp* remains the same as in the last section of Chapter 5. Furthermore, the functions *smartHomeSystemInit()* and *smartHomeSystemUpdate()*, called from the *main()* function, have no changes. Those functions call the functions *userInterfaceInit()* and *userInterfaceUpdate()*, respectively, and these are the ones that make the corresponding calls to the functions of the *display* module, as detailed below.

Implementation of the Proposed Solution

In Table 6.4, the sections where lines have been added to the file *user_interface.cpp* are summarized. Besides the definition of DISPLAY_REFRESH_TIME_MS and the declaration of the two functions that will be explained below, it should be noted that *fire_alarm.h* and *display.h* have been included.

Table 6.4 *Sections in which lines were added to user_interface.cpp.*

Section or function	Lines that were added
Libraries	`#include "fire_alarm.h"` `#include "display.h"`
Definitions	`#define DISPLAY_REFRESH_TIME_MS 1000`
Declarations (prototypes) of private functions	`static void userInterfaceDisplayInit();` `static void userInterfaceDisplayUpdate();`

As previously mentioned, the functions *userInterfaceInit()* and *userInterfaceUpdate()* are modified in order to include the initialization and update of the display, respectively, as can be seen in Code 6.1 and Code 6.2.

```
1   void userInterfaceInit()
2   {
3       incorrectCodeLed = OFF;
4       systemBlockedLed = OFF;
5       matrixKeypadInit( SYSTEM_TIME_INCREMENT_MS );
6       userInterfaceDisplayInit();
7   }
```

Code 6.1 *New implementation of the function userInterfaceInit(), including userInterfaceDisplayInit().*

```
1   void userInterfaceUpdate()
2   {
3       userInterfaceMatrixKeypadUpdate();
4       incorrectCodeIndicatorUpdate();
5       systemBlockedIndicatorUpdate();
6       userInterfaceDisplayUpdate();
7   }
8
```

Code 6.2 *New implementation of the function userInterfaceUpdate(), including userInterfaceDisplayUpdate().*

The implementation of the function *userInterfaceDisplayInit()* is shown in Code 6.3. It is declared as a private function by means of the reserved word *static* on line 1 of the corresponding code. On line 3, the display is initialized by means of the function *displayInit()*. The details of the implementation of *displayInit()* will be shown below this example.

In Code 6.3, the functions *displayCharPositionWrite()* and *displayStringWrite()* are used to move the cursor to a given position and write a given string in that position. In this way, the strings "Temperature", "Gas", and "Alarm" are written in specific positions of the display. The way in which the corresponding positions of those strings are indicated using *x* and *y* coordinates is shown in Figure 6.12. These coordinates are the parameters of *displayCharPositionWrite()*, as discussed below. The details of the implementation of *displayStringWrite()* are also discussed below.

 NOTE: The messages in lines 6, 9, and 12 are strings because the '\0' (null character) is automatically added to the end of an array of char when it is written between quotes, as, for example, in "Temperature:".

```
1   static void userInterfaceDisplayInit()
2   {
3       displayInit();
4
5       displayCharPositionWrite ( 0,0 );
6       displayStringWrite( "Temperature:" );
7
8       displayCharPositionWrite ( 0,1 );
9       displayStringWrite( "Gas:" );
10
11      displayCharPositionWrite ( 0,2 );
12      displayStringWrite( "Alarm:" );
13  }
```

Code 6.3 Implementation of the function userInterfaceDisplayInit().

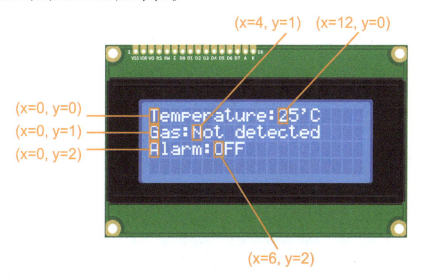

Figure 6.12 Position of the strings that are placed in the character LCD display.

The implementation of the function *userInterfaceDisplayUpdate()* is shown in Code 6.4. On lines 3 and 4, two variables are declared: a static int *accumulatedDisplayTime* that is initialized to 0, and a char array *temperatureString*, which has three positions because it is considered that the temperature will be in the range of 0 to 40 °C (a third char position is reserved for the null character). On line 6, a check is made whether *accumulatedDisplayTime* has reached the value established by DISPLAY_REFRESH_TIME_MS, which is defined in *user_interface.cpp* as 1000. If so, the present temperature value, the state of the gas detector, and the state of the alarm are updated on the display by means of the code on lines 6 to 31. In this way, the display is updated every 1000 ms. The corresponding (*x*, *y*) positions of the temperature value, the gas detection, and the alarm state can be seen in Figure 6.12. Finally, if *accumulatedDisplayTime* is lower than DISPLAY_REFRESH_TIME_MS, then the value of *accumulatedDisplayTime* is incremented by SYSTEM_TIME_INCREMENT_MS (lines 33 to 36).

NOTE: The function *sprintf*, used in line 11 of Code 6.4, was introduced in Chapter 4. This function creates a string (an array of char ending with a null character, '\0') in the indicated destination (in this case *temperatureString*), following the indicated format (in this case "%.0f", a float displayed without decimals) using as input the stated value (the return value of the function *temperatureSensorReadCelsius()*).

```
1   static void userInterfaceDisplayUpdate()
2   {
3       static int accumulatedDisplayTime = 0;
4       char temperatureString[3] = "";
5
6       if( accumulatedDisplayTime >=
7           DISPLAY_REFRESH_TIME_MS ) {
8
9           accumulatedDisplayTime = 0;
10
11          sprintf(temperatureString, "%.0f", temperatureSensorReadCelsius());
12          displayCharPositionWrite ( 12,0 );
13          displayStringWrite( temperatureString );
14          displayCharPositionWrite ( 14,0 );
15          displayStringWrite( "'C" );
16
17          displayCharPositionWrite ( 4,1 );
18
19          if ( gasDetectorStateRead() ) {
20              displayStringWrite( "Detected    " );
21          } else {
22              displayStringWrite( "Not Detected" );
23          }
24
25          displayCharPositionWrite ( 6,2 );
26
27          if ( sirenStateRead() ) {
28              displayStringWrite( "ON " );
29          } else {
30              displayStringWrite( "OFF" );
31          }
32
33      } else {
34          accumulatedDisplayTime =
35              accumulatedDisplayTime + SYSTEM_TIME_INCREMENT_MS;
36      }
37  }
```

Code 6.4 Implementation of the function userInterfaceDisplayUpdate().

The implementation of the function *displayInit()* is shown in Code 6.5. It follows the initialization procedure that was introduced in Figure 6.11. In line 3, there is a 50-millisecond delay in order to have a safety margin above the 40 millisecond wait after power on. In line 5, *displayCodeWrite()* is used to send the first "Function Set" instruction to the display. The implementation of this function is discussed below, but it can be seen that the first parameter (DISPLAY_RS_INSTRUCTION) is used to indicate that the code corresponds to an instruction, while the second parameter indicates that it is a DISPLAY_IR_FUNCTION_SET instruction, and the third parameter (DISPLAY_IR_FUNCTION_SET_8BITS) indicates that the 8-bit interface bit is set.

The statements between lines 8 and 42 follow the steps indicated in Figure 6.11. The only difference is that at the end the display is turned on (lines 44 to 49).

```
1   void displayInit()
2   {
3       delay( 50 );
4
5       displayCodeWrite( DISPLAY_RS_INSTRUCTION,
6                         DISPLAY_IR_FUNCTION_SET |
7                         DISPLAY_IR_FUNCTION_SET_8BITS );
8       delay( 5 );
9
10      displayCodeWrite( DISPLAY_RS_INSTRUCTION,
11                        DISPLAY_IR_FUNCTION_SET |
12                        DISPLAY_IR_FUNCTION_SET_8BITS );
13      delay( 1 );
14
15      displayCodeWrite( DISPLAY_RS_INSTRUCTION,
16                        DISPLAY_IR_FUNCTION_SET |
17                        DISPLAY_IR_FUNCTION_SET_8BITS );
18      delay( 1 );
19
20      displayCodeWrite( DISPLAY_RS_INSTRUCTION,
21                        DISPLAY_IR_FUNCTION_SET |
22                        DISPLAY_IR_FUNCTION_SET_8BITS |
23                        DISPLAY_IR_FUNCTION_SET_2LINES |
24                        DISPLAY_IR_FUNCTION_SET_5x8DOTS );
25      delay( 1 );
26
27      displayCodeWrite( DISPLAY_RS_INSTRUCTION,
28                        DISPLAY_IR_DISPLAY_CONTROL |
29                        DISPLAY_IR_DISPLAY_CONTROL_DISPLAY_OFF |
30                        DISPLAY_IR_DISPLAY_CONTROL_CURSOR_OFF |
31                        DISPLAY_IR_DISPLAY_CONTROL_BLINK_OFF );
32      delay( 1 );
33
34      displayCodeWrite( DISPLAY_RS_INSTRUCTION,
35                        DISPLAY_IR_CLEAR_DISPLAY );
36      delay( 1 );
37
38      displayCodeWrite( DISPLAY_RS_INSTRUCTION,
39                        DISPLAY_IR_ENTRY_MODE_SET |
40                        DISPLAY_IR_ENTRY_MODE_SET_INCREMENT |
41                        DISPLAY_IR_ENTRY_MODE_SET_NO_SHIFT );
42      delay( 1 );
43
44      displayCodeWrite( DISPLAY_RS_INSTRUCTION,
45                        DISPLAY_IR_DISPLAY_CONTROL |
46                        DISPLAY_IR_DISPLAY_CONTROL_DISPLAY_ON |
47                        DISPLAY_IR_DISPLAY_CONTROL_CURSOR_OFF |
48                        DISPLAY_IR_DISPLAY_CONTROL_BLINK_OFF );
49      delay( 1 );
50  }
```

Code 6.5 Implementation of the function displayInit().

Code 6.6 shows the #defines that are used by *displayCodeWrite()*. The corresponding values follow the information that was summarized in Table 6.3. The OR bitwise operator (|) is used to set the values of the corresponding bits of the code. For example, "DISPLAY_IR_FUNCTION_SET | DISPLAY_IR_ FUNCTION_ SET_8BITS" implies the OR bitwise operator between the binary values 0b00100000 and 0b00010000, which is equal to 0b00110000. This value corresponds to the first value that should be sent over the data bus after power on, according to Figure 6.11.

```
1   #define DISPLAY_IR_CLEAR_DISPLAY     0b00000001
2   #define DISPLAY_IR_ENTRY_MODE_SET    0b00000100
3   #define DISPLAY_IR_DISPLAY_CONTROL   0b00001000
4   #define DISPLAY_IR_FUNCTION_SET      0b00100000
5   #define DISPLAY_IR_SET_DDRAM_ADDR    0b10000000
6
7   #define DISPLAY_IR_ENTRY_MODE_SET_INCREMENT 0b00000010
8   #define DISPLAY_IR_ENTRY_MODE_SET_DECREMENT 0b00000000
9   #define DISPLAY_IR_ENTRY_MODE_SET_SHIFT     0b00000001
10  #define DISPLAY_IR_ENTRY_MODE_SET_NO_SHIFT  0b00000000
11
12  #define DISPLAY_IR_DISPLAY_CONTROL_DISPLAY_ON  0b00000100
13  #define DISPLAY_IR_DISPLAY_CONTROL_DISPLAY_OFF 0b00000000
14  #define DISPLAY_IR_DISPLAY_CONTROL_CURSOR_ON   0b00000010
15  #define DISPLAY_IR_DISPLAY_CONTROL_CURSOR_OFF  0b00000000
16  #define DISPLAY_IR_DISPLAY_CONTROL_BLINK_ON    0b00000001
17  #define DISPLAY_IR_DISPLAY_CONTROL_BLINK_OFF   0b00000000
18
19  #define DISPLAY_IR_FUNCTION_SET_8BITS     0b00010000
20  #define DISPLAY_IR_FUNCTION_SET_4BITS     0b00000000
21  #define DISPLAY_IR_FUNCTION_SET_2LINES    0b00001000
22  #define DISPLAY_IR_FUNCTION_SET_1LINE     0b00000000
23  #define DISPLAY_IR_FUNCTION_SET_5x10DOTS  0b00000100
24  #define DISPLAY_IR_FUNCTION_SET_5x8DOTS   0b00000000
25
26  #define DISPLAY_20x4_LINE1_FIRST_CHARACTER_ADDRESS 0
27  #define DISPLAY_20x4_LINE2_FIRST_CHARACTER_ADDRESS 64
28  #define DISPLAY_20x4_LINE3_FIRST_CHARACTER_ADDRESS 20
29  #define DISPLAY_20x4_LINE4_FIRST_CHARACTER_ADDRESS 84
30
31  #define DISPLAY_RS_INSTRUCTION 0
32  #define DISPLAY_RS_DATA        1
33
34  #define DISPLAY_RW_WRITE 0
35  #define DISPLAY_RW_READ  1
```

Code 6.6 Defines that are used by the displayCodeWrite() function.

The implementation of *displayCodeWrite()* is shown in Code 6.7. It has two parameters; the first is used to indicate the type of code to be written, and the second is to indicate the value that should be loaded into the data bus (DB7 to DB0). Line 3 assesses if *type* corresponds to DISPLAY_RS_INSTRUCTION. In that case, in line 4 the RS pin is assigned a value of 0 by means of the function *displayPinWrite()*. This function receives two parameters, the pin that should be written and the value that should be written into that pin. If *type* is not DISPLAY_RS_INSTRUCTION, then the RS pin is assigned a value of 1 (DISPLAY_RS_DATA) in line 6.

In line 7, the R/W pin is assigned a value of 0 using the *displayPinWrite()* function and the definition DISPLAY_RW_WRITE. Lastly, in line 8 the values of DB7 to DB0 are written into the data bus using *displayDataBusWrite()*. This function also generates the pulse in the E pin, as will be discussed below.

```
1  static void displayCodeWrite( bool type, uint8_t dataBus )
2  {
3      if ( type == DISPLAY_RS_INSTRUCTION )
4          displayPinWrite( DISPLAY_PIN_RS, DISPLAY_RS_INSTRUCTION);
5      else
6          displayPinWrite( DISPLAY_PIN_RS, DISPLAY_RS_DATA);
7      displayPinWrite( DISPLAY_PIN_RW, DISPLAY_RW_WRITE );
8      displayDataBusWrite( dataBus );
9  }
```

Code 6.7 Implementation of the function displayCodeWrite().

 NOTE: The *if-else* structure in Code 6.7 is intentionally written without using { } in order to show that if only one statement is used (as in line 4 and line 6), then the braces are not mandatory.

Code 6.8 shows the implementation of *displayPinWrite()*. The parameter *value* is assigned to a DigitalOut object indicated by the parameter *pinName*. Code 6.9 shows the DigitalOut objects that are declared. In Code 6.10, the #defines used in this function are shown (the numbers follow the pin numeration).

It can be seen that in the case of *pinName* equal to DISPLAY_PIN_RW, no DigitalOut object is assigned because the R/W pin of the display is connected to GND (only write operations can be made on the display).

```
1  static void displayPinWrite( uint8_t pinName, int value )
2  {
3      switch( pinName ) {
4          case DISPLAY_PIN_D0: displayD0 = value;    break;
5          case DISPLAY_PIN_D1: displayD1 = value;    break;
6          case DISPLAY_PIN_D2: displayD2 = value;    break;
7          case DISPLAY_PIN_D3: displayD3 = value;    break;
8          case DISPLAY_PIN_D4: displayD4 = value;    break;
9          case DISPLAY_PIN_D5: displayD5 = value;    break;
10         case DISPLAY_PIN_D6: displayD6 = value;    break;
11         case DISPLAY_PIN_D7: displayD7 = value;    break;
12         case DISPLAY_PIN_RS: displayRS = value;    break;
13         case DISPLAY_PIN_EN: displayEN = value;    break;
14         case DISPLAY_PIN_RW: break;
15         default: break;
16     }
17 }
```

Code 6.8 Implementation of the function displayPinWrite().

```
1   DigitalOut displayD0( D0 );
2   DigitalOut displayD1( D1 );
3   DigitalOut displayD2( D2 );
4   DigitalOut displayD3( D3 );
5   DigitalOut displayD4( D4 );
6   DigitalOut displayD5( D5 );
7   DigitalOut displayD6( D6 );
8   DigitalOut displayD7( D7 );
9   DigitalOut displayRS( D8 );
10  DigitalOut displayEN( D9 );
```

Code 6.9 Declaration of public global objects in display.cpp.

```
1    #define DISPLAY_PIN_RS   4
2    #define DISPLAY_PIN_RW   5
3    #define DISPLAY_PIN_EN   6
4    #define DISPLAY_PIN_D0   7
5    #define DISPLAY_PIN_D1   8
6    #define DISPLAY_PIN_D2   9
7    #define DISPLAY_PIN_D3  10
8    #define DISPLAY_PIN_D4  11
9    #define DISPLAY_PIN_D5  12
10   #define DISPLAY_PIN_D6  13
11   #define DISPLAY_PIN_D7  14
```

Code 6.10 Defines that are used by the displayPinWrite() function.

The implementation of *displayDataBusWrite()* is shown in Code 6.11. In line 3, the E pin is assigned a low state. From line 4 to line 11, the pins of the data bus are written. For this purpose the AND bitwise operator (&) is used with a value expressed in binary format. For example, line 4 uses "& 0b10000000", which implies that a high state (1) will be written into DISPLAY_PIN_D7 if the most significant bit of *dataBus* is 1, while a low state (0) will be written into DISPLAY_PIN_D7 if the most significant bit of *dataBus* is 0.

The code in lines 12 to 15 is used to generate a pulse in the E pin, as was explained in section 6.2.2.

 NOTE: Every time *displayDataBusWrite()* is executed, there is an extra delay of 2 milliseconds (lines 13 and 15) incorporated into *smartHomeSystemUpdate()*. Given that the execution rate of *smartHomeSystemUpdate()* is controlled using a 10-millisecond delay, this 2-millisecond extra delay impacts on how many times per second the function *smartHomeSystemUpdate()* is executed (approximately 16% fewer times).

```
1    static void displayDataBusWrite( uint8_t dataBus )
2    {
3        displayPinWrite( DISPLAY_PIN_EN, OFF );
4        displayPinWrite( DISPLAY_PIN_D7, dataBus & 0b10000000 );
5        displayPinWrite( DISPLAY_PIN_D6, dataBus & 0b01000000 );
6        displayPinWrite( DISPLAY_PIN_D5, dataBus & 0b00100000 );
7        displayPinWrite( DISPLAY_PIN_D4, dataBus & 0b00010000 );
8        displayPinWrite( DISPLAY_PIN_D3, dataBus & 0b00001000 );
9        displayPinWrite( DISPLAY_PIN_D2, dataBus & 0b00000100 );
10       displayPinWrite( DISPLAY_PIN_D1, dataBus & 0b00000010 );
11       displayPinWrite( DISPLAY_PIN_D0, dataBus & 0b00000001 );
12       displayPinWrite( DISPLAY_PIN_EN, ON );
13       delay( 1 );
14       displayPinWrite( DISPLAY_PIN_EN, OFF );
15       delay( 1 );
16   }
```

Code 6.11 Implementation of the function displayDataBusWrite().

In Code 6.12, the implementation of the function *displayCharPositionWrite()*, which was used in Code 6.4, is shown. This function has two parameters: the position in *x* and *y* coordinates. In line 3, there is a switch over *charPositionY*. Depending on the value of *charPositionY*, *displayCodeWrite()* is called using different parameters. The first parameter of *displayCodeWrite()* is used to indicate that it is an instruction that should be written to the instruction register. The second parameter is used to indicate that it is a "Set DDRAM address" instruction and the value that should be loaded in the DDRAM address.

For example, if *charPositionY* is 0 (line 4), the DDRAM address value is obtained as "DISPLAY_20x4_LINE1_ FIRST_CHARACTER_ADDRESS + charPositionX", where DISPLAY_20x4_LINE1_FIRST_CHARACTER_ ADDRESS is defined as 0, as was shown in Code 6.6. If *charPositionY* is 1 (line 12), the DDRAM address value is obtained as "DISPLAY_20x4_LINE2_FIRST_CHARACTER_ADDRESS + charPositionX", where DISPLAY_20x4_LINE2_FIRST_CHARACTER_ ADDRESS is defined as 64, as was shown in Code 6.6.

> **NOTE:** There are other ways to implement *displayCharPositionWrite()* that lead to shorter code. However, the implementation shown in Code 6.12 was chosen because the program code is easy to understand.

The other function of the *display* module used in Code 6.4 is *displayStringWrite()*. The implementation of this function is shown in Code 6.13. It has only one parameter, a *pointer* to a string (i.e., char* str). As was mentioned in previous chapters, a string is an array of characters ending with a null character ('\0'). When, for example, *displayStringWrite("Detected")* is written in the program code, the pointer *points* to the first element of *"Detected"*, in this case the character "D". Then, in the *while* loop (line 3 of Code 6.13), the positions in the array are read one after the other, until the null element is found (remember that a null character is added at the end of an array of char when it is written between quotes, as in "Detected").

In this way, *displayCodeWrite()* is called on line 4. In this case, the first parameter is DISPLAY_RS_DATA to indicate that the value in the data bus should be written to the data register. The second parameter is the character pointed by the pointer *str*. Thus, the corresponding character is written on the display. The pointer is incremented to the next position of the string on line 5. In this way, one after the other the characters of the string are written on the display until the null character ('\0') is found (that is, *str is equal to '\0').

> **NOTE:** The str++ operation in line 4 of Code 6.13 is the first time in the book that a mathematical operation has been made on a pointer. As discussed in Chapter 4, the modification of the value of a pointer should be done carefully, because otherwise improper access to a memory address can be made.

```
1  void displayCharPositionWrite( uint8_t charPositionX, uint8_t charPositionY )
2  {
3      switch( charPositionY ) {
4          case 0:
5              displayCodeWrite( DISPLAY_RS_INSTRUCTION,
6                                DISPLAY_IR_SET_DDRAM_ADDR |
7                                ( DISPLAY_20x4_LINE1_FIRST_CHARACTER_ADDRESS +
8                                  charPositionX ) );
9              delay( 1 );
10             break;
11
12         case 1:
13             displayCodeWrite( DISPLAY_RS_INSTRUCTION,
14                               DISPLAY_IR_SET_DDRAM_ADDR |
15                               ( DISPLAY_20x4_LINE2_FIRST_CHARACTER_ADDRESS +
16                                 charPositionX ) );
17             delay( 1 );
18             break;
19
20         case 2:
21             displayCodeWrite( DISPLAY_RS_INSTRUCTION,
22                               DISPLAY_IR_SET_DDRAM_ADDR |
23                               ( DISPLAY_20x4_LINE3_FIRST_CHARACTER_ADDRESS +
24                                 charPositionX ) );
25             delay( 1 );
26             break;
27
28         case 3:
29             displayCodeWrite( DISPLAY_RS_INSTRUCTION,
30                               DISPLAY_IR_SET_DDRAM_ADDR |
31                               ( DISPLAY_20x4_LINE4_FIRST_CHARACTER_ADDRESS +
32                                 charPositionX ) );
33             delay( 1 );
34             break;
35     }
36 }
```

Code 6.12 Implementation of the function displayCharPositionWrite().

```
1  void displayStringWrite( const char* str )
2  {
3      while (*str) {
4          displayCodeWrite(DISPLAY_RS_DATA, *str++);
5          str++;
6      }
7  }
```

Code 6.13 Implementation of the function displayStringWrite().

Proposed Exercises

1. How can a string "Smart Home" be placed in the center of the fourth line of the display?

2. How can the symbol "°" be placed in the position ($x = 14$, $y = 0$) to indicate the degree sign?

Answers to the Exercises

1. The fourth line of the display corresponds to $y = 3$, and the string "Smart Home" has 10 characters; so, in order to be centered the string must be placed at $x = 5$. The following statements could be used:

```
displayCharPositionWrite ( 5,3 );
displayStringWrite( "Smart Home"  );
```

2. The code for the "°" symbol in Table 6.1 is 223, so an array *char buffer[3];* can be declared, and in line 15 of Code 6.4 the following statements can be used:

```
sprintf (buffer, "%cC", 223);
displayStringWrite( buffer );
```

Example 6.2: Use of a 4-Bit Mode to Send Commands and Data to the Display

Objective

Introduce the use of a character LCD display by means of a GPIO connection with fewer wires.

Summary of the Expected Behavior

The expected behavior is the same as in the previous example, the only difference being that a reduced number of connections is used between the display and the NUCLEO board, as shown in Figure 6.13.

Test the Proposed Solution on the Board

Import the project "Example 6.2" using the URL available in [3], build the project, and drag the *.bin* file onto the NUCLEO board. The behavior should be the same as that discussed in Example 6.1.

Discussion of the Proposed Solution

In Code 6.5 of Example 6.1, the configuration "DISPLAY_IR_FUNCTION_SET_8BITS" was used. By reading the datasheet of the character LCD display driver [2], the reader may notice that there is also a 4-bit mode available, which uses only the D4 to D7 pins of the display instead of using D0 to D7. In this example, the *display* module is modified in order to allow the use of both the 8-bit mode and the 4-bit mode connection.

 NOTE: Only the functions that are modified are shown. All the other code remains the same.

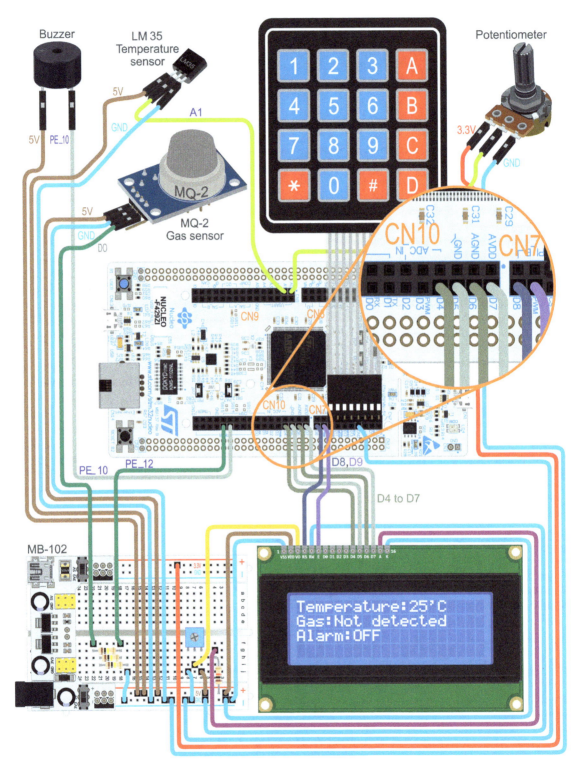

Figure 6.13 The smart home system connected to the character LCD display using 4-bit mode interface.

The transfer timing sequence of writing instructions when a 4-bit interface is configured is shown in Figure 6.14. It can be seen that first the four bits are transferred and then the last four bits are transferred. The only case where the transfer timing sequence shown in Figure 6.13 is not followed is at the beginning of the 4-bit interface initialization procedure, shown in Figure 6.15, that is described in [2]. It can be seen that the initialization procedure is very similar to the 8-bit interface initialization procedure that was introduced in Figure 6.11. The main difference is that now transfers are done using only the D4 to D7 pins of the LCD display and that the "Function Set" instruction is executed five times.

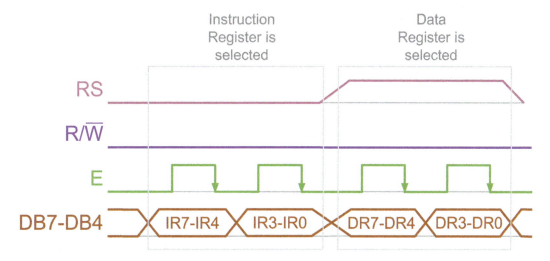

Figure 6.14 Transfer timing sequence of writing instructions when a 4-bit interface is configured.

Implementation of the Proposed Solution

In Code 6.14, the new implementation of *userInterfaceDisplayInit()* is shown. It can be seen on line 4 that *displayInit()* now has a parameter, which in this case is DISPLAY_CONNECTION_GPIO_4BITS.

```
1   static void userInterfaceDisplayInit()
2   {
3       displayInit( DISPLAY_CONNECTION_GPIO_4BITS );
4
5       displayCharPositionWrite ( 0,0 );
6       displayStringWrite( "Temperature:" );
7
8       displayCharPositionWrite ( 0,1 );
9       displayStringWrite( "Gas:" );
10
11      displayCharPositionWrite ( 0,2 );
12      displayStringWrite( "Alarm:" );
13  }
14
```

Code 6.14 Implementation of the function userInterfaceDisplayInit().

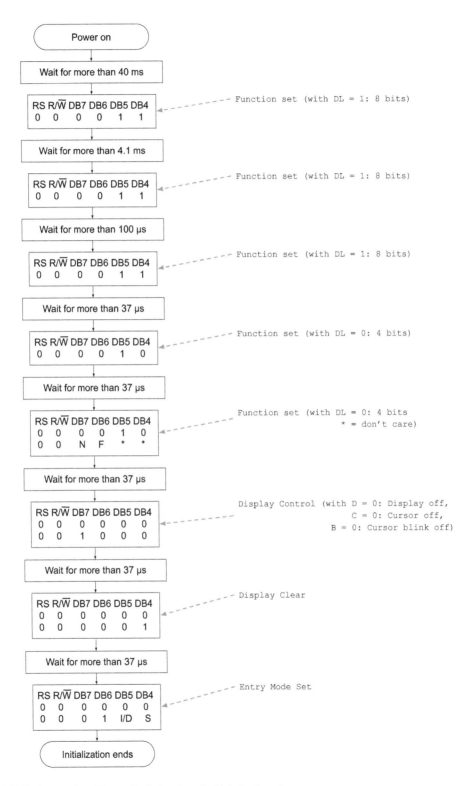

Figure 6.15 Initialization procedure of the graphic display when a 4-bit interface is used.

In Code 6.15 and Code 6.16, the new implementation of *displayInit()* is shown. On line 3 of Code 6.15, a static variable of theuser-defined type displayConnection_t named *displayConnection* is declared. This type is defined in *display.h* and can have only two values: DISPLAY_CONNECTION_GPIO_4BITS and DISPLAY_CONNECTION_GPIO_8BITS.

On line 5, a new private global Boolean variable named *initial8BitCommunicationIsCompleted*, that is declared in *display.cpp*, is assigned false. In this way, it is indicated that the transfer timing sequence must be made according to Figure 6.11 (only one E pin pulse per data transfer and only one data bus set of values).

From lines 7 to 22, the program code remains the same as in the previous implementation of *displayInit()*. This is because the first three instructions on Figure 6.11 and Figure 6.15 are the same, the only difference being that in one case the D7 to D0 pins of the LCD display are connected to the NUCLEO board, while in the other case only the D7 to D4 pins of the LCD display are connected to the NUCLEO board.

On line 24, there is a switch statement over *display.connection*. In the case of DISPLAY_ CONNECTION_GPIO_ 8BITS, the code between lines 25 and 32 is executed; it corresponds to the fourth instruction shown on Figure 6.11. In the case of DISPLAY_CONNECTION_GPIO_4BITS, the code between lines 34 and 48 is executed; it corresponds to the fourth and fifth instructions shown on Figure 6.15. It is important to note that in line 40, *initial8BitCommunicationIsCompleted* is assigned true. In this way, it is indicated that from now on the transfer should be following the timing sequence shown in Figure 6.14. Consequently, the fifth instruction shown in Figure 6.15 is transferred using two E pin pulses per display instruction.

The second part of *displayInit()*, which is shown in Code 6.16, is the same as in Code 6.5, because the last part of Figure 6.11 is equal to the last part of Figure 6.15. The only difference is how the instructions are sent to the display: in the first case the D7 to D0 pins are used, while in the second case only the D7 to D4 pins are used. The new implementation of *displayDataBusWrite()* deals with this.

Code 6.17 shows the new implementation of *displayDataBusWrite()*. Lines 3 to 7 are the same as in the previous implementation (Code 6.11). In line 8, there is a switch statement over *display.connection*. In the case of DISPLAY_CONNECTION_GPIO_8BITS, lines 10 to 13 are executed, which are the same as lines 8 to 11 of Code 6.11. In the case of DISPLAY_CONNECTION_GPIO_4BITS, the *if* statement on line 17 is evaluated. If *initial8BitCommunicationIsCompleted* is true (it is set true on line 40 of Code 6.15), a pulse on the E pin is generated (lines 18 to 21) and then the *DigitalOut* objects D7 to D4 are written with the values of DB3 to DB0 (lines 22 to 25). For example, on line 22 the statement is *displayPinWrite(DISPLAY_PIN_D7, dataBus & 0b00001000)*, which implies that the fourth bit from the left of *dataBus* (that is, DB3) is written into DISPLAY_PIN_D7.

Finally, in lines 30 to 33, a pulse is generated in the E pin. This pulse performs the transfer of the data, either the data corresponding to lines 4 to 13, or 22 to 25, depending on the value of *display.connection*.

```
1   void displayInit( displayConnection_t connection )
2   {
3       display.connection = connection;
4
5           initial8BitCommunicationIsCompleted = false;
6
7       delay( 50 );
8
9       displayCodeWrite( DISPLAY_RS_INSTRUCTION,
10                        DISPLAY_IR_FUNCTION_SET |
11                        DISPLAY_IR_FUNCTION_SET_8BITS );
12      delay( 5 );
13
14      displayCodeWrite( DISPLAY_RS_INSTRUCTION,
15                        DISPLAY_IR_FUNCTION_SET |
16                        DISPLAY_IR_FUNCTION_SET_8BITS );
17      delay( 1 );
18
19      displayCodeWrite( DISPLAY_RS_INSTRUCTION,
20                        DISPLAY_IR_FUNCTION_SET |
21                        DISPLAY_IR_FUNCTION_SET_8BITS );
22      delay( 1 );
23
24      switch( display.connection ) {
25          case DISPLAY_CONNECTION_GPIO_8BITS:
26              displayCodeWrite( DISPLAY_RS_INSTRUCTION,
27                                DISPLAY_IR_FUNCTION_SET |
28                                DISPLAY_IR_FUNCTION_SET_8BITS |
29                                DISPLAY_IR_FUNCTION_SET_2LINES |
30                                DISPLAY_IR_FUNCTION_SET_5x8DOTS );
31              delay( 1 );
32              break;
33
34          case DISPLAY_CONNECTION_GPIO_4BITS:
35              displayCodeWrite( DISPLAY_RS_INSTRUCTION,
36                                DISPLAY_IR_FUNCTION_SET |
37                                DISPLAY_IR_FUNCTION_SET_4BITS );
38              delay( 1 );
39
40              initial8BitCommunicationIsCompleted = true;
41
42              displayCodeWrite( DISPLAY_RS_INSTRUCTION,
43                                DISPLAY_IR_FUNCTION_SET |
44                                DISPLAY_IR_FUNCTION_SET_4BITS |
45                                DISPLAY_IR_FUNCTION_SET_2LINES |
46                                DISPLAY_IR_FUNCTION_SET_5x8DOTS );
47              delay( 1 );
48              break;
49      }
```

Code 6.15 New implementation of the function displayInit() (Part 1/2).

```
1      displayCodeWrite( DISPLAY_RS_INSTRUCTION,
2                        DISPLAY_IR_DISPLAY_CONTROL |
3                        DISPLAY_IR_DISPLAY_CONTROL_DISPLAY_OFF |
4                        DISPLAY_IR_DISPLAY_CONTROL_CURSOR_OFF |
5                        DISPLAY_IR_DISPLAY_CONTROL_BLINK_OFF );
6      delay( 1 );
7
8      displayCodeWrite( DISPLAY_RS_INSTRUCTION,
9                        DISPLAY_IR_CLEAR_DISPLAY );
10     delay( 1 );
11
12         displayCodeWrite( DISPLAY_RS_INSTRUCTION,
13                           DISPLAY_IR_ENTRY_MODE_SET |
14                           DISPLAY_IR_ENTRY_MODE_SET_INCREMENT |
15                           DISPLAY_IR_ENTRY_MODE_SET_NO_SHIFT );
16     delay( 1 );
17
18     displayCodeWrite( DISPLAY_RS_INSTRUCTION,
19                       DISPLAY_IR_DISPLAY_CONTROL |
20                           DISPLAY_IR_DISPLAY_CONTROL_DISPLAY_ON |
21                           DISPLAY_IR_DISPLAY_CONTROL_CURSOR_OFF |
22                           DISPLAY_IR_DISPLAY_CONTROL_BLINK_OFF );
23     delay( 1 );
24  }
```

Code 6.16 New implementation of the function displayInit() (Part 2/2).

```
1   static void displayDataBusWrite( uint8_t dataBus )
2   {
3       displayPinWrite( DISPLAY_PIN_EN, OFF );
4       displayPinWrite( DISPLAY_PIN_D7, dataBus & 0b10000000 );
5       displayPinWrite( DISPLAY_PIN_D6, dataBus & 0b01000000 );
6       displayPinWrite( DISPLAY_PIN_D5, dataBus & 0b00100000 );
7       displayPinWrite( DISPLAY_PIN_D4, dataBus & 0b00010000 );
8       switch( display.connection ) {
9           case DISPLAY_CONNECTION_GPIO_8BITS:
10              displayPinWrite( DISPLAY_PIN_D3, dataBus & 0b00001000 );
11              displayPinWrite( DISPLAY_PIN_D2, dataBus & 0b00000100 );
12              displayPinWrite( DISPLAY_PIN_D1, dataBus & 0b00000010 );
13              displayPinWrite( DISPLAY_PIN_D0, dataBus & 0b00000001 );
14              break;
15
16          case DISPLAY_CONNECTION_GPIO_4BITS:
17              if ( initial8BitCommunicationIsCompleted == true) {
18                  displayPinWrite( DISPLAY_PIN_EN, ON );
19                  delay( 1 );
20                  displayPinWrite( DISPLAY_PIN_EN, OFF );
21                  delay( 1 );
22                  displayPinWrite( DISPLAY_PIN_D7, dataBus & 0b00001000 );
23                  displayPinWrite( DISPLAY_PIN_D6, dataBus & 0b00000100 );
24                  displayPinWrite( DISPLAY_PIN_D5, dataBus & 0b00000010 );
25                  displayPinWrite( DISPLAY_PIN_D4, dataBus & 0b00000001 );
26              }
27              break;
28
29          }
30      displayPinWrite( DISPLAY_PIN_EN, ON );
31      delay( 1 );
32      displayPinWrite( DISPLAY_PIN_EN, OFF );
33      delay( 1 );
34  }
```

Code 6.17 New implementation of the function displayDataBusWrite().

NOTE: There are other ways to implement *displayDataBusWrite()* that lead to shorter code. However, the implementation shown in Code 6.17 was chosen because the program code is easy to understand.

The new implementation of *displayPinWrite()* is shown in Code 6.18. In line 3, there is a switch statement over *display.connection*. In the case of DISPLAY_CONNECTION_GPIO_8BITS, the code from lines 5 to 18 is executed, which corresponds to the same code as in Code 6.8. In the case of DISPLAY_CONNECTION_GPIO_4BITS, the code between lines 21 and 30 is executed, which is very similar to the code from lines 6 to 18, the difference being that the DigitalOut objects *displayD0* to *displayD3* are never assigned a value.

```
1   static void displayPinWrite( uint8_t pinName, int value )
2   {
3       switch( display.connection ) {
4           case DISPLAY_CONNECTION_GPIO_8BITS:
5               switch( pinName ) {
6                   case DISPLAY_PIN_D0: displayD0 = value;    break;
7                   case DISPLAY_PIN_D1: displayD1 = value;    break;
8                   case DISPLAY_PIN_D2: displayD2 = value;    break;
9                   case DISPLAY_PIN_D3: displayD3 = value;    break;
10                  case DISPLAY_PIN_D4: displayD4 = value;    break;
11                  case DISPLAY_PIN_D5: displayD5 = value;    break;
12                  case DISPLAY_PIN_D6: displayD6 = value;    break;
13                  case DISPLAY_PIN_D7: displayD7 = value;    break;
14                  case DISPLAY_PIN_RS: displayRS = value;    break;
15                  case DISPLAY_PIN_EN: displayEN = value;    break;
16                  case DISPLAY_PIN_RW: break;
17                  default: break;
18              }
19              break;
20          case DISPLAY_CONNECTION_GPIO_4BITS:
21              switch( pinName ) {
22                  case DISPLAY_PIN_D4: displayD4 = value;    break;
23                  case DISPLAY_PIN_D5: displayD5 = value;    break;
24                  case DISPLAY_PIN_D6: displayD6 = value;    break;
25                  case DISPLAY_PIN_D7: displayD7 = value;    break;
26                  case DISPLAY_PIN_RS: displayRS = value;    break;
27                  case DISPLAY_PIN_EN: displayEN = value;    break;
28                  case DISPLAY_PIN_RW: break;
29                  default: break;
30              }
31              break;
32      }
33  }
```

Code 6.18 New implementation of the function displayPinWrite().

Proposed Exercise

1. How can Code 6.14 be modified in order to use an 8-bit mode connection?

Answer to the Exercise

1. Line 3 should be modified as follows:

```
displayInit( DISPLAY_CONNECTION_GPIO_8BITS );
```

 WARNING: If an 8-bit mode connection is set, then the eight data pins of the display (D0 to D7) should be connected, as shown in Figure 6.2.

 NOTE: An 8-bit mode connection implies less time to transfer data to the display and code that is easier to read when compared with a 4-bit mode connection. However, given that data transfer time between the microcontroller and the display is not usually an issue, 4-bit mode may be more convenient due to the reduced number of connections.

6.2.3 Connect a Character LCD Display to the Smart Home System using the I2C Bus

In the previous sections, many GPIOs and cables were used to connect the character-based LCD display to the NUCLEO board. It might be more convenient to employ a setup that uses fewer cables to connect the character-based LCD display with the NUCLEO board. The proposed solution is shown in Figure 6.16. It can be seen that a module based on the PCF8574 8-bit I/O expander for I2C bus is used, which is described in [6]. This module provides 8 GPIO pins, which are controlled by means of a two-wire I2C bus connection, as summarized in Figure 6.17. The aim of this setup is to reduce the number of cables that are necessary to connect to the NUCLEO board to control the character-based LCD display.

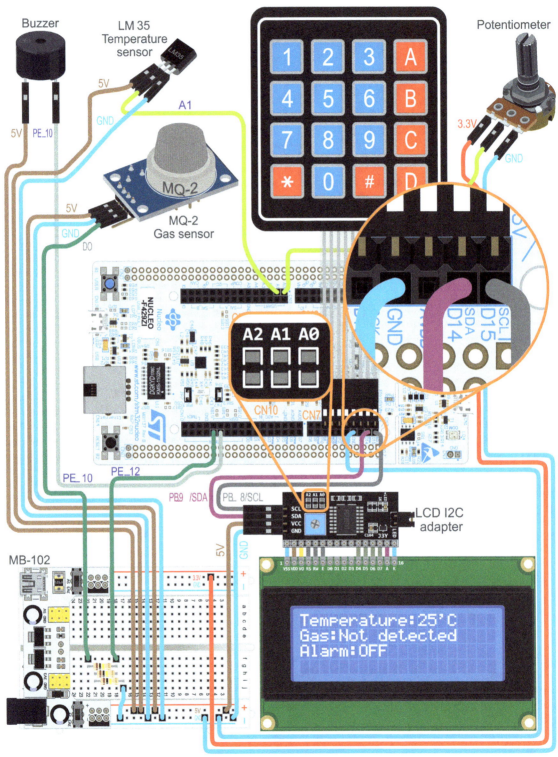

Figure 6.16 The smart home system is now connected to the character LCD display using the I2C bus.

The I2C bus is used to implement a serial communication between the NUCLEO board and the module based on the PCF8574. The PCF8574 LCD module receives, by means of the I2C bus, the commands and data that the NUCLEO board delivers to the character-based LCD display and places those bits in its own GPIOs. These are connected to the character LCD display, as shown in Figure 6.17.

 NOTE: The jumper JP1 is used to connect or disconnect the anode of the LCD from the 5 V supply provided in the VCC pin of the PCF8574. The functionality of the A0, A1, and A2 pads is discussed below.

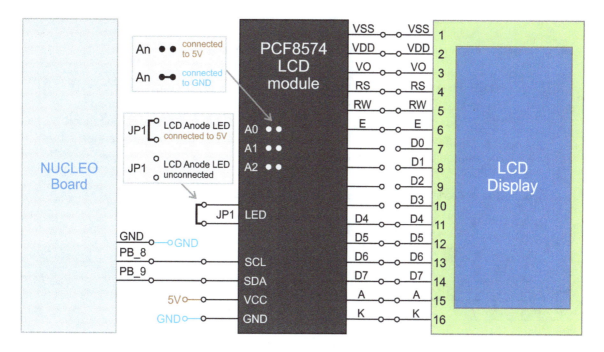

Figure 6.17 Diagram of the connections between the character LCD display and the NUCLEO board using the I2C bus.

A simplified block diagram of the PCF8574, together with its connections to the display, is shown in Figure 6.18. The state of D7, D6, D5, D4, A, E, R/W, and RS is controlled using the I2C bus. For example, if the binary value 0b10001001 is written into the PCF8574, then D7, A, and RS will be in high state, while D6, D5, D4, E, and R/W will be in low state. The pins A0, A1, and A2 are used to set the address of the PCF8574 module, as shown in Table 6.5. If those pins are left unconnected, as in Figure 6.16, they are in high state because of pull-up resistors located in the module, and then the I2C bus 8-bit write address 78 is configured.

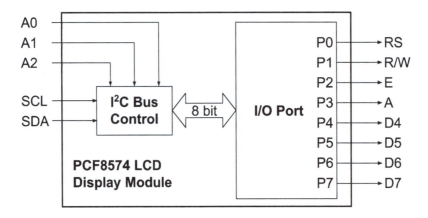

Figure 6.18 Simplified block diagram of the PCF8574 together with its connections to the LCD display.

 NOTE: The concept of "I2C bus 8-bit addresses" is used because addresses are defined in this way in [7]. However, the way in which addresses are defined in the I2C bus is discussed in more detail in section 6.2.4, and it is explained that it might be more appropriate to talk about 7-bit addresses, as they are defined in the corresponding standard, as can be seen in [8].

Table 6.5 Address reference of the PCF8574 module. The addresses used in the proposed setup are highlighted.

Inputs			I2C Bus 8-bit Write Address	I2C Bus 8-bit Read Address
A2	A1	A0		
Low	Low	Low	64	65
Low	Low	High	66	67
Low	High	Low	68	69
Low	High	High	70	71
High	Low	Low	72	73
High	Low	High	74	75
High	High	Low	76	77
High	High	High	78	79

The reader might notice in Figure 6.16 that the cables and connections are simpler than in Figure 6.2 and Figure 6.13 and that the resistor and the potentiometer have been removed from the breadboard. The PCF8574 LCD module provides a potentiometer that can be used to adjust the contrast of the character LCD display.

 WARNING: Other modules based on the PCF8574 are available on the market, as shown in Figure 6.19. Those modules are not convenient for this application because they do not include the potentiometer and resistor that are necessary to connect the character LCD display and, therefore, require more elements.

Figure 6.19 Examples of other PCF8574 modules that do not include the potentiometer and the resistors.

TIP: If the reader has two 20 × 4 character LCD displays, the character LCD display connected as shown in Figure 6.13 can be kept, and a second character LCD display may be connected as shown in Figure 6.16. Only one display will be active, depending on the program code, but it will be easier to compare how they work.

To test if the character LCD display is working, the *.bin* file of the program "Subsection 6.2.3" should be downloaded from the URL available in [3] and dragged onto the NUCLEO board. After power on, the most pertinent information about the smart home system should be shown on the character LCD display.

6.2.4 Fundamentals of the Inter-Integrated Circuit (I2C) Communication Protocol

The I2C bus that is used in the proposed setup is described in [8]. This bus has some similarities and differences to the UART communication that was introduced in Chapter 2. Firstly, on each device there is only one pin that is used to exchange data with other devices, called SDA (*Serial Data Line*), while in the UART serial port each device has a TxD pin to transmit data and an RxD pin to receive data. Secondly, there is a pin called SCL (*Serial Clock Line*), which is used to establish a common *clock signal* used to control the timing of the data interchange. In this way, the I2C bus establishes a *synchronous communication* (because the clock signal is delivered), and it is not necessary to agree the transmission rate in advance, as in the UART interface, which does not have a clock signal and, therefore, is based on *asynchronous communication*.

A third point, which is very important to highlight, is that UART connection only allows a point-to-point connection between two devices, while an I2C bus allows up to 127 devices to be connected together using only the two connections, SDA and SCL. This idea is illustrated in Figure 6.20, where two pull-up resistors are included because the I2C bus standard establishes that the SDA and SCL outputs are open drain.

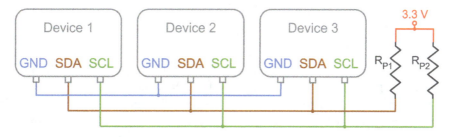

Figure 6.20 Example of a typical I2C bus connection between many devices.

In order to implement the connection of multiple devices using only two wires, a method to unequivocally identify each device must be implemented. In this way, the manager can send a message to any device, and it can be guaranteed that the destination device will recognize that the message is for it alone.

The address of each device is configured by means of a fixed base address plus an optional offset that is modifiable by means of wired connections. In this way, the PCF8574 module can be configured with any 8-bit address in the range of 64/65 to 78/79. The three connections shown in Figure 6.16 on the PCF8574 module (A0, A1, and A2) are used for this purpose, as was shown in Table 6.5.

When a device is not transmitting, it does not establish either a low or high state in its SDA and SCL pins. If no device is transmitting, the SDA and SCL lines are in high state, because of the pull-up resistors (Rp1 and Rp2) that can be seen in Figure 6.20. Therefore, a manager that wants to transmit data establishes a start bit condition on the bus by setting SDA to a low state when the signal in SCL is high, as can be seen in Figure 6.21. The same figure also shows how the stop bit condition is established.

Figure 6.21 Example of I2C bus start and stop conditions.

The first message that the transmitting device sends is the address of the device for which the message is intended. This message is depicted in Figure 6.22. The transmitting device establishes, one after the other, the seven bits of the address of the device for which the message is intended (A6 to A0). This is followed by an R/W bit that indicates if the message is a read or a write operation (it is high if it is a read operation and low if it is a write operation). The ACK (acknowledge) bit (shown in blue) is established by the destination device to confirm that it has received the message.

Figure 6.22 Example of a typical I2C bus address message.

Figure 6.23 shows the typical sequence of an I2C communication. Firstly, the device that starts the communication, called the *manager* device, establishes the start sequence, followed by the address message corresponding to another I2C device, called the *subordinate*. Note that the SCL signal is generated by the manager. In Figure 6.23, the first R/W bit indicates that a read operation is to be made. The subordinate acknowledges in the ninth clock pulse (shown in blue). Then, the manager indicates which register of the subordinate it wants to read using D7 to D0. Note that this is followed by another start bit without any prior stop bit, after which the manager repeats the address of the subordinate, using the R/W bit to indicate that a read operation is being made. After that, the subordinate writes the 8 bits (indicated in blue) corresponding to the register data following the SCL pulses that are established by the manager. Finally, the manager generates the ACK bit (indicated in brown) and the stop bit.

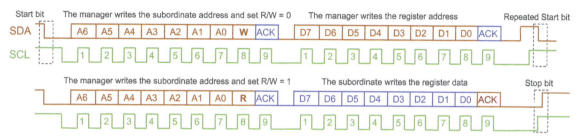

Figure 6.23 Example of a typical I2C bus communication.

 NOTE: In a read operation, if the subordinate is not ready to send the data it is allowed to hold the SCL line low. The manager should wait until the SCL line goes high before continuing.

NOTE: The I2C bus allows more than one manager on the bus, but only one manager can use the bus at any one time. For this purpose there is an established arbitration mechanism that is not covered in this book. For further details, the reader is referred to [8].

The examples below will show how to implement I2C communications in order to control the character display using the PCF8574. Given that only write operations will be used, the sequence will be simpler than the one shown in Figure 6.23, and the subordinate will never hold the SCL line low.

Figure 6.24 shows the sequence to write the port pins value of the PCF8574 LCD module. The first four bits of the address, 1000, are fixed and cannot be changed. The next three bits, 111, correspond to A2, A1, and A0, as explained above. The last bit, 0, indicates that it is a write operation. In this way, the 8-bit address value 0b10001110 is obtained, which corresponds to 78 (in decimal notation). Lastly, it can be seen in Figure 6.24 that the port pin values are written (P7–P0). In this way, the display pins D7–D4, A, E, R/W, and RS are established.

Figure 6.24 Example of a writing operation to the PCF8574.

257

> **NOTE:** 8-bit addresses are obtained considering as a whole the bits A6 to A0 (7 bits) and the R/W bit. It will be seen in the example that considering 8-bit addresses (as was shown in Table 6.5) simplifies the code. However, in most I2C literature, addresses are defined using only bits A6 to A0 (without considering the R/W bit) and, therefore, addresses have 7 bits. In this way, up to 127 different addresses can be used ($2^7 - 1$).

Example 6.3: Control the Character LCD Display by means of the I2C Bus

Objective

Introduce the usage of the I2C bus.

Summary of the Expected Behavior

The expected behavior is exactly the same as in the previous example (Example 6.2), although the connection with the character LCD display has been changed from GPIOs to the I2C bus.

Test the Proposed Solution on the Board

Import the project "Example 6.3" using the URL available in [3], build the project, and drag the .*bin* file onto the NUCLEO board. Follow the same steps as indicated in the section "Test the Proposed Solution on the Board" of Example 6.1. The present temperature, gas detector, and alarm state should be shown on the display.

Discussion of the Proposed Solution

The proposed solution is based on changes introduced in the *display* module. This time, the functions are modified in order to allow the selection of the communication type with the display, the available options being 8-bit GPIO, 4-bit GPIO, or I2C bus by means of the PCF8574 LCD module. All the other characteristics remain the same, as will be shown in the code below. In this way, the concept of a *Hardware Abstraction Layer* is introduced.

Implementation of the Proposed Solution

The new implementation of the function *userInterfaceDisplayInit()* is shown in Code 6.19. It can be seen that the only change is on line 3, where the first parameter is used to indicate how to establish communication with the display. All the other functions and parameters remain the same as in Code 6.3, although the communication with the display has changed. This is possible thanks to the hardware abstraction approach used in the design of the functions of the *display* module.

```
 1   static void userInterfaceDisplayInit()
 2   {
 3       displayInit( DISPLAY_CONNECTION_I2C_PCF8574_IO_EXPANDER );
 4
 5       displayCharPositionWrite ( 0,0 );
 6       displayStringWrite( "Temperature:" );
 7
 8       displayCharPositionWrite ( 0,1 );
 9       displayStringWrite( "Gas:" );
10
11       displayCharPositionWrite ( 0,2 );
12       displayStringWrite( "Alarm:" );
13   }
```

Code 6.19 New implementation of the function userInterfaceDisplayInit().

The implementation of the function *userInterfaceDisplayUpdate()* is shown in Code 6.20. The reader should note that the code remains exactly the same as in Code 6.4, although the interface with the display has changed. Again, this is possible thanks to the hardware abstraction approach followed in the design of the functions of the *display* module. In this way, the maintainability of the code is improved, as well as the possibility of using this same code in other projects, even if other interfaces are used in order to communicate with the display.

```
 1   static void userInterfaceDisplayUpdate()
 2   {
 3       static int accumulatedDisplayTime = 0;
 4       char temperatureString[3] = "";
 5
 6       if( accumulatedDisplayTime >=
 7           DISPLAY_REFRESH_TIME_MS ) {
 8
 9           accumulatedDisplayTime = 0;
10
11           sprintf(temperatureString, "%.0f", temperatureSensorReadCelsius());
12           displayCharPositionWrite ( 12,0 );
13           displayStringWrite( temperatureString );
14           displayCharPositionWrite ( 14,0 );
15           displayStringWrite( "'C" );
16
17           displayCharPositionWrite ( 4,1 );
18
19           if ( gasDetectorStateRead() ) {
20               displayStringWrite( "Detected    " );
21           } else {
22               displayStringWrite( "Not Detected" );
23           }
24
25           displayCharPositionWrite ( 6,2 );
26
27           if ( sirenStateRead() ) {
28               displayStringWrite( "ON " );
29           } else {
30               displayStringWrite( "OFF" );
31           }
32
33       } else {
34           accumulatedDisplayTime =
35               accumulatedDisplayTime + SYSTEM_TIME_INCREMENT_MS;
36       }
37   }
```

Code 6.20 Implementation of the function userInterfaceDisplayUpdate().

In Code 6.21, the new #defines that are used in *display.cpp* are shown. In line 1, DISPLAY_PIN_A_PCF8574 is defined as 3. In lines 3 and 4, the pins PB_9 and PB_8 used for the I2C connection are defined as I2C1_SDA and I2C1_SCL, respectively. In line 6, PCF8574_I2C_BUS_8BIT_WRITE_ADDRESS is defined as 78.

```
1    #define DISPLAY_PIN_A_PCF8574 3
2
3    #define I2C1_SDA PB_9
4    #define I2C1_SCL PB_8
5
6    #define PCF8574_I2C_BUS_8BIT_WRITE_ADDRESS 78
```

Code 6.21 Declaration of new private #defines in display.cpp.

Code 6.22 shows the declaration of the new public global object that is used for the I2C bus communication, as it is declared in *display.cpp*.

```
1    I2C i2cPcf8574( I2C1_SDA, I2C1_SCL );
```

Code 6.22 Declaration of the public global object used to implement the I2C bus communication.

A new private data type, shown in Code 6.23, is declared in *display.cpp* in order to implement the control of the LCD pins using the PCF8574 LCD module.

```
1    typedef struct{
2        int address;
3        char data;
4        bool displayPinRs;
5        bool displayPinRw;
6        bool displayPinEn;
7        bool displayPinA;
8        bool displayPinD4;
9        bool displayPinD5;
10       bool displayPinD6;
11       bool displayPinD7;
12   } pcf8574_t;
```

Code 6.23 New private data type used to implement the control of the LCD pins using the PCF8574 LCD module.

A private variable of type *pcf8574_t* is declared in *display.cpp*, as shown in Code 6.24.

```
1    static pcf8574_t pcf8574;
```

Code 6.24 Declaration of a private variable of type pcf8574_t.

The implementation of *displayInit()* is shown in Code 6.25 and Code 6.26. In line 3 of Code 6.25, *display.connection* is assigned and in line 5 it is evaluated to establish if it is equal to DISPLAY_CONNECTION_I2C_PCF8574_IO_EXPANDER. If so, *pcf8574.address* and *pcf8574.data* are assigned (lines 6 and 7), *i2cPcf8574* frequency is configured as 100,000 Hz (line 8), and the display anode is set to high (line 9).

The remaining lines of Code 6.25 and Code 6.26 are as in the previous version of *displayInit()*, except line 42 of Code 6.25, which is new. The reader might notice that the case of DISPLAY_CONNECTION_ I2C_PCF8574_IO_EXPANDER is treated in the same way as DISPLAY_CONNECTION_GPIO_4BITS. This is due to the fact that they involve the same data transfer, despite data being transferred from the NUCLEO board to the character LCD display using the I2C bus in one setup, and GPIOs in the other setup.

For the same reason, *displayDataBusWrite()* (Code 6.27) is the same as in the previous implementation, except line 17, where the case DISPLAY_CONNECTION_I2C_PCF8574_IO_EXPANDER has been added.

In Code 6.28, the new implementation of *displayPinWrite()* is shown. Line 32 starts the case for DISPLAY_CONNECTION_I2C_PCF8574_IO_EXPANDER. Firstly (line 33), it is assessed if *value* is true. If so, the corresponding field of the pcf8574 is set to ON between lines 35 and 43. Otherwise, the corresponding pin is set to OFF between lines 48 and 56.

In line 59, *pcf8574.data* is assigned with 0b00000000. Then, one after the other, the pins fields of *pcf8574* are evaluated. If they are ON, then the corresponding bit of *pcf8574.data* is turned on. For example, in line 60 it is assessed if *pcf8574.displayPinRs* is true. If so, *pcf8574.data* is set to 0b00000001 by means of the OR bitwise operation *pcf8574.data* |= 0b00000001.

Finally, in line 65 the corresponding value is transferred using *i2cPcf8574.write(pcf8574.address, &pcf8574.data, 1)*. The first parameter is the address, the second parameter is the data to be transferred (which must be preceded by the reference operator (&)), and the third parameter (1) is used to indicate that only one byte of data is to be transferred.

```
1   void displayInit( displayConnection_t connection )
2   {
3       display.connection = connection;
4
5       if( display.connection == DISPLAY_CONNECTION_I2C_PCF8574_IO_EXPANDER) {
6           pcf8574.address = PCF8574_I2C_BUS_8BIT_WRITE_ADDRESS;
7           pcf8574.data = 0b00000000;
8           i2cPcf8574.frequency(100000);
9           displayPinWrite( DISPLAY_PIN_A_PCF8574,  ON );
10      }
11
12      initial8BitCommunicationIsCompleted = false;
13
14      delay( 50 );
15
16      displayCodeWrite( DISPLAY_RS_INSTRUCTION,
17                        DISPLAY_IR_FUNCTION_SET |
18                        DISPLAY_IR_FUNCTION_SET_8BITS );
19      delay( 5 );
20
21      displayCodeWrite( DISPLAY_RS_INSTRUCTION,
22                        DISPLAY_IR_FUNCTION_SET |
23                        DISPLAY_IR_FUNCTION_SET_8BITS );
```

```
24          delay( 1 );
25
26          displayCodeWrite( DISPLAY_RS_INSTRUCTION,
27                            DISPLAY_IR_FUNCTION_SET |
28                            DISPLAY_IR_FUNCTION_SET_8BITS );
29          delay( 1 );
30
31          switch( display.connection ) {
32              case DISPLAY_CONNECTION_GPIO_8BITS:
33                  displayCodeWrite( DISPLAY_RS_INSTRUCTION,
34                                    DISPLAY_IR_FUNCTION_SET |
35                                    DISPLAY_IR_FUNCTION_SET_8BITS |
36                                    DISPLAY_IR_FUNCTION_SET_2LINES |
37                                    DISPLAY_IR_FUNCTION_SET_5x8DOTS );
38                  delay( 1 );
39                  break;
40
41              case DISPLAY_CONNECTION_GPIO_4BITS:
42              case DISPLAY_CONNECTION_I2C_PCF8574_IO_EXPANDER:
43                  displayCodeWrite( DISPLAY_RS_INSTRUCTION,
44                                    DISPLAY_IR_FUNCTION_SET |
45                                    DISPLAY_IR_FUNCTION_SET_4BITS );
46                  delay( 1 );
47
48                  initial8BitCommunicationIsCompleted = true;
49
50                  displayCodeWrite( DISPLAY_RS_INSTRUCTION,
51                                    DISPLAY_IR_FUNCTION_SET |
52                                    DISPLAY_IR_FUNCTION_SET_4BITS |
53                                    DISPLAY_IR_FUNCTION_SET_2LINES |
54                                    DISPLAY_IR_FUNCTION_SET_5x8DOTS );
55                  delay( 1 );
56                  break;
57          }
```

Code 6.25 New implementation of the function displayInit() (Part 1/2).

```
1          displayCodeWrite( DISPLAY_RS_INSTRUCTION,
2                            DISPLAY_IR_DISPLAY_CONTROL |
3                            DISPLAY_IR_DISPLAY_CONTROL_DISPLAY_OFF |
4                            DISPLAY_IR_DISPLAY_CONTROL_CURSOR_OFF |
5                            DISPLAY_IR_DISPLAY_CONTROL_BLINK_OFF );
6      delay( 1 );
7
8      displayCodeWrite( DISPLAY_RS_INSTRUCTION,
9                        DISPLAY_IR_CLEAR_DISPLAY );
10     delay( 1 );
11
12         displayCodeWrite( DISPLAY_RS_INSTRUCTION,
13                           DISPLAY_IR_ENTRY_MODE_SET |
14                           DISPLAY_IR_ENTRY_MODE_SET_INCREMENT |
15                           DISPLAY_IR_ENTRY_MODE_SET_NO_SHIFT );
16     delay( 1 );
17
18     displayCodeWrite( DISPLAY_RS_INSTRUCTION,
19                       DISPLAY_IR_DISPLAY_CONTROL |
20                           DISPLAY_IR_DISPLAY_CONTROL_DISPLAY_ON |
21                           DISPLAY_IR_DISPLAY_CONTROL_CURSOR_OFF |
22                           DISPLAY_IR_DISPLAY_CONTROL_BLINK_OFF );
23     delay( 1 );
24 }
```

Code 6.26 New implementation of the function displayInit() (Part 2/2).

```
1   static void displayDataBusWrite( uint8_t dataBus )
2   {
3       displayPinWrite( DISPLAY_PIN_EN, OFF );
4       displayPinWrite( DISPLAY_PIN_D7, dataBus & 0b10000000 );
5       displayPinWrite( DISPLAY_PIN_D6, dataBus & 0b01000000 );
6       displayPinWrite( DISPLAY_PIN_D5, dataBus & 0b00100000 );
7       displayPinWrite( DISPLAY_PIN_D4, dataBus & 0b00010000 );
8       switch( display.connection ) {
9           case DISPLAY_CONNECTION_GPIO_8BITS:
10              displayPinWrite( DISPLAY_PIN_D3, dataBus & 0b00001000 );
11              displayPinWrite( DISPLAY_PIN_D2, dataBus & 0b00000100 );
12              displayPinWrite( DISPLAY_PIN_D1, dataBus & 0b00000010 );
13              displayPinWrite( DISPLAY_PIN_D0, dataBus & 0b00000001 );
14              break;
15
16          case DISPLAY_CONNECTION_GPIO_4BITS:
17          case DISPLAY_CONNECTION_I2C_PCF8574_IO_EXPANDER:
18              if ( initial8BitCommunicationIsCompleted == true) {
19                  displayPinWrite( DISPLAY_PIN_EN, ON );
20                  delay( 1 );
21                  displayPinWrite( DISPLAY_PIN_EN, OFF );
22                  delay( 1 );
23                  displayPinWrite( DISPLAY_PIN_D7, dataBus & 0b00001000 );
24                  displayPinWrite( DISPLAY_PIN_D6, dataBus & 0b00000100 );
25                  displayPinWrite( DISPLAY_PIN_D5, dataBus & 0b00000010 );
26                  displayPinWrite( DISPLAY_PIN_D4, dataBus & 0b00000001 );
27              }
28              break;
29
30          }
31      displayPinWrite( DISPLAY_PIN_EN, ON );
32      delay( 1 );
33      displayPinWrite( DISPLAY_PIN_EN, OFF );
34      delay( 1 );
35  }
```

Code 6.27 New implementation of the function displayDataBusWrite().

```
1   static void displayPinWrite( uint8_t pinName, int value )
2   {
3       switch( display.connection ) {
4           case DISPLAY_CONNECTION_GPIO_8BITS:
5               switch( pinName ) {
6                   case DISPLAY_PIN_D0: displayD0 = value;    break;
7                   case DISPLAY_PIN_D1: displayD1 = value;    break;
8                   case DISPLAY_PIN_D2: displayD2 = value;    break;
9                   case DISPLAY_PIN_D3: displayD3 = value;    break;
10                  case DISPLAY_PIN_D4: displayD4 = value;    break;
11                  case DISPLAY_PIN_D5: displayD5 = value;    break;
12                  case DISPLAY_PIN_D6: displayD6 = value;    break;
13                  case DISPLAY_PIN_D7: displayD7 = value;    break;
14                  case DISPLAY_PIN_RS: displayRS = value;    break;
15                  case DISPLAY_PIN_EN: displayEN = value;    break;
16                  case DISPLAY_PIN_RW: break;
17                  default: break;
18              }
19              break;
20          case DISPLAY_CONNECTION_GPIO_4BITS:
21              switch( pinName ) {
22                  case DISPLAY_PIN_D4: displayD4 = value;    break;
23                  case DISPLAY_PIN_D5: displayD5 = value;    break;
24                  case DISPLAY_PIN_D6: displayD6 = value;    break;
```

```
25                case DISPLAY_PIN_D7: displayD7 = value;    break;
26                case DISPLAY_PIN_RS: displayRS = value;    break;
27                case DISPLAY_PIN_EN: displayEN = value;    break;
28                case DISPLAY_PIN_RW: break;
29                default: break;
30            }
31          break;
32        case DISPLAY_CONNECTION_I2C_PCF8574_IO_EXPANDER:
33          if ( value ) {
34              switch( pinName ) {
35                  case DISPLAY_PIN_D4: pcf8574.displayPinD4 = ON; break;
36                  case DISPLAY_PIN_D5: pcf8574.displayPinD5 = ON; break;
37                  case DISPLAY_PIN_D6: pcf8574.displayPinD6 = ON; break;
38                  case DISPLAY_PIN_D7: pcf8574.displayPinD7 = ON; break;
39                  case DISPLAY_PIN_RS: pcf8574.displayPinRs = ON; break;
40                  case DISPLAY_PIN_EN: pcf8574.displayPinEn = ON; break;
41                  case DISPLAY_PIN_RW: pcf8574.displayPinRw = ON; break;
42                  case DISPLAY_PIN_A_PCF8574: pcf8574.displayPinA = ON; break;
43                  default: break;
44              }
45          }
46          else {
47              switch( pinName ) {
48                  case DISPLAY_PIN_D4: pcf8574.displayPinD4 = OFF; break;
49                  case DISPLAY_PIN_D5: pcf8574.displayPinD5 = OFF; break;
50                  case DISPLAY_PIN_D6: pcf8574.displayPinD6 = OFF; break;
51                  case DISPLAY_PIN_D7: pcf8574.displayPinD7 = OFF; break;
52                  case DISPLAY_PIN_RS: pcf8574.displayPinRs = OFF; break;
53                  case DISPLAY_PIN_EN: pcf8574.displayPinEn = OFF; break;
54                  case DISPLAY_PIN_RW: pcf8574.displayPinRw = OFF; break;
55                  case DISPLAY_PIN_A_PCF8574: pcf8574.displayPinA = OFF; break;
56                  default: break;
57              }
58          }
59          pcf8574.data = 0b00000000;
60          if ( pcf8574.displayPinRs ) pcf8574.data |= 0b00000001;
61          if ( pcf8574.displayPinRw ) pcf8574.data |= 0b00000010;
62          if ( pcf8574.displayPinEn ) pcf8574.data |= 0b00000100;
63          if ( pcf8574.displayPinA  ) pcf8574.data |= 0b00001000;
64          if ( pcf8574.displayPinD4 ) pcf8574.data |= 0b00010000;
65          if ( pcf8574.displayPinD5 ) pcf8574.data |= 0b00100000;
66          if ( pcf8574.displayPinD6 ) pcf8574.data |= 0b01000000;
67          if ( pcf8574.displayPinD7 ) pcf8574.data |= 0b10000000;
68          i2c_pcf8574.write( pcf8574.address, &pcf8574.data, 1);
69          break;
70      }
71  }
```

Code 6.28 New implementation of the function displayPinWrite().

Proposed Exercise

1. How can a second display be connected using the same I2C bus?

Answer to the Exercise

1. A second PCF8574 module should be connected using the signals SDA and SCL of the same bus, and a different address should be configured for this PCF8574 module, changing the configuration of A2, A1, and A0 (as shown in Figure 6.16). Then, when using this module, that address must be used. Note that using this approach, up to eight character-based LCD displays can be connected to the same I2C bus.

6.2.5 Connect a Graphical LCD Display to the Smart Home System using the SPI Bus

In the previous sections, a character-based LCD display was connected to the NUCLEO board using GPIOs and the I2C bus. In this section, a 128 × 64 pixel graphical LCD display is connected using the SPI bus, as shown in Figure 6.25. The connections that must be made are summarized in Figure 6.26.

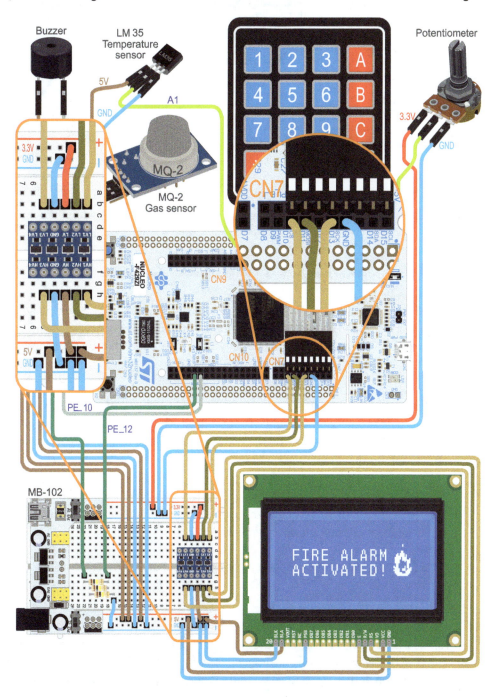

Figure 6.25 The smart home system is now connected to the graphical LCD display using the SPI bus.

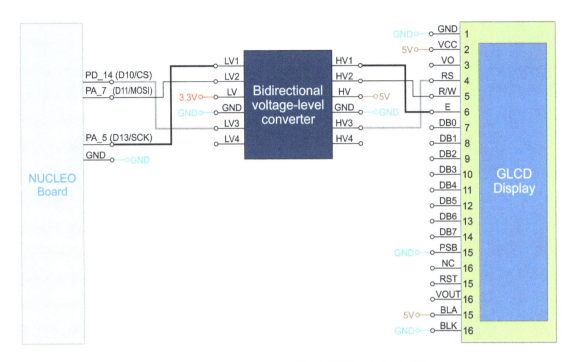

Figure 6.26 Diagram of the connections between the graphical LCD display and the NUCLEO board using the SPI bus.

 TIP: The display (or displays) that were previously connected as shown in Figure 6.13 and Figure 6.16 can be kept, and the graphical LCD display connected as shown in Figure 6.25. Only one display will be active at a time, depending on the program code, but it will be easier to compare how they work.

The 4-bit voltage-level converter, which is connected as shown in Figure 6.25, is necessary because the NUCLEO board provides 3.3 V outputs, while the graphical LCD display expects to receive 5 V signals on its E, R/W, and RS pins. The 4-bit voltage-level converter is specially designed to solve this problem.

 NOTE: In this case, a voltage divider, as used to connect the MQ-2 Gas Sensor with the NUCLEO board, cannot be used to solve the problem, because the voltage does not need to be attenuated, but augmented.

NOTE: The graphical LCD display can be configured to receive 3.3 V signals, but this requires soldering some SMD (surface-mount device) components, which is beyond the scope of this book.

To test if the graphical LCD display is working, the *.bin* file of the program "Subsection 6.2.5" should be downloaded from the URL available in [3] and dragged onto the NUCLEO board. After power on, the most pertinent information of the smart home system should be shown on the graphical LCD display.

6.2.6 Basics Principles of Graphical LCD Displays

The graphical LCD display module that is used [9] is based on the ST7920 LCD controller [10]. This controller provides all the functionality provided by the character-based LCD display that was used in the previous examples, plus additional functionality, which is possible thanks to the 128 × 64 pixel arrangement of the graphical LCD display. Every individual pixel is addressable; hence, the display offers graphic capabilities (in this case, monochrome).

The graphical LCD display can be configured in character mode and in graphic mode. If character mode is selected, the LCD display behaves as a 16 × 4 display that follows the DDRAM map shown in Figure 6.27, where each address stores two characters and each character has 8 × 16 dots. For example, address 0 stores one 8 × 16 dot character that is printed in the position indicated as 0L (left) and another 8 × 16 dot character that is printed in the position indicated as 0R (right). This is because the ST7920 LCD controller is optimized for Chinese characters, which have a square shape (e.g., 米 or 光) and, therefore, occupy two display positions for a single character (e.g., 0L and 0R). Note that 16 × 4 by 8 × 16 results in 128 × 64 pixels.

Figure 6.27 Addresses corresponding to each of the positions of a graphical LCD display in character mode.

It is possible to write a single Latin character (e.g., "a" or "b") in the left half of a position (for example, 0_L, 1_L, etc.). For that purpose, the corresponding DDRAM address must be set (for example, 0, 1, etc.) and then the character transferred. However, it is not possible to write a Latin character only on the right half of a position (for example, 0_R, 1_R, etc.). To write a character in the right half of a position, first a character must be written in the left half of the position and then the desired character must be written in the right half. For example, to write "Gas:" at the beginning of the second row, the address 16 must be written into the DDRAM and then, one after the other, the characters "G", "a", "s", ":" are transferred. To write "Not detected" just next to "Gas:", address 18 must be set and the characters "N", "o", "t", " ", "D", "e", "t", "e", "c", "t", "e", "d" transferred.

NOTE: In the ST7920 datasheet, "high" and "low" are used in place of "left" and "right", respectively.

NOTE: In previous examples, the coordinate (4,1) was used to write "Not detected" in the DDRAM address 68. This address was calculated as 4 added to the first character address of line 2 (64). For the reasons explained above, in order to write "Not detected" in the same display position, the coordinate (4,1) is used in the examples below, and the corresponding address (18) is calculated as the first character address of line 2 (16) increased by the x coordinate (4) divided by 2. In this way, 18 is obtained as "16 + 4/2".

The instructions to initialize the graphical LCD display and to transfer the characters are summarized in Table 6.6. They are almost the same as the instructions that were used in previous sections to control the character LCD display. The differences are highlighted in blue. It can be seen that a bit is not used to set the number of lines (N). There is a bit used to set the instruction set (RE); this bit must be set to 0 during the initialization in order to select the basic instruction set. The bit G is used to activate graphic mode.

Table 6.6 Summary of the graphical LCD display instructions that are used in this chapter.

Instruction	Code										Description	Execution time
	RS	R/W	DB7	DB6	DB5	DB4	DB3	DB2	DB1	DB0		
Clear display	0	0	0	0	0	0	0	0	0	1	Clears entire display and sets DDRAM address 0 in address counter.	1.52 ms
Entry mode set	0	0	0	0	0	0	0	1	I/D	S	Sets cursor move direction and specifies display shift.	1.52 ms
Display control	0	0	0	0	0	0	1	D	C	B	Sets entire display (D) on/off, cursor on/off (C), and blinking of cursor (B).	37 µs
Function set	0	0	0	0	1	DL	*	RE	G	*	Sets interface data length (DL), **instruction set (RE), and graphic display (G).**	37 µs
Set DDRAM address	0	0	1	A6	A5	A4	A3	A2	A1	A0	Sets DDRAM address.	37 µs
Write data to DDRAM	1	0	D7	D6	D5	D4	D3	D2	D1	D0	Writes data into DDRAM.	37 µs

I/D = 1: Increment, I/D = 0: Decrement DL = 1: 8 bits, DL = 0: 4 bits
S = 1: Accompany display shift, **RE = 1: Extended, RE = 0: Basic (instruction set)**
S = 0: Don't accompany display shift, **G = 1: Graphics on, G = 0: Graphics off**
D = 1: Display on, D = 0: Display off * = don't care
C = 1: Cursor on, C = 0: Cursor off A6 ... A0 = Address
B = 1: Cursor blink on, B = 0: Cursor blink off D7 ... D0 = Data

The PSB pin (Parallel/Serial Bus configuration) of the graphical LCD display is used to select its interface. If PSB is connected to 5 V, then 8/4-bit parallel bus mode is selected, and the data transfer is made exactly as in the character LCD display (Figure 6.11 and Figure 6.13). If PSB is connected to GND (as in Figure 6.25), then a serial communication interface based on the SPI (Serial Peripheral Interface) bus is selected.

In the serial interface mode, the RS, R/W, and E pins play a different role than the ones discussed in the previous sections. This is summarized in Table 6.7.

Table 6.7 Connections of the graphical LCD display used in this book when the serial bus option is selected.

Pin label	Pin functionality in serial mode	Description
RS	CS	Chip select (high: chip enable, low: chip disable)
R/W	SID	Serial data input
E	SCLK	Serial clock

The data transfer is made following the timing diagram shown in Figure 6.28. CS must be high during the data transfer. The SCLK signal is used to implement the clock of the transmission (in a similar way as the SCL signal of the I2C bus). The SID signal is used to transfer the data to the LCD display. First, a synchronizing bit string (0b11111) is sent, followed by the state of RW and the state of RS. Then, a 0 state is sent. Next, D7 to D4 are sent, followed by four zeros. Lastly, D3 to D0 are sent, followed by four zeros.

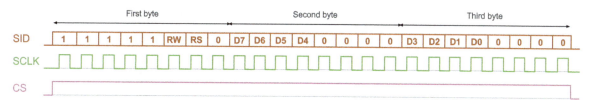

Figure 6.28 Transfer timing sequence of the graphical LCD display when the serial mode is configured.

As has been mentioned, the G bit is used to activate graphic mode. RE and G cannot be altered in the same instruction, so RE is changed first and G later. The examples below show how this is done.

Once the display is in graphic mode, the structure of the data transfer completely changes, and instead of DDRAM, the Graphic Display RAM (GDRAM) is used. The way in which data loaded into the GDRAM is shown in the display is very particular and is closely related to the way in which data is organized in Figure 6.27.

Data organization in Figure 6.27 suggests that it can be thought of as a 32 × 2 character display, where each character has 8 × 16 bits, and whose two rows are "cut" at the middle and reorganized as a 16 × 4 display. This is actually the case, because the ST7920 has 32 common signal driver pins and 64 segment signal driver pins. To drive a 64 × 128 dot matrix LCD panel, the ST7920 controls two ST7921 chips, as shown in Figure 6.29. Each ST7921 is capable of driving 96 segments. In this way, a

ST7920 is used to control a 32 × 256 dot matrix LCD. In the graphical LCD display module used in this chapter, the dots of this matrix are arranged in two 32 × 128 dot layouts, one over the other, as shown in Figure 6.30.

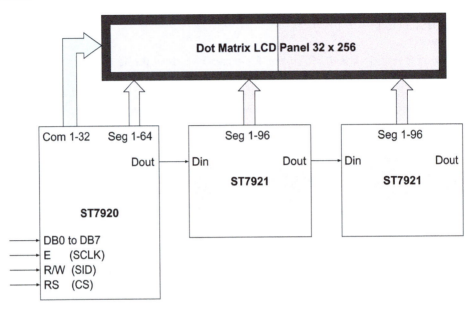

Figure 6.29 Simplified block diagram of an ST7920 and two ST7921 used to drive a 32 × 256 dot matrix LCD panel.

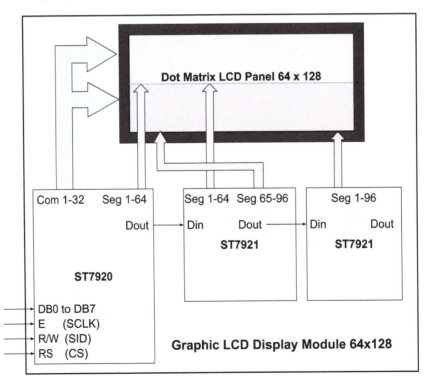

Figure 6.30 Simplified block diagram of an ST7920 and two ST7921 used to drive a 64 × 128 dot matrix LCD panel.

For this reason, the correspondence between the GDRAM addresses and the display pixels is as shown in Figure 6.31. Each GDRAM address stores 16 bits and is identified by a horizontal and a vertical address. To load the content of a given GDRAM address, the transfer procedure is as follows:

1. Set vertical address (Y) for GDRAM

2. Set horizontal address (X) for GDRAM

3. Write the bits b15 to b8 to GDRAM (first byte)

4. Write the bits b7 to b0 to GDRAM (second byte)

The "Set DDRAM address" instruction code shown in Table 6.6 is used to set the vertical and horizontal address, and the "Write data to DDRAM" instruction code shown in Table 6.6 is used to write the GDRAM bits.

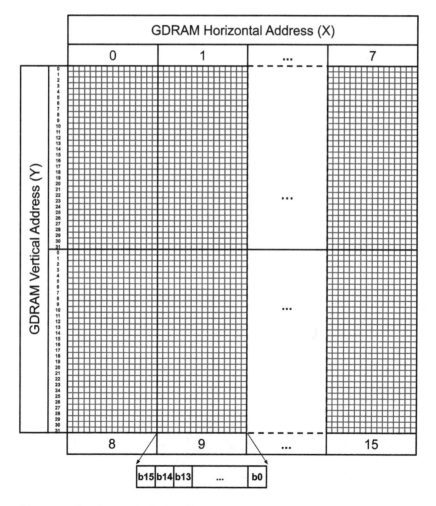

Figure 6.31 Diagram of the correspondence between the GDRAM addresses and the display pixels.

NOTE: The ST7920 includes other functionality that is not discussed here for space reasons and because meaningful programs can be made using the functionality that has been presented in this section, as is shown in the examples below.

NOTE: The HD44780 used in previous sections has 16 common signal driver pins and 40 segment signal driver pins, as shown in [2]. Also in [2], it is shown how the connections are made inside character LCD modules in order to control LCD displays having different layouts using a single HD44780.

6.2.7 Fundamentals of the Serial Peripheral Interface (SPI) Communication Protocol

The transfer timing sequence shown in Figure 6.28 is a special (reduced) implementation of the SPI bus [11]. The SPI bus is implemented by means of four signals, as shown in Table 6.8. It can be seen that the graphical LCD display has completely different pin designations than the signals shown in Table 6.8. The CS, SID, and SCLK signals in Table 6.7 correspond to the SS, MOSI, and SCLK signals, respectively.

Table 6.8 Signals of the SPI bus.

Signal name	Function
SS (Subordinate Select)	The manager sets this to low to select only one subordinate at a time.
SCLK (Clock)	The manager drives this signal, which is common to all the subordinates.
MOSI (Manager Output Subordinate Input)	The manager sends data to one subordinate at a time using this signal.
MISO (Manager Input Subordinate Output)	The manager receives data from one subordinate at a time using this signal.

It can also be seen that the graphical LCD display does not have a signal equivalent to the MISO signal (i.e., the graphical LCD is not able to output data to the NUCLEO board when the serial bus configuration option is used). The SPI signals that are provided by the NUCLEO board are summarized in Table 6.9.

Table 6.9 Summary of the NUCLEO board pins that are used to implement the SPI bus communication.

NUCLEO board	SPI bus signal
PD_14	CS
PA_7	MOSI
PA_5	SCK

In Figure 6.32, a typical SPI connection between a manager and several subordinates can be seen. There is only one SCLK signal, only one MOSI signal, and only one MISO signal, but as many SS signals as subordinates. In this way, the manager controls which subordinate is active on the bus. It should be noted that there can be only one manager in an SPI bus network.

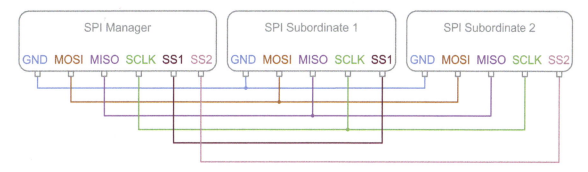

Figure 6.32 Example of a typical SPI bus connection between many devices.

 NOTE: If a single subordinate device is used, the SS pin may be fixed to logic low, as shown in Figure 6.25.

Finally, it should be noted that, unlike the I2C bus, the SPI bus does not have a start bit, a stop bit, or an ACK bit. Moreover, there is no definition for how many bits there are in a message, although 8-bit messages are the most common. There is also no unique option for the *clock polarity* and *clock phase* with respect to the data; thus, there are four possible situations, each of which is known as an SPI mode, as shown in Figure 6.33. The corresponding SPI mode should be configured, as will be shown in the examples below.

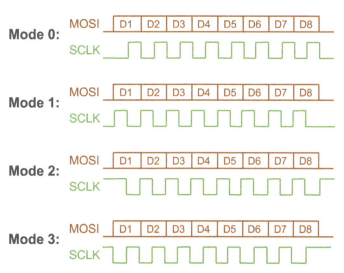

Figure 6.33 Diagram of the four possible SPI modes, depending on the clock polarity and clock phase.

 NOTE: In Figure 6.33, only the MOSI signal and the SCLK signal are shown. However, once SPI mode is configured, the MISO signal must respect the same clock polarity and phase as the MOSI signal.

Example 6.4: Control the Graphical LCD Display by means of the SPI Bus

Objective

Introduce the use of the SPI bus.

Summary of the Expected Behavior

The expected behavior is exactly the same as in Examples 6.1, 6.2, and 6.3, although a graphical LCD display is now being used and that connection with the display is implemented using the SPI bus.

Test the Proposed Solution on the Board

Import the project "Example 6.4" using the URL available in [3], build the project, and drag the *.bin* file onto the NUCLEO board. Follow the same steps as indicated in the section "Test the Proposed Solution on the Board" of Example 6.1. The present temperature, gas detector, and alarm state should be shown on the display.

Discussion of the Proposed Solution

The functions of the *display* module are modified in order to allow communication with a graphical LCD display by means of the SPI bus. All the other characteristics of the functions remain the same, as will be shown. In this way, the concept of a *Hardware Abstraction Layer* is applied one more time.

 NOTE: The graphical features of the graphical LCD display are not used in this example. Those features are introduced in Example 6.5.

Implementation of the Proposed Solution

The new implementation of the function *userInterfaceDisplayInit()* is shown in Code 6.29. It can be seen that the function *displayInit()* on line 3 has been changed in order to include the display type and the type of connection. It can also be seen that all the other functions and parameters from lines 10 to 17 remain the same as in Code 6.19, although the communication with the display has changed, as well as the type of display being used.

```
1   static void userInterfaceDisplayInit()
2   {
3       displayInit( DISPLAY_TYPE_GLCD_ST7920, DISPLAY_CONNECTION_SPI);
4
5       displayCharPositionWrite ( 0,0 );
6       displayStringWrite( "Temperature:" );
7
8       displayCharPositionWrite ( 0,1 );
9       displayStringWrite( "Gas:" );
10
11      displayCharPositionWrite ( 0,2 );
12      displayStringWrite( "Alarm:" );
13  }
```

Code 6.29 New implementation of the function userInterfaceDisplayInit().

The public data types to implement the parameters used in line 3 of Code 6.29 are declared in *display.h*, as shown in Code 6.30. The data type *displayType_t* has two possible values, DISPLAY_TYPE_LCD_ HD44780 and DISPLAY_TYPE_GLCD_ST7920. The data type *displayConnection_t* (lines 6 to 11) was used in previous examples. In this example, the value DISPLAY_CONNECTION_SPI is included. Using these data types, the struct *display_t* is declared (lines 13 to 16), having two fields, *connection* and *type*.

The new private #defines that are declared in *display.cpp* are shown in Code 6.31. The corresponding values were discussed in section 6.2.6. SPI1_MISO is defined because it is required by the SPI object, but it is left unconnected. ST7920_SPI_SYNCHRONIZING_BIT_STRING is defined as 0b11111000 and will be used to implement the first five bits, shown in Figure 6.28. By means of the definitions shown in lines 13 to 17, the state of the RS and RW bits shown in Figure 6.28 will be implemented.

```
1   typedef enum {
2         DISPLAY_TYPE_LCD_HD44780,
3         DISPLAY_TYPE_GLCD_ST7920,
4   } displayType_t;
5
6   typedef enum {
7         DISPLAY_CONNECTION_GPIO_4BITS,
8         DISPLAY_CONNECTION_GPIO_8BITS,
9         DISPLAY_CONNECTION_I2C_PCF8574_IO_EXPANDER,
10        DISPLAY_CONNECTION_SPI
11  } displayConnection_t;
12
13  typedef struct {
14      displayConnection_t connection;
15      displayType_t type;
16  } display_t;
```

Code 6.30 Public data types defined in display.h.

```
1    #define SPI1_MOSI PA_7
2    #define SPI1_MISO PA_6
3    #define SPI1_SCK  PA_5
4    #define SPI1_CS   PD_14
5
6    #define DISPLAY_ST7920_LINE1_FIRST_CHARACTER_ADDRESS 0
7    #define DISPLAY_ST7920_LINE2_FIRST_CHARACTER_ADDRESS 16
8    #define DISPLAY_ST7920_LINE3_FIRST_CHARACTER_ADDRESS 8
9    #define DISPLAY_ST7920_LINE4_FIRST_CHARACTER_ADDRESS 24
10
11   #define ST7920_SPI_SYNCHRONIZING_BIT_STRING 0b11111000
12
13   #define ST7920_SPI_RS_INSTRUCTION 0b000000000
14   #define ST7920_SPI_RS_DATA        0b000000010
15
16   #define ST7920_SPI_RW_WRITE 0b000000000
17   #define ST7920_SPI_RW_READ  0b000000100
```

Code 6.31 New private defines that are declared in display.cpp.

Two new public objects are declared, as shown in Code 6.32. DigitalOut object *spiSt7920ChipSelect* is used to generate the CS signal, according to Figure 6.28. The SPI object allows the implementation of the SCLK and SID signals, as shown in the same figure.

```
1  DigitalOut spiSt7920ChipSelect(SPI1_CS);
2  SPI spiSt7920(SPI1_MOSI, SPI1_MISO, SPI1_SCK);
```

Code 6.32 New public objects that are declared in display.cpp.

 NOTE: The SPI object could also be defined as *SPI spiSt7920(SPI1_MOSI, SPI1_MISO, SPI1_SCK, SPI1_CS)*, and the *DigitalOut* object *spiSt7920ChipSelect(SPI1_CS)* would not be necessary. However, when using that definition of the *SPI* object, only one SPI device can be connected to the SPI bus, while defining Chip Select pin as a *DigitalOut* object means that many devices can be connected to the same SPI bus.

The implementation of the function *userInterfaceDisplayUpdate()* used in this example is exactly the same as in Examples 6.1, 6.2, and 6.3. This fact is quite remarkable, considering that in this example a graphical LCD display is being used and that the communication with the display is implemented by means of an SPI bus connection. In this way, it can be appreciated how powerful a Hardware Abstraction Layer (HAL) can be in terms of code reusability and maintainability. For this reason, the HAL must be carefully designed.

The HAL implemented in this chapter is shown in Figure 6.34. It can be seen that the *display* module allows the use of different types of connections without changing the program code. In this way, a graphical display in character mode connected using the SPI bus can be controlled using the same functions (i.e., *displayCharPositionWrite()* and *displayStringWrite()*) as the character display connected using either 4-bit GPIO, 8-bit GPIO, or I2C bus.

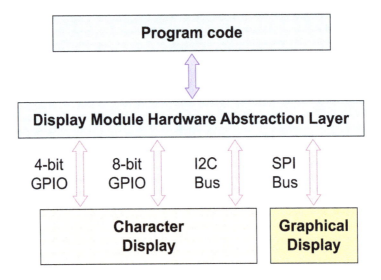

Figure 6.34 Diagram of the Hardware Abstraction Layer that is implemented in the display module.

In this context, for the sake of completeness, the program code should be written in such a way that it becomes clear what every function will do according to the selected type of display and connection. For this reason, the lines shown in Code 6.33 are included at the end of *displayPinWrite()* and *displayDataBusWrite()* to make clear that no action will be made by those functions if they are called when *display.connection* is set to DISPLAY_CONNECTION_SPI. This is because when the SPI bus connection is used, the only way to write information in the display is using the scheme introduced in Figure 6.28 (i.e., it is not possible to write into a single pin or to write only to the data bus).

```
1          case DISPLAY_CONNECTION_SPI:
2          break;
```

Code 6.33 Lines added to displayPinWrite() and displayDataBusWrite().

The new implementation of the function *displayInit()* is shown in Code 6.34 and Code 6.35. In line 3 of Code 6.34, the value of the parameter type is set to *display.type*, and on line 4, the value of the parameter *connection* is assigned to *display.connection*. The new lines in Code 6.34 are lines 13 to 16 and line 39. In line 14, *spiSt7920* is configured with 8 bits per transfer and mode 3, as discussed in Figure 6.33. In line 15, the SPI object is configured to 1,000,000 Hz (1 MHz). Line 39 indicates that the SPI initialization implies the same instructions as the 8-bit parallel mode. Code 6.35 is exactly the same as in previous examples.

```
1   void displayInit( displayType_t type, displayConnection_t connection )
2   {
3       display.type = type;
4       display.connection = connection;
5
6   if( display.connection == DISPLAY_CONNECTION_I2C_PCF8574_IO_EXPANDER) {
7           pcf8574.address = PCF8574_I2C_BUS_8BIT_WRITE_ADDRESS;
8           pcf8574.data = 0b00000000;
9           i2cPcf8574.frequency(100000);
10          displayPinWrite( DISPLAY_PIN_A_PCF8574,  ON );
11      }
12
13  if( display.connection == DISPLAY_CONNECTION_SPI) {
14          spiSt7920.format( 8, 3 );
15          spiSt7920.frequency( 1000000 );
16      }
17
18  initial8BitCommunicationIsCompleted = false;
19
20      delay( 50 );
21
22      displayCodeWrite( DISPLAY_RS_INSTRUCTION,
23                        DISPLAY_IR_FUNCTION_SET |
24                        DISPLAY_IR_FUNCTION_SET_8BITS );
25      delay( 5 );
26
27      displayCodeWrite( DISPLAY_RS_INSTRUCTION,
28                        DISPLAY_IR_FUNCTION_SET |
29                        DISPLAY_IR_FUNCTION_SET_8BITS );
30      delay( 1 );
31
32      displayCodeWrite( DISPLAY_RS_INSTRUCTION,
```

```
33                                  DISPLAY_IR_FUNCTION_SET |
34                                  DISPLAY_IR_FUNCTION_SET_8BITS );
35          delay( 1 );
36
37          switch( display.connection ) {
38              case DISPLAY_CONNECTION_GPIO_8BITS:
39              case DISPLAY_CONNECTION_SPI:
40                  displayCodeWrite( DISPLAY_RS_INSTRUCTION,
41                                    DISPLAY_IR_FUNCTION_SET |
42                                    DISPLAY_IR_FUNCTION_SET_8BITS |
43                                    DISPLAY_IR_FUNCTION_SET_2LINES |
44                                    DISPLAY_IR_FUNCTION_SET_5x8DOTS );
45                  delay( 1 );
46                  break;
47
48              case DISPLAY_CONNECTION_GPIO_4BITS:
49              case DISPLAY_CONNECTION_I2C_PCF8574_IO_EXPANDER:
50                  displayCodeWrite( DISPLAY_RS_INSTRUCTION,
51                                    DISPLAY_IR_FUNCTION_SET |
52                                    DISPLAY_IR_FUNCTION_SET_4BITS );
53                  delay( 1 );
54
55                  initial8BitCommunicationIsCompleted = true;
56
57                  displayCodeWrite( DISPLAY_RS_INSTRUCTION,
58                                    DISPLAY_IR_FUNCTION_SET |
59                                    DISPLAY_IR_FUNCTION_SET_4BITS |
60                                    DISPLAY_IR_FUNCTION_SET_2LINES |
61                                    DISPLAY_IR_FUNCTION_SET_5x8DOTS );
62                  delay( 1 );
63                  break;
64          }
```

Code 6.34 New implementation of the function displayInit() (Part 1/2).

```
1           displayCodeWrite( DISPLAY_RS_INSTRUCTION,
2                             DISPLAY_IR_DISPLAY_CONTROL |
3                             DISPLAY_IR_DISPLAY_CONTROL_DISPLAY_OFF |
4                             DISPLAY_IR_DISPLAY_CONTROL_CURSOR_OFF |
5                             DISPLAY_IR_DISPLAY_CONTROL_BLINK_OFF );
6           delay( 1 );
7
8           displayCodeWrite( DISPLAY_RS_INSTRUCTION,
9                             DISPLAY_IR_CLEAR_DISPLAY );
10          delay( 1 );
11
12              displayCodeWrite( DISPLAY_RS_INSTRUCTION,
13                                DISPLAY_IR_ENTRY_MODE_SET |
14                                DISPLAY_IR_ENTRY_MODE_SET_INCREMENT |
15                                DISPLAY_IR_ENTRY_MODE_SET_NO_SHIFT );
16          delay( 1 );
17
18          displayCodeWrite( DISPLAY_RS_INSTRUCTION,
19                            DISPLAY_IR_DISPLAY_CONTROL |
20                                DISPLAY_IR_DISPLAY_CONTROL_DISPLAY_ON |
21                                DISPLAY_IR_DISPLAY_CONTROL_CURSOR_OFF |
22                                DISPLAY_IR_DISPLAY_CONTROL_BLINK_OFF );
23          delay( 1 );
24      }
```

Code 6.35 New implementation of the function displayInit() (Part 2/2).

In Code 6.36, the new implementation of *displayCodeWrite()* is shown. The new code is between lines 15 and 30, where the case of DISPLAY_CONNECTION_SPI is addressed. On line 16, *spi.lock()* is used to acquire exclusive access to the SPI bus. On line 17, *spiSt7920ChipSelect* is set to ON. Line 18 assesses if the code corresponds to an instruction. If so, lines 19 to 21 are used to write the first byte to the SPI bus, following the format that was introduced in Figure 6.28. Otherwise, lines 23 to 25 are executed, to transfer the first byte with the RS bit set to 1 because ST7920_SPI_RS_DATA is defined as 0b000000010.

Line 26 is used to send the second byte using *"dataBus & 0b11110000"*. In this way, only the D7 to D4 bits of *dataBus* are transferred, followed by four zeros. Line 27 is used to send the third byte by means of *"(dataBus<<4) & 0b11110000"*. The <<4 bitwise operation is used to shift the bits of dataBus four positions to the left. In this way, the D3 to D0 bits are placed in the first part of the byte, as shown in the third byte of Figure 6.28. Line 28 is used to set *spiSt7920ChipSelect* to OFF. Finally, on line 29, *spiSt7920.unlock()* is used to release exclusive access to this SPI bus.

In Code 6.37 and Code 6.38, the implementation of *displayCharPositionWrite()* is shown. In line 3, an *if* statement is used to evaluate if *display.type* is DISPLAY_TYPE_LCD_HD44780. If so, the switch statement of line 4 is executed, which has the same code as in previous examples. Line 9 of Code 6.38 evaluates if *display.type* is DISPLAY_TYPE_GLCD_ST7920; in that case, the *switch* statement of line 10 is executed. It is important to note that *charPositionX/2* is used in lines 15, 23, 31, and 39. This is due to the reasons explained regarding Figure 6.27.

 NOTE: In this example, the implementation of *displayStringWrite()* is not shown, since this function was not modified in this example. The modifications introduced in *displayPinWrite()* and *displayDataBusWrite()* were already discussed in Code 6.33.

```
1    static void displayCodeWrite( bool type, uint8_t dataBus )
2    {
3        switch( display.connection ) {
4            case DISPLAY_CONNECTION_GPIO_8BITS:
5            case DISPLAY_CONNECTION_GPIO_4BITS:
6            case DISPLAY_CONNECTION_I2C_PCF8574_IO_EXPANDER:
7                if ( type == DISPLAY_RS_INSTRUCTION )
8                    displayPinWrite( DISPLAY_PIN_RS, DISPLAY_RS_INSTRUCTION);
9                else
10                   displayPinWrite( DISPLAY_PIN_RS, DISPLAY_RS_DATA);
11               displayPinWrite( DISPLAY_PIN_RW, DISPLAY_RW_WRITE );
12               displayDataBusWrite( dataBus );
13               break;
14
15           case DISPLAY_CONNECTION_SPI:
16               spiSt7920.lock();
17               spiSt7920ChipSelect = ON;
18               if ( type == DISPLAY_RS_INSTRUCTION )
19                   spiSt7920.write( ST7920_SPI_SYNCHRONIZING_BIT_STRING |
20                                    ST7920_SPI_RW_WRITE |
21                                    ST7920_SPI_RS_INSTRUCTION );
22               else
23                   spiSt7920.write( ST7920_SPI_SYNCHRONIZING_BIT_STRING |
24                                    ST7920_SPI_RW_WRITE |
```

```
25                                          ST7920_SPI_RS_DATA );
26                spiSt7920.write( dataBus & 0b11110000 );
27                spiSt7920.write( (dataBus<<4) & 0b11110000 );
28                spiSt7920ChipSelect = OFF;
29                spiSt7920.unlock();
30                break;
31        }
32  }
```

Code 6.36 New implementation of the function displayCodeWrite().

```
1  void displayCharPositionWrite( uint8_t charPositionX, uint8_t charPositionY )
2  {
3      if( display.type == DISPLAY_TYPE_LCD_HD44780 ) {
4          switch( charPositionY ) {
5              case 0:
6                  displayCodeWrite( DISPLAY_RS_INSTRUCTION,
7                                    DISPLAY_IR_SET_DDRAM_ADDR |
8                                    ( DISPLAY_20x4_LINE1_FIRST_CHARACTER_ADDRESS +
9                                      charPositionX ) );
10                 delay( 1 );
11                 break;
12
13             case 1:
14                 displayCodeWrite( DISPLAY_RS_INSTRUCTION,
15                                   DISPLAY_IR_SET_DDRAM_ADDR |
16                                   ( DISPLAY_20x4_LINE2_FIRST_CHARACTER_ADDRESS +
17                                     charPositionX ) );
18                 delay( 1 );
19                 break;
20
21             case 2:
22                 displayCodeWrite( DISPLAY_RS_INSTRUCTION,
23                                   DISPLAY_IR_SET_DDRAM_ADDR |
24                                   ( DISPLAY_20x4_LINE3_FIRST_CHARACTER_ADDRESS +
25                                     charPositionX ) );
26                 delay( 1 );
27                 break;
```

Code 6.37 New implementation of the function displayCharPositionWrite() (Part 1/2).

```
1              case 3:
2                  displayCodeWrite( DISPLAY_RS_INSTRUCTION,
3                                    DISPLAY_IR_SET_DDRAM_ADDR |
4                                    ( DISPLAY_20x4_LINE4_FIRST_CHARACTER_ADDRESS +
5                                      charPositionX ) );
6                  delay( 1 );
7                  break;
8          }
9      } else if( display.type == DISPLAY_TYPE_GLCD_ST7920 ) {
10         switch( charPositionY ) {
11             case 0:
12                 displayCodeWrite( DISPLAY_RS_INSTRUCTION,
13                                   DISPLAY_IR_SET_DDRAM_ADDR |
14                                   ( DISPLAY_ST7920_LINE1_FIRST_CHARACTER_ADDRESS +
15                                     charPositionX/2 ) );
16                 delay( 1 );
17                 break;
18
```

```
19              case 1:
20                  displayCodeWrite( DISPLAY_RS_INSTRUCTION,
21                              DISPLAY_IR_SET_DDRAM_ADDR |
22                              ( DISPLAY_ST7920_LINE2_FIRST_CHARACTER_ADDRESS +
23                                  charPositionX/2 ) );
24                  delay( 1 );
25                  break;
26
27              case 2:
28                  displayCodeWrite( DISPLAY_RS_INSTRUCTION,
29                              DISPLAY_IR_SET_DDRAM_ADDR |
30                              ( DISPLAY_ST7920_LINE3_FIRST_CHARACTER_ADDRESS +
31                                  charPositionX/2 ) );
32                  delay( 1 );
33                  break;
34
35              case 3:
36                  displayCodeWrite( DISPLAY_RS_INSTRUCTION,
37                              DISPLAY_IR_SET_DDRAM_ADDR |
38                              ( DISPLAY_ST7920_LINE4_FIRST_CHARACTER_ADDRESS +
39                                  charPositionX/2 ) );
40                  delay( 1 );
41                  break;
42          }
43      }
44  }
```

Code 6.38 New implementation of the function displayCharPositionWrite() (Part 2/2).

Proposed Exercise

1. How should *displayInit()* be called if a character LCD display is used with a 4-bit mode connection?

Answer to the Exercise

1. The function call should be made as follows:

```
displayInit ( DISPLAY_TYPE_LCD_HD44780, DISPLAY_CONNECTION_GPIO_4BITS );
```

Example 6.5: Use of the Graphic Capabilities of the Graphical LCD Display

Objective

Introduce the use of the graphic mode of the graphical LCD display.

Summary of the Expected Behavior

The expected behavior is similar to the previous examples, the difference being that when the alarm is activated the display is changed to graphic mode, and an animation of a fire burning, together with a "FIRE ALARM ACTIVATED!" legend, is shown. When the alarm is deactivated, the display is configured again to character mode and its behavior returns to the behavior of the previous examples.

Test the Proposed Solution on the Board

Import the project "Example 6.5" using the URL available in [3], build the project, and drag the *.bin* file onto the NUCLEO board. Follow the same steps as indicated in the section "Test the Proposed Solution on the Board" of Example 6.1. The present temperature, gas detector, and alarm states should be shown on the display. When the alarm is activated, an animation composed of the four images shown in Figure 6.35 should be displayed.

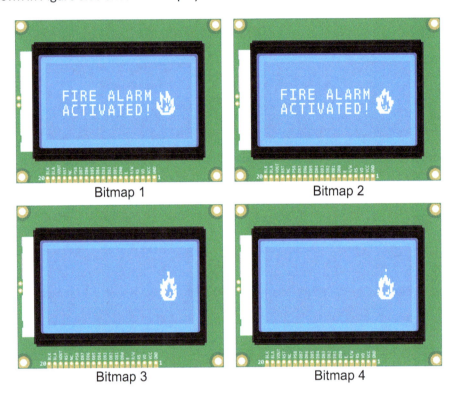

Figure 6.35 Frames of the animation that are shown when the alarm is activated.

Discussion of the Proposed Solution

In this example, the functions *displayModeWrite()* and *displayBitmapWrite()* are included. The former allows selecting between character mode and graphic mode, while the latter is used to send a bitmap to the graphical LCD display.

Implementation of the Proposed Solution

In Table 6.10, the sections where lines were added to the file *user_interface.cpp* are summarized. It can be seen that the file *GLCD_fire_alarm.h* has been included. This file has the bitmaps shown in Figure 6.35. There are also two new #defines, which are used to control the refresh time of the display: DISPLAY_REFRESH_TIME_REPORT_MS, which replaces the previous #define (removed), as shown in Table 6.11, and DISPLAY_REFRESH_TIME_ALARM_MS, which is used when the animation is shown.

Table 6.10 also shows the declaration of a new data type, *displayState_t*, which is used to control the display, as will be shown below. Three private global variables are declared, as shown in Table 6.10. Finally, four private functions are declared, which will be explained below.

Table 6.10 Sections in which lines were added to user_interface.cpp.

Section or function	Lines that were added
Libraries	`#include "GLCD_fire_alarm.h"`
Definitions	`#define DISPLAY_REFRESH_TIME_REPORT_MS 1000` `#define DISPLAY_REFRESH_TIME_ALARM_MS 300`

Declaration of private data types	`typedef enum{`
	`    DISPLAY_ALARM_STATE,`
	`    DISPLAY_REPORT_STATE`
	`} displayState_t;`

Declaration and initialization of private global variables	`static displayState_t displayState = DISPLAY_REPORT_STATE;`
	`static int displayAlarmGraphicSequence = 0;`
	`static int displayRefreshTimeMs = DISPLAY_REFRESH_TIME_REPORT_MS;`

Declarations (prototypes) of private functions	`static void userInterfaceDisplayReportStateInit();`
	`static void userInterfaceDisplayReportStateUpdate();`
	`static void userInterfaceDisplayAlarmStateInit();`
	`static void userInterfaceDisplayAlarmStateUpdate();`

Table 6.11 Sections in which lines were removed from user_interface.cpp.

Section or function	Lines that were removed
Definitions	`#define DISPLAY_REFRESH_TIME_MS 1000`

In Code 6.39, the new public data type *displayMode_t* is shown. It has two valid values, DISPLAY_MODE_CHAR and DISPLAY_MODE_GRAPHIC. This data type is incorporated into the *display_t*, as shown in Code 6.39.

```
1  typedef enum {
2       DISPLAY_MODE_CHAR,
3       DISPLAY_MODE_GRAPHIC
4  } displayMode_t;
5
6  typedef struct {
7     displayConnection_t connection;
8     displayType_t type;
9     displayMode_t mode;
10 } display_t;
```

Code 6.39 New private data types declared in display.h.

In Code 6.40, the new #defines that are introduced in *display.cpp* are shown. DISPLAY_IR_SET_GDRAM_ADDR is used to establish the GDRAM address. The other #defines are used to implement the instructions shown in blue in Table 6.6.

```
1   #define DISPLAY_IR_SET_GDRAM_ADDR   0b10000000
2
3   #define DISPLAY_IR_FUNCTION_SET_EXTENDED_INSTRUCION_SET  0b00000100
4   #define DISPLAY_IR_FUNCTION_SET_BASIC_INSTRUCION_SET     0b00000000
5   #define DISPLAY_IR_FUNCTION_SET_GRAPHIC_DISPLAY_ON       0b00000010
6   #define DISPLAY_IR_FUNCTION_SET_GRAPHIC_DISPLAY_OFF      0b00000000
```

Code 6.40 Declaration of new private #defines in display.cpp.

In Code 6.41, the new implementation of the function *userInterfaceDisplayUpdate()* is shown. It is now divided into two different states. In the case of DISPLAY_REPORT_STATE, the behavior is similar to the previous examples, except that the Alarm ON state is not shown. In order to implement this functionality, the new function *userInterfaceDisplayReportStateUpdate()* is used.

When the siren is active, *userInterfaceDisplayAlarmStateInit()* is called (line 15), which changes the state of the variable *displayState* to DISPLAY_ALARM_STATE and makes the display change to graphic mode.

When the siren is not activated, the function *userInterfaceDisplayReportStateInit()* is called (line 23). As discussed below, this function changes the state of the variable *displayState* to DISPLAY_REPORT_STATE and also makes the display change to character mode.

Finally, note that *displayRefreshTimeMs* is configured in *userInterfaceDisplayAlarmStateInit()* and *userInterfaceDisplayReportStateInit()*, because different refresh time values are used depending on the state of the display (DISPLAY_ALARM_STATE or DISPLAY_REPORT_STATE).

```
1   static void userInterfaceDisplayUpdate()
2   {
3       static int accumulatedDisplayTime = 0;
4
5       if( accumulatedDisplayTime >=
6           displayRefreshTimeMs ) {
7
8           accumulatedDisplayTime = 0;
9
10          switch ( displayState ) {
11              case DISPLAY_REPORT_STATE:
12                  userInterfaceDisplayReportStateUpdate();
13
14                  if ( sirenStateRead() ) {
15                      userInterfaceDisplayAlarmStateInit();
16                  }
17                  break;
18
19              case DISPLAY_ALARM_STATE:
20                  userInterfaceDisplayAlarmStateUpdate();
21
22                  if ( !sirenStateRead() ) {
23                      userInterfaceDisplayReportStateInit();
24                  }
25                  break;
```

```
26
27                  default:
28                      userInterfaceDisplayReportStateInit();
29                      break;
30              }
31
32      } else {
33          accumulatedDisplayTime =
34              accumulatedDisplayTime + SYSTEM_TIME_INCREMENT_MS;
35      }
36  }
```

Code 6.41 New implementation of the function userInterfaceDisplayUpdate().

The function *userInterfaceDisplayInit()*, shown in Code 6.42, is simpler than in the previous examples, as some parts of the initialization are made in *userInterfaceDisplayReportStateInit()*. Note that in the previous examples the strings "Temperature:", "Gas:", and "Alarm:" were written once at the beginning and not modified again. In this example, those strings should be output whenever the display returns to the DISPLAY_REPORT_STATE.

In this example, the implementation of *displayInit()* is not shown, as there is only one new line, which is used to set the new field *mode* of the variable *display* to DISPLAY_MODE_CHAR. The display is always initialized in character mode, and *displayModeWrite()* should be used to change to graphic mode.

```
1   static void userInterfaceDisplayInit()
2   {
3       displayInit( DISPLAY_TYPE_GLCD_ST7920, DISPLAY_CONNECTION_SPI );
4       userInterfaceDisplayReportStateInit();
5   }
```

Code 6.42 New implementation of the function userInterfaceDisplayInit().

In Code 6.43, the new function *userInterfaceDisplayReportStateInit()* is shown. It has some statements that were previously in the function *userInterfaceDisplayInit()*. This function also configures the display state, the refresh time, and the display to char mode, which is established by means of *displayModeWrite()* on line 6. It can be seen that there is also a new function, *displayClear()*, which is used to clear everything that might be written on the display.

```
1   static void userInterfaceDisplayReportStateInit()
2   {
3       displayState = DISPLAY_REPORT_STATE;
4       displayRefreshTimeMs = DISPLAY_REFRESH_TIME_REPORT_MS;
5
6       displayModeWrite( DISPLAY_MODE_CHAR );
7
8       displayClear();
9
10      displayCharPositionWrite ( 0,0 );
11      displayStringWrite( "Temperature:" );
12
13      displayCharPositionWrite ( 0,1 );
14      displayStringWrite( "Gas:" );
15
16      displayCharPositionWrite ( 0,2 );
17      displayStringWrite( "Alarm:" );
18  }
19
```

Code 6.43 Implementation of the function userInterfaceDisplayReportStateInit().

The public function *displayClear()* is implemented in *display.cpp*, as shown in Code 6.44. In line 3, *displayCodeWrite()* is used to send the "Display Clear" instruction to the display. In line 5, a 2-millisecond delay is implemented.

```
1   void displayClear( void )
2   {
3       displayCodeWrite( DISPLAY_RS_INSTRUCTION,
4                         DISPLAY_IR_CLEAR_DISPLAY );
5       delay( 2 );
6   }
```

Code 6.44 Implementation of the function displayClear().

In Code 6.45, *userInterfaceDisplayReportStateUpdate()* is shown. It mostly includes code that previously was in *userInterfaceDisplayUpdate()*.

```
1   static void userInterfaceDisplayReportStateUpdate()
2   {
3       char temperatureString[3] = "";
4
5       sprintf(temperatureString, "%.0f", temperatureSensorReadCelsius());
6       displayCharPositionWrite ( 12,0 );
7       displayStringWrite( temperatureString );
8       displayCharPositionWrite ( 14,0 );
9       displayStringWrite( "'C" );
10
11      displayCharPositionWrite ( 4,1 );
12
13      if ( gasDetectorStateRead() ) {
14          displayStringWrite( "Detected      " );
15      } else {
16          displayStringWrite( "Not Detected" );
17      }
18      displayCharPositionWrite ( 6,2 );
19      displayStringWrite( "OFF" );
20  }
```

Code 6.45 Implementation of the function userInterfaceDisplayReportStateUpdate().

The implementation of *userInterfaceDisplayAlarmStateInit()* is shown in Code 6.46. This function initializes the display by means of configuring the state of the display to DISPLAY_ALARM_STATE, changing the refresh time, clearing the display, and changing to graphic mode. The variable *displayAlarmGraphicSequence*, which is related to the animation that is displayed, is also initialized.

```
1   static void userInterfaceDisplayAlarmStateInit()
2   {
3       displayState = DISPLAY_ALARM_STATE;
4       displayRefreshTimeMs = DISPLAY_REFRESH_TIME_ALARM_MS;
5
6       displayClear();
7
8       displayModeWrite( DISPLAY_MODE_GRAPHIC );
9
10      displayAlarmGraphicSequence = 0;
11  }
```

Code 6.46 Implementation of the function userInterfaceDisplayAlarmStateInit().

The images that comprise the fire burning animation are declared in a new filename, *GLCD_fire_alarm.h*, which is now included in the *display* module. The most relevant lines of this file are shown in Code 6.47 and Code 6.48. Code 6.47 shows the declaration of the array *GLCD_ClearScreen*. It has 1024 elements in correspondence with the 8 columns, each having two bytes, and 64 rows that were introduced in Figure 6.31 (i.e., 1024 = 8 × 2 × 64). All its elements are declared as zero using hexadecimal notation (0x00). For the sake of brevity, only some of the elements are shown.

In Code 6.48, the declaration of *GLCD_fire_alarm* is shown. It has four parts, each having 1024 elements, as is indicated in line 1. For the sake of brevity, only some of the elements are shown with the aim of illustrating that each of the four images that compose the fire burning animation is defined using a different set of bytes.

```
1    uint8_t GLCD_ClearScreen[1024] = {
2    0x00, 0x00, 0x00, 0x00, 0x00, 0x00, 0x00, 0x00, 0x00, 0x00, 0x00, 0x00, 0x00, 0x00,
3    0x00, 0x00, 0x00, 0x00, 0x00, 0x00, 0x00, 0x00, 0x00, 0x00, 0x00, 0x00, 0x00, 0x00,
4    ...
5    0x00, 0x00, 0x00, 0x00, 0x00, 0x00, 0x00, 0x00, 0x00, 0x00, 0x00, 0x00, 0x00, 0x00,
6    };
```

Code 6.47 Summary of the content of GLCD_fire_alarm.h (Part 1/2).

```
1    uint8_t GLCD_fire_alarm[4][1024] = {
2    {
3    0x00, 0x00, 0x00, 0x00, 0x00, 0x00, 0x00, 0x00, 0x00, 0x00, 0x00, 0x00, 0x00, 0x00,
4    ...
5    0x00, 0x01, 0xF1, 0xF1, 0xE1, 0xF0, 0x00, 0x41, 0x00, 0x41, 0xE1, 0x10, 0x00, 0x00,
6    ...
7    0x00, 0x00, 0x00, 0x00, 0x00, 0x00, 0x00, 0x00, 0x00, 0x00, 0x00, 0x00, 0x00, 0x00,
8    },
9    {
10   0x00, 0x00, 0x00, 0x00, 0x00, 0x00, 0x00, 0x00, 0x00, 0x00, 0x00, 0x00, 0x00, 0x00,
11   ...
12   0x00, 0x01, 0x00, 0x41, 0x11, 0x00, 0x00, 0xA1, 0x00, 0xA1, 0x11, 0x10, 0x00, 0xC0,
13   ...
14   0x00, 0x00, 0x00, 0x00, 0x00, 0x00, 0x00, 0x00, 0x00, 0x00, 0x00, 0x00, 0x00, 0x00,
15   },
16   {
17   0x00, 0x00, 0x00, 0x00, 0x00, 0x00, 0x00, 0x00, 0x00, 0x00, 0x00, 0x00, 0x00, 0x00,
18   ...
19   0x00, 0x00, 0x04, 0x7E, 0x00, 0x00, 0x00, 0x00, 0x00, 0x00, 0x00, 0x00, 0x00, 0x00,
20   ...
21   0x00, 0x00, 0x00, 0x00, 0x00, 0x00, 0x00, 0x00, 0x00, 0x00, 0x00, 0x00, 0x00, 0x00,
22   },
23   {
24   0x00, 0x00, 0x00, 0x00, 0x00, 0x00, 0x00, 0x00, 0x00, 0x00, 0x00, 0x00, 0x00, 0x00,
25   ...
26   0x00, 0x00, 0x1F, 0x79, 0x00, 0x00, 0x00, 0x00, 0x00, 0x00, 0x00, 0x00, 0x00, 0x00
27   ...
28   0x00, 0x00, 0x00, 0x00, 0x00, 0x00, 0x00, 0x00, 0x00, 0x00, 0x00, 0x00, 0x00, 0x00,
29   }
30   };
```

Code 6.48 Summary of the content of GLCD_fire_alarm.h (Part 2/2).

The function *userInterfaceDisplayAlarmStateUpdate()*, shown in Code 6.49, writes each of the four images that comprise the fire burning animation to the LCD shown in Figure 6.35. It can be seen that the function *displayBitmapWrite()* is used to write each of the images, which are defined in the *GLCD_fire_alarm.h* file.

```
1   static void userInterfaceDisplayAlarmStateUpdate()
2   {
3       switch( displayAlarmGraphicSequence ){
4           case 0:
5               displayBitmapWrite( GLCD_fire_alarm[0] );
6               displayAlarmGraphicSequence++;
7               break;
8           case 1:
9               displayBitmapWrite( GLCD_fire_alarm[1] );
10              displayAlarmGraphicSequence++;
11              break;
12          case 2:
13              displayBitmapWrite( GLCD_fire_alarm[2] );
14              displayAlarmGraphicSequence++;
15              break;
16          case 3:
17              displayBitmapWrite( GLCD_fire_alarm[3] );
18              displayAlarmGraphicSequence = 0;
19              break;
20          default:
21              displayBitmapWrite( GLCD_ClearScreen  );
22              displayAlarmGraphicSequence = 1;
23              break;
24      }
25  }
```

Code 6.49 Implementation of the function userInterfaceDisplayAlarmStateUpdate().

In Code 6.50, the implementation of the function *displayBitmapWrite()* of the *display* module is shown. The *for* loop on line 4 is used to increase the y coordinate of the image. If y is less than 32 (line 5), the top half of the screen is drawn using the *for* loop in lines 6 to 17. In extended instruction mode, vertical and horizontal coordinates must be specified before sending data. The vertical coordinate of the screen is specified first (line 7), then the horizontal coordinate of the screen is specified (line 10). On lines 13 and 15, the upper and lower bytes are sent to the coordinate (as shown in Figure 6.31). If y is not less than 32, then the operation is very similar, but the addresses are changed as shown in lines 20 and 23 of Code 6.50, following the ideas that were introduced in Figure 6.31.

```
1   void displayBitmapWrite( uint8_t* bitmap )
2   {
3       uint8_t x, y;
4       for( y=0; y<64; y++ ) {
5           if ( y < 32 ) {
6               for( x = 0; x < 8; x++ ) {
7                   displayCodeWrite( DISPLAY_RS_INSTRUCTION,
8                                     DISPLAY_IR_SET_GDRAM_ADDR |
9                                     y );
10                  displayCodeWrite( DISPLAY_RS_INSTRUCTION,
11                                    DISPLAY_IR_SET_GDRAM_ADDR |
12                                    x );
13                  displayCodeWrite(DISPLAY_RS_DATA,
```

```
14                                    bitmap[16*y + 2*x] );
15                 displayCodeWrite(DISPLAY_RS_DATA,
16                                    bitmap[16*y + 2*x+1] );
17             }
18         } else {
19             for( x = 0; x < 8; x++ ) {
20                 displayCodeWrite( DISPLAY_RS_INSTRUCTION,
21                                    DISPLAY_IR_SET_GDRAM_ADDR |
22                                    (y-32) );
23                 displayCodeWrite( DISPLAY_RS_INSTRUCTION,
24                                    DISPLAY_IR_SET_GDRAM_ADDR |
25                                    (x+8) );
26                 displayCodeWrite(DISPLAY_RS_DATA,
27                                    bitmap[16*y + 2*x]);
28                 displayCodeWrite(DISPLAY_RS_DATA,
29                                    bitmap[16*y + 2*x+1]);
30             }
31         }
32     }
33 }
```

Code 6.50 Implementation of the function displayBitmapWrite().

 NOTE: The function *displayBitmapWrite()* involves sending hundreds of bytes to the graphical display, which interferes with the time management of the strobe light and the siren. In this way, when gas and over temperature are detected, the time off and on of the strobe light and the siren is not always 100 ms as expected. This problem will be addressed in the next chapters as new concepts are introduced.

In Code 6.51, the implementation of *displayModeWrite()* is shown. On line 3, the *mode* parameter is compared to DISPLAY_MODE_GRAPHIC. If they are equal, the display is configured to graphic mode by means of the statements between lines 5 and 15. Otherwise, if *mode* is equal to DISPLAY_MODE_CHAR, then the display is configured to character mode by means of the statements in lines 17 to 22.

```
1  void displayModeWrite( displayMode_t mode )
2  {
3      if ( mode == DISPLAY_MODE_GRAPHIC )
4      {
5          displayCodeWrite( DISPLAY_RS_INSTRUCTION,
6                            DISPLAY_IR_FUNCTION_SET   |
7                            DISPLAY_IR_FUNCTION_SET_8BITS |
8                            DISPLAY_IR_FUNCTION_SET_EXTENDED_INSTRUCION_SET );
9          delay(1);
10         displayCodeWrite( DISPLAY_RS_INSTRUCTION,
11                           DISPLAY_IR_FUNCTION_SET   |
12                           DISPLAY_IR_FUNCTION_SET_8BITS |
13                           DISPLAY_IR_FUNCTION_SET_EXTENDED_INSTRUCION_SET |
14                           DISPLAY_IR_FUNCTION_SET_GRAPHIC_DISPLAY_ON   );
15         delay(1);
16     } else if ( mode == DISPLAY_MODE_CHAR ) {
17         displayCodeWrite( DISPLAY_RS_INSTRUCTION,
18                           DISPLAY_IR_FUNCTION_SET |
19                           DISPLAY_IR_FUNCTION_SET_8BITS |
20                           DISPLAY_IR_FUNCTION_SET_BASIC_INSTRUCION_SET |
21                           DISPLAY_IR_FUNCTION_SET_GRAPHIC_DISPLAY_OFF);
22         delay(1);
23     }
24 }
```

Code 6.51 Implementation of the function displayModeWrite().

Proposed Exercise

1. How can a blank screen be added at the end of the animation shown when the alarm is activated?

Answer to the Exercise

1. The function *userInterfaceDisplayAlarmStateUpdate()* should be modified as shown in Code 6.52.

```
1   static void userInterfaceDisplayAlarmStateUpdate()
2   {
3       switch( displayAlarmGraphicSequence ){
4           case 0:
5               displayBitmapWrite( GLCD_fire_alarm[0] );
6               displayAlarmGraphicSequence++;
7               break;
8           case 1:
9               displayBitmapWrite( GLCD_fire_alarm[1] );
10              displayAlarmGraphicSequence++;
11              break;
12          case 2:
13              displayBitmapWrite( GLCD_fire_alarm[2] );
14              displayAlarmGraphicSequence++;
15              break;
16          case 3:
17              displayBitmapWrite( GLCD_fire_alarm[3] );
18              displayAlarmGraphicSequence++;
19              break;
20          case 4:
21              displayCommandWrite( GLCD_ClearScreen );
22              delay(2);
23              displayAlarmGraphicSequence = 0;
24              break;
25          default:
26              displayBitmapWrite( GLCD_ClearScreen );
27              displayAlarmGraphicSequence = 1;
28              break;
29      }
30  }
```

Code 6.52 Implementation of the function userInterfaceDisplayAlarmStateUpdate().

6.3 Under the Hood

6.3.1 Comparison between UART, SPI, and I2C

A comparison between the UART (which was introduced in chapter 2) and the SPI and I2C buses that were introduced in this chapter is shown in Table 6.12. It should be noted that all these communication interfaces require a wired connection between the devices. In Chapters 10 and 11, wireless communications will be introduced.

Table 6.12 Comparison between UART, SPI, and I2C.

	UART	SPI	I2C
Connectivity characteristics	Point-to-point connection (GND, TxD, and RxD connections)	Difficult to connect many devices (GND, SCLK, MOSI, MISO, SS)	Easy to chain many devices (GND, SCL, and SDA)
Maximum devices	2	Not defined (usually less than 10)	127
Maximum distance	Highest (up to 50 feet / 15 meters)	Lowest (up to 10 feet / 3 meters)	Medium (up to 33 feet / 10 meters)
Maximum data rate	Lowest (up to 460 kbps)	Highest (up to 20 Mbps)	Medium (up to 3.4 Mbps)
Number of managers	None	One	One or more
Parity bit	Available	No	No
Acknowledge bit	No	No	Yes
Advantages	Simplicity	Fastest of all these alternatives	Only two wires are required
Disadvantages	Can only connect two devices	Requires multiple SS wires	Slower when compared to SPI

 NOTE: The values shown in Table 6.12 might not be available in some devices and/or might not be attainable in real-life implementations.

 WARNING: There is usually a trade-off between distance and data rate. For example, the maximum length of an I2C link is about 1 meter at 100 kbps and about 10 meters at 10 kbps.

Proposed Exercises

1. What bus would seem to be the most appropriate for a wired connection of 20 sensors to three microcontrollers?

2. A 1 kbps data rate sensor is placed 12 meters away from the microcontroller. Which bus best suits this situation?

3. Which bus seems most appropriate to connect a 10 GB SD memory card to a microcontroller?

Answers to the Exercises

1. According to Table 7.3, the most appropriate bus seems to be I2C. The data rate of the sensors should be checked.

2. Given that there is only one sensor connected at a low data rate and considering the large distance, UART is most appropriate.

3. In this case, the data rate is critical, while the distance is very short, so SPI is the most appropriate, as will be seen in Chapter 9.

6.4 Case Study

6.4.1 LCD Usage in Mbed-Based Projects

In this chapter, a character-based LCD display and a graphical LCD display were connected to the NUCLEO board using 4-bit and 8-bit modes, the I2C bus, and the SPI bus. In Figure 6.36, some examples of other systems based on Mbed that make use of LCD displays are shown.

Figure 6.36 Examples of other systems based on Mbed that make use of LCD displays.

The system on the left of Figure 6.36 is a solar charge controller that makes use of a character-based LCD display [12]. It is interesting to note that it is provided with a matrix keypad, and its information can be accessed by means of a smartphone application. In Chapter 10, the smart home system will be configured with a BLE connection and a smartphone app.

The system on the right of Figure 6.36 is a game console with a graphical LCD display [13]. The game console is the first example in this book where the power supply is a set of batteries. Power consumption becomes a critical issue in this type of system.

Proposed Exercises

1. What is the resolution of the graphical LCD display that is used in the game console? How does this resolution compare to the resolution of the graphical LCD used in the smart home system?

2. What batteries are used by the game console? How long will these batteries last if the current consumption is about 70 mA and the batteries are rated as 600 mAh?

Answers to the Exercises

1. In one of the images available in [13] it can be seen that the resolution of the LCD graphic display of the game console is 220 × 176. This resolution is greater than the resolution of the LCD graphic display of the smart home system (128 × 64).

2. The game console uses Li-Po batteries, according to one of the images available in [13]. In that image, it is also indicated that the battery life is about eight to ten hours. Considering a current consumption of 70 mA, a battery rated as 600 mAh will last for about 8 hours (600 mAh/70 mA).

References

[1] "16x2 LCD Module_ Pinout, Diagrams, Description & Datasheet" Accessed July 9, 2021.
https://components101.com/displays/16x2-lcd-pinout-datasheet

[2] "HD44780U (LCD-II) (Dot Matrix Liquid Crystal Display Controller/Driver)". Accessed July 9, 2021.
https://www.sparkfun.com/datasheets/LCD/HD44780.pdf

[3] "GitHub - armBookCodeExamples/Directory". Accessed July 9, 2021.
https://github.com/armBookCodeExamples/Directory/

[4] "NUCLEO-F429ZI | Mbed". Accessed July 9, 2021.
https://os.mbed.com/platforms/ST-Nucleo-F429ZI/

[5] "ASCII | Wikipedia". Accessed July 9, 2021.
https://en.wikipedia.org/wiki/ASCII

[6] "I2C Serial Interface Adapter Module for LCD". Accessed July 9, 2021.
https://components101.com/modules/i2c-serial-interface-adapter-module

[7] "PCF8574 Remote 8-Bit I/O Expander for I2C Bus". Accessed July 9, 2021.
https://www.ti.com/lit/ds/symlink/pcf8574.pdf

[8] "Addressing - I2C Bus". Accessed July 9, 2021.
https://www.i2c-bus.org/addressing/

[9] "ST7290 GLCD Pinout, Features, Interfacing & Datasheet". Accessed July 9, 2021.
https://components101.com/displays/st7290-graphical-lcd

[10] "ST7920 Chinese Fonts built in LCD controller/driver". Accessed July 9, 2021.
https://pdf1.alldatasheet.es/datasheet-pdf/view/326219/SITRONIX/ST7920.html

[11] "KeyStone Architecture | Serial Peripheral Interface (SPI)". Accessed July 9, 2021.
https://www.ti.com/lit/ug/sprugp2a/sprugp2a.pdf

[12] "Solar Charge Controller | Mbed". Accessed July 9, 2021.
https://os.mbed.com/built-with-mbed/solar-charge-controller/

[13] "Game Console | Mbed". Accessed July 9, 2021.
https://os.mbed.com/built-with-mbed/game-console/

Chapter 7

DC Motor Driving using Relays
and Interrupts

7.1 Roadmap

7.1.1 What You Will Learn

After you have studied the material in this chapter, you will be able to:

- Summarize the fundamentals of relay modules and use them to control a DC motor.

- Develop programs to get and manage interrupts with the NUCLEO board.

- Summarize how LEDs are connected and used in electronic circuits.

- Describe how to connect a PIR sensor to the NUCLEO board using a digital input.

- Design and generate modifications of existing code to include new functionality.

7.1.2 Review of Previous Chapters

In previous chapters, a broad set of modules were connected to the smart home system. In order to deal with all those modules, different functions were called based on a *polling cycle*: at predefined intervals the states of the different elements of the system were checked. In this chapter, a different technique based on hardware interrupts is introduced in order to avoid the overhead of cyclically checking for a given condition. It is shown how to combine the polling cycle technique with the technique based on hardware interrupts.

7.1.3 Contents of This Chapter

In this chapter, a direct current (DC) motor will be connected to the smart home system by means of a relay module. The motion of the DC motor will be controlled with a set of buttons. In order to introduce the concept of a *hardware interrupt*, these buttons will not be polled at periodic intervals as in previous chapters. Instead, an *interrupt service routine* will be used to handle the button detection. As part of the implementation, it will be explained how to connect a pair of LEDs to indicate the rotation direction of the DC motor.

To explore the use of interrupts in further detail, a PIR-based motion sensor will be used. The output signal of this sensor will be tracked using interrupts.

Finally, some modifications of the existing code will be made in order to include a new alarm source in the smart home system: the detection of an intruder by means of the PIR sensor. A new alarm message will be shown on the display, and a different configuration for the strobe time of the light and the siren will be defined.

7.2 Motion Detection and DC Motor Control using Relays and Interrupts

7.2.1 Connect a DC Motor and a PIR Sensor to the Smart Home System

In this chapter, a PIR sensor, a motor, four buttons, and two LEDs are connected to the smart home system in order to implement the behavior shown in Figure 7.1. The PIR sensor is used to detect intruders. In that event, the alarm is activated. The motor is used to move a gate, which is activated by means of two buttons on the Gate control panel labeled "Open" and "Close", as shown in Figure 7.1. The LEDs (green and red) are used to indicate if the gate is opening or closing.

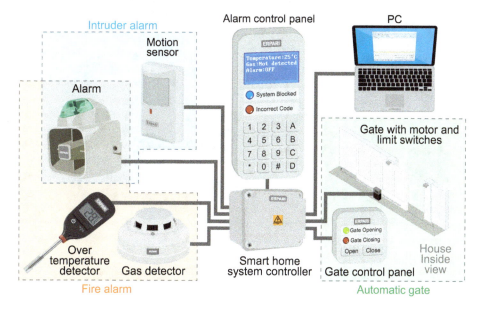

Figure 7.1 The smart home system is now connected to an LCD display.

The other two buttons that are connected in this chapter are used to simulate the limit switches that are activated when the gate is completely opened or closed (Figure 7.2). In this way, the motor is stopped when the gate reaches its travel limits.

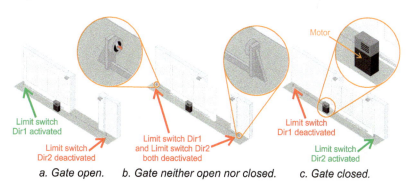

a. Gate open.   *b. Gate neither open nor closed.*   *c. Gate closed.*

Figure 7.2 Diagram of the limit switches that are considered in this chapter.

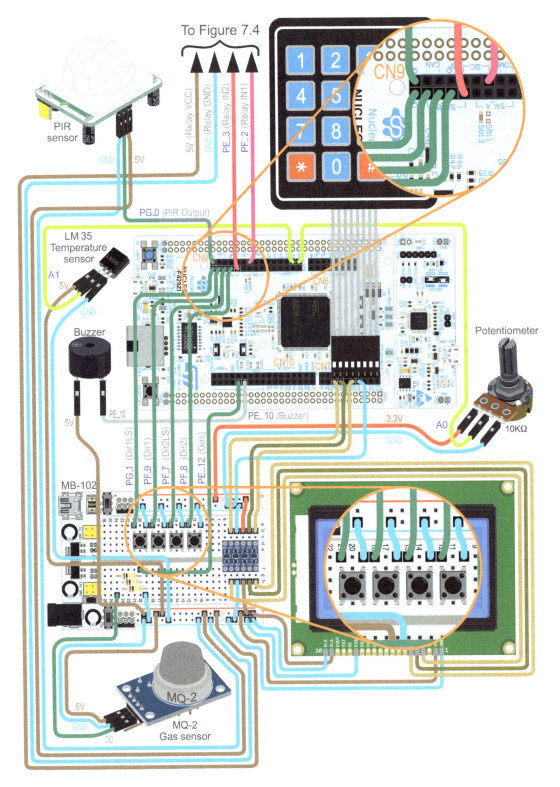

Figure 7.3 *The smart home system is now connected to a PIR sensor and a set of four buttons.*

In this chapter, a 5 V DC motor, similar to the motor shown in [1], and a HC-SR501 PIR sensor, described in [2], are connected to the smart home system, as shown in Figure 7.3 and Figure 7.4. The aim is to introduce the use of *interrupts*.

Figure 7.4 shows that a second MB102 is incorporated in the setup in order to supply the motor with an independent power supply. One of the main reasons for using relay modules in embedded systems is to turn on and off a load (such as an AC or DC motor, or a lamp) by means of a signal that is applied at the input of the relay module by a microcontroller that does not share the same power supply as the load. In this way, microcontrollers are kept safe from high voltages that might be necessary to power the load and are also *isolated* from electrical noise that could be generated when the load is activated.

 WARNING: The GND pin of the second MB102 (indicated as "GNDmotor" in Figure 7.4) is not connected to the GND of the smart home system. In this way, the power supply of the motor is properly isolated.

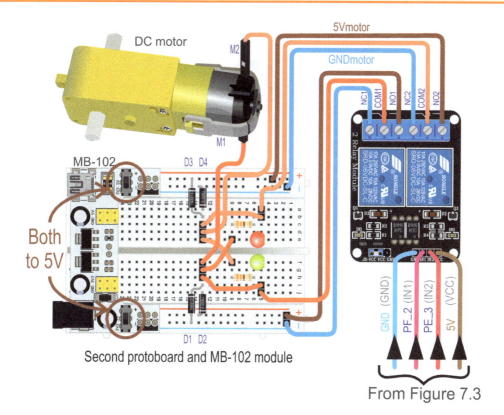

Figure 7.4 The smart home system is now connected to a 5 V DC motor using a relay module.

Figure 7.5 shows a conceptual diagram of the circuit that is used to activate the DC motor, LED1, and LED2. The circuit is based on two relays, RL1 and RL2. When IN1 is set to GND, the COM1 terminal of RL1 is connected to NO1 (Normally Open 1). This connects 5Vmotor to the M1 connector of the DC motor. When IN1 is left unconnected, the COM1 terminal of RL1 is connected to NC1 (Normally Closed 1). This connects GNDmotor to the M1 connector of the DC motor. The same behavior is obtained with RL2 when applying GND to IN2 and when IN2 is left unconnected, respectively. In this way, the DC motor can be activated and its rotation direction controlled, as shown in Table 7.1.

NOTE: The diagram shown in Figure 7.5 is presented only to illustrate the operation of the circuit. In the actual circuit, the inputs IN1 and IN2 are not directly connected to the relay; circuitry is used in between. The details of the actual circuit are discussed in the Under the Hood section of this chapter.

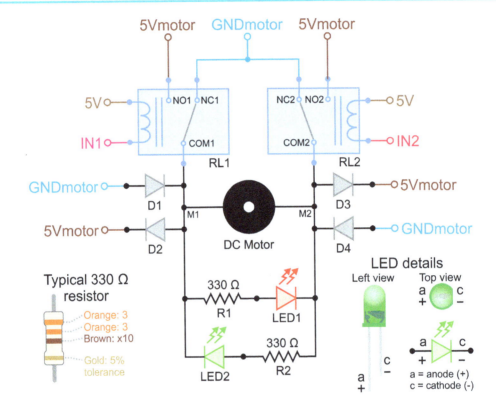

Figure 7.5 Conceptual diagram of the circuit that is used to activate the DC motor, LED1, and LED2.

Table 7.1 Summary of the signals applied to the motor depending on IN1 and IN2, and the resulting behavior.

IN1	M1	IN2	M2	Behavior
GND	5Vmotor	GND	5Vmotor	The motor does not turn (M2 – M1 = 0 V)
Unconnected	GNDmotor	GND	5Vmotor	The motor turns in one direction (M2 – M1 = +5 V)
GND	5Vmotor	Unconnected	GNDmotor	The motor turns in the other direction (M2 – M1 = –5 V)
Unconnected	GNDmotor	Unconnected	GNDmotor	The motor does not turn (M2 – M1 = 0 V)

The reader might note that by means of IN1 and IN2, the voltage of M1 and M2 is controlled. The aim of the relay is to *isolate* the *input* from the *output*. In this way, just a few micro-amperes are drained by IN1 and IN2, while about 100 milliamperes are provided to the DC motor by means of the connections to GNDmotor and 5Vmotor through the relay.

The diodes D1–D4 are to absorb inductive spikes from the motor inductance. In this way, positive spikes will be conducted to 5Vmotor and negative spikes to GNDmotor. The 1N5819 diode can be used for D1–D4.

This circuit can be used to control powerful DC motors that work with higher voltages and currents by replacing the 5Vmotor voltage supply with an appropriate power supply. Even alternating current (AC) motors can be controlled by means of relay-based circuits, although this topic is beyond the scope of this book.

The connections between the NUCLEO board and the relay module are summarized in Table 7.2, while the connections between the relay module and the breadboard are summarized in Table 7.3.

 WARNING: In some relay modules, the connections VCC and GND are labeled DC+ and DC-, respectively.

Table 7.2 Summary of the connections between the NUCLEO board and the relay module.

NUCLEO board	Relay module
PF_2	IN1
PE_3	IN2

Table 7.3 Summary of other connections that should be made to the relay module.

Relay module	Element
VCC	5V
GND	GND
NO1	5Vmotor
COM1	M1
NC2	GNDmotor
NO2	5Vmotor
COM2	M2
NC2	GNDmotor

In Figure 7.5, it can be seen that there are two LEDs, LED1 and LED2, connected in opposite directions (i.e., LED1 *points* from M1 to M2, while LED2 *points* from M2 to M1). These LEDs are to indicate the motor's turning direction. An LED turns on only if the voltage at its anode is higher than the voltage at its cathode. In Figure 7.5, a detailed drawing of an LED is shown, which helps to identify its anode and cathode. Given the connections shown in Figure 7.5, LED1 will turn on when the voltage in M1 is greater than the voltage in M2 ($V_{M1} > V_{M2}$), while LED2 will turn when $V_{M2} > V_{M1}$. The resistors R1 and R2 are used to limit the current across the LED. Figure 7.5 shows how to identify a typical 330 Ω resistor that has a tolerance of 5% of its value.

WARNING: Be sure to use 330 Ω resistors and to connect LED1 and LED2 as indicated in Figure 7.5. Otherwise, the LEDs may be damaged and/or not turn on as expected. The tolerance of the resistor and its maximum power dissipation are not relevant. Nor is it relevant whether it is a carbon or metal film resistor.

The *passive infrared sensor* (PIR sensor) works on the basis that all objects emit heat energy in the form of radiation at infrared wavelengths. This radiation is not visible to the human eye but can be detected by electronic devices. A PIR sensor detects changes in the amount of infrared radiation impinging upon it, which varies depending on the temperature and surface characteristics of the objects in front of the sensor.

The term *passive* refers to the fact that PIR devices do not radiate energy for detection purposes but work by detecting infrared radiation (radiant heat) *emitted by* or *reflected from* objects. PIR sensors are commonly used in security alarms and automatic lighting applications.

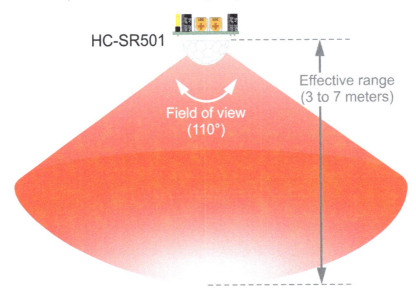

Figure 7.6 Diagram of the field of view and the effective range of the HC-SR501 PIR sensor.

For instance, when a person passes in front of a garden, the temperature at that point in the sensor's field of view will rise from the grass temperature to the body temperature. The sensor converts the change in the incoming infrared radiation into a change in its output voltage. The emitted radiation not only depends on the object's temperature but also on its surface characteristics, which can also be used to detect objects.

The most common PIR sensors have an effective range of approximately 10 meters (30 feet) and a field of view of approximately 180°. PIR sensors with a longer effective range and wider fields of view are available, as well as PIRs with very narrow coverage. The HC-SR501 PIR sensor that is used in this chapter has an effective range that is adjustable to between three and seven meters, and a field of view of 110°, as shown in Figure 7.6.

In Figure 7.7, the adjustments and the connection pins of the HC-SR501 PIR sensor are shown. The *sensitivity adjust* potentiometer can be used to set the effective range between three and seven meters. The *time delay adjust* allows configuration of the output signal duration (pulse duration) in the range of three seconds to five minutes. The jumper allows a setting of whether triggering signals are ignored when the output is active (*single trigger*) or are considered (*repeat trigger*). Note that the *repeat trigger* mode must be selected, as shown in Figure 7.7. Some HC-SR501 PIR sensors have this selection made from the factory using bond pads.

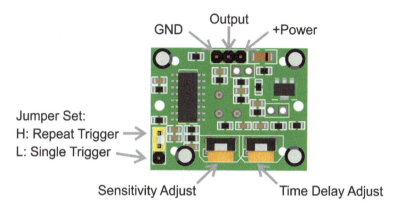

Figure 7.7 Adjustments and connector of the HC-SR501 PIR sensor.

The connection between the NUCLEO board and the HC-SR501 PIR sensor is shown in Table 7.4, while the connections between the HC-SR501 PIR sensor and the breadboard are summarized in Table 7.5.

Table 7.4 Summary of the connections between the NUCLEO board and the HC-SR501 PIR sensor.

HC-SR501 PIR sensor	NUCLEO board
Output	PG_0

Table 7.5 Summary of connections to the breadboard that should be made on the HC-SR501 PIR sensor.

HC-SR501 PIR sensor	Breadboard
GND	GND
+Power	5 V

 WARNING: It will take up to a minute for the HC-SR501 PIR sensor to stabilize after power-on. Additionally, after the output signal turns inactive, there will be a three-second delay before it can be triggered again.

To test if the HC-SR501 PIR sensor and the motor are working properly, the *.bin* file of the program "Subsection 7.2.1" should be downloaded from the URL available in [3] and loaded onto the NUCLEO board. When the HC-SR501 PIR sensor detects a movement, its output signal will become active and remain active for a time t_{Delay} given by the *time delay adjust* (as shown in Figure 7.7). The motor will turn in one direction, and one of the LEDs will turn on while the output signal of the HC-SR501 PIR sensor is active. Once the motor stops, if the sensor is activated again, the motor will turn in the other direction and the other LED will turn on. This behavior continues indefinitely.

> **WARNING:** Ignore all the other elements of the setup during the proposed test (Alarm LED, display, etc.).

> **NOTE:** Given that the repeat trigger option is selected (as indicated in Figure 7.7) during t_{Delay}, the sensor can be triggered again by a movement being detected. If that happens, the output signal will be kept active and the counting of t_{Delay} will start again from that point.

> **TIP:** This test program can be used to adjust the HC-SR501 *Time Delay Adjust*. It is convenient to select the *Single Trigger* option, as indicated in Figure 7.7, and wave a hand over the HC-SR501 PIR sensor. The motor will turn for a time of t_{Delay}. Using a screwdriver, the Time Delay Adjust can be set to make t_{Delay} last for an appropriate time, for example five seconds.

In Table 7.6, the buttons that are connected in Figure 7.3 are summarized. In many applications, such as 3D printers, limit switches are used to detect the end of travel of an object. In Figure 7.8, a typical limit switch is shown. In this chapter, tactile switches are used to represent limit switches.

Table 7.6 Summary of the buttons that are connected in Figure 7.3.

Button name	NUCLEO board
Dir1 (Direction 1)	PF_9
Dir1LS (Direction 1 Limit Switch)	PG_1
Dir2 (Direction 2)	PF_8
Dir2LS (Direction 2 Limit Switch)	PF_7

Figure 7.8 A typical limit switch. Note the connectors on the bottom: common, normally open and normally closed.

WARNING: In order to show that internal pull-up resistors can also be used to connect the buttons (instead of pull-down resistors, as in previous chapters), buttons are connected in a different way than in Chapter 1. Follow the connection diagram shown in Figure 7.3, otherwise the buttons will not work as expected.

 NOTE: *Dir1LS* and *Dir2LS* are conceived as limit switches used to deactivate the motor when a gate or tool moved by the motor reaches the end of its travel. For this reason, once *Dir1LS* is activated, the motor will not be allowed to move again in Direction 1 until it has first moved in Direction 2.

To test the buttons, press button *Dir1*. The motor should turn in one direction, and one of the LEDs should turn on. Then press button *Dir1LS*. The motor should stop, and the LED should turn off. Next, press button *Dir2*. The motor should turn in the other direction, and the other LED should turn on. Finally, press button *Dir2LS*. The motor should stop, and the LED should turn off.

7.2.2 Fundamentals of Interrupt Service Routines

Embedded systems can be configured in order to promptly execute a piece of code when a given condition takes place. This behavior is called an *interrupt*, because the normal flow of the program is altered (i.e., *interrupted*). For example, an electronically controlled lathe must prioritize a halt button related to the safety of the operator over any other functionality. If the halt button is pressed, the electronic controller must alter its normal execution flow in order to execute a given *interrupt service routine* (ISR), as shown in Figure 7.9.

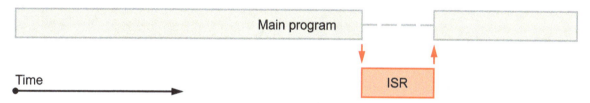

Figure 7.9 Conceptual diagram of the normal flow of a program altered by an interrupt service routine.

An interrupt can be caused by an electrical condition. For example, an interrupt is triggered when a signal connected to a microcontroller pin becomes 3.3 V. In this way, a microcontroller may have dozens of interrupt sources that might even be activated simultaneously. For this reason, it must be decided how to proceed when each of the events that can trigger an interrupt occurs. Table 7.7 shows a simplified representation of this concept. It can be seen that some interrupt sources might be active, while others are inactive, and that every active interrupt has an assigned priority and code to be executed when it is triggered.

Table 7.7 Example of an interrupt service table.

Interrupt	Assigned pin	Active/Inactive	Priority	ISR function
External hardware interrupt (INT0)	D13	Active	1	*ISRInt0()*
External hardware interrupt (INT1)	D17	Active	2	*ISRInt1()*
UART0 received byte interrupt	–	Inactive	–	*ISRUart0()*
UART1 received byte interrupt	–	Inactive	–	–
Timer0 elapsed time interrupt	–	Active	3	*ISRTimer0()*

In Table 7.7, it can be seen that interrupts can be triggered by UARTs and timers. If an interrupt from a UART is activated when a new byte (i.e., a character) is received by the UART, a given function will be executed (i.e., *ISRUart0()*). This behavior can be used to avoid *polling* the UART at regular times, as in the examples in previous chapters.

One ISR can be interrupted by another ISR, as shown in Figure 7.10. It should be noted that the priority number is used to determine which interrupt must be attended to first. In the example, ISR1 has a higher priority than ISR2. ISR1 is not interrupted by the occurrence of ISR2 (left of Figure 7.10), while ISR2 is interrupted by the occurrence of ISR1 (right of Figure 7.10).

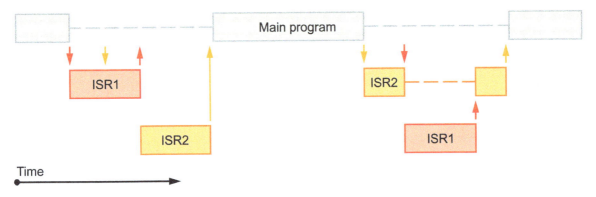

Figure 7.10 Conceptual diagram of the normal flow of a program altered by two interrupt service routines.

 NOTE: Given that one ISR can be interrupted by another ISR, and given that the normal flow of the program will be altered when an ISR is called, the complexity and operation time of the ISRs must be kept as small as possible.

Besides hardware interrupts, there are other types of interrupts, such as software interrupt instructions or software exceptions. For example, if a division by zero is executed, then a software interrupt can take place. If this occurs, the programmer may provide a piece of code to be executed to attempt to overcome the issue. This specific piece of code, also called an ISR, may be responsible for notifying the user that a division by zero is not allowed or may just set a given Boolean variable in order to later, when possible, notify the user that a division by zero is not allowed.

In the examples below, interrupts will be used to detect when buttons *Dir1*, *Dir2*, *Dir1LS*, and *Dir2LS* are pressed, as well as to detect when the PIR motion detector is activated.

> **NOTE:** The situations described in this chapter (for example, intruder detection or motor activation) might also be implemented without using interrupts. Interrupts are chosen here with the aim of introducing the topic.

Example 7.1: Control a DC Motor using Interrupts

Objective

Introduce the use of a direct current motor.

Summary of the Expected Behavior

By means of buttons *Dir1* and *Dir2*, the rotation direction of the motor is controlled. Two LEDs are used to indicate the direction in which the motor is turning.

Test the Proposed Solution on the Board

Import the project "Example 7.1" using the URL available in [3], build the project, and drag the *.bin* file onto the NUCLEO board. Press "m" on the PC keyboard. A message indicating "The motor is stopped" should be displayed on the PC. Press button *Dir1*. The motor should turn in one direction, and one of the LEDs should turn on. Press "m" again on the PC keyboard. A message indicating "The motor is turning in direction 1" should be displayed on the PC. Press button *Dir2*. The motor should turn in the other direction, and the other LED should turn on. Press "m" again on the PC keyboard. A message indicating "The motor is turning in direction 2" should be displayed on the PC.

Discussion of the Proposed Solution

The proposed solution is based on a new software module named *motor* and some new lines in the *user_interface* module. The motor is controlled by means of a new set of ISRs, which are triggered by the buttons *Dir1* and *Dir2*.

Implementation of the Proposed Solution

The initialization of the *motor* module is done at the beginning of the program by calling the function *motorControlInit()* from *smartHomeSystemInit()*, as can be seen on line 6 of Code 7.1. The function *motorControlUpdate()* is included in *smartHomeSystemUpdate()* (line 15). In order to implement these calls, the library *motor* is included in *smart_home_system.cpp*, as can be seen in Table 7.8.

```
1   void smartHomeSystemInit()
2   {
3       userInterfaceInit();
4       fireAlarmInit();
5       pcSerialComInit();
6       motorControlInit();
7   }
8
9   void smartHomeSystemUpdate()
10  {
11      userInterfaceUpdate();
12      fireAlarmUpdate();
13      pcSerialComUpdate();
14      eventLogUpdate();
15      motorControlUpdate();
16      delay(SYSTEM_TIME_INCREMENT_MS);
17  }
```

Code 7.1 New implementation of the functions smartHomeSystemInit() and smartHomeSystemUpdate().

Table 7.8 Sections in which lines were added to smart_home_system.cpp.

Section	Lines that were added
Libraries	#include "motor.h"

The implementation of *motor.cpp* is shown in Code 7.2 and Code 7.3. The libraries that are included are shown from line 3 to line 6 of Code 7.2. On line 10, the motor update time is defined. On lines 14 and 15, the global objects that will control the motor are created and assigned to available pins. It is necessary to declare these objects as *DigitalInOut* to allow the pin to be configured as *unconnected*. This is achieved by using the *.mode(OpenDrain)* configuration. On lines 19 and 20, two variables of the data type *motorDirection_t* (defined in *motor.h*) are declared.

 NOTE: For the sake of brevity, only the file sections that have some content are shown in the Code. The full versions of the files are available in [3].

```
1   //=====[Libraries]===================================================
2
3   #include "mbed.h"
4   #include "arm_book_lib.h"
5
6   #include "motor.h"
7
8   //=====[Declaration of private defines]==============================
9
10  #define MOTOR_UPDATE_TIME 9
11
12  //=====[Declaration and initialization of public global objects]=====
13
14  DigitalInOut motorM1Pin(PF_2);
15  DigitalInOut motorM2Pin(PE_3);
16
17  //=====[Declaration and initialization of public global variables]===
18
```

```
19   motorDirection_t motorDirection;
20   motorDirection_t motorState;
21
22   //=====[Implementations of public functions]===================================
23
24   void motorControlInit()
25   {
26       motorM1Pin.mode(OpenDrain);
27       motorM2Pin.mode(OpenDrain);
28
29       motorM1Pin.input();
30       motorM2Pin.input();
31
32       motorDirection = STOPPED;
33       motorState = STOPPED;
34   }
35
36   motorDirection_t motorDirectionRead()
37   {
38       return motorDirection;
39   }
40
41   void motorDirectionWrite( motorDirection_t direction )
42   {
43       motorDirection = direction;
44   }
```

Code 7.2 Implementation of motor.cpp file (Part 1/2).

On lines 24 to 34, the implementation of the function *motorControlInit()* is shown. On lines 26 and 27, the pins connected to the motor are configured as *open drain* and on lines 29 and 30 as input. In this way, both pins are in a *high impedance* state (which can be considered as unconnected), so the relays that control the motor are not energized. On lines 32 and 33, *motorDirection* and *motorState* are initialized as STOPPED. From lines 36 to 44, the implementations of the functions *motorDirectionRead()*, which returns the value of the variable *motorDirection*, and *motorDirectionWrite*, which assigns the received parameter (*Direction*) to *motorDirection*, are shown.

In Code 7.3, the implementation of the function *motorControlUpdate()* is shown. This function is responsible for the operation of the motor depending on the value of the variable *motorState*. The finite-state machine that controls the motor is executed every 100 ms, taking into account the value of MOTOR_UPDATE_TIME and the fact that *motorControlUpdate()* is called every 10 ms. If the value of *motorState* is DIRECTION_1 (the motor is turning in DIRECTION_1) and the value of *motorDirection* is DIRECTION_2 or STOPPED (lines 13 and 14), then the motor is stopped by putting both motor pins in high impedance (lines 15 and 16). The same behavior is implemented for the other direction (lines 21 to 28).

In the STOPPED state (lines 30 to 45), the direction of the motor is defined depending on the value of *motorDirection*. The pin that corresponds to the received direction is configured as output (lines 34 and 41), and LOW is assigned to it in order to activate the motor (lines 35 and 42), while the other pin is configured in high impedance (lines 33 and 40). In this way, only the relay that corresponds to the pin of the selected direction will be energized. In all cases, the variable *motorState* is updated (lines 17, 26, 36, and 43).

```
1   void motorControlUpdate()
2   {
3       static int motorUpdateCounter = 0;
4
5       motorUpdateCounter++;
6
7       if ( motorUpdateCounter > MOTOR_UPDATE_TIME ) {
8
9           motorUpdateCounter = 0;
10
11          switch ( motorState ) {
12              case DIRECTION_1:
13                  if ( motorDirection == DIRECTION_2 ||
14                       motorDirection == STOPPED ) {
15                      motorM1Pin.input();
16                      motorM2Pin.input();
17                      motorState = STOPPED;
18                  }
19                  break;
20
21              case DIRECTION_2:
22                  if ( motorDirection == DIRECTION_1 ||
23                       motorDirection == STOPPED ) {
24                      motorM1Pin.input();
25                      motorM2Pin.input();
26                      motorState = STOPPED;
27                  }
28                  break;
29
30              case STOPPED:
31              default:
32                  if ( motorDirection == DIRECTION_1 ) {
33                      motorM2Pin.input();
34                      motorM1Pin.output();
35                      motorM1Pin = LOW;
36                      motorState = DIRECTION_1;
37                  }
38
39                  if ( motorDirection == DIRECTION_2 ) {
40                      motorM1Pin.input();
41                      motorM2Pin.output();
42                      motorM2Pin = LOW;
43                      motorState = DIRECTION_2;
44                  }
45                  break;
46          }
47      }
48  }
```

Code 7.3 Implementation of motor.cpp file (Part 2/2).

In Code 7.4, the implementation of *motor.h* is shown. It can be seen that the data type *motorDirection_t* is defined on lines 8 to 12, and the prototypes of the public functions implemented in Code 7.3 are declared on lines 16 to 21.

```
1   //=====[#include guards - begin]================================================
2
3   #ifndef _MOTOR_H_
4   #define _MOTOR_H_
5
6   //=====[Declaration of public data types]=========================================
7
8   typedef enum {
9       DIRECTION_1,
10      DIRECTION_2,
11      STOPPED
12  } motorDirection_t;
13
14  //=====[Declarations (prototypes) of public functions]============================
15
16  void motorControlInit();
17  void motorDirectionWrite( motorDirection_t direction );
18
19  motorDirection_t motorDirectionRead();
20
21  void motorControlUpdate();
22
23  //=====[#include guards - end]====================================================
24
25  #endif // _MOTOR_H_
```

Code 7.4 Implementation of motor.h file.

In Table 7.9, the sections in which lines were added to *user_interface.cpp* are shown. It can be seen that *motor.h* has been included, and the public global objects of type InterruptIn *motorDirection1Button* and *motorDirection2Button* were assigned to the pins PF_9 and PF_8, respectively. The private functions *motorDirection1ButtonCallback()* and *motorDirection2ButtonCallback()* are declared.

Table 7.9 Sections in which lines were added to user_interface.cpp.

Section	Lines that were added
Libraries	`#include "motor.h"`
Declaration and initialization of public global objects	`InterruptIn motorDirection1Button(PF_9);` `InterruptIn motorDirection2Button(PF_8);`
Declarations (prototypes) of private functions	`static void motorDirection1ButtonCallback();` `static void motorDirection2ButtonCallback();`

In Code 7.5, the new implementation of the function *userInterfaceInit()* of the module *user_interface* is shown. On lines 3 and 4, the two buttons that will control the direction of the motors are configured with an internal pull-up resistor. On lines 6 and 7, the interrupt is configured for these two buttons.

Whenever a transition from high to low state (*falling edge*) is detected in those pins, a *callback function* is called. These functions are referred to as the *handlers* for the interrupts related to *motorDirection1Button.fall* and *motorDirection2Button.fall*. For pin PF_9, the callback function is *motorDirection1ButtonCallback()*, and for pin PF_8 the callback function is *motorDirection2ButtonCallback()*. Note that the callback functions are preceded by the reference operator (&). Lines 9 to 12 remain unchanged from the previous version of this function.

```
1  void userInterfaceInit()
2  {
3      motorDirection1Button.mode(PullUp);
4      motorDirection2Button.mode(PullUp);
5
6      motorDirection1Button.fall(&motorDirection1ButtonCallback);
7      motorDirection2Button.fall(&motorDirection2ButtonCallback);
8
9      incorrectCodeLed = OFF;
10     systemBlockedLed = OFF;
11     matrixKeypadInit( SYSTEM_TIME_INCREMENT_MS );
12     userInterfaceDisplayInit();
13 }
```

Code 7.5 New implementation of the function userInterfaceInit().

In Code 7.6, the implementation of the callbacks *motorDirection1ButtonCallback()* and *motorDirection2ButtonCallback()* is shown. Each of these functions calls *motorDirectionWrite()* (shown in Code 7.3) with the parameter DIRECTION_1 (line 3) or DIRECTION_2 (line 8).

```
1  static void motorDirection1ButtonCallback()
2  {
3      motorDirectionWrite( DIRECTION_1 );
4  }
5
6  static void motorDirection2ButtonCallback()
7  {
8      motorDirectionWrite( DIRECTION_2 );
9  }
```

Code 7.6 Implementation of the functions motorDirection1ButtonCallback() and motorDirection2ButtonCallback().

To implement the new command "m", the lines shown in Table 7.10 were added to *pcSerialComCommandUpdate()* and *availableCommands()* in *pc_serial_com.cpp*. In Table 7.11, the sections in which lines were added to *pc_serial_com.cpp* are shown. It can be seen that a new private function, *commandShowCurrentMotorState()*, is declared.

Table 7.10 Functions in which lines were added in pc_serial_com.cpp.

Functions	Lines that were added
static void pcSerialComCommandUpdate(char receivedChar)	`case 'm': case 'M': commandShowCurrentMotorState();` `break;`
static void availableCommands()	`pcSerialComStringWrite( "Press 'm' or 'M' to show the` `motor status\r\n" );`

Table 7.11 Sections in which lines were added in pc_serial_com.cpp.

Section	Lines that were added
Libraries	`#include "motor.h"`
Declarations (prototypes) of private functions	`static void commandShowCurrentMotorState();`

When "m" is pressed on the PC keyboard, the function *commandShowCurrentMotorState()* shown in Code 7.7 is called. On line 3, the function *motorDirectionRead()* (shown in Code 7.2) is called. One of three different messages is sent to the PC console (lines 5 to 9) depending on the returned value.

```
1   static void commandShowCurrentMotorState()
2   {
3       switch ( motorDirectionRead() ) {
4           case STOPPED:
5               pcSerialComStringWrite( "The motor is stopped\r\n" ); break;
6           case DIRECTION_1:
7               pcSerialComStringWrite( "The motor is turning in direction 1\r\n" ); break;
8           case DIRECTION_2:
9               pcSerialComStringWrite( "The motor is turning in direction 2\r\n" ); break;
10      }
11  }
```

Code 7.7 Implementation of the function commandShowCurrentMotorState().

Proposed Exercise

1. How can the program be modified in order to include a new button that stops the motor, regardless of which direction it is turning?

Answer to the Exercise

1. A new button should be included, and code should be implemented following the same procedure as the direction buttons, with the difference that the callback function should use the function *motorDirectionWrite* with STOPPED as the parameter.

Example 7.2: Use a DC Motor to Open and Close a Gate

Objective

Expand the functionality of the external interrupts and modify the code to include a gate.

Summary of the Expected Behavior

By means of the buttons *Dir1* and *Dir2*, the motor rotation direction is controlled. The buttons *Dir1LS* and *Dir2LS* are used to indicate that a gate has reached a *Limit Switch*. In that situation, the motor should stop.

 NOTE: In the implementation proposed in this example, the actual gate is not included; this gate might be the gate of a house or any other gate that the user might choose.

Test the Proposed Solution on the Board

Import the project "Example 7.2" using the URL available in [3], build the project, and drag the *.bin* file onto the NUCLEO board. Press button *Dir1*. The motor should turn in a given direction, and one of the

LEDs should turn on. Press "g" on the PC keyboard. A message indicating "The gate is opening" should be displayed on the PC. Press the button *Dir1LS*. The motor should stop, and LED1 should turn off. Press "g" again on the PC keyboard. A message indicating "The gate is open" should be displayed on the PC.

Press button *Dir2*. The motor should turn in the other direction, and the other LED should turn on. Press "g" again on the PC keyboard. A message indicating "The gate is closing" should be displayed on the PC. Press button *Dir2LS*. The motor should stop, and LED2 should turn off. Press "g" again on the PC keyboard. A message indicating "The gate is closed" should be displayed on the PC.

Discussion of the Proposed Solution

The proposed solution is based on a new module, named *gate*. The motor and the gate are controlled by means of a new set of ISRs, which are triggered by the buttons *Dir1LS* and *Dir2LS*.

Implementation of the Proposed Solution

The initialization of the *gate* module is done at the beginning of the program by means of a call to the function *gateInit()* from *smartHomeSystemInit()*, as can be seen on line 7 of Code 7.8. In order to implement this call, the library *gate* is included in *smart_home_system.cpp*, as can be seen in Table 7.12.

```
1   void smartHomeSystemInit()
2   {
3       userInterfaceInit();
4       fireAlarmInit();
5       pcSerialComInit();
6       motorControlInit();
7       gateInit();
8   }
```

Code 7.8 New implementation of the function smartHomeSystemInit().

Table 7.12 Sections in which lines were added to smart_home_system.cpp.

Section	Lines that were added
Libraries	#include "gate.h"

Since, in this example, the motor is associated with a gate, some modifications in the code are needed in the module *user_interface*. The user will open or close a gate instead of turning a motor in direction 1 or 2. To account for this change, the variables and functions related to the motor are renamed as shown in Table 7.13 and Table 7.14 and in the new implementation of *userInterfaceInit()* shown in Code 7.9 (lines 3 to 7).

Table 7.13 Public global objects that were renamed in user_interface.cpp.

Object name in Example 7.1	Object name in Example 7.2
InterruptIn motorDirection1Button(PF_9);	InterruptIn gateOpenButton(PF_9);
InterruptIn motorDirection2Button(PF_8);	InterruptIn gateCloseButton(PF_8);

Table 7.14 Private functions that were renamed in user_interface.cpp.

Function name in Example 7.1	Function name in Example 7.2
static void motorDirection1ButtonCallback();	static void gateOpenButtonCallback();
static void motorDirection2ButtonCallback();	static void gateCloseButtonCallback();

```
1   void userInterfaceInit()
2   {
3        gateOpenButton.mode(PullUp);
4        gateCloseButton.mode(PullUp);
5
6        gateOpenButton.fall(&gateOpenButtonCallback);
7        gateCloseButton.fall(&gateCloseButtonCallback);
8
9        incorrectCodeLed = OFF;
10       systemBlockedLed = OFF;
11       matrixKeypadInit( SYSTEM_TIME_INCREMENT_MS );
12       userInterfaceDisplayInit();
13   }
```

Code 7.9 New implementation of the function userInterfaceInit().

Code 7.6 from Example 7.1 is modified as shown in Code 7.10. In this example, the rotation direction of the motor represents the opening or closing of the gate, so the functions *gateOpen()* and *gateClose()* from the Gate module are used. In order to use these functions, *gate.h* is included as shown in Table 7.15.

```
1   static void gateOpenButtonCallback()
2   {
3        gateOpen();
4   }
5
6   static void gateCloseButtonCallback()
7   {
8        gateClose();
9   }
```

Code 7.10 Changes in the name and implementation of functions of user_interface.cpp file.

Table 7.15 Sections in which lines were added to user_interface.cpp.

Section	Lines that were added
Libraries	#include "gate.h"

The implementation of *gate.cpp* is shown in Code 7.11 and Code 7.12. The libraries that are included are shown from lines 3 to 7 of Code 7.11. The external interrupts are assigned to pins PG_1 and PF_7 and declared on lines 11 and 12, respectively. On lines 16 and 17, two private global variables are created that will store the state of each limit switch when they are pressed. The interrupt handlers of each of the external interrupts are declared on lines 23 and 24.

The function *gateInit()* is shown on lines 28 to 39 of Code 7.11. The pins that simulate the limit switches of the gate are configured with internal pull-up resistors on lines 30 and 31, and the callbacks are defined on lines 33 and 34. Finally, on lines 36 to 38, the variables that store the status of the limit switches and the gate are initialized, setting the gate to closed.

 NOTE: If the gate is not closed during the initialization, the system will synchronize with the limit switches as soon as the gate open limit switch or the gate close limit switch is activated.

```
1   //=====[Libraries]============================================================
2
3   #include "mbed.h"
4   #include "arm_book_lib.h"
5
6   #include "gate.h"
7   #include "motor.h"
8
9   //=====[Declaration and initialization of public global objects]===============
10
11  InterruptIn gateOpenLimitSwitch(PG_1);
12  InterruptIn gateCloseLimitSwitch(PF_7);
13
14  //=====[Declaration and initialization of private global variables]===========
15
16  static bool gateOpenLimitSwitchState;
17  static bool gateCloseLimitSwitchState;
18
19  static gateStatus_t gateStatus;
20
21  //=====[Declarations (prototypes) of private functions]=======================
22
23  static void gateOpenLimitSwitchCallback();
24  static void gateCloseLimitSwitchCallback();
25
26  //=====[Implementations of public functions]==================================
27
28  void gateInit()
29  {
30      gateOpenLimitSwitch.mode(PullUp);
31      gateCloseLimitSwitch.mode(PullUp);
32
33      gateOpenLimitSwitch.fall(&gateOpenLimitSwitchCallback);
34      gateCloseLimitSwitch.fall(&gateCloseLimitSwitchCallback);
35
36      gateOpenLimitSwitchState = OFF;
37      gateCloseLimitSwitchState = ON;
38      gateStatus = GATE_CLOSED;
39  }
```

Code 7.11 Implementation of gate.cpp file (Part 1/2).

In Code 7.12, the implementations of the functions *gateOpen()* and *gateClose()* are shown from lines 1 to 17. If the state of the limit switch is OFF (lines 3 and 12), the motor is set to the requested direction (lines 4 and 13), the status of the gate is updated (lines 5 and 14), and the opposite limit switch is set to OFF (lines 6 and 15). Lines 19 to 22 show the implementation of the function *gateStatusRead()*, which returns the value of the variable *gateStatus*.

The implementation of the private functions that handle the interrupts is shown from lines 26 to 42. These handlers have similarities with the implementations of the functions *gateOpen()* and *gateClose()*. If the motor is turning in the direction that corresponds to the callback (lines 28 and 37), then the motor is stopped (lines 29 and 38), the status of the gate is updated (lines 30 and 39), and the limit switch is set to ON (lines 31 and 40).

```
1   void gateOpen()
2   {
3       if ( !gateOpenLimitSwitchState ) {
4           motorDirectionWrite( DIRECTION_1 );
5           gateStatus = GATE_OPENING;
6           gateCloseLimitSwitchState = OFF;
7       }
8   }
9
10  void gateClose()
11  {
12      if ( !gateCloseLimitSwitchState ) {
13          motorDirectionWrite( DIRECTION_2 );
14          gateStatus = GATE_CLOSING;
15          gateOpenLimitSwitchState = OFF;
16      }
17  }
18
19  gateStatus_t gateStatusRead()
20  {
21      return gateStatus;
22  }
23
24  //=====[Implementations of private functions]=========================
25
26  static void gateOpenLimitSwitchCallback()
27  {
28      if ( motorDirectionRead() == DIRECTION_1 ) {
29          motorDirectionWrite(STOPPED);
30          gateStatus = GATE_OPEN;
31          gateOpenLimitSwitchState = ON;
32      }
33  }
34
35  static void gateCloseLimitSwitchCallback()
36  {
37      if ( motorDirectionRead() == DIRECTION_2 ) {
38          motorDirectionWrite(STOPPED);
39          gateStatus = GATE_CLOSED;
40          gateCloseLimitSwitchState = ON;
41      }
42  }
```

Code 7.12 Implementation of gate.cpp file (Part 2/2).

In Code 7.13, the implementation of *gate.h* is shown. It can be seen that the data type *gateStatus_t* is defined on lines 8 to 13, and the prototypes of the public functions defined in Code 7.11 and Code 7.12 are declared on lines 17 to 22.

```
1    //=====[#include guards - begin]===============================================
2
3    #ifndef _GATE_H_
4    #define _GATE_H_
5
6    //=====[Declaration of public data types]=======================================
7
8    typedef enum {
9        GATE_CLOSED,
10       GATE_OPEN,
11       GATE_OPENING,
12       GATE_CLOSING,
13   } gateStatus_t;
14
15   //=====[Declarations (prototypes) of public functions]==========================
16
17   void gateInit();
18
19   void gateOpen();
20   void gateClose();
21
22   gateStatus_t gateStatusRead();
23
24   //=====[#include guards - end]==================================================
25
26   #endif // _GATE_H_
```

Code 7.13 Implementation of gate.h file.

To implement the new command "g", the lines shown in Table 7.16 are added to *pcSerialComCommand Update()* and *availableCommands()* in *pc_serial_com.cpp*. In Table 7.17, the sections in which lines are added to *pc_serial_com.cpp* are shown. It can be seen that a new private function, *commandShowCurrentMotorState()*, is declared.

Table 7.16 Functions in which lines were added in pc_serial_com.cpp.

Function	Lines that were added
static void pcSerialComCommandUpdate(char receivedChar)	`case 'g': case 'G': commandShowCurrentGateState();` `break;`
static void availableCommands()	`pcSerialComStringWrite( "Press 'g' or 'G' to show the` `gate status\r\n" );`

Table 7.17 Sections in which lines were added to pc_serial_com.cpp.

Section	Lines that were added
Libraries	`#include "gate.h"`
Declarations (prototypes) of private functions	`static void commandShowCurrentGateState();`

When "g" is pressed on the PC keyboard, the function *commandShowCurrentGateState()* shown in Code 7.14 is called. On line 3, the function *gateStatusRead()* (shown in Code 7.12) is called and, depending on the returned value, one of four different messages is sent to the PC console (lines 4 to 7).

```
1    static void commandShowCurrentGateState()
2    {
3        switch ( gateStatusRead() ) {
4            case GATE_CLOSED: pcSerialComStringWrite( "The gate is closed\r\n" ); break;
5            case GATE_OPEN: pcSerialComStringWrite( "The gate is open\r\n" ); break;
6            case GATE_OPENING: pcSerialComStringWrite( "The gate is opening\r\n" ); break;
7            case GATE_CLOSING: pcSerialComStringWrite( "The gate is closing\r\n" ); break;
8        }
9    }
```

Code 7.14 Implementation of the function commandShowCurrentGateState().

Proposed Exercise

1. What should be changed in the code to detect the buttons if they are now connected to 3.3 V instead of GND?

Answer to the Exercise

1. In Code 7.11, lines 30 and 31 should be modified to use the *pullDown* parameter, and lines 33 and 34 should use the *rise* interrupt type.

Example 7.3: Use of a PIR Sensor to Detect Intruders

Objective

Introduce the reading of a PIR sensor using interrupts.

Summary of the Expected Behavior

Intruders are detected by the PIR sensor, and the corresponding event is registered in the event log.

Test the Proposed Solution on the Board

Import the project "Example 7.3" using the URL available in [3], build the project, and drag the *.bin* file onto the NUCLEO board. Wave a hand over the PIR sensor. A message indicating "MOTION_ON" should be displayed on the serial terminal. Then, after a time defined by t_{Delay}, a message indicating "MOTION_OFF" should be displayed on the serial terminal. Press "h" on the PC keyboard or "B" on the matrix keypad. The system will stop tracking the PIR sensor. Press "i" on the PC keyboard or "A" on the matrix keypad. The system will restart its tracking of the PIR sensor.

NOTE: If key "h" or "B" is pressed just when the PIR sensor has detected a movement, the message "The motion sensor has been deactivated" followed by "MOTION_ON" can be seen on the serial terminal. After this last activation, the PIR sensor will not be activated again until key "i" or "A" is pressed. If key "h" or "B" is pressed many times, "The motion sensor has been deactivated" will be printed many times. If "i" or "A" is pressed many times, "The motion sensor has been activated" will be printed many times.

Discussion of the Proposed Solution

The proposed solution is based on a new module named *motion_sensor*. This module makes use of an interrupt to detect the pulse that the PIR sensor generates when it detects movement. An interrupt is triggered by a rising edge of the PIR sensor output signal. To detect the end of the pulse, an interrupt that is triggered when the signal transitions from high to low state (*falling edge*) is enabled. Figure 7.11 illustrates the initialization of the *motion_sensor* module (i.e., *motionSensorInit()*), the pulse generated when motion is detected, the content of the interrupt callback triggered (i.e., *motionDetected()*), and the content of the callback triggered when the pulse ceases (i.e., *motionCeased()*).

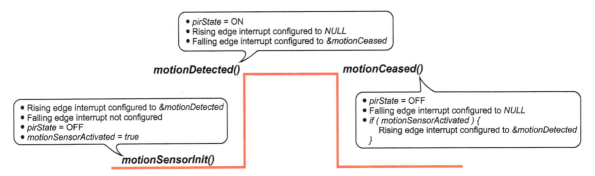

Figure 7.11 Pulse generated by PIR sensor when motion is detected and the corresponding initialization and callbacks.

In the initialization, the callback of the rising edge interrupt of *pirOutputSignal* (i.e., PG_0) is configured to *motionDetected()*, the callback of its falling edge interrupt is not configured, the Boolean variable *pirState* is assigned the OFF state, and *motionSensorActivated* is assigned true. When motion is detected by the PIR sensor, a rising edge pulse is generated on *pirOutputSignal*, which triggers the rising edge interrupt. This interrupt calls its callback function, *motionDetected()*, which assigns ON to *pirState*, disables the rising edge interrupt (i.e., NULL is assigned), activates the *pirOutputSignal* falling edge interrupt, and configures its callback to *motionCeased()*. Lastly, when motion ceases, a falling edge pulse is generated on *pirOutputSignal*, which triggers the falling edge interrupt. This interrupt calls its callback function, *motionCeased()*, which assigns OFF to *pirState*, disables the falling edge interrupt (i.e., NULL is assigned), and, if *motionSensorActivated* is true, then activates the *pirOutputSignal* rising edge interrupt and configures its callback to *motionDetected()*.

In the implementation introduced in this example, it is possible to deactivate the motion sensor detection at any time by pressing keys "h" or "B", even when the PIR sensor is detecting motion. In that situation, as was seen in the "Test the Proposed Solution on the Board" section, the message "The motion sensor has been deactivated" will be shown on the serial terminal, and the PIR sensor will not be activated again until keys "i" or "A" are pressed. Note that if the motion sensor detection is deactivated when the PIR sensor is detecting motion, then the falling edge interrupt will be disabled when *motionCeased()* is called as a consequence of the falling edge on *pirOutputSignal*. This is discussed below as the corresponding program code is shown.

Implementation of the Proposed Solution

Code 7.15 shows the new implementation of the function *smartHomeSystemInit()*. It can be seen that the function *motionSensorInit()* is called on line 8 to initialize the *motion_sensor* module.

```
1  void smartHomeSystemInit()
2  {
3      userInterfaceInit();
4      fireAlarmInit();
5      pcSerialComInit();
6      motorControlInit();
7      gateInit();
8      motionSensorInit();
9  }
```

Code 7.15 Details of the new implementation of the function smartHomeSystemInit().

In Table 7.18, the sections in which lines were added to *smart_home_system.cpp* are shown. It can be seen that *motion_sensor.h* has been included.

Table 7.18 Sections in which lines were added to smart_home_system.cpp.

Section	Lines that were added
Libraries	`#include "motion_sensor.h"`

To implement the new commands "i" and "h", the lines shown in Table 7.19 were added to *pcSerialComCommandUpdate()* and *availableCommands()* in *pc_serial_com.cpp*. In Table 7.19, the sections in which lines were added to *pc_serial_com.cpp* are shown. It can be seen that two new private functions are declared: *commandMotionSensorActivate()* and *commandMotionSensorDeactivate()*.

Table 7.19 Functions in which lines were added in pc_serial_com.cpp

Function	Lines that were added

static void pcSerialComCommandUpdate(char receivedChar)	`case 'i': case 'I': commandMotionSensorActivate();`
	`    break;`
	`case 'h': case 'H': commandMotionSensorDeactivate();`
	`    break;`

static void availableCommands()	`pcSerialComStringWrite( "Press 'i' or 'I' to`
	`    activate the motion sensor\r\n" );`
	`pcSerialComStringWrite( "Press 'h' or 'H' to`
	`    deactivate the motion sensor\r\n" );`

Table 7.20 Sections in which lines were added in pc_serial_com.cpp.

Section	Lines that were added
Libraries	`#include "motion_sensor.h"`
Declarations (prototypes) of private functions	`static void commandMotionSensorActivate();` `static void commandMotionSensorDeactivate();`

In Code 7.16, the implementations of *commandMotionSensorActivate()* and *commandMotionSensor Deactivate()* are shown. These functions call *motionSensorActivate()* and *motionSensorDeactivate()*, respectively.

```
1   static void commandMotionSensorActivate()
2   {
3       motionSensorActivate();
4   }
5
6   static void commandMotionSensorDeactivate()
7   {
8       motionSensorDeactivate();
9   }
```

Code 7.16 Implementation of commandMotionSensorActivate() and commandMotionSensorDeactivate().

The implementation of *motion_sensor.cpp* is shown in Code 7.17 and Code 7.18. The libraries that are included are shown from lines 3 to 7. On line 11, a public global object of type InterruptIn named *pirOutputSignal* is declared and assigned to the pin PG_0. This pin will be used to detect the pulse generated by the PIR sensor when it identifies movement, as was explained using Figure 7.11. This pulse will be processed by the private functions *motionDetected()* and *motionCeased()*, declared on lines 20 and 21, respectively. It will modify the state of the global private variable named *pirState*, which is declared on line 15. Finally, another global private variable named *motionSensorActivated*, which is declared on line 16, will define whether the tracking of the motion sensor is active.

```
1   //=====[Libraries]=========================================================
2
3   #include "mbed.h"
4   #include "arm_book_lib.h"
5
6   #include "motion_sensor.h"
7   #include "pc_serial_com.h"
8
9   //=====[Declaration and initialization of public global objects]===============
10
11  InterruptIn pirOutputSignal(PG_0);
12
13  //=====[Declaration and initialization of private global variables]============
14
15  static bool pirState;
16  static bool motionSensorActivated;
17
18  //=====[Declarations (prototypes) of private functions]=======================
19
20  static void motionDetected();
21  static void motionCeased();
```

Code 7.17 Details of the implementation of motion_sensor.cpp (Part 1/2).

The implementation of public and private functions of the *motion_sensor* module is shown in Code 7.18. From lines 3 to 8, the function *motionSensorInit()* is implemented. On line 5, the callback function of *pirOutputSignal* interrupt is configured with the function *motionDetected()* when there is a rising edge on PG_0 (i.e., when there is a rising edge on PG_0 the function *motionDetected()* is called).

On line 6, *pirState* is initialized to OFF because it is assumed that at the beginning the PIR sensor is inactive. On line 7, *motionSensorActivated* is initialized to true in order to activate the motion sensor. Therefore, the tracking of this sensor will be active, since the smart home system is initialized. From lines 10 to 13, the public function *motionSensorRead()* is implemented. This function returns the value of *pirState*.

On line 15, *motionSensorActivate()* is implemented. First, it assigns true to *motionSensorActivated*. Then, if *pirState* is OFF (line 18), it configures an interrupt associated with a rising edge on *pirOutputSignal* with *motionDetected()* as its callback. Note that if *pirState* is ON, this rising edge interrupt will be configured by the callback associated with the falling edge interrupt, as discussed above (Figure 7.11). Finally, this function sends the string "The motion sensor has been activated" to the serial terminal (line 21).

On line 24, *motionSensorDeactivate()* is implemented. First, it assigns false to *motionSensorActivated*. Then, if *pirState* is OFF (line 27), it disables the interrupt associated with a rising edge on *pirOutputSignal* (line 28). Note that if *pirState* is ON, this rising edge interrupt will be configured by the callback associated with the rising edge interrupt, as discussed above (Figure 7.11). Lastly, this function sends the string "The motion sensor has been deactivated" to the serial terminal (line 30).

```
1    //=====[Implementations of public functions]===================================
2
3    void motionSensorInit()
4    {
5        pirOutputSignal.rise(&motionDetected);
6        pirState = OFF;
7        motionSensorActivated = true;
8    }
9
10   bool motionSensorRead()
11   {
12       return pirState;
13   }
14
15   void motionSensorActivate()
16   {
17       motionSensorActivated = true;
18       if ( !pirState ) {
19           pirOutputSignal.rise(&motionDetected);
20       }
21       pcSerialComStringWrite( "The motion sensor has been activated\r\n" );
22   }
23
24   void motionSensorDeactivate()
25   {
26       motionSensorActivated = false;
27       if ( !pirState ) {
28           pirOutputSignal.rise(NULL);
29       }
30       pcSerialComStringWrite("The motion sensor has been deactivated\r\n");
31   }
32
```

```
33   //=====[Implementations of private functions]==================================
34
35   static void motionDetected()
36   {
37       pirState = ON;
38       pirOutputSignal.rise(NULL);
39       pirOutputSignal.fall(&motionCeased);
40   }
41
42   static void motionCeased()
43   {
44       pirState = OFF;
45       pirOutputSignal.fall(NULL);
46       if ( motionSensorActivated ) {
47           pirOutputSignal.rise(&motionDetected);
48       }
49   }
```

Code 7.18 Details of the implementation of motion_sensor.cpp (Part 2/2).

As was mentioned earlier, when a rising edge is detected on *pirOutputSignal* (pin PG_0), the function *motionDetected()* is called (recall the interrupt that is configured on lines 5 and 19). This function sets *pirState* to ON (line 37) to keep track of the state of the PIR sensor, deactivates the rising edge interrupt (line 38), and configures a falling edge interrupt that triggers the function *motionCeased()* (line 39).

The function *motionCeased()*, from lines 42 to 49, first sets *pirState* to OFF on line 44. Then, on line 45, the falling edge interrupt is deactivated. On line 46, if *motionSensorActivated* is true, then *pirOutputSignal.rise(&motionDetected)* on line 47 is used to configure an interrupt to be triggered by a rising edge on PG_0 and to assign *motionDetected()* as its handler. In this way, it is established what to do when *pirOutputSignal* becomes active again. Note that if *motionSensorActivated* is false, then the rising interrupt is not enabled. Thus, the falling and the rising edge interrupts will be disabled and, therefore, the motion sensor is deactivated. To activate the motion sensor, "i" can be pressed on the PC keyboard. This causes *motionSensorActivate()* to be called, as was explained above.

In Code 7.19, the implementation of *motion_sensor.h* is shown. The prototypes of the public functions are declared from lines 8 to 11. The implementation of these functions was shown in Code 7.18.

```
1    //=====[#include guards - begin]====================================
2
3    #ifndef _MOTION_SENSOR_H_
4    #define _MOTION_SENSOR_H_
5
6    //=====[Declarations (prototypes) of public functions]=============
7
8    void motionSensorInit();
9    bool motionSensorRead();
10   void motionSensorActivate();
11   void motionSensorDeactivate();
12
13   //=====[#include guards - end]=====================================
14
15   #endif // _MOTION_SENSOR_H_
```

Code 7.19 Details of the implementation of motion_sensor.h.

Code 7.20 shows the new implementation of the function *eventLogUpdate()*. It can be seen that lines 23 to 25 have been added in order to determine if the state of the PIR sensor has changed since the last update. If a change has taken place, then the corresponding message is displayed on the serial terminal (line 24), and the state of *motionLastState* is updated (line 26).

```
1   void eventLogUpdate()
2   {
3       bool currentState = sirenStateRead();
4       eventLogElementStateUpdate( sirenLastState, currentState, "ALARM" );
5       sirenLastState = currentState;
6
7       currentState = gasDetectorStateRead();
8       eventLogElementStateUpdate( gasLastState, currentState, "GAS_DET" );
9       gasLastState = currentState;
10
11      currentState = overTemperatureDetectorStateRead();
12      eventLogElementStateUpdate( tempLastState, currentState, "OVER_TEMP" );
13      tempLastState = currentState;
14
15      currentState = incorrectCodeStateRead();
16      eventLogElementStateUpdate( ICLastState, currentState, "LED_IC" );
17      ICLastState = currentState;
18
19      currentState = systemBlockedStateRead();
20      eventLogElementStateUpdate( SBLastState ,currentState, "LED_SB" );
21      SBLastState = currentState;
22
23      currentState = motionSensorRead();
24      eventLogElementStateUpdate( motionLastState ,currentState, "MOTION" );
25      motionLastState = currentState;
26  }
```

Code 7.20 Details of the new implementation of the function eventLogUpdate().

In Table 7.21, the sections in which lines were added to *event_log.cpp* are shown. It can be seen that *motion_sensor.h* has been included, and the private Boolean variable *motionLastState* has been declared and initialized to OFF.

Table 7.21 Sections in which lines were added to event_log.cpp.

Section	Lines that were added
Libraries	#include "motion_sensor.h"
Declaration and initialization of private global variables	static bool motionLastState = OFF;

The matrix keypad can be used in order to activate or deactivate the tracking of the PIR sensor. In Table 7.22, the line added to *user_interface.cpp* to include the library *motion_sensor.h* is shown.

Table 7.22 Sections in which lines were added to user_interface.cpp.

Section	Lines that were added
Libraries	#include "motion_sensor.h"

In Code 7.21, the new implementation of *userInterfaceMatrixKeypadUpdate()* is shown. The new code is from lines 27 to 34. If the system is not blocked (line 27), then if the "A" key is pressed (line 28), *motionSensorActivate()* is called (line 29), and if the "B" key is pressed (line 30), *motionSensorDeactivate()* is called (line 32).

```
1   static void userInterfaceMatrixKeypadUpdate()
2   {
3       static int numberOfHashKeyReleased = 0;
4       char keyReleased = matrixKeypadUpdate();
5
6       if( keyReleased != '\0' ) {
7
8           if( sirenStateRead() && !systemBlockedStateRead() ) {
9               if( !incorrectCodeStateRead() ) {
10                  codeSequenceFromUserInterface[numberOfCodeChars] = keyReleased;
11                  numberOfCodeChars++;
12                  if ( numberOfCodeChars >= CODE_NUMBER_OF_KEYS ) {
13                      codeComplete = true;
14                      numberOfCodeChars = 0;
15                  }
16              } else {
17                  if( keyReleased == '#' ) {
18                      numberOfHashKeyReleased++;
19                      if( numberOfHashKeyReleased >= 2 ) {
20                          numberOfHashKeyReleased = 0;
21                          numberOfCodeChars = 0;
22                          codeComplete = false;
23                          incorrectCodeState = OFF;
24                      }
24                  }
26              }
27          } else if ( !systemBlockedStateRead() ) {
28              if( keyReleased == 'A' ) {
29                  motionSensorActivate();
30              }
31              if( keyReleased == 'B' ) {
32                  motionSensorDeactivate();
33              }
34          }
35      }
36  }
```

Code 7.21 New implementation of userInterfaceMatrixKeypadUpdate().

Proposed Exercises

1. How can the code be changed in order to use more than one PIR sensor?

2. Why are the new module in this example and its public functions called *motion_sensor* instead of *pir*?

3. Why are the functions *commandMotionSensorActivate()* and *commandMotionSensorDeactivate()* used in the module *pc_serial_com* instead of calling the public functions *motionSensorActivate()* and *motionSensorDeactivate()* directly?

Answers to the Exercises

1. In *motion_sensor.cpp*, new InterruptIn objects must be declared and the corresponding functions to handle each interrupt must be written.

2. Because in this way, any code calling the module can treat its functions as independent of the implementation of the sensor. In this case a PIR sensor was used, but different technologies could be used to provide the same functionality for the smart home system; in this scenario, the public functions of the module would need to be rewritten, but their names would remain unchanged, as would any calling functions.

3. The functions *commandMotionSensorActivate()* and *commandMotionSensorDeactivate()* are used in the module *pc_serial_com* to make the implementation similar to the implementation used in the other commands.

Example 7.4: Use of the PIR Sensor as an Intruder Detection Alarm

Objective

Trigger the alarm when an intruder is detected.

Summary of the Expected Behavior

The siren and the alarm are also triggered by the PIR sensor.

Test the Proposed Solution on the Board

Import the project "Example 7.4" using the URL available in [3], build the project, and drag the *.bin* file onto the NUCLEO board. Wave a hand over the PIR sensor. The siren and the strobe light will turn on and off every 1000 milliseconds, and the display will show "Intruder Detected". Deactivate the alarm using the matrix keypad or the PC keyboard in the same way as in previous chapters. Press the B1 User button (from now on it will be called "Fire alarm test button"). The siren and the strobe light will turn on and off every 500 milliseconds, and the display will show "Fire Alarm Activated!". Wave a hand over the PIR sensor. The siren and the strobe light will turn on and off every 100 milliseconds. The display will indicate "Fire Alarm Activated!" because during a fire the smoke is also registered as movement by the PIR sensor.

 NOTE: As discussed in the previous chapter, the on and off time of the siren and the strobe light are not always 100 ms. In the next chapter, a technique will be introduced to tackle this.

Discussion of the Proposed Solution

The proposed solution is based on the modification of several parts of the code and on new software modules called *alarm* and *intruder_alarm*. The modifications are needed because in previous versions of the code, the alarm was only related to the fire detection subsystem. The *alarm* module will be responsible for checking if any of the alarm sources are active.

Implementation of the Proposed Solution

In Table 7.23, the sections in which lines were added to *smart_home_system.cpp* are shown. It can be seen that *alarm.h* and *intruder_alarm.h* have been included.

Table 7.23 Sections in which lines were added to smart_home_system.cpp.

Section	Lines that were added
Libraries	`#include "alarm.h"` `#include "intruder_alarm.h"`

Code 7.22 shows the new implementation of the functions *smartHomeSystemInit()* and *smartHomeSystemUpdate()*. It can be seen that the new functions *alarmInit()* and *intruderAlarmInit()* are called on lines 8 and 10, respectively, and *motionSensorInit()* has been removed, since this function is called by *intruderAlarmInit()*. The functions *intruderAlarmUpdate()* and *alarmUpdate()* are included in *smartHomeSystemUpdate()* (lines 18 and 19).

```
1   //=====[Implementations of public functions]====================================
2
3   void smartHomeSystemInit()
4   {
5       userInterfaceInit();
6       alarmInit();
7       fireAlarmInit();
8       intruderAlarmInit();
9       pcSerialComInit();
10      motorControlInit();
11      gateInit();
12  }
13
14  void smartHomeSystemUpdate()
15  {
16      userInterfaceUpdate();
17      fireAlarmUpdate();
18      intruderAlarmUpdate();
19      alarmUpdate();
20      eventLogUpdate();
21      pcSerialComUpdate();
22      delay(SYSTEM_TIME_INCREMENT_MS);
23  }
```

Code 7.22 New implementation of the function smartHomeSystemInit and smartHomeSystemUpdate.

The new module *alarm* is presented in Code 7.23, Code 7.24, Code 7.25, and Code 7.26. This module contains functionality that was previously carried out by the *fire_alarm* module. In Code 7.23, in lines 3 to 12, the libraries used in this module are included. The variable *alarmState* on line 22 and the private function *alarmDeactivate()* on line 26 are declared.

The strobe time of the siren and the strobe light, which was previously defined in the *fire_alarm* module, is defined in this module after the modifications to the code. Additionally, the different strobe times have new meanings. If only the intruder alarm is activated, the strobe time has a value of 1000 milliseconds. If only the fire alarm is activated, then the strobe time has a value of 500 milliseconds. Finally, if both the intruder alarm and the fire alarm are activated, the strobe time has a value of 100 milliseconds. These differences can be seen in the declaration of private #defines on lines 16 to 18 and the implementations of the private function *alarmStrobeTime()* (lines 12 to 27 in Code 7.25).

```
1   //=====[Libraries]=============================================================
2
3   #include "mbed.h"
4   #include "arm_book_lib.h"
5
6   #include "alarm.h"
7   #include "siren.h"
8   #include "strobe_light.h"
9   #include "code.h"
10  #include "matrix_keypad.h"
11  #include "fire_alarm.h"
12  #include "intruder_alarm.h"
13
14  //=====[Declaration of private defines]==================================
15
16  #define STROBE_TIME_INTRUDER_ALARM            1000
17  #define STROBE_TIME_FIRE_ALARM                 500
18  #define STROBE_TIME_FIRE_AND_INTRUDER_ALARM    100
19
20  //=====[Declaration and initialization of private global variables]=========
21
22  static bool alarmState;
23
24  //=====[Declarations (prototypes) of private functions]==================
25
26  static void alarmDeactivate();
```

Code 7.23 Details of the implementation of alarm.cpp (Part 1/3).

The implementation of public and private functions is shown in Code 7.24. The function *alarmInit()* (lines 3 to 7) is used to initialize the variable *alarmState* and the siren and strobe light using its public functions. The deactivation of the alarm, which was previously included in *fireAlarmDeactivationUpdate()*, has moved to the function *alarmUpdate()* (lines 10 to 30).

If a correct code is entered, then the function *alarmDeactivate()* is called (line 15). The function *alarmUpdate()* also updates the strobe time of the siren and the strobe light by means of the functions *sirenUpdate()* (line 19) and *strobeLightUpdate()* (line 20). Depending on the state of the alarm sources – gas, over temperature and intruder detection (lines 20 to 23) – *alarmState* (line 26), *sirenState* (line 27), and *strobeLightState* (line 28) are updated. Finally, the public function *alarmStateRead()* (lines 32 to 35) returns the value of *alarmState*.

The private function *alarmDeactivate()* (lines 3 to 10 of Code 7.25) implements the functionality that was previously located in *fireAlarmDeactivate()*, taking into account the new alarm source.

In Code 7.26, the implementation of *alarm.h* is shown. It can be seen that the prototypes of the public functions are declared from lines 8 to 10.

```
1    //=====[Implementations of public functions]=======================================
2
3    void alarmInit()
4    {
5        alarmState = OFF;
6        sirenInit();
7        strobeLightInit();
8    }
9
10   void alarmUpdate()
11   {
12       if ( alarmState ) {
13
14           if ( codeMatchFrom(CODE_KEYPAD) ||
15               codeMatchFrom(CODE_PC_SERIAL) ) {
16               alarmDeactivate();
17           }
18
19           sirenUpdate( alarmStrobeTime() );
20           strobeLightUpdate( alarmStrobeTime() );
21
22       } else if ( gasDetectedRead() ||
23                   overTemperatureDetectedRead() ||
24                   intruderDetectedRead() )   {
25
26           alarmState = ON;
27           sirenStateWrite(ON);
28           strobeLightStateWrite(ON);
29       }
30   }
31
32   bool alarmStateRead()
33   {
34       return alarmState;
35   }
```

Code 7.24 Details of the implementation of alarm.cpp (Part 2/3).

```
1    //=====[Implementations of private functions]=======================================
2
3    static void alarmDeactivate()
4    {
5        alarmState = OFF;
6        sirenStateWrite(OFF);
7        strobeLightStateWrite(OFF);
8        intruderAlarmDeactivate();
9        fireAlarmDeactivate();
10   }
11
12   static int alarmStrobeTime()
13   {
14       if ( ( gasDetectedRead() || overTemperatureDetectedRead() ) &&
15               intruderDetectedRead() ) {
16           return STROBE_TIME_FIRE_AND_INTRUDER_ALARM;
17
18       } else if ( gasDetectedRead() || overTemperatureDetectedRead() ) {
19           return STROBE_TIME_FIRE_ALARM;
20
21       } else if ( intruderDetectedRead() ) {
22           return STROBE_TIME_INTRUDER_ALARM;
23
24       } else {
25           return 0;
26       }
27   }
```

Code 7.25 Details of the implementation of alarm.cpp (Part 3/3).

```
1   //=====[#include guards  - begin]===============================================
2
3   #ifndef _ALARM_H_
4   #define _ALARM_H_
5
6   //=====[Declarations (prototypes) of public functions]===========================
7
8   void alarmInit();
9   void alarmUpdate();
10  bool alarmStateRead();
11
12  //=====[#include guards - end]===================================================
13
14  #endif // _ALARM_H_
```

Code 7.26 Details of the implementation of alarm.h.

The new module *intruder_alarm* is shown in Code 7.27 and Code 7.28. The reader will note that this module is similar to the new implementation of the module *fire_alarm*, which is presented in Code 7.29, Code 7.30, and Code 7.31. The main differences between these two modules are that *fire_alarm* has two sensors (gas and temperature), *intruder_alarm* has only one sensor (PIR sensor), and *fire_alarm* has a test button, which after the modifications in the code is called *fireAlarmTestButton*.

In Code 7.27, the libraries used in the *intruder_alarm* module are included on lines 3 to 7. Two private global variables are declared and initialized on lines 11 and 12: *intruderDetected* and *intruderDetectorState*. In Code 7.27 and Code 7.30, the implementation of the public functions of the modules *fire_alarm* and *intruder_alarm* is shown. These two modules are described together to emphasize their similarities.

The functions that end with "Init" (lines 3 to 6 of Code 7.27 and lines 3 to 8 of Code 7.30) call the functions that initialize the sensors associated with the alarm. The functions that end with "Read" (lines 30 to 38 of Code 7.27 and lines 34 to 52 of Code 7.30) return the values of private variables. The functions that end with "Update" (lines 21 to 28 of Code 7.27 and lines 10 to 32 of Code 7.30) read the sensors and update the variables that end with "Detected" (used to activate the alarm) and "DetectorState". Finally, the functions that end with "Deactivate" (lines 40 to 43 of Code 7.27 and lines 54 to 58 of Code 7.30) assign OFF to the variables that end with "Detected" in order to turn off the alarm.

In Code 7.29, the libraries used in the new implementation of the *fire_alarm* module are included on lines 3 to 11. It is important to note that the libraries *code.h* and *matrix_keypad.h* are no longer needed after the modifications in this module. In the declaration of private #defines, the constants related to the strobe time of the siren are removed. Also, due to the module modifications, the private functions are removed in this new implementation.

The file headers of *intruder_alarm* and *fire_alarm* are shown in Code 7.28 and Code 7.31. It can be seen that the prototypes of the public functions are declared (lines 8 to 13 in Code 7.28 and lines 8 to 16 in Code 7.31).

```
1   //=====[Libraries]=================================================
2
3   #include "mbed.h"
4   #include "arm_book_lib.h"
5
6   #include "intruder_alarm.h"
7   #include "motion_sensor.h"
8
9   //=====[Declaration and initialization of private global variables]=============
10
11  static bool intruderDetected = OFF;
12  static bool intruderDetectorState = OFF;
13
14  //=====[Implementations of public functions]===========================
15
16  void intruderAlarmInit()
17  {
18      motionSensorInit();
19  }
20
21  void intruderAlarmUpdate()
22  {
23      intruderDetectorState = motionSensorRead();
24
25      if ( intruderDetectorState ) {
26          intruderDetected = ON;
27      }
28  }
29
30  bool intruderDetectorStateRead()
31  {
32      return intruderDetectorState;
33  }
34
35  bool intruderDetectedRead()
36  {
37      return intruderDetected;
38  }
39
40  void intruderAlarmDeactivate()
41  {
42      intruderDetected = OFF;
43  }
```

Code 7.27 Details of the implementation of intruder_alarm.cpp.

```
1   //=====[#include guards - begin]===================================
2
3   #ifndef _INTRUDER_ALARM_H_
4   #define _INTRUDER_ALARM_H_
5
6   //=====[Libraries]=================================================
7
8   void intruderAlarmInit();
9   void intruderAlarmUpdate();
10  void intruderAlarmDeactivate();
11
12  bool intruderDetectorStateRead();
13  bool intruderDetectedRead();
14
15  //=====[#include guards - end]=====================================
16
17  #endif // _INTRUDER_ALARM_H_
```

Code 7.28 Details of the implementation of intruder_alarm.h.

```
1    //=====[Libraries]==============================================
2
3    #include "mbed.h"
4    #include "arm_book_lib.h"
5
6    #include "fire_alarm.h"
7
8    #include "user_interface.h"
9    #include "date_and_time.h"
10   #include "temperature_sensor.h"
11   #include "gas_sensor.h"
12
13   //=====[Declaration of private defines]=========================
14
15   #define TEMPERATURE_C_LIMIT_ALARM              50.0
16
17   //=====[Declaration and initialization of public global objects]===============
18
19   DigitalIn fireAlarmTestButton(BUTTON1);
20
21   //=====[Declaration and initialization of private global variables]============
22
23   static bool gasDetected                 = OFF;
24   static bool overTemperatureDetected     = OFF;
25   static bool gasDetectorState            = OFF;
26   static bool overTemperatureDetectorState = OFF;
```

Code 7.29 Details of the new implementation of fire_alarm.cpp (Part 1/2).

```
1    //=====[Implementations of public functions]====================
2
3    void fireAlarmInit()
4    {
5        temperatureSensorInit();
6        gasSensorInit();
7        fireAlarmTestButton.mode(PullDown);
8    }
9
10   void fireAlarmUpdate()
11   {
12       temperatureSensorUpdate();
13       gasSensorUpdate();
14
15       overTemperatureDetectorState = temperatureSensorReadCelsius() >
16                                      TEMPERATURE_C_LIMIT_ALARM;
17
18       if ( overTemperatureDetectorState ) {
19           overTemperatureDetected = ON;
20       }
21
22       gasDetectorState = !gasSensorRead();
23
24       if ( gasDetectorState ) {
25           gasDetected = ON;
26       }
27
28       if( fireAlarmTestButton ) {
29           overTemperatureDetected = ON;
30           gasDetected = ON;
31       }
32   }
33
34   bool gasDetectorStateRead()
35   {
36       return gasDetectorState;
```

```
37   }
38
39   bool overTemperatureDetectorStateRead()
40   {
41       return overTemperatureDetectorState;
42   }
43
44   bool gasDetectedRead()
45   {
46       return gasDetected;
47   }
48
49   bool overTemperatureDetectedRead()
50   {
51       return overTemperatureDetected;
52   }
53
54   void fireAlarmDeactivate()
55   {
56       overTemperatureDetected = OFF;
57       gasDetected             = OFF;
58   }
```

Code 7.30 Details of the new implementation of fire_alarm.cpp (Part 2/2).

```
 1   //=====[#include guards - begin]===================================================
 2
 3   #ifndef _FIRE_ALARM_H_
 4   #define _FIRE_ALARM_H_
 5
 6   //=====[Declarations (prototypes) of public functions]============================
 7
 8   void fireAlarmInit();
 9   void fireAlarmUpdate();
10   void fireAlarmDeactivate();
11
12   bool gasDetectorStateRead();
13   bool gasDetectedRead();
14
15   bool overTemperatureDetectorStateRead();
16   bool overTemperatureDetectedRead();
17
18   //=====[#include guards - end]=====================================================
19
20   #endif // _FIRE_ALARM_H_
```

Code 7.31 Details of the new implementation of fire_alarm.h.

Because there are two alarm sources, the display should show two different messages. In Code 7.32, the new implementation of the function *userInterfaceDisplayAlarmStateUpdate()* of the *user_interface* module is modified to account for this change. If the alarm is related to the gas detector or the temperature sensor (line 3), then the message is the same as in previous examples (lines 4 to 25). If the alarm is related to the intruder detector (line 26), then a new message is displayed: "Intruder Detected" (lines 27 to 40). If both alarm sources are active, the display will show the fire alarm message.

```
1    static void userInterfaceDisplayAlarmStateUpdate()
2    {
3        if ( ( gasDetectedRead() ) || ( overTemperatureDetectedRead() ) ) {
4            switch( displayFireAlarmGraphicSequence ) {
5            case 0:
6                displayBitmapWrite( GLCD_fire_alarm[0] );
7                displayFireAlarmGraphicSequence++;
8                break;
9            case 1:
10               displayBitmapWrite( GLCD_fire_alarm[1] );
11               displayFireAlarmGraphicSequence++;
12               break;
13           case 2:
14               displayBitmapWrite( GLCD_fire_alarm[2] );
15               displayFireAlarmGraphicSequence++;
16               break;
17           case 3:
18               displayBitmapWrite( GLCD_fire_alarm[3] );
19               displayFireAlarmGraphicSequence = 0;
20               break;
21           default:
22               displayBitmapWrite( GLCD_ClearScreen );
23               displayFireAlarmGraphicSequence = 0;
24               break;
25           }
26       } else if ( intruderDetectedRead() ) {
27           switch( displayIntruderAlarmGraphicSequence ) {
28           case 0:
29               displayBitmapWrite( GLCD_intruder_alarm );
30               displayIntruderAlarmGraphicSequence++;
31               break;
32           case 1:
33           default:
34               displayBitmapWrite( GLCD_ClearScreen );
35               displayIntruderAlarmGraphicSequence = 0;
36               break;
37           }
38       }
39   }
```

Code 7.32 New implementation of the function userInterfaceDisplayAlarmStateUpdate().

In Table 7.24, the sections in which lines were added to *user_interface.cpp* are shown. It can be seen that *alarm.h* and *intruder_alarm.h* have been included. A file *GLCD_intruder_alarm.h*, which contains the message that the display will show when an intruder is detected, is also included. The file *GLCD_clear_screen.h* contains the values for a blank screen that were previously included in *GLCD_intruder_alarm.h*.

The private global variable *displayIntruderAlarmGraphicSequence* is used to make the message appear on the display, and the variable name of *displayAlarmGraphicSequence* has been replaced by *displayFireAlarmGraphicSequence*, as shown in Table 7.25.

Table 7.24 Sections in which lines were added to user_interface.cpp.

Section	Lines that were added

Libraries	`#include "alarm.h"`
	`#include "intruder_alarm.h"`
	`#include "GLCD_intruder_alarm.h"`
	`#include "GLCD_clear_screen.h"`

Declaration and initialization of private global variables	`static int displayIntruderAlarmGraphicSequence = 0;`

Table 7.25 Variables that were renamed in user_interface.cpp.

Variable name in Example 7.3	Variable name in Example 7.4
displayAlarmGraphicSequence	displayFireAlarmGraphicSequence

Proposed Exercise

1. How can the code be changed to activate the intruder alarm *only* when the PIR sensor is active for more than four seconds?

Answer to the Exercise

1. The function *intruderAlarmUpdate()* should be modified. In Code 7.33, the proposed implementation is shown. Because *intruderAlarmUpdate()* is called every 10 milliseconds, when *intruderDetectorCount* reaches a value of 400, the PIR sensor has been active for roughly 4 seconds.

```
1   void intruderAlarmUpdate()
2   {
3       static int intruderDetectorCount = 0;
4
5       intruderDetectorState = motionSensorRead();
6
7       if ( intruderDetectorState ) {
8           intruderDetectorCount++;
9       } else {
10          intruderDetectorCount = 0;
11      }
12
13      if ( intruderDetectorCount > 400 ) {
14          intruderDetected = ON;
15      }
16  }
```

Code 7.33 New implementation of intruderAlarmUpdate() that solves the proposed exercise.

7.3 Under the Hood

7.3.1 Basic Principles of a Relay Module

In this chapter, a relay module was used to control a DC motor. Figure 7.12 shows a diagram of a typical circuit that is used in a relay module. As was mentioned in subsection 7.2.1, the aim of this circuit is to isolate the input (i.e., IN1 and 5 V) from the output (i.e., COM1, NC1, and NO1). It is also designed to use an output of the microcontroller to drive IN1. This implies that IN1 can take only three possible states: GND, 3.3 V, or unconnected, and is expected to drain or sink a current as small as possible from the microcontroller.

For these reasons, the optocoupler shown in Figure 7.12 is used, as well as the optional JDVCC power supply connection. When GND is applied to IN1, there will be a current established from VCC that will go through R1, the LED inside the optocoupler, and LED1. In this way, LED1 will turn on, and the LED inside the optocoupler will activate the transistor. This transistor will allow current to flow from

JVDCC to R2 through the base (B) of the T1 transistor. In this way, the T1 transistor is activated, which allows a current to flow between its collector terminal (C) and its emitter terminal (E). This current activates the coil of the relay, which causes its internal switch to connect COM1 and NO1.

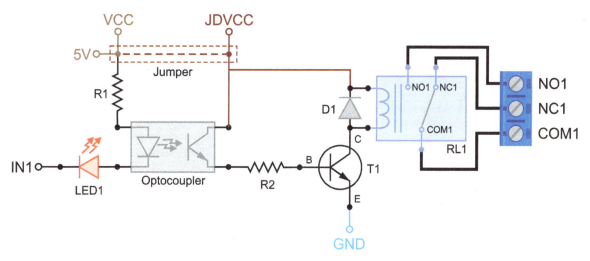

Figure 7.12 Diagram of a typical circuit that is used in a relay module.

Once IN1 is left unconnected, the optocoupler is unenergized, which causes the T1 transistor to turn off and the current through the coil of the RL1 relay to be cut off. This makes the internal switch of the relay move back via a spring in order to connect COM1 and NC1. It causes a high reverse voltage over the terminals of the coil. In order to prevent this voltage from damaging the circuit, the D1 diode is put in place, which prevents sparks from occurring.

TIP: In typical low-power applications, a jumper can be connected between VCC and JDVCC in order to avoid the need for an extra power supply. Note that in this case, the purpose of the optocoupler (i.e., to isolate the 5 V supply and the IN1 input from the stage composed by R2, T1, and D1) is voided. In any case, the relay RL1 isolates the output of the relay module (NO1, NC1, and COM1) from the rest of the circuit.

Proposed Exercise

1. How can a relay module be used to control an AC motor?

Answer to the Exercise

1. The proposed circuit connection is shown in Figure 7.13.

WARNING: The circuit shown in Figure 7.13 can be used with 110 or 220 V AC, but special care must be taken when working with voltages above 50 V.

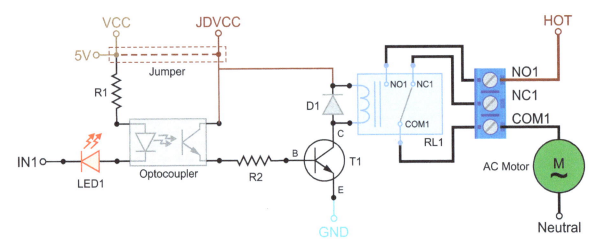

Figure 7.13 Diagram of a typical circuit that is used to turn on and off an AC motor using a relay module.

7.4 Case Study

7.4.1 Smart Street Lighting

In this chapter, a PIR sensor was connected to the NUCLEO board, and a DC motor was controlled using a relay module. This allowed a gate to be closed when intruders were detected. A smart street lighting system, built with Mbed and containing some similar features, can be found in [4]. In Figure 7.14, a diagram of the whole system is shown.

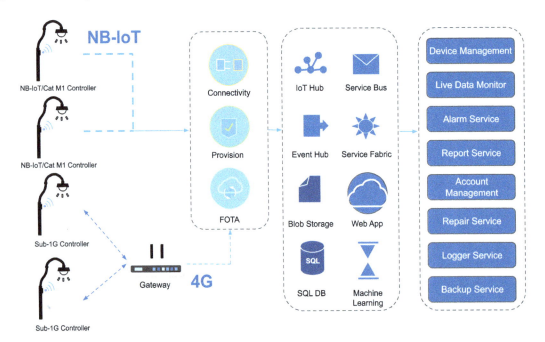

Figure 7.14 A diagram of the Smart Street Lighting system.

The smart street lighting system provides advanced dimming and on/off schedules that can be configured to optimize energy consumption during off-peak hours. In addition, using a built-in light sensor, the light is able to automatically switch off when daylight is detected. The system also provides fault detection and operator alerting via text or email, which allows for timely maintenance.

It might be noticed that the principle of operation of the light level sensor that is placed on each lamp of the smart street lighting system is very similar to the principle of operation of the PIR sensor that was used in this chapter. The lamps can be controlled using relay modules, such as the one used in this chapter, or solid-state relays, depending on the specific features of the lamp and the control system. Moreover, the smart street lighting system uses a set of tools to monitor and control the state of the lamps over the internet, having behavior and resources that are very similar to the tools used in this chapter.

> **NOTE:** In the next chapter, a light level sensor will be included in the smart home system.

Proposed Exercise

1. How can an AC lamp be turned on and off using a relay module?

Answer to the Exercise

1. The proposed circuit connection is shown in Figure 7.15. It can be seen that it is very similar to the circuit used in Figure 7.13. Different AC-powered devices can be controlled using a relay module.

> **WARNING:** The circuit shown in Figure 7.15 can be used with 110 or 220 V AC, but special care must be taken when working with voltages above 50 V.

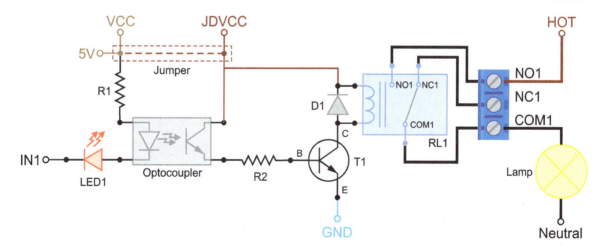

Figure 7.15 Diagram of a typical circuit that is used to turn on and off an AC lamp using a relay module.

References

[1]   "Toy/Hobby DC Motor Pinout Wiring, Specifications, Uses Guide and Datasheet". Accessed July 9, 2021.
https://components101.com/motors/toy-dc-motor

[2]   "HC-SR501 PIR Sensor Working, Pinout & Datasheet". Accessed July 9, 2021.
https://components101.com/sensors/hc-sr501-pir-sensor

[3]   "GitHub - armBookCodeExamples/Directory". Accessed July 9, 2021.
https://github.com/armBookCodeExamples/Directory/

[4]   "Smart Street Lighting | Mbed". Accessed July 9, 2021.
https://os.mbed.com/built-with-mbed/smart-street-lighting/

Chapter 8

Advanced Time Management,
Pulse-Width Modulation, Negative
Feedback Control, and Audio
Message Playback

8.1 Roadmap

8.1.1 What You Will Learn

After you have studied the material in this chapter, you will be able to:

- Describe how to connect RGB LEDs to the NUCLEO board using digital output pins.

- Describe how to connect a light sensor to the NUCLEO board using an analog input pin.

- Develop programs to control the brightness of the RGB LED using pulse-width modulation.

- Summarize the fundamentals of timers that are integrated into a typical microcontroller.

- Implement time management on embedded systems using microcontroller timers.

- Generate an audio message using pulse-width modulation.

- Develop a simple negative feedback control system.

8.1.2 Review of Previous Chapters

In Chapter 3, the *delay()* function was used to vary the blinking rate of LED LD1 to indicate which element had triggered the fire alarm. In that chapter, the behavior was implemented first by means of a continuous delay (100 ms, 500 ms, or 1000 ms depending on the source of the alarm) and then by a delay built up from a set of 10 ms delays, in order to improve the responsiveness of the program. In this chapter, a new way of managing time intervals will be introduced, which will improve the responsiveness even more.

8.1.3 Contents of This Chapter

In this chapter, the use of integrated timers that are found in a typical microcontroller is explained. By means of these timers, time management will be implemented in order to control the behavior of the system. It will be shown that time control based on integrated timers provides a precise and responsive behavior in embedded system implementations.

Pulse-width modulation (PWM) is also introduced, by means of which the brightness level of an RGB LED can be controlled. An RGB (red, green, and blue) LED allows for the implementation of a wide variety of colors by appropriately combining the brightness level of each of the red, green, and blue elements of the RGB LED. It will be explained how to obtain an audio signal (an analog output voltage level that can be heard using headphones) by means of a PWM signal and an appropriate low pass filter.

Finally, the fundamentals of control theory are introduced through an example wherein light is sensed using a LDR (light-dependent resistor or photoresistor), and the brightness of an RGB LED is adjusted using PWM in order to achieve the brightness level, which is set using a potentiometer.

8.2 Analog Signal Generation with the NUCLEO Board

8.2.1 Connect an RGB LED, a Light Sensor, and an Audio Plug to the Smart Home System

In this chapter, the smart home system is provided with a decorative RGB light, a light sensor, and the capability to playback an audio message that says, "Welcome to the Smart Home System." A conceptual diagram of this setup is shown in Figure 8.1. The aim of this setup is to introduce the use of timers and the fundamentals of control theory.

The audio message and the signal to control the RGB light are generated using the PWM technique, as will be discussed in the examples below. The LDR sensor is used to measure the RGB light in order to be able to adjust its intensity to a value that is set using the potentiometer, which is now incorporated in the Gate control panel (Figure 8.1).

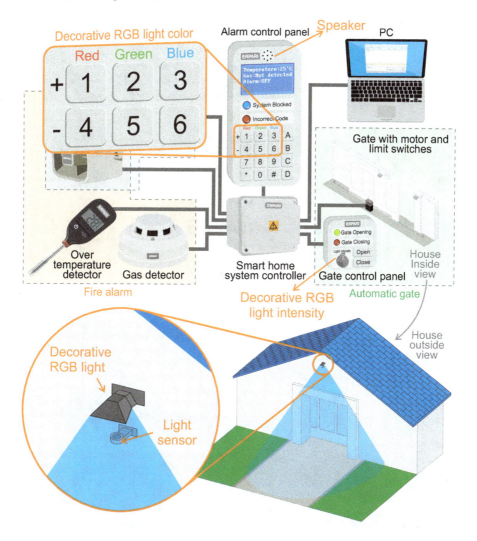

Figure 8.1 The smart home system is now connected to an LCD display.

Figure 8.2 shows the connections of the RGB LED [1], LDR light sensor [2], RC (resistor-capacitor) low pass filter [3], and the headphones that are connected to the smart home system in this chapter.

NOTE: In the implementation detailed in this chapter, the speaker is replaced by headphones, while the potentiometer that was connected in previous chapters is used to control the RGB intensity.

NOTE: The buzzer is now connected to the pin PC_9. In the following pages it will be explained why this is the case.

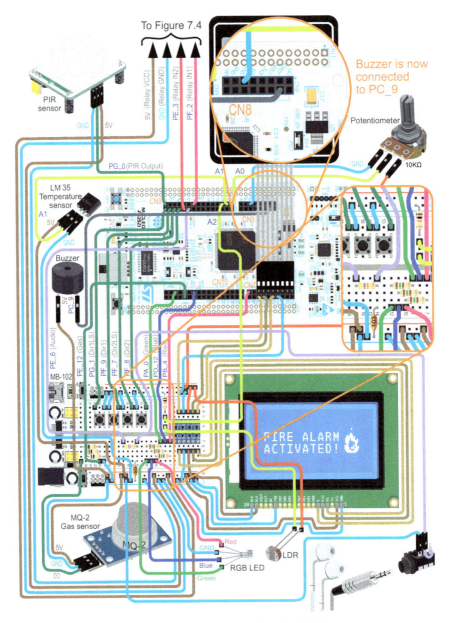

Figure 8.2 The smart home system now has an RGB LED, a light sensor, and a circuit for audio playback.

Figure 8.3 shows a diagram of the RGB LED connections and how to identify each of the pins of the RGB LED. The 150 Ω resistors are used to limit the current through each of the LEDs. The red, blue, and green LEDs are all built inside the package of the RGB LED.

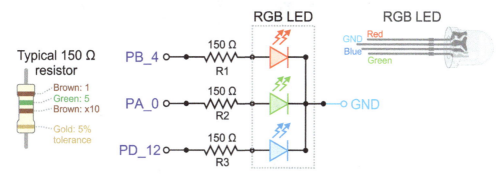

Figure 8.3 Diagram of the connection of the RGB LED.

Turning the different LEDs on and off obtains the set of colors shown in Figure 8.4. If the light intensity of each LED is modulated, a palette of millions of colors can be obtained. This behavior can be achieved by using the *pulse-width modulation* (PWM) technique, which is explained in subsection 8.2.2.

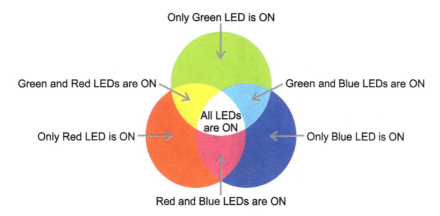

Figure 8.4 Diagram of the light colors that result dependent on the LEDs that are turned on.

To test if the RGB LED is working, the *.bin* file of the program "Subsection 8.2.1.a" should be downloaded from the URL available in [4] and loaded onto the NUCLEO board. The program should vary the color of the RGB LED through the palette shown in Figure 8.4 and all the intermediate colors as the button B1 USER is pressed. At the same time, the intensity of each of the LEDs of the RGB LED is printed on the serial terminal on a scale from 0 to 1.

 NOTE: In Figure 8.5 it can be seen that PB_4, PA_0, and PD_12 are associated with PWM3/1, PWM2/1, and PWM4/1, respectively, which means PWM timer 3/channel 1, PWM timer 2/channel 1, and PWM timer 4/channel 1. By connecting each LED to a different PWM timer, it is possible to control their intensities independently, as will be shown in the examples below.

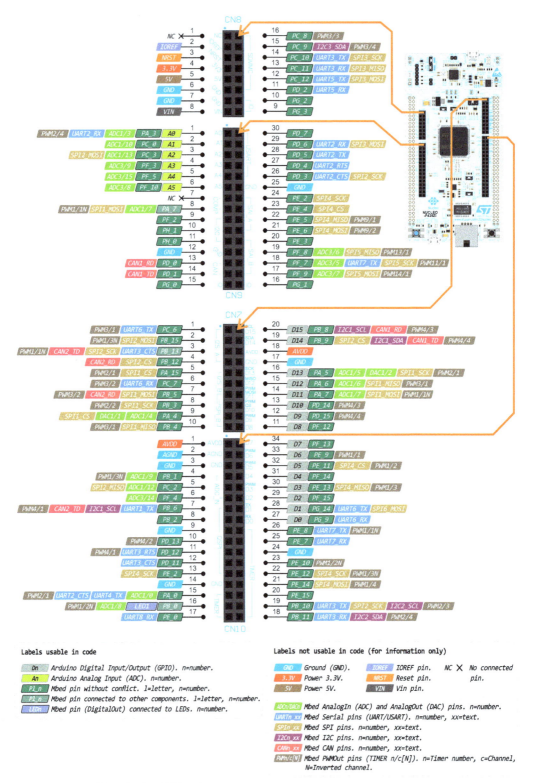

Figure 8.5 ST Zio connectors of the NUCLEO-F429ZI board.

Figure 8.6 shows the connections of a circuit used to sense light intensity by means of an LDR. This component varies its resistance depending on the amount of light sensed. In this way, the voltage at the analog input A2 varies as the light intensity over the LDR varies.

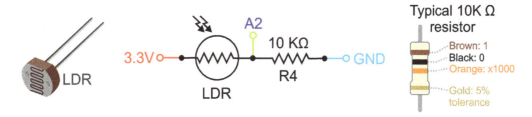

Figure 8.6 Diagram of the connection of the LDR.

 TIP: The LDR pins are identical, so the LDR can be connected either way around.

Figure 8.7 shows the RC circuit that is used to obtain the analog audio signal from a digital signal at pin PE_6 by using PWM (associated to PWM9/2, as can be seen in Figure 8.5). The resistor R5 and the capacitor C1 make up a *low pass filter*. Subsection 8.2.2 explains how this setup works.

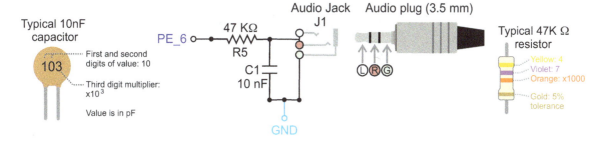

Figure 8.7 Diagram of the connection of the low pass filter and the audio jack.

 TIP: If the components shown in Figure 8.7 are not available, then the values of R5 and C1 can be modified without noticeably degrading the audio signal. For example, a 39 KΩ or 56 KΩ resistor can be used for R5, while a 4.7 nF or 22 nF capacitor can be used for C1. The power dissipation of the resistors and the capacitor voltage rate are not relevant because of the low current and low voltage of this application.

To test if the LDR and the low pass filter are working properly, the *.bin* file of the program "Subsection 8.2.1.b" should be downloaded from the URL available in [4] and loaded onto the NUCLEO board. Plug headphones into the audio jack, and an audio message "Welcome to the smart home system" should be heard just after the NUCLEO board powers up. To listen to the message again, reset the NUCLEO board by means of the Reset B2 button.

NOTE: The audio level is not very loud. To get a louder audio level, an audio amplifier should be used.

 TIP: Ignore all the other elements of the setup during the proposed test (Alarm LED, display, etc.).

Also, as the knob of the potentiometer is turned, the *set point* of the brightness level is modified. The set point is indicated by a message on the serial terminal where the reading of the potentiometer is shown on a scale from 0 to 1 (it is indicated as "SP", as shown in Figure 8.8). The program uses the LDR to sense the light intensity. The reading of the LDR is shown on a scale from 0 to 1 (Figure 8.8). When the light that impinges on the LDR is blocked, the reading shown on the serial terminal should diminish.

 NOTE: Example 8.5 will explain in detail the concept of *set point* and how the brightness of the RGB LED can be controlled by means of the readings of the potentiometer and the LDR, as in the conceptual diagram shown on Figure 8.1.

```
SP: 0.7369 | LDR: 0.7046
SP: 0.7374 | LDR: 0.7151
SP: 0.7361 | LDR: 0.7232
SP: 0.7352 | LDR: 0.7342
SP: 0.7369 | LDR: 0.7384
```

Figure 8.8 Information shown on the serial terminal when program "Subsection 8.2.1.b" is running.

It was mentioned in Example 6.5 that the function *displayBitmapWrite()* requires sending hundreds of bytes of data to the graphical display, which may interfere with the time management of the strobe light and the siren implemented by means of LD1 and the buzzer, respectively. Due to this, when gas and over temperature are detected, the time the siren and the strobe light are on and off is not always 100 ms as expected. This problem is addressed in this chapter by means of using PWM to control the siren and the strobe light.

In order to use the PWM technique to control the siren and the strobe light, it should be noted in Figure 8.5 that PB_0 is connected to LED1 of the NUCLEO board (the one labeled as LD1 that is used to mock the strobe light). It should also be noted that PB_0 is associated with PWM1/2N. This means that the strobe light (LD1) can be controlled using channel 2 of PWM timer 1 (the N stands for inverted, which means that the true state is implemented with 0 V).

In Figure 8.5, it can be seen that the pin PE_10 that was used in previous chapters to activate the buzzer (which simulates the siren) is also related to PWM1/2N. In this way, if PWM timer 1 is used to control LD1 and the buzzer, then both will be driven by the same signal. In this particular case this is a problem, because LD1 is turned off by placing a low state on this LED, while the buzzer is turned off by placing a high state on the corresponding pin. In other words, it will not be possible to turn off both LD1 and the buzzer at the same time using the PWM1/2N signal to control both elements. Therefore, a different PWM timer should be used to control the siren, because the connection of LD1 cannot be modified.

In Table 8.1, it can be seen that all of the PWM timers available in Figure 8.5 are already occupied. In order to solve this problem, *alternative peripheral instances* must be used to assign a PWM timer to the buzzer.

Table 8.1 Summary of the PWM timers that are already in use or occupied by other functionalities.

PWM timer	Used by	Pin	PWM used
1	LD1	PB_0	PWM1/2N
2	RGB LED (G)	PA_0	PWM2/1
3	RGB LED (R)	PB_4	PWM3/1
4	RGB LED (B)	PD_12	PWM4/1
5	Not available in Figure 8.5	–	–
6	Not available in Figure 8.5	–	–
7	Not available in Figure 8.5	–	–
8	Not available in Figure 8.5	–	–
9	Audio playback	PE_6	PWM9/2
10	Not available in Figure 8.5	–	–
11	Button Dir2LS	PF_7	–
12	Not available in Figure 8.5	–	–
13	Button Dir2	PF_8	–
14	Button Dir1	PF_9	–

Alternative peripheral instances are explained in [5]. The idea is that all pins are defined in the *PinNames.h* file of each board. For example, the pins corresponding to the NUCLEO-F429ZI board can be found in [6]. Code 8.1 shows the first part of this file. It can be seen that alternative possibilities that use other hardware peripheral instances are mentioned. In particular, it is highlighted that these alternative possibilities can be used as any other "normal" pin and that these pins are not displayed on the board pinout image shown in Figure 8.5.

```
 1  //=================================================================================
 2  // Notes
 3  //
 4  // - The pins mentioned Px_y_ALTz are alternative possibilities which use other
 5  //   HW peripheral instances. You can use them the same way as any other "normal"
 6  //   pin (i.e. PwmOut pwm(PA_7_ALT0);). These pins are not displayed on the board
 7  //   pinout image on mbed.org.
 8  //
 9  // - The pins which are connected to other components present on the board have
10  //   the comment "Connected to xxx". The pin function may not work properly in this
11  //   case. These pins may not be displayed on the board pinout image on mbed.org.
12  //   Please read the board reference manual and schematic for more information.
13  //
14  // - Warning: pins connected to the default STDIO_UART_TX and STDIO_UART_RX pins are
15  //   commented
16  //   See https://os.mbed.com/teams/ST/wiki/STDIO for more information.
17  //
18  //=================================================================================
```

Code 8.1 Notes on the PinNames.h file of the NUCLEO-F429ZI board.

Code 8.2 and Code 8.3 show the section of *PinNames.h* regarding PWM pins. For example, on line 4 of Code 8.2, it can be seen that PA_0 is related to PWM2 and channel 1 (channel 1 is indicated by the 1 that is the penultimate value of line 4), which is used to control the green LED of the RGB LED (see Figure 8.3). This "normal" functionality of PA_0 is shown in Figure 8.5. In line 1 of Code 8.3, it can be seen that PB_0 is related to PWM1 and channel 2, with inverted behavior (ultimate value 1 of line 1). Inverted behavior means that a logic true is set by a 0 V value, as was explained above. This functionality is also shown on Figure 8.5.

```
 1  //*** PWM ***
 2
 3  MSTD_CONSTEXPR_OBJ_11 PinMap PinMap_PWM[] = {
 4      {PA_0,       PWM_2, STM_PIN_DATA_EXT(STM_MODE_AF_PP, GPIO_NOPULL, GPIO_AF1_TIM2, 1, 0)},
 5      {PA_1,       PWM_2, STM_PIN_DATA_EXT(STM_MODE_AF_PP, GPIO_NOPULL, GPIO_AF1_TIM2, 2, 0)},
 6      {PA_2,       PWM_2, STM_PIN_DATA_EXT(STM_MODE_AF_PP, GPIO_NOPULL, GPIO_AF1_TIM2, 3, 0)},
 7      {PA_2_ALT0,  PWM_9, STM_PIN_DATA_EXT(STM_MODE_AF_PP, GPIO_NOPULL, GPIO_AF3_TIM9, 1, 0)},
 8      {PA_3,       PWM_2, STM_PIN_DATA_EXT(STM_MODE_AF_PP, GPIO_NOPULL, GPIO_AF1_TIM2, 4, 0)},
 9      {PA_3_ALT0,  PWM_9, STM_PIN_DATA_EXT(STM_MODE_AF_PP, GPIO_NOPULL, GPIO_AF3_TIM9, 2, 0)},
10      {PA_5,       PWM_2, STM_PIN_DATA_EXT(STM_MODE_AF_PP, GPIO_NOPULL, GPIO_AF1_TIM2, 1, 0)},
11      {PA_5_ALT0,  PWM_8, STM_PIN_DATA_EXT(STM_MODE_AF_PP, GPIO_NOPULL, GPIO_AF3_TIM8, 1, 1)},
12      {PA_6,       PWM_3, STM_PIN_DATA_EXT(STM_MODE_AF_PP, GPIO_NOPULL, GPIO_AF2_TIM3, 1, 0)},
13      {PA_6_ALT0,  PWM_13, STM_PIN_DATA_EXT(STM_MODE_AF_PP, GPIO_NOPULL, GPIO_AF9_TIM13, 1, 0)},
14      {PA_7,       PWM_1, STM_PIN_DATA_EXT(STM_MODE_AF_PP, GPIO_NOPULL, GPIO_AF1_TIM1, 1, 1)},
15      {PA_7_ALT0,  PWM_3,  STM_PIN_DATA_EXT(STM_MODE_AF_PP, GPIO_NOPULL, GPIO_AF2_TIM3, 2, 0)},
16      {PA_7_ALT1,  PWM_8,  STM_PIN_DATA_EXT(STM_MODE_AF_PP, GPIO_NOPULL, GPIO_AF3_TIM8, 1, 1)},
17      {PA_7_ALT2,  PWM_14, STM_PIN_DATA_EXT(STM_MODE_AF_PP, GPIO_NOPULL, GPIO_AF9_TIM14, 1, 0)},
18      {PA_8,       PWM_1,  STM_PIN_DATA_EXT(STM_MODE_AF_PP, GPIO_NOPULL, GPIO_AF1_TIM1, 1, 0)},
19      {PA_9,       PWM_1,  STM_PIN_DATA_EXT(STM_MODE_AF_PP, GPIO_NOPULL, GPIO_AF1_TIM1, 2, 0)},
20      {PA_10,      PWM_1,  STM_PIN_DATA_EXT(STM_MODE_AF_PP, GPIO_NOPULL, GPIO_AF1_TIM1, 3, 0)},
21      {PA_11,      PWM_1,  STM_PIN_DATA_EXT(STM_MODE_AF_PP, GPIO_NOPULL, GPIO_AF1_TIM1, 4, 0)},
22      {PA_15,      PWM_2,  STM_PIN_DATA_EXT(STM_MODE_AF_PP, GPIO_NOPULL, GPIO_AF1_TIM2, 1, 0)},
```

Code 8.2 Notes on the PinNames.h file of the NUCLEO-F429ZI board.

It can be seen that PWM functionality is available as alternative functionality in more pins indicated as Px_y_ALTz, which are not shown in Figure 8.5. For example, PWM timer 8 is available in PA_5_ALT0 (line 11 of Code 8.2). However, PA_5 is already occupied by the SPI1_SCK functionality used by the graphical

LCD display and, therefore, PA_5 cannot be used without interfering with the display. PWM timer 8 is also available in PA_7_ALT1 (line 20 of Code 8.2), but PA_7 is used by SPI1_MOSI, also used by the graphical LCD display. PWM timer 8 is also available in PB_0_ALT1, PB_1_ALT1, PB_14_ALT0, PB_15_ALT0, PC_6_ALT0, PC_7_ALT0, PC_8_ALT0, and PC_9_ALT0 (Code 8.3). Some of these pins are not being used, as, for example, PC_9. For this reason, the buzzer is connected to PC_9 (see Figure 8.2). In the program code in the examples, a PWM object will be created and assigned to PC_9_ALT0. In this way, this pin will be associated with PWM8/4 (PWM timer 8/channel 4), as can be seen in line 32 of Code 8.3.

```
 1        {PB_0,        PWM_1,   STM_PIN_DATA_EXT(STM_MODE_AF_PP, GPIO_NOPULL, GPIO_AF1_TIM1,  4, 1)},
 2        {PB_0_ALT0,   PWM_3,   STM_PIN_DATA_EXT(STM_MODE_AF_PP, GPIO_NOPULL, GPIO_AF2_TIM3,  3, 0)},
 3        {PB_0_ALT1,   PWM_8,   STM_PIN_DATA_EXT(STM_MODE_AF_PP, GPIO_NOPULL, GPIO_AF3_TIM8,  2, 1)},
 4        {PB_1,        PWM_1,   STM_PIN_DATA_EXT(STM_MODE_AF_PP, GPIO_NOPULL, GPIO_AF1_TIM1,  3, 1)},
 5        {PB_1_ALT0,   PWM_3,   STM_PIN_DATA_EXT(STM_MODE_AF_PP, GPIO_NOPULL, GPIO_AF2_TIM3,  4, 0)},
 6        {PB_1_ALT1,   PWM_8,   STM_PIN_DATA_EXT(STM_MODE_AF_PP, GPIO_NOPULL, GPIO_AF3_TIM8,  3, 1)},
 7        {PB_3,        PWM_2,   STM_PIN_DATA_EXT(STM_MODE_AF_PP, GPIO_NOPULL, GPIO_AF1_TIM2,  2, 0)},
 8        {PB_4,        PWM_3,   STM_PIN_DATA_EXT(STM_MODE_AF_PP, GPIO_NOPULL, GPIO_AF2_TIM3,  1, 0)},
 9        {PB_5,        PWM_3,   STM_PIN_DATA_EXT(STM_MODE_AF_PP, GPIO_NOPULL, GPIO_AF2_TIM3,  2, 0)},
10        {PB_6,        PWM_4,   STM_PIN_DATA_EXT(STM_MODE_AF_PP, GPIO_NOPULL, GPIO_AF2_TIM4,  1, 0)},
11        {PB_7,        PWM_4,   STM_PIN_DATA_EXT(STM_MODE_AF_PP, GPIO_NOPULL, GPIO_AF2_TIM4,  2, 0)},
12        {PB_8,        PWM_4,   STM_PIN_DATA_EXT(STM_MODE_AF_PP, GPIO_NOPULL, GPIO_AF2_TIM4,  3, 0)},
13        {PB_8_ALT0,   PWM_10,  STM_PIN_DATA_EXT(STM_MODE_AF_PP, GPIO_NOPULL, GPIO_AF3_TIM10, 1, 0)},
14        {PB_9,        PWM_4,   STM_PIN_DATA_EXT(STM_MODE_AF_PP, GPIO_NOPULL, GPIO_AF2_TIM4,  4, 0)},
15        {PB_9_ALT0,   PWM_11,  STM_PIN_DATA_EXT(STM_MODE_AF_PP, GPIO_NOPULL, GPIO_AF3_TIM11, 1, 0)},
16        {PB_10,       PWM_2,   STM_PIN_DATA_EXT(STM_MODE_AF_PP, GPIO_NOPULL, GPIO_AF1_TIM2,  3, 0)},
17        {PB_11,       PWM_2,   STM_PIN_DATA_EXT(STM_MODE_AF_PP, GPIO_NOPULL, GPIO_AF1_TIM2,  4, 0)},
18        {PB_13,       PWM_1,   STM_PIN_DATA_EXT(STM_MODE_AF_PP, GPIO_NOPULL, GPIO_AF1_TIM1,  1, 1)},
19        {PB_14,       PWM_1,   STM_PIN_DATA_EXT(STM_MODE_AF_PP, GPIO_NOPULL, GPIO_AF1_TIM1,  2, 1)},
20        {PB_14_ALT0,  PWM_8,   STM_PIN_DATA_EXT(STM_MODE_AF_PP, GPIO_NOPULL, GPIO_AF3_TIM8,  2, 1)},
21        {PB_14_ALT1,  PWM_12,  STM_PIN_DATA_EXT(STM_MODE_AF_PP, GPIO_NOPULL, GPIO_AF9_TIM12, 1, 0)},
22        {PB_15,       PWM_1,   STM_PIN_DATA_EXT(STM_MODE_AF_PP, GPIO_NOPULL, GPIO_AF1_TIM1,  3, 1)},
23        {PB_15_ALT0,  PWM_8,   STM_PIN_DATA_EXT(STM_MODE_AF_PP, GPIO_NOPULL, GPIO_AF3_TIM8,  3, 1)},
24        {PB_15_ALT1,  PWM_12,  STM_PIN_DATA_EXT(STM_MODE_AF_PP, GPIO_NOPULL, GPIO_AF9_TIM12, 2, 0)},
25        {PC_6,        PWM_3,   STM_PIN_DATA_EXT(STM_MODE_AF_PP, GPIO_NOPULL, GPIO_AF2_TIM3,  1, 0)},
26        {PC_6_ALT0,   PWM_8,   STM_PIN_DATA_EXT(STM_MODE_AF_PP, GPIO_NOPULL, GPIO_AF3_TIM8,  1, 0)},
27        {PC_7,        PWM_3,   STM_PIN_DATA_EXT(STM_MODE_AF_PP, GPIO_NOPULL, GPIO_AF2_TIM3,  2, 0)},
28        {PC_7_ALT0,   PWM_8,   STM_PIN_DATA_EXT(STM_MODE_AF_PP, GPIO_NOPULL, GPIO_AF3_TIM8,  2, 0)},
29        {PC_8,        PWM_3,   STM_PIN_DATA_EXT(STM_MODE_AF_PP, GPIO_NOPULL, GPIO_AF2_TIM3,  3, 0)},
30        {PC_8_ALT0,   PWM_8,   STM_PIN_DATA_EXT(STM_MODE_AF_PP, GPIO_NOPULL, GPIO_AF3_TIM8,  3, 0)},
31        {PC_9,        PWM_3,   STM_PIN_DATA_EXT(STM_MODE_AF_PP, GPIO_NOPULL, GPIO_AF2_TIM3,  4, 0)},
32        {PC_9_ALT0,   PWM_8,   STM_PIN_DATA_EXT(STM_MODE_AF_PP, GPIO_NOPULL, GPIO_AF3_TIM8,  4, 0)},
33        {PD_12,       PWM_4,   STM_PIN_DATA_EXT(STM_MODE_AF_PP, GPIO_NOPULL, GPIO_AF2_TIM4,  1, 0)},
34        {PD_13,       PWM_4,   STM_PIN_DATA_EXT(STM_MODE_AF_PP, GPIO_NOPULL, GPIO_AF2_TIM4,  2, 0)},
35        {PD_14,       PWM_4,   STM_PIN_DATA_EXT(STM_MODE_AF_PP, GPIO_NOPULL, GPIO_AF2_TIM4,  3, 0)},
36        {PD_15,       PWM_4,   STM_PIN_DATA_EXT(STM_MODE_AF_PP, GPIO_NOPULL, GPIO_AF2_TIM4,  4, 0)},
37        {PE_5,        PWM_9,   STM_PIN_DATA_EXT(STM_MODE_AF_PP, GPIO_NOPULL, GPIO_AF3_TIM9,  1, 0)},
38        {PE_6,        PWM_9,   STM_PIN_DATA_EXT(STM_MODE_AF_PP, GPIO_NOPULL, GPIO_AF3_TIM9,  2, 0)},
39        {PE_8,        PWM_1,   STM_PIN_DATA_EXT(STM_MODE_AF_PP, GPIO_NOPULL, GPIO_AF1_TIM1,  1, 1)},
40        {PE_9,        PWM_1,   STM_PIN_DATA_EXT(STM_MODE_AF_PP, GPIO_NOPULL, GPIO_AF1_TIM1,  1, 0)},
41        {PE_10,       PWM_1,   STM_PIN_DATA_EXT(STM_MODE_AF_PP, GPIO_NOPULL, GPIO_AF1_TIM1,  2, 1)},
42        {PE_11,       PWM_1,   STM_PIN_DATA_EXT(STM_MODE_AF_PP, GPIO_NOPULL, GPIO_AF1_TIM1,  2, 0)},
42        {PE_12,       PWM_1,   STM_PIN_DATA_EXT(STM_MODE_AF_PP, GPIO_NOPULL, GPIO_AF1_TIM1,  3, 1)},
43        {PE_13,       PWM_1,   STM_PIN_DATA_EXT(STM_MODE_AF_PP, GPIO_NOPULL, GPIO_AF1_TIM1,  3, 0)},
44        {PE_14,       PWM_1,   STM_PIN_DATA_EXT(STM_MODE_AF_PP, GPIO_NOPULL, GPIO_AF1_TIM1,  4, 0)},
45        {PF_6,        PWM_10,  STM_PIN_DATA_EXT(STM_MODE_AF_PP, GPIO_NOPULL, GPIO_AF3_TIM10, 1, 0)},
46        {PF_7,        PWM_11,  STM_PIN_DATA_EXT(STM_MODE_AF_PP, GPIO_NOPULL, GPIO_AF3_TIM11, 1, 0)},
47        {PF_8,        PWM_13,  STM_PIN_DATA_EXT(STM_MODE_AF_PP, GPIO_NOPULL, GPIO_AF9_TIM13, 1, 0)},
48        {PF_9,        PWM_14,  STM_PIN_DATA_EXT(STM_MODE_AF_PP, GPIO_NOPULL, GPIO_AF9_TIM14, 1, 0)},
49        {NC, NC, 0}
50     };
```

Code 8.3 Notes on the PinNames.h file of the NUCLEO-F429ZI board.

TIP: To augment the strobe light functionality, an optional external high-brightness LED can be connected by means of a transistor, as shown in Figure 8.9. This high-brightness LED cannot be connected directly to a NUCLEO board pin, as the NUCLEO board pin cannot provide the current that the LED needs to turn on at its maximum brightness. For this reason, transistor T1 is used, which acts as a controlled switch allowing the higher current to flow through the high-brightness LED when the NUCLEO board pin is set to 3.3 V, and blocking the current through the high-brightness LED when the NUCLEO board pin is set to 0 V.

Note that this circuit is activated with high state and deactivated with low state, the same logic as the NUCLEO board LD1 LED, which is internally connected to the PB_0 pin. Therefore, if the NUCLEO board pin of this circuit is connected to the PB_0 pin of the NUCLEO board, then the high-brightness LED will turn on and off concurrently with the NUCLEO board LD1 LED without needing to modify the code and with a much higher brightness.

The resistor RB is used to limit the current sourced from the NUCLEO board pin. The resistor RC is used to limit the current flow through the high-brightness LED. The brightness of the high-brightness LED can be augmented by reducing the value of RC. This should be done with caution, however, because if the value used is too low, then the high-brightness LED or the transistor T1 (or both) could be damaged.

The maximum current that the BC548C transistor can handle is 100 mA. If a high-brightness LED that demands a higher current is used, then a transistor with a higher maximum current should be used.

If a brighter light is needed for a specific application, the circuit introduced in Figure 7.12 can be used, with the proviso that the warning detailed in Chapter 7 is heeded. It is not recommended to switch a relay more than once a second or its lifetime can be severely reduced.

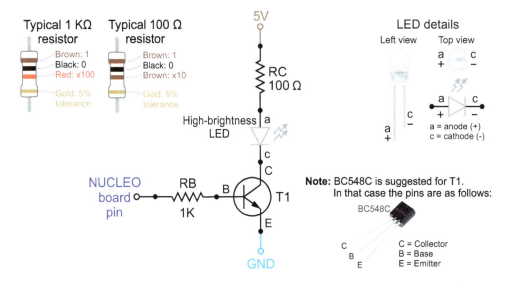

Figure 8.9 Connection of a high-brightness LED to a NUCLEO board pin (optional).

8.2.2 Fundamentals of Timers, Pulse-Width Modulation, and Audio Message Playback

This subsection explains how to use the timers of a microcontroller to generate periodic events. Also, based on these periodic events, it is explained how to use the *pulse-width modulation (PWM)* technique to control the brightness of an LED and to generate audio signals.

Timers are the basis of time management in microcontrollers. The *delay()* function used in Chapter 3 is based on the timers of the microcontroller. In that case, no other code was able to be executed when *delay()* was taking place. This led to the code having low responsiveness, and it was concluded that in order to overcome this issue, it was better to implement a long delay by means of many consecutive short delays. This allowed some other tasks to be attended to in the gaps between these short delays. However, this solution results in inaccurate durations of the delays and many calls to the delay functions.

Implementing the delays with a timer linked to an *interrupt service routine* means that the processor can do other things during the counting. This leads to more accurate and repeatable delays.

In Figure 8.10, a basic diagram of a timer is shown. On the left, it can be seen that the clock signal can be internal or external, which is configured by writing into special locations of the microcontroller internal memory known as *registers* that control the multiplexor selection. Then, there is a *"Down Counter"* module that decrements its value each time there is a pulse of the selected clock. Once this counter reaches zero, an interrupt can be triggered, depending on the control configuration. The timer can also be configured to automatically load the "Initial value" and restart the count from there each time it reaches zero.

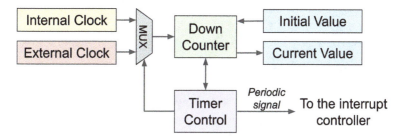

Figure 8.10 Simplified diagram of a timer.

In this way, the periodic signal can be configured by changing the "Initial value" register. The current value of the timer count can be read any time by means of reading the "Current value" register.

Microcontrollers' timers can be used to generate periodic signals, known as *tickers*, as shown in Figure 8.11. The period of the tickers can be adjusted by writing into special registers. There are also registers that are used to enable or disable the tickers, as well as to enable or disable *interrupts* related to the tickers' signals. When writing programs in the C/C++ language, the compiler takes care of all the details regarding the registers.

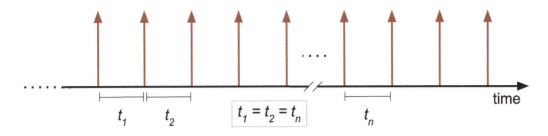

Figure 8.11 Periodic signal generated by the built-in timer of a microcontroller.

Most timers inside microcontrollers are also equipped with special hardware that allows easy implementation of PWM. To see what PWM is and how it can be used to dim the brightness of an LED, download the *.bin* file of the program "Subsection 8.2.2" from [4] and load it onto the NUCLEO board. The program will make LEDs LD1, LD2, and LD3 turn on and off according to the time intervals shown in Table 8.2. When pressing button *Dir1*, connected to pin PF_9, it will be clear to see when the LEDs are on and off. In the case of pressing button *Dir2*, connected to pin PF_8, it will still be appreciated when they are on and off. However, in the case of pressing button *Dir2LS*, connected to pin PF_7, it will not be appreciated when the LEDs are on or off. Instead, the LEDs will appear to shine just a little bit (exactly 20% of full brightness, given that they are on 2 ms and off 8 ms; 2 ms / (2 ms + 8ms) = 0.2).

Table 8.2 On time and off time of the LEDs used in the program "Subsection 8.2.2".

Button	On time	Off time
Button Dir1 connected to pin PF_9	200 milliseconds	800 milliseconds
Button Dir2 connected to pin PF_8	20 milliseconds	80 milliseconds
Button Dir2LS connected to pin PF_7	2 milliseconds	8 milliseconds

Figure 8.12 shows how the brightness of an LED varies as the *duty cycle* of the signal varies.

In frame (d) of Figure 8.13, the waveform of the message "Welcome to the Smart Home System" is shown. This message lasts for three seconds, and the amplitude of the analog signal is sampled regularly (every 125 μs, or 8000 samples per second). Each sample is quantized to the nearest value within a range of digital steps with 8-bit resolution. This is known as *pulse-code modulation* (PCM) and is the standard form of digital audio in computers, compact discs, digital telephony, and other digital audio applications.

In this way, an array of 24,000 values (samples) named *welcomeMessageData* is obtained. In the (a) frame of Figure 8.13, four consecutive values of this array are shown: [n], [n+1], [n+2], and [n+3]. In this example these values are 191, 127, 64, and 120, which corresponds to 75%, 50%, 25%, and 47% of the maximum value obtainable using the 8 bits resolution (255).

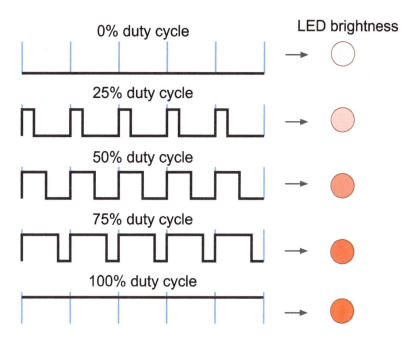

Figure 8.12 Example of the variation of LED brightness by the pulse width modulation technique.

Frame (c) of Figure 8.13 shows how the duty cycle of a PWM digital signal is *modulated* using the data of *welcomeMessageData*, normalized to 255. The period of the signal is 25 µs, so every 5 periods (125 µs), its duty cycle is adjusted according to a new value read from the *welcomeMessageData* array.

Frame (b) of Figure 8.13 shows the analog output signal that is obtained when the signal shown in (b) is filtered by the low pass filter introduced in Figure 8.7. It can be seen that in this way a 500 µs piece out of the three seconds' length audio signal is obtained.

By means of repeating this process for the whole set of values of the array *welcomeMessageData*, the message "Welcome to the smart home system" is obtained.

 NOTE: The value of V_{Max} (in frame (c) of Figure 8.13) varies depending on several factors.

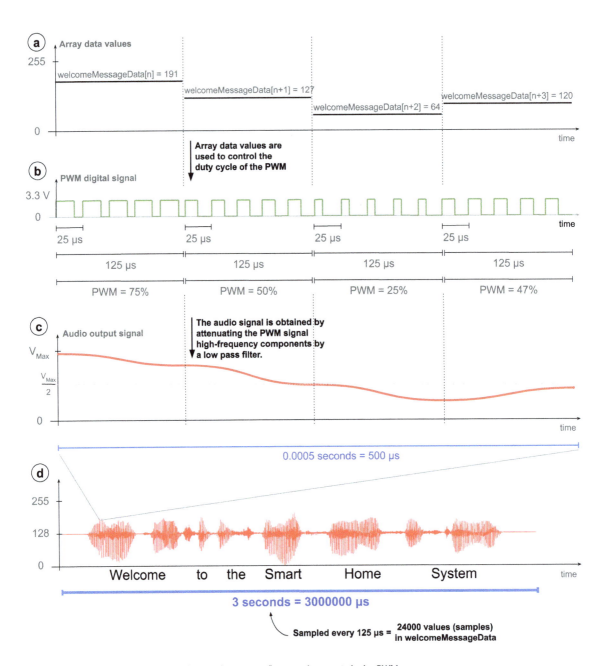

Figure 8.13 *Detail on how the "Welcome to the smart home system" message is generated using PWM.*

Example 8.1: Implementation of PWM to Control the Brightness of an RGB LED

Objective

Introduce an implementation of pulse-width modulation (PWM).

Summary of the Expected Behavior

The brightness of the RGB LED should change as the knob of the potentiometer is rotated.

Test the Proposed Solution on the Board

Import the project "Example 8.1" using the URL available in [4], build the project, and drag the .*bin* file onto the NUCLEO board. Rotate the knob of the potentiometer gradually and observe how the RGB LED turns on in a white color, and its brightness changes as the knob of the potentiometer is rotated.

Discussion of the Proposed Solution

The proposed solution is based on three new modules: *light_system*, responsible for updating the duty cycle of the PWM; *bright_control*, responsible for generating the PWM signal with a given duty cycle; and *light_level_control*, responsible for the reading of the potentiometer. In this way, if the element that controls the light level is changed (for instance, using a set of buttons instead of the potentiometer), only the *light_level_control* module needs to be changed, and there is no need to update the *light_system* module.

Implementation of the Proposed Solution

The initialization of the *light_system* module is done at the beginning of the program by means of a call to the function *lightSystemInit()* from *smartHomeSystemInit()*, as can be seen on line 10 of Code 8.4. The function *lightSystemUpdate()* is included in *smartHomeSystemUpdate()* (line 21) to periodically update the duty cycle of the PWM signal. In order to implement these calls, the library *light_system.h* is included in *smart_home_system.cpp*, as can be seen in Table 8.3.

```
1   void smartHomeSystemInit()
2   {
3       userInterfaceInit();
4       alarmInit();
5       fireAlarmInit();
6       intruderAlarmInit();
7       pcSerialComInit();
8       motorControlInit();
9       gateInit();
10      lightSystemInit();
11  }
12
13  void smartHomeSystemUpdate()
14  {
15      userInterfaceUpdate();
16      fireAlarmUpdate();
17      intruderAlarmUpdate();
18      alarmUpdate();
19      eventLogUpdate();
20      pcSerialComUpdate();
21      lightSystemUpdate();
22      delay(SYSTEM_TIME_INCREMENT_MS);
23  }
```

Code 8.4 New implementation of the functions smartHomeSystemInit and smartHomeSystemUpdate.

Table 8.3 Sections in which lines were added to smart_home_system.cpp.

Section	Lines that were added
Libraries	#include "light_system.h"

The assignment of the *sirenPin* was modified for the reasons that were discussed on section 8.2.1. This change is summarized on Table 8.4.

Table 8.4 Lines that were modified in siren.cpp.

Section	Previous line	New line
Declaration and initialization of public global objects	DigitalOut sirenPin(PE_10);	DigitalOut sirenPin(PC_9);

The new module *light_system* is shown in Code 8.5 and Code 8.6. The libraries that are included are shown from lines 3 to 7 of Code 8.5. On line 11, a private global variable name *dutyCycle* is declared and initialized. From lines 15 to 18, the implementation of the function *lightSystemInit()* is shown. This calls the function that initializes the module *bright_control* (line 17). Finally, the function *lightSystemUpdate()*, which reads the value of the potentiometer (line 22) and updates the duty cycle for each of the three LEDs (lines 24 to 26), is shown.

```
1   //=====[Libraries]==========================================================
2
3   #include "arm_book_lib.h"
4
5   #include "light_system.h"
6   #include "bright_control.h"
7   #include "light_level_control.h"
8
9   //=====[Declaration and initialization of private global variables]=============
10
11  static float dutyCycle = 0.5;
12
13  //=====[Implementations of public functions]====================================
14
15  void lightSystemInit()
16  {
17      brightControlInit();
18  }
19
20  void lightSystemUpdate()
21  {
22      dutyCycle = lightLevelControlRead();
23
24      setDutyCycle( RGB_LED_RED, dutyCycle );
25      setDutyCycle( RGB_LED_GREEN, dutyCycle );
26      setDutyCycle( RGB_LED_BLUE, dutyCycle );
27  }
```

Code 8.5 Details of the implementation of light_system.cpp.

In Code 8.6, the implementation of *light_system.h* is shown. It can be seen that the data type *lightSystem_t* and the prototypes of the public functions are declared on lines 8 to 12 and 16 to 17, respectively.

```
1   //=====[#include guards - begin]=================================================
2
3   #ifndef _LIGHT_SYSTEM_H_
4   #define _LIGHT_SYSTEM_H_
5
6   //=====[Declaration of public data types]=========================================
7
8   typedef enum {
9       RGB_LED_RED,
10      RGB_LED_GREEN,
11      RGB_LED_BLUE,
12  } lightSystem_t;
13
14  //=====[Declarations (prototypes) of public functions]============================
15
16  void lightSystemInit();
17  void lightSystemUpdate();
18
19  //=====[#include guards - end]====================================================
20
21  #endif // _LIGHT_SYSTEM_H_
```

Code 8.6 Details of the implementation of light_system.h.

The implementation of the new module *light_level_control* is presented in Code 8.7. The libraries that are included are shown from lines 3 to 6. On line 10, the public global object *potentiometer*, related to the potentiometer connected to the analog input 2 (A0), is declared. The reader may notice that the public functions implementation (from lines 14 to 21) is quite simple. In this case, no average is applied to the analog signal samples as the voltage is more stable than when reading sensors; this was explained in Chapter 3. In this case, a small variation in the reading due to noise has no significant impact on the system behavior. The functions *lightLevelControlInit()* (line 14) and *lightLevelControlUpdate()* (line 16) are kept to maintain the same structure used as, for example, in the *temperature_sensor* module.

```
1   //=====[Libraries]================================================================
2
3   #include "arm_book_lib.h"
4
5   #include "smart_home_system.h"
6   #include "light_level_control.h"
7
8   //=====[Declaration and initialization of public global objects]=================
9
10  AnalogIn potentiometer(A0);
11
12  //=====[Implementations of public functions]=====================================
13
14  void lightLevelControlInit() { }
15
16  void lightLevelControlUpdate() { }
17
18  float lightLevelControlRead()
19  {
20      return potentiometer.read();
21  }
22
23  //=====[Implementations of private functions]====================================
```

Code 8.7 Details of the implementation of light_level_control.cpp.

Code 8.8 shows the implementation of *light_level_control.h*. The prototypes of the public functions are declared from lines 8 to 10.

```
1    //=====[#include guards - begin]============================================
2
3    #ifndef _LIGHT_LEVEL_CONTROL_H_
4    #define _LIGHT_LEVEL_CONTROL_H_
5
6    //=====[Declarations (prototypes) of public functions]=====================
7
8    void lightLevelControlInit();
9    void lightLevelControlUpdate();
10   float lightLevelControlRead();
11
12   //=====[#include guards - end]=============================================
13
14   #endif // _LIGHT_LEVEL_CONTROL_H_
```

Code 8.8 Details of the implementation of light_level_control.h.

The new module *bright_control* is presented in Code 8.9, Code 8.10, and Code 8.11. From lines 3 to 8 of Code 8.9, the libraries used in this module are included. A private definition of LEDS_QUANTITY is declared on line 12. On line 18, the public global array object *RGBLed* of DigitalOut, relating to each of the colors of the RGB LED (PB_4 for red, PA_0 for green, and PD_12 for blue), is declared. These LEDs represent the lights of the smart home system that will be controlled using PWM, with a duty cycle that will be defined by the light level control (represented by a potentiometer).

```
1    //=====[Libraries]=========================================================
2
3    #include "arm_book_lib.h"
4
5    #include "bright_control.h"
6
7    #include "light_level_control.h"
8    #include "pc_serial_com.h"
9
10   //=====[Declaration of private defines]====================================
11
12   #define LEDS_QUANTITY 3
13
14   //=====[Declaration and initialization of public global objects]===========
15
16   DigitalOut RGBLed[] = {(PB_4), (PA_0), (PD_12)};
17
18   Ticker tickerBrightControl;
19
20   //=====[Declaration and initialization of private global variables]========
21
22   static int onTime[LEDS_QUANTITY];
23   static int offTime[LEDS_QUANTITY];
24
25   static int tickRateMsBrightControl = 1;
26   static int tickCounter[LEDS_QUANTITY];
27
28   static float periodSFloat[LEDS_QUANTITY];
29
30   //=====[Declarations (prototypes) of private functions]====================
31
32   static void setPeriod( lightSystem_t light, float period );
33   static void tickerCallbackBrightControl( );
```

Code 8.9 Details of the implementation of bright_control.cpp (Part 1/2).

In this example, the PWM signal will be generated using a timer interrupt associated with a ticker. The private global object *tickerBrightControl* of type ticker is declared on line 18. The global variables that account for the on and off time of the RGB LEDs are declared on lines 22 and 23, respectively. On line 25, *tickRateMsBrightControl* is declared and initialized, which will be used to set the tick rate to 1 ms to control the brightness.

Line 26 declares an array of int to account for the ticks of the ticker. On line 28, an array of type float is declared to store the period of each LED expressed in seconds. Each position of this array stores the period of each of the RGB LEDs' PWM signals.

The prototype of the function *setPeriod()* is declared on line 32. This function will be used to set the period of each of the LEDs. The callback function *tickerCallbackBrightControl()* is declared on line 33. This callback function will be called once every millisecond, as discussed below.

Code 8.10 shows the implementation of *brightControlInit()*. In line 5, *tickerBrightControl* is configured. The first parameter indicates that *tickerCallbackBrightControl()* must be called at the tick rate expressed in seconds by the second parameter, *(float) tickRateMsBrightControl) / 1000.0*. The variable is divided by 1000 and the result is *cast* to a float in order to get 0.001 (which corresponds to one millisecond).

```
1   //=====[Implementations of public functions]==================================
2
3   void brightControlInit()
4   {
5       tickerBrightControl.attach( tickerCallbackBrightControl,
6                                 ( (float) tickRateMsBrightControl) / 1000.0 );
7
8       setPeriod( RGB_LED_RED, 0.01f );
9       setPeriod( RGB_LED_GREEN, 0.01f );
10      setPeriod( RGB_LED_BLUE, 0.01f );
11
12      setDutyCycle( RGB_LED_RED, 0.5f );
13      setDutyCycle( RGB_LED_GREEN, 0.5f );
14      setDutyCycle( RGB_LED_BLUE, 0.5f );
15  }
16
17  void setDutyCycle( lightSystem_t light, float dutyCycle )
18  {
19      onTime[light] = int ( ( periodSFloat[light] * dutyCycle ) * 1000 );
20      offTime[light] = int ( periodSFloat[light] * 1000) - onTime[light];
21  }
22
23  //=====[Implementations of private functions]=================================
24
25  void setPeriod( lightSystem_t light, float period )
26  {
27      periodSFloat[light] = period;
28  }
29
30  static void tickerCallbackBrightControl( )
31  {
32      int i;
33
34      for (i = 0 ; i < LEDS_QUANTITY ; i++) {
35          tickCounter[i]++;
36          if ( RGBLed[i].read() == ON ) {
```

```
37              if( tickCounter[i] > onTime[i] ) {
38                  tickCounter[i] = 1;
39                  if ( offTime[i] ) RGBLed[i] = OFF;
40
41              }
42          } else {
43              if( tickCounter[i] > offTime[i] ) {
44                  tickCounter[i] = 1;
45                  if ( onTime[i] ) RGBLed[i] = ON;
46              }
47          }
48      }
49  }
```

Code 8.10 Details of the implementation of bright_control.cpp (Part 2/2).

For all three LEDs, a period of 10 milliseconds (0.01 f) is set from lines 8 to 10 using the private function *setPeriod()*. An initial duty cycle of 50% (0.5 f) is set from lines 12 to 14, using the public function *setDutyCycle()*.

The function *setDutyCycle()* is shown on lines 17 to 21 of Code 8.10. This function receives a parameter named *light* of type *lightSystem_t*, defined in *light_system.h* (Code 8.6), and a float named *dutyCycle*. Because the handler of *tickerBrightControl* is called once a millisecond, the duty cycle needs to be converted from a percentage to a time expressed in milliseconds. This implies a truncation that affects the PWM signal accuracy and resolution. To set the on time, the period defined for each of the LEDs is multiplied in line 19 by the duty cycle received as a parameter. Because the period is defined in seconds, it is multiplied by 1000 to get the value in milliseconds. Finally, the result is *cast* (forcing one data type to be converted into another) to an int variable. On line 20, the off time is computed.

> **NOTE:** The cast operation removes the decimals of the result, so if the result before the cast is 2.9, the value after the cast will be 2. As the reader may notice, this operation degrades the accuracy and resolution of the PWM signal. In the next example, a way to tackle this issue will be presented.

In Code 8.10, the implementation of *setPeriod()* is shown on lines 25 to 28. This function receives a parameter named *light* of type *lightSystem_t* and a float named *period*. The value of *period* is stored in the position *light* of the array *periodSFloat* declared on line 28 of Code 8.9.

The implementation of the callback function *tickerCallbackBrightControl()* is shown on lines 30 to 49 of Code 8.10. A *for* loop is used to update the state of the pins connected to each of the colors of the RGB LEDs. The array *tickCounter* counts the milliseconds elapsed since the last transition (low to high or high to low) of each color and is incremented in each call (line 35). If the RGB LED color pin being compared is ON (line 36), then the *tickCounter* is compared with the stored value of *onTime* (line 37). Otherwise, when it is OFF (line 42), the *tickCounter* is compared with the stored value of *offTime* (line 43). When these values are reached, the *tickCounter* is reset (lines 38 and 44), and the corresponding RGB LED color pin is toggled if the duration of the next time (*onTime* or *offTime)* is different from zero (lines 39 and 45).

In Code 8.11, the implementation of *bright_control.h* is shown. In this particular case, a library is included on line 8, because the user-defined type *lightSystem_t* that is used in this module is defined in *light_system.h*. It can be seen that the prototypes of the public functions are declared on lines 16 and 17.

```
1   //=====[#include guards - begin]================================================
2
3   #ifndef _BRIGHT_CONTROL_H_
4   #define _BRIGHT_CONTROL_H_
5
6   //=====[Libraries]==============================================================
7
8   #include "light_system.h"
9
10  //=====[Declarations (prototypes) of public functions]==========================
11
12  void brightControlInit();
13  void setDutyCycle( lightSystem_t light, float dutyCycle );
14
15  //=====[#include guards - end]==================================================
16
17  #endif // _BRIGHT_CONTROL_H_
```

Code 8.11 Details of the implementation of bright_control.h.

The initialization of the *light_level_control* module is added to *userInterfaceInit()* (line 14 of Code 8.12), and *lightLevelControlUpdate()* is called in *userInterfaceUpdate()* (line 23 of Code 8.12). As described, these functions have no functionality and are only included to maintain the same structure as in previous implementations. In order to make these calls, the library *bright_control.h* is included in *user_interface.cpp*, as can be seen in Table 8.5.

```
1   void userInterfaceInit()
2   {
3       gateOpenButton.mode(PullUp);
4       gateCloseButton.mode(PullUp);
5
6       gateOpenButton.fall(&gateOpenButtonCallback);
7       gateCloseButton.fall(&gateCloseButtonCallback);
8
9       incorrectCodeLed = OFF;
10      systemBlockedLed = OFF;
11      matrixKeypadInit( SYSTEM_TIME_INCREMENT_MS );
12      userInterfaceDisplayInit();
13
14      lightLevelControlInit();
15  }
16
17  void userInterfaceUpdate()
18  {
19      userInterfaceMatrixKeypadUpdate();
20      incorrectCodeIndicatorUpdate();
21      systemBlockedIndicatorUpdate();
22      userInterfaceDisplayUpdate();
23      lightLevelControlUpdate();
24  }
```

Code 8.12 New implementation of the functions userInterfaceInit and userInterfaceUpdate.

Table 8.5 Sections in which lines were added to user_interface.cpp.

Section	Lines that were added
Libraries	`#include "bright_control.h"`

Proposed Exercises

1. How can the PWM resolution be improved?

2. Why is the function *setPeriod()* private to the module *bright_control*, while the function *setDutyCycle()* is public?

Answers to the Exercises

1. A larger period could be defined for each of the PWM signals (lines 8 to 10 of Code 8.10). The period can be increased until the LED starts blinking instead of changing its brightness; then the maximum period has been reached.

2. The function *setPeriod()* is private because it is only used by the module *bright_control*, and the function *setDutyCycle()* is public because it is used by other modules.

Example 8.2: Implementation of PWM using the PwmOut Class

Objective

Use the PwmOut class to control the period and duty cycle of a PWM signal.

Summary of the Expected Behavior

The behavior should be the same as the previous example, although the reader may notice that the accuracy and the resolution of the PWM signal is improved.

Test the Proposed Solution on the Board

Import the project "Example 8.2" using the URL available in [4], build the project, and drag the *.bin* file onto the NUCLEO board. Rotate the knob of the potentiometer gradually, and observe how the RGB LED turns on in a white color, and its brightness changes as the knob of the potentiometer is rotated.

Discussion of the Proposed Solution

The proposed solution modifies the module *bright_control* to use the *PwmOut* object.

Implementation of the Proposed Solution

In Code 8.13, the new implementation of *bright_control.cpp* is shown. An object of the *class* PwmOut is used in line 11 to declare each of the pins connected to the colors of the RGB LED *PwmOut*. The reader should notice that in Code 8.9, an array of DigitalOut objects was used to declare the pins connected to the RGB LED.

As a consequence, the reader may notice that the code is now far simpler than in the previous example, by comparing Code 8.13 with Code 8.9 and Code 8.10. In Table 8.6, the sections in which lines were removed from *bright_control.cpp* are shown. Functions in which lines were removed are shown on Table 8.7. All the other lines remain the same. The implementations of *setPeriod()* and *setDutyCycle()* are reduced in Code 8.13 to a single line. In *setDutyCycle()*, the duty cycle is set on line 32, and in *setPeriod()*, the period is configured on line 39. The on and off times of the PWM signal are not truncated in this implementation, so the accuracy and resolution are improved.

Table 8.6 Sections in which lines were removed from bright_control.cpp.

Section	Lines that were removed
Declaration of private defines	`#define LEDS_QUANTITY 3`
Declaration and initialization of public global objects	`Ticker tickerBrightControl;`

Declaration and initialization of private global variables	`static int onTime[LEDS_QUANTITY];`
	`static int offTime[LEDS_QUANTITY];`
	`int tickRateMSBrightControl = 1;`
	`static int tickCounter[LEDS_QUANTITY];`
	`static float periodSFloat[LEDS_QUANTITY];`

Declarations (prototypes) of private functions	`static void tickerCallbackBrightControl( );`

Table 8.7 Functions in which lines were removed from bright_control.cpp.

Section	Lines that were removed

void brightControlInit()	`atickerBrightControl.attach(`
	`    tickerCallbackBrightControl,`
	`( (float) tickRateMSBrightControl) / 1000.0 );`

static void tickerCallbackBrightControl()	This function was removed.

The reader may also notice that because of modularization and the use of functions, a different implementation of PWM was introduced, and the only changes were in the bright control module. All the other new modules presented in the previous examples are *abstracted* from the way the PWM is implemented.

```
1   //=====[Libraries]==================================================
2
3   #include "arm_book_lib.h"
4
5   #include "bright_control.h"
6
7   #include "light_level_control.h"
8
9   //=====[Declaration and initialization of public global objects]===============
10
11  PwmOut RGBLed[] = {(PB_4), (PA_0), (PD_12)};
12
13  //=====[Declaration and initialization of private global variables]============
14
15  static void setPeriod( lightSystem_t light, float period );
16
17  //=====[Implementations of public functions]===================================
18
19  void brightControlInit()
20  {
21      setPeriod( RGB_LED_RED, 0.01f );
22      setPeriod( RGB_LED_GREEN, 0.01f );
23      setPeriod( RGB_LED_BLUE, 0.01f );
24
25      setDutyCycle( RGB_LED_RED, 0.5 );
26      setDutyCycle( RGB_LED_GREEN, 0.5 );
27      setDutyCycle( RGB_LED_BLUE, 0.5 );
28  }
29
30  void setDutyCycle( lightSystem_t light, float dutyCycle )
31  {
32      RGBLed[light].write(dutyCycle);
33  }
34
35  //=====[Implementations of private functions]==================================
36
37  static void setPeriod( lightSystem_t light, float period )
38  {
39      RGBLed[light].period(period);
40  }
```

Code 8.13 Details of the implementation of bright_control.cpp.

Proposed Exercise

1. How can the code of Examples 8.1 and 8.2 be compared, considering that their functionality is the same?

Answer to the Exercise

1. In Example 8.1, the PWM technique was implemented using a *ticker* object and a set of functions that were implemented, like *setDutyCycle()*, *setPeriod()*, and *tickerCallbackBrightControl()*. In Example 8.2, the object *PwmOut* was used, which simplifies the usage of the PWM technique. Having implemented all the details in Example 8.1 helps in understanding what is going on in the background when the object *PwmOut* is used.

Example 8.3: Control the Siren and Strobe Light using PWM

Objective

Use the PwmOut object to control the siren and the strobe light.

Summary of the Expected Behavior

The behavior should be the same as the previous example, although the problem related to the timing of the strobe light and siren not always being 100 ms is addressed.

Test the Proposed Solution on the Board

Import the project "Example 8.3" using the URL available in [4], build the project, and drag the .*bin* file onto the NUCLEO board. Activate the motion sensor and the fire alarm, and observe that the time for which the strobe light and siren are on and off is always 100 ms.

Discussion of the Proposed Solution

The proposed solution modifies the module *siren* and *strobe_light* to use the PwmOut object. In this way, there is not a DigitalOut object that is set on and off, as was the case in the previous implementation, but a PwmOut object that is configured to alternate its state over time or to remain in the off state all the time, depending on the value of the variable *sirenState*.

Implementation of the Proposed Solution

The proposed new implementation of *siren.cpp* and *strobe_light.cpp* is shown in Code 8.14 and Code 8.15, respectively. These two implementations are identical except for the use of *siren* and *strobeLight* in each case, and the value of the parameter in lines 24 and 46.

On line 12, the object is changed from DigitalOut to PwmOut. In order to avoid changes in other files, the prototypes of all the public functions were left unmodified. When the function *sirenUpdate()* or *strobeLightUpdate()* is called, the current strobe time (declared on line 17: *currentStrobeTime*) is compared with the received parameter (line 40). If they are different, then the received strobe time is multiplied by two (because the strobe time accounts only for the time the alarm must be in ON state, while *sirenPin.period* is the sum of the time it is on and off), converted from milliseconds to seconds (i.e., multiplied by 1000), and cast to float to set the PWM period (line 41). Then, the PWM signal duty cycle is set to 50% (line 42), and the current strobe time is updated (line 43).

In order to turn off the siren, a 100% duty cycle is set (line 46 of Code 8.14) because the buzzer is turned off with a high state signal. In the case of the strobe light, a 0% duty cycle is set (line 46 of Code 8.15) because LD1 is turned off with a low state signal. The current strobe time is set to 0 in both programs (line 47). The initialization of each module is implemented by setting a period of 1 second (line 23) with a 100% duty cycle (line 24) (in the case of the *strobe light*, a 0% duty cycle is set).

```
1   //=====[Libraries]===============================================================
2
3   #include "mbed.h"
4   #include "arm_book_lib.h"
5
6   #include "siren.h"
7
8   #include "smart_home_system.h"
9
10  //=====[Declaration and initialization of public global objects]================
11
12  PwmOut sirenPin(PC_9_ALT0);
13
14  //=====[Declaration and initialization of private global variables]============
15
16  static bool sirenState = OFF;
17  static int currentStrobeTime = 0;
18
19  //=====[Implementations of public functions]====================================
20
21  void sirenInit()
22  {
23      sirenPin.period(1.0f);
24      sirenPin.write(1.0f);
25  }
26
27  bool sirenStateRead()
28  {
29      return sirenState;
30  }
31
32  void sirenStateWrite( bool state )
33  {
34      sirenState = state;
35  }
36
37  void sirenUpdate( int strobeTime )
38  {
39      if( sirenState ) {
40          if (currentStrobeTime != strobeTime) {
41              sirenPin.period( (float) strobeTime * 2 / 1000 );
42              sirenPin.write(0.5f);
43              currentStrobeTime = strobeTime;
44          }
45      } else {
46          sirenPin.write(1.0f);
47          currentStrobeTime = 0;
48      }
49  }
```

Code 8.14 Details of the new implementation of siren.cpp.

```cpp
1   //=====[Libraries]================================================
2
3   #include "mbed.h"
4   #include "arm_book_lib.h"
5
6   #include "strobe_light.h"
7
8   #include "smart_home_system.h"
9
10  //=====[Declaration and initialization of public global objects]================
11
12  PwmOut strobeLight(LED1);
13
14  //=====[Declaration and initialization of private global variables]============
15
16  static bool strobeLightState = OFF;
17  static int currentStrobeTime = 0;
18
19  //=====[Implementations of public functions]===============================
20
21  void strobeLightInit()
22  {
23      strobeLight.period(1.0f);
24      strobeLight.write(0.0f);
25  }
26
27  bool strobeLightStateRead()
28  {
29      return strobeLightState;
30  }
31
32  void strobeLightStateWrite( bool state )
33  {
34      strobeLightState = state;
35  }
36
37  void strobeLightUpdate( int strobeTime )
38  {
39      if( strobeLightState ) {
40          if (currentStrobeTime != strobeTime) {
41              strobeLight.period( (float) strobeTime * 2 / 1000 );
42              strobeLight.write(0.5f);
43              currentStrobeTime = strobeTime;
44          }
45      } else {
46          strobeLight.write(0.0f);
47          currentStrobeTime = 0;
48      }
49  }
```

Code 8.15 Details of the new implementation of strobe_light.cpp.

Example 8.4: Adjustment of the Color of the Decorative RGB LED

Objective

Upgrade the code to allow independent control of each LED.

Summary of the Expected Behavior

The color of the decorative RGB LED is configured using the matrix keypad.

Test the Proposed Solution on the Board

Import the project "Example 8.4" using the URL available in [4], build the project, and drag the .*bin* file onto the NUCLEO board. Rotate the knob of the potentiometer and set the maximum brightness of the RGB LED. Press button 4 five times on the matrix keypad and observe how gradually the red color of the RGB LED turns off. Press button 5 five times on the matrix keypad and observe how gradually the green color of the RGB LED turns off. Press button 6 five times on the matrix keypad and observe how gradually the blue color of the RGB LED turns off. Now press buttons 1, 2, and 3 several times in order to see how the red, green, and blue colors of the RGB LED turn on. Rotate the knob of the potentiometer to see that the light color of the RGB LED remains unchanged, while the brightness increases and decreases.

 NOTE: Buttons 1 through 6 of the matrix keypad are only available to use for this functionality when the alarm is OFF.

Discussion of the Proposed Solution

The proposed solution modifies only the modules *user_interface* and *light_system*. An independent factor for each color is introduced in order to multiply the duty cycle that is configured using the potentiometer. In this way, each color can be varied independently.

Implementation of the Proposed Solution

In Code 8.16, the new implementation of the function *userInterfaceMatrixKeypadUpdate()* is shown. A new set of options is included using the *if* statement from lines 34 to 51. In each of these options, the function *lightSystemBrightnessChangeRGBFactor()* is called with all the possible combinations of colors and true or false.

```
1   static void userInterfaceMatrixKeypadUpdate()
2   {
3       static int numberOfHashKeyReleased = 0;
4       char keyReleased = matrixKeypadUpdate();
5
6       if( keyReleased != '\0' ) {
7
8           if( alarmStateRead() && !systemBlockedStateRead() ) {
9               if( !incorrectCodeStateRead() ) {
10                  codeSequenceFromUserInterface[numberOfCodeChars] = keyReleased;
11                  numberOfCodeChars++;
12                  if ( numberOfCodeChars >= CODE_NUMBER_OF_KEYS ) {
13                      codeComplete = true;
14                      numberOfCodeChars = 0;
15                  }
16              } else {
17                  if( keyReleased == '#' ) {
18                      numberOfHashKeyReleased++;
19                      if( numberOfHashKeyReleased >= 2 ) {
20                          numberOfHashKeyReleased = 0;
21                          numberOfCodeChars = 0;
22                          codeComplete = false;
23                          incorrectCodeState = OFF;
24                      }
25                  }
26              }
27          } else if ( !systemBlockedStateRead() ) {
28              if( keyReleased == 'A' ) {
29                  motionSensorActivate();
30              }
31              if( keyReleased == 'B' ) {
32                  motionSensorDeactivate();
33              }
34              if( keyReleased == '1' ) {
35                  lightSystemBrightnessChangeRGBFactor( RGB_LED_RED, true );
36              }
37              if( keyReleased == '2' ) {
38                  lightSystemBrightnessChangeRGBFactor( RGB_LED_GREEN, true );
39              }
40              if( keyReleased == '3' ) {
41                  lightSystemBrightnessChangeRGBFactor( RGB_LED_BLUE, true );
42              }
43              if( keyReleased == '4' ) {
44                  lightSystemBrightnessChangeRGBFactor( RGB_LED_RED, false );
45              }
46              if( keyReleased == '5' ) {
47                  lightSystemBrightnessChangeRGBFactor( RGB_LED_GREEN, false );
48              }
49              if( keyReleased == '6' ) {
50                  lightSystemBrightnessChangeRGBFactor( RGB_LED_BLUE, false );
51              }
52          }
53      }
54  }
```

Code 8.16 Details of the new implementation of userInterfaceMatrixKeypadUpdate().

In order to make these calls, the library *light_system.h* is included in *user_interface.cpp*, as can be seen in Table 8.8.

Table 8.8 Sections in which lines were added to user_interface.cpp.

Section	Lines that were added
Libraries	`#include "light_system.h"`

The new implementation of the function *lightSystemUpdate()* is shown in Code 8.17. On lines 5 to 7, the function *setDutyCycle()* now includes an independent brightness factor for each color. These variables are declared and initialized to 0.5 f in *light_system.cpp*, as can be seen in Table 8.9.

The new function *lightSystemBrightnessChangeRGBFactor()* is shown in Code 8.17. Depending on the value of the parameters *light* and *state*, the brightness factor of each color is increased or decreased by 0.1. *If* statements are used to keep the brightness factor values between 0 and 1. The prototype of this function is included in *light_system.h*, as shown in Table 8.10.

```
1   void lightSystemUpdate()
2   {
3       dutyCycle = lightLevelControlRead();
4
5       setDutyCycle( RGB_LED_RED, brightnessRGBLedRedFactor*dutyCycle );
6       setDutyCycle( RGB_LED_GREEN, brightnessRGBLedGreenFactor*dutyCycle );
7       setDutyCycle( RGB_LED_BLUE, brightnessRGBLedBlueFactor*dutyCycle );
8   }
9
10  void lightSystemBrightnessChangeRGBFactor( lightSystem_t light, bool state )
11  {
12      switch( light ) {
13          case RGB_LED_RED:
14              if ( state ) brightnessRGBLedRedFactor+=0.1;
15                  else brightnessRGBLedRedFactor-=0.1;
16              if ( brightnessRGBLedRedFactor > 1) brightnessRGBLedRedFactor=1.0;
17              if ( brightnessRGBLedRedFactor < 0) brightnessRGBLedRedFactor=0.0;
18          break;
19          case RGB_LED_GREEN:
20              if ( state ) brightnessRGBLedGreenFactor+=0.1;
21                  else brightnessRGBLedGreenFactor-=0.1;
22              if ( brightnessRGBLedGreenFactor > 1) brightnessRGBLedGreenFactor=1.0;
23              if ( brightnessRGBLedGreenFactor < 0) brightnessRGBLedGreenFactor=0.0;
24          break;
25          case RGB_LED_BLUE:
26              if ( state ) brightnessRGBLedBlueFactor+=0.1;
27                  else brightnessRGBLedBlueFactor-=0.1;
28              if ( brightnessRGBLedBlueFactor > 1) brightnessRGBLedBlueFactor=1.0;
29              if ( brightnessRGBLedBlueFactor < 0) brightnessRGBLedBlueFactor=0.0;
30          break;
31          default:
32          break;
33      }
34  }
```

Code 8.17 Details of the new implementation of lightSystemUpdate() and the implementation of lightSystemBrightnessChangeRGBFactor().

Table 8.9 Sections in which lines were added to light_system.cpp.

Section	Lines that were added

Declaration and initialization of private global variables	`static float brightnessRGBLedRedFactor = 0.5f;`
	`static float brightnessRGBLedGreenFactor = 0.5f;`
	`static float brightnessRGBLedBlueFactor = 0.5f;`

Table 8.10 Sections in which lines were added to light_system.h.

Section	Lines that were added
Declarations (prototypes) of public functions	`void lightSystemBrightnessChangeEnable( lightSystem_t light, bool state );`

Proposed Exercises

1. How many different colors can be obtained by means of the implemented functionality?

2. How can the number of obtainable colors be increased?

Answers to the Exercises

1. Each color factor can take 11 intensity values (from 0.0 to 1.0). Therefore, $11 \times 11 \times 11 = 1331$ different colors can be obtained.

2. By means of modifying the 0.1 factor that is used in *lightSystemBrightnessChangeRGBFactor()*. For example, if this value is changed to 0.05, then $21 \times 21 \times 21 = 9621$ different colors can be obtained.

Example 8.5: Use of the Light Sensor Reading to Control the RGB LED

Objective

Introduce the basics of a negative feedback control.

Summary of the Expected Behavior

The brightness of the RGB LEDs is governed by the LDR reading.

 NOTE: The LDR should be placed as close as possible to the RGB LED, and ambient light should be reduced as much as possible.

Test the Proposed Solution on the Board

Import the project "Example 8.5" using the URL available in [4], build the project, and drag the *.bin* file onto the NUCLEO board. Set the potentiometer to mid-way through its range. Change the lighting conditions of the LDR. Observe how the RGB LED responds to these changes.

WARNING: If the RGB LED does not respond as expected, it is recommended to wait a few seconds until the system stabilizes. If after waiting a few seconds the problem is not solved, in the Proposed Exercises subsection an implementation will be shown that will allow the reader to understand what is happening.

Discussion of the Proposed Solution

The proposed solution is based on a new module called *ldr_sensor* and the implementation of a *negative feedback control system*. The potentiometer is used to establish a *set point* in the range of 0 to 1, and the light intensity is measured by means of the LDR circuit introduced in Figure 8.6, obtaining a value in the range of 0 to 1. The duty cycle of the RGB LED is increased or decreased in order to make the reading of the LDR sensor as similar as possible to the set point established using the potentiometer.

Implementation of the Proposed Solution

A new module called *ldr_sensor* is created, with its implementation shown in Code 8.18 and Code 8.19. Because the implementation is similar to the module *light_level_sensor*, no explanation will be included.

```
1   //=====[Libraries]=======================================================
2
3   #include "arm_book_lib.h"
4
5   #include "smart_home_system.h"
6   #include "ldr_sensor.h"
7
8   //=====[Declaration and initialization of public global objects]===============
9
10  AnalogIn LDR(A2);
11
12  //=====[Implementations of public functions]===================================
13
14  void ldrSensorInit() { }
15
16  void ldrSensorUpdate() { }
17
18  float ldrSensorRead()
19  {
20      return LDR.read();
21  }
```

Code 8.18 Details of the implementation of ldr_sensor.cpp.

In Code 8.8, the implementation of *light_level_control.h* is shown. It can be seen that the prototypes of the public functions are declared in lines 14 to 16.

```
1   //=====[#include guards - begin]==============================================
2
3   #ifndef _LDR_SENSOR_H_
4   #define _LDR_SENSOR_H_
5
6   //=====[Declarations (prototypes) of public functions]======================
7
8   void ldrSensorInit();
9   void ldrSensorUpdate();
10  float ldrSensorRead();
11
12  //=====[#include guards - end]==============================================
13
14  #endif // _LDR_SENSOR_H_
```

Code 8.19 Details of the implementation of ldr_sensor.h.

In Code 8.20, the new implementation of the function *lightSystemUpdate()* is shown. The only difference appears on lines 3 and 4, where a negative feedback control system is implemented. The basics of negative feedback control theory are explained in the Under the Hood section. For now, it is enough to explain that the difference between the reading of the LDR sensor and the set point (line 4) is multiplied by a gain factor (line 5) and added to the previous value of the duty cycle. In this way, the duty cycle is increased or decreased until the difference between the LDR sensor reading and the set point becomes negligible.

Note that if the set point or the LDR sensor reading is modified (for example, the potentiometer knob is rotated), then the difference changes, so the duty cycle is modified again in order to reduce this difference.

In order to make the call to *LDRSensorRead()*, the library *ldr_sensor.h* is included in *light_system.cpp*, as can be seen in Table 8.11. In the same table, a variable named *lightSystemLoopGain* is declared and initialized.

```
1   void lightSystemUpdate()
2   {
3       dutyCycle = dutyCycle + lightSystemLoopGain
4                           * (lightLevelControlRead() - ldrSensorRead());
5
6       setDutyCycle( RGB_LED_RED, brightnessRGBLedRedFactor*dutyCycle );
7       setDutyCycle( RGB_LED_GREEN, brightnessRGBLedGreenFactor*dutyCycle );
8       setDutyCycle( RGB_LED_BLUE, brightnessRGBLedBlueFactor*dutyCycle );
9   }
```

Code 8.20 Details of the new implementation of the function lightSystemUpdate().

Table 8.11 Sections in which lines were added to light_system.cpp.

Section	Lines that were added
Libraries	`#include "ldr_sensor.h"`
Declaration and initialization of private global variables	`static float lightSystemLoopGain = 0.01;`

Proposed Exercises

1. How can the code be modified to monitor the variables related to the negative feedback control system?

2. How can the duty cycle value be limited to the range 0 to 1, in order to improve the system behavior?

Answers to the Exercises

1. Lines 3, 4, and 13 to 34 could be added to the function *lightSystemUpdate()*, as shown in Code 8.21. Ten positions were assigned to str (line 4) for safety reasons because *dutyCycle* is not limited in size, as discussed below.

```
1   void lightSystemUpdate()
2   {
3       static int i = 0;
4       char str[10];
5
6       dutyCycle = dutyCycle + lightSystemLoopGain
7                           * (lightLevelControlRead() - ldrSensorRead());
8
9       setDutyCycle( RGB_LED_RED, brightnessRGBLedRedFactor*dutyCycle );
10      setDutyCycle( RGB_LED_GREEN, brightnessRGBLedGreenFactor*dutyCycle );
11      setDutyCycle( RGB_LED_BLUE, brightnessRGBLedBlueFactor*dutyCycle );
12
13      if (i > 100) {
14          i=0;
15
16          pcSerialComStringWrite("SP: ");
17          sprintf( str, "%0.4f", lightLevelControlRead() );
18          pcSerialComStringWrite( str );
19          pcSerialComStringWrite(" | ");
20          pcSerialComStringWrite("LDR: ");
21          sprintf( str, "%0.4f", ldrSensorRead() );
22          pcSerialComStringWrite( str );
23          pcSerialComStringWrite(" | ");
24          pcSerialComStringWrite("Duty: ");
25          sprintf( str, "%0.4f", dutyCycle );
26          pcSerialComStringWrite( str );
27          pcSerialComStringWrite(" | ");
28          pcSerialComStringWrite("Added: ");
29          sprintf( str, "%0.4f", lightSystemLoopGain
30                              * (lightLevelControlRead() - ldrSensorRead()) );
31          pcSerialComStringWrite( str );
32          pcSerialComStringWrite("\r\n");
33      }
34      i++;
35  }
```

Code 8.21 Details of the new implementation of the function lightSystemUpdate().

In this way, an output similar to the one presented in Figure 8.14 should appear on the serial terminal.

NOTE: The line numbers in Figure 8.14 have been added for pedagogical purposes only.

WARNING: Ambient light should be reduced as much as possible when testing this program.

In Figure 8.14, as shown in Code 8.21, *SP* stands for *set point* (the reading of the potentiometer), *LDR* shows the reading of the LDR, *Duty* shows the *dutyCycle* (where 0 stands for 0% and 1 for 100%), and *Added* shows the value added in each call of the variable *dutyCycle*.

NOTE: These parameters are shown once every 100 calls of *lightSystemUpdate()* (approximately once every second), as defined on line 12 of Code 8.21.

There are some interesting things to highlight in the output presented in Figure 8.14:

- From lines 1 to 5, the loop appears to be stable despite the noise of the LDR reading.

- From lines 6 to 11, the LDR is exposed to external light. This can be identified by an increase in its value. The negative feedback control system tries to compensate for this change by reducing *dutyCycle*, but because there are no limits, starting from line 8 the duty cycle moves into negative values.

WARNING: Duty cycles cannot have negative values. The negative values are a consequence of the implementation of the negative feedback control system. The interface PwmOut assigns 0 in these cases.

- From lines 12 to 21, the LDR is not exposed to external light. This can be identified by a decrease in its value. The negative feedback control system is able to minimize the error, and the duty cycle presents values between 0 and 1 starting from line 17.

- From lines 21 to 27, the LDR is again exposed to external light, and the potentiometer is turned to the extremes of its rotation. The negative feedback control system tries to compensate for this change by increasing *dutyCycle* but, again because there are no limits, starting from line 23 the duty cycle takes values bigger than 1.

WARNING: Duty cycles cannot have values beyond 100%. Values beyond 1 are a consequence of the implementation of the negative feedback control system. The interface PwmOut assigns 1 in these cases.

1	SP: 0.2369 | LDR: 0.2046 | Duty: 0.2678 | Added: 0.0010
2	SP: 0.2374 | LDR: 0.1951 | Duty: 0.3121 | Added: 0.0010
3	SP: 0.2361 | LDR: 0.1832 | Duty: 0.3605 | Added: 0.0002
4	SP: 0.2352 | LDR: 0.2042 | Duty: 0.4100 | Added: 0.0001
5	SP: 0.2369 | LDR: 0.1954 | Duty: 0.4613 | Added: -0.0017
6	SP: 0.2354 | LDR: 0.4303 | Duty: 0.3605 | Added: -0.0032
7	SP: 0.2381 | LDR: 0.5067 | Duty: 0.1212 | Added: -0.0021
8	SP: 0.2374 | LDR: 0.4281 | Duty: -0.0811 | Added: -0.0019
9	SP: 0.2369 | LDR: 0.4300 | Duty: -0.2743 | Added: -0.0019
10	SP: 0.2342 | LDR: 0.4313 | Duty: -0.4704 | Added: -0.0020
11	SP: 0.2347 | LDR: 0.4379 | Duty: -0.6724 | Added: -0.0020
12	SP: 0.2352 | LDR: 0.0525 | Duty: -0.8133 | Added: 0.0018
13	SP: 0.2359 | LDR: 0.0364 | Duty: -0.6107 | Added: 0.0020
14	SP: 0.2359 | LDR: 0.0344 | Duty: -0.4080 | Added: 0.0020
15	SP: 0.2357 | LDR: 0.0371 | Duty: -0.2055 | Added: 0.0020
16	SP: 0.2369 | LDR: 0.0371 | Duty: -0.0041 | Added: 0.0020
17	SP: 0.2386 | LDR: 0.1438 | Duty: 0.1236 | Added: 0.0014
18	SP: 0.2371 | LDR: 0.1683 | Duty: 0.2022 | Added: 0.0012
19	SP: 0.2364 | LDR: 0.1768 | Duty: 0.2594 | Added: 0.0011
20	SP: 0.2376 | LDR: 0.1766 | Duty: 0.3355 | Added: 0.0002
21	SP: 0.2357 | LDR: 0.1766 | Duty: 0.4040 | Added: -0.0017
22	SP: 0.9990 | LDR: 0.4965 | Duty: 0.7392 | Added: 0.0071
23	SP: 0.9961 | LDR: 0.5026 | Duty: 1.2705 | Added: 0.0050
24	SP: 0.9949 | LDR: 0.5021 | Duty: 1.7722 | Added: 0.0050
25	SP: 0.9988 | LDR: 0.5023 | Duty: 2.2741 | Added: 0.0050
26	SP: 0.9993 | LDR: 0.5016 | Duty: 2.7758 | Added: 0.0050
27	SP: 0.9978 | LDR: 0.5023 | Duty: 3.2778 | Added: 0.0049

Figure 8.14 Output of serial terminal generated by proposed example 8.4.

2. The duty cycle values can be limited within the 0 to 1 range by means of including lines 9 and 10 shown in Code 8.22. This implementation is a first step towards *saturation arithmetic*, which is a version of arithmetic in which all operations such as addition and multiplication are limited to a fixed range between a minimum and maximum value. This is very important in the context of *control systems*, such as the one implemented in this example.

```
1   void lightSystemUpdate()
2   {
3       static int i = 0;
4       char str[100] = "";
5
6       dutyCycle = dutyCycle + lightSystemLoopGain
7                           * (lightLevelControlRead() - ldrSensorRead());
8
9       if ( dutyCycle > 1 ) dutyCycle = 1;
10      if ( dutyCycle < 0 ) dutyCycle = 0;
11
12      setDutyCycle( RGB_LED_RED, brightnessRGBLedRedFactor*dutyCycle );
13      setDutyCycle( RGB_LED_GREEN, brightnessRGBLedGreenFactor*dutyCycle );
14      setDutyCycle( RGB_LED_BLUE, brightnessRGBLedBlueFactor*dutyCycle );
15
16      if (i > 100) {
17          i=0;
18
19          pcSerialComStringWrite("SP: ");
20          sprintf( str, "%0.4f", lightLevelControlRead() );
21          pcSerialComStringWrite( str );
22          pcSerialComStringWrite(" | ");
23          pcSerialComStringWrite("LDR: ");
24          sprintf( str, "%0.4f", ldrSensorRead() );
25          pcSerialComStringWrite( str );
26          pcSerialComStringWrite(" | ");
27          pcSerialComStringWrite("Duty: ");
28          sprintf( str, "%0.4f", dutyCycle );
29          pcSerialComStringWrite( str );
30          pcSerialComStringWrite(" | ");
31          pcSerialComStringWrite("Added: ");
32          sprintf( str, "%0.4f", lightSystemLoopGain
33                          * (lightLevelControlRead() - ldrSensorRead()) );
34          pcSerialComStringWrite( str );
35          pcSerialComStringWrite("\r\n");
36      }
37      i++;
38  }
```

Code 8.22 Details of the new implementation of the function lightSystemUpdate().

Example 8.6: Playback of an Audio Message using the PWM Technique

Objective

Introduce the basics of how to obtain analog signals using the PWM technique.

Summary of the Expected Behavior

Play back a "Welcome to the Smart Home System" message during the smart home system power up.

Test the Proposed Solution on the Board

Import the project "Example 8.6" using the URL available in [4], build the project, and drag the *.bin* file onto the NUCLEO board. Plug headphones into the audio jack. The "Welcome to the Smart Home System" message should be heard every time the NUCLEO board is restarted.

Discussion of the Proposed Solution

The proposed solution is based on a new module named *audio* and the usage of the PWM technique together with an appropriate low pass filter and a digitized audio signal, as discussed in subsection 8.2.2. The new module has three files: *audio.h*, *audio.cpp*, and *welcome_message.h*. The information about the digitized audio signal is stored in *welcome_message.h*, as explained below.

Implementation of the Proposed Solution

In Code 8.23, the new implementation of *smart_home_system.cpp* is shown. The *audio* module is included in line 17, and the function *audioInit()* is called on line 23.

In Code 8.24, the implementation of *audio.h* is shown. The only public function of this module is *audioInit()*.

The implementation of *audio.cpp* is shown in Code 8.25. On lines 6 and 8, the files *welcome_message.h* and *audio.h* are included. On line 12, AUDIO_SAMPLE_DURATION is defined with the value of 125. On line 16, an object of type *PwmOut* named *audioOut* is declared and assigned to PE_6. On line 20, the private function *welcomeMessage()* is declared. The implementation of the public function *audioInit()* is shown on line 24, which only makes a call to *welcomeMessage()* on line 25 and then returns.

The implementation of the private function *welcomeMessage()* is shown on line 32. On line 34, the float variable *audioDutyCycle* is declared and initialized at zero. On line 36, the period of *audioOut* is set to 25 microseconds, as shown in Figure 8.13. On line 38, the integer variable *i* is declared, and on line 39 it is used in a *for* loop.

On line 40, *audioDutyCycle* is assigned with the value of *welcomeMessageData[i]* divided by 255. Note that the (float) cast is used, otherwise this value will always be zero because *welcomeMessageData* is an array of unsigned char, as will be seen below.

On line 41, the duty cycle of *audioOut* is set to *audioDutyCycle*, and on line 42, the Mbed OS function *wait_us()* is called in order to introduce a delay of length AUDIO_SAMPLE_DURATION (125 microseconds). In this way, five periods of the PWM are generated with the same duty cycle, as illustrated in Figure 8.13.

In Code 8.26, the first lines of *welcome_message.h* are shown. On line 1, the *constant* integer variable *welcomeMessageLength* is defined. The *const* keyword is used to prevent overriding the variable's value. On line 3, the first part of the constant array of type unsigned char named *welcomeMessageData* is shown.

```
1   //=====[Libraries]=================================================
2
3   #include "arm_book_lib.h"
4
5   #include "smart_home_system.h"
6
7   #include "alarm.h"
8   #include "user_interface.h"
9   #include "fire_alarm.h"
10  #include "intruder_alarm.h"
11  #include "pc_serial_com.h"
12  #include "event_log.h"
13  #include "motion_sensor.h"
14  #include "motor.h"
15  #include "gate.h"
16  #include "light_system.h"
17  #include "audio.h"
18
19  //=====[Implementations of public functions]=======================
20
21  void smartHomeSystemInit()
22  {
23      audioInit();
24      userInterfaceInit();
25      alarmInit();
26      fireAlarmInit();
27      intruderAlarmInit();
28      pcSerialComInit();
29      motorControlInit();
30      gateInit();
31      lightSystemInit();
32  }
33
34  void smartHomeSystemUpdate()
35  {
36      userInterfaceUpdate();
37      fireAlarmUpdate();
38      intruderAlarmUpdate();
39      alarmUpdate();
40      eventLogUpdate();
41      pcSerialComUpdate();
42      lightSystemUpdate();
43      delay(SYSTEM_TIME_INCREMENT_MS);
44  }
```

Code 8.23 Details of the new implementation of the smart_home_system.cpp.

```
1   //=====[#include guards - begin]===================================
2
3   #ifndef _AUDIO_H_
4   #define _AUDIO_H_
5
6   //=====[Libraries]=================================================
7
8   void audioInit();
9
10  //=====[#include guards - end]=====================================
11
12  #endif // _AUDIO_H_
```

Code 8.24 Details of the implementation of the audio.h.

```
1    //=====[Libraries]=======================================================
2
3    #include "mbed.h"
4    #include "arm_book_lib.h"
5
6    #include "welcome_message.h"
7
8    #include "audio.h"
9
10   //=====[Declaration of private defines]==================================
11
12   #define AUDIO_SAMPLE_DURATION   125
13
14   //=====[Declaration and initialization of public global objects]=========
15
16   PwmOut audioOut(PE_6);
17
18   //=====[Declarations (prototypes) of private functions]==================
19
20   static void welcomeMessage();
21
22   //=====[Implementations of public functions]=============================
23
24   void audioInit()
25   {
26       welcomeMessage();
27       return;
28   }
29
30   //=====[Implementations of private functions]============================
31
32   static void welcomeMessage()
33   {
34       float audioDutyCycle = 0.0;
35
36       audioOut.period(0.000025f);
37
38       int i = 0;
39       for( i=1; i<welcomeMessageLength; i++ ) {
40           audioDutyCycle = (float) welcomeMessageData[i]/255;
41           audioOut.write(audioDutyCycle);
42           wait_us(AUDIO_SAMPLE_DURATION);
43       }
44
45       return;
46   }
```

Code 8.25 Details of the implementation of audio.cpp.

```
1    const int welcomeMessageLength=24000;
2
3    const unsigned char welcomeMessageData[] = {128, 128, 128, 128, 128, 128, ...
```

Code 8.26 Details of the implementation of welcome_message.h.

Proposed Exercise

1. How can the welcome message be modified?

Answer to the Exercise

1. The file *welcome_message.h* should be modified with the data corresponding to the new message.

 TIP: Many online "text to speech" tools are available on the internet, as well as many wav to C converters. These enable different messages to be generated, even in different languages.

8.3 Under the Hood

8.3.1 Fundamentals of Control Theory

In this chapter, the brightness of an RGB LED was controlled by means of the NUCLEO board considering a *set point reference* established using a potentiometer and reading the light intensity using an LDR. This implementation can be analyzed using *control theory*. In Figure 8.15, a diagram is shown of a *negative feedback control system*. It is based on a feedback loop, which controls the process variable by comparing it with a desired value (the reference) and applying the difference (measured error) as an error signal to generate a control output to reduce or eliminate the error.

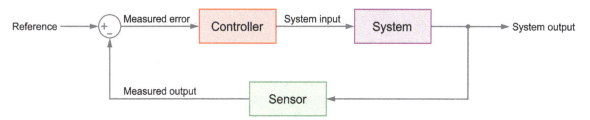

Figure 8.15 Diagram of a negative feedback control system.

The model shown in Figure 8.15 can be applied to the setup used in Example 8.6, as shown in Figure 8.16, where the duty cycle of the PWM signal was obtained by adding the current value of the duty cycle to the product of a given gain and the difference between the reading of the analog conversion of A0 and A2:

dutyCycle = dutyCycle + lightSystemLoopGain * (lightLevelControlRead − LDRSensorRead)   (1)

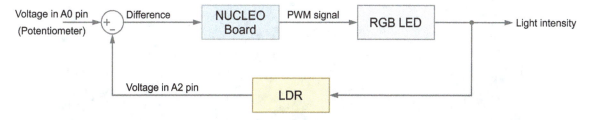

Figure 8.16 Diagram of the negative feedback control system implemented in Example 8.5.

In Example 8.6, different values can be tested with the controller gain, and it will be seen that, depending on the values, the response of the controller can be appropriate, or can be unstable or too slow.

If the control system is implemented using a microcontroller, as in the example above, it is referred to as *digital control*, and its behavior is adjusted by the values of the parameters used in the computation. If the control system is implemented using analog components, such as *operational amplifiers*, it is called *analog control*, and the system behavior depends on the values of resistors, capacitors, etc. Usually, a digital controller is more resistant to noise, more power efficient, and needs less maintenance, because digital devices do not tend to degrade or get damaged over time or need to be calibrated, which is often the case with analog devices.

Proposed Exercise

1. In the Example 8.5 implementation, is the *measured error* signal obtained outside the controller?

Answer to the Exercise

1. No, it can be seen that in Example 8.5 the *measured error* is computed by the microcontroller.

8.4 Case Study

8.4.1 Smart City Bike Lights

In this chapter, an RGB LED and a light sensor were connected to the NUCLEO board. In this way, the brightness of the RGB LED was controlled using PWM. An example of smart city bike lights, built with Mbed with similar features, can be found in [7]. In Figure 8.17, the smart city bike light is shown mounted on a bike (red rear light, on the left), and the set of front and rear lights is shown with the smartphone application (on the right).

Figure 8.17 On the left, smart city bike light mounted on a bike. On the right, rear and front lights and the mobile app.

The smart city bike light system can adjust its brightness level based on ambient light to conserve battery life. It also flashes brighter and faster depending on a set of conditions to make sure that the cyclist stands out. It is also provided with accelerometers to monitor various conditions such as swerving, sudden braking, road surface condition, and falls. It contains two different types of LEDs (focused and dispersed beam) to make it visible up to 3 km away and also gives 270° of side visibility. The mobile app lets the cyclist personalize light settings and gives low battery alerts straight to the phone.

The smart city bike light uses the PWM technique introduced in this chapter to adjust the brightness level. The sensor used in this chapter to measure ambient light is also very similar to the sensor used by the smart city bike light. Moreover, the system is connected to a smartphone using Bluetooth Low Energy in the same way as will be shown for the smart home system in Chapter 10.

Proposed Exercise

1. The smart city bike light states that it has 300 lumens of luminous flux in the rear and 400 lumens in the front. How does this compare with the maximum light intensity that an RGB LED such as the one used in this chapter can provide?

Answer to the Exercise

1. The luminous flux Φ_v in lumens (lm) is related to the luminous intensity I_v in candela (cd) and the apex angle θ in degrees (°) by means of the following formula:

$$\Phi_{v(lm)} = I_{v(cd)} \times (2\pi(1 - \cos(\theta/2))) \qquad (2)$$

Considering that the RGB LED has three LEDs and that altogether can provide up to 5 cd over a typical viewing angle of 45°, as shown in [1], the luminous flux results in about 2.5 lumens. This value is about a hundred times smaller than the luminous flux provided by the smart city bike light rear and front lights.

References

[1] "RGB LED Pinout, Features, Circuit & Datasheet". Accessed July 9, 2021.
https://components101.com/diodes/rgb-led-pinout-configuration-circuit-datasheet

[2] "LDR Pinout, Working, Applications & Datasheet". Accessed July 9, 2021.
https://components101.com/resistors/ldr-datasheet

[3] "Low-pass filter - Wikipedia". Accessed July 9, 2021.
https://en.wikipedia.org/wiki/Low-pass_filter#RC_filter

[4] "GitHub - armBookCodeExamples/Directory". Accessed July 9, 2021.
https://github.com/armBookCodeExamples/Directory/

[5] "pinout_labels - | Mbed". Accessed July 9, 2021.
https://os.mbed.com/teams/ST/wiki/pinout_labels

[6] "mbed-os/PeripheralPinMaps.h at master · ARMmbed/mbed-os · GitHub". Accessed July 9, 2021.
https://github.com/ARMmbed/mbed-os/blob/master/targets/TARGET_STM/TARGET_STM32F4/
TARGET_STM32F429xI/TARGET_NUCLEO_F429ZI/PeripheralPinMaps.h

[7] "Smart City Bike Lights | Mbed". Accessed July 9, 2021.
https://os.mbed.com/built-with-mbed/smart-city-bike-lights/

Chapter 9

File Storage on SD Cards and
Usage of Software Repositories

9.1 Roadmap

9.1.1 What You Will Learn

After you have studied the material in this chapter, you will be able to:

- Describe how to connect an SD card to the NUCLEO board using an SPI bus interface.

- Develop programs to manage files on an SD card with the NUCLEO board.

- Implement a revision control system using repositories.

- Summarize the fundamentals of filesystems.

9.1.2 Review of Previous Chapters

In the previous chapters, many sensors and actuators were included in the smart home system. Different events were detected, for example over temperature or the presence of intruders. These events were reported using the serial terminal, as well as the display, a range of lights, and the siren, which was simulated using a buzzer. However, once the system is turned off, there is no record of the events that took place. This can be inconvenient, as after a fire alarm or an intruder detection, the system manager might wish to analyze what happened even if there was a power outage in between.

9.1.3 Contents of This Chapter

In this chapter, an SD card (*Secure Digital memory card*) is used to store a copy of the events log of the smart home system. In this way, events can be recorded over time on the SD card, even after turning off the power supply of the smart home system. In addition, the files stored in the SD card can be read by any device provided with an SD card reader, such as a PC or a smartphone.

For this purpose, the concept of a *filesystem* will be introduced as a way to organize the storage capacity of the SD card into *files* and *folders*. The files on the SD card will be able to be created, written, read, modified, and deleted.

9.2 File Storage with the NUCLEO Board

9.2.1 Connect an SD Card to the Smart Home System

In this chapter, a micro-SD card, such as the one described in [1], is connected to the smart home system, as shown in Figure 9.1. The aim of this setup is to store the events log on the SD card (for the sake of brevity, we use "SD card" to refer to the micro-SD card).

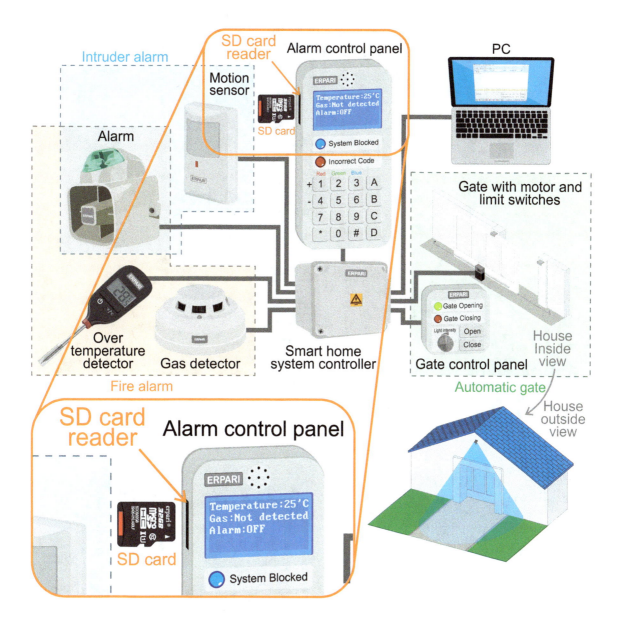

Figure 9.1 The smart home system is now connected to an SD card.

The connections that should be made are shown in Figure 9.2 and summarized in Table 9.1. The reader may notice that an SPI bus is used to connect the NUCLEO board with the SD card.

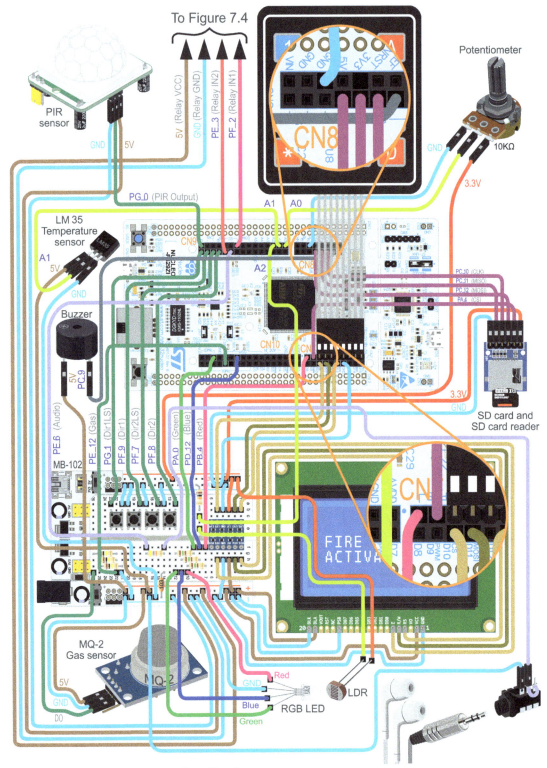

Figure 9.2 The smart home system is now connected to an SD card.

Table 9.1 Summary of the connections between the NUCLEO board and the SD card.

NUCLEO board	SD card
3.3 V	3V3
PA_4	CS
PC_12	MOSI
PC_10	CLK
PC_11	MISO
GND	GND

 NOTE: In Figure 8.5 it can be seen that PC_10, PC_11, PC_12, and PA_4 correspond to SPI3_SCK, SPI3_MISO, SPI3_MOSI, and SPI3_CS, respectively. In Chapter 6, in order to connect the graphical display, the pins PA_5, PA_6, PA_7, and PD_14 (SPI1_SCK, SP1_MISO, SPI1_MOSI, and SPI1_CS) were used. The graphical LCD display does not ignore the SPI MOSI and SCK signals even if its CS signal is inactive. Therefore, if the same SPI bus was used for both devices, the display would show glitches every time the program used the SD card.

In Figure 9.3, the details of the SD card module pins are shown. It can be seen that they correspond to the SPI bus signals that were introduced in section 6.2.4. Figure 9.3 also shows how to properly insert the SD card into the SD card module.

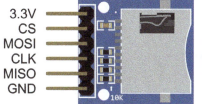 

Figure 9.3 Details of the SD card module pins and how to insert the SD card into the module.

 WARNING: It is important to use an SD card properly formatted as FAT32. To format the SD card, it is recommended to use a notebook provided with an SD card slot and the *format tool* of its operating system.

WARNING: Some SD card modules have a different pinout. Follow the 3.3V, CS, MOSI, CLK, MISO and GND labels of the module when making the connections. Be sure to use a module that can be powered using 3.3 V and that supports the SD card memory size you are using.

To test if the SD card is working correctly, the *.bin* file of the program "Subsection 9.2.1" should be downloaded from the URL available in [2] and loaded onto the NUCLEO board. Press "w" on the PC keyboard to create a file called *Hello.txt* on the SD card connected to the NUCLEO board. Then press "l" to get a list of all the files in the root directory of the SD card. The file *Hello.txt* should be in the listing, as well as other files and folders contained on the SD card.

TIP: Ignore all the other elements of the setup during the proposed test (Alarm LED, display, etc.).

9.2.2 A Filesystem to Control how Data is Stored and Retrieved

Data are usually stored on devices such as SD cards or hard disk drives. Without appropriate organization, the data placed on those devices would be one single body of useless bits with no way to determine where each element of data begins and ends. In order to organize the data, a *filesystem* is used.

In a filesystem, each group of data is called a *file*. The logical rules and structure used to manage the data and their names is called a filesystem. Typically, a filesystem consists of two or three layers, as shown in Figure 9.4. The *logical layer* provides access to files and directories, among other operations. It is usually accessed by means of an *Application Programming Interface* (API), using functions such as *open*, *read*, *write*, *close*, etc. The reader might notice that the modularization implemented in Chapter 5 and many of the names of the functions introduced in that chapter follow this logic. Examples include *eventLogRead()* and *eventLogWrite()*.

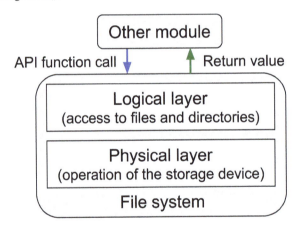

Figure 9.4 Diagram of a typical organization of a filesystem.

The second layer shown in Figure 9.4 is the *physical layer*. This layer is concerned with the physical operation of the storage device, for example an SD card. It is responsible for the physical placement of data in specific locations on the storage medium, and for retrieving the data when needed.

The filesystem is responsible for organizing files and directories and keeping track of which areas of the media belong to which file and which are not being used. The data are usually stored in *allocation units* of a given size. This results in unused space when a file is not an exact multiple of the allocation unit. Choosing an allocation size based on the average size of the files expected to be in the filesystem can minimize the amount of unusable space.

There are different kinds of filesystems, each having different advantages and disadvantages. The family of *File Allocation Table* (FAT) filesystems is simpler than other technologies and is supported by almost all operating systems for personal computers. For that reason, it is used in this chapter to store data on the SD card. It is based on a table (the file allocation table) stored on the device in which the areas associated with each file are identified.

Example 9.1: Create a File with the Event Log on the SD Card

Objective

Introduce the usage of filesystems and repositories.

Summary of the Expected Behavior

When pressing the "w" key on the PC keyboard, a *.txt* text file with a copy of the current event log (containing up to twenty events) should be created on the SD card.

Test the Proposed Solution on the Board

Import the project "Example 9.1" using the URL available in [2], build the project, and drag the *.bin* file onto the NUCLEO board. Press "s" on the PC keyboard in order to configure the date and time of the RTC of the NUCLEO board. Press "t" on the PC keyboard to confirm that the RTC is working properly. Use the Fire alarm test button (B1 button) to activate the alarm. Press "e" on the PC keyboard to get the date and time of the alarm activation. Press "w" on the PC keyboard to write a file with the events log onto the SD card connected to the NUCLEO board. A message indicating that the file was successfully written on the SD card should be shown on the serial terminal, as shown in Figure 9.5.

```
Storing event 1 in file 2021_07_09_05_25_26.txt
Storing event 2 in file 2021_07_09_05_25_26.txt
Storing event 3 in file 2021_07_09_05_25_26.txt
Storing event 4 in file 2021_07_09_05_25_26.txt
File successfully written
```

Figure 9.5 Example of events storage messages.

NOTE: Jan 1, 1970, 00:00 hours will be the date and time if the RTC is not configured, as was explained in Chapter 4.

The content of the event file after storing the four events corresponding to Figure 9.5 is shown in Figure 9.6. It can be seen that the content of the *.txt* file shown in Figure 9.6 is the same as the message that is shown on the serial terminal if the letter "e" is pressed on the PC keyboard. This *.txt* file can be opened using a PC or a smartphone if the SD card is inserted into those devices, provided they are properly formatted as FAT32.

```
Event = ALARM_ON
Date and Time = Fri Jul 9 05:25:24 2021

Event = GAS_DET_ON
Date and Time = Fri Jul 9 05:25:24 2021

Event = GAS_DET_OFF
Date and Time = Fri Jul 9 05:25:25 2021

Event = ALARM_OFF
Date and Time = Fri Jul 9 05:25:25 2021
```

Figure 9.6 Example of the content of an event file stored on the SD card as a .txt file.

Discussion of the Proposed Solution

The proposed solution is based on a new module named *sd_card*. This module is composed of two files, *sd_card.cpp* and *sd_card.h*, following the modularized structure discussed in previous chapters. In addition, some Mbed OS libraries to manage FAT filesystems and SD devices that are available in [3] are included in *sd_card.cpp* (*FATFileSystem.h*, *SDBlockDevice.h*, and *mbed_retarget.h*). Also, the *mbed_app.json* file is used by the Mbed OS to configure the SD card, so it was modified as shown in Code 9.1.

```
{
    "target_overrides": {
        "*": {
            "platform.stdio-convert-newlines": 1,
            "target.features_add": ["STORAGE"],
            "target.components_add": ["SD"],
            "sd.INIT_FREQUENCY": 350000,
            "target.printf_lib": "std"
        }
    }
}
```

Code 9.1 Content of the mbed_app.json file.

The line "target.printf_lib": "std" was already in the *mbed_app.json* file that was introduced in Chapter 3. By means of the other parameters that are now on the *mbed_app.json* file, the SD card is configured. For more information, see [3].

Implementation of the Proposed Solution

In Table 9.2 and Table 9.3, the sections where lines were added to *pc_serial_com.h* and *pc_serial_com.cpp* are shown. It can be seen that the library sd_card.h is now included, as well as the new functions *pcSerialComIntWrite()* and *commandEventLogSaveToSdCard()*. In Table 9.4, the lines that were added in *pcSerialComCommandUpdate()* and *availableCommands()* in order to implement the "w" command are shown.

Table 9.2 Sections in which lines were added to pc_serial_com.h.

Section	Lines that were added
Declarations (prototypes) of public functions	`void pcSerialComIntWrite( int number );`

Table 9.3 Sections in which lines were added to pc_serial_com.cpp.

Section	Lines that were added
Libraries	`#include "sd_card.h"`
Declarations (prototypes) of private functions	`static void commandEventLogSaveToSdCard();`

Table 9.4 Functions in which lines were added in pc_serial_com.cpp.

Section	Lines that were added
static void pcSerialComCommandUpdate(char receivedChar)	`case 'w': case 'W': commandEventLogSaveToSdCard();` `    break;`
static void availableCommands()	`pcSerialComStringWrite( "Press 'w' or 'W' to store` `    the events log in the SD card\r\n" );`

In Code 9.2, the implementation of the function *pcSerialComIntWrite()* is shown. This function is used to show on the serial terminal the number of the event that has been stored on the SD card.

```
1   void pcSerialComIntWrite( int number )
2   {
3       char str[4] = "";
4       sprintf( str, "%d", number );
5       pcSerialComStringWrite( str );
6   }
```

Code 9.2 Implementation of the function pcSerialComIntWrite().

In Code 9.3, the implementation of the function *commandEventLogSaveToSdCard()* is shown. This function is called when the "w" key is pressed on the PC keyboard. As can be seen in Code 9.3, it only calls the function *eventLogSaveToSdCard()*.

```
1   static void commandEventLogSaveToSdCard()
2   {
3       eventLogSaveToSdCard();
4   }
```

Code 9.3 Implementation of the function commandEventLogSaveToSdCard().

In Table 9.5 and Table 9.6, the sections in which lines were added to *event_log.h* and *event_log.cpp* are shown. It can be seen that *commandEventLogSaveToSdCard()* has been declared as a public function, and that the library sd_card has been included.

Table 9.5 Sections in which lines were added to event_log.h.

Section	Lines that were added
Declarations (prototypes) of public functions	`bool eventLogSaveToSdCard();`

Table 9.6 Sections in which lines were added to event_log.cpp.

Section	Lines that were added
Libraries	`#include "sd_card.h"`

In Code 9.4, the implementation of the new function *eventLogSaveToSdCard()* is shown. On lines 3 and 4, two char arrays, *fileName* and *eventStr* are declared and initialized. The former is used to store the name of the file, while the latter is used to store a string corresponding to the event to be stored. The Boolean variable *eventsStored* on line 5 is used to indicate whether events have been stored. On lines 7 and 8, two more variables that are used in this example are declared, *seconds* and *i*.

On line 10, the RTC of the NUCLEO board is read, and the current time is stored in the variable *seconds*. On line 12, the name of the new file to be created is generated by means of the function *strftime()* provided by Mbed OS. For this purpose, the value of the variable *seconds* is used. This value is converted into the "YYYY MM DD HH MM SS" format by means of the function *localtime()*. The value of SD_CARD_FILENAME_MAX_LENGTH (that is defined in *sd_card.h*) is used to limit the number of characters that are used in *fileName*. On line 14, the file extension *.txt* is appended to the fileName by means of *strcat()*.

The *for* loop on line 16 is used to read all the events that are stored in memory, and one after the other these events are stored in the string *eventStr* (line 17).

On line 18, the function *sdCardWriteFile()* is called to write the event log onto the SD card. This function receives two parameters, the filename and a string corresponding to the event to be stored. There is an *if* statement on line 18 as the function *sdCardWriteFile()* returns true if it can successfully write the event in the file, and false if not.

Lines 19 to 23 are used to display a message on the serial terminal showing the event that has been written, as shown in Figure 9.5.

Note that if there are no events in the log, then the function *eventLogNumberOfStoredEvents()* returns 0 on line 16 and, therefore, the *for* loop is never executed. If this is the case, the variable *eventsStored* remains false and the message "There are no events to store or SD card is not available" is shown, as can be seen on line 31 of Code 9.4.

```
1   bool eventLogSaveToSdCard()
2   {
3       char fileName[SD_CARD_FILENAME_MAX_LENGTH] = "";
4       char eventStr[EVENT_STR_LENGTH] = "";
5       bool eventsStored = false;
6
7       time_t seconds;
8       int i;
9
10      seconds = time(NULL);
11
12      strftime( fileName, SD_CARD_FILENAME_MAX_LENGTH,
13              "%Y_%m_%d_%H_%M_%S", localtime(&seconds) );
14      strcat( fileName, ".txt" );
15
16      for (i = 0; i < eventLogNumberOfStoredEvents(); i++) {
17          eventLogRead( i, eventStr );
18          if ( sdCardWriteFile( fileName, eventStr ) ){
19              pcSerialComStringWrite("Storing event ");
20              pcSerialComIntWrite(i+1);
21              pcSerialComStringWrite(" in file ");
22              pcSerialComStringWrite(fileName);
23              pcSerialComStringWrite("\r\n");
24              eventsStored = true;
25          }
26      }
27
28      if ( eventsStored ) {
29          pcSerialComStringWrite("File successfully written\r\n\r\n");
30      } else {
31          pcSerialComStringWrite("There are no events to store ");
32          pcSerialComStringWrite("or SD card is not available\r\n\r\n");
33      }
34
35      return true;
36  }
```

Code 9.4 Implementation of the function eventLogSaveToSdCard().

Code 9.5 shows the content of the *sd_card.h* file. On line 8 it can be seen that the #define SD_CARD_FILENAME_MAX_LENGTH that is used in the function *eventLogSaveToSdCard()* has the value 32. It can also be seen on lines 12 and 13 that two public functions are declared, *sdCardInit()* and *sdCardWriteFile()*.

```
1   //=====[#include guards - begin]====================================
2
3   #ifndef _SD_CARD_H_
4   #define _SD_CARD_H_
5
6   //=====[Libraries]==================================================
7
8   #define SD_CARD_FILENAME_MAX_LENGTH 32
9
10  //=====[Declarations (prototypes) of public functions]=============
11
12  bool sdCardInit();
13  bool sdCardWriteFile( const char* fileName, const char* writeBuffer );
14
15  //=====[#include guards - end]======================================
16
17  #endif // _SD_CARD_H_
```

Code 9.5 Content of the sd_card.h file.

In Code 9.6, the first part of the file *sd_card.cpp* is shown. From lines 3 to 15 all the libraries that are used in the *sd_card* module can be seen. It can also be seen that *mbed_retarget.h*, *FATFileSystem.h*, and *SDBlockDevice.h* are included. These are libraries that are used to work with files on the SD card.

On lines 19 to 22 the pins used to connect the SD card are defined. These pins are related to SPI3, and it is important to note that an alternative pin (PA_4_ALT0) is used on line 22 for the *chip select* pin (SPI3_CS).

 NOTE: It is not necessary to use the SPI port-specific pin for chip select; a DigitalOut can be used and controlled by software. In Chapter 6, PD_14 was used instead of pin PA_4, which is the SPI1 port-specific chip select pin. In this case, the specific pin for SPI3 is used in order to show a usage example of the alternative pins that were introduced in Chapter 8. More information about alternative pins and port-specific pins for peripherals can be found in [4] and [5].

Finally, on lines 26 and 28, two objects are declared; the former is used in the communication with the SD card, and the latter is used to implement the filesystem.

```
1   //=====[Libraries]==============================================================
2
3   #include "mbed.h"
4   #include "arm_book_lib.h"
5
6   #include "sd_card.h"
7
8   #include "event_log.h"
9   #include "date_and_time.h"
10  #include "pc_serial_com.h"
11
12  #include "FATFileSystem.h"
13  #include "SDBlockDevice.h"
14
15  #include "platform/mbed_retarget.h"
16
17  //=====[Declaration of private defines]=========================================
18
19  #define SPI3_MOSI    PC_12
20  #define SPI3_MISO    PC_11
21  #define SPI3_SCK     PC_10
22  #define SPI3_CS      PA_4_ALT0
23
24  //=====[Declaration and initialization of public global objects]================
25
26  SDBlockDevice sd( SPI3_MOSI, SPI3_MISO, SPI3_SCK, SPI3_CS );
27
28  FATFileSystem sdCardFileSystem("sd", &sd);
```

Code 9.6 Content of the sd_card.cpp file (Part 1/2).

NOTE: An SPI object is not declared as in Chapter 6 despite the fact that the SD card is connected to the NUCLEO board using an SPI bus. Recall that in Chapter 6 the objects *SPI spiSt7920(SPI1_MOSI, SPI1_MISO, SPI1_SCK)* and *DigitalOut spiSt7920ChipSelect(SPI1_CS)* were declared, the SPI bus was configured by means of *SPI_ST9720.format(8,3)* and *SPI_ST9720.frequency(1000000)*, and this was used by *SPI_ST9720.write()*. In this chapter, the objects *SDBlockDevice sd(SPI3_MOSI, SPI3_MISO, SPI3_SCK, SPI3_CS)* and *FATFileSystem sdCardFileSystem("sd", &sd)* are declared to control the SD card using the SPI bus, following the format established by Mbed OS.

In Code 9.7, the second part of the *sd_card.cpp* file is shown. Lines 1 to 16 show the implementation of the function *sdCardInit()*. It can be seen that a message is first displayed indicating that it is looking for a filesystem (line 3). On line 4, *mount()* is used to get the information of the FAT filesystem of the SD card into the object *sdCardFileSystem*. On line 5, the function *opendir()*, which is declared and implemented in the Mbed OS, is used to get the list of directories on the SD card. If the list of directories can be successfully read, then it is stored in the object *sdCardListOfDirectories*; otherwise NULL is stored in *sdCardListOfDirectories*. On line 6, the value of *sdCardListOfDirectories* is checked in order to determine if there is a FAT filesystem mounted on the SD card. If so, the message shown on line 7 is shown and the directory is closed by means of line 8.

```cpp
1   bool sdCardInit()
2   {
3       pcSerialComStringWrite("Looking for a filesystem in the SD card... \r\n");
4       sdCardFileSystem.mount(&sd);
5       DIR *sdCardListOfDirectories = opendir("/sd/");
6       if ( sdCardListOfDirectories != NULL ) {
7           pcSerialComStringWrite("Filesystem found in the SD card.\r\n");
8           closedir(sdCardListOfDirectories);
9           return true;
10      } else {
11          pcSerialComStringWrite("Filesystem not mounted. \r\n");
12          pcSerialComStringWrite("Insert an SD card and ");
13          pcSerialComStringWrite("reset the NUCLEO board.\r\n");
14          return false;
15      }
16  }
17
18  bool sdCardWriteFile( const char* fileName, const char* writeBuffer )
19  {
20      char fileNameSD[SD_CARD_FILENAME_MAX_LENGTH+4] = "";
21
22      fileNameSD[0] = '\0';
23      strcat( fileNameSD, "/sd/" );
24      strcat( fileNameSD, fileName );
25
26      FILE *sdCardFilePointer = fopen( fileNameSD, "a" );
27
28      if ( sdCardFilePointer != NULL ) {
29          fprintf( sdCardFilePointer, "%s", writeBuffer );
30          fclose( sdCardFilePointer );
31          return true;
32      } else {
33          return false;
34      }
35  }
```

Code 9.7 Content of the sd_card.cpp file (Part 2/2).

If an appropriate FAT filesystem is not found on the SD card, then lines 10 to 15 are executed in order to indicate this to the user.

 WARNING: The messages on lines 11 to 13 will be displayed in any of the following situations:
- The SD card is not connected.
- The SD card module is not properly connected.
- The SD card is not working properly (i.e., it is damaged).
- The filesystem format of the SD Card is not FAT32 as expected.

On line 18 of Code 9.7, the implementation of the function *sdCardWriteFile()* is shown. The first parameter that this function receives (*fileName*) is the filename, and the second parameter (*writeBuffer*) is the data to be written. Lines 22 to 24 are used to write the prefix "/sd/" in fileNameSD, which is necessary in order to indicate that this is the root folder of the SD card. On line 26, the object *sdCardFilePointer* of type FILE is declared and is assigned a pointer to the file that is opened by means of *fopen()*. The parameter "a" on line 26 is used to indicate that new content will be appended to the opened file. It is important to note that the use of the "a" parameter implies that if the file doesn't exist, then it must be created.

 NOTE: Recall that a pointer is an object that stores a memory address, usually corresponding to a variable. Pointers will be discussed in detail in Chapter 10 and an example will be implemented using pointers.

Line 28 assesses whether the file was correctly opened and, if so, the content of *writeBuffer* is written to the file by means of *fprintf()* (line 29). Then, the file is closed (line 30) and the *Boolean* value true is returned (line 31). If the content of *writeBuffer* was not successfully appended to the file, then false is returned (line 33).

Lastly, in Code 9.8 the new implementation of *smartHomeSystemInit()* is shown. It can be seen that *sdCardInit()* was added on line 12.

```
1   void smartHomeSystemInit()
2   {
3       audioInit();
4       userInterfaceInit();
5       alarmInit();
6       fireAlarmInit();
7       intruderAlarmInit();
8       pcSerialComInit();
9       motorControlInit();
10      gateInit();
11      lightSystemInit();
12      sdCardInit();
13  }
```

Code 9.8 New implementation of the function smartHomeSystemInit.

Proposed Exercise

1. What should be modified in order to connect the SD card to a different set of pins of the NUCLEO board?

Answer to the Exercise

1. The pins' assignment in *sd_card.cpp* (line 28 of Code 9.6) should be modified to use the SPI_4. For example, the following assignment can be used:

```
#define SPI4_MOSI    PE_14
#define SPI4_MISO    PE_5
#define SPI4_SCK     PE_2
#define SPI4_CS      PE_4

SDBlockDevice sd( SPI4_MOSI, SPI4_MISO, SPI4_SCK, SPI4_CS );
```

Example 9.2: Save a File on the SD Card with only New Events that were not Previously Saved

Objective

Introduce functionality regarding the management of data storage in files.

Summary of the Expected Behavior

When pressing the key "w" on the PC keyboard, a *.txt* file with a copy of events that were not saved previously is stored on the SD card. In this way, multiple copies of the same events in different files are avoided.

Test the Proposed Solution on the Board

Import the project "Example 9.2" using the URL available in [2], build the project, and drag the *.bin* file onto the NUCLEO board. Repeat the steps in Example 9.1 in order to write a log file onto the SD card such as the one shown in Figure 9.6. Use the Fire alarm test button (B1 button) to activate the alarm again. Press "e" on the PC keyboard to get the date and time of the alarm activation. Press "w" on the PC keyboard to write the events log onto the SD card. A message indicating that the file was successfully written on the SD card with only the new events that were not previously stored should be shown on the serial terminal, as in Figure 9.7.

```
Storing event 5 in file 2021_07_09_08_12_54.txt
Storing event 6 in file 2021_07_09_08_12_54.txt
Storing event 7 in file 2021_07_09_08_12_54.txt
Storing event 8 in file 2021_07_09_08_12_54.txt
New events successfully stored in the SD card
```

Figure 9.7 Example of events storage messages.

The content of the event file after storing the new events corresponding to Figure 9.7 is shown in Figure 9.8. The *.txt* file has only the new events corresponding to the second time the Fire alarm test button was pressed (i.e., event 5 to event 8). Note that in Example 9.1, a new file was created each time the "w" key was pressed on the PC keyboard, logging all events, not only new events.

```
Event = ALARM_ON
Date and Time = Fri Jul 9 08:12:51 2021

Event = GAS_DET_ON
Date and Time = Fri Jul 9 08:12:51 2021

Event = GAS_DET_OFF
Date and Time = Fri Jul 9 08:12:53 2021

Event = ALARM_OFF
Date and Time = Fri Jul 9 08:12:53 2021
```

Figure 9.8 Example of the content of an event file stored on the SD card as a .txt file.

Finally, press "w" again. It will show a message "No new events to store in SD card." In this way, it is seen that now a file is created only if there are events that were not previously stored.

Discussion of the Proposed Solution

Due to the modularization that has been followed in the program structure, the proposed modification can be done by means of only changing the *event_log.cpp* file. The corresponding details are shown below.

Implementation of the Proposed Solution

In order to identify which events were already stored on the SD card, a new *member* is included in the data structure *systemEvent_t*, which is defined in the *event_log.cpp* file. This member is named *storedInSd*, as shown in Code 9.9. The value *storedInSd* of an element will be set as false if the corresponding event was not stored on the SD card and will be set to true when it has been successfully stored on the SD card.

```
1  typedef struct systemEvent {
2      time_t seconds;
3      char typeOfEvent[EVENT_LOG_NAME_MAX_LENGTH];
4      bool storedInSd;
5  } systemEvent_t;
```

Code 9.9 New declaration of the data structure systemEvent_t.

Code 9.10 shows the new implementation of the function *eventLogWrite()*. It may be noted that only line 14 has been incorporated. This line is used to set to false the Boolean member *storedInSd* of the corresponding element of *arrayOfStoredEvents* (indicated by *eventsIndex*) each time a new event is added to the log.

The new implementation of *eventLogSaveToSdCard()* is shown in Code 9.11. An *if* statement has been included on line 17 in order to evaluate the value of *arrayOfStoredEvents[i].storedInSd*. If the value is false, then the event is stored on the SD card and then is set to true (line 20) in order to avoid storing it again in the future. The messages on lines 32 and 34 were also modified to indicate whether events were stored or not.

```
1   void eventLogWrite( bool currentState, const char* elementName )
2   {
3       char eventAndStateStr[EVENT_LOG_NAME_MAX_LENGTH] = "";
4
5       strcat( eventAndStateStr, elementName );
6       if ( currentState ) {
7           strcat( eventAndStateStr, "_ON" );
8       } else {
9           strcat( eventAndStateStr, "_OFF" );
10      }
11
12      arrayOfStoredEvents[eventsIndex].seconds = time(NULL);
13      strcpy( arrayOfStoredEvents[eventsIndex].typeOfEvent, eventAndStateStr );
14      arrayOfStoredEvents[eventsIndex].storedInSd = false;
15      if ( eventsIndex < EVENT_LOG_MAX_STORAGE - 1 ) {
16          eventsIndex++;
17      } else {
18          eventsIndex = 0;
19      }
20
21      pcSerialComStringWrite(eventAndStateStr);
22      pcSerialComStringWrite("\r\n");
23  }
```

Code 9.10 New implementation of the function eventLogWrite().

```
1   bool eventLogSaveToSdCard()
2   {
3       char fileName[SD_CARD_FILENAME_MAX_LENGTH] = "";
4       char eventStr[EVENT_STR_LENGTH] = "";
5       bool eventsStored = false;
6
7       time_t seconds;
8       int i;
9
10      seconds = time(NULL);
11
12      strftime( fileName, SD_CARD_FILENAME_MAX_LENGTH,
13               "%Y_%m_%d_%H_%M_%S", localtime(&seconds) );
14      strcat( fileName, ".txt" );
15
16      for (i = 0; i < eventLogNumberOfStoredEvents(); i++) {
17          if ( !arrayOfStoredEvents[i].storedInSd ) {
18              eventLogRead( i, eventStr );
19              if ( sdCardWriteFile( fileName, eventStr ) ){
20                  arrayOfStoredEvents[i].storedInSd = true;
21                  pcSerialComStringWrite("Storing event ");
22                  pcSerialComIntWrite(i+1);
23                  pcSerialComStringWrite(" in file ");
24                  pcSerialComStringWrite(fileName);
25                  pcSerialComStringWrite("\r\n");
26                  eventsStored = true;
27              }
28          }
29      }
30
31      if ( eventsStored ) {
32          pcSerialComStringWrite("New events successfully stored in the SD card\r\n\r\n");
33      } else {
34          pcSerialComStringWrite("No new events to store in the SD card\r\n\r\n");
35      }
36      return true;
37  }
```

Code 9.11 New implementation of the function eventLogSaveToSdCard().

Proposed Exercise

1. How can the code be modified in order to name the files using the year, month, and day?

Answer to the Exercise

1. Line 13 of Code 9.11 can be replaced by:

```
strftime( fileName, SD_CARD_FILENAME_MAX_LENGTH,
        "%Y_%m_%d_%H_%M_%S", localtime(&seconds));
```

Example 9.3: Get the List of Event Log Files Stored on the SD Card

Objective

Introduce more advanced functionality of the filesystem.

Summary of the Expected Behavior

When pressing the "l" key on the PC keyboard, a list of the event log files stored on the SD card should be displayed on the serial monitor.

Test the Proposed Solution on the Board

Import the project "Example 9.3" using the URL available in [2], build the project, and drag the .*bin* file onto the NUCLEO board. Press "l" on the PC keyboard to get the list of all the event log files stored on the SD card. A message similar to the one shown in Figure 9.9 should be displayed on the serial monitor.

```
Printing all filenames:
hello.txt
image.jpg
1970_01_01_00_04_13.txt
2021_07_09_05_25_26.txt
2021_07_09_08_12_54.txt
```

Figure 9.9 Example of the file listing that is shown on the PC.

Discussion of the Proposed Solution

The proposed solution is based on the function *sdCardListFiles()*, which is used to retrieve the listing of the files that are stored on the SD card. The list of the files is then shown on the serial monitor.

Implementation of the Proposed Solution

Table 9.7 shows that the private function *commandSdCardListFiles()* was added to *pc_serial_com.cpp*. In Table 9.8, the lines that were added in *pcSerialComCommandUpdate()* and *availableCommands()* in order to implement the "l" command are shown.

Table 9.7 Sections in which lines were added to pc_serial_com.cpp.

Section	Lines that were added
Declarations (prototypes) of private functions	`static void commandSdCardListFiles();`

Table 9.8 Functions in which lines were added in pc_serial_com.cpp.

Section	Lines that were added
static void pcSerialComCommandUpdate(char receivedChar)	`case 'l': case 'L': commandSdCardListFiles(); break;`

static void availableCommands()	`pcSerialComStringWrite( "Press 'l' or 'L' to list all`
	`                the files " );`
	`pcSerialComStringWrite( "in the root directory of the SD`
	`                card\r\n" );`

In Code 9.12, the implementation of the function *commandSdCardListFiles()* is shown. On line 3, the array of char *fileListBuffer* is declared with the appropriate size to store a list of up to ten files (SD_CARD_MAX_FILE_LIST is defined as 10) in the situation of all the filenames having a length of 32 bytes (SD_CARD_FILENAME_MAX_LENGTH is defined as 32). On line 4, *sdCardListFiles()* is called in order to load up to a maximum of ten filenames into *fileListBuffer*. On line 6, the list of files is sent to the serial terminal, followed by "\r\n", as can be seen on line 7.

```
1  static void commandSdCardListFiles()
2  {
3      char fileListBuffer[SD_CARD_MAX_FILE_LIST*SD_CARD_FILENAME_MAX_LENGTH] = "";
4      sdCardListFiles( fileListBuffer,
5                       SD_CARD_MAX_FILE_LIST*SD_CARD_FILENAME_MAX_LENGTH );
6      pcSerialComStringWrite( fileListBuffer );
7      pcSerialComStringWrite( "\r\n" );
8  }
```

Code 9.12 Implementation of the function commandSdCardListFiles().

In Table 9.9, the sections where lines were added to *sd_card.h* are shown. It can be seen that SD_CARD_MAX_FILE_LIST was defined, and the new public function *sdCardListFiles()* has been declared. The corresponding code is shown in Code 9.13.

Table 9.9 Sections in which lines were added to sd_card.h.

Section	Lines that were added
Declaration of private defines	`#define SD_CARD_MAX_FILE_LIST        10`
Declarations (prototypes) of public functions	`bool sdCardListFiles( char* fileNamesBuffer,` `                      int fileNamesBufferSize );`

```
1   bool sdCardListFiles( char* fileNamesBuffer, int fileNamesBufferSize )
2   {
3       int NumberOfUsedBytesInBuffer = 0;
4       struct dirent *sdCardDirectoryEntryPointer;
5
6       DIR *sdCardListOfDirectories = opendir("/sd/");
7
8       if ( sdCardListOfDirectories != NULL ) {
9           pcSerialComStringWrite("Printing all filenames:\r\n");
10          sdCardDirectoryEntryPointer = readdir(sdCardListOfDirectories);
11
12          while ( ( sdCardDirectoryEntryPointer != NULL ) &&
13                  ( NumberOfUsedBytesInBuffer + strlen(sdCardDirectoryEntryPointer->d_name)
14                      < fileNamesBufferSize) ) {
15              strcat( fileNamesBuffer, sdCardDirectoryEntryPointer->d_name );
16              strcat( fileNamesBuffer, "\r\n" );
17              NumberOfUsedBytesInBuffer = NumberOfUsedBytesInBuffer +
18                                  strlen(sdCardDirectoryEntryPointer->d_name);
19              sdCardDirectoryEntryPointer = readdir(sdCardListOfDirectories);
20          }
21
22          closedir(sdCardListOfDirectories);
23
24          return true;
25      } else {
26          pcSerialComStringWrite("Insert an SD card and ");
27          pcSerialComStringWrite("reset the NUCLEO board.\r\n");
28          return false;
29      }
31  }
```

Code 9.13 Implementation of the function sdCardListFiles().

On line 3 of Code 9.13, it can be seen that a variable called *NumberOfUsedBytesInBuffer* is declared and initialized to zero. This variable will be used to keep track of the number of bytes used to store the list of files on the SD card. On line 4, a pointer named *sdCardDirectoryEntryPointer* of the type dirent (directory entry) is declared.

On line 6, the root directory of the SD card is opened by means of the function *opendir()*, and a pointer to it is stored in the object *sdCardListOfDirectories*. Line 8 evaluates if the root directory was successfully opened by means of evaluating the content of *sdCardListOfDirectories*. If the directory was successfully opened, then the message on line 9 is shown on the serial monitor. Then, the list of files in the directory is retrieved by means of *readdir()* on line 10 and stored in *sdCardDirectoryEntryPointer*.

The *while* loop shown on line 12 is used to (i) check that *sdCardDirectoryEntryPointer* is not NULL (in that case it implies that all the files were already explored) and (ii) that the memory usage is below the limit given by the expression "*(bufferNumberUsedBytes + strlen(sdCardDirectoryEntryPointer->d_name)*

< fileNamesBufferSize)". This expression assesses if the number of bytes that has already been used (*NumberOfUsedBytesInBuffer*) plus the size in bytes of the next filename to be read (given by *strlen(sdCardDirectoryEntryPointer->d_name)*) is smaller than the maximum number of available bytes (*fileNamesBufferSize*).

> **NOTE:** The (->) arrow operator is used to dereference the address a pointer contains (in this example sdCardDirectoryEntryPointer points to the next directory entry) to get or set the value stored in the variable itself. This operator will be discussed in detail in Chapter 10.

On lines 15 and 16, the file names are written one after the other into *fileNamesBuffer*. On line 17, the value of the *NumberOfUsedBytesInBuffer* is updated by means of adding the size of the filename (i.e., *strlen(sdCardDirectoryEntryPointer->d_name)*) to be appended to the list of files. On line 19, the pointer *sdCardDirectoryEntryPointer* is pointed to the next file in the directory in order to be ready to start a new iteration of the *while* loop.

After finishing the *while* loop, the directory is closed on line 22 and the value *true* is returned on line 24.

If the statement on line 8 is false (i.e., the root directory was not successfully opened), then the statements on lines 26 and 27 are executed in order to instruct the user to insert an SD card, just like in the previous examples.

Proposed Exercise

1. What will happen if the SCK signal of the SD card module is disconnected before pressing the "l" key?

Answer to the Exercise

1. The message "Insert an SD card and reset the board." will be shown on the PC screen.

Example 9.4: Choose and Display One of the Event Log Files Stored on the SD Card

Objective

Introduce more advanced functionality regarding the filesystem.

Summary of the Expected Behavior

When pressing the "o" key on the PC keyboard, a filename can be entered. After pressing the Enter key on the PC keyboard, the content of the corresponding file is shown on the serial terminal.

Test the Proposed Solution on the Board

Import the project "Example 9.4" using the URL available in [2], build the project, and drag the *.bin* file onto the NUCLEO board. Press "l" on the PC keyboard to get a list of all the event log files stored on the SD card. A message with the listing should be displayed on the PC. Then, press "o" on the PC keyboard and type in the name of the file that will be opened, and then press Enter. The contents of the file should be shown on the serial terminal.

In Figure 9.10, the result of executing the "o" command is shown for two different situations. First, the name of a file that does exist (*2021_01_27_17_05_06.txt*) is entered and then the name of a file that does not exist (*2021_01_27_17_00_00.txt*) is entered.

```
Please enter the file name
2021_01_27_17_05_06.txt
Opening file: /sd/2021_01_27_17_05_06.txt
The file content is:
Event = ALARM_ON
Date and Time = Wed Jan 27 17:04:47 2021
Event = MOTION_ON
Date and Time = Wed Jan 27 17:04:47 2021
Event = MOTION_OFF
Date and Time = Wed Jan 27 17:04:51 2021
Event = ALARM_OFF
Date and Time = Wed Jan 27 17:04:54 2021

Please enter the file name
2021_01_27_17_00_00.txt
File not found
```

Figure 9.10 Two examples of opening a file: first, when the file exists, and second, when the file does not exist.

Discussion of the Proposed Solution

The proposed solution is based on the function *sdCardReadFile()*, which is used to read the content of a file on the SD card that is opened once its name has been entered by means of the PC keyboard.

Implementation of the Proposed Solution

In Table 9.10, the sections where lines were added to *pc_serial_com.cpp* are shown. It can be seen that two private global variables are declared: an integer variable named *numberOfCharsInFileName* and a char array named *fileName* of size SD_CARD_FILENAME_MAX_LENGTH (i.e., 32, which was introduced in Code 9.5). In addition, four new private functions are declared: *pcSerialComCharWrite()*, *pcSerialComGetFileName()*, *pcSerialComShowSdCardFile()*, and *commandGetFileName()*. The implementation of these functions is discussed below.

In Table 9.11, the lines that were added in *pcSerialComCommandUpdate()* and *availableCommands()* in order to implement the "o" command are shown.

Table 9.10 Sections in which lines were added to pc_serial_com.cpp.

Section	Lines that were added
Declaration and initialization of private global variables	`static int numberOfCharsInFileName = 0;` `static char fileName[SD_CARD_FILENAME_MAX_LENGTH] = "";`

Declarations (prototypes) of private functions	`static void pcSerialComCharWrite( char chr );`
	`static void pcSerialComGetFileName( char receivedChar );`
	`static void pcSerialComShowSdCardFile( char * fileName );`
	`static void commandGetFileName();`

Table 9.11 Functions in which lines were added in pc_serial_com.cpp.

Function	Lines that were added
static void pcSerialComCommandUpdate(char receivedChar)	`case 'o': case 'O': commandGetFileName(); break;`
static void availableCommands()	`pcSerialComStringWrite( "Press 'o' or 'O' to show an SD` `       Card file contents\r\n" );`

The implementation of the function *commandGetFileName()*, which is called when the "o" key is pressed, is presented in Code 9.14. On line 3, it can be seen that a message is shown in order to indicate that a filename should be entered. Then, on line 4, the variable *pcSerialComMode* is assigned by PC_SERIAL_GET_FILE_NAME. This new mode is introduced in the new definition of *pcSerialComMode_t*, as can be seen on line 2 of Code 9.15. The new mode is used in a similar way to the other modes used in *pcSerialComUpdate()*, as can be seen on lines 6 to 8 of Code 9.16.

Finally, it is important to mention that the value of *numberOfCharsInFileName* is set to zero on line 5 of *commandGetFileName()*, as can be seen in Code 9.14. This is done in order to prepare the variable *numberOfCharsInFileName* to receive a new filename.

NOTE: When *pcSerialComMode* is in the PC_SERIAL_GET_FILE_NAME mode, the smart home system will not accept new commands until the filename is entered.

```
1   static void commandGetFileName()
2   {
3       pcSerialComStringWrite( "Please enter the file name \r\n" );
4       pcSerialComMode = PC_SERIAL_GET_FILE_NAME ;
5       numberOfCharsInFileName = 0;
6   }
```

Code 9.14 Implementation of the function commandGetFileName().

```
1   typedef enum{
2       PC_SERIAL_GET_FILE_NAME,
3       PC_SERIAL_COMMANDS,
4       PC_SERIAL_GET_CODE,
5       PC_SERIAL_SAVE_NEW_CODE,
6   } pcSerialComMode_t;
```

Code 9.15 New declaration of the type definition pcSerialComMode_t.

```
1   void pcSerialComUpdate()
2   {
3       char receivedChar = pcSerialComCharRead();
4       if( receivedChar != '\0' ) {
5           switch ( pcSerialComMode ) {
6               case PC_SERIAL_GET_FILE_NAME:
7                   pcSerialComGetFileName( receivedChar );
8               break;
9               case PC_SERIAL_COMMANDS:
10                  pcSerialComCommandUpdate( receivedChar );
11              break;
12              case PC_SERIAL_GET_CODE:
13                  pcSerialComGetCodeUpdate( receivedChar );
14              break;
15              case PC_SERIAL_SAVE_NEW_CODE:
16                  pcSerialComSaveNewCodeUpdate( receivedChar );
17              break;
18              default:
19                  pcSerialComMode = PC_SERIAL_COMMANDS;
20              break;
21          }
22      }
23  }
```

Code 9.16 New implementation of the function pcSerialComUpdate().

In Code 9.17, the implementation of the function *pcSerialComGetFileName()*, which is called on line 7 of the function *pcSerialComUpdate()*, is shown. On lines 3 and 4, it can be seen that the entered character is checked to find out if it is '\r' (i.e., the "Enter" key on the PC keyboard), and it is also checked to see if the length of the filename is smaller than the maximum filename length. If so, then PC_SERIAL_COMMANDS is assigned to *pcSerialComMode* in order to be ready to receive new commands. Then, a null character is written at the last position of fileName in order to finalize the string (line 6), and *numberOfCharsInFileName* is set to zero in order to be ready to get a new filename the next time the function *pcSerialComGetFileName()* is called. Finally, the *pcSerialComShowSdCardFile()* function is used to display the contents of the file on the serial terminal.

In the event that the key pressed is not "Enter" and the length of the filename is smaller than the maximum filename length, the *else* statement shown on line 9 of Code 9.17 is executed. It can be seen that the received character is stored in the last position of fileName (line 10), the received character is printed on the serial terminal (line 11), and then the number of characters in the filename is incremented.

```
1   static void pcSerialComGetFileName( char receivedChar )
2   {
3       if ( (receivedChar == '\r') &&
4           (numberOfCharsInFileName < SD_CARD_FILENAME_MAX_LENGTH) ) {
5           pcSerialComMode = PC_SERIAL_COMMANDS;
6           fileName[numberOfCharsInFileName] = '\0';
7           numberOfCharsInFileName = 0;
8           pcSerialComShowSdCardFile( fileName );
9       } else {
10          fileName[numberOfCharsInFileName] = receivedChar;
11          pcSerialComCharWrite( receivedChar );
12          numberOfCharsInFileName++;
13      }
14  }
```

Code 9.17 Implementation of the function pcSerialComGetFileName().

The implementation of *pcSerialComShowSdCardFile()* is shown in Code 9.18. On line 3, the array of char *fileContentBuffer* is declared with the appropriate size to store a file with twenty events, as discussed below. Then, "\r\n" is written to the PC screen in order to start a new line. After this, the new function *sdCardReadFile()* that is included in the *sd_card* module is called. This function copies the content of the file whose name is indicated by *fileName* to *fileContentBuffer*, up to a maximum number of bytes indicated by its third parameter, EVENT_STR_LENGTH*EVENT_LOG_MAX_STORAGE (line 6). If the file exists, then *sdCardReadFile()* returns true, lines 7 to 9 are executed, and the file content is shown on the serial monitor. If that file doesn't exist, then *sdCardReadFile()* returns false, and lines 7 to 9 are not executed.

```
1   static void pcSerialComShowSdCardFile( char* fileName )
2   {
3       char fileContentBuffer[EVENT_STR_LENGTH*EVENT_LOG_MAX_STORAGE] = "";
4       pcSerialComStringWrite( "\r\n" );
5       if ( sdCardReadFile( fileName, fileContentBuffer,
6                           EVENT_STR_LENGTH*EVENT_LOG_MAX_STORAGE ) ) {
7           pcSerialComStringWrite( "The file content is:\r\n");
8           pcSerialComStringWrite( fileContentBuffer );
9           pcSerialComStringWrite( "\r\n" );
10      }
11  }
```

Code 9.18 Implementation of the function pcSerialComShowSdCardFile().

The implementation of *pcSerialComCharWrite()* is shown on Code 9.19. Note that its parameter, *chr*, is of type char, instead of the parameter of the function *pcSerialComStringWrite()*, which is of type const char*, as was discussed in previous chapters. Because of this, *pcSerialComStringWrite()* cannot be used on line 11 of Code 9.17 instead of *pcSerialComCharWrite()*.

```
1   static void pcSerialComCharWrite( char chr )
2   {
3       char str[2] = "";
4       sprintf (str, "%c", chr);
5       uartUsb.write( str, strlen(str) );
6   }
```

Code 9.19 Implementation of the function pcSerialComCharWrite().

In Table 9.12, the lines that were added to *sd_card.h* are shown. It can be seen that the public function *sdCardReadFile()* has been included.

Table 9.12 Sections in which lines were added to sd_card.h.

Section	Lines that were added
Declarations (prototypes) of public functions	`bool sdCardReadFile( const char* fileName, char *` `readBuffer, int readBufferSize );`

In Code 9.20, the implementation of the function *sdCardReadFile()* as can be seen in *sd_card.cpp* is shown. Lines 3 to 8 are similar to previous examples. The aim of these lines is to append /sd/ to the filename and store this in the string *fileNameSD*. For that reason, this string is declared with four more positions (i.e., +4).

On line 10, the chosen file is opened and a pointer to the file is stored in *sdCardFilePointer*. It should be noted that the parameter "r" is used when the file is opened, which states that the file is to be opened with read privileges only. If the file has been successfully opened, then *sdCardFilePointer* is not NULL and lines 13 to 24 are executed.

By means of lines 13 to 15, the name of the file that is being opened is shown. The *while* loop on line 18 is used to read all of the characters in the file sequentially and copy them to the *readBuffer* array until the end of the file is reached (in that event the return value by *feof(sdCardFilePointer)* becomes true and the *while* loop is finished) or the size of the read buffer has been reached (in that event the *while* loop is finished, too).

The function *fread()* on line 19 has the following four parameters: a pointer to a block of memory where the read bytes are stored (&*readBuffer[i]* in this example), the size in bytes of each element to be read (1 in this example, because the elements are of type char), the number of elements to read (1 in this example, because the characters of the file are read one after the other), and, finally, a pointer to a FILE object that specifies the input stream (*sdCardFilePointer* in this example).

On line 22, the null character is written into *readBuffer* in order to indicate the end of the data, and on line 23 the file is closed.

If the file does not exist, then *sdCardFilePointer* is assigned the NULL value. In that case, the *else* condition of the *if* statement on line 12 is executed in order to indicate that the file was not found.

NOTE: In summary, in this example the reading of the file was ended because of one of these reasons:
- i) It was not possible to open the file (i.e., *sdCardFilePointer* == NULL)
- ii) The end of the file was reached (i.e., *feof(sdCardFilePointer)* == true)
- iii) The maximum size of the buffer was reached (i.e., *i* == *readBufferSize* - 1)

For the sake of simplicity, the situation of an error on the file, which is assessed using *ferror()*, is not considered in Code 9.19.

```
1   bool sdCardReadFile( const char* fileName, char * readBuffer, int readBufferSize )
2   {
3       char fileNameSD[SD_CARD_FILENAME_MAX_LENGTH+4] = "";
4       int i;
5
6       fileNameSD[0] = '\0';
7       strcat( fileNameSD, "/sd/" );
8       strcat( fileNameSD, fileName );
9
10      FILE *sdCardFilePointer = fopen( fileNameSD, "r" );
11
12      if ( sdCardFilePointer != NULL ) {
13          pcSerialComStringWrite( "Opening file: " );
14          pcSerialComStringWrite( fileNameSD );
15          pcSerialComStringWrite( "\r\n" );
16
17          i = 0;
18          while ( ( !feof(sdCardFilePointer) ) && ( i < readBufferSize - 1 ) ) {
19              fread( &readBuffer[i], 1, 1, sdCardFilePointer );
20              i++;
21          }
22          readBuffer[i-1] = '\0';
23          fclose( sdCardFilePointer );
24          return true;
25      } else {
26          pcSerialComStringWrite( "File not found\r\n" );
27          return false;
28      }
29  }
```

Code 9.20 Implementation of the function sdCardReadFile().

Proposed Exercises

1. What will happen if an event log file with no events is selected?

2. How can the code be modified in order to automatically generate a daily backup of the events?

Answers to the Exercises

1. The smart home system will not store event log files with no events.

2. The *eventLogUpdate()* function can be modified in order to keep track of the current day, and once it detects that the day has changed, it generates a new file with the corresponding events of the day.

9.3 Under the Hood

9.3.1 Fundamentals of Software Repositories

All the programs used in this book are imported from [2] to the Keil Studio Cloud. This program sharing is done by means of a set of links and buttons, which are the *front end* (the presentation layer) of a *software repository* that is being used in the *back end* (the data access layer) to support the file sharing.

A software repository is a storage location for software. At the user side, a *package manager* (such as some tools provided by Keil Studio Cloud) usually helps to manage the repositories. The server side is typically provided by organizations, either free of charge or for a subscription fee. For example, major Linux distributions have many repositories around the world that mirror the main repository.

A repository provides a revision control system, which includes a historical record of changes in the repository together with the corresponding committed objects. The user of a repository usually has access to basic information about the repository, such as that shown in Table 9.13.

Table 9.13 Summary of typical information available about a repository.

Information	Used to
Versions available	Indicate current and previous versions
Dependencies	Indicate other elements that the current element depends on
Dependants	Specify other elements that depend on the current element
License	Govern the use or redistribution of the element
Build date and time	Be able to trace each specific version
Metrics	Indicate some properties of the element

Some functionality that is provided by most repositories is to add, edit, and delete content; show the elements using different sorting properties; search for different types of elements and data; provide access control; and import and export elements.

By means of this functionality, a repository can evolve as shown in Figure 9.11. It can be seen that there is a main project (indicated in green) with different *tags* (1, 3, and 7 in Figure 9.11) from which branches (indicated in yellow) can be created. The branches can be merged with the main project, as shown in red, in order to create a new version of the software. They could, alternatively, become a discontinued development branch, such as the one indicated in violet.

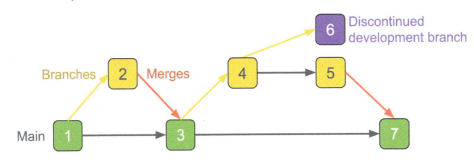

Figure 9.11 Diagram of a typical evolution of a repository.

The use of repositories provides many advantages, among which the following can be highlighted:

▣ Allows many programmers to work in the same repository without interrupting one another.

▣ Indicates when changes in the repository (*commits*) have been introduced by other programmers.

The Keil Studio Cloud provides an easy-to-use environment where most of these things can be done, as described in [6]:

- Set a remote repository

- Branch a repository

- Edit files from a repository

- Stage changes of a repository

- Commit to a repository

- Push to a repository

Proposed Exercises

1. How can the revision history of a given project be accessed using Keil Studio Cloud?

2. How can the changes between selected revisions be seen using Keil Studio Cloud?

3. How can changes made on a program be committed?

4. How can a program be shared with other people?

 WARNING: In order to do some of the proposed exercises, it is important to set credentials for GitHub in Keil Studio Cloud as described step-by-step in [6].

Answers to the Exercises

1. The project should be selected as the active project and then the "History" view selected (its shortcut is Alt+H). The "Revision History" window will open, showing all the information corresponding to the commits that were made along the project history.

2. In the "Revision History" window, click once on any of the commits shown in order to select it. Click for a second time on the same commit in order to display the list of changed files. Double-click on one of the selected files. A window will open where the changes between revisions are shown in different colors.

3. The reader is encouraged to make a change in Example 9.4; for example, in *sdCardReadFile()*, change the line *pcSerialComStringWrite("File not found\r\n");* to *pcSerialComStringWrite("File not found in the SD Card\r\n")*. Then, select the "Source Control" window (Ctrl+Shift+G). Select the file *sd_card.cpp*

and press the "+" sign. The file should be listed in the "Staged changes" list. Enter a commit message and press the "Commit" button (its drawing is a check mark). Press the "More Actions..." button (represented by three small dots). A menu will be displayed. Select "Push". A message indicating that the reader does not have permission to push will be shown.

In order to commit the changes, the reader can fork to their own GitHub account but will first need to connect the Mbed account to their GitHub account, following the instructions shown by Keil Studio Cloud. If it was not previously connected, follow the step-by-step instructions indicated in [6]. Once the Mbed account is connected to the GitHub account of the reader, press "Push" again. A message indicating that the reader does not have permission to push will be shown. This time, the option to "Fork on GitHub" will be shown. After doing so, a message indicating that the fork has been created will be shown. In this way, the changes will be committed to the GitHub repository of the reader.

4. The reader should use a web browser to access GitHub and open the repository related to the project. Then, be sure that the repository access is configured as "public" and copy the URL of the repository in order to share the created repository with other people.

9.4 Case Study

9.4.1 Repository Usage in Mbed-Based Projects

In this chapter, the fundamentals of repositories and their usage was introduced. It is interesting to explore how repositories are used in Mbed-based projects. As an example, the game console provided with a graphical LCD display [7] that was introduced in the Case Study of Chapter 6 can be used.

A representation of the system is shown in Figure 9.12. On that web page, similar to the one in [8], a basic example of the game console "Pokitto" is shown, named "Hello World!" It can be seen that the current version is indicated by a label (where it says "Files at revision"). All the previous versions are available in the "History" tab.

At the bottom of Figure 9.12, it can be seen that there are three files in the repository: *My_settings.h*, *PokittoLib.lib*, and *main.cpp*. This file structure is similar to the one used in the first chapters of this book. By clicking on the "Revisions" link at the right of each file, the details of the corresponding revisions can be seen.

In the "Repository details" frame at the right of Figure 9.12, some interesting information can be seen. For example, it shows how many forks have been made of this repository, as well as how many commits were made to the repository. At the bottom of the frame, the whole repository can be downloaded.

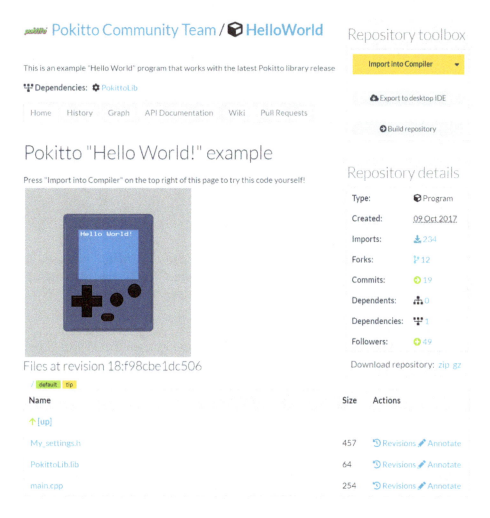

Figure 9.12 Repository of an example of a game console based on Mbed.

Proposed Exercises

1. Are there any other examples of Pokitto programs available in repositories on the Mbed OS web page?

2. How could a copy of the Pokitto "Hello World!" example be copied into the reader's personal repository?

Answers to the Exercises

1. About thirty examples are available in [9], all having the same organization as shown in Figure 9.12.

2. In order to make a copy of the example "Hello World!", the "Import into Compiler" button must be pressed.

References

[1] "microSD Card Pinout, Features & Datasheet". Accessed July 9, 2021.
https://components101.com/misc/microsd-card-pinout-datasheet

[2] "GitHub - armBookCodeExamples/Directory". Accessed July 9, 2021.
https://github.com/armBookCodeExamples/Directory/

[3] "Data storage - API references and tutorials | Mbed OS 6 Documentation". Accessed July 9, 2021.
https://os.mbed.com/docs/mbed-os/v6.12/apis/data-storage.html

[4] "pinout_labels - | Mbed". Accessed July 9, 2021.
https://os.mbed.com/teams/ST/wiki/pinout_labels

[5] "mbed-os/PeripheralPinMaps.h at master · ARMmbed/mbed-os · GitHub". Accessed July 9, 2021.
https://github.com/ARMmbed/mbed-os/blob/master/targets/TARGET_STM/TARGET_STM32F4/
TARGET_STM32F429xI/TARGET_NUCLEO_F429ZI/PeripheralPinMaps.h

[6] "Arm Keil Studio Cloud User Guide". Accessed July 9, 2021.
https://developer.arm.com/documentation/102497/1-5/Source-control/Work-with-Git

[7] "Game Console | Mbed". Accessed July 9, 2021.
https://os.mbed.com/built-with-mbed/game-console/

[8] "HelloWorld - This is an example "Hello World" program that w... | Mbed". Accessed July 9, 2021.
https://os.mbed.com/teams/Pokitto-Community-Team/code/HelloWorld/

[9] "Pokitto Community Team | Mbed". Accessed July 9, 2021.
https://os.mbed.com/teams/Pokitto-Community-Team/

Chapter 10

Bluetooth Low Energy
Communication with a
Smartphone

10.1 Roadmap

10.1.1 What You Will Learn

After you have studied the material in this chapter, you will be able to:

▪ Describe how to connect Bluetooth Low Energy (BLE) modules to the NUCLEO board using a UART.

▪ Develop programs to exchange data between the NUCLEO board and a smartphone using a BLE connection.

▪ Summarize the fundamentals of a BLE connection.

▪ Describe the fundamentals of C++ objects.

10.1.2 Review of Previous Chapters

In previous chapters, the smart home system was provided with many functions, implemented by means of a set of sensors and actuators. This functionality was configured by the user using different interfaces, including a matrix keypad, an LCD display, and a PC. These interfaces were appropriate for this project, but often there are other interfaces that are more convenient, more flexible, or allow a better presentation of the information.

10.1.3 Contents of This Chapter

In this chapter, it will be explained how to enable communication between the NUCLEO board and a smartphone using a BLE connection. This will be achieved by using an HM-10 module connected to one of the UARTs of the NUCLEO board available in the ST ZIO connectors. In this way, relevant information from the smart home system will be shown on the smartphone. In addition, the gate will be controlled using the smartphone.

The fundamentals of object-oriented programming (OOP) will be introduced. It will be explained how OOP can be used to increase code modularity, reusability, flexibility, and effectiveness. Some details about the Mbed OS library objects that were used in previous chapters will be discussed.

Finally, a new way of implementing delays using interrupts and pointers will be shown. The delay in the main loop will be replaced by a *non-blocking delay*. This will be useful to avoid blocking the processor and keep it executing instructions while waiting for the expiration of the delay time.

10.2 Bluetooth Low Energy Communication between a Smartphone and the NUCLEO Board

10.2.1 Connect the Smart Home System to a Smartphone

In this chapter, the smart home system will be connected to a smartphone using Bluetooth Low Energy (BLE), as shown in Figure 10.1. The aim of this setup is to monitor relevant information from the smart home system and control the gate from the smartphone.

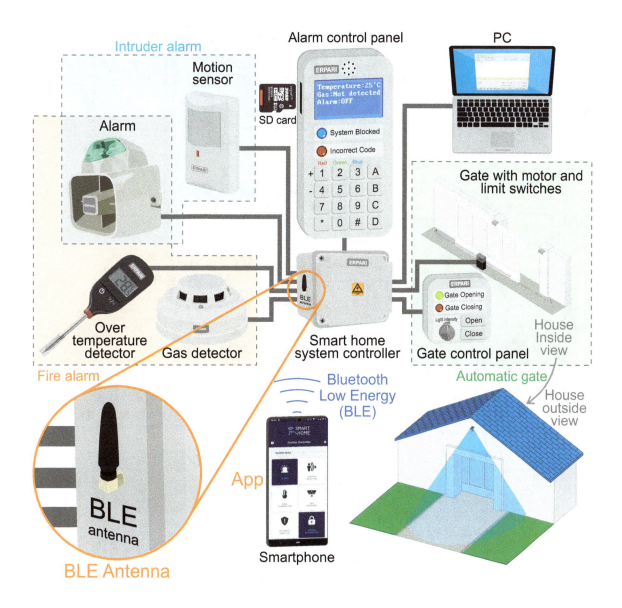

Figure 10.1 The smart home system will be connected to a smartphone via Bluetooth Low Energy.

In order to connect the NUCLEO board to a smartphone, two elements are required:

1. A module that provides the NUCLEO board with BLE communication capabilities.

2. A specifically prepared application running on a smartphone.

Figure 10.2 shows how to connect the HM-10 Bluetooth module, which is described in [1], to the NUCLEO board. These connections are summarized in Table 10.1.

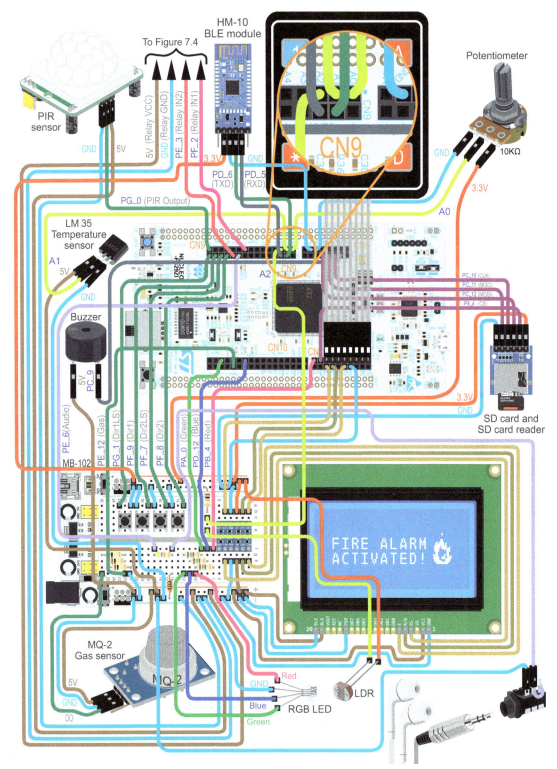

Figure 10.2 Connections to be made between the NUCLEO board and the HM-10 module.

Table 10.1 Summary of the connections between the NUCLEO board and the HM-10 module.

NUCLEO board	HM-10 module
3V3	VCC
GND	GND
PD_6 (UART2_RX)	TXD
PD_5 (UART2_TX)	RXD

In Figure 10.3, the pins of the HM-10 module are shown. The STATE pin is the *connection status*. It is in LOW when not connected and in HIGH when connected. The BRK pin is the Break pin. When there is an active connection, bringing the BRK pin LOW breaks the connection. These two pins are not used in this book.

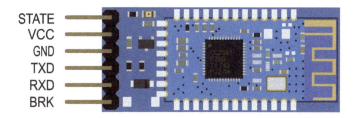

STATE
VCC
GND
TXD
RXD
BRK

Figure 10.3 Basic functionality of the HM-10 module pins.

The HM-10 module is connected to the NUCLEO board by means of the pins PD_5 and PD_6, which are the TXD and RXD signals of a UART on the NUCLEO board; this is shown in Figure 8.5 and Table 10.1. The HM-10 module is responsible for the communication with the smartphone using a BLE connection. Using a UART serial communication, such as the one explained in Chapter 2, the information is exchanged between the NUCLEO board and the HM-10 module.

On the other side of the connection, a BLE module inside the smartphone implements the communication with the HM-10 module. The smartphone routes the messages from the smart home system to the application "Smart Home System App."

To test the HM-10 module, download the *.bin* file of the program "Subsection 10.2.1" from the URL available in [2] and load it onto the NUCLEO board. The application to be used on the smartphone is named "Smart Home System App" and should be downloaded from Google Play or the App Store (depending on the operating system of the smartphone the user owns) and installed on the smartphone as usual.

Open the application. The "Connect to the Smart Home System" screen is displayed. Click on the magnifying glass located at the bottom of the screen (Figure 10.4). Some BLE connections should be listed on the smartphone. Select the "BT05" connection (Figure 10.4). Once the connection is established, different icons will be displayed on the screen, and the status of the connection will be indicated in the top right corner (Figure 10.4). Wave a hand over the PIR sensor. The "ALARM" and "MOTION DETECTOR" indicators of the "Smart Home System App" should change their color. Press the "OPEN THE GATE" and "CLOSE THE GATE" buttons of the "Smart Home System App." The motor should rotate in one direction and then the other. If so, the reader is ready to move forward to the first example of this chapter.

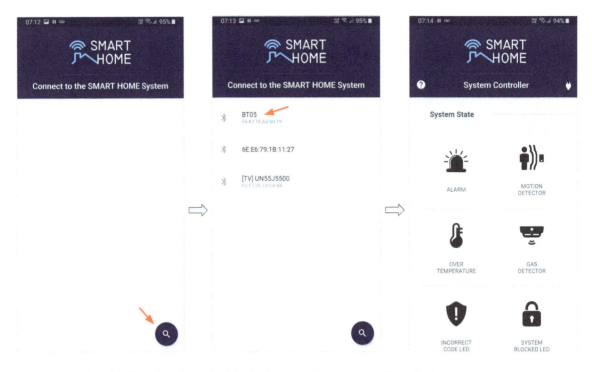

Figure 10.4 Screenshots of the "Smart Home System App," showing the sequence to connect and use the application.

WARNING: Ignore all the other elements of the setup during the proposed test (Alarm LED, display, etc.).

TIP: If the BLE connection is not established, check if all the wires are properly connected. If there are no mistakes in the connections detailed in Table 10.1, try using another HM-10 module or smartphone.

10.2.2 Messages Exchanged with the Smartphone Application

In order to exchange information between the program running on the NUCLEO board and the smartphone application, the list of messages that the smartphone application is prepared to receive and send by means of the BLE connection must be known.

NOTE: The code used to implement the application running on the smartphone is beyond the scope of this book and, therefore, is not analyzed. However, the reader may download from Google Play or the App Store a "Bluetooth terminal" application and use it on the smartphone to receive and send the messages detailed below in a similar way as messages are received and sent to the PC using the serial terminal. In that case, the "Smart Home System App" behavior can be emulated using a Bluetooth terminal. "CR+LF" should be configured in "newline receive settings" and "None" in "newline send settings."

All the messages that can be sent from the NUCLEO board to the application are listed in Table 10.2. These messages force a given element in the application to turn on or off.

Table 10.2 Summary of the messages from the NUCLEO board to the application.

Message	Meaning
ALARM_ON	Turn on the state indicator of the alarm in the application
ALARM_OFF	Turn off the state indicator of the alarm in the application
GAS_DET_ON	Turn on the state indicator of the gas detector in the application
GAS_DET_OFF	Turn off the state indicator of the gas detector in the application
OVER_TEMP_ON	Turn on the state indicator of the over temperature detector in the application
OVER_TEMP_OFF	Turn off the state indicator of the over temperature detector in the application
LED_IC_ON	Turn on the state indicator of the Incorrect code LED in the application
LED_IC_OFF	Turn off the state indicator of the Incorrect code LED in the application
LED_SB_ON	Turn on the state indicator of the System blocked LED in the application
LED_SB_OFF	Turn off the state indicator of the System blocked LED in the application
MOTION_ON	Turn on the state indicator of the motion sensor in the application
MOTION_OFF	Turn off the state indicator of the motion sensor in the application

All the messages that can be sent from the application to the NUCLEO board are listed in Table 10.3. The aim of these messages is to inform the board that a given button has been pressed or released in the application or to request the current state of all the system events that are shown by the smartphone.

Table 10.3 Summary of the messages from the application to the NUCLEO board.

Message	Meaning
O	The "Open the gate" button was pressed in the application
C	The "Close the gate" button was pressed in the application
b	The application requested the current state of all the system events shown in Table 10.2

> **NOTE:** In order to simplify the software implementation, only one letter is used in the messages from the application to the NUCLEO board, as can be seen in Table 10.3. Messages having more letters, as in Table 10.2, could be used. However, in that case the program becomes more complex.

In the following examples, the messages in Table 10.2 and Table 10.3 will be gradually introduced as more functionality regarding the smartphone application is incorporated into the smart home system.

Example 10.1: Control the Gate Opening and Closing from a Smartphone

Objective

Introduce the use of a BLE module to receive data sent from a smartphone application to the NUCLEO board.

Summary of the Expected Behavior

If the "Open the gate" button is pressed in the application, it is reported to the NUCLEO board, which in turn opens the gate if it is not already opened. If the "Close the gate" button is pressed in the application, it is reported to the NUCLEO board, which closes the gate if it is not already closed.

Test the Proposed Solution on the Board

Import the project "Example 10.1" using the URL available in [2], build the project, and drag the *.bin* file onto the NUCLEO board. Open the application "Smart Home System App" on the smartphone. Connect the application to the NUCLEO board. Press the "Open the gate" button in the application. If the gate is not already opened, then it should be opened by the NUCLEO board. Press the "Close the gate" button in the application. The gate should close.

Discussion of the Proposed Solution

The proposed solution is based on the BLE communication that is established between the HM-10 module and the application running on the smartphone. The fundamentals of BLE communication are described in the Under the Hood section at the end of this chapter. In this example, only the code that runs on the STM32 microcontroller is explained.

A new module named *ble_com* is included in order to receive commands from the smartphone application.

Implementation of the Proposed Solution

The function *bleComUpdate()* is included in *smartHomeSystemUpdate()* (line 10 of Code 10.1) to periodically check if a new command is received from the smartphone. In order to implement this call, the library *ble_com.h* is included in *smart_home_system.cpp*, as can be seen in Table 10.4.

```
 1   void smartHomeSystemUpdate()
 2   {
 3       userInterfaceUpdate();
 4       fireAlarmUpdate();
 5       intruderAlarmUpdate();
 6       alarmUpdate();
 7       eventLogUpdate();
 8       pcSerialComUpdate();
 9       lightSystemUpdate();
10       bleComUpdate();
11       delay(SYSTEM_TIME_INCREMENT_MS);
12   }
```

Code 10.1 Details of the new implementation of smart_home_system.cpp.

Table 10.4 Sections in which lines were added to smart_home_system.cpp.

Section	Lines that were added
Libraries	#include "ble_com.h"

The new module *ble_com* is shown in Code 10.2 and Code 10.3. The libraries that are included are shown from lines 3 to 6 of Code 10.2. On line 10, the public global object *uartBle* is declared. On line 14, the prototype of the private function *bleComCharRead()* is declared.

The implementation of the public function *bleComUpdate()* is shown on lines 18 to 27 of Code 10.2. The reader may notice that this is similar to the function *pcSerialComCommandUpdate()* of the *pc_serial_com* module. On line 20, the private function *bleComCharRead()* (implemented on lines 31 to 38) is used to read characters that the smartphone application sends. If the application does not send a character, then the function returns the null character ('\0').

On lines 21 to 26, if a new character is received from the smartphone application, a switch statement is used to call *gateOpen()* or *gateClose()* from the module *gate* if the character is "O" or "C", respectively.

```
 1   //=====[Libraries]=============================================
 2
 3   #include "mbed.h"
 4
 5   #include "ble_com.h"
 6   #include "gate.h"
 7
 8   //=====[Declaration and initialization of public global objects]=================
 9
10   UnbufferedSerial uartBle(PD_5, PD_6, 9600);
11
12   //=====[Declarations (prototypes) of private functions]===================
13
14   static char bleComCharRead();
15
16   //=====[Implementations of public functions]===================
17
18   void bleComUpdate()
19   {
20       char receivedChar = bleComCharRead();
```

```
21        if( receivedChar != '\0' ) {
22            switch (receivedChar) {
23                case 'O': gateOpen(); break;
24                case 'C': gateClose(); break;
25            }
26        }
27    }
28
29    //=====[Implementations of private functions]================================
30
31    static char bleComCharRead()
32    {
33        char receivedChar = '\0';
34        if( uartBle.readable() ) {
35            uartBle.read(&receivedChar,1);
36        }
37        return receivedChar;
38    }
```

Code 10.2 Details of the implementation of the ble_com.h.

 NOTE: The program code implemented in this example does not include the response of the "b" message that was introduced in Table 10.3. This will be addressed in Example 10.3.

Finally the implementation of the file *ble_com.h* is shown in Code 10.3.

```
1    //=====[#include guards - begin]=============================================
2
3    #ifndef _BLE_COM_H_
4    #define _BLE_COM_H_
5
6    //=====[Declarations (prototypes) of public functions]======================
7
8    void bleComUpdate();
9
10   //=====[#include guards - end]===============================================
11
12   #endif // _BLE_COM_H_
```

Code 10.3 Implementation of the file ble_com.h.

Proposed Exercise

1. How can the Fire alarm test button functionality be implemented by means of a button press on the smartphone application?

Answer to the Exercise

1. A "Fire alarm test button" should be included in the application, and a character (such as "A") should be sent from the smartphone to the NUCLEO board when this button is pressed. The program running on the NUCLEO board should process this message and trigger the corresponding actions in order to set the variables *overTemperatureDetected* and *gasDetected* to ON.

Example 10.2: Report the Smart Home System State to a Smartphone

Objective

Use of a BLE module to send data from the NUCLEO board to the smartphone.

Summary of the Expected Behavior

The states of different elements of the smart home system (alarm, gas detector, over temperature detector, Incorrect code indicator, System blocked indicator, and motion sensor) are communicated to the application running on the smartphone.

Test the Proposed Solution on the Board

Import the project "Example 10.2" using the URL available in [2], build the project, and drag the .*bin* file onto the NUCLEO board. Make sure that the alarm is not active. Open the smartphone application "Smart Home System App." Connect the application to the NUCLEO board. Press the Fire alarm test button (B1 User button). The state of the alarm should be displayed in the application. Wave a hand over the PIR sensor. The application should notify the user that motion has been detected.

Discussion of the Proposed Solution

The proposed solution is again based on the BLE communication established between the HM-10 module and the application running on the smartphone. New functionality is included in the *ble_com* module in order to implement the expected behavior.

Implementation of the Proposed Solution

The states of the alarm, gas detector, over temperature detector, Incorrect code indicator, System block indicator, and motion sensor are to be reported. To send the states to the smartphone application, the function *eventLogWrite()* from the module *event_log* is modified. The new implementation can be seen in Code 10.4.

```
1   void eventLogWrite( bool currentState, const char* elementName )
2   {
3       char eventAndStateStr[EVENT_LOG_NAME_MAX_LENGTH]) = "";
4
5       strcat( eventAndStateStr, elementName );
6       if ( currentState ) {
7           strcat( eventAndStateStr, "_ON" );
8       } else {
9           strcat( eventAndStateStr, "_OFF" );
10      }
11
12      arrayOfStoredEvents[eventsIndex].seconds = time(NULL);
13      strcpy( arrayOfStoredEvents[eventsIndex].typeOfEvent, eventAndStateStr );
14      if ( eventsIndex < EVENT_LOG_MAX_STORAGE - 1 ) {
15          eventsIndex++;
16      } else {
17          eventsIndex = 0;
```

```
18          }
19
20          arrayOfStoredEvents[eventsIndex].storedInSd = false;
21
22          pcSerialComStringWrite(eventAndStateStr);
23          pcSerialComStringWrite("\r\n");
24
25          bleComStringWrite(eventAndStateStr);
26          bleComStringWrite("\r\n");
27
28          eventAndStateStrSent = true;
29  }
```

Code 10.4 New implementation of the function eventLogWrite().

The function *eventLogWrite()* already sends the messages shown in Table 10.2 to the serial terminal (lines 22 and 23). Following a similar procedure, lines 25 and 26 are added to call the new function *bleComStringWrite()*. In order to implement this call, the library *ble_com.h* is included in *event_log.cpp*, as can be seen in Table 10.5. When the function *eventLogWrite()* is called, the variable *eventAndStateStrSent* is set to true (line 28). This variable is declared in *event_log.cpp*, as can be seen in Table 10.5, and its meaning will be explained in Code 10.5.

The new implementation of the function *eventLogUpdate()* can be seen in Code 10.5. This function is called approximately every 10 milliseconds (depending on the delays executed in the other function calls of *smartHomeSystemUpdate()*). The application running on the smartphone needs some time between received messages in order to process each command. For this reason, *eventLogUpdate()* is modified in order to send only one message in each call. To accomplish this, the variable *eventAndStateStrSent* is set to false in line 3. The event states will be updated only if this variable is false (lines 6 to 41).

As explained for Code 10.4, *eventAndStateStrSent* is set to true when a message is sent to the smartphone. This is because *eventLogWrite()* is called if there are changes in the state of any event. Then, if more than one event changes its state simultaneously, there will be at least a 10-millisecond delay between the corresponding messages. For instance, the ALARM_ON and GAS_DET_ON events occur almost simultaneously. Also, the LED_SB_ON and LED_IC_ON events occur simultaneously. In any of these cases, the corresponding messages will be sent to the smartphone with a gap of at least 10 milliseconds.

```
1   void eventLogUpdate()
2   {
3           eventAndStateStrSent = false;
4           bool currentState;
5
6           if ( !eventAndStateStrSent ) {
7               currentState = sirenStateRead();
8               eventLogElementStateUpdate( sirenLastState, currentState, "ALARM" );
9               sirenLastState = currentState;
10          }
11
12          if ( !eventAndStateStrSent ) {
13              currentState = gasDetectorStateRead();
14              eventLogElementStateUpdate( gasLastState, currentState, "GAS_DET" );
```

```
15            gasLastState = currentState;
16      }
17
18      if ( !eventAndStateStrSent ) {
19          currentState = overTemperatureDetectorStateRead();
20          eventLogElementStateUpdate( tempLastState, currentState, "OVER_TEMP" );
21          tempLastState = currentState;
22      }
23
24      if ( !eventAndStateStrSent ) {
25          currentState = incorrectCodeStateRead();
26          eventLogElementStateUpdate( ICLastState, currentState, "LED_IC" );
27          ICLastState = currentState;
28      }
29
30      if ( !eventAndStateStrSent ) {
31          currentState = systemBlockedStateRead();
32          eventLogElementStateUpdate( SBLastState ,currentState, "LED_SB" );
33          SBLastState = currentState;
34      }
35
36      if ( !eventAndStateStrSent ) {
37          currentState = motionSensorRead();
38          eventLogElementStateUpdate( motionLastState ,currentState, "MOTION" );
39          motionLastState = currentState;
40      }
41 }
```

Code 10.5 New implementation of the function eventLogUpdate().

Table 10.5 Sections in which lines were added to event_log.cpp.

Section	Lines that were added
Libraries	`#include "ble_com.h"`
Declaration and initialization of private global variables	`static bool eventAndStateStrSent;`

The implementation of the new public function *bleComStringWrite()* from module ble_com is shown in Code 10.6, and its prototype is declared in *ble_com.h*, as shown in Table 10.6.

```
1  void bleComStringWrite( const char* str )
2  {
3      uartBle.write( str, strlen(str) );
4  }
```

Code 10.6 New function bleComStringWrite() in ble_com.cpp.

Table 10.6 Sections in which lines were added to ble_com.h.

Section	Lines that were added
Declarations (prototypes) of public functions	`void bleComStringWrite( const char* str );`

Proposed Exercise

1. Given that the modules *pc_serial_com* and *ble_com* have many similarities, why was a function named *bleComInit()* not included in *smartHomeSystemInit()*?

Answer to the Exercise

1. The HM-10 module automatically initializes itself after power on, so no initialization is required. However, as stated in other chapters, this function may have been included in order to follow the same pattern as in other modules even though no functionality is needed in the BLE communication.

Example 10.3: Implement the Smart Home System State Report Using Objects

Objective

Introduce the use of object-oriented programming.

 NOTE: The C language does not support object-oriented programming. The C++ language is a superset of C that introduces the concept of classes and objects, among other features. Given that objects are used in all of the program code of this book (for example, DigitalIn, DigitalOut, etc.), the C language is not sufficient to interpret the code. The IDE (*Integrated Development Environment*, such as Keil Studio Cloud) infers that C++ is being used because the files have the extension *.cpp* ("C plus plus", C++).

Summary of the Expected Behavior

The behavior of this example will remain exactly the same as that in Example 10.2, but some changes are included to improve the smartphone application functionality. Also, the code will be refactored in order to introduce the use of object-oriented programming.

Test the Proposed Solution on the Board

Import the project "Example 10.3" using the URL available in [2], build the project, and drag the *.bin* file onto the NUCLEO board. Open the smartphone application "Smart Home System App." Connect the application to the NUCLEO board. Press the Fire alarm test button (B1 User button). The state of the alarm should be displayed in the application. Reset the NUCLEO board. Note that the alarm turns off on the NUCLEO board but in the smartphone application it remains on. Press the button "System Controller" in the smartphone application, which is used to send a request to the NUCLEO board for the updated state of the system events. The alarm should turn off.

Discussion of the Proposed Solution

Throughout this book, the concept of *object* has been mentioned several times. In this example, a class named *system_event* is created. Several instances of this class are declared to implement part of the functionality of the *event_log* module. Each instance of the *system_event* class is called an object. How to implement methods and create attributes to use the *system_event* objects that are created is shown below.

Implementation of the Proposed Solution

A new module called *system_event* is created. The implementation is shown in Code 10.7 and Code 10.8. In Code 10.7, the library *event_log.h* is included because the definition of EVENT_LOG_NAME_MAX_LENGTH is used on line 20. The declaration of the new class *systemEvent* can be seen on lines 12 to 21 of file *system_event.h*. The objects of this class will provide the functionality that is needed to implement the events that are logged and reported by the module *event_log*.

The class is divided into *public* (line 17) and *private* (line 22) *members*. The public members (from lines 14 to 17) are accessible outside the class, and the private members (from lines 19 to 21) are neither accessible nor viewable from outside the class. The concept is similar to the concepts of public and private that were introduced in Chapter 5. The variables and functions that belong to the class alone are called *attributes* and *methods*, respectively.

The public method declared on line 14 is a special method that every class must have, called the *constructor*. The constructor is a method with the same name as the class, which is automatically called to initialize an object of a class when it is created. The constructor may execute statements or call functions.

The implementation of the other methods and use of the attributes of this class is shown in Code 10.8 from lines 10 to 39. The difference in the implementation of functions is that the name of the class and "::" should precede the name of the method.

```
1   //======[#include guards - begin]===================================================
2
3   #ifndef _SYSTEM_EVENT_H_
4   #define _SYSTEM_EVENT_H_
5
6   //======[Libraries]=================================================================
7
8   #include "event_log.h"
9
10  //======[Declaration of public classes]============================================
11
12  class systemEvent {
13      public:
14          systemEvent(const char* eventLabel);
15          void stateUpdate( bool state );
16          bool lastStateRead( );
17          char* getLabel( );
18      private:
19          void lastStateUpdate(bool state);
20          char label[EVENT_LABEL_MAX_LENGTH];
21          bool lastState;
22  };
23
24  //======[#include guards - end]====================================================
25
26  #endif // _SYSTEM_EVENT_H_
```

Code 10.7 Details of the implementation of the file system_event.h.

If the current state of the event is different from the previous state (line 32), then the function *eventLogWrite()* is called (line 33). Finally, the last state of the event is stored (line 35). The keyword *this* is an expression whose value is the memory address of the object on which the member function is being called.

The methods *lastStateRead()*, *getLabel()*, and *lastStateUpdate()* are shown in Code 10.8. The implementation of these methods is very straightforward: *lastStateRead()* returns the last state, while *getLabel()* returns a pointer to the label. The method *lastStateUpdate()* assigns the value of the parameter *state* to the *lastState* private variable of the object of the class *systemEvent*.

In Code 10.9, some sections of the file *event_log.cpp* are shown. The names of the struct and data types previously named *systemEvent* and *systemEvent_t* were renamed to *storedEvents* and *storedEvents_t*, respectively (lines 3 and 7). Line 21 was modified to account for this change. Also, the private function *eventLogElementStateUpdate()* was removed from this module.

The objects related to each of the events shown in Table 10.2 are declared on lines 11 to 16. When each of these objects is created, the constructor is called and the *eventLabel* attribute is assigned to the created object (line 12 of Code 10.8). Then, the private attribute *lastState* is initialized to OFF on line 13 of Code 10.8. In order to make use of the class *systemEvent*, the library *system_event.h* is included in *event_log.cpp*, as indicated in Table 10.7. Also in Table 10.7 the declarations of the function prototype *eventLabelReduce* and the private definition EVENT_LOG_NAME_SHORT_MAX_LENGTH are shown. In Table 10.8, the lines added to *event_log.h* are shown.

Table 10.7 Sections in which lines were added to event_log.cpp.

Section	Lines that were added
Libraries	`#include "system_event.h"`
Declarations (prototypes) of private functions	`void eventLabelReduce(char * eventLogReportStr, systemEvent * event);`
Declaration of private defines	`#define EVENT_LOG_NAME_SHORT_MAX_LENGTH   22`

Table 10.8 Sections in which lines were added to event_log.h.

Section	Lines that were added
Declarations (prototypes) of public functions	`void eventLogReport();`
Declaration of public definitions	`#define EVENT_LABEL_MAX_LENGTH   10`

```
1   //=====[Libraries]=======================================================
2
3   #include "mbed.h"
4   #include "arm_book_lib.h"
5
6   #include "system_event.h"
7
8   //=====[Implementations of public methods]===============================
9
10  systemEvent::systemEvent(const char* eventLabel)
11  {
12      strcpy( label, eventLabel );
13      lastState = OFF;
14  }
15
16  void systemEvent::stateUpdate( bool state )
17  {
18      if ( state != this->lastStateRead() ) {
19          eventLogWrite( state, this->getLabel() );
20      }
21      this->lastStateUpdate( state );
22  }
23
24  bool systemEvent::lastStateRead( )
25  {
26      return lastState;
27  }
28
29  char* systemEvent::getLabel( )
30  {
31      return label;
32  }
33
34  //=====[Implementations of private methods]==============================
35
36  void systemEvent::lastStateUpdate(bool state)
37  {
38      lastState = state;
39  }
```

Code 10.8 Details of the implementation of the file system_event.cpp.

```
1   //=====[Declaration of private data types]===============================
2
3   typedef struct storedEvent {
4       time_t seconds;
5       char typeOfEvent[EVENT_LOG_NAME_MAX_LENGTH];
6       bool storedInSd;
7   } storedEvent_t;
8
9   //=====[Declaration and initialization of public global objects]=========
10
11  systemEvent alarmEvent("ALARM");
12  systemEvent gasEvent("GAS_DET");
13  systemEvent overTempEvent("OVER_TEMP");
14  systemEvent ledICEvent("LED_IC");
15  systemEvent ledSBEvent("LED_SB");
16  systemEvent motionEvent("MOTION");
17
18  //=====[Declaration and initialization of private global variables]=======
19
20  static int eventsIndex      = 0;
21  static storedEvent_t arrayOfStoredEvents[EVENT_LOG_MAX_STORAGE];
22  static bool eventAndStateStrSent;
```

Code 10.9 Details of the new implementation of some sections of the file event_log.cpp.

The new implementation of the public function *eventLogUpdate()* is shown in Code 10.10. The method *stateUpdate()* is called for each system event if *eventAndStateStrSent* is false (lines 5 to 13) and replaces the functionality of the private function *eventLogElementStateUpdate()*, which was removed from *event_log.cpp*.

```
1   void eventLogUpdate()
2   {
3       eventAndStateStrSent = false;
4
5       if ( !eventAndStateStrSent ) alarmEvent.stateUpdate( sirenStateRead() );
6       if ( !eventAndStateStrSent ) gasEvent.stateUpdate(  gasDetectorStateRead() );
7       if ( !eventAndStateStrSent )
8           overTempEvent.stateUpdate(  overTemperatureDetectorStateRead() );
9       if ( !eventAndStateStrSent )
10          ledICEvent.stateUpdate(  incorrectCodeStateRead() );
11      if ( !eventAndStateStrSent )
12          ledSBEvent.stateUpdate( systemBlockedStateRead() );
13      if ( !eventAndStateStrSent ) motionEvent.stateUpdate( motionSensorRead() );
14  }
```

Code 10.10 Details of the implementation of the ble_com.h.

By comparing lines 11 to 16 of Code 10.9 and Code 10.10 with Code 7.20, it can be seen how the code modularity, reusability, flexibility, and effectiveness is increased by the use of object-oriented programming (OOP).

> **NOTE:** Some other features of OOP, such as polymorphism, inheritance, encapsulation, and abstraction, are beyond the scope of this book and are, therefore, not discussed here.
>
> **NOTE:** The objects defined by the Mbed OS that were introduced in previous chapters, such as DigitalIn, DigitalOut, UnbufferedSerial, etc. are used in a very similar way to the object introduced in this example. All those Mbed OS objects have a constructor and a set of publicly defined methods and can be instantiated as many times as needed, just like the *systemEvent* Object.

In order to improve the experience of using the smartphone application, the NUCLEO board now responds to the character "b" sent from the smartphone application. When this character is received, the function *eventLogReport()* is called, as shown in the new implementation of *bleComUpdate()* (line 8 of Code 10.11).

```
 1   void bleComUpdate()
 2   {
 3       char receivedChar = bleComCharRead();
 4       if( receivedChar != '\0' ) {
 5           switch (receivedChar) {
 6               case 'O': gateOpen(); break;
 7               case 'C': gateClose(); break;
 8               case 'b': eventLogReport(); break;
 9           }
10       }
11   }
```

Code 10.11 Details of the implementation of the bleComUpdate().

The implementation of *eventLogReport()* in the module *event_log* is shown in Code 10.12. This function sends a string to the smartphone application that contains the state of the system events, separated by commas. Because there is a limitation in the length of the string, each event label and state is sent using only a character; for instance, the string "AF,GF,TF,IF,SF,MF" means that all the system events are off. From lines 5 to 20, this string (*eventLogReportStr*) is prepared using the function *eventLabelReduce()*, and on lines 22 to 23, *eventLogReportStr* is sent using *bleComStringWrite()*.

```
 1   void eventLogReport()
 2   {
 3       char eventLogReportStr[EVENT_LOG_NAME_SHORT_MAX_LENGTH] = "";
 4
 5       eventLabelReduce( eventLogReportStr, &alarmEvent );
 6       strcat( eventLogReportStr, "," );
 7
 8       eventLabelReduce( eventLogReportStr, &gasEvent );
 9       strcat( eventLogReportStr, "," );
10
11       eventLabelReduce( eventLogReportStr, &overTempEvent );
12       strcat( eventLogReportStr, "," );
13
14       eventLabelReduce( eventLogReportStr, &ledICEvent );
15       strcat( eventLogReportStr, "," );
16
17       eventLabelReduce( eventLogReportStr, &ledSBEvent );
18       strcat( eventLogReportStr, "," );
19
20       eventLabelReduce( eventLogReportStr, &motionEvent );
21
22       bleComStringWrite(eventLogReportStr);
23       bleComStringWrite("\r\n");
24   }
```

Code 10.12 Details of the implementation of the function eventLogReport().

The implementation of the function *eventLabelReduce()* is shown in Code 10.13. This function concatenates onto the string *eventLogReportStr* a character that represents the event (lines 4, 6, 8, 10, 12, and 14) by using *strcmp* to compare the label of the event received with each event string (lines 3, 5, 7, 9, 11, and 13). Then, it checks the last state of the event (line 17) and appends a character that represents the state (lines 18 or 20).

```
1   static void eventLabelReduce(char * eventLogReportStr, systemEvent * event)
2   {
3       if (strcmp(event->getLabel(), "ALARM") == 0) {
4           strcat(eventLogReportStr,"A");
5       } else if (strcmp(event->getLabel(), "GAS_DET") == 0) {
6           strcat(eventLogReportStr,"G");
7       } else if(strcmp(event->getLabel(), "OVER_TEMP") == 0) {
8           strcat(eventLogReportStr,"T");
9       } else if(strcmp(event->getLabel(), "LED_IC") == 0) {
10          strcat(eventLogReportStr,"I");
11      } else if(strcmp(event->getLabel(), "LED_SB") == 0) {
12          strcat(eventLogReportStr,"S");
13      } else if(strcmp(event->getLabel(), "MOTION") == 0) {
14          strcat(eventLogReportStr,"M");
15      }
16
17      if ( event->lastStateRead() ) {
18          strcat( eventLogReportStr, "N" );
19      } else {
20          strcat( eventLogReportStr, "F" );
21      }
22  }
```

Code 10.13 Details of the implementation of the function eventLabelReduce().

Proposed Exercise

1. How can a *systemEvent* object be created in order to monitor the state of the strobe light?

Answer to the Exercise

1. A possible implementation may be by means of declaring the object in Code 10.9 as:

systemEvent strobeLightEvent("STROBE_LIGHT");

and then incorporating the following lines in Code 10.10:

strobeLightEvent.stateUpdate(strobeLightStateRead());

Example 10.4: Implement Non-Blocking Delays using Pointers and Interrupts

Objective

Introduce the use of non-blocking delays and review the concepts of pointer and interrupt.

Summary of the Expected Behavior

The behavior of this example will remain exactly the same as that in Example 10.3. However, the delay used in the main loop of the program will be replaced by a non-blocking delay.

Test the Proposed Solution on the Board

Import the project "Example 10.4" using the URL available in [2], build the project, and drag the *.bin* file onto the NUCLEO board. The behavior should be exactly the same as in Example 10.3.

Discussion of the Proposed Solution

The proposed solutions implemented throughout the examples in the book use blocking delays. This means that the processor waits until the expiration of the delay time without executing other instructions. Using non-blocking delays allows the program to check the condition of the delay time expiration with an *if* statement. In this way, the processor can execute other instructions while waiting for the delay time to expire.

Implementation of the Proposed Solution

Code 10.14 shows the new implementations of *smartHomeSystemInit()* and *smartHomeSystemUpdate()*. The blocking delay of the function *smartHomeSystemUpdate()* is replaced by the function *nonBlockingDelayRead()*. This function is called using *smartHomeSystemDelay* as a parameter.

The "&" operator before the parameter is called the *reference operator* and it is defined as the "*memory address of...*". This operator brings an important concept: *parameter passing* to functions. In this book, the two most common methods are used: *pass-by-value* and *pass-by-reference*. In the former, a local copy of the variable used as a parameter is created and used inside the function, as introduced in Chapter 3. Therefore, the value of the variable used as a parameter is not modified, only the local copy. In the latter, the memory address of the variable used as a parameter is passed, and the function can change its value. In this way, if the value of the variable used as a parameter is modified inside the function, its value outside the function scope is also modified. Some examples are shown in Table 10.9.

Table 10.9 Examples of functions with parameters passed by reference and by value.

Parameter passing method	Example
pass-by-value	`static void setPeriod( lightSystem_t light, float period );`
pass-by-reference	`bool sdCardWriteFile( const char* fileName, const char* writeBuffer )`

The function *nonBlockingDelayRead()* that is used on line 19 of Code 10.14 checks if the time configured on line 14 of Code 10.14 (*SYSTEM_TIME_INCREMENT_MS*) to the variable *smartHomeSystemDelay* using *nonBlockingDelayInit()* is reached and returns true in that case or false otherwise. In this way, the processor is able to execute other instructions while waiting for the delay time to expire.

On line 3, the function *tickInit()* is called to configure the interrupt service routine (ISR) used to account time by the *non_blocking_delay* module. This function is based on a ticker, in a very similar way to the *brightControlInit()* function that was introduced in Example 8.1, as discussed below. The library *non_blocking_delay.h* is included to implement these function calls, and the variable *smartHomeSystemDelay* of type *nonBlockingDelay_t* is declared, as can be seen in Table 10.10.

NOTE: Recall the concept of interrupt service routines (ISRs), which was introduced in Chapter 7.

```
1   void smartHomeSystemInit()
2   {
3       tickInit();
4       audioInit();
5       userInterfaceInit();
6       alarmInit();
7       fireAlarmInit();
8       intruderAlarmInit();
9       pcSerialComInit();
10      motorControlInit();
11      gateInit();
12      lightSystemInit();
13      sdCardInit();
14      nonBlockingDelayInit( &smartHomeSystemDelay, SYSTEM_TIME_INCREMENT_MS );
15  }
16
17  void smartHomeSystemUpdate()
18  {
19      if( nonBlockingDelayRead(&smartHomeSystemDelay) ) {
20          userInterfaceUpdate();
21          fireAlarmUpdate();
22          intruderAlarmUpdate();
23          alarmUpdate();
24          eventLogUpdate();
25          pcSerialComUpdate();
26          motorControlUpdate();
27          lightSystemUpdate();
28          bleComUpdate();
29      }
30  }
```

Code 10.14 New implementation of the functions smartHomeSystemInit and smartHomeSystemUpdate.

Table 10.10 Sections in which lines were added to smart_home_system.cpp.

Section	Lines that were added
Libraries	`#include "non_blocking_delay.h"`
Declaration and initialization of public global objects	`static nonBlockingDelay_t smartHomeSystemDelay;`

The implementation of *non_blocking_delay.cpp* is shown in Code 10.15 and Code 10.16. The library that is included is shown on line 3 of Code 10.15. On line 7, the global object that will be used for the ISR that is triggered by the ticker is created, and on line 8, the variable *tickCounter* is declared. Finally, the prototype of the function *tickerCallback()* is declared on line 12, and the prototype of *tickRead()* is declared on line 13.

```
1   //=====[Libraries]=================================================
2
3   #include "non_blocking_delay.h"
4
5   //=====[Declaration and initialization of private global variables]=============
6
7   static Ticker ticker;
8   static tick_t tickCounter;
9
10  //=====[Declarations (prototypes) of private functions]=========================
11
12  void tickerCallback();
13  tick_t tickRead();
```

Code 10.15 Details of the implementation of the file non_blocking_delay.cpp (1/2).

Code 10.16 shows the implementation of the public functions. On lines 3 to 6, the timer interrupt is configured in the function *tickInit()*. The callback function *tickerCallback* will be called once every millisecond. This function, implemented from lines 40 to 43, increments the variable *tickCounter* by one in each call.

The function used to initialize the non-blocking delays is implemented from lines 8 to 12. As was mentioned before, the first parameter of type *nonBlockingDelay_t* is *passed-by-reference*. For this reason, the operator "*" should be included before *delay* (line 8 of Code 10.16). The operator "*" is called the *dereference operator* and it is defined as "the content pointed to by... ".

Because *delay* is a pointer to the type *nonBlockingDelay_t* and *nonBlockingDelay_t* is a *struct*, its members are accessed using the "->" operator. When line 14 of Code 10.14 is executed, the value *SYSTEM_TIME_INCREMENT_MS* is assigned to the member *duration* (line 10 of Code 10.16), and false is assigned to the member *isRunning* of the content pointed by *delay* (line 11), that is, the variable *smartHomeSystemDelay* (Code 10.14). As has been explained, the function modifies the passed variable directly.

The parameters of the function *nonBlockingDelayRead()* are also *passed-by-reference*. On line 16, a local bool variable named *timeArrived* is declared and initialized with false. If the member *isRunning* of the content pointed by *delay* is true, then the delay time has not expired. This condition is checked by an *if-else* statement. If it is not running (line 19), then the non-blocking delay is started (lines 20 and 21). If it is running (line 22), the elapsed time is obtained as the difference between *tickCounter* and *delay->startTime* (line 23). Line 24 assesses if *elapsedTime* has reached the delay duration. If so, true is assigned to *timeArrived* on line 25, and the member *isRunning* of the content pointed by *delay* is set to false (line 26). Finally, the local variable *timeArrived* is returned by the function *nonBlockingDelayRead()* on line 28.

```
1   //=====[Implementations of public functions]=====================================
2
3   void tickInit()
4   {
5       ticker.attach( tickerCallback, ((float) 0.001 ));
6   }
7
8   void nonBlockingDelayInit( nonBlockingDelay_t * delay, tick_t durationValue )
9   {
10      delay->duration = durationValue;
11      delay->isRunning = false;
12  }
13
14  bool nonBlockingDelayRead( nonBlockingDelay_t * delay )
15  {
16      bool timeArrived = false;
17      tick_t elapsedTime;
18
19      if( !delay->isRunning ) {
20          delay->startTime = tickCounter;
21          delay->isRunning = true;
22      } else {
23          elapsedTime = tickCounter - delay->startTime
24          if ( elapsedTime >= delay->duration ) {
25              timeArrived = true;
26              delay->isRunning = false;
27          }
28      }
29
30      return timeArrived;
31  }
32
33  void nonBlockingDelayWrite( nonBlockingDelay_t * delay, tick_t durationValue )
34  {
35      delay->duration = durationValue;
36  }
37
38  //=====[Implementations of private functions]=====================================
39
40  void tickerCallback( void )
41  {
42      tickCounter++;
43  }
```

Code 10.16 Details of the implementation of the file non_blocking_delay.cpp (2/2).

The function *nonBlockingDelayWrite()* implemented from lines 33 to 36 of Code 10.16 assigns the parameter *durationValue* (*passed-by-value* as the second parameter of the function) to the member *duration* of the content pointed by *delay*.

The implementation of *non_blocking_delay.h* is shown in Code 10.17. The library *mbed.h* (line 8) is included because the new data type tick_t is defined using an unsigned integer of 64 bits: *uint64_t* (line 14). This definition will allow the implementation of large delays without overflow.

TIP: In some applications, a ticker is used to implement a very precise measurement with a high resolution of time elapsed between events (for example, the time between the transmission of a signal and the reception of the response). In those cases, the ticker interval can be specified in microseconds, as can be seen in [3].

The other data type in this module is defined from lines 16 to 20: *nonBlockingDelay_t*. Finally, the prototypes of public functions are declared from lines 24 to 26.

```
1    //=====[#include guards - begin]===========================================
2
3    #ifndef _NON_BLOCKING_DELAY_H_
4    #define _NON_BLOCKING_DELAY_H_
5
6    //==================[Libraries]============================================
7
8    #include "mbed.h"
9
10   //=====[Declaration of public data types]=================================
11
12   typedef uint64_t tick_t;
13
14   typedef struct{
15       tick_t startTime;
16       tick_t duration;
17       bool isRunning;
18   } nonBlockingDelay_t;
19
20   //=====[Declarations (prototypes) of public functions]====================
21
22   void tickInit();
23
24   void nonBlockingDelayInit( nonBlockingDelay_t* delay, tick_t durationValue );
25   bool nonBlockingDelayRead( nonBlockingDelay_t* delay );
26   void nonBlockingDelayWrite( nonBlockingDelay_t* delay, tick_t durationValue );
27
28   //=====[#include guards - end]============================================
29
30   #endif // _NON_BLOCKING_DELAY_H_
31
32
```

Code 10.17 Details of the implementation of the file non_blocking_delay.h.

NOTE: The proposed implementation of the non-blocking delay is based on a software module of the *sAPI library*. The *sAPI (simple Application Programming Interface) library* is an open-source library written by Eric Pernia and other collaborators for *Proyecto CIAA*. Many ideas in the sAPI library were used as a starting point for many of the code examples in this book. The reader is encouraged to explore the *sAPI library* in [4], where a broad set of useful functions is available, ranging from step motor drivers to LED dimming code, as well as information about Proyecto CIAA (Computadora Industrial Abierta Argentina, Argentine Open Industrial Computer), which is the context in which the sAPI library was written.

Proposed Exercise

1. How can a blocking delay be implemented using the tick interrupt?

Answer to the Exercise

1. A module similar to *non_blocking_delay* might be implemented with a function *blockingDelay()*, as shown in Code 10.18.

```
1   void blockingDelay( tick_t durationMs )
2   {
3       tick_t startTime = tickCounter;
4       tick_t elapsedTime;
5
6       while ( elapsedTime < durationMs ) {
7           elapsedTime = tickCounter - startTime;
8       }
9   }
```

Code 10.18 Details of the implementation of the function blockingDelay().

10.3 Under the Hood

10.3.1 Basic Principles of Bluetooth Low Energy Communication

In this chapter, the connection between the NUCLEO board and the smartphone was made using Bluetooth Low Energy (BLE) by means of an HM-10 module. Firstly, it should be noted that classic Bluetooth and BLE are two different technologies. There are many differences, but the most relevant is that BLE is designed for low energy consumption.

 NOTE: In BLE, the low energy consumption is achieved by using smaller data packets that are transmitted only when necessary. BLE is not designed for continuous connections and large amounts of data. When large amounts of data need to be transmitted, it is more convenient to use classic Bluetooth, which maintains a continuous connection.

In this chapter, a connection of the type *Central + Peripheral* was used. In this configuration, a peripheral advertises itself at startup and waits for a central device to connect to it. A peripheral is usually a small device like a smart sensor. A central device is usually a smartphone that is scanning for devices. After a peripheral makes a connection, it is called the *subordinate*. After a central makes a connection, it is called the *manager*. This is illustrated in Figure 10.5.

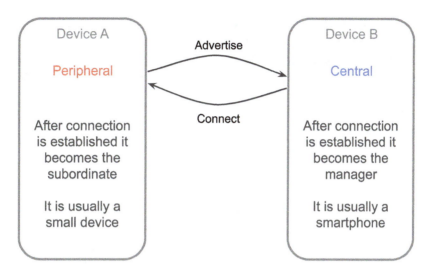

Figure 10.5 Illustration of the names and behaviors of each device in the BLE startup process.

After a BLE connection has been established, the more typical names and behaviors are as shown in Figure 10.6. The client is usually the manager, and the server is usually the subordinate.

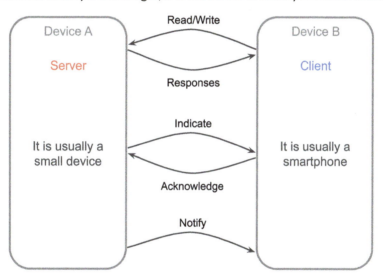

Figure 10.6 Illustration of the names and behaviors of each device in a typical BLE communication.

 NOTE: The data exchange shown in Figure 10.5 and Figure 10.6 is automatically managed by the HM-10 module. Therefore, the C/C++ code to use the BLE communication does not have to tackle this task.

A server provides resources to the client. For example, in this chapter the NUCLEO board with the HM-10 module is the server. It provides the states of the alarm, the gas detector, the over temperature detector, the Incorrect code LED, the System blocked LED, and the motion detector to the client (the smartphone).

 NOTE: It must be mentioned that a client is usually the manager, but a client could instead be the subordinate. Conversely, a server is usually the subordinate, but a server could be the manager. This role change is not necessary for basic setups and, therefore, is neither used nor explained further in this book.

As can be seen in Figure 10.6, there are three possible ways in which data can be exchanged between the client and the server:

- A client sends *Read/Write* operations to the server, and the server responds with data; if appropriate, the server changes its local data or configuration.

- A server sends an *Indicate* operation to the client, which is acknowledged by the client.

- A server sends a *Notify* operation to the client, which is not acknowledged by the client.

In this chapter, the connection implemented was based on Notify and Read/Write operations over a *personalized service* of the HM-10 module. The messages sent by the NUCLEO board to the smartphone (Table 10.2) correspond to Notify operations. The messages sent by the smartphone to the NUCLEO board (Table 10.3) are Read/Write operations, even if there is no response from the NUCLEO board.

BLE operates in the spectrum range of 2.400–2.4835 GHz, as does classic Bluetooth technology. It uses a different set of channels, however. Instead of classic Bluetooth's 79 1-MHz channels, BLE has 40 2-MHz channels. In order to avoid communication collisions between different clients and servers, each client–server pair should use a different channel. BLE also uses *frequency hopping* to counteract narrowband interference problems.

Within a channel, data is transmitted using Gaussian frequency shift modulation, similar to classic Bluetooth's Basic Rate scheme. The bit rate is between 1 Mbit/s and 2 Mbit/s, depending on the BLE version. Further details are given in Volume 6 Part A (Physical Layer Specification) of the Bluetooth Core Specification V4.0 [5].

 NOTE: In advanced setups, a device can be the central device to up to eight other devices that are acting as peripherals. A device can also be a central and peripheral simultaneously to different devices.

Proposed Exercises

1. It was discussed in the proposed exercises of subsection "2.3.1 Basic Principles of Serial Communication" how one device can be sure that another device has received information with no errors. It was concluded that both devices must be involved in the process of checking the integrity of the information. Is it possible to find this kind of process in Figure 10.6?

2. It was concluded in the proposed exercises subsection "2.3.1 Basic Principles of Serial Communication" that using 115,200 bps serial communication, such as that used in Chapter 2, it will take about 86 seconds to transfer a 1 MB file. How much time will it take to transfer a 1 MB file using the BLE connection under optimal conditions?

Answers to the Exercises

1. In Figure 10.6 it can be seen that the *Indicate* operation has an acknowledgement. This acknowledgement contains information that is used to check the integrity of the information.

2. 1 MB is equal to 8 Mbits. Considering a 1 Mbit/s physical layer bit rate and assuming that this reflects the actual data rate (which is not true), it will take 8 seconds to transfer a 1 MB file. This is about ten times less than the 86 seconds that was obtained in the calculation of subsection 2.3.1 for the UART connection at 115,200 bps.

 WARNING: It is important to note that optimal conditions (namely, no interference from other devices, maximum possible speed with every device, etc.) are not easy to achieve, so in practical situations the real bit rate is lower than the aforementioned 1 Mbit/s. In the implementation of this chapter, the transfer speed of 1 Mbit/s cannot be reached because the communication with the HM-10 is at 9600 bps.

10.4 Case Study

10.4.1 Wireless Bolt

In this chapter, the NUCLEO board communicated with a smartphone by means of a BLE connection implemented with an HM-10 module. By using an application, it was possible to access the state of the elements and control the gate through the smartphone. A brief of a commercial "wireless bolt" built with Mbed, containing some similar features, can be found in [5]. An image of this is shown in Figure 10.7.

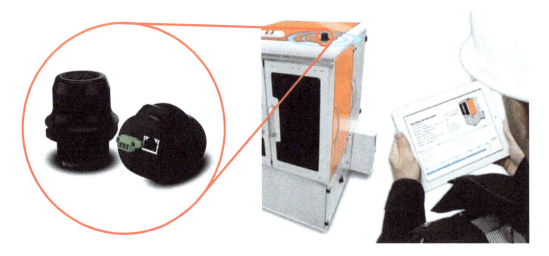

Figure 10.7 "Anybus wireless bolt" built with Mbed contains elements introduced in this chapter.

The wireless bolt shown in Figure 10.7 is designed to be mounted on an industrial device, machine, or cabinet and to enable wireless access via Bluetooth or wireless LAN. The system is made up of two elements: the black device shown inside the circle in Figure 10.7, and an application that runs on a tablet, laptop, or smartphone. By connecting the appropriate signals to the wireless bolt and properly configuring the application, it is possible to save the cost of buying an HMI (Human–Machine Interface). Another typical use is connecting the wireless bolt to an existing infrastructure or an external cloud service.

It can be appreciated that the functionality shown in Figure 10.7 is very similar to the functionality implemented in this chapter (to monitor and configure a device from a smartphone application using BLE). In the following chapter, it will be explained how to implement a Wi-Fi connection to the NUCLEO board, as well as looking at some other technologies that are mentioned in [6], such as TCP/UDP.

Proposed Exercises

1. If the Anybus wireless bolt were to be connected to the smart home system, what elements might it be used to observe?

2. What are the main differences between the smart home system developed so far and the Anybus wireless bolt?

Answers to the Exercises

1. It might be used to observe the state of the alarm, the gas detector, and the over temperature detector, for example.

2. The smart home system is intended to be used to monitor and control certain specific elements. Conversely, Anybus wireless bolt allows monitoring and control of various elements, according to

need in each case. Furthermore, the smart home system developed so far supports few connectivity options, just USB and Bluetooth, while the Anybus wireless bolt supports many connectivity options. In the next chapter, the connectivity of the smart home system will be increased.

References

[1] "HM-10 Bluetooth Module Pinout, Features, Interfacing & Datasheet". Accessed July 9, 2021.
     https://components101.com/wireless/hm-10-bluetooth-module

[2] "GitHub - armBookCodeExamples/Directory". Accessed July 9, 2021.
     https://github.com/armBookCodeExamples/Directory

[3] "Ticker - API references and tutorials | Mbed OS 6 Documentation". Accessed July 9, 2021.
     https://os.mbed.com/docs/mbed-os/v6.12/apis/ticker.html

[4] "sAPI library for microcontrollers". Accessed July 9, 2021.
     https://github.com/epernia/firmware_v3/blob/master/libs/sapi/documentation/api_reference_en.md

[5] Bluetooth Core Specification V4.0
     https://www.bluetooth.com/specifications/bluetooth-core-specification/

[6] "Anybus® Wireless Bolt™ | Mbed". Accessed July 9, 2021.
     https://os.mbed.com/built-with-mbed/anybus-wireless-bolt/

Chapter 11

Embedded Web Server
over a Wi-Fi Connection

11.1 Roadmap

11.1.1 What You Will Learn

After you have studied the material in this chapter, you will be able to:

- ▨ Describe how to connect a Wi-Fi module to the NUCLEO board.

- ▨ Develop programs to serve a web page using the NUCLEO board and a Wi-Fi module.

- ▨ Summarize the fundamentals of AT commands and TCP/IP connections.

11.1.2 Review of Previous Chapters

In the previous chapter, the smart home system was provided with a BLE (Bluetooth Low Energy) connection by means of which it was possible to get some information on the state of the system using a smartphone, as well as to control the opening and closing of the gate. A limitation is that the BLE range is just a few meters, and sometimes it is useful to monitor the state of the system from a greater distance. This could be, for example, a web browser that is running on a PC or a smartphone. Also, in certain applications, a high data rate over a wireless connection is needed, as well as error-checked delivery of data, error-detection, and retransmission, among other capabilities that are limited if BLE is used.

11.1.3 Contents of This Chapter

In this chapter, the process of serving a web page using a Wi-Fi module is carried out step-by-step by the reader in subsection 11.2.2. The reader enters each command one after the other. The process is then gradually automated through the examples. In this way, the aim is to give an insight into the process in order to separate understanding of what should be done (the commands and the logic around those commands) from the automation of those commands and the corresponding logic on the NUCLEO board.

Some basic AT commands will be introduced (the *de facto* standard to communicate with different types of modems, Wi-Fi modules, GPS modules, cellular modules, etc.). Some basic concepts about TCP connections and Wi-Fi communications will also be discussed. In addition, the implementation of a *parser* will be shown, in order to analyze the responses of the Wi-Fi module to the AT commands sent by the NUCLEO board.

11.2 Serve a Web Page with the NUCLEO Board

11.2.1 Connect a Wi-Fi Module to the Smart Home System

In this chapter, the smart home system is provided with the capability of serving a web page using Wi-Fi, as shown in Figure 11.1. In this way, the information can be accessed using a smartphone or a PC.

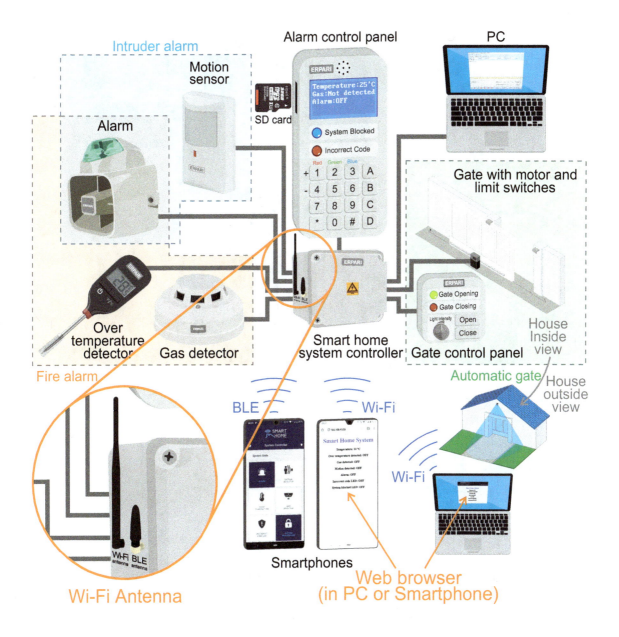

Figure 11.1 The smart home system is now able to serve a web page.

The Wi-Fi connection is implemented using an ESP-01 module, which is described in [1] and shown in Figure 11.2, and which is part of a broad family of Wi-Fi modules based on the ESP8266 chipset [2].

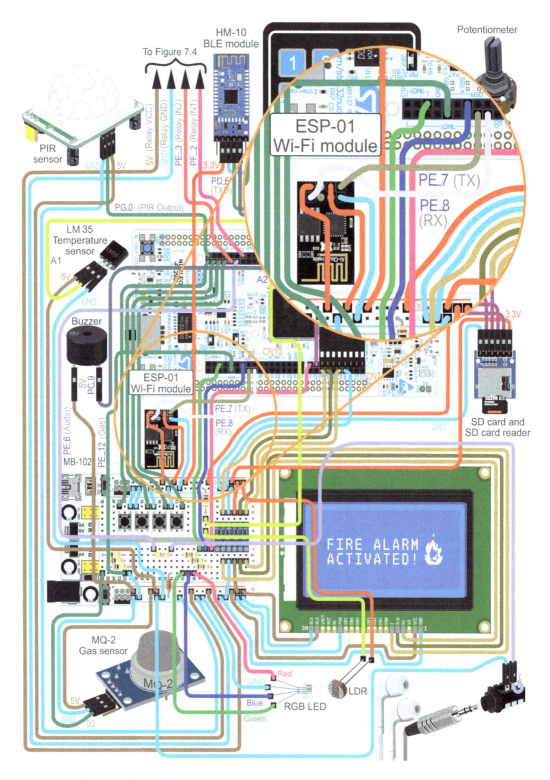

Figure 11.2 The smart home system is now connected to a ESP-01 module.

In Figure 11.3, the basic functions of the ESP-01 module pins are shown. Besides the GND and VCC power supply pins, the RST (reset) pin, and the EN (chip enabled) pin, it can be seen that there are two UART pins (RXD and TXD) and two GPIO pins (IO0 and IO2). The UART pins are used in this chapter to connect the ESP-01 module and the NUCLEO board, while the GPIO pins are not used in this book.

NOTE: More information about the broad set of functions of the ESP-01 module is available in [1].

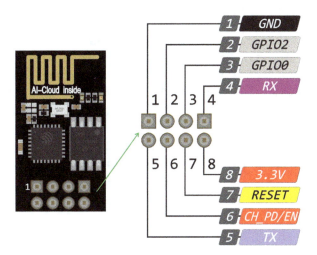

Figure 11.3 Basic functionality of the ESP-01 module pins.

The connections between the NUCLEO board and the ESP-01 module are summarized in Table 11.1, while the connections between the ESP-01 module and the breadboard are summarized in Table 11.2.

Table 11.1 Summary of the connections between the NUCLEO board and the ESP-01 module.

NUCLEO board	ESP-01 module
PE_8 (UART7_TX)	RXD
PE_7 (UART7_RX)	TXD

Table 11.2 Summary of other connections that should be made to the ESP-01.

ESP-01 module	Breadboard
GND	GND
EN	3.3 V
VCC	3.3 V

WARNING: The ESP-01 module has soldered pins on its bottom side. The connections in Figure 11.2 are for illustrative purposes only. The soldered pins on its bottom side must be used to connect the module.

To test if the ESP-01 module is working, the setup shown in Figure 11.4 will be used. In this setup, there is a smartphone or PC with a web browser that is connected to an access point by means of a Wi-Fi connection. The test program that runs on the NUCLEO board uses the connection to a PC, where the serial terminal is running. The program that runs on the NUCLEO board also uses a connection to the ESP-01 module, as shown in Figure 11.4. As discussed below, the ESP-01 module runs a TCP server (*Transmission Control Protocol* server), while the NUCLEO board runs an HTML server, which is implemented in this chapter.

During the test, the user is asked for the SSID (Service Set IDentifier) and password of the access point, and the test program configures the ESP-01 module using these credentials. This allows it to connect to the same access point as the smartphone or PC with the web browser. The ESP-01 module internally runs a TCP server, which receives requests from other devices connected to the access point – in this case the smartphone or PC. The ESP-01 module reports the requests to the test program that runs on the NUCLEO board, which provides the ESP-01 module with the HTML document to use in the response. The HTML document contains relevant information about the smart home system.

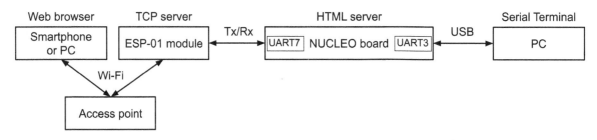

Figure 11.4 Diagram of the communication that is implemented between the different devices.

Download the *.bin* file of the program "Subsection 11.2.1" from the URL available in [3] and load it onto the NUCLEO board. This program uses the setup illustrated in Figure 11.4. After powering on, the NUCLEO board will ask the user to enter the SSID and the password of the Wi-Fi access point. It will then indicate the IP (Internet Protocol) address assigned to the ESP-01 module by the Wi-Fi access point, as shown in Figure 11.5.

```
*Subsection 11.2.1 test program*

Please provide the SSID of the Wi-Fi Access Point and press the Enter key
> mySSID
Wi-Fi Access Point SSID configured

Please provide the Password of the Wi-Fi Access Point and press the Enter
key
> **********
Wi-Fi Access Point password configured

Wi-Fi communication started, please wait...

IP address assigned correctly

Enter 192.168.43.53 as the URL in the web browser
```

Figure 11.5 Steps to follow in the test program used in this subsection.

Open the web browser on a PC or smartphone connected to the same access point as the ESP-01 module, and in the address bar enter the IP indicated on the serial terminal, as shown in Figure 11.6. A web page such as the one shown in Figure 11.6 should be displayed in the web browser. If so, the ESP-01 module is connected and working properly. Otherwise, review the connections of the module and the access point, and check that the ESP-01 is connected to the same access point as the PC or smartphone where the web browser runs.

Figure 11.6 Web page served by the ESP-01 module.

11.2.2 Fundamentals of the Web Server to be Implemented

In this subsection, the fundamentals of web servers are introduced in order to allow the reader to understand the main concepts that are used in the examples that are discussed in this chapter.

The web page that was displayed in subsection 11.2.1 is provided by a *web server* that is composed of a TCP server that runs on the ESP-01 module and an HTML server that runs on the NUCLEO board. The primary function of a web server is to store, process, and deliver web pages to *clients*. Usually, a client is a web browser, which initiates the communication by making a request for a specific web page using the *Hypertext Transfer Protocol* (HTTP). The web server then responds with the web page content or with an error message if it is unable to retrieve the requested web page.

The web pages delivered are most frequently *Hypertext Markup Language (HTML) documents*, which may include images, style sheets, and scripts in addition to the textual content. The received HTML documents are rendered by the web browser. For this purpose, HTML documents can be assisted by technologies such as *Cascading Style Sheets (CSS)* used for describing the presentation of a web page (colors, fonts, etc.) and scripting languages such as *JavaScript* to enable interactive behavior.

It is also important to mention that the ESP8266 chipset, on which the ESP-01 module is based, can be configured as a server, as a client, and as server and client at the same time. When it is configured as a server, it serves HTML documents that in the proposed setup are retrieved by the NUCLEO board, as shown in subsection 11.2.1. When it is configured as a client, it retrieves HTML documents from a server.

The configuration of the ESP8266 chipset is done by means of *AT commands*. These commands were originally defined by Hayes Microcomputer Products in the early 1980s to be used to configure and operate modems. The AT commands consist of short texts that can be combined to produce commands for operations such as changing the parameters of a connection or connecting to a given IP address. In this subsection and in the examples below, some basic AT commands are used to configure the ESP8266 chipset. More information about the ESP8266 AT commands can be found in [4].

In order to get an idea about how all these concepts are used, a step-by-step example is shown, where AT commands are used to implement an embedded web server that serves a basic web page to a web browser.

First, download the *.bin* file of the program "Subsection 11.2.2" from the URL available in [3] and load it onto the NUCLEO board.

Next, the command "*AT*" (which stands for *attention*) should be typed into the serial terminal and the "Enter" key pressed on the PC keyboard. This AT command is forwarded by the NUCLEO board to the ESP-01 module, which should reply "*OK*". The NUCLEO board will forward this "OK" message to the serial terminal, as shown in Figure 11.7. This step is only to confirm that the most basic AT command works.

Figure 11.7 The "AT" command (attention) is sent to the ESP-01 module, which replies "OK".

The user should then type "*AT+CWMODE=1*" (standing for Change Wi-Fi mode) in order to configure the operation mode of the ESP-01 module as a station. This indicates that it should connect to an access point in order to get an IP address, after which it should reply "*OK*", as shown in Figure 11.8.

Figure 11.8 The "AT+CWMODE=1" command (mode configuration) is sent to the ESP-01 module, which replies "OK".

The next step is to connect the ESP-01 module to an available Wi-Fi access point, by means of entering the corresponding SSID and password. For example, if the SSID name is "mySSID" and the password is "abcd1234", then the user should type: *AT+CWJAP="mySSID","abcd1234"* (note: for clarity, the quotes around commands issued to the ESP=01 module are omitted here and in the remainder of this section). This stands for *Join Access Point*, as shown in Figure 11.9. The ESP-01 module should reply *"WIFI CONNECTED"*, *"WIFI GOT IP"*, and *"OK"*, and the NUCLEO board should forward these messages to the serial terminal, as shown in Figure 11.9.

```
AT+CWJAP="mySSID","abcd1234"
WIFI CONNECTED
WIFI GOT IP

OK
```

Figure 11.9 The "AT+CWJAP" command (Join Access Point) is sent to the ESP-01 module.

The user should then type *AT+CIFSR* in order to retrieve the IP address that has been assigned to the ESP-01 module. The response of the ESP-01 module will be forwarded by the NUCLEO board and will look as in Figure 11.10, where the IP address 192.168.43.53 has been assigned to the ESP-01 module.

```
AT+CIFSR
+ CIFSR:STAIP,"192.168.43.53"
+ CIFSR:STAMAC,"84:f3:eb:b7:34:84"

OK
```

Figure 11.10 The "AT+CIFSR" command (Get IP Address) is sent to the ESP-01 module.

 NOTE: In Figure 11.10, STAIP stands for Station IP, and STAMAC stands for Station MAC. The MAC (*Media Access Control*) address is a unique identifier assigned to each network interface controller.

Next, the command *AT+CIPMUX=1* should be entered in order to enable multiple connections with the ESP-01 module using the assigned IP. The ESP-01 module should reply "OK", as shown in Figure 11.11.

```
AT+CIPMUX=1

OK
```

Figure 11.11 The "AT+CIPMUX=1" command to enable multiple connections is sent to the ESP-01 module.

The command *AT+CIPSERVER=1,80* should then be typed into the serial terminal to create a TCP server on the ESP-01 module. The "1" indicates that the command is to create a TCP server, and "80" is the port number assigned. This is the default HTTP port number. This TCP server is able to receive and respond to requests from different clients, for example web browsers. The ESP-01 module replies "OK", as shown in Figure 11.12.

```
AT+CIPSERVER=1,80

OK
```

Figure 11.12 The "AT+CIPSERVER=1,80" command (creates a TCP server) is sent to the ESP-01 module.

 NOTE: The TCP server can only be created if multiple connections were first activated (AT+CIPMUX=1).

At this point, the TCP server is already running on the ESP-01 module. Therefore, whenever a client sends a request to the server IP address (in this case 192.168.43.53), the TCP server will keep a record that a TCP connection request has been received and will also keep some details of the request content.

To assess if a request has been received by the TCP server, the command *AT+CIPSTATUS* must be sent to the ESP-01 module. Figure 11.13 shows the response when no request has been received yet. All the possible values of STATUS are shown in Table 11.3. When the ESP-01 module has an assigned IP address and has received a TCP connection request, it will return "STATUS:3". In this way, it can be confirmed that a request has been received by the TCP server that is embedded in the ESP-01 module.

```
AT+CIPSTATUS

STATUS:2

OK
```

Figure 11.13 The "AT+CIPSTATUS" command shows the connection status of the ESP-01 module.

Table 11.3 Summary of the AT+CIPSTATUS return values.

STATUS value	Meaning
0	The ESP-01 module is not initialized
1	The ESP-01 module is initialized, but Wi-Fi connection has not been started yet
2	The ESP-01 module is connected to an access point and has an assigned IP address
3	The ESP-01 module has an assigned IP address and has received a TCP connection request
4	All of the TCP/UDP/SSL connections of the ESP device station are disconnected
5	The ESP-01 module is not connected to an access point

To show how the process works, the next step is to connect a PC or a smartphone to the same Wi-Fi access point as the ESP-01 module. The IP address assigned to the ESP-01 module (i.e., 192.168.43.53 in this case, as shown in Figure 11.10) should be entered into the address bar of a web browser on the PC or smartphone, as shown in Figure 11.14.

Figure 11.14 A request to the ESP-01 module is sent by a web browser.

The TCP server that is running on the ESP-01 module receives this request and informs the NUCLEO board that it has received a request by means of sending the messages that are shown in Figure 11.15.

```
0,CONNECT

+IPD,0,479:GET / HTTP/1.1
Host: 192.168.43.53
Connection: keep-alive
Upgrade-Insecure-Requests: 1
User-Agent: Mozilla/5.0 (Windows NT 10.0; Win64; x64) AppleWebKit/537.36
  (KHTML, like Gecko) Chrome/85.0.4183.102 Safari/537.36
Accept: text/html,application/xhtml+xml,application/xml;q=0.9,image/avif,
  image/webp,image/apng,/;q=0.8,application/signed-exchange;v=b3;q=0.9
Accept-Encoding: gzip, deflate
Accept-Language: en-US,en;q=0.9,es-AR;q=0.8,es;q=0.7
```

Figure 11.15 The ESP-01 module indicates that a network connection with ID of 0 has been established.

NOTE: The messages shown in Figure 11.15 are sent to the NUCLEO board by the ESP-01 module using a UART (as in Figure 11.4) and are then displayed on the serial terminal. This is only because the program that is running on the NUCLEO board forwards every character that it receives from the ESP-01 module to the PC by means of another UART (again, recall Figure 11.4).

In the first line of Figure 11.15, the ESP-01 module indicates that a TCP connection with ID 0 has been established. The other lines between *+IPD* and *q=0.7* are details about the connection that has been established and are not discussed here in order to keep this explanation as short as possible. For more information, please refer to [4].

At this point, if the command *AT+CIPSTATUS* is sent to the ESP-01 module, the response shown in Figure 11.16 is obtained. By means of "STATUS: 3", it is indicated that a TCP connection request has been received by the TCP server (recall Table 11.3). The details in Figure 11.16 follow the next sequence: +CIPSTATUS:<link ID>,<"type">,<"remote IP">,<remote port>,<local port>,<tetype>, as shown in [5].

```
AT+CIPSTATUS

STATUS:3
+CIPSTATUS:0,"TCP","192.168.77.198",60297,80,1.1

OK
```

Figure 11.16 The "AT+CIPSTATUS" command shows the connection status of the ESP-01 module.

The way in which the NUCLEO board indicates to the ESP-01 module how to respond to the web browser request is by loading the answer into the TCP server. In this case, the response will be an HTML document that must be loaded into the TCP server. In this step-by-step example, this is done by means of *AT+CIPSEND=0,52*, where "0" is the ID (identifier) of the connection with the TCP server and "52" is the length of the message in bytes that will be sent to the TCP server. Then, the ESP-01 module replies "OK" and sends the prompt symbol, ">", to the NUCLEO board in order to indicate that it is waiting for the HTML document, as shown in Figure 11.17.

```
AT+CIPSEND=0,52

OK
>
```

Figure 11.17 The "AT+CIPSEND=0,52" command (sends data) is sent to the ESP-01 module, and it responds ">".

The next step is to load the HTML document into the TCP server. In this particular example, the program that is loaded on the NUCLEO board will sequentially send the 52 bytes of the HTML document to the TCP server. The characters these bytes represent are shown in Code 11.1 and are sent when the "h" key is pressed on the PC keyboard.

```
<!doctype html> <html> <body> Hello! </body> </html>
```

Code 11.1 The code of the HTML document that is loaded in the TCP server when the "h" key is pressed.

The first part of the code, *<!doctype html>*, is used to indicate that it is an HTML document. Then, the tag *<html>* is used to indicate the beginning of the HTML code, and the *<body>* tag is used to indicate the beginning of the body of the HTML code. This is the part of the HTML document that the web browser renders on the screen. In this case, the body is just "Hello!" The last tags, (*</body>* and *</html>*), are used to close the previous tags.

Once the "h" key has been pressed on the PC keyboard, the 52 bytes are sent from the NUCLEO board to the ESP-01 module. The response of the ESP-01 module will be forwarded to the serial terminal using UART3 and, if everything goes well, the response will be as shown in Figure 11.18. This indicates that the 52 bytes were received correctly by the TCP server that is running on the ESP-01 module.

```
Recv 52 bytes

SEND OK

OK
```

Figure 11.18 The "AT+CIPSEND=0,52" command (sends data) is sent to the ESP-01 module.

Finally, the TCP connection between the ESP-01 module and the NUCLEO board should be closed by means of typing *AT+CIPCLOSE=0*, as shown in Figure 11.19. This is done in order to close the TCP connection with the web browser. In this way, the TCP server knows that no more data will be sent as a response to the web browser request.

```
AT+CIPCLOSE=0

0,CLOSED

OK
```

Figure 11.19 The "AT+CIPCLOSE=0" command (close a TCP connection) is sent to the ESP-01 module.

Now the TCP server has the response that should be sent to the web browser (i.e., the HTML document that has just been loaded to it) and sends the 52 bytes to the web browser. As a consequence, the web browser receives the 52 bytes, identifies it as an HTML document (because of the tag <!doctype html>), and displays the text "Hello!" as shown in Figure 11.20.

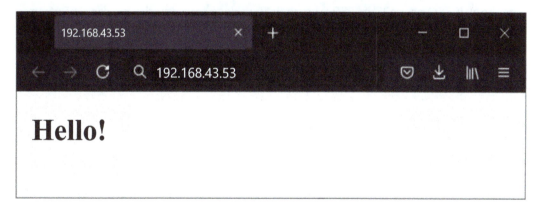

Figure 11.20 Web page served by the ESP-01 module.

 NOTE: By means of using more complex HTML code, together with other resources such as JavaScript and CSS, more appealing and meaningful web pages can be created. These topics are beyond the scope of this book.

WARNING: Do not worry if a "Not secure" message is indicated by the web browser. The web page has no harmful elements. This message can be avoided if a TLS (Transport Layer Security) connection is provided, which is beyond the scope of this book.

In the following examples, all the steps that were followed in this section are automated by means of a new software module that is gradually incorporated into the smart home system program.

Example 11.1: Implement the AT Command to Detect the Wi-Fi Module

Objective

Introduce the Finite-State Machine (FSM) that is used to control the ESP-01 module using AT commands.

Summary of the Expected Behavior

The NUCLEO board will send the command "AT" to the ESP-01 module and will wait five seconds to receive the reply "OK". If this reply is received correctly by the NUCLEO board, then "AT command responded correctly" will be shown on the serial terminal. If this message is not received within 10 seconds, then "AT command not responded correctly" will be shown on the serial terminal.

Test the Proposed Solution on the Board

Import the project "Example 11.1" using the URL available in [3], build the project, and drag the *.bin* file onto the NUCLEO board. If the ESP-01 module is working correctly, the message "AT command responded correctly" should appear on the serial terminal after 10 seconds. If this does not happen, check the connections, the ESP-01 module, and the access point and try again by pressing "a" on the PC keyboard.

Discussion of the Proposed Solution

The proposed solution is based on a new module named *wifi_com*. This module will manage all the communications with the ESP-01 module.

Implementation of the Proposed Solution

Code 11.2 shows the new implementation of *smartHomeSystemInit()* and *smartHomeSystemUpdate()*. On line 14, the *wifi_com* module is initialized by means of *wifiComInit()*. On line 15, the non-blocking delay is initialized using SYSTEM_TIME_INCREMENT_MS, which is equal to 10 milliseconds, as in Example 10.4.

```
 1   void smartHomeSystemInit()
 2   {
 3       tickInit();
 4       audioInit();
 5       userInterfaceInit();
 6       alarmInit();
 7       fireAlarmInit();
 8       intruderAlarmInit();
 9       pcSerialComInit();
10       motorControlInit();
11       gateInit();
12       lightSystemInit();
13       sdCardInit();
14       wifiComInit();
15       nonBlockingDelayInit( &smartHomeSystemDelay, SYSTEM_TIME_INCREMENT_MS );
16   }
17
18   void smartHomeSystemUpdate()
19   {
20       if( nonBlockingDelayRead(&smartHomeSystemDelay) ) {
21           userInterfaceUpdate();
22           fireAlarmUpdate();
23           intruderAlarmUpdate();
24           alarmUpdate();
25           eventLogUpdate();
26           pcSerialComUpdate();
27           motorControlUpdate();
28           lightSystemUpdate();
29           bleComUpdate();
30       }
31       wifiComUpdate();
32   }
```

Code 11.2 New implementation of the functions smartHomeSystemInit() and smartHomeSystemUpdate().

Given that the communication with the ESP-01 module will be established using a UART at a relatively high speed (115,200 bps) and there will be a relatively large number of bytes, the ESP-01 module must be read as fast as possible. For this purpose, the function *wifiComUpdate()* is called on line 31 outside the *if* statement that checks the non-blocking delay. In this way, *smartHomeSystemUpdate()* will call the functions from line 21 to line 29 every 10 milliseconds, while *wifiComUpdate()* will be called at a much higher rate. The reader is encouraged to compare how *smartHomeSystemUpdate()* is implemented in Code 11.2 and in Example 10.4.

In Table 11.4, the new library *wifi_com.h* that was added to *smart_home_system.cpp* is shown. The implementation of *wifi_com.h* is shown in Code 11.3. It can be seen that the public functions *wifiComRestart()*, *wifiComInit()*, and *wifiComUpdate()* are declared from line 8 to line 10.

Table 11.4 Sections in which lines were added to smart_home_system.cpp.

Section	Lines that were added
Libraries	#include "wifi_com.h"

```
1   //=====[#include guards - begin]===========================================
2
3   #ifndef _WIFI_COM_
4   #define _WIFI_COM_
5
6   //=====[Declarations (prototypes) of public functions]=====================
7
8   void wifiComRestart();
9   void wifiComInit();
10  void wifiComUpdate();
11
12  //=====[#include guards - end]=============================================
13
14  #endif /* _WIFI_COM_ */
```

Code 11.3 Implementation of wifi_com.h.

The library *wifi_com.h* was added to *pc_serial_com.cpp*, as shown in Table 11.5. The table also shows that the private function *commandRestartWifiCom()* was declared in *pc_serial_com.cpp*. In order to implement this function, the lines shown in Table 11.6 were added in *pcSerialComCommandUpdate()* and *availableCommands()*. In this way, the command "a" is incorporated into the *pc_serial_com* module. This command calls the function *commandRestartWifiCom()*.

The implementation of *commandRestartWifiCom()* is shown in Code 11.4. This function sends "Wi-Fi communication restarted" to *uartUsb* (line 3) and calls the function *wifiComRestart()* of the *wifi_com* module (line 4).

Table 11.5 Sections in which lines were added to pc_serial_com.cpp.

Section	Lines that were added
Libraries	`#include "wifi_com.h"`
Declarations (prototypes) of private functions	`static void commandRestartWifiCom();`

Table 11.6 Functions in which lines were added in pc_serial_com.cpp.

Function	Lines that were added
static void pcSerialComCommandUpdate(char receivedChar)	`case 'a': case 'A': commandRestartWifiCom(); break;`
static void availableCommands()	`pcSerialComStringWrite( "Press 'a' or 'A' to restart the  Wi-Fi communication\r\n" );`

```
1   static void commandRestartWifiCom()
2   {
3       pcSerialComStringWrite( "Wi-Fi communication restarted \r\n" );
4       wifiComRestart();
5   }
```

Code 11.4 Implementation of commandRestartWifiCom().

From Code 11.5 to Code 11.7, the implementation of *wifi_com.cpp* is shown. On lines 3 to 8 of Code 11.5, the libraries used by the *wifi_com* module are included. On line 12, DELAY_5_SECONDS is defined as 5000. A data type named *wifiComState_t* is declared in lines 16 to 22. This data type is used to implement an FSM that is used to control the ESP-01 module. A serial object is declared on line 27 in order to implement the communication with the ESP-01 module.

Line 30 declares a private array of char named *responseOk*. Because it is declared using the reserved word *const*, its content cannot be modified later in the program. Line 32 declares a pointer to a char type named *wifiComExpectedResponse*, which will be used to point to a string holding the expected response.

```
1    //=====[Libraries]=====================================================
2
3    #include "arm_book_lib.h"
4
5    #include "wifi_com.h"
6
7    #include "non_blocking_delay.h"
8    #include "pc_serial_com.h"
9
10   //=====[Declaration of private defines]===============================
11
12   #define DELAY_5_SECONDS        5000
13
14   //=====[Declaration of private data types]===========================
15
16   typedef enum {
17       WIFI_STATE_INIT,
18       WIFI_STATE_SEND_AT,
19       WIFI_STATE_WAIT_AT,
20       WIFI_STATE_IDLE,
21       WIFI_STATE_ERROR
22   } wifiComState_t;
23
24   //=====[Declaration and initialization of public global objects]=======
25
26   UnbufferedSerial uartWifi( PE_8, PE_7, 115200 );
27
28   //=====[Declaration and initialization of private global variables]======
29
30   static const char responseOk[] = "OK";
31
32   static const char* wifiComExpectedResponse;
33   static wifiComState_t wifiComState;
34
35   static nonBlockingDelay_t wifiComDelay;
36
37   //=====[Declarations (prototypes) of private functions]================
38
39   static bool isExpectedResponse();
40   bool wifiComCharRead( char* receivedChar );
41   void wifiComStringWrite( const char* str );
```

Code 11.5 Details of the implementation of the file wifi_com.cpp (Part 1/3).

NOTE: The UART communication with the ESP-01 module uses the default configuration, which is 8 bits, no parity, and one stop bit. For this reason, these parameters are not configured.

On line 33, the variable *wifiComState* of type *wifiComState_t*, is declared, while on line 35, the variable *wifiComDelay* of type *nonBlockingDelay_t* is declared. The prototypes of the private functions *isExpectedResponse()*, *wifiComCharRead()*, and *wifiComStringWrite()* are declared from line 39 to line 41.

In Code 11.6, the implementation of *wifiComInit()* is shown on line 3. This function sets *wifiComState* to WIFI_STATE_INIT. On line 8, the implementation of *wifiComRestart()* can be seen, which only sets *wifiComState* to WIFI_STATE_INIT.

Line 13 shows the implementation of *wifiComUpdate()*. On line 15, *receivedCharWifiCom* is declared, which is a char variable that preserves its value between one call and another of *wifiComUpdate()* because it is declared as static. The FSM starts on line 17, with a switch over *wifiComState*. If its value is WIFI_STATE_INIT, then a non-blocking delay of five seconds is configured, and *wifiComState* is assigned with the value WIFI_STATE_SEND_AT.

```
1   //=====[Implementations of public functions]===================================
2
3   void wifiComInit()
4   {
5       wifiComState = WIFI_STATE_INIT;
6   }
7
8   void wifiComRestart()
9   {
10      wifiComState = WIFI_STATE_INIT;
11  }
12
13  void wifiComUpdate()
14  {
15      switch (wifiComState) {
16
17          case WIFI_STATE_INIT:
18              nonBlockingDelayWrite(&wifiComDelay, DELAY_5_SECONDS);
19              wifiComState = WIFI_STATE_SEND_AT;
20          break;
21
22          case WIFI_STATE_SEND_AT:
23              if (nonBlockingDelayRead(&wifiComDelay)) {
24                  wifiComStringWrite( "AT\r\n" );
25                  wifiComExpectedResponse = responseOk;
26                  nonBlockingDelayWrite(&wifiComDelay, DELAY_5_SECONDS);
27                  wifiComState = WIFI_STATE_WAIT_AT;
28              }
29          break;
30
31          case WIFI_STATE_WAIT_AT:
```

```
32              if (isExpectedResponse()) {
33                  nonBlockingDelayWrite(&wifiComDelay, DELAY_5_SECONDS);
34                  pcSerialComStringWrite("AT command responded ");
35                  pcSerialComStringWrite("correctly\r\n");
36                  wifiComState = WIFI_STATE_IDLE;
37              }
38              if (nonBlockingDelayRead(&wifiComDelay)) {
39                  pcSerialComStringWrite("AT command not responded ");
40                  pcSerialComStringWrite("correctly\r\n");
41                  wifiComState = WIFI_STATE_ERROR;
42              }
43          break;
44
45          case WIFI_STATE_IDLE:
46          case WIFI_STATE_ERROR:
47          break;
48      }
49  }
```

Code 11.6 Details of the implementation of the file wifi_com.cpp (Part 2/3).

On line 22, the state WIFI_STATE_SEND_AT is implemented. If the non-blocking delay of five seconds has elapsed, then the command AT is written (line 24) and "OK" is assigned to *wifiComExpectedResponse* (line 25). A non-blocking delay of five seconds is initialized on line 26, and *wifiComState* is set to WIFI_STATE_WAIT_AT on line 27.

The implementation of WIFI_STATE_WAIT_AT is shown from line 31 to line 43. First, it is assessed whether there is a response and whether it is the expected response (line 32). If so, in lines 33 to 36 a new five-second non-blocking delay is started, the corresponding message is sent to the PC, and *wifiComState* is assigned to WIFI_STATE_IDLE. Otherwise, it is checked on line 38 if the five-second delay has expired. If so, the corresponding message is sent to the PC, and *wifiComState* is set to WIFI_STATE_ERROR. On lines 45 and 46, it can be seen that no actions are assigned to the WIFI_STATE_IDLE or WIFI_STATE_ERROR states.

Code 11.7 shows the implementation of some of the remaining functions of *wifi_com.cpp*. On line 3, it can be seen that *wifiComCharRead()* first checks if a character was received on *uartWifi* (connected to the ESP8266) (line 6), and if so, it writes the corresponding content on the memory address pointed by *receivedChar* (line 8). The returned value of *wifiComCharRead()* depends on whether there was a character available to be read (line 9) or not (line 11).

The function *wifiComStringWrite()* on line 14 is used to write the string pointed by its parameter *str* to the *uartWifi* object.

The implementation of *isExpectedResponse()* is shown between lines 19 and 37. First, three variables are declared: *responseStringPositionIndex*, to track the index of the position in the string corresponding to the response (note that it is declared as static); *charReceived*, to store the received char; and the Boolean variable *moduleResponse*, which is assigned the false state.

```
1    //=====[Implementations of private functions]======================================
2
3    bool wifiComCharRead( char* receivedChar )
4    {
5        char receivedCharLocal = '\0';
6        if( uartWifi.readable() ) {
7            uartWifi.read(&receivedCharLocal,1);
8            *receivedChar = receivedCharLocal;
9            return true;
10       }
11       return false;
12   }
13
14   void wifiComStringWrite( const char* str )
15   {
16       uartWifi.write( str, strlen(str) );
17   }
18
19   static bool isExpectedResponse()
20   {
21       static int responseStringPositionIndex = 0;
22       char charReceived;
23       bool moduleResponse = false;
24
25       if( wifiComCharRead(&charReceived) ){
26           if (charReceived == wifiComExpectedResponse[responseStringPositionIndex]) {
27               responseStringPositionIndex++;
28               if (wifiComExpectedResponse[responseStringPositionIndex] == '\0') {
29                   responseStringPositionIndex = 0;
30                   moduleResponse = true;
31               }
32           } else {
33               responseStringPositionIndex = 0;
34           }
35       }
36       return moduleResponse;
37   }
```

Code 11.7 Details of the implementation of the file wifi_com.cpp (Part 3/3).

Line 25 assesses whether there is a char available to be read on the *uartWifi* object. If so, line 26 assesses whether the received char is equal to the char that is expected at the corresponding position of the string *wifiComExpectedResponse*, and on line 27, *responseStringPositionIndex* is incremented by one. Line 28 assesses whether the current position of *wifiComExpectedResponse* is the null character. If so, *responseStringPositionIndex* is set to zero, and *moduleResponse* is set to the true state. If the received char is not the expected char (line 32), *responseStringPositionIndex* is set to zero. Finally, on line 36, *moduleResponse* is returned. Its value will be true if the expected response was received (recall line 30), and false otherwise.

Proposed Exercise

1. How can more AT commands be added to the *wifi_com* module?

Answer to the Exercise

1. In order to add more AT commands, the corresponding states should be added to *wifiComState_t* (line 16 of Code 11.5), and the corresponding state should be incorporated into *wifiComUpdate()*. This is shown in Example 11.2.

Example 11.2: Configure the Credentials to Connect to the Wi-Fi Access Point

Objective

Include AT commands in the FSM in order to implement the connection with the Wi-Fi access point.

Summary of the Expected Behavior

The NUCLEO board will send the commands "*AT*", "*AT+CWMODE=1*", "*AT+CWJAP*", and "*AT+CIFSR*" to the ESP-01 module (recall Section 11.2.2). It will be indicated on the serial terminal if the expected responses are received correctly by the NUCLEO board or not.

Test the Proposed Solution on the Board

Import the project "Example 11.2" using the URL available in [3], build the project, and drag the *.bin* file onto the NUCLEO board. Press "d" on the PC keyboard to set the Wi-Fi SSID of the access point that is to be used, and press "r" to set the Wi-Fi password. Then, press "a" to restart the Wi-Fi communication. If everything has worked correctly, after a few seconds the message "IP address assigned correctly" should appear on the serial terminal, and by pressing "p", the assigned IP address will be shown on the serial terminal. If this does not happen, check the connections, the access point, and the Wi-Fi credentials, and press "a" again to retry.

Discussion of the Proposed Solution

The proposed solution is based on new states that are incorporated into the FSM of the *wifi_com* module. These new states implement the steps shown in Figure 11.8 to Figure 11.10.

Implementation of the Proposed Solution

Table 11.7 shows the lines that were added to *pc_serial_com.cpp*. It can be seen that the private variables *numberOfCharsInApCredentials*, *ApSsid*, and *ApPassword* are created to manage the access point (AP) credentials. AP_SSID_MAX_LENGTH and AP_PASSWORD_MAX_LENGTH are defined in *wifi.h*, as shown below. Also, five new prototypes of private functions are declared in order to configure the SSID and the password and to get the assigned IP address.

In Table 11.8, the new lines that were added to *pcSerialComCommandUpdate()* and *availableCommands()* are shown. These lines are used to inform the user how to set the AP credentials and get the assigned IP address.

Table 11.7 Sections in which lines were added to pc_serial_com.cpp.

Section	Lines that were added

Declaration and initialization of private global variables	`static int numberOfCharsInApCredentials = 0;`
	`static char ApSsid[AP_SSID_MAX_LENGTH] = "";`
	`static char ApPassword[AP_PASSWORD_MAX_LENGTH] = "";`

Declarations (prototypes) of private functions	`static void pcSerialComGetWiFiComApSsid( char receivedChar );`
	`static void pcSerialComGetWiFiComApPassword( char receivedChar );`
	`static void commandSetWifiComApSsid();`
	`static void commandSetWifiComApPassword();`
	`static void commandGetWifiComAssignedIp();`

Table 11.8 Functions in which lines were added in pc_serial_com.cpp.

Function	Lines that were added

static void pcSerialComCommandUpdate(char receivedChar)	`case 'd': case 'D': commandSetWifiComApSsid(); break;`
	`case 'r': case 'R': commandSetWifiComApPassword(); break;`
	`case 'p': case 'P': commandGetWifiComAssignedIp(); break;`

static void availableCommands()	`pcSerialComStringWrite( "Press 'd' or 'D' to set Wi-Fi AP SSID\r\n" );`
	`pcSerialComStringWrite( "Press 'r' or 'R' to set Wi-Fi AP Password\r\n" );`
	`pcSerialComStringWrite( "Press 'p' or 'P' to get Wi-Fi assigned IP\r\n" );`

The new declaration of the user-defined type *pcSerialComMode_t* is shown in Code 11.8. Two new valid values are incorporated: PC_SERIAL_GET_WIFI_AP_CREDENTIALS_SSID and PC_SERIAL_GET_WIFI_AP_CREDENTIALS_PASSWORD.

```
1  typedef enum{
2      PC_SERIAL_GET_FILE_NAME,
3      PC_SERIAL_COMMANDS,
4      PC_SERIAL_GET_CODE,
5      PC_SERIAL_SAVE_NEW_CODE,
6      PC_SERIAL_GET_WIFI_AP_CREDENTIALS_SSID,
7      PC_SERIAL_GET_WIFI_AP_CREDENTIALS_PASSWORD,
8  } pcSerialComMode_t;
```

Code 11.8 New declaration of the type definition pcSerialComMode_t.

The new implementation of *pcSerialComUpdate()* is shown in Code 11.9. The new program code is between lines 18 and 23. It is used to get the AP credentials using the functions *pcSerialComGetWiFiComApSsid()* and *pcSerialComGetWiFiComApPassword()*, which are discussed below.

```
1   void pcSerialComUpdate()
2   {
3       char receivedChar = pcSerialComCharRead();
4       if( receivedChar != '\0' ) {
5           switch ( pcSerialComMode ) {
6               case PC_SERIAL_GET_FILE_NAME:
7                   pcSerialComGetFileName( receivedChar );
8                   break;
9               case PC_SERIAL_COMMANDS:
10                  pcSerialComCommandUpdate( receivedChar );
11                  break;
12              case PC_SERIAL_GET_CODE:
13                  pcSerialComGetCodeUpdate( receivedChar );
14                  break;
15              case PC_SERIAL_SAVE_NEW_CODE:
16                  pcSerialComSaveNewCodeUpdate( receivedChar );
17                  break;
18              case PC_SERIAL_GET_WIFI_AP_CREDENTIALS_SSID:
19                  pcSerialComGetWiFiComApSsid( receivedChar );
20                  break;
21              case PC_SERIAL_GET_WIFI_AP_CREDENTIALS_PASSWORD:
22                  pcSerialComGetWiFiComApPassword( receivedChar );
23                  break;
24              default:
25                  pcSerialComMode = PC_SERIAL_COMMANDS;
26                  break;
27          }
28      }
29  }
```

Code 11.9 Implementation of new cases in Serial_com pcSerialComUpdate().

In Code 11.10, the new functions that are incorporated into *pc_serial_com.cpp* are shown. The functions *pcSerialComGetWiFiComApSsid()* and *pcSerialComGetWiFiComApPassword()* are both called from *pcSerialComUpdate()*, as was shown in Code 11.9. These functions are used to ask the user for the AP credentials, which are stored in *ApSsid* and *ApPassword*. The credentials are configured into the ESP-01 module using the functions *wifiComSetWiFiComApSsid()* and *wifiComSetWiFiComApPassword()*, which are discussed below. The number of characters is stored in *numberOfCharsInApCredentials*.

The implementation of the functions that were mentioned in Table 11.8 are shown in Code 11.10. These functions are used to ask the user for the SSID and the password of the AP, and also to report the assigned IP address. To get the assigned IP address, the function *wifiComGetIpAddress()* is used, which is discussed below. Notice that *pcSerialComMode* is set in *commandSetWifiComApSsid()* and *commandSetWifiComApPassword()*, and *numberOfCharsInApCredentials* is set to zero in both functions.

```
1   static void commandSetWifiComApSsid()
2   {
3       pcSerialComStringWrite("\r\nPlease provide the SSID of the Wi-Fi ");
4       pcSerialComStringWrite("Access Point and press the Enter key\r\n");
5       pcSerialComStringWrite("> ");
6       pcSerialComMode = PC_SERIAL_GET_WIFI_AP_CREDENTIALS_SSID;
7       numberOfCharsInApCredentials = 0;
8   }
9
10  static void commandSetWifiComApPassword()
11  {
12      pcSerialComStringWrite("\r\nPlease provide the Password of the Wi-Fi ");
13      pcSerialComStringWrite("Access Point and press the Enter key\r\n");
14      pcSerialComStringWrite("> ");
15      pcSerialComMode = PC_SERIAL_GET_WIFI_AP_CREDENTIALS_PASSWORD;
16      numberOfCharsInApCredentials = 0;
17  }
18
19  static void commandGetWifiComAssignedIp()
20  {
21      pcSerialComStringWrite( "The assigned IP is: " );
22      pcSerialComStringWrite( wifiComGetIpAddress() );
23      pcSerialComStringWrite( "\r\n" );
24  }
25
26  static void pcSerialComGetWiFiComApSsid( char receivedChar )
27  {
28      if ( (receivedChar == '\r') &&
29           (numberOfCharsInApCredentials < AP_SSID_MAX_LENGTH) ) {
30          pcSerialComMode = PC_SERIAL_COMMANDS;
31          ApSsid[numberOfCharsInApCredentials] = '\0';
32          wifiComSetWiFiComApSsid(ApSsid);
33          pcSerialComStringWrite( "\r\nWi-Fi Access Point SSID configured\r\n\r\n" );
34      } else {
35          ApSsid[numberOfCharsInApCredentials] = receivedChar;
36          pcSerialComCharWrite( receivedChar );
37          numberOfCharsInApCredentials++;
38      }
39  }
40
41  static void pcSerialComGetWiFiComApPassword( char receivedChar )
42  {
43      if ( (receivedChar == '\r') &&
44           (numberOfCharsInApCredentials < AP_PASSWORD_MAX_LENGTH) ) {
45          pcSerialComMode = PC_SERIAL_COMMANDS;
46          ApPassword[numberOfCharsInApCredentials] = '\0';
47          wifiComSetWiFiComApPassword(ApPassword);
48          pcSerialComStringWrite( "\r\nWi-Fi Access Point password configured\r\n\r\n" );
49      } else {
50          ApPassword[numberOfCharsInApCredentials] = receivedChar;
51          pcSerialComStringWrite( "*" );
52          numberOfCharsInApCredentials++;
53      }
54  }
```

Code 11.10 Implementation of new private functions in pc_serial_com.cpp.

In Code 11.11 the new implementation of *wifi_com.h* is shown. The definitions that were used in Table 11.7 are shown on lines 8 and 9. It can be seen that the three public functions that were introduced in Code 11.10 are declared in lines 13 to 15. The implementation of these three functions is in the file *wifi_com.cpp* and is shown in Code 11.12. It can be seen that *wifiComSetWiFiComApSsid()* uses the function *strncpy()* to copy the content of the string *ApSsid* into the string *wifiComApSsid* in order to avoid the user input causing buffer overflow issues, as discussed in Chapter 4. The function *wifiComSetWiFiComApPassword()* makes a copy of *ApPassword* into *wifiComApPassword*. Finally, *wifiComGetIpAddress()* returns a pointer to the string *wifiComIpAddress*, which is introduced below.

```
1    //=====[#include guards - begin]=================================================
2
3    #ifndef _WIFI_COM_
4    #define _WIFI_COM_
5
6    //=====[Declaration of public defines]===========================================
7
8    #define AP_SSID_MAX_LENGTH      (32 + 1)
9    #define AP_PASSWORD_MAX_LENGTH  (63 + 1)
10
11   //=====[Declarations (prototypes) of public functions]===========================
12
13   void wifiComSetWiFiComApSsid( char * ApSsid );
14   void wifiComSetWiFiComApPassword( char * ApPassword );
15   char * wifiComGetIpAddress();
16
17   void wifiComRestart();
18   void wifiComInit();
19   void wifiComUpdate();
20
21   //=====[#include guards - end]===================================================
22
23   #endif /* _WIFI_COM_ */
```

Code 11.11 New implementation of wifi_com.h.

```
1    void wifiComSetWiFiComApSsid( char * ApSsid )
2    {
3        strncpy(wifiComApSsid, ApSsid, AP_SSID_MAX_LENGTH);
4    }
5
6    void wifiComSetWiFiComApPassword( char * ApPassword )
7    {
8        strncpy(wifiComApPassword, ApPassword, AP_PASSWORD_MAX_LENGTH );
9    }
10
11   char * wifiComGetIpAddress()
12   {
13       return wifiComIpAddress;
14   }
```

Code 11.12 Implementation of the public functions of the wifi_com module.

The lines that were added to *wifi_com.cpp* are shown in Table 11.9. A definition of DELAY_10_SECONDS as 10000 is added, as well as a definition of IP_MAX_LENGTH. Also seven private global strings are declared. Four of them are used to implement specific steps of the FSM, as discussed below. The other three are used to store information regarding the AP, also discussed below.

Table 11.9 Sections in which lines were added to wifi_com.cpp.

Section	Lines that were added
Declaration of private defines	`#define DELAY_10_SECONDS     10000` `#define IP_MAX_LENGTH        (15 + 1)`

Declaration and initialization of private global variables	`static const char responseCwjapOk[] = "+CWJAP:";`
	`static const char responseCwjap1[] = "WIFI CONNECTED";`
	`static const char responseCwjap2[] = "WIFI GOT IP";`
	`static const char responseCifsr[] = "+CIFSR:STAIP,\"";`
	`static char wifiComApSsid[AP_SSID_MAX_LENGTH] = "";`
	`static char wifiComApPassword[AP_PASSWORD_MAX_LENGTH] = "";`
	`static char wifiComIpAddress[IP_MAX_LENGTH];`

As was mentioned in the section "Summary of the Expected Behavior," in this example the NUCLEO board sends the commands "*AT*", "*AT+CWMODE=1*", "*AT+CWJAP*", and "*AT+CIFSR*" to the ESP-01 module. To handle this functionality, new states are incorporated into the FSM, as shown in Code 11.13 (lines 5 to 14).

```
1   typedef enum {
2       WIFI_STATE_INIT,
3       WIFI_STATE_SEND_AT,
4       WIFI_STATE_WAIT_AT,
5       WIFI_STATE_SEND_CWMODE,
6       WIFI_STATE_WAIT_CWMODE,
7       WIFI_STATE_SEND_CWJAP_IS_SET,
8       WIFI_STATE_WAIT_CWJAP_IS_SET,
9       WIFI_STATE_SEND_CWJAP_SET,
10      WIFI_STATE_WAIT_CWJAP_SET_1,
11      WIFI_STATE_WAIT_CWJAP_SET_2,
12      WIFI_STATE_SEND_CIFSR,
13      WIFI_STATE_WAIT_CIFSR,
14      WIFI_STATE_LOAD_IP,
15      WIFI_STATE_IDLE,
16      WIFI_STATE_ERROR
17  } wifiComState_t;
```

Code 11.13 New declaration of the user-defined type wifiComState_t.

The new implementation of the FSM is shown in Code 11.14 to Code 11.16. On lines 3 and 4 of Code 11.14, two new static variables are declared: *receivedCharWifiCom* and *IpStringPositionIndex*. Lines 6 to 32 of Code 11.14 are the same as in Example 11.1 (Code 11.6). The "*AT+CWMODE=1*" command is implemented from lines 34 to 41. The corresponding response is expected using the FSM that is implemented from lines 43 to 53. Note that the program code that is used to implement the "*AT+CWMODE=1*" command is very similar to the program code used to implement the "*AT*" command that was discussed in Example 11.1. For this reason, lines 34 to 53 are not further discussed here.

The implementation of the "*AT+CWJAP*" command is shown between lines 55 and 62 of Code 11.14 and in lines 1 to 51 of Code 11.15. Firstly, the state WIFI_STATE_SEND_CWJAP_IS_SET sends "*AT+CWJAP?*" to the ESP-01 module in order to determine if the AP credentials are configured. Next, the WIFI_STATE_WAIT_CWJAP_IS_SET state assesses if the response is "OK". If so, the next state is WIFI_STATE_SEND_CIFSR. Otherwise, the next state is WIFI_STATE_SEND_CWJAP_SET, where the AP credentials are sent to the ESP-01, the expected response is set in line 20 of Code 11.15 to *responseCwjap1*, which is "WIFI CONNECTED", and the next state is set to WIFI_STATE_WAIT_CWJAP_SET_1. The WIFI_STATE_WAIT_CWJAP_SET_1 state assesses if "WIFI CONNECTED" is received. If so, the expected response is set to *responseCwjap2*, which is "WIFI GOT IP", and the next state is set to WIFI_STATE_WAIT_CWJAP_SET_2. Finally, the WIFI_STATE_WAIT_CWJAP_SET_2 state assesses if "WIFI GOT IP" is received. If so, the next state is set to WIFI_STATE_SEND_CIFSR.

The implementation of the "*AT+CIFSR*" command is shown between lines 53 and 60 of Code 11.15 and in lines 1 to 24 of Code 11.16. First, the state WIFI_STATE_SEND_CIFSR sends "*AT+CIFSR*" to the ESP-01 module in order to receive the assigned IP address. The expected response is set in line 56 to *responseCifsr*, which is "+CIFSR:STAIP,\", and the next state is set to WIFI_STATE_WAIT_CIFSR. Next, the WIFI_STATE_WAIT_CIFSR state assesses if "+CIFSR:STAIP,\" is received. If so, the next state is set to WIFI_STATE_LOAD_IP, and *IpStringPositionIndex* is set to zero. In the state WIFI_STATE_LOAD_IP, the assigned IP address is read and loaded into *wifiComIpAddress*. The assessment "*IpStringPositionIndex < IP_MAX_LENGTH*" is used to avoid buffer overflow issues, as discussed in Chapter 4, if for any reason the ESP-01 module sends more IP characters than expected. Then, the message "IP address assigned correctly" is sent to the serial terminal (line 20).

Lastly, lines 26 to 28 of Code 11.16 are the same as in the previous implementation of *wifiComUpdate()* in Example 11.1. In this way, the FSM will remain in WIFI_STATE_IDLE or case WIFI_STATE_ERROR if those states are reached. Note that no specific message is displayed in these situations, in order to simplify the implementation of this example.

```
1   void wifiComUpdate()
2   {
3       static char receivedCharWifiCom;
4       static int IpStringPositionIndex;
5
6       switch (wifiComState) {
7
8         case WIFI_STATE_INIT:
9             nonBlockingDelayWrite(&wifiComDelay, DELAY_5_SECONDS);
10            wifiComState = WIFI_STATE_SEND_AT;
11            break;
12
13        case WIFI_STATE_SEND_AT:
14            if (nonBlockingDelayRead(&wifiComDelay)) {
15                wifiComStringWrite( "AT\r\n" );
16                wifiComExpectedResponse = responseOk;
17                nonBlockingDelayWrite(&wifiComDelay, DELAY_5_SECONDS);
18                wifiComState = WIFI_STATE_WAIT_AT;
19            }
20            break;
21
22        case WIFI_STATE_WAIT_AT:
23            if (isExpectedResponse()) {
24                nonBlockingDelayWrite(&wifiComDelay, DELAY_5_SECONDS);
25                wifiComState = WIFI_STATE_SEND_CWMODE;
26            }
27            if (nonBlockingDelayRead(&wifiComDelay)) {
28                pcSerialComStringWrite("AT command not responded ");
```

```
29              pcSerialComStringWrite("correctly\r\n");
30              wifiComState = WIFI_STATE_ERROR;
31          }
32          break;
33
34      case WIFI_STATE_SEND_CWMODE:
35          if (nonBlockingDelayRead(&wifiComDelay)) {
36              wifiComStringWrite( "AT+CWMODE=1\r\n" );
37              wifiComExpectedResponse = responseOk;
38              nonBlockingDelayWrite(&wifiComDelay, DELAY_5_SECONDS);
39              wifiComState = WIFI_STATE_WAIT_CWMODE;
40          }
41          break;
42
43      case WIFI_STATE_WAIT_CWMODE:
44          if (isExpectedResponse()) {
45              nonBlockingDelayWrite(&wifiComDelay, DELAY_5_SECONDS);
46              wifiComState = WIFI_STATE_SEND_CWJAP_IS_SET;
47          }
48          if (nonBlockingDelayRead(&wifiComDelay)) {
49              pcSerialComStringWrite("AT+CWMODE=1 command not ");
50              pcSerialComStringWrite("responded correctly\r\n");
51              wifiComState = WIFI_STATE_ERROR;
52          }
53          break;
54
55      case WIFI_STATE_SEND_CWJAP_IS_SET:
56          if (nonBlockingDelayRead(&wifiComDelay)) {
57              wifiComStringWrite( "AT+CWJAP?\r\n" );
58              wifiComExpectedResponse = responseCwjapOk;
59              nonBlockingDelayWrite(&wifiComDelay, DELAY_5_SECONDS);
60              wifiComState = WIFI_STATE_WAIT_CWJAP_IS_SET;
61          }
62          break;
```

Code 11.14 New implementation of wifiComUpdate() (Part 1/3).

```
1       case WIFI_STATE_WAIT_CWJAP_IS_SET:
2           if (isExpectedResponse()) {
3               wifiComExpectedResponse = responseOk;
4               wifiComState = WIFI_STATE_SEND_CIFSR;
5           }
6           if (nonBlockingDelayRead(&wifiComDelay)) {
7               nonBlockingDelayWrite(&wifiComDelay, DELAY_5_SECONDS);
8               wifiComState = WIFI_STATE_SEND_CWJAP_SET;
9           }
10          break;
11
12      case WIFI_STATE_SEND_CWJAP_SET:
13          if (nonBlockingDelayRead(&wifiComDelay)) {
14              wifiComStringWrite( "AT+CWJAP=\"" );
15              wifiComStringWrite( wifiComApSsid );
16              wifiComStringWrite( "\",\"" );
17              wifiComStringWrite( wifiComApPassword );
18              wifiComStringWrite( "\"" );
19              wifiComStringWrite( "\r\n" );
20              wifiComExpectedResponse = responseCwjap1;
21              nonBlockingDelayWrite(&wifiComDelay, DELAY_10_SECONDS);
22              wifiComState = WIFI_STATE_WAIT_CWJAP_SET_1;
23          }
```

```
24              break;
25
26          case WIFI_STATE_WAIT_CWJAP_SET_1:
27              if (isExpectedResponse()) {
28                  wifiComExpectedResponse = responseCwjap2;
29                  wifiComState = WIFI_STATE_WAIT_CWJAP_SET_2;
30              }
31              if (nonBlockingDelayRead(&wifiComDelay)) {
32                  pcSerialComStringWrite("Error in state: ");
33                  pcSerialComStringWrite("WIFI_STATE_WAIT_CWJAP_SET_1\r\n");
34                  pcSerialComStringWrite("Check Wi-Fi AP credentials ");
35                  pcSerialComStringWrite("and restart\r\n");
36                      wifiComState = WIFI_STATE_ERROR;
37              }
38              break;
39
40          case WIFI_STATE_WAIT_CWJAP_SET_2:
41              if (isExpectedResponse()) {
42                  wifiComState = WIFI_STATE_SEND_CIFSR;
43              }
44              if (nonBlockingDelayRead(&wifiComDelay)) {
45                  pcSerialComStringWrite("Error in state: ");
46                  pcSerialComStringWrite("WIFI_STATE_WAIT_CWJAP_SET_2\r\n");
47                  pcSerialComStringWrite("Check Wi-Fi AP credentials ");
48                  pcSerialComStringWrite("and restart\r\n");
49                  wifiComState = WIFI_STATE_ERROR;
50              }
51          break;
52
53          case WIFI_STATE_SEND_CIFSR:
54              if (nonBlockingDelayRead(&wifiComDelay)) {
55                  wifiComStringWrite( "AT+CIFSR\r\n" );
56                  wifiComExpectedResponse = responseCifsr;
57                  nonBlockingDelayWrite(&wifiComDelay, DELAY_5_SECONDS);
58                  wifiComState = WIFI_STATE_WAIT_CIFSR;
59              }
60              break;
```

Code 11.15 New implementation of wifiComUpdate() (Part 2/3).

```
1           case WIFI_STATE_WAIT_CIFSR:
2               if (isExpectedResponse()) {
3                   wifiComState = WIFI_STATE_LOAD_IP;
4                   IpStringPositionIndex = 0;
5               }
6               if (nonBlockingDelayRead(&wifiComDelay)) {
7                   pcSerialComStringWrite("AT+CIFSR command not responded ");
8                   pcSerialComStringWrite("correctly\r\n");
9                   wifiComState = WIFI_STATE_ERROR;
10              }
11          break;
12
13          case WIFI_STATE_LOAD_IP:
14              if (wifiComCharRead(&receivedCharWifiCom)) {
15                  if ( (receivedCharWifiCom != '"') &&
16                       (IpStringPositionIndex < IP_MAX_LENGTH) ) {
17                      wifiComIpAddress[IpStringPositionIndex] = receivedCharWifiCom;
18                      IpStringPositionIndex++;
19                  } else {
20                      wifiComIpAddress[IpStringPositionIndex] = '\0';
21                      pcSerialComStringWrite("IP address assigned correctly\r\n\r\n");
```

```
22                        wifiComState = WIFI_STATE_IDLE;
23                   }
24              }
25        break;
26
27        case WIFI_STATE_IDLE:
28        case WIFI_STATE_ERROR:
29        break;
30     }
31  }
```

Code 11.16 New implementation of wifiComUpdate() (Part 3/3).

Proposed Exercise

1. Once the ESP-01 module is connected to the AP, what should be done in order to serve a web page?

Answer to the Exercise

1. The AT commands shown from Figure 11.11 to Figure 11.19 must be implemented. This is shown in Example 11.3.

Example 11.3: Serve a Simple Web Page using the Wi-Fi Connection

Objective

Include AT commands in the FSM in order to serve a web page using the Wi-Fi access point.

Summary of the Expected Behavior

The NUCLEO board will send the commands *"AT"*, *"AT+CWMODE=1"*, *"AT+CWJAP"*, *"AT+CIFSR"*, *"AT+CIPMUX=1"*, *"AT+CIPSERVER=1,80"*, *"AT+CIPSTATUS"*, *"AT+CIPSEND"*, the HTML document, and the command *"AT+CIPCLOSE"* to the ESP-01 module (recall Section 11.2.2). It will be indicated on the serial terminal if the expected responses are received correctly by the NUCLEO board or not. If everything works as expected, the web page that was shown in Figure 11.20 should be displayed on the web browser.

Test the Proposed Solution on the Board

Import the project "Example 11.3" using the URL available in [3], build the project, and drag the *.bin* file onto the NUCLEO board. Repeat the same steps as in Example 11.2. Press "p" to get the IP address assigned to the ESP-01 module. Enter this IP in a web browser. The web page that was shown in Figure 11.20 should be displayed in the web browser. If this does not happen, check the connections and press "a" to retry.

Discussion of the Proposed Solution

The proposed solution is based on new states that are incorporated into the FSM of the *wifi_com* module. These new states implement the steps shown in Figure 11.11 to Figure 11.19.

Implementation of the Proposed Solution

In this example, the *wifi_com* module incorporates many AT commands. To handle this functionality, new states are incorporated into the FSM as shown in Code 11.17 (lines 15 to 29).

```
1   typedef enum {
2       WIFI_STATE_INIT,
3       WIFI_STATE_SEND_AT,
4       WIFI_STATE_WAIT_AT,
5       WIFI_STATE_SEND_CWMODE,
6       WIFI_STATE_WAIT_CWMODE,
7       WIFI_STATE_SEND_CWJAP_IS_SET,
8       WIFI_STATE_WAIT_CWJAP_IS_SET,
9       WIFI_STATE_SEND_CWJAP_SET,
10      WIFI_STATE_WAIT_CWJAP_SET_1,
11      WIFI_STATE_WAIT_CWJAP_SET_2,
12      WIFI_STATE_SEND_CIFSR,
13      WIFI_STATE_WAIT_CIFSR,
14      WIFI_STATE_LOAD_IP,
15      WIFI_STATE_SEND_CIPMUX,
16      WIFI_STATE_WAIT_CIPMUX,
17      WIFI_STATE_SEND_CIPSERVER,
18      WIFI_STATE_WAIT_CIPSERVER,
19      WIFI_STATE_SEND_CIPSTATUS,
20      WIFI_STATE_WAIT_CIPSTATUS_STATUS_3,
21      WIFI_STATE_WAIT_CIPSTATUS,
22      WIFI_STATE_WAIT_GET_ID,
23      WIFI_STATE_WAIT_CIPSTATUS_OK,
24      WIFI_STATE_SEND_CIPSEND,
25      WIFI_STATE_WAIT_CIPSEND,
26      WIFI_STATE_SEND_HTML,
27      WIFI_STATE_WAIT_HTML,
28      WIFI_STATE_SEND_CIPCLOSE,
29      WIFI_STATE_WAIT_CIPCLOSE
30      WIFI_STATE_IDLE,
31      WIFI_STATE_ERROR
32  } wifiComState_t;
```

Code 11.17 New declaration of the user-defined type wifiComState_t.

Two new variables are declared in *wifiComUpdate()*, as shown in Table 11.10. The variable *lengthOfHtmlCode* is used together with the "*AT+CIPSEND*" command in order to indicate the length in bytes of the HTTP that is being sent to the web browser (recall Figure 11.17). The array *strToSend* is used as a string where the message to be sent is stored in the cases of the "*AT+CIPSEND*" and "*AT+CIPCLOSE*" commands, because these commands require some parameters (recall Figure 11.17 and Figure 11.19).

Table 11.10 Functions in which lines were added in wifi_com.cpp.

Function	Lines that were added
void wifiComUpdate()	`int lengthOfHtmlCode;` `char strToSend[50] = "";`

In Table 11.11, the new private global variables that are declared in *wifi_com.cpp* are shown. The strings stored in *responseStatus3* and *responseCipstatus* are used to implement the command *"AT+CIPSTATUS"*. The string *responseSendOk* is used to implement the command *"AT+CIPSEND"*, while the string *responseCipclose* is used to implement the *"AT+CIPCLOSE=0"* command. The integer variable *currentConnectionId* is used to get the identifier (ID) of the connection that is established. Lastly, the HTML code that is used to implement the web page that is shown in the web browser is stored in the string *htmlCode* (recall Code 11.1, where this HTML is introduced).

Table 11.11 Sections in which lines were added to wifi_com.cpp.

Section	Lines that were added

Declaration and initialization of private global variables	`static const char responseStatus3[] = "STATUS:3";`
	`static const char responseCipstatus[] = "+CIPSTATUS:";`
	`static const char responseSendOk[] = "SEND OK";`
	`static const char responseCipclose[] = "CLOSED";`
	`static int currentConnectionId;`
	`static const char htmlCode [] =`
	`    "<!doctype html> <html> <body> Hello! </body> </html>"`

The implementation of the new states of the FSM in *wifiComUpdate()* is shown in Code 11.18 to Code 11.20. In Code 11.18, the implementation of *"AT+CIPMUX=1"* and *"AT+CIPSERVER=1,80"* is shown. The implementation of these commands is not further discussed because it is very similar to the implementation of *"AT+CWMODE=1"*, which was explained in Example 11.2.

Code 11.19 shows the implementation of the *"AT+CIPSTATUS"* command. The sequence is as shown in Figure 11.16: first, *"AT+CIPSTATUS"* is sent to the ESP-01 module (line 3), then it is assessed whether the expected response *"STATUS:3"* is obtained (line 11). After this, it is assessed if the ESP-01 module sends the message *"+CIPSTATUS:"* (line 23), then the current connection ID is read (line 34), and, finally, it is checked if *"OK"* has been sent by the ESP-01 module.

Code 11.20 shows the implementation of the *"AT+CIPSEND"* and *"AT+CIPCLOSE"* commands. On line 3, the *"AT+CIPSEND"* command is prepared with the corresponding parameters (recall Figure 11.17). For this purpose, the current connection ID and the length in bytes of the HTML web page code, which is obtained in line 2 using *strlen()*, are used. The *"AT+CIPSEND"* command is sent on line 5. Line 11 checks if the ESP-01 module response is *"OK"*. If so, the FSM moves to the WIFI_STATE_SEND_HTML state (line 13). Otherwise, it returns to the WIFI_STATE_SEND_CIPSTATUS state (line 17).

The HTML document is sent on line 22, and the "SEND OK" response is checked on line 28. If this response is obtained, it moves to the state WIFI_STATE_SEND_CIPCLOSE (line 30). If it is not obtained, the FSM moves back to the WIFI_STATE_SEND_CIPSEND state (line 34). The "*AT+CIPCLOSE*" command is implemented between lines 38 and 57. It is important to note that if everything works as expected (i.e., "OK" is received), the next state is set to WIFI_STATE_SEND_CIPSTATUS (line 51); if not, the next state is also set to WIFI_STATE_SEND_CIPSTATUS (line 55). This is done this way because in either scenario the next step is to wait for a new web page request, and this is done in WIFI_STATE_SEND_CIPSTATUS by means of asking the ESP-01 module about the CIPSTATUS.

```
1      case WIFI_STATE_SEND_CIPMUX:
2          if (nonBlockingDelayRead(&wifiComDelay)) {
3              wifiComStringWrite( "AT+CIPMUX=1\r\n" );
4              wifiComExpectedResponse = responseOk;
5              nonBlockingDelayWrite(&wifiComDelay, DELAY_5_SECONDS);
6              wifiComState = WIFI_STATE_WAIT_CIPMUX;
7          }
8          break;
9
10     case WIFI_STATE_WAIT_CIPMUX:
11         if (isExpectedResponse()) {
12             nonBlockingDelayWrite(&wifiComDelay, DELAY_5_SECONDS);
13             wifiComState = WIFI_STATE_SEND_CIPSERVER;
14         }
15         if (nonBlockingDelayRead(&wifiComDelay)) {
16             pcSerialComStringWrite("AT+CIPMUX=1 command not responded ");
17             pcSerialComStringWrite("correctly\r\n\r\n");
18             wifiComState = WIFI_STATE_ERROR;
19         }
20         break;
21
22     case WIFI_STATE_SEND_CIPSERVER:
23         if (nonBlockingDelayRead(&wifiComDelay)) {
24             wifiComStringWrite( "AT+CIPSERVER=1,80\r\n" );
25             wifiComExpectedResponse = responseOk;
26             nonBlockingDelayWrite(&wifiComDelay, DELAY_5_SECONDS);
27             wifiComState = WIFI_STATE_WAIT_CIPSERVER;
28         }
29         break;
30
31     case WIFI_STATE_WAIT_CIPSERVER:
32         if (isExpectedResponse()) {
33             nonBlockingDelayWrite(&wifiComDelay, DELAY_5_SECONDS);
34             wifiComState = WIFI_STATE_SEND_CIPSTATUS;
35         }
36         if (nonBlockingDelayRead(&wifiComDelay)) {
37             pcSerialComStringWrite("AT+CIPSERVER=1,80 command not responded ");
38             pcSerialComStringWrite("correctly\r\n\r\n");
39             wifiComState = WIFI_STATE_ERROR;
40         }
41         break;
```

Code 11.18 Implementation of the new states in wifiComUpdate() (Part 1/3).

```
1    case WIFI_STATE_SEND_CIPSTATUS:
2        if (nonBlockingDelayRead(&wifiComDelay)) {
3            wifiComStringWrite( "AT+CIPSTATUS\r\n" );
4            wifiComExpectedResponse = responseStatus3;
5            nonBlockingDelayWrite(&wifiComDelay, DELAY_5_SECONDS);
6            wifiComState = WIFI_STATE_WAIT_CIPSTATUS_STATUS_3;
7        }
8        break;
9
10   case WIFI_STATE_WAIT_CIPSTATUS_STATUS_3:
11       if (isExpectedResponse()) {
12           nonBlockingDelayWrite(&wifiComDelay, DELAY_5_SECONDS);
13           wifiComExpectedResponse = responseCipstatus;
14           wifiComState = WIFI_STATE_WAIT_CIPSTATUS;
15       }
16       if (nonBlockingDelayRead(&wifiComDelay)) {
17           nonBlockingDelayWrite(&wifiComDelay, DELAY_5_SECONDS);
18           wifiComState = WIFI_STATE_SEND_CIPSTATUS;
19       }
20       break;
21
22   case WIFI_STATE_WAIT_CIPSTATUS:
23       if (isExpectedResponse()) {
24           wifiComState = WIFI_STATE_WAIT_GET_ID;
25       }
26       if (nonBlockingDelayRead(&wifiComDelay)) {
27           nonBlockingDelayWrite(&wifiComDelay, DELAY_5_SECONDS);
28           wifiComState = WIFI_STATE_SEND_CIPSTATUS;
29       }
30       break;
31
32   case WIFI_STATE_WAIT_GET_ID:
33       if( wifiComCharRead(&receivedCharWifiCom) ){
34           currentConnectionId = receivedCharWifiCom;
35           wifiComExpectedResponse = responseOk;
36           wifiComState = WIFI_STATE_WAIT_CIPSTATUS_OK;
37       }
38       break;
39
40   case WIFI_STATE_WAIT_CIPSTATUS_OK:
41       if (isExpectedResponse()) {
42           wifiComState = WIFI_STATE_SEND_CIPSEND;
43       }
44       if (nonBlockingDelayRead(&wifiComDelay)) {
45           nonBlockingDelayWrite(&wifiComDelay, DELAY_5_SECONDS);
46           wifiComState = WIFI_STATE_SEND_CIPSTATUS;
47       }
48       break;
```

Code 11.19 Implementation of the new states in wifiComUpdate() (Part 2/3).

```
1        case WIFI_STATE_SEND_CIPSEND:
2            lengthOfHtmlCode = (strlen(htmlCode));
3            sprintf( strToSend, "AT+CIPSEND=%c,%d\r\n", currentConnectionId,
4                                                 lengthOfHtmlCode );
5            wifiComStringWrite( strToSend );
6            wifiComState = WIFI_STATE_WAIT_CIPSEND;
7            wifiComExpectedResponse = responseOk;
8            break;
9
10       case WIFI_STATE_WAIT_CIPSEND:
11           if (isExpectedResponse()) {
12               nonBlockingDelayWrite(&wifiComDelay, DELAY_5_SECONDS);
13               wifiComState = WIFI_STATE_SEND_HTML;
14           }
15           if (nonBlockingDelayRead(&wifiComDelay)) {
16               nonBlockingDelayWrite(&wifiComDelay, DELAY_5_SECONDS);
17               wifiComState = WIFI_STATE_SEND_CIPSTATUS;
18           }
19           break;
20
21       case WIFI_STATE_SEND_HTML:
22           wifiComStringWrite( htmlCode );
23           wifiComState = WIFI_STATE_WAIT_HTML;
24           wifiComExpectedResponse = responseSendOk;
25           break;
26
27       case WIFI_STATE_WAIT_HTML:
28           if (isExpectedResponse()) {
29               nonBlockingDelayWrite(&wifiComDelay, DELAY_5_SECONDS);
30               wifiComState = WIFI_STATE_SEND_CIPCLOSE;
31           }
32           if (nonBlockingDelayRead(&wifiComDelay)) {
33               nonBlockingDelayWrite(&wifiComDelay, DELAY_5_SECONDS);
34               wifiComState = WIFI_STATE_SEND_CIPSEND;
35           }
36           break;
37
38       case WIFI_STATE_SEND_CIPCLOSE:
39           if (nonBlockingDelayRead(&wifiComDelay)) {
40               sprintf( strToSend, "AT+CIPCLOSE=%c\r\n", currentConnectionId );
41               wifiComStringWrite( strToSend );
42               wifiComExpectedResponse  = responseCipclose;
43               nonBlockingDelayWrite(&wifiComDelay, DELAY_5_SECONDS);
44               wifiComState = WIFI_STATE_WAIT_CIPCLOSE;
45           }
46           break;
47
48       case WIFI_STATE_WAIT_CIPCLOSE:
49           if (isExpectedResponse()) {
50               nonBlockingDelayWrite(&wifiComDelay, DELAY_5_SECONDS);
51               wifiComState = WIFI_STATE_SEND_CIPSTATUS;
52           }
53           if (nonBlockingDelayRead(&wifiComDelay)) {
54               nonBlockingDelayWrite(&wifiComDelay, DELAY_5_SECONDS);
55               wifiComState = WIFI_STATE_SEND_CIPSTATUS;
56           }
57           break;
58
59       case WIFI_STATE_IDLE:
60       case WIFI_STATE_ERROR:
61           break;
62       }
63   }
```

Code 11.20 Implementation of the new states in wifiComUpdate() (Part 3/3).

Proposed Exercise

1. How can the web page be configured in order to show some relevant data about the smart home system?

Answer to the Exercise

1. The HTML document that is served must be modified in order to include some information about the smart home system. This is shown in Example 11.4.

Example 11.4: Serve a Web Page that Shows the Smart Home System Information

Objective

Include in the web page the status of different elements of the smart home system.

Summary of the Expected Behavior

The NUCLEO board will serve a web page, as in Example 11.3, but in this case the web page will contain relevant information about the smart home system: the temperature expressed in degrees Celsius; the status of the over temperature, gas, and motion detectors; and the status of the alarm, Incorrect code LED, and System blocked LED, as shown in Figure 11.6.

Test the Proposed Solution on the Board

Import the project "Example 11.4" using the URL available in [3], build the project, and drag the *.bin* file onto the NUCLEO board. Follow the same steps as in Example 11.3. If everything worked correctly, the web page that was introduced in Figure 11.6 should be displayed in the web browser. Otherwise, check the connections and the access point credentials, and press "a" to retry.

Discussion of the Proposed Solution

The proposed solution is based on the same states of the FSM that were introduced in previous examples. The difference is that in this example more information is shown in the web page served by the smart home system.

Implementation of the Proposed Solution

In order to show more information in the web page served by the smart home system, some lines were added in different sections of *wifi_com.cpp*, as shown in Table 11.12. It can be seen that the libraries regarding the temperature sensor, siren, fire alarm, motion sensor, and user interface were included. Two new definitions are also made: BEGIN_USER_LINE and END_USER_LINE. The former is used to indicate the beginning of a paragraph by means of <p>. The latter is used to indicate the ending of the paragraph by means of </p>.

Table 11.12 Sections in which lines were added to wifi_com.cpp.

Section	Lines that were added

Libraries	```#include "temperature_sensor.h"```
	```#include "siren.h"```
	```#include "fire_alarm.h"```
	```#include "motion_sensor.h"```
	```#include "user_interface.h"```

Declaration of private defines	```#define BEGIN_USER_LINE "<p>"``` ```#define END_USER_LINE "</p>"```

Declaration and initialization of private global variables	```static char stateString[4] = "";```
	```static const char htmlCodeHeader [] =```
	``` "<!doctype html>"```
	``` "<html> <head> <title>Smart Home System</title> </head>"```
	``` "<body style=\"text-align: center;\">"```
	``` "<h1 style=\"color: #0000ff;\">Smart Home System</h1>"```
	``` "<div style=\"font-weight: bold\">";```
	```static const char htmlCodeFooter [] = "</div> </body> </html>";```
	```static char htmlCodeBody[450] = "";```

Declarations (prototypes) of private functions	```void wifiComWebPageDataUpdate();``` ```char * stateToString(bool state);```

Table 11.12 shows that some new private variables were declared. *stateString* will be used to store a string that will indicate the status of the different elements of the smart home system (i.e., "ON" or "OFF"). *htmlCodeHeader* is used to store the header of the HTML code. Its first lines (*"<!doctype html> <html> <head>"*) are the same as in Example 11.3. Next, *"<title>Smart Home System</title>"* is used to assign a title to the web page. Then, center-aligned text is configured for the body of the document. After this, "Smart Home System" is printed using heading size 1 (i.e., h1) and blue color (#0000ff). A division or section in the HTML code is opened where bold font is set. The *htmlCodeFooter* string is used to close the *<div>*, *<body>*, and *<html>* tags that were opened in *htmlCodeHeader*. Finally, the string *htmlCodeBody* is used to store the body of the HTML code. The prototypes of the new private functions *wifiComWebPageDataUpdate()* and *stateToString()* are declared in *wifi_com.cpp*, and are discussed below.

Table 11.13 shows that the string *htmlCode* was removed from *wifi_com.cpp*. In Table 11.14, the implementation of the FSM states that were modified are shown. In WIFI_STATE_WAIT_CIPSTATUS_OK, the function *wifiComWebPageDataUpdate()* is now used to prepare the web page, as discussed below.

Table 11.13 Sections in which lines were removed from wifi_com.cpp.

Section	Lines that were removed
Declaration and initialization of private global variables	```static const char htmlCode [] =``` ``` "<!doctype html> <html> <body> Hello! </body> </html>"```

Table 11.14 States of the FSM that were modified in wifi_com.cpp.

Previous implementation of the state	New implementation of the state
```case WIFI_STATE_WAIT_CIPSTATUS_OK: if (isExpectedResponse()) { wifiComState = WIFI_STATE_SEND_CIPSEND; } if (nonBlockingDelayRead(&wifiComDelay)) { nonBlockingDelayWrite(&wifiComDelay, DELAY_5_SECONDS); wifiComState = WIFI_STATE_SEND_CIPSTATUS; } break;```	```case WIFI_STATE_WAIT_CIPSTATUS_OK: if (isExpectedResponse()) { wifiComState = WIFI_STATE_SEND_CIPSEND; wifiComWebPageDataUpdate(); } if (nonBlockingDelayRead(&wifiComDelay)) { nonBlockingDelayWrite(&wifiComDelay, DELAY_5_SECONDS); wifiComState = WIFI_STATE_SEND_ CIPSTATUS; } break;```
```case WIFI_STATE_SEND_CIPSEND: lengthOfHtmlCode = (strlen(htmlCode)); sprintf(strToSend, "AT+CIPSEND=%c,%d\r\n", currentConnectionId, lengthOfHtmlCode); wifiComStringWrite(strToSend); wifiComState = WIFI_STATE_WAIT_CIPSEND; wifiComExpectedResponse = responseOk; break;```	```case WIFI_STATE_SEND_CIPSEND: lengthOfHtmlCode = (strlen(htmlCodeHeader) + strlen(htmlCodeBody) + strlen(htmlCodeFooter)); sprintf(strToSend, "AT+CIPSEND=%c,%d\r\n", currentConnectionId, lengthOfHtmlCode); wifiComStringWrite(strToSend); wifiComState = WIFI_STATE_WAIT_CIPSEND; wifiComExpectedResponse = responseOk; break;```
```case WIFI_STATE_SEND_HTML: wifiComStringWrite(htmlCode); wifiComState = WIFI_STATE_WAIT_HTML; wifiComExpectedResponse = responseSendOk; break;```	```case WIFI_STATE_SEND_HTML: wifiComStringWrite(htmlCodeHeader); wifiComStringWrite(htmlCodeBody); wifiComStringWrite(htmlCodeFooter); wifiComState = WIFI_STATE_WAIT_HTML; wifiComExpectedResponse = responseSendOk; break;```

In WIFI_STATE_SEND_CIPSEND, the length of the HTML code to send is obtained by summing the length in bytes of *htmlCodeHeader*, *htmlCodeBody*, and *htmlCodeFooter*.

In WIFI_STATE_SEND_HTML, it can be seen that the HTML code that is sent is composed of *htmlCodeHeader*, followed by *htmlCodeBody*, and finally *htmlCodeFooter*.

In Code 11.21, it can be seen how *htmlCodeBody* is structured. One after the other, the different values to be shown in the web page are appended onto *htmlCodeBody*. Note that *sprintf* is used to append the values, by means of an offset given by + *strlen(htmlCodeBody)*. In order to separate the information into different lines, BEGIN_USER_LINE and END_USER_LINE are used when appending the string corresponding to each element. Note that in order to print the degrees symbol "°", the HTML predefined character entity "º" is used in line 3. Lastly, note that to append the information corresponding to different elements as an "ON" or "OFF" string, the function *stateToString()* is used.

```
1   void wifiComWebPageDataUpdate()
2   {
3       sprintf( htmlCodeBody, "%s Temperature: %.2f &ordm;C %s",
4               BEGIN_USER_LINE, temperatureSensorReadCelsius(), END_USER_LINE );
5
6       sprintf( htmlCodeBody + strlen(htmlCodeBody),
7               "%s Over temperature detected: %s %s", BEGIN_USER_LINE,
8               stateToString( overTemperatureDetectorStateRead() ), END_USER_LINE );
9
10      sprintf( htmlCodeBody + strlen(htmlCodeBody), "%s Gas detected: %s %s",
11              BEGIN_USER_LINE, stateToString( gasDetectorStateRead() ),
12              END_USER_LINE );
13
14      sprintf( htmlCodeBody + strlen(htmlCodeBody),
15              "%s Motion detected: %s %s", BEGIN_USER_LINE,
16              stateToString( motionSensorRead() ), END_USER_LINE );
17
18      sprintf( htmlCodeBody + strlen(htmlCodeBody), "%s Alarm: %s %s",
19              BEGIN_USER_LINE, stateToString( sirenStateRead() ), END_USER_LINE );
20
21      sprintf( htmlCodeBody + strlen(htmlCodeBody),
22              "%s Incorrect code LED: %s %s", BEGIN_USER_LINE,
23              stateToString( incorrectCodeStateRead() ), END_USER_LINE );
24
25      sprintf( htmlCodeBody + strlen(htmlCodeBody),
26              "%s System blocked LED: %s %s", BEGIN_USER_LINE,
27              stateToString( systemBlockedStateRead() ), END_USER_LINE );
28  }
```

Code 11.21 Implementation of wifiComWebPageDataUpdate().

 NOTE: Recall Chapter 3, where it was explained that the file *mbed_app.json* was introduced in order to enable the *%.2f* format that is used in Code 11.21. For more information, please refer to [6].

Code 11.22 shows the implementation of the function *stateToString()*. It returns "ON" or "OFF" depending on the value of its only parameter (*state*).

```
1   char * stateToString( bool state )
2   {
3       if ( state ) {
4           strcpy( stateString, "ON");
5       } else {
6           strcpy( stateString, "OFF");
7       }
8       return stateString;
9   }
```

Code 11.22 Implementation of stateToString().

In this way, the HTML code served by the smart home system looks like the example shown in Code 11.23.

```
1    <!doctype html>
2    <html>
3      <head>
4        <title>Smart Home System</title>
5      </head>
6      <body style="text-align: center;">
7        <h1 style="color: #0000ff;">Smart Home System</h1>
8        <div style="font-weight: bold">
9          <p>Temperature: 10 &ordm;C</p>
10         <p>Over temperature detected: OFF</p>
11         <p>Gas detected: OFF</p>
12         <p>Motion detected: OFF</p>
13         <p>Alarm: OFF</p>
14         <p>Incorrect code LED: OFF</p>
15         <p>System blocked LED: OFF</p>
16        </div>
17      </body>
18   </html>
```

Code 11.23 Example of the HTML code served by the smart home system.

Proposed Exercises

1. What should be modified in order to include more information in the web page served by the smart home system?

2. How can the HTML code be modified in order to auto refresh the data every ten seconds?

Answers to the Exercises

1. The function *wifiComWebPageDataUpdate()* should be modified in order to include more information in *htmlCodeBody*.

2. Table 11.15 shows how to modify *htmlCodeHeader* in *wifi_com.cpp*. The meta tag should be included with the parameters \"refresh\" and content=\"10\". In this way, the web browser will automatically ask the smart home system for the web page every ten seconds.

Table 11.15 Sections in which lines were modified in wifi_com.cpp.

Section	Lines that were added
Declaration and initialization of private global variables	```static const char htmlCodeHeader [] = "<!doctype html>" "<html> <head> <title>Smart Home System</title>" "<meta http-equiv=\"refresh\" content=\"10\" /> </head>" "<body> <h1 style=\"text-align: center;\">" "<font color=\"#0000ff\">Smart Home System</font></h1>"```

11.3 Under the Hood

11.3.1 Basic Principles of Wi-Fi and TCP Connections

In this chapter, a Wi-Fi connection was used to serve a web page. In fact, Wi-Fi is a family of wireless network protocols based on the IEEE 802.11 family of standards, which are commonly used for local area networking of devices and sharing internet access. Different versions of Wi-Fi are specified that use different radio bands and technologies, which determine their maximum ranges and achievable speeds.

The ESP-01 module used in this chapter uses the same 2.4 GHz band as the HM-10 module that was introduced in Chapter 3. The 2.4 GHz band is currently the most popular band for Wi-Fi connections, together with the 5 GHz band. Each Wi-Fi band is divided into multiple channels in the same way as in Bluetooth communication, as was explained in Chapter 10. Channels can be shared between networks, but only one transmitter can transmit on a channel at any given moment in time.

The set of channels and techniques used to avoid narrowband interference problems varies depending on the Wi-Fi version, as does the maximum bit rate that is reachable under optimal conditions. Wi-Fi equipment frequently supports multiple versions of Wi-Fi. For example, the ESP-01 module supports Wi-Fi 1 (802.11b), Wi-Fi 3 (802.11g), and Wi-Fi 4 (802.11n), as described in [1]. The main characteristics of each Wi-Fi version are listed in Table 11.16.

Table 11.16 Summary of the main characteristics of the Wi-Fi versions.

Generation (Standard)	Maximum Link Rate	Adopted	Frequency
Wi-Fi 6E (802.11ax)	600 to 9608 Mbit/s	2019	6 GHz
Wi-Fi 6 (802.11ax)	600 to 9608 Mbit/s	2019	2.4/5 GHz
Wi-Fi 5 (802.11ac)	433 to 6933 Mbit/s	2014	5 GHz
Wi-Fi 4 (802.11n)	72 to 600 Mbit/s	2009	2.4/5 GHz
Wi-Fi 3 (802.11g)	3 to 54 Mbit/s	2003	2.4 GHz
Wi-Fi 2 (802.11a)	1.5 to 54 Mbit/s	1999	5 GHz
Wi-Fi 1 (802.11b)	1 to 11 Mbit/s	1999	2.4 GHz

NOTE: Wi-Fi is a trademark of the non-profit Wi-Fi Alliance, integrated by hundreds of companies around the world. For more information about Wi-Fi technology and the Wi-Fi Alliance, please refer to [7].

In the examples in this chapter, a TCP server was used to implement the communications between the ESP-01 module and the web browser. As mentioned earlier, TCP stands for Transmission Control Protocol and is one of the main communications protocols used on the internet and similar computer networks.

TCP provides reliable, ordered, and error-checked delivery of data between applications running on devices that communicate using a network, where every device has a unique IP (Internet Protocol) identifier. Thus, the entire suite is commonly referred to as TCP/IP. Major internet applications such as the World Wide Web, email, and file transfer all rely on TCP.

TCP is connection-oriented, and a connection between client and server has to be established before data can be sent, as was shown in subsection 11.2.2. The server must be listening for connection requests from clients before a connection is established.

TCP includes different techniques in order to improve the reliability of the communication, such as error-detection, retransmission, etc. However, it has some vulnerabilities that can be exploited by hackers. For this reason, among others, TCP has been used in the first two versions of the Hypertext Transfer Protocol (HTTP in 1996 and HTTP/2 in 2015) but is not used by the latest standard (HTTP/3 (2020)).

Proposed Exercise

1. Which technology allows a higher data transfer rate, Bluetooth Low Energy (BLE) or Wi-Fi?

Answer to the Exercise

1. In Chapter 10, it was shown that depending on the BLE version, the maximum achievable bit rate is between 1 Mbit/s and 2 Mbit/s. Looking at Table 11.16, it can be seen that Wi-Fi allows a higher data transfer rate.

11.4 Case Study

11.4.1 Indoor Environment Monitoring

In this chapter, a web server was incorporated into the smart home system. In this way, the user is able to access the information of the smart home system by means of a web browser. In [8], an Mbed-based indoor environment monitoring system is shown that allows facilities managers to measure environmental factors such as humidity, light levels, CO_2, and occupancy, by means of a web service that offers real-time insights, alerts, and reports relating to building performance. A representation of the system is shown in Figure 11.21.

Figure 11.21 Example of an Mbed-based system having a web service with real-time insights, alerts and reports.

There are many similarities between the functionality of the indoor environment monitoring system and the functionality of the smart home system, such as:

■ Gas detection

■ Alert generation

■ Occupancy monitoring

■ Light level measurement

■ Real-time information

Proposed Exercise

1. How can a plan of the home be added to the web page provided by the smart home system?

Answer to the Exercise

1. The code of the web page must be modified in order to allow the user to upload a home plan.

References

[1] "ESP-01/07/12 Series Modules User's Manual". Accessed July 9, 2021.
     https://docs.ai-thinker.com/_media/esp8266/esp8266_series_modules_user_manual_en.pdf

[2] "esp8266-module-family [ESP8266 Support WIKI]". Accessed July 9, 2021.
     https://www.esp8266.com/wiki/doku.php?id=esp8266-module-family

[3] "GitHub - armBookCodeExamples/Directory". Accessed July 9, 2021.
     https://github.com/armBookCodeExamples/Directory

[4] "AT Command Set — ESP-AT User Guide documentation". Accessed July 9, 2021.
     https://docs.espressif.com/projects/esp-at/en/latest/AT_Command_Set/index.html

[5] "TCP_IP AT Commands — ESP-AT User Guide documentation". Accessed July 9, 2021.
     https://docs.espressif.com/projects/esp-at/en/latest/AT_Command_Set/TCP-IP_AT_Commands.
     html#cmd-status

[6] "mbed-os_README.md at master · ARMmbed_mbed-os · GitHub". Accessed July 9, 2021.
     https://github.com/ARMmbed/mbed-os/blob/master/platform/source/minimal-printf/README.
     md#usage

[7] "Wi-Fi Alliance". Accessed July 9, 2021.
     https://www.wi-fi.org/

[8] "Indoor Environment Monitoring | Mbed". Accessed July 9, 2021.
     https://os.mbed.com/built-with-mbed/indoor-environment-monitoring/

Chapter 12

Guide to Designing and Implementing an Embedded System Project

12.1 Roadmap

12.1.1 What You Will Learn

After you have studied the material in this chapter, you will be able to:

- Describe how an embedded system project can be developed following an ordered process.

- Design and implement a prototype of an embedded system, including its hardware and software.

- Summarize the fundamentals of the concepts of verification and validation.

- Develop the final documentation of an embedded system.

12.1.2 Review of Previous Chapters

Throughout this book, a smart home system provided with a broad variety of functionalities has been implemented. The NUCLEO board was used as the system core, and many hardware modules and elements were connected to it. A learn-by-doing approach was used, by means of which several embedded system programming concepts were introduced.

The smart home system project was started from scratch in Chapter 1, and functionality was gradually added through the chapters as different hardware modules and elements were incorporated. This approach led to a single file having hundreds of lines, after which the idea of software modularization was introduced in Chapter 5. From then on, in Chapters 6 to 11, many software modules were included as more hardware was incorporated into the system.

The reader may have noticed that, for pedagogical reasons, the features and functionalities of the smart home system were not established at the beginning. This made it possible to introduce the topics gradually, but also led to many changes during its implementation. As a consequence, it can be concluded that it would be more convenient to adopt a structured process to efficiently design and implement an embedded system. This process should include a step at the beginning where the features and functionality of the system are defined.

12.1.3 Contents of This Chapter

In this chapter, a structured process will be introduced to efficiently design and implement an embedded system. The proposed process consists of ten steps, including the selection of the project, its definition, design, implementation, and final documentation. The hardware and software aspects are tackled, following an approach that guarantees consistency between the initial objectives and the obtained results.

In order to illustrate how each of the proposed steps is carried out, a project is implemented within this chapter. For the sake of brevity, a system with a reduced number of sensors and actuators is used in the examples, although this does not limit the introduction of the important concepts.

The proposed process benefits from all the concepts that were introduced throughout this book, while also helping to introduce other important concepts such as *requirements, verification*, and *validation*. This chapter constitutes a summary of the book, while introducing important new concepts.

12.2 Fundamentals of Embedded System Design and Implementation

12.2.1 Proposed Steps to Design and Implement an Embedded System Project

The proposed process to design and implement embedded systems is summarized in Table 12.1. It can be seen that it consists of ten steps, ranging from the selection of the project that will be implemented to its design, implementation, and final documentation, as was mentioned in the previous section.

Table 12.1 Summary of the proposed steps to design and implement an embedded system project.

Step	Outcome
1. Select the project that will be implemented	A rationale that leads to an appropriate project to implement
2. Elicit project requirements and use cases	A concise and structured description of what will be implemented
3. Design the hardware	Diagram of hardware modules, connections, and bill of materials
4. Design the software	Diagram of the software design and description of the modules
5. Implement the user interface	Software implementation
6. Implement the reading of the sensors	Software implementation
7. Implement the driving of the actuators	Software implementation
8. Implement the system behavior	Software implementation
9. Check the system behavior	Assessment of accomplishment of requirements and use cases
10. Develop the final documentation	A reference to the most relevant documentation of the project

The proposed steps include a gradual implementation of the software. First, the user interface is implemented in step 5. The aim is to have a way to read the system information and to enter commands. In this step, the reading of the sensors is replaced by *stub* code that temporarily substitutes the *yet-to-be-developed* code to read the sensors. In step 6, the reading of the sensors is implemented and the corresponding values shown on the user interface. In step 7, the actuators are driven, but stub code is used to trigger their activation. In step 8, the complete system behavior is implemented, so no more stub code remains in the software.

In the examples below, the ten proposed steps are introduced by means of a given project that is developed from start to end, following a *top-down* approach. This starts by formulating an overview design of the system, and goes on to gradually define and implement each part in detail.

TIP: Through the examples, the reader is encouraged to think of their own project and to develop that project as each step is introduced, by adapting each example to their own requirements. It is recommended that the reader choose a simple project to avoid complications that will distract from the main aim of this chapter, which is to understand and adopt the proposed steps.

NOTE: There are many other possible approaches to tackling the design and implementation of an embedded system, depending on the characteristics of the project, as well as on the size and skills of the developing team. The proposed steps correspond to the implementation of an embedded system prototype by a single developer or a very reduced team. A more complex project may suggest an iterative approach, where the outcomes of the steps are revised and improved more than once.

Example 12.1: Select the Project that will be Implemented

Objective

Introduce the idea that the project to be implemented should result from a decision process.

Summary of the Expected Outcome

As a result of this step, a rationale about the most appropriate project to be implemented should be obtained.

NOTE: This step is particularly important because the results can lead to either a valuable project or a questionable project (in terms of learning, benefits, etc.).

Discussion on How to Implement this Step

In order to select the project, it should first be established which aspects will be analyzed in the decision process. Those aspects will vary depending on the developer profile and skills, the organization where the developer is studying or working, and many other aspects. However, a table summarizing the aspects to be analyzed, as well as the score of each proposed project in each aspect, seems to be a reasonable way to decide which project to implement.

Implementation of this Proposed Step

First, the aspects that will be considered in the decision process should be determined. For the sake of brevity, just a few aspects will be considered in this example. However, an important idea is introduced: different aspects may have different weights in the decision process. To factor all these ideas into the decision process, a quantitative approach will be followed.

Some aspects that could be considered in the decision process are as follows:

- Availability of the hardware

- Utility of the project

- Implementation time

In the particular context of this book, the hardware availability might be considered an important aspect, given that it is convenient for the reader to reuse the hardware from previous chapters. The usefulness of the project could be considered less relevant, because in this context the reader is more concerned about learning than using the project in a real-life application. Finally, the implementation time can be considered an important aspect, given that the aim is to choose a simple project that can be completed in a single chapter.

Some possible projects that could be analyzed include the following:

- A mobile robot that avoids obstacles

- A flying drone fitted with a camera

- A home irrigation system for indoor plants

In this way, Table 12.2 can be obtained, which includes the possible projects and all the proposed aspects with given weights, as per the above discussion. A weighted score for each project is obtained.

The mobile robot that avoids obstacles will require hardware that was not used in this book (wheels, structure, motors, obstacle sensors, etc.), and for that reason was awarded a score of three out of ten points in the hardware availability aspect. The utility of this project is questionable, and for that reason this project again obtains three out of ten points in the corresponding aspect. Finally, this project will take a reasonable implementation time and, therefore, obtains five points in that aspect. Consequently, considering that the aspects are weighted by a factor of ten, five, and eight, respectively, the weighted scores are obtained (30, 15, and 40), and the sum of weighted scores is 85, as can be seen in the last column of Table 12.2.

The flying drone fitted with a camera will require even more specific and complex hardware than the mobile robot, and for that reason it gets two points in the hardware availability aspect. The utility of this project might be considered higher than the utility of the mobile robot, and therefore it gets five points in that aspect. Finally, this project will demand a considerable implementation time and, therefore, this project scores two points in that aspect. As a result, this project gets a sum of weighted scores of 61.

NOTE: The implementation time aspect gets a lower score when the time demand is bigger.

A typical home irrigation system allows the user to set how often and for how long the plants are irrigated. It can be implemented by means of a few buttons, an LCD display, a moisture sensor, and an on/off electro-valve, as will be discussed in Example 12.3. Most of this hardware is already available to the reader or is easy to obtain and use. Therefore, this project gets eight points in the hardware availability aspect. This project can be useful if the reader has some indoor plants, and therefore it gets seven points in the utility of the project aspect. Finally, this project can be implemented with limited effort, and, therefore, it gets eight points in the implementation time aspect. As a result, this project gets a sum of weighted scores of 179.

The home irrigation system for indoor plants project is chosen, as it gets the highest value in the sum of weighted scores, as can be seen in the last column of Table 12.2.

Table 12.2 Selection of the project to be implemented.

Project		Hardware availability (weight: 10)	Utility of the project (weight: 5)	Implementation time (weight: 8)	Sum of weighted scores
Mobile robot that avoids obstacles	Score on each aspect:	3	3	5	–
	Weighted score:	30	15	40	85
Flying drone provided with a camera	Score on each aspect:	2	5	2	–
	Weighted score:	20	25	16	61
Home irrigation system for indoor plants	Score on each aspect:	8	7	8	–
	Weighted score:	80	35	64	179

 NOTE: The score in each aspect, as well as the weight of each aspect, is an approximate value only. It should be noted that, in general, a small variation in an aspect score for a given project, or in an aspect weighting, does not modify which project obtains the highest sum of weighted scores shown in Table 12.2.

Proposed Exercise

1. How can the reader use the concepts that were introduced in this chapter to select a project to implement?

Answer to the Exercise

1. The reader should first establish a list of aspects that they would like to consider in the selection of a project. Then, the weighting of each aspect should be determined, and finally the different projects should be scored.

 TIP: Consider including aspects such as "How fun the project is," "What will be learned," or "Profitability" as a way to guarantee that the selection reflects the reader's personal motivations.

Example 12.2: Elicit Project Requirements and Use Cases

Objective

Introduce the concepts of *requirements* and *use cases*.

Summary of the Expected Outcome

As a result of this step, the project to be implemented should be clearly defined. This will be done by means of a list of requirements and use cases.

Discussion of How to Implement this Step

This step is based on the concepts of requirements and use cases.

DEFINITION: In product development, a *requirement* is a singular documented physical, functional, or non-functional need that a particular design, product, or process aims to satisfy.

DEFINITION: In software and systems engineering, a *use case* is a list of actions or event steps typically defining the interactions between an actor (for example, a user) and a system to achieve a goal.

The requirements are the basis on which a project is to be developed. Therefore, there are many important criteria that a developer should apply when writing the requirements. Some of these criteria are frequently summarized using the "SMART" mnemonic acronym, as shown in Table 12.3.

Table 12.3 Summary of the SMART mnemonic acronym.

Letter	Term adopted in this book	Meaning
S	Specific	Clearly defined
M	Measurable	Able to be measured
A	Achievable	Able to be achieved
R	Relevant	Targets a significant need
T	Time-bound	Has a time limit or deadline

NOTE: SMART is sometimes used to refer to other criteria. For example, the letter "A" is frequently related to the term "agreed," meaning that the requirements must be agreed with the client.

WARNING: In professional *project management*, every project should have a due date. Therefore, the time-bound criterion applies to the whole project and can also be applied to each requirement. In this example, it is established that the whole project (all the requirements) should be completed in one week.

A use case can be defined in multiple ways. In the scope of this book, the elements shown in Table 12.4 will be used. The reader should note that alongside each is a simplified approach that is appropriate for many projects.

Table 12.4 Elements that will be used to define a use case.

Use case element	Meaning
ID	A unique number that represents a use case
Title	The title that is associated with the use case
Trigger	What event triggers this use case
Precondition	What must be met before this use case can start
Basic flow	The events that occur when there are no errors or exceptions
Alternate flows	The most significant alternatives and exceptions

Lastly, in most cases there are already products on the market that implement the same functionality as the embedded system project that will be designed. Many of those products may be very successful. Therefore, it is recommended to analyze and summarize those products before writing the requirements and use cases of a new embedded system project, as per the example below.

Implementation of this Proposed Step

First, some examples of home irrigation systems are analyzed, as was suggested in the previous paragraph. Table 12.5 summarizes the main characteristics of two products. Based on those characteristics, the requirements indicated in Table 12.6 are established with consideration of what can be achieved.

 NOTE: The requirements in Table 12.6 are preliminary requirements that may be modified as the project evolves. If requirements are modified, then the modifications should be clearly indicated in order to avoid misunderstandings.

Table 12.5 Summary of the main characteristics of two home irrigation systems currently available on the market.

Characteristics	Product A	Product B
Water-in port	½-inch connector	½-inch connector
Irrigation circuits	Controls two independent irrigation circuits	Controls one irrigation circuit
Operation modes	Continuous: water flow is controlled by a button Programmed irrigation: irrigation is time-controlled	Continuous: water flow is controlled by a button Programmed irrigation: irrigation is time-controlled
Configuration	The parameters "how often" to irrigate and "how long" to irrigate can be configured for each circuit	The parameters "how often" to irrigate and "how long" to irrigate can be configured
User interface	A rotary control key, two buttons, and a display	A set of buttons and a set of LEDs
Power supply	Two AA batteries	Four AA batteries
Sensors	None	None
Price	80 USD	60 USD

Table 12.6 Initial requirements defined for the home irrigation system.

Req. Group	Req. ID	Description
1. Water	1.1	The system will have one water-in port based on a ½-inch connector
	1.2	The system will control one irrigation circuit by means of a solenoid valve
2. Modes	2.1	The system will have a continuous mode in which a button will enable the water flow
	2.2	The system will have a programmed irrigation mode based on a set of configurations:
	2.2.1	Irrigation will be enabled only if moisture is below the "Minimum moisture level" value
	2.2.2	Irrigation will be enabled every H hours with H being the "How often" configuration
	2.2.3	Irrigation will be enabled for S seconds, with S being the "How long" configuration
	2.2.4	Irrigation will be skipped if "How long" is configured to 0 (zero)
3. Configuration	3.1	The system configuration will be done by means of a set of buttons:
	3.1.1	The "Mode" button will change between "Programmed irrigation" and "Continuous irrigation"
	3.1.2	The "How often" button will increase the time between irrigations in programmed mode by one hour
	3.1.3	The "How long" button will increase the irrigation time in programmed mode by ten seconds
	3.1.4	The "Moisture" button will increase the "Minimum moisture level" configuration by 5%
	3.1.5	The maximum values will be: "How often": 24 h; "How long": 90 s; "Moisture": 95%
	3.1.6	"How long" and "Moisture" will be set to 0 (zero) if the maximum is reached and the button is pressed
	3.1.7	"How often" will be set to 1 if the maximum is reached and the button is pressed
4. Display	4.1	The system will have an LCD display:
	4.1.1	The LCD display will show the current operation mode: Continuous or Programmed
	4.1.2	The LCD display will show the values of "How often", "How long", and "Minimum moisture level"
5. Sensor	5.1	The system will measure soil moisture at one point with an accuracy better than 5%
6. Power supply	6.1	The system will be powered using two AA batteries
7. Due date	7.1	The system will be finished one week after starting (this includes buying the parts)
8. Cost	8.1	The components for the prototype should cost less than 60 USD
9. Documents	9.1	The prototype should be accompanied by a list of parts, a connection diagram, the code repository, and a table indicating the accomplishment of requirements and use cases

Finally, three use cases are defined, as can be seen in Table 12.7, Table 12.8, and Table 12.9.

Table 12.7 Use Case #1 – Title: The user wants to irrigate plants immediately for a couple of minutes.

Use case element	Definition
Trigger	The user realizes that the plants need irrigation immediately
Precondition	The system must be powered on, and the water supply should be connected. The system is not irrigating the plants.
Basic flow	The user presses the "Mode" button to set "Continuous" irrigation. Water starts to flow to the plants. After a couple of minutes, the user presses the "Mode" button to set "Programmed" irrigation. Water irrigation stops.
Alternate flows	1.a. There is no water supply. The user presses the "Mode" button to set "Continuous" irrigation. The solenoid valve is activated, but the plants are not irrigated. 1.b. The user presses the "Mode" button. The user notes that the water is overflowing the plant pot. The user presses the "Mode" button and irrigation stops.

Table 12.8 Use Case #2 – Title: The user wants to program irrigation to take place for ten seconds every six hours.

Use case element	Definition
Trigger	The user wants to establish an irrigation program
Precondition	The system must be powered on, and the water supply should be connected. The system is not irrigating the plants.
Basic flow	The user presses the "How often" button until the value "6 hours" is shown on the display. The user presses the "How long" button until the value "10 seconds" is shown on the display. Irrigation will start in six hours and will last for ten seconds if the measured moisture is below the "Minimum moisture level" configured.
Alternate flows	2.a. There is no water supply. The solenoid valve will be activated, but the plants will not be irrigated.

Table 12.9 Use Case #3 – Title: The user wants the plants not to be irrigated.

Use case element	Definition
Trigger	The user wants the plants to not be irrigated
Precondition	The system must be powered on, and water supplied should be connected. The system is not irrigating the plants.
Basic flow	The user presses the "How long" button until "How long" is set to 0 (zero). Irrigation is skipped, and a legend indicating "Programmed-Skip" is shown.
Alternate flows	3.a. Plants will not be irrigated even if the measured moisture is below the "Minimum moisture level" configured.

Proposed Exercise

1. Define the requirements and three use cases for the project that was selected in the "Proposed Exercise" of Example 12.1.

Answer to the Exercise

1. It is strongly recommended to start by analyzing and summarizing some products that are available on the market. Based on the characteristics of those products and the reader's own ideas, the initial requirements may be established following the format shown in Table 12.6. The use cases can be defined following the format shown in Table 12.7.

TIP: When defining the requirements, keep in mind the SMART criteria discussed above. In particular, consider the time available to implement the project and the relevancy and achievability of each requirement. Moreover, try to clearly define each requirement, and use measurable quantities if possible.

Example 12.3: Design the Hardware

Objective

Design hardware that fulfills the requirements and can be used to implement the software functionality.

Summary of the Expected Outcome

The outcomes of this step are expected to include:

- a diagram of the hardware modules showing all of their interconnections,

- a rationale that argues the most appropriate components with which to implement the hardware modules,

- a connection diagram of the selected components and tables summarizing their interconnections, and

- a bill of materials that includes all the necessary elements to implement the prototype.

Discussion of How to Implement this Step

A reasonable approach for this step might be to start by analyzing designs made by other developers to implement similar requirements; this also includes the previous chapters of this book. A diagram following the ideas shown in Chapter 1 will be the starting point. After this diagram is created, the parts can be selected and their interconnections defined. The final step will be to create the bill of materials.

Implementation of this Proposed Step

Figure 12.1 shows a first proposal for the hardware modules of the irrigation system prototype. It is based on the elements introduced in previous chapters, as well as the assumption that it will be possible to find an appropriate moisture sensor and a suitable solenoid valve, which converts electrical energy into mechanical energy and, in turn, opens or closes the valve mechanically.

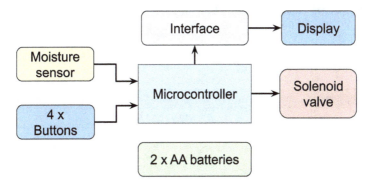

Figure 12.1 First proposal of the hardware modules of the irrigation system.

In the prototype implementation, it is reasonable to use the NUCLEO board for the microcontroller module. The reader already owns this board and knows that it is capable of implementing all the software functionality.

For the display, any of the options introduced in Chapter 6 can be used. For the sake of simplicity, and considering the hardware costs, the character-based LCD display is selected using 4-bit mode.

The buttons will be implemented using a breadboard and tactile switches, as in Chapter 1. Therefore, all that is needed is to define how to implement the moisture sensor, the solenoid valve, and the battery power supply.

In Table 12.10, three moisture sensor modules are shown. After this comparison, it seems reasonable to use the HL-69 in this first prototype due to its price. It also seems very difficult to accomplish Requirement 5.1, related to having an accuracy of better than 5%, as accuracy is not specified for any of the sensors.

Table 12.10 Comparison of moisture sensors.

Sensor name	Technology	Accuracy	Interface	Unit price [USD]
HL-69	Resistive	Not specified	VCC, GND, Digital Output, Analog Output	2
SEN-13322	Resistive	Not specified	VCC, GND, Analog Output	5
Moisture v1.2	Capacitive	Not specified	VCC, GND, Analog Output	2

In Table 12.11, three solenoid valves are shown. After this comparison, it seems reasonable to use an FPD-270A in the first prototype. Given that the solenoid valve must be powered using 12 V, a relay module will need to be used to control its activation. In order to keep this first design simple, a 12 V power supply can be included in the system. Consequently, in this prototype, the NUCLEO board can be supplied using the USB connection, as it has throughout this book.

 NOTE: In a future version of the system, it might be considered to use a switching step-up power supply connected to two AA batteries to provide 12 V for the solenoid and 5 V for the NUCLEO board.

Table 12.11 Comparison of solenoid valves.

Solenoid name	Water-in connector	Activation method	Unit price [USD]
FPD-270A	½-inch	12 V / 0.25 A	9
USS-NSV00003	½-inch	12 V / 1 A	35
VA-8H	½-inch	12 V / 0.5 A	45

The resulting final version of the hardware modules of the irrigation system is shown in Figure 12.2.

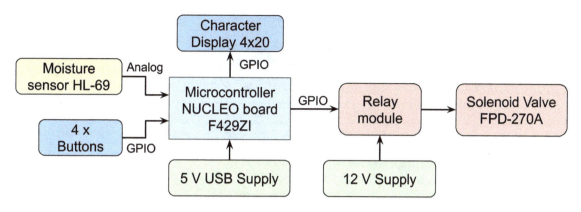

Figure 12.2 Final version of the hardware modules of the irrigation system.

 NOTE: In the hardware design shown in Figure 12.2, an MB102 module is not used because the 300 mA maximum current consumption from the 5 V USB supply discussed in Chapter 4 is not reached.

The proposed connection diagram of all the hardware elements is shown in Figure 12.3. From Table 12.12 to Table 12.17, the corresponding connections are summarized. For the pin assignments, the diagram available in [1] has been used, while the connections used in previous chapters were kept whenever possible.

Table 12.12 Summary of the connections between the NUCLEO board and the character-based LCD display.

NUCLEO board	Character LCD display
D4	D4
D5	D5
D6	D6
D7	D7
D8	RS
D9	E

Table 12.13 Summary of other connections that should be made to the character-based LCD display.

Character LCD display	Voltage/Element
VSS	GND
VDD	5 V
VO	10 kΩ potentiometer
R/W	GND
A	1 kΩ resistor to 5 V
K	GND

Table 12.14 Summary of the connections between the NUCLEO board and the buttons.

NUCLEO board	Button
PG_1	"Mode"
PF_9	"How Often"
PF_7	"How Long"
PF_8	"Moisture"

Table 12.15 Summary of connections that should be made to the HL-69 moisture sensor.

HL-69 moisture sensor	Voltage/Element
GND	GND
VCC	3.3 V
DO	Unconnected
AO	A3 pin - NUCLEO board

Table 12.16 Summary of connections that should be made to the relay module.

Relay module	Voltage/Element
VCC	5 V
GND	GND
IN1	PF_2
NO1	FPD-270A (Terminal 1)
COM1	12 V
NC1	Unconnected
IN2	Unconnected
NO2	Unconnected
COM2	Unconnected
NC2	Unconnected

Table 12.17 Summary of connections that should be made to the FPD-270A.

FPD-270A	Voltage/Element
Terminal 1	Relay module (NO1)
Terminal 2	GND12

 NOTE: The GND terminal of the 12 V power supply (named *GND12*) was intentionally kept isolated from the GND of the 5 V USB power supply. This is done to prevent any potential damage to the microcontroller caused by the 12 V voltage, and also to diminish the electrical noise interference over the microcontroller that could be generated when the load is activated, as was explained in Chapter 7.

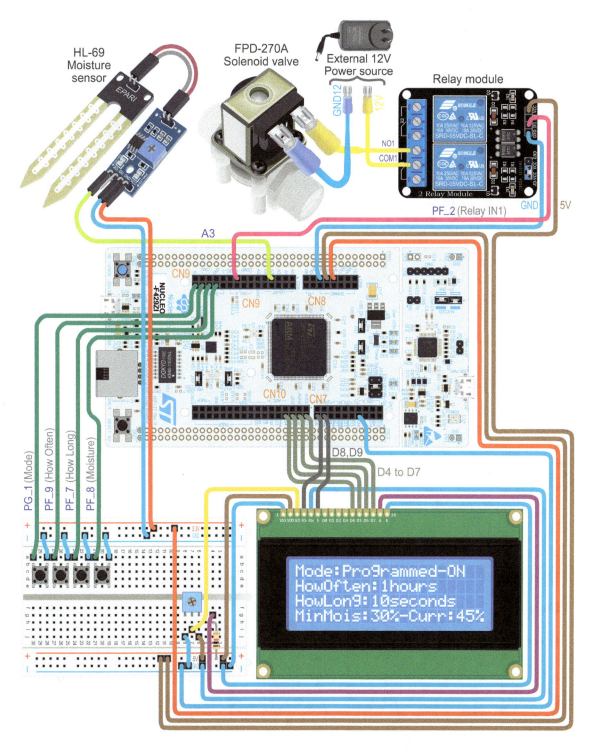

Figure 12.3 Connection diagram of all the hardware elements of the irrigation system.

NOTE: The connections used in previous chapters have been kept whenever possible. In this way, the setup shown in Figure 12.3 can be promptly implemented from the setup used in previous chapters.

TIP: In order to be able to use the program codes of Chapters 6 to 11 again without delay, the elements connected in those chapters can be left connected to the NUCLEO board and to the breadboard (they will not cause any interference in this chapter). In that case, disconnect the wire that connects the 3.3 V output of the NUCLEO board with the breadboard, and use the MB102 module to supply 3.3 V to the system.

Finally, in Table 12.18, the bill of materials is shown. It can be seen that the estimated cost is below 60 USD, and therefore requirement 8.1, which was established in Table 12.6, is fulfilled. Note that if this prototype were to be produced in quantity, a redesign would have to be done. This would lower some costs (e.g., a bespoke design of the microcontroller board will save cost), while it would increase other costs (e.g., container, printed circuit board, time required).

Table 12.18 Bill of materials.

Item	Quantity	Price [USD]
NUCLEO Board F429ZI	1	25
Moisture sensor HL-69	1	2
FPD-270A solenoid valve	1	9
Character display 4 × 20	1	15
Relay module	1	5
Tactile switches	4	0.1
	Total:	56.4

Proposed Exercise

1. Design the hardware of the project that was selected in the "Proposed Exercise" of Example 12.1. Create a diagram of the connections and tables indicating all the details. A bill of materials will also be very useful.

Answer to the Exercise

1. It is strongly recommended to start by reusing as much as possible from the previous chapters of this book. A search of the internet may help to find appropriate components and circuits for the remaining parts of the project.

Example 12.4: Design the Software

Objective

Design software that fulfills the functionality described in the requirements and the use cases.

Summary of the Expected Outcome

The results of this step are expected to include:

- a diagram of the software modules indicating all their interconnections,
- a table indicating the variables and objects of each of the software modules,
- a table indicating the functions of each of the software modules that will be used, and
- a diagram of the finite-state machine (FSM) that will be used to implement the functionality.

Discussion of How to Implement this Step

Given the set of requirements, the software design is not necessarily unique. The design will depend on the developer's experience and preferences. A reasonable approach to this step might be to start by analyzing designs made by other developers to implement similar requirements. This also includes the previous chapters of this book. A diagram using the ideas shown in Chapter 5 can be the starting point. After this, a set of tables showing the variables, objects, and functions of each of the software modules can be prepared. Finally, a diagram of the FSM that will be used to implement the functionality can be drawn, as well as a sketch of the proposed layout for the display.

Implementation of this Proposed Step

Since the functionality of the system does not require any high-speed reactions, a very simple approach such as the one shown in Figure 12.4 can be followed. It can be seen that there is an initialization of all the modules and then an update every 100 milliseconds. The reader might notice that it is very similar to the approach followed in Chapter 5 of this book. However, a non-blocking delay will be used to obtain more accurate timing behavior.

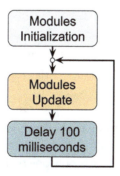

Figure 12.4 Software design of the irrigation system program.

The next step will be to determine the software modules. Figure 12.5 shows a proposal based on software modules introduced in previous chapters (display, relay, etc.), as well as the assumption that it will be possible to implement a *Moisture sensor* module. An *Irrigation timer* module has been included to account for the *waiting time* between irrigations, and to account for the *irrigation time* during the irrigation. Finally, an *Irrigation control* module has been included to implement an FSM to control the irrigation.

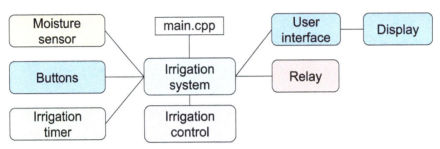

Figure 12.5 Software modules of the irrigation system program.

The proposed organization of folders and files to implement the software is shown in Figure 12.6. It can be appreciated that it is very similar to the organization introduced in Chapter 5.

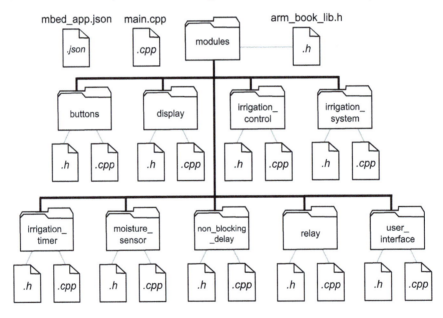

Figure 12.6 Diagram of the .cpp and .h files of the irrigation system software.

In Table 12.19, there is a brief description of each of the modules shown in Figure 12.5. Note that the proposed implementation is very simple, with the aim of keeping the attention on the proposed steps to implement a project. For this reason, there is only one driver that is used to manage the display, which uses the same files introduced in Chapter 6 and will be used without any modification.

Table 12.19 Functionalities and roles of the home irrigation system modules.

Module	Description of its functionality	Role
irrigation_system	Calls initialization and update functions of other modules	System
moisture_sensor	Reads the HL-69 moisture sensor and processes the readings	Subsystem
buttons	Detects buttons pressed and accounts for the configurations	Subsystem
irrigation_timer	Accounts for waiting and irrigation time in programmed mode	Subsystem
irrigation_control	Controls irrigation based on the mode and the timer	Subsystem
relay	Controls relay activation	Subsystem
user_interface	Sends information to be printed to the display driver	Subsystem
display	Receives commands from the user_interface module	Driver

NOTE: In the proposed implementation, the *buttons* module detects the buttons that are pressed by the user. It also processes the information to determine the current value of the configurations that were detailed in Table 12.6: "How often", "How long", and "Minimum moisture level". In addition, it detects when the Mode button is pressed and informs the *irrigation_control* module, which determines the current operation mode.

The proposed next step is to define the private variables and objects of each of the subsystem modules. These are shown in Table 12.20 to Table 12.25.

Table 12.20 Private objects and variables of the moisture_sensor module.

Name of the element	Type	Description of its functionality
hl69	AnalogIn object	Is used to read the A3 analog input of the NUCLEO board where the HL-69 is connected.
hl69AveragedValue	Float variable	Is used to process the reading to avoid noise problems. It is the average of the last ten readings.
hl69ReadingsArray	Float variable	Is used to store the last ten readings of the HL-69 moisture sensor.

Table 12.21 Private objects and variables of the buttons module.

Name of the element	Type	Description of its functionality
changeModeButton	DigitalIn object	Is used to read the PG_1 digital input of the NUCLEO board, which indicates when the current mode has to be changed.
howOftenButton	DigitalIn object	Is used to read the PF_9 digital input of the NUCLEO board, by means of which the "how often" configuration is changed.
howLongButton	DigitalIn object	Is used to read the PF_7 digital input of the NUCLEO board, by means of which the "how long" configuration is changed.
moistureButton	DigitalIn object	Is used to read the PF_8 digital input of the NUCLEO board, by means of which the "minimum moisture level" is changed.
buttonsStatus	Typedef	Is used to store the configuration status. Its members are changeMode, howOften, howLong, and moisture.

Table 12.22 Private objects and variables of the irrigation_timer module.

Name of the element	Type	Description of its functionality
irrigationTimer	Typedef	Used to track the status of the timers. Its members are *waitedTime* and *irrigatedTime*, both integer variables.

Table 12.23 Private objects and variables of the irrigation_control module.

Name of the element	Type	Description of its functionality
irrigationControlStatus	Typedef	Used to inform the state of the FSM that is implemented in this module and also used to indicate when to reset the timers of the irrigation_timer module. Its members are: • *irrigationState*: Enum type defined, with valid states: INITIAL_MODE_ASSESSMENT, CONTINUOUS_MODE_IRRIGATING, PROGRAMMED_MODE_WAITING_TO_IRRIGATE, PROGRAMMED_MODE_IRRIGATION_SKIPPED, and PROGRAMMED_MODE_IRRIGATING. • *waitedTimeMustBeReset*: a Boolean variable. • *irrigatedTimeMustBeReset*: a Boolean variable.

Table 12.24 Private objects and variables of the user_interface module.

Name of the element	Type	Description of its functionality
–	–	This module has no private objects or variables.

Table 12.25 Private objects and variables of the relay module.

Name of the element	Type	Description of its functionality
relayControlPin	DigitalInOut object	Used to write the PF_2 pin of the NUCLEO board. When it is 0, the relay is activated.

From Table 12.26 to Table 12.32, the proposed public functions for each of the modules are detailed.

Table 12.26 Public functions of the irrigation_system module.

Name of the function	Description of its functionality	File that uses it
irrigationSystemInit()	Initializes the subsystems of the irrigation system and the non-blocking delay.	main.cpp
irrigationSystemUpdate()	Calls the functions that update the modules when the corresponding time of non-blocking delay has elapsed.	main.cpp

Table 12.27 Public functions of the moisture_sensor module.

Name of the function	Description of its functionality	Modules that use it
moistureSensorInit()	Has no functionality.	–
moistureSensorUpdate()	Updates the value of *hl69ProcessedValue*.	irrigation_system
moistureSensorRead()	Returns *hl69ProcessedValue*.	irrigation_control user_interface

Table 12.28 Public functions of the buttons module.

Name of the function	Description of its functionality	Modules that use it
buttonsInit()	Configures all buttons in pull-up mode and sets initial configuration of the system after power on.	irrigation_system
buttonsUpdate()	Updates the values of *buttonsStatus*.	irrigation_system
buttonsRead()	Returns the values of *buttonsStatus*.	irrigation_control user_interface

Table 12.29 Public functions of the irrigation_timer module.

Name of the function	Description of its functionality	Modules that use it
irrigationTimerInit()	Sets initial values of *irrigationTimer*.	irrigation_system
irrigationTimerUpdate()	Updates the values of *irrigationTimer*.	irrigation_system
irrigationTimerRead()	Returns the values of *irrigationTimer*.	irrigation_control

Table 12.30 Public functions of the irrigation_control module.

Name of the function	Description of its functionality	Modules that use it
irrigationControlInit()	*IrrigationState* is set to "INITIAL_MODE_ASSESSMENT"; *waitedTimeMustBeReset* and *waitedTimeMustBeReset* are set to true.	irrigation_system
irrigationControlUpdate()	Updates the FSM of the *irrigation_control* module.	irrigation_system
irrigationControlRead()	Returns the values of *irrigationControlStatus*.	user_interface irrigation_timer relay

Table 12.31 Public functions of the display module.

Name of the function	Description of its functionality	Modules that use it
userInterfaceInit()	Calls *displayInit()* and prints the text that does not change over time on the display.	irrigation_system
userInterfaceUpdate()	Updates the current values of mode and configurations in the display by means of the display driver.	irrigation_system
userInterfaceRead()	Has no functionality.	-

Table 12.32 Public functions of the relay module.

Name of the function	Description of its functionality	Modules that use it
relayInit()	Initializes the value of *relayControlPin*.	irrigation_system
relayUpdate()	Updates the value of *relayControlPin*.	irrigation_system
relayRead()	Has no functionality.	-

In Figure 12.7, the proposed FSM is shown. After the start, the first state is INITIAL_MODE_ ASSESSMENT. In this mode, the state of the Mode button is read (it is indicated as the *changeMode* variable in Figure 12.7). If it is pressed (*changeMode* is true), *irrigationControlStatus.irrigationState* (introduced in Table 12.23) is set to CONTINUOUS_MODE_IRRIGATING. If the Mode button is not being pressed (*changeMode* is false), then *irrigationControlStatus.irrigationState* is set to PROGRAMMED_MODE_WAITING_TO_IRRIGATE, and *irrigationControlStatus.waitedTimeMustBeReset* (Table 12.23) is set to true.

In the CONTINUOUS_MODE_IRRIGATING state, the Mode button is checked. If it is not pressed (*changeMode* is false), then *irrigationControlStatus.irrigationState* is not modified, and the FSM remains in the CONTINUOUS_MODE_IRRIGATING state. If the Mode button is pressed (*changeMode* is true), *irrigationControlStatus.irrigationState* is set to PROGRAMMED_MODE_WAITING_TO_IRRIGATE, and *irrigationControlStatus.waitedTimeMustBeReset* is set to true.

> **NOTE:** The relay is controlled by the *relay* module based on the return value of *irrigationControlRead()*. If the read state is CONTINUOUS_MODE_IRRIGATING or PROGRAMMED_MODE_IRRIGATING, the relay will be activated, and it will be deactivated if the read state is INITIAL_MODE_ASSESSMENT, PROGRAMMED_ MODE_WAITING_TO_IRRIGATE, or PROGRAMMED_MODE_IRRIGATION_ SKIPPED.

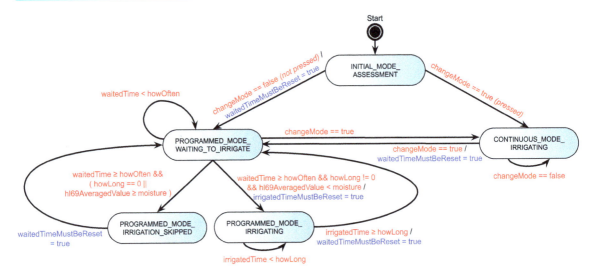

Figure 12.7 Diagram of the proposed FSM.

In the state PROGRAMMED_MODE_WAITING_TO_IRRIGATE, the first step is to set *irrigationControlStatus.waitedTimeMustBeReset* to false, because once in this state *irrigationTimer.waitedTime* (introduced in Table 12.22) has already been reset by the *irrigation_timer* module (see the Note below). Next, it is assessed whether the Mode button is pressed.

If it is (*changeMode* is true), *irrigationControlStatus.irrigationState* is set to CONTINUOUS_MODE_IRRIGATING. If the Mode button is not pressed, it is checked if *irrigationTimer.waitedTime* is smaller than *howOften*. If so, the FSM remains in PROGRAMMED_MODE_WAITING_TO_IRRIGATE. If *irrigationTimer.waitedTime* is equal to or greater than *howOften*, then the other conditions are checked.

NOTE: In the code to be implemented, if the FSM is in PROGRAMMED_MODE_WAITING _TO_IRRIGATE, the value of *irrigationTimer.waitedTime* will be increased by the *irrigation_timer* module each time *irrigationTimerUpdate()* is executed, and will be reset by the *irrigation_timer* module when it detects, by means of the return value of *irrigationControlRead()*, that *irrigationControlStatus.waitedTimeMustBeReset* is true. If the current state is PROGRAMMED_MODE_IRRIGATING, the *irrigation_timer* module will increase *irrigationTimer.irrigatedTime* (introduced in Table 12.22) each time *irrigationTimerUpdate()* is executed and will reset *irrigationTimer.irrigatedTime* if it detects that *irrigationControlStatus.irrigatedTimeMustBeReset* is true, by means of the return value of *irrigationControlRead()*. In this way, the modularization principle will not be violated, because only the *irrigation_timer* module will modify the irrigation and waiting timers.

If *hl69AveragedValue* is greater than or equal to the minimum moisture level configuration (*moisture*) or *irrigationtimer.howLong* is zero, then *irrigationControlStatus.irrigationState* is set to PROGRAMMED_MODE_IRRIGATION_SKIPPED. If *howLong* is not zero and *hl69AveragedValue* is smaller than the minimum moisture level configuration (*moisture*), then *irrigationControlStatus.irrigationState* is set to PROGRAMMED_MODE_IRRIGATING, and *irrigationControlStatus.irrigatedTimeMustBeReset* is set to true.

The state PROGRAMMED_MODE_IRRIGATION_SKIPPED is only used to show on the display that the irrigation was skipped. This is done by the *user_interface* module, which reads the value of *irrigationControlStatus.irrigationState* using *irrigationControlRead()*. In this state, *irrigationControlStatus.waitedTimeMustBeReset* is set to true, and *irrigationControlStatus.irrigationState* is set to PROGRAMMED_MODE_WAITING_TO_IRRIGATE.

In the state PROGRAMMED_MODE_IRRIGATING, *irrigationControlStatus.irrigatedTimeMustBeReset* is first set to false. Then, it assesses if *irrigationTimer.irrigatedTime* is smaller than *howLong*. After the irrigation is completed, it sets *irrigationControlStatus.waitedTimeMustBeReset* to true and *irrigationControlStatus.IrrigationState* to PROGRAMMED_MODE_WAITING_TO_IRRIGATE.

To conclude this step, in Figures 12.8 to 12.11 some sketches of the proposed layout of the LCD display are shown. On the first line of the display, the current irrigation mode is shown. It is also indicated whether the system is irrigating or not in the case of the Programmed irrigation mode. On the second and third lines of the display, the values of the "How Often" and "How Long" configurations are shown. On the fourth line, the minimum moisture level below which irrigation will be activated in the Programmed irrigation mode is shown on the left, and the current moisture measurement is shown on the right.

Figure 12.8 Layout of the LCD for the Programmed irrigation mode when the system is waiting to irrigate.

Figure 12.9 Layout of the LCD for the Programmed irrigation mode when the system is irrigating.

Figure 12.10 Layout of the LCD for the Programmed irrigation mode when irrigation is skipped.

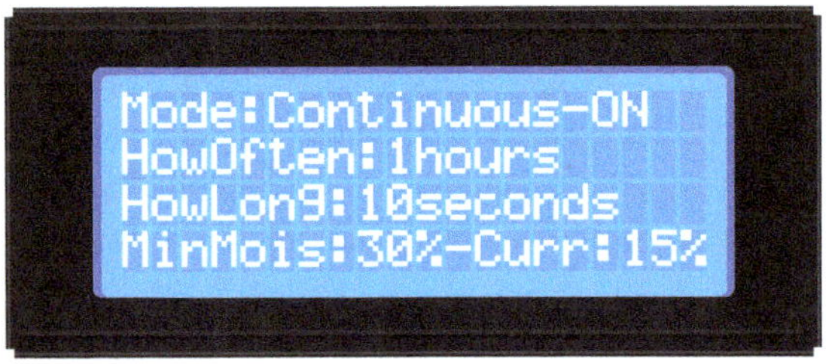

Figure 12.11 Layout of the LCD for the Continuous irrigation mode.

Proposed Exercise

1. Design the software for the project that was selected in the "Proposed Exercise" of Example 12.1. Produce a diagram of the module interconnections and tables indicating all of the details. Include a diagram of the FSM designed to implement the functionality.

Answer to the Exercise

1. It is strongly recommended to start by reusing as much as possible from the previous chapters of this book. Using the internet may help to find more ideas for the remaining parts of the software.

Example 12.5: Implement the User Interface

Objective

Implement the system's user interfaces, as designed in step 4.

Summary of the Expected Outcome

The result of this step is expected to be a set of folders and .h and .cpp files that implement the user interface.

Discussion on how to Implement this Step

In this step, the software should be implemented as a set of .h and .cpp files. The layout of the software should follow the design that was created previously unless there are strong rationales to introduce changes. In the irrigation system, the user interface consists of four buttons and a character-based LCD display. Therefore, only the corresponding functionality is implemented in this step.

Implementation of this Proposed Step

In Code 12.1, *main.cpp* is shown. On line 3, the library *irrigation_system.h* is included. The *main()* function is presented on lines 7 to 14. On line 9, the function *irrigationSystemInit()* is called, and on lines 10 to 13 the *superloop* is implemented. The function *irrigationSystemUpdate()* is called inside the superloop.

```
1   //=====[Libraries]============================================================
2
3   #include "irrigation_system.h"
4
5   //=====[Main function, the program entry point after power on or reset]========
6
7   int main()
8   {
9       irrigationSystemInit();
10      while (true) {
11          irrigationSystemUpdate();
12      }
13  }
14
```

Code 12.1 Implementation of main.cpp.

In Code 12.2, the implementation of *irrigation_system.h* is shown. On line 8, SYSTEM_TIME_INCREMENT_MS is defined, and the public functions *irrigationSystemInit()* and *irrigationSystemUpdate()* are declared.

```
1   //=====[#include guards - begin]==============================================
2
3   #ifndef _IRRIGATION_SYSTEM_H_
4   #define _IRRIGATION_SYSTEM_H_
5
6   //=====[Declaration of public defines]========================================
7
8   #define SYSTEM_TIME_INCREMENT_MS    100
9
10  //=====[Declarations (prototypes) of public functions]========================
11
12  void irrigationSystemInit();
13  void irrigationSystemUpdate();
14
15  //=====[#include guards - end]================================================
16
17  #endif // _IRRIGATION_SYSTEM_H_
```

Code 12.2 Implementation of irrigation_system.h.

In Code 12.3, the implementation of *irrigation_system.cpp* is shown. From lines 3 to 7, libraries
are included. On line 11, the private variable *irrigationSystemDelay* of type *nonBlockingDelay_t* is
declared. This variable will be used to implement the non-blocking delay. On line 15, the function
irrigationSystemInit() is implemented. First, *tickInit()* is called. Then, *buttonsInit()* and *userInterfaceInit()*
are called. Finally, on line 20, the non-blocking delay is initialized to SYSTEM_TIME_INCREMENT_MS.

On line 23, *irrigationSystemUpdate()* is implemented. Line 25 assesses whether *irrigationSystemDelay*
has reached the value set by *nonBlockingDelayInit()*. In that case, *buttonsUpdate()* and
userInterfaceUpdate() are called.

 NOTE: For the sake of brevity, only the file sections that have some content are shown
in the Codes. The full versions of the files are available in [2].

```
1   //=====[Libraries]===========================================================
2
3   #include "irrigation_system.h"
4
5   #include "buttons.h"
6   #include "user_interface.h"
7   #include "non_blocking_delay.h"
8
9   //=====[Declaration and initialization of public global variables]=============
10
11  static nonBlockingDelay_t irrigationSystemDelay;
12
13  //=====[Implementations of public functions]=================================
```

```
14
15   void irrigationSystemInit()
16   {
17       tickInit();
18       buttonsInit();
19       userInterfaceInit();
20       nonBlockingDelayInit( &irrigationSystemDelay, SYSTEM_TIME_INCREMENT_MS );
21   }
22
23   void irrigationSystemUpdate()
24   {
25       if( nonBlockingDelayRead(&irrigationSystemDelay) ) {
26           buttonsUpdate();
27           userInterfaceUpdate();
28       }
29   }
```

Code 12.3 Implementation of irrigation_system.cpp.

In Code 12.4, the implementation of *buttons.h* is shown. From line 8 to line 16, nine definitions are introduced. They are used to implement requirements 3.1.2 to 3.1.7, as shown in Table 12.33. On line 20, the type definition of the struct named *buttonsStatus_t* is shown. This struct has four members: *changeMode*, which is used to keep track of the mode; *howOften*, which is used to keep track of the value of the "How often" configuration; *howLong*, which is used to keep track of the value of the "How long" configuration; and *moisture*, which used to keep track of the value of the "Minimum moisture level" configuration. On lines 29 to 31, the three public functions of this module are declared: *buttonsInit()*, *buttonsUpdate()*, and *buttonsRead()*. The latter is the only one that has a return value, which is of type *buttonsStatus_t*.

In Code 12.5, the implementation of *buttons.cpp* is shown. On lines 10 to 13, the private DigitalIn objects *changeModeButton*, *howOftenButton*, *howLongButton*, and *moistureButton* are declared and assigned to PG_1, PF_9, PF_7, and PF_8, respectively. On line 17, the private variable *buttonsStatus* of the type *buttonsStatus_t* is declared. On line 21, *buttonsInit()* is implemented. First, all of the buttons are configured with pull-up resistors (lines 23 to 26) and then the members of *buttonsStatus* are set to an initial value (lines 28 to 31).

 NOTE: In previous chapters, objects were declared public in order to simplify the software implementation. In this chapter, objects are declared private to improve the software modularity.

```
1    //=====[#include guards - begin]=================================================
2
3    #ifndef _BUTTONS_H_
4    #define _BUTTONS_H_
5
6    //=====[Declaration of public defines]============================================
7
8    #define HOW_OFTEN_INCREMENT    1
9    #define HOW_OFTEN_MIN          1
10   #define HOW_OFTEN_MAX          24
11   #define HOW_LONG_INCREMENT     10
```

```
12    #define HOW_LONG_MIN          0
13    #define HOW_LONG_MAX          90
14    #define MOISTURE_INCREMENT     5
15    #define MOISTURE_MIN           0
16    #define MOISTURE_MAX          95
17
18    //=====[Declaration of public data types]=======================================
19
20    typedef struct buttonsStatus {
21        bool changeMode;
22        int howOften;
23        int howLong;
24        int moisture;
25    } buttonsStatus_t;
26
27    //=====[Declarations (prototypes) of public functions]==========================
28
29    void buttonsInit();
30    void buttonsUpdate();
31    buttonsStatus_t buttonsRead();
32
33    //=====[#include guards - end]==================================================
34
35    #endif // _BUTTONS_H_
```

Code 12.4 Implementation of buttons.h.

Table 12.33 Some of the initial requirements defined for the home irrigation system.

Req. Group	Req. ID	Description
3. Configuration	3.1	The system configuration will be done by means of a set of buttons:
	3.1.1	The "Mode" button will change between "Programmed irrigation" and "Continuous irrigation".
	3.1.2	The "How often" button will increase the time between irrigations in programmed mode by one hour.
	3.1.3	The "How long" button will increase the irrigation time in programmed mode by ten seconds.
	3.1.4	The "Moisture" button will increase the "Minimum moisture level" configuration by 5%.
	3.1.5	The maximum values are: "How often": 24 h; "How long": 90 s; "Moisture": 95%.
	3.1.6	"How long" and "Moisture" will be set to 0 (zero) if they reach the maximum and the button is pressed.
	3.1.7	"How often" will be set to 1 if it reaches its maximum value and the button is pressed.

On line 34, the function *buttonsUpdate()* is implemented. First, *buttonsStatus.changeMode* is assigned the value of *!changeModeButton* because *changeModeButton* is configured with a pull-up resistor. On line 38, *howOftenButton* is assessed. If it is pressed (*howOftenButton* is false), then *buttonsStatus. howOften* is incremented by HOW_OFTEN_INCREMENT in line 39. On line 40, it is assessed if *buttonsStatus.howOften* is greater than or equal to HOW_OFTEN_MAX + HOW_OFTEN_INCREMENT. If so, it is assigned HOW_OFTEN_MIN on line 41.

The code on lines 45 to 50, and the code on lines 52 to 57, are very similar to the code from lines 38 to 43 and, therefore, are not discussed line by line.

Finally, on lines 60 to 63, the function *buttonsRead()* is implemented. This function returns the value of the private variable *buttonsStatus*. In this way, other modules can get the values of the *buttonsStatus* members *changeMode, howOften, howLong,* and *moisture* without violating the principle of modularization.

```cpp
1    //=====[Libraries]=================================================
2
3    #include "mbed.h"
4    #include "arm_book_lib.h"
5
6    #include "buttons.h"
7
8    //=====[Declaration and initialization of private global objects]================
9
10   static DigitalIn changeModeButton(PG_1);
11   static DigitalIn howOftenButton(PF_9);
12   static DigitalIn howLongButton(PF_7);
13   static DigitalIn moistureButton(PF_8);
14
15   //=====[Declaration and initialization of private global variables]============
16
17   static buttonsStatus_t buttonsStatus;
18
19   //=====[Implementations of public functions]================================
20
21   void buttonsInit()
22   {
23       changeModeButton.mode(PullUp);
24       howOftenButton.mode(PullUp);
25       howLongButton.mode(PullUp);
26       moistureButton.mode(PullUp);
27
28       buttonsStatus.changeMode = OFF;
29       buttonsStatus.howOften = HOW_OFTEN_MIN;
30       buttonsStatus.howLong = HOW_LONG_MIN;
31       buttonsStatus.moisture = MOISTURE_MIN;
32   }
33
34   void buttonsUpdate()
35   {
36       buttonsStatus.changeMode = !changeModeButton;
37
38       if ( !howOftenButton ) {
39           buttonsStatus.howOften = buttonsStatus.howOften + HOW_OFTEN_INCREMENT;
40           if ( buttonsStatus.howOften >= HOW_OFTEN_MAX + HOW_OFTEN_INCREMENT) {
41               buttonsStatus.howOften = HOW_OFTEN_MIN;
42           }
43       }
44
45       if ( !howLongButton ) {
46           buttonsStatus.howLong = buttonsStatus.howLong + HOW_LONG_INCREMENT;
47           if ( buttonsStatus.howLong >= HOW_LONG_MAX + HOW_LONG_INCREMENT) {
48               buttonsStatus.howLong = HOW_LONG_MIN;
49           }
50       }
51
52       if ( !moistureButton ) {
53           buttonsStatus.moisture = buttonsStatus.moisture + MOISTURE_INCREMENT;
54           if ( buttonsStatus.moisture >= MOISTURE_MAX + MOISTURE_INCREMENT) {
55               buttonsStatus.moisture = MOISTURE_MIN;
56           }
57       }
58   }
59
60   buttonsStatus_t buttonsRead()
61   {
62       return buttonsStatus;
63   }
```

Code 12.5 Implementation of buttons.cpp.

In Code 12.6, the implementation of *user_interface.h* is shown. The private functions *userInterfaceInit()*, *userInterfaceUpdate()*, and *userInterfaceRead()* are declared on lines 8 to 10.

```
1    //=====[#include guards - begin]========================================
2
3    #ifndef _USER_INTERFACE_H_
4    #define _USER_INTERFACE_H_
5
6    //=====[Declarations (prototypes) of public functions]==================
7
8    void userInterfaceInit();
9    void userInterfaceUpdate();
10   void userInterfaceRead();
11
12   //=====[#include guards - end]==========================================
13
14   #endif // _USER_INTERFACE_H_
```

Code 12.6 Implementation of user_interface.h.

In Code 12.7, the first part of the implementation of *user_interface.cpp* is shown. On lines 3 to 9, the libraries are included. From lines 13 to 27, the function *userInterfaceInit()* is implemented. On line 15, *displayInit()* is used to establish that a character-based display in 4-bit mode is used. On line 17, *displayClear()* is used to clear the display. Lines 19 to 25 are used to write some text on the display following the design introduced in Figure 12.8. This text does not change in this example, even if the buttons are pressed.

```
1    //=====[Libraries]======================================================
2
3    #include "mbed.h"
4    #include "arm_book_lib.h"
5
6    #include "user_interface.h"
7
8    #include "display.h"
9    #include "buttons.h"
10
11   //=====[Implementations of public functions]============================
12
13   void userInterfaceInit()
14   {
15       displayInit( DISPLAY_TYPE_LCD_HD44780,DISPLAY_CONNECTION_GPIO_4BITS );
16
17       displayClear();
18       displayCharPositionWrite( 0, 0 );
19       displayStringWrite( "Mode:Programmed-Wait" );
20       displayCharPositionWrite( 0, 1 );
21       displayStringWrite( "HowOften:   hours" );
22       displayCharPositionWrite( 0, 2 );
23       displayStringWrite( "HowLong:   seconds" );
24       displayCharPositionWrite( 0, 3 );
25       displayStringWrite( "MinMois:  %-Curr:15%" );
26   }
```

Code 12.7 Implementation of user_interface.cpp (Part 1/2).

From lines 1 to 20 of Code 12.8, the function *userInterfaceUpdate()* is implemented. On line 3, an array of char named *number* is declared. On line 5, a variable named *buttonsStatusLocalCopy* of type *buttonsStatus_t* is declared. On line 7, *buttonsStatusLocalCopy* is assigned the return value of *buttonsRead()*. Lines 9 to 11 are used to write the value of *buttonsStatusLocalCopy.howOften* to location (9,1) of the display. The format tag prototype "%02d" is used to indicate that two characters should be used for the value. If the value to be written has less than two characters, the result is padded with leading zeros. A very similar approach is used to write *buttonsStatusLocalCopy.howLong* (lines 13 to 15) and *buttonsStatusLocalCopy.moisture* (lines 17 to 19). Lastly, on line 22, it can be seen that *userInterfaceRead()* has no functionality.

```
1   void userInterfaceUpdate()
2   {
3       char number[3];
4
5       buttonsStatus_t buttonsStatusLocalCopy;
6
7       buttonsStatusLocalCopy = buttonsRead();
8
9       displayCharPositionWrite( 9, 1 );
10      sprintf( number, "%02d", buttonsStatusLocalCopy.howOften );
11      displayStringWrite( number );
12
13      displayCharPositionWrite( 8, 2 );
14      sprintf( number, "%02d", buttonsStatusLocalCopy.howLong );
15      displayStringWrite( number );
16
17      displayCharPositionWrite( 8, 3 );
18      sprintf( number, "%02d", buttonsStatusLocalCopy.moisture );
19      displayStringWrite( number );
20  }
21
22  void userInterfaceRead()
23  {
24  }
```

Code 12.8 Implementation of user_interface.cpp (Part 2/2).

Finally, given that the pins used to connect the display (Table 12.12) are the same pins used in Chapter 6, it is not necessary to modify the pins assignment used in *display.cpp*. If the display were to be connected to other pins, then *displayEN*, *displayRS*, *displayD4*, *displayD5*, *displayD6*, and *displayD7* would have to be assigned with the corresponding pins.

Proposed Exercise

1. Implement the system's user interface for the project that was selected in the "Proposed Exercise" of Example 12.1. Write all the corresponding *.h* and *.cpp* files.

Answer to the Exercise

1. It is strongly recommended to start by reusing as much as possible from the previous chapters of this book, or even from this example.

Example 12.6: Implement the Reading of the Sensors

Objective

Implement the reading of the sensors, as designed in step 4.

Summary of the Expected Outcome

As a result of this step, it is expected to have a set of *.h* and *.cpp* files that implement the user interface and the reading of the sensors.

Discussion on How to Implement this Step

As was previously mentioned, the layout of the software should follow the design that was done in step 4 unless there are strong rationales to introduce changes. The irrigation system has only one sensor, the moisture sensor. Therefore, only the corresponding functionality is implemented in this step.

Implementation of this Proposed Step

For the sake of brevity, in this example only new files or files that have changes are shown. The full set of files for this example are available in [2]. In particular, new lines are introduced in *irrigation_system.cpp*, as can be seen in Code 12.9. The library *moisture_sensor.h* is included on line 8, and the functions *moistureSensorInit()* and *moistureSensorUpdate()* are called on lines 21 and 30, respectively.

There are also a few new lines in *user_interface.cpp*, as can be seen in Code 12.10. On line 10, the library *moisture_sensor.h* is included. On line 26, "MinMois: %-Curr: %" is written. On line 34, the float variable *hl69AveragedValueLocalCopy* is declared, and on line 37 it is assigned the return value of *moistureSensorRead()*. Lines 51 to 53 are included in order to write the reading of the moisture sensor.

```
1   //=====[Libraries]==========================================================
2
3   #include "irrigation_system.h"
4
5   #include "buttons.h"
6   #include "user_interface.h"
7   #include "non_blocking_delay.h"
8   #include "moisture_sensor.h"
9
10  //=====[Declaration and initialization of public global variables]==============
11
12  static nonBlockingDelay_t irrigationSystemDelay;
13
14  //=====[Implementations of public functions]===============================
15
16  void irrigationSystemInit()
17  {
18      tickInit();
19      buttonsInit();
20      userInterfaceInit();
```

```
21        moistureSensorInit();
22        nonBlockingDelayInit( &irrigationSystemDelay, SYSTEM_TIME_INCREMENT_MS );
23    }
24
25    void irrigationSystemUpdate()
26    {
27        if( nonBlockingDelayRead(&irrigationSystemDelay) ) {
28            buttonsUpdate();
29            userInterfaceUpdate();
30            moistureSensorUpdate();
31        }
32    }
```

Code 12.9 New implementation of irrigation_system.cpp.

```
1    //=====[Libraries]=========================================================
2
3    #include "mbed.h"
4    #include "arm_book_lib.h"
5
6    #include "user_interface.h"
7
8    #include "display.h"
9    #include "buttons.h"
10   #include "moisture_sensor.h"
11
12   //=====[Implementations of public functions]==============================
13
14   void userInterfaceInit()
15   {
16       displayInit( DISPLAY_TYPE_LCD_HD44780,DISPLAY_CONNECTION_GPIO_4BITS );
17
18       displayClear();
19       displayCharPositionWrite( 0, 0 );
20       displayStringWrite( "Mode:Programmed-Wait" );
21       displayCharPositionWrite( 0, 1 );
22       displayStringWrite( "HowOften:  hours" );
23       displayCharPositionWrite( 0, 2 );
24       displayStringWrite( "HowLong:  seconds" );
25       displayCharPositionWrite( 0, 3 );
26       displayStringWrite( "MinMois:  %-Curr:  %" );
27   }
28
29   void userInterfaceUpdate()
30   {
31       char number[3];
32
33       buttonsStatus_t buttonsStatusLocalCopy;
34       float hl69AveragedValueLocalCopy;
35
36       buttonsStatusLocalCopy = buttonsRead();
37       hl69AveragedValueLocalCopy = moistureSensorRead();
38
39       displayCharPositionWrite( 9, 1 );
40       sprintf( number, "%02d", buttonsStatusLocalCopy.howOften );
41       displayStringWrite( number );
42
43       displayCharPositionWrite( 8, 2 );
44       sprintf( number, "%02d", buttonsStatusLocalCopy.howLong );
45       displayStringWrite( number );
46
```

```
47        displayCharPositionWrite( 8, 3 );
48        sprintf( number, "%02d", buttonsStatusLocalCopy.moisture );
49        displayStringWrite( number );
50
51        displayCharPositionWrite( 17, 3 );
52        sprintf( number, "%2.0f", 100*hl69AveragedValueLocalCopy );
53        displayStringWrite( number );
54   }
55
56   void userInterfaceRead()
57   {
58   }
```

Code 12.10 New implementation of user_interface.cpp.

In Code 12.11, the implementation of *moisture_sensor.h* is shown. It can be seen that the public functions *moistureSensorInit()*, *moistureSensorUpdate()*, and *moistureSensorRead()* are declared.

```
1    //=====[#include guards - begin]=============================================
2
3    #ifndef _MOISTURE_SENSOR_H_
4    #define _MOISTURE_SENSOR_H_
5
6    //=====[Declarations (prototypes) of public functions]=======================
7
8    void moistureSensorInit();
9    void moistureSensorUpdate();
10   float moistureSensorRead();
11
12   //=====[#include guards - end]===============================================
13
14   #endif // _MOISTURE_SENSOR_H_
```

Code 12.11 Implementation of moisture_sensor.h.

In Code 12.12, the first part of the implementation of *moisture_sensor.cpp* is shown. From lines 3 to 6, the libraries are included. On line 10, NUMBER_OF_AVERAGED_SAMPLES is defined as 10. On line 14, the AnalogIn object *hl69* is declared and assigned to the A3 pin. On line 18, the private float variable *hl69AveragedValue*, which will be used to store the average of the last NUMBER_OF_AVERAGED_ SAMPLES, is declared and initialized. The private array of float variable *hl69ReadingsArray* is declared on line 19. On line 23, the implementation of the function *moistureSensorInit()* is shown. As can be seen, it has no functionality.

In Code 12.13, the implementation of the function *moistureSensorUpdate()* is shown on lines 1 to 18. Note that it is very similar to the way in which the LM35 sensor was read earlier in this book. On line 3, a static integer variable named *hl69SampleIndex* is declared. On line 4, an integer variable *i* is declared. On line 6, the result of 1 minus the reading of the HL-69 sensor is assigned to the corresponding position of *hl69ReadingsArray*. The assignment is done this way because the sensor retrieves 1 when the moisture is 0%. On lines 8 to 12, *hl69AveragedValue* is computed. On lines 14 to 17, the value of *hl69SampleIndex* is updated. Finally, the function *moistureSensorRead()* is implemented on lines 20 to 23.

```
1   //=====[Libraries]==================================================
2
3   #include "mbed.h"
4   #include "arm_book_lib.h"
5
6   #include "moisture_sensor.h"
7
8   //=====[Declaration of private defines]=============================
9
10  #define NUMBER_OF_AVERAGED_SAMPLES     10
11
12  //=====[Declaration and initialization of private global objects]====
13
14  static AnalogIn hl69(A3);
15
16  //=====[Declaration and initialization of private global variables]====
17
18  static float hl69AveragedValue = 0.0;
19  static float hl69ReadingsArray[NUMBER_OF_AVERAGED_SAMPLES];
20
21  //=====[Implementations of public functions]=========================
22
23  void moistureSensorInit()
24  {
25  }
```

Code 12.12 Implementation of moisture_sensor.cpp (Part 1/2).

```
1   void moistureSensorUpdate()
2   {
3       static int hl69SampleIndex = 0;
4       int i;
5
6       hl69ReadingsArray[hl69SampleIndex] = 1 - hl69.read();
7
8       hl69AveragedValue = 0.0;
9       for (i = 0; i < NUMBER_OF_AVERAGED_SAMPLES; i++) {
10          hl69AveragedValue = hl69AveragedValue + hl69ReadingsArray[i];
11      }
12      hl69AveragedValue = hl69AveragedValue / NUMBER_OF_AVERAGED_SAMPLES;
13
14      hl69SampleIndex++;
15      if ( hl69SampleIndex >= NUMBER_OF_AVERAGED_SAMPLES) {
16          hl69SampleIndex = 0;
17      }
18  }
19
20  float moistureSensorRead()
21  {
22      return hl69AveragedValue;
23  }
```

Code 12.13 Implementation of moisture_sensor.cpp (Part 2/2).

 NOTE: The fact that the positions of the *hl69ReadingsArray* are not initialized and *hl69AveragedValue* is calculated using those values does not lead to incorrect behavior, as this situation lasts for only the first second after power on, during which the Programmed mode is still waiting to irrigate.

Proposed Exercise

1. Implement the reading of the sensors for the project that was selected in the "Proposed Exercise" of Example 12.1. Write all the corresponding *.h* and *.cpp* files.

Answer to the Exercise

1. It is strongly recommended to start by reusing as much as possible from the previous chapters of this book, or even from this example.

Example 12.7: Implement the Driving of the Actuators

Objective

Implement the drivers for the actuators, as designed in step 4.

Summary of the Expected Outcome

As a result of this step, it is expected to have a set of *.h* and *.cpp* files that implement the user interface, the reading of the sensors, and the drivers for the actuators.

Discussion of How to Implement this Step

The irrigation system has only one actuator, the solenoid valve, which is activated by means of a relay module. In this example, the activation of this relay module is implemented.

Implementation of this Proposed Step

New lines are introduced in *irrigation_system.cpp*, as can be seen on lines 9, 23, and 33 of Code 12.14. The other files that were introduced in previous examples are not changed.

In Code 12.15, the implementation of *relay.h* is shown. It can be seen that the public functions *relayInit()*, *relayUpdate()*, and *relayRead()* are declared.

```
1    //=====[Libraries]=============================================================
2
3    #include "irrigation_system.h"
4
5    #include "buttons.h"
6    #include "user_interface.h"
7    #include "non_blocking_delay.h"
8    #include "moisture_sensor.h"
9    #include "relay.h"
10
11   //=====[Declaration and initialization of public global variables]==============
12
13   static nonBlockingDelay_t irrigationSystemDelay;
14
```

```
15   //=====[Implementations of public functions]===================================
16
17   void irrigationSystemInit()
18   {
19       tickInit();
20       buttonsInit();
21       userInterfaceInit();
22       moistureSensorInit();
23       relayInit();
24       nonBlockingDelayInit( &irrigationSystemDelay, SYSTEM_TIME_INCREMENT_MS );
25   }
26
27   void irrigationSystemUpdate()
28   {
29       if( nonBlockingDelayRead(&irrigationSystemDelay) ) {
30           buttonsUpdate();
31           userInterfaceUpdate();
32           moistureSensorUpdate();
33           relayUpdate();
34       }
35   }
```

Code 12.14 New implementation of irrigation_system.cpp.

```
1    //=====[#include guards - begin]==========================================
2
3    #ifndef _RELAY_H_
4    #define _RELAY_H_
5
6    //=====[Declarations (prototypes) of public functions]====================
7
8    void relayInit();
9    void relayUpdate();
10   float relayRead();
11
12   //=====[#include guards - end]============================================
13
14   #endif // _RELAY_H_
```

Code 12.15 Implementation of relay.h.

In Code 12.16, the Implementation of *relay.cpp* is shown. On lines 3 to 8, the libraries are included. On line 12, a private DigitalInOut object named *relayControlPin* is declared and assigned PF_2. The function *relayInit()* initializes *relayControlPin* as an input, which turns off the relay.

 NOTE: This same type of initialization and use was implemented in previous chapters to control the buzzer using the relay, given that buzzers are 5 V devices, and it is not advised to turn them on directly using a digitalOut object.

```
1    //=====[Libraries]=========================================================
2
3    #include "mbed.h"
4    #include "arm_book_lib.h"
5
6    #include "relay.h"
7
8    #include "buttons.h"
9
10   //=====[Declaration and initialization of private global objects]===========
11
12   static DigitalInOut relayControlPin(PF_2);
13
14   //=====[Implementations of public functions]================================
15
16   void relayInit()
17   {
18       relayControlPin.mode(OpenDrain);
19       relayControlPin.input();
20   }
21
22   void relayUpdate()
23   {
24       buttonsStatus_t buttonsStatusLocalCopy;
25
26       buttonsStatusLocalCopy = buttonsRead();
27
28     if( buttonsStatusLocalCopy.changeMode ) {
29           relayControlPin.output();
30           relayControlPin = LOW;
31       } else {
32               relayControlPin.input();
33       }
34   }
35
36   void relayRead()
37   {
38   }
```

Code 12.16 Implementation of relay.cpp.

The implementation of the function *relayUpdate()* is shown from lines 22 to 34. On line 24, *buttonsStatusLocalCopy*, a variable of type *buttonsStatus_t*, is declared. On line 26, *buttonsRead()* is used to load the status of the buttons into this variable. On line 28, *buttonsStatusLocalCopy.changeMode* is assessed. If it is true, then the relay is turned on by means of the statements on lines 29 and 30. Otherwise, the relay is turned off on line 32. In this way, the relay should become active each time the Mode button is pressed.

The function *relayRead()*, which has no functionality, is shown on lines 36 to 38.

NOTE: The behavior implemented in this example only has the purpose of testing the activation of the relay. The behavior will be changed in the next example as the remaining modules of the software are incorporated in the system implementation.

Proposed Exercise

1. Implement the drivers of the actuators for the project that was selected in the "Proposed Exercise" of Example 12.1. Write all the corresponding *.h* and *.cpp* files.

Answer to the Exercise

1. It is strongly recommended to start by reusing as much as possible from the previous chapters of this book, or even from this example. Remember that a quick look on the internet may help to find more ideas for the remaining parts of the software.

Example 12.8: Implement the Behavior of the System

Objective

Implement the behavior of the system as established in previous steps (Table 12.6 and Figure 12.7).

Summary of the Expected Outcome

As a result of this step, it is expected to have a set of *.h* and *.cpp* files that implement the complete behavior of the system.

Discussion on How to Implement this Step

In this step, the last two remaining modules, *irrigation_timer* and *irrigation_control*, are included in the system, and all the functionality described in the requirements is implemented.

Implementation of this Proposed Step

New lines are introduced in *irrigation_system.cpp*, as can be seen on lines 10, 11, 25, 26, 37, and 38 of Code 12.17. In this new implementation, *userInterfaceInit()* and *userInterfaceUpdate()* are called after all the other initialization and update function calls to properly implement the logic introduced in Example 12.4.

```
1   //=====[Libraries]=============================================================
2
3   #include "irrigation_system.h"
4
5   #include "buttons.h"
6   #include "user_interface.h"
7   #include "non_blocking_delay.h"
8   #include "moisture_sensor.h"
9   #include "relay.h"
10  #include "irrigation_control.h"
11  #include "irrigation_timer.h"
12
13  //=====[Declaration of private defines]========================================
14
```

```
15    static nonBlockingDelay_t irrigationSystemDelay;
16
17    //=====[Implementations of public functions]====================================
18
19    void irrigationSystemInit()
20    {
21        tickInit();
22        buttonsInit();
23        moistureSensorInit();
24        relayInit();
25        irrigationControlInit();
26        irrigationTimerInit();
27        userInterfaceInit();
28        nonBlockingDelayInit( &irrigationSystemDelay, SYSTEM_TIME_INCREMENT_MS );
29    }
30
31    void irrigationSystemUpdate()
32    {
33        if( nonBlockingDelayRead(&irrigationSystemDelay) ) {
34            buttonsUpdate();
35            moistureSensorUpdate();
36            relayUpdate();
37            irrigationControlUpdate();
38            irrigationTimerUpdate();
39            userInterfaceUpdate();
40        }
41    }
```

Code 12.17 New implementation of irrigation_system.cpp.

In Code 12.18, the implementation of *irrigation_control.h* is shown. On line 8, TO_SECONDS is defined as 10. This #define will be used to convert from a number of counts of 100 milliseconds to seconds. On line 9, TO_HOURS is defined as 36000. This #define will be used to convert from a number of counts of 100 milliseconds to hours.

On line 13, the public data type *irrigationState_t* is declared. As can be seen on lines 14 to 18, it can have five possible values. On line 21, the public data type *irrigationControlStatus_t* is declared. Its first member is *irrigationState*, of type *irrigationState_t*. The other two members are the Boolean variables, *waitedTimeMustBeReset* and *irrigatedTimeMustBeReset*. On lines 29 to 31, the prototypes of the public functions *irrigationControlInit()*, *irrigationControlUpdate()*, and *irrigationControlRead()* are declared.

```
1     //=====[#include guards - begin]===============================================
2
3     #ifndef _IRRIGATION_CONTROL_H_
4     #define _IRRIGATION_CONTROL_H_
5
6     //=====[Declaration of public defines]=========================================
7
8     #define TO_SECONDS    10
9     #define TO_HOURS      36000
10
11    //=====[Declaration of public data types]======================================
12
13    typedef enum {
14        INITIAL_MODE_ASSESSMENT,
```

```
15        CONTINUOUS_MODE_IRRIGATING,
16        PROGRAMMED_MODE_WAITING_TO_IRRIGATE,
17        PROGRAMMED_MODE_IRRIGATION_SKIPPED,
18        PROGRAMMED_MODE_IRRIGATING
19   } irrigationState_t;
20
21   typedef struct irrigationControlStatus {
22        irrigationState_t irrigationState;
23        bool waitedTimeMustBeReset;
24        bool irrigatedTimeMustBeReset;
25   } irrigationControlStatus_t;
26
27   //=====[Declarations (prototypes) of public functions]=========================
28
29   void irrigationControlInit();
30   void irrigationControlUpdate();
31   irrigationControlStatus_t irrigationControlRead();
32
33   //=====[#include guards - end]==================================================
34
35   #endif // _IRRIGATION_CONTROL_H_
```

Code 12.18 Implementation of irrigation_control.h.

In Code 12.19 and Code 12.20, the implementation of *irrigation_control.cpp* is shown. The libraries are included on lines 3 to 10 of Code 12.19. A private global variable named *irrigationControlStatus* is declared on line 14. The function *irrigationControlInit()*, declared on line 18, is used to initialize the members of *irrigationControlStatus*. The function *irrigationControlUpdate()*, shown from lines 25 to 65 of Code 12.19 and 1 to 40 of Code 12.20, implements the FSM discussed in Example 12.4. It is, therefore, not discussed here. Finally, in Code 12.20, the function *irrigationControlRead()* is implemented on lines 42 to 45 of Code 12.20.

 NOTE: FSM transitions corresponding to *waitedTime < howOften, irrigatedTime < howLong, changeMode* == false (see Figure 12.7) are to the same state, so there is no need to include code to implement them. Lines 8 to 10 of Code 12.20 are included only to improve code clarity but can be replaced by *else irrigationControlStatus. irrigationState* = PROGRAMMED_MODE_IRRIGATION_SKIPPED.

```
1    //=====[Libraries]=============================================================
2
3    #include "mbed.h"
4    #include "arm_book_lib.h"
5
6    #include "irrigation_control.h"
7
8    #include "buttons.h"
9    #include "irrigation_timer.h"
10   #include "moisture_sensor.h"
11
12   //=====[Declaration and initialization of private global variables]=============
13
14   static irrigationControlStatus_t irrigationControlStatus;
15
```

```
16    //=====[Implementations of public functions]========================================
17
18    void irrigationControlInit()
19    {
20        irrigationControlStatus.irrigationState = INITIAL_MODE_ASSESSMENT;
21        irrigationControlStatus.waitedTimeMustBeReset = true;
22        irrigationControlStatus.irrigatedTimeMustBeReset = true;
23    }
24
25    void irrigationControlUpdate()
26    {
27        buttonsStatus_t buttonsStatusLocalCopy;
28        irrigationTimer_t irrigationTimerLocalCopy;
29        float hl69AveragedValueLocalCopy;
30
31        buttonsStatusLocalCopy = buttonsRead();
32        irrigationTimerLocalCopy = irrigationTimerRead();
33        hl69AveragedValueLocalCopy = moistureSensorRead();
34
35        switch( irrigationControlStatus.irrigationState ) {
36
37            case INITIAL_MODE_ASSESSMENT:
38
39                if( buttonsStatusLocalCopy.changeMode ) {
40                    irrigationControlStatus.irrigationState = CONTINUOUS_MODE_IRRIGATING;
41                } else {
42                    irrigationControlStatus.irrigationState =
43                                            PROGRAMMED_MODE_WAITING_TO_IRRIGATE;
44                    irrigationControlStatus.waitedTimeMustBeReset = true;
45                }
46                break;
47
48            case CONTINUOUS_MODE_IRRIGATING:
49
50                if( buttonsStatusLocalCopy.changeMode ) {
51                    irrigationControlStatus.irrigationState =
52                                            PROGRAMMED_MODE_WAITING_TO_IRRIGATE;
53                    irrigationControlStatus.waitedTimeMustBeReset = true;
54                }
55                break;
56
57            case PROGRAMMED_MODE_WAITING_TO_IRRIGATE:
58
59                irrigationControlStatus.waitedTimeMustBeReset = false;
60                if( buttonsStatusLocalCopy.changeMode ) {
61                    irrigationControlStatus.irrigationState =
62                                            CONTINUOUS_MODE_IRRIGATING;
63                }
64                else if( irrigationTimerLocalCopy.waitedTime >= (
65                        buttonsStatusLocalCopy.howOften * TO_HOURS) ) {
```

Code 12.19 Implementation of irrigation_control.cpp (Part 1/2).

```
 1                        if( ( buttonsStatusLocalCopy.howLong != 0 ) &&
 2                            ( (int) (100*hl69AveragedValueLocalCopy) <
 3                                buttonsStatusLocalCopy.moisture ) ) {
 4                        irrigationControlStatus.irrigationState =
 5                                            PROGRAMMED_MODE_IRRIGATING;
 6                        irrigationControlStatus.irrigatedTimeMustBeReset = true;
 7                        }
 8                        else if ( ( buttonsStatusLocalCopy.howLong == 0 ) ||
 9                            ( (int) (100*hl69AveragedValueLocalCopy) >=
10                                buttonsStatusLocalCopy.moisture ) ) {
11                        irrigationControlStatus.irrigationState =
12                                        PROGRAMMED_MODE_IRRIGATION_SKIPPED;
13                        }
14                    }
15
16            case PROGRAMMED_MODE_IRRIGATION_SKIPPED:
17
18                irrigationControlStatus.waitedTimeMustBeReset = true;
19                irrigationControlStatus.irrigationState =
20                                    PROGRAMMED_MODE_WAITING_TO_IRRIGATE;
21
22                break;
23
24            case PROGRAMMED_MODE_IRRIGATING:
25
26                irrigationControlStatus.waitedTimeMustBeReset = false;
27
28                if( irrigationTimerLocalCopy.irrigatedTime >= (
29                    buttonsStatusLocalCopy.howLong * TO_SECONDS) ) {
30                    irrigationControlStatus.irrigationState =
31                                    PROGRAMMED_MODE_WAITING_TO_IRRIGATE;
32                    irrigationControlStatus.waitedTimeMustBeReset = true;
33                }
34                break;
35
36            default:
37                irrigationControlInit();
38                break;
39        }
40 }
41
42 irrigationControlStatus_t irrigationControlRead()
43 {
44     return irrigationControlStatus;
45 }
```

Code 12.20 Implementation of irrigation_control.cpp (Part 2/2).

In Code 12.21, the implementation of *irrigation_timer.h* is shown. On line 8, the defined type *irrigationTimer_t* is declared. It has two members, *waitedTime* and *irrigatedTime*, used to account for the time elapsed while waiting to irrigate and the time elapsed while irrigating. On lines 15 to 17, the public functions are declared.

In Code 12.22, the implementation of *irrigation_timer.cpp* is shown. Libraries are included on lines 3 to 8. On line 12, the defined type variable *irrigationTimer* is declared. On lines 16 to 20, *irrigationTimerInit()* is implemented. It can be seen that *irrigationTimer.waitedTime* and *irrigationTimer.irrigatedTime* are both set to 0. On lines 22 to 45, *irrigationTimerUpdate()* is implemented. The variable *irrigationControlStatusLocalCopy* is declared on line 24, and it is assigned the return value of *irrigationControlRead()* on line 26. Line 28 assesses whether *irrigationTimer.waitedTime* must be reset by evaluating *irrigationControlStatusLocalCopy.waitedTimeMustBeReset*. Line 32 assesses whether *irrigationTimer.irrigatedTime* must be reset.

Line 36 assesses whether *irrigationTimer.waitedTime* must be incremented, which is true if *irrigationControlStatusLocalCopy.irrigationState* is equal to PROGRAMMED_MODE_WAITING_TO_ IRRIGATE. Line 41 assesses whether *irrigationTimer.irrigatedTime* must be incremented, which is true if *irrigationControlStatusLocalCopy.irrigationState* is equal to PROGRAMMED_MODE_IRRIGATING. Finally, on lines 47 to 50, *irrigationTimerRead()* is implemented.

```c
1    //=====[#include guards - begin]===================================
2
3    #ifndef _IRRIGATION_TIMER_H_
4    #define _IRRIGATION_TIMER_H_
5
6    //=====[Declaration of public data types]==========================
7
8    typedef struct irrigationTimer {
9        int waitedTime;
10       int irrigatedTime;
11   } irrigationTimer_t;
12
13   //=====[Declarations (prototypes) of public functions]=============
14
15   void irrigationTimerInit();
16   void irrigationTimerUpdate();
17   irrigationTimer_t irrigationTimerRead();
18
19   //=====[#include guards - end]=====================================
20
21   #endif // _IRRIGATION_TIMER_H_
```

Code 12.21 Implementation of irrigation_timer.h.

```c
1    //=====[Libraries]=================================================
2
3    #include "mbed.h"
4    #include "arm_book_lib.h"
5
6    #include "irrigation_timer.h"
7
8    #include "buttons.h"
9
10   //=====[Declaration and initialization of private global variables]=============
11
12   static irrigationTimer_t irrigationTimer;
13
14   //=====[Implementations of public functions]=======================
15
16   void irrigationTimerInit()
17   {
18       irrigationTimer.waitedTime = 0;
19       irrigationTimer.irrigatedTime = 0;
20   }
21
22   void irrigationTimerUpdate()
23   {
24       irrigationControlStatus_t irrigationControlStatusLocalCopy;
```

```
25
26          irrigationControlStatusLocalCopy = irrigationControlRead();
27
28          if ( irrigationControlStatusLocalCopy.waitedTimeMustBeReset ) {
29              irrigationTimer.waitedTime = 0;
30          }
31
32          if ( irrigationControlStatusLocalCopy.irrigatedTimeMustBeReset ) {
33              irrigationTimer.irrigatedTime = 0;
34          }
35
36          if ( irrigationControlStatusLocalCopy.irrigationState ==
37              PROGRAMMED_MODE_WAITING_TO_IRRIGATE ) {
38              irrigationTimer.waitedTime++;
39          }
40
41          if ( irrigationControlStatusLocalCopy.irrigationState ==
42              PROGRAMMED_MODE_IRRIGATING ) {
43              irrigationTimer.irrigatedTime++;
44          }
45      }
46
47      irrigationTimer_t irrigationTimerRead()
48      {
49          return irrigationTimer;
50      }
```

Code 12.22 Implementation of irrigation_timer.cpp.

In Code 12.23 and Code 12.24, the new implementation of *user_interface.cpp* is shown. In Code 12.23, libraries are included on lines 3 to 11, and line 21 is modified to only write "Mode:". On line 9 of Code 12.24, the display position after "Mode:" is written (i.e., "5,0"). Then, a switch statement is used on *irrigationControlStatusLocalCopy.irrigationState* to write the corresponding text on the display.

```
1   //=====[Libraries]===========================================================
2
3   #include "mbed.h"
4   #include "arm_book_lib.h"
5
6   #include "user_interface.h"
7
8   #include "display.h"
9   #include "buttons.h"
10  #include "moisture_sensor.h"
11  #include "irrigation_control.h"
12
13  //=====[Implementations of public functions]===================================
14
15  void userInterfaceInit()
16  {
17      displayInit( DISPLAY_TYPE_LCD_HD44780,DISPLAY_CONNECTION_GPIO_4BITS );
18
19      displayClear();
20      displayCharPositionWrite( 0, 0 );
21      displayStringWrite( "Mode:" );
22      displayCharPositionWrite( 0, 1 );
23      displayStringWrite( "HowOften:  hours" );
24      displayCharPositionWrite( 0, 2 );
```

```
25      displayStringWrite( "HowLong:    seconds" );
26      displayCharPositionWrite( 0, 3 );
27      displayStringWrite( "MinMois:  %-Curr:  %" );
28  }
29
30  void userInterfaceUpdate()
31  {
32      char number[3];
33
34      buttonsStatus_t buttonsStatusLocalCopy;
35      float hl69AveragedValueLocalCopy;
36      irrigationControlStatus_t irrigationControlStatusLocalCopy;
37
38      buttonsStatusLocalCopy = buttonsRead();
39      hl69AveragedValueLocalCopy = moistureSensorRead();
40      irrigationControlStatusLocalCopy = irrigationControlRead();
41
42      displayCharPositionWrite( 9, 1 );
43      sprintf( number, "%02d", buttonsStatusLocalCopy.howOften );
44      displayStringWrite( number );
45
46      displayCharPositionWrite( 8, 2 );
47      sprintf( number, "%02d", buttonsStatusLocalCopy.howLong );
48      displayStringWrite( number );
49
```

Code 12.23 New implementation of user_interface.cpp (Part 1/2).

```
1       displayCharPositionWrite( 8, 3 );
2       sprintf( number, "%02d", buttonsStatusLocalCopy.moisture );
3       displayStringWrite( number );
4
5       displayCharPositionWrite( 17, 3 );
6       sprintf( number, "%2.0f", 100*hl69AveragedValueLocalCopy );
7       displayStringWrite( number );
8
9       displayCharPositionWrite( 5, 0 );
10
11      switch( irrigationControlStatusLocalCopy.irrigationState ) {
12
13          case INITIAL_MODE_ASSESSMENT:
14              displayStringWrite( "Initializing..." );
15              break;
16
17          case CONTINUOUS_MODE_IRRIGATING:
18              displayStringWrite( "Continuous-ON   " );
19              break;
20
21          case PROGRAMMED_MODE_WAITING_TO_IRRIGATE:
22              displayStringWrite( "Programmed-Wait" );
23              break;
24
25          case PROGRAMMED_MODE_IRRIGATION_SKIPPED:
26              displayStringWrite( "Programmed-Skip" );
27              break;
28
29          case PROGRAMMED_MODE_IRRIGATING:
30              displayStringWrite( "Programmed-ON   " );
31              break;
32
33          default:
34              displayStringWrite( "Non-supported   " );
35              break;
36      }
37
38  void userInterfaceRead()
39  {
40  }
```

Code 12.24 New implementation of user_interface.cpp (Part 2/2).

In Code 12.25, the new implementation of *relay.cpp* is shown. Libraries are included on lines 3 to 8. Note that *buttons.h* is not included anymore. The private DigitalInOut object *relayControlPin* is declared on line 12 and assigned to pin PF_2. The function *relayInit()* is declared on line 16. This function turns off the relay by configuring *relayControlPin* as an input, so no energy is supplied to the relay.

On lines 22 to 56, the implementation of *relayUpdate()* is shown. On line 24, *irrigationControlStatusLocalCopy* is declared and assigned the return value of *irrigationControlRead()* on line 26. On line 28, there is a switch over *irrigationControlStatusLocalCopy.irrigationState*. Depending on the value of *irrigationControlStatusLocalCopy.irrigationState*, the relay is turned on or off. For example, in the irrigation state CONTINUOUS_MODE_IRRIGATING, the relay should be turned on, and, therefore, *relayControlPin* is configured as output and LOW is assigned to the pin (remember that the relay is turned on by assigning 0 V to the pin PF_2).

Finally, the function *relayRead()* is shown on lines 57 to 61.

```
1    //=====[Libraries]=========================================================
2
3    #include "mbed.h"
4    #include "arm_book_lib.h"
5
6    #include "relay.h"
7
8    #include "irrigation_control.h"
9
10   //=====[Declaration and initialization of public global objects]===========
11
12   static DigitalInOut relayControlPin(PF_2);
13
14   //=====[Implementations of public functions]===============================
15
16   void relayInit()
17   {
18       relayControlPin.mode(OpenDrain);
19       relayControlPin.input();
20   }
21
22   void relayUpdate()
23   {
24       irrigationControlStatus_t irrigationControlStatusLocalCopy;
25
26       irrigationControlStatusLocalCopy = irrigationControlRead();
27
28       switch( irrigationControlStatusLocalCopy.irrigationState ) {
29
30           case INITIAL_MODE_ASSESSMENT:
31               relayControlPin.input();
32               break;
33
34           case CONTINUOUS_MODE_IRRIGATING:
35               relayControlPin.output();
36               relayControlPin = LOW;
37               break;
38
39           case PROGRAMMED_MODE_WAITING_TO_IRRIGATE:
40               relayControlPin.input();
```

```
41                    break;
42
43           case PROGRAMMED_MODE_IRRIGATION_SKIPPED:
44                relayControlPin.input();
45                break;
46
47           case PROGRAMMED_MODE_IRRIGATING:
48                relayControlPin.output();
49                relayControlPin = LOW;
50                break;
51
52           default:
53                relayControlPin.input();
54                break;
55        }
56 }
57
58 void relayRead()
59 {
60 }
```

Code 12.25 New implementation of relay.cpp.

Proposed Exercise

1. Implement the behavior for the project that was selected in the "Proposed Exercise" of Example 12.1. Write all the corresponding *.h* and *.cpp* files.

Answer to the Exercise

1. The implementation of the behavior might be a difficult task. For that reason, some tips are presented below.

TIP: It is strongly recommended to start by implementing a reduced set of the system functionality. In this way, the code is easier to revise and test. For example, in Code 12.26, it is shown how a first version of *irrigationControlUpdate()* could be written to include only three of the states.

```
1  void irrigationControlUpdate()
2  {
3      buttonsStatus_t buttonsStatusLocalCopy;
4
5      buttonsStatusLocalCopy = buttonsRead();
6
7      switch( irrigationControlStatus.irrigationState ) {
8
9         case INITIAL_MODE_ASSESSMENT:
10
11             if( buttonsStatusLocalCopy.changeMode ) {
12                 irrigationControlStatus.irrigationState = CONTINUOUS_MODE_IRRIGATING;
13             } else {
14                 irrigationControlStatus.irrigationState =
15                                         PROGRAMMED_MODE_WAITING_TO_IRRIGATE;
16             }
```

```
17                    break;
18
19            case CONTINUOUS_MODE_IRRIGATING:
20
21                if( buttonsStatusLocalCopy.changeMode ) {
22                    irrigationControlStatus.irrigationState =
23                                    PROGRAMMED_MODE_WAITING_TO_IRRIGATE;
24                }
25            break;
26
27            case PROGRAMMED_MODE_WAITING_TO_IRRIGATE:
28                if( buttonsStatusLocalCopy.changeMode ) {
29                    irrigationControlStatus.irrigationState =
30                                    CONTINUOUS_MODE_IRRIGATING;
31                }
32            break;
33
34        default:
35                irrigationControlInit();
36            break;
37        }
38 }
```

Code 12.26 Simplified implementation of irrigation_control.cpp.

 TIP: It is also recommended to consider showing some additional information on the user interface to have a better understanding of what is going on. For example, lines 59 to 65 of Code 12.27 are used to print on the display the values of *waitedTime* and *irrigatedTime*. By means of these lines, as well as the values of TO_SECONDS and TO_HOUR shown in Table 12.34, the behavior of the system can be tested in a shorter amount of time by having more information on hand.

```
1  void userInterfaceUpdate()
2  {
3      char number[3];
4
5      buttonsStatus_t buttonsStatusLocalCopy;
6      float hl69AveragedValueLocalCopy;
7      irrigationControlStatus_t irrigationControlStatusLocalCopy;
8      irrigationTimer_t irrigationTimerLocalCopy;
9
10     buttonsStatusLocalCopy = buttonsRead();
11     hl69AveragedValueLocalCopy = moistureSensorRead();
12     irrigationControlStatusLocalCopy = irrigationControlRead();
13     irrigationTimerLocalCopy = irrigationTimerRead();
14
15     displayCharPositionWrite( 9, 1 );
16     sprintf( number, "%02d", buttonsStatusLocalCopy.howOften );
17     displayStringWrite( number );
18
19     displayCharPositionWrite( 8, 2 );
20     sprintf( number, "%02d", buttonsStatusLocalCopy.howLong );
21     displayStringWrite( number );
22
23     displayCharPositionWrite( 8, 3 );
24     sprintf( number, "%02d", buttonsStatusLocalCopy.moisture );
25     displayStringWrite( number );
```

```
26
27        displayCharPositionWrite( 17, 3 );
28        sprintf( number, "%2.0f", 100*hl69AveragedValueLocalCopy );
29        displayStringWrite( number );
30
31        displayCharPositionWrite( 5, 0 );
32        switch( irrigationControlStatusLocalCopy.irrigationState ) {
33
34            case INITIAL_MODE_ASSESSMENT:
35                displayStringWrite( "Initializing..." );
36                break;
37
38            case CONTINUOUS_MODE_IRRIGATING:
39                displayStringWrite( "Continuous-ON  " );
40                break;
41
42            case PROGRAMMED_MODE_WAITING_TO_IRRIGATE:
43                displayStringWrite( "Programmed-Wait" );
44                break;
45
46            case PROGRAMMED_MODE_IRRIGATION_SKIPPED:
47                displayStringWrite( "Programmed-Skip" );
48                break;
49
50            case PROGRAMMED_MODE_IRRIGATING:
51                displayStringWrite( "Programmed-ON  " );
52                break;
53
54            default:
55                displayStringWrite( "Non-supported  " );
56                break;
57        }
58
59        displayCharPositionWrite( 18, 1 );
60        sprintf( number, "%02d", irrigationTimerLocalCopy.waitedTime );
61        displayStringWrite( number );
62
63        displayCharPositionWrite( 18, 2 );
64        sprintf( number, "%02d", irrigationTimerLocalCopy.irrigatedTime );
65        displayStringWrite( number );
66 }
```

Code 12.27 Alternative version of the implementation of user_interface.cpp, where more information is shown.

Table 12.34 Sections in which lines were modified in irrigation_control.h.

Section	Lines that were added
Declaration of public defines	#define TO_SECONDS 1 #define TO_HOURS 1

 WARNING: The UART connection with the PC over USB can be used to print the values of *waitedTime* and *irrigatedTime* on the serial terminal. In this case, it should be remembered that there is a delay for each character that is sent to the PC (recall the Under the Hood section of Chapter 2), and this may alter the system behavior.

Example 12.9: Check the System Behavior

Objective

Check the behavior of the system against the requirements and use cases defined in step 2.

Summary of the Expected Outcome

The results of this step are expected to be:

- a table listing all the requirements, indicating whether they were accomplished or not, and

- a table listing all the use cases, indicating whether the system behaves as expected or not.

Discussion of How to Implement this Step

In step 2 (Example 12.2), the requirements were established, as well as the use cases. In this step, the accomplishment of each requirement and use case will be analyzed. In the case of non-compliance, it will be explained why it was not possible to accomplish the requirement and what the proposed solution is.

Implementation of this Proposed Step

In Table 12.35, the accomplishment of the requirements is assessed. It can be seen that out of 24 requirements, only 2 were not accomplished (Req. 5.1 and 6.1). In the case of Req. 5.1, the moisture sensor that was used is not, and cannot be, calibrated. Perhaps in a future version of the system the sensor can be changed or calibrated. Regarding Req. 6.1, it was noticed that the available solenoid valves operate with 12 V, and for the sake of simplicity in this version it was decided not to use an extra circuit (e.g., a step-up DC/DC converter) to obtain 12 V out of two AA batteries.

Table 12.35 Accomplishment of the requirements defined for the home irrigation system.

Req. ID	Description	Accomplished?
1.1	The system will have one water-in port based on a ½-inch connector.	✓
1.2	The system will control one irrigation circuit by means of a solenoid valve.	✓
2.1	The system will have a continuous mode in which a button will enable the water flow.	✓
2.2	The system will have a programmed irrigation mode based on a set of configurations:	✓
2.2.1	Irrigation will be enabled only if moisture is below the "Minimum moisture level" value.	✓
2.2.2	Irrigation will be enabled every H hours, with H being the "How often" configuration.	✓
2.2.3	Irrigation will be enabled for S seconds, with S being the "How long" configuration.	✓
2.2.4	Irrigation will be skipped if "How long" is configured to 0 (zero).	✓
3.1	The system configuration will be done by means of a set of buttons:	✓
3.1.1	The "Mode" button will change between "Programmed irrigation" and "Continuous irrigation".	✓
3.1.2	The "How often" button will increase the time between irrigations in programmed mode by one hour.	✓
3.1.3	The "How long" button will increase the irrigation time in programmed mode by ten seconds.	✓

Req. ID	Description	Accomplished?
3.1.4	The "Moisture" button will increase the "Minimum moisture level" configuration by 5%.	✓
3.1.5	The maximum values are: "How often": 24 h; "How long": 90 s; "Moisture": 95%.	✓
3.1.6	"How long" and "Moisture" will be set to 0 (zero) if they reach the maximum and the button is pressed.	✓
3.1.7	"How often" will be set to 1 if it reaches its maximum value and the button is pressed.	✓
4.1	The system will have an LCD display:	✓
4.1.1	The LCD display will show the current operation mode: Continuous or Programmed.	✓
4.1.2	The LCD display will show the value of "How often", "How long", and "Moisture".	✓
5.1	The system will measure soil moisture with an accuracy better than 5%.	✗
6.1	The system will be powered using two AA batteries.	✗
7.1	The system should be finished one week after starting (this includes buying the parts).	✓
8.1	The components for the prototype should cost less than 60 USD.	✓
9.1	The prototype should be accompanied with a list of parts, a connection diagram, the code repository, a table indicating the accomplishment of requirements, and use cases.	✓

 NOTE: Req. 7.1 is considered accomplished based on an estimation of the time that it will take the reader to complete this project, considering the skills acquired through this book and six hours/day of work.

In Table 12.36, the set of use cases that were established in Example 12.2 are shown, as is an assessment of whether they have been accomplished. It can be seen that the three use cases were fully accomplished.

Table 12.36 Accomplishment of the use cases defined for the home irrigation system.

Use case	Title	Accomplished?
#1	The user wants to irrigate plants immediately for a couple of minutes.	✓
#2	The user wants to program irrigation to take place for ten seconds every six hours.	✓
#3	The user wants the plants not to be irrigated.	✓

Considering that 92% of the requirements and 100% of the use cases were accomplished, it can be considered that the project was successfully developed.

Lastly, this helps to introduce two important concepts, which are frequently confused with each other: *verification* and *validation* [3].

 DEFINITION: *Verification* asks the question, "Are we building the product right?" That is, does the software conform to its specifications? (As a house conforms to its blueprints.)

DEFINITION: *Validation* asks the question, "Are we building the right product?" That is, does the software do what the user really requires? (As a house conforms to what the owner wants.)

After these definitions, and given the accomplishment results shown above, it can be stated that:

- It was verified that the system that was developed accomplished almost all of its specifications.

- Given that users were not asked about their needs, at this point validation cannot be assessed.

It can be concluded that it is of capital importance to involve the users at an early stage of the system development process in order to be able to adjust the system specifications to their actual needs. Otherwise, a product can be built that works as expected but is not useful for the users.

Proposed Exercise

1. Analyze the accomplishment of the requirements and use cases of the project that was selected in the "Proposed Exercise" of Example 12.1. Document them by means of tables, as has been shown in this example.

Answer to the Exercise

1. Table 12.35 and Table 12.36 can be used as templates to list all the requirements and use cases and the corresponding assessment of their accomplishment.

Example 12.10: Develop the Documentation of the System

Objective

Provide a set of documents that summarize the final outcome of the project.

Summary of the Expected Outcome

The results of this step are expected to be:

- a set of tables, drawings, and rationales summarizing the results of the project, and

- a list of proposed steps that could be followed in order to continue and improve the project.

Discussion of How to Implement this Step

Throughout the examples, many tables, drawings, and rationales about the project were shown. In this final step, all those documents can be presented as a final summary of the project. Additionally, based on the experience obtained during the project implementation, proposals can be made about how to continue and improve the project.

Implementation of this Proposed Step

In Table 12.37, a set of elements that summarize the most important information about the home irrigation system design and implementation are presented. It can be seen that by analyzing this information, a developer can understand most of the project details. A user manual and complementary documents can be added to this list, depending on the specific characteristics of the project.

Table 12.37 Elements that summarize the most important information about the home irrigation system.

Element	Reference
Rationale explaining why the project was selected	Example 12.1
Requirements of the project	Table 12.6
Use cases of the project	Table 12.7
Diagram of the hardware modules of the system	Figure 12.2
Connection diagram of all the hardware elements	Figure 12.3
Bill of materials	Table 12.18
Diagram of the software design	Figure 12.4, Figure 12.5
Definition of the software modules (public functions, variables, etc.)	Table 12.19 to Table 12.32
Diagram of the proposed finite-state machine	Figure 12.7
Software implementation	[2]
Assessment of the accomplishment of the requirements	Table 12.35
Assessment of the accomplishment of the use cases	Table 12.36
Proposal for next steps	Example 12.10
Final conclusions	Example 12.10

Based on the experience obtained during the project design and implementation, the following next steps can be addressed:

- A step-up module might be included in the design in order to provide the 5 V supply for the NUCLEO board and the 12 V supply for the solenoid using two AA batteries.

- A calibration process can be implemented to determine the correspondence between the output signal of the HL-69 sensor and the moisture level.

Moreover, in order to achieve a commercial version of the design, the following items can be considered:

- The development board might be replaced by a bespoke design on a printed circuit board (PCB), which should reduce the cost and size of the system.

- A case can be designed for the irrigation system in order to make it portable and usable for final users.

- The reliability of the system can be tested in order to determine if more improvements are required.

As a final conclusion for this project, it can be seen that the software design proved to be appropriate for implementing a project with a certain complexity. Therefore, the approach can be reused in future projects, such as the mobile robot that avoids obstacles or the flying drone equipped with a camera, which were mentioned in Example 12.1.

Proposed Exercise

1. Develop a list of the relevant documentation regarding the project which was selected in the "Proposed Exercise" of Example 12.1. Document the project by means of tables, as has been shown in this example. Recommend a set of future steps for the project, and finally develop a brief conclusion.

Answer to the Exercise

1. Table 12.37 can be used as a template to list all of the relevant documentation. The next steps and the final conclusion can be similar to the ones presented in this example.

12.3 Final Words

12.3.1 The Projects to Come

Throughout this book, many concepts have been introduced. At this point, the reader is capable of implementing a broad set of embedded systems. Moreover, the reader now has many keys that will open the doors to "projects to come." Those projects will include some technologies and techniques that were introduced and discussed in this book, and probably some other elements that are beyond the scope of this book. In any case, the reader now has a solid basis into which new knowledge can be incorporated.

For example, the HC-SR04 ultrasonic module shown in Figure 12.12 is very popular. It uses the principle of sonar (sound navigation ranging) to determine the distance to an object in the same way that bats do. It has four pins: VCC, Trig, Echo, and GND. The Trig pin is used to trigger a high-frequency sound. When the signal is reflected, the echo pin changes its state. The time between the transmission and reception of the signal allows us to calculate the distance to an object, which is useful, for example, in parking systems or in autonomous vehicles. Note that the knowledge to implement the appropriate software module to use this sensor was introduced within this book (i.e., look at the Tip on Example 10.4).

Figure 12.12 Image of the HC-SR04 ultrasonic module.

A microphone module, as shown in Figure 12.13, can be easily used by applying the concepts introduced in this book. The module has a digital output pin (DO) and analog output pin (AO). The digital output sends a high signal when the sound intensity reaches a certain threshold, which is adjusted using the potentiometer on the sensor. The analog output can be sampled and stored in an array using an appropriate sampling rate, in order to be reproduced later, for example in a public address system. The procedure is similar to that applied to the temperature sensor.

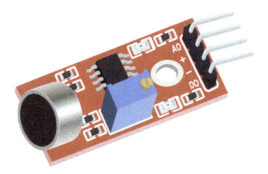

Figure 12.13 Image of a microphone module.

In Figure 12.14, a digital barometric pressure module is shown, used to measure the absolute pressure of the environment. By converting the pressure measures into altitude, the height of a drone can be estimated. The sensor also measures temperature and humidity and has an I2C bus interface, such as the one introduced in Chapter 6.

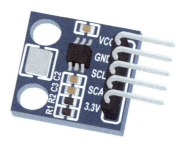

Figure 12.14 Image of a digital barometric pressure module.

There are many other sensor modules available, as well as many actuators that the reader is ready to use. For example, the micro servo motor shown in Figure 12.15 has three pins: GND, VCC, and Signal. The angle of the motor axis angle is controlled in the range 0 to 180° by the duty cycle of the signal delivered at the Signal pin. The reader is encouraged to explore actuators that allow tiny movements, such as stepper motors.

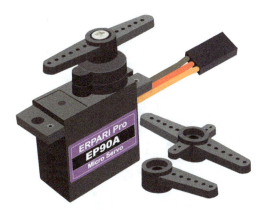

Figure 12.15 Image of a micro servo motor.

GPS (global positioning system) modules, such as the one shown in Figure 12.16, are also very popular. They are commanded using AT commands, in a very similar way to the ESP-01 module introduced in Chapter 11.

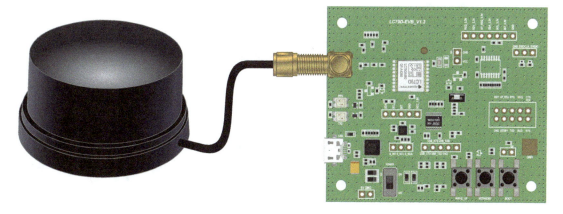

Figure 12.16 Image of a GPS module. Note the GPS antenna on the left.

Finally, in Figure 12.17, an NB-IoT (Narrow Band Internet of Things) cellular module is shown. These modules are also controlled using AT commands and can be used to implement communications based on 4G, 5G, LoRa, or SigFox, for example.

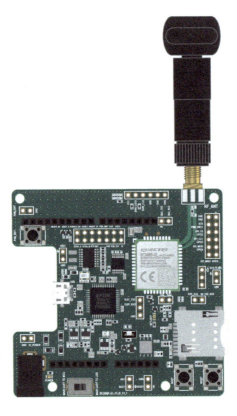

Figure 12.17 Image of an NB-IoT cellular module. Note the SIM card slot on the right.

Given the vast range of modules that are available, the aim of this section is just to give an overview of how most of them, maybe even all of them, can be used by applying the techniques and concepts introduced in this book.

Enjoy the projects to come!

 TIP: Never forget that good engineering is based on following processes, keeping things as simple as possible, dividing problems into small pieces, and solving trade-off situations.

Proposed Exercise

1. How can a micro servo motor be controlled using the techniques introduced in this book?

Answer to the Exercise

1. As explained above, the motor axis angle is controlled by the duty cycle of the signal delivered at the Signal pin. Thus, the PWM technique that was introduced in Chapter 8 can be used.

References

[1] "NUCLEO-F429ZI | Mbed". Accessed July 9, 2021.
https://os.mbed.com/platforms/ST-Nucleo-F429ZI/#zio-and-arduino-compatible-headers

[2] "GitHub - armBookCodeExamples/Directory". Accessed July 9, 2021.
https://github.com/armBookCodeExamples/Directory

[3] Pham, H. (1999). Software Reliability. John Wiley & Sons, Inc. p. 567. ISBN 9813083840.

Glossary of Abbreviations

4G	Fourth Generation
A	Anode
AC	Alternating Current
ACK	Acknowledge
ACSE	Asociación Civil para la Investigación, Promoción y Desarrollo de Sistemas Electrónicos Embebidos, Civil Association for Research, Promotion and Development of Embedded Electronic Systems
ADC	Analog to Digital Converter
ALT	Alternative
AOUT, AO	Analog Output
API	Application Programming Interface
ASCII	American Standard Code For Information Interchange
AT	Attention
BLE	Bluetooth Low Energy
BRK	Break
CADIEEL	Cámara Argentina de Industrias Electrónicas, Electromecánicas y Luminotécnicas, Argentine Chamber of Electronic, Electromechanical and Lighting Industries
CGRAM	Custom Generated Random-Access Memory
CIAA	Computadora Industrial Abierta Argentina, Argentine Open Industrial Computer
CO_2	Carbon Dioxide
COM	Communication

CONICET	Consejo Nacional de Investigaciones Científicas y Técnicas, National Scientific and Technical Research Council of Argentina
CPU	Central Processing Unit
CR	Carriage Return
CS	Chip Select
CSS	Cascading Style Sheets
DAC	Digital to Analog Converter
DB	Data Bus
DC	Direct Current
DDRAM	Display Data Random Access Memory
DL	Display Lines
DO-LED	Digital Output Light Emitting Diode
DOUT, DO	Digital Output
E	Enable
ESP	Espressif Systems
FAT	File Allocation Table
FAT32	File Allocation Table 32
FPU	Floating-Point Unit
FSM	Finite-State Machine
GB	GigaByte
GDRAM	Graphic Display RAM
GLCD	Graphical Liquid Crystal Display
GND	Ground

GPIO	General Purpose Input Output
GPS	Global Positioning System
HAL	Hardware Abstraction Layer
HDMI	High-Definition Multimedia Interface
HMI	Human–Machine Interface
HTML	Hypertext Markup Language
HTTP	Hypertext Transfer Protocol
HV	High Voltage
I/D	Increment/Decrement
I/O or IO	Input/Output
I2C	Inter Integrated Circuit
IC	Integrated Circuit
ICC	Iterative Conversion Controller
IDE	Integrated Development Environment
IEEE	Institute of Electrical and Electronics Engineers
IoT	Internet of Things
IP	Internet Protocol
IR	Infrared
ISA	Instruction Set Architecture
ISR	Interrupt Service Routine
K	Cathode
K&R	Kernighan & Ritchie

kbps	Kilobits per second
LCD	Liquid Crystal Display
LDR	Light-Dependent Resistor
LED	Light-Emitting Diode
LF	Line Feed
Li-Po	Lithium Polymer
LoRa	Long Range
LS	Limit Switch
LSb	Least Significant bit
LV	Low Voltage
MAC	Media Access Control
Mbps	Megabits per second
MCU	Microcontroller
MISO	Manager Input Subordinate Output
MOSI	Manager Output Subordinate Input
MSb	Most Significant bit
NB-IoT	Narrow Band Internet of Things
NC	Normally Closed
NO	Normally Opened
OOP	Object-Oriented Programming
PC	Personal Computer
PCM	Pulse-Code Modulation

PIR	Passive Infrared Sensor
PSB	Parallel/Serial Bus
PWM	Pulse-Width Modulation
RC	Resistor-Capacitor
RGB	Red, Green and Blue
RS	Register Select
RST	Reset
RTC	Real-Time Clock
RTOS	Real-Time Operating System
RW	Read/Write
RxD	Received Data
SAR	Successive Approximation Register
SCL	Serial Clock Line
SCLK	Serial Clock
SD	Secure Digital
SDA	Serial Data Line
SID	Serial Input Data
SMART	Specific, Measurable, Achievable, Relevant, and Time-bound
SMD	Surface-Mount Device
SONAR	Sound Navigation Ranging
SPI	Serial Peripheral Interface
SS	Subordinate Select

SSID	Service Set IDentifier
SSL	Secure Sockets Layer
ST	STMicroelectronics
STAMAC	Station MAC
TCP	Transmission Control Protocol
Trimpot	Trimmer Potentiometer
TxD	Transmitted Data
UART	Universal Asynchronous Receiver Transmitter
UBA	Universidad de Buenos Aires, University of Buenos Aires
UDP	User Datagram Protocol
UNLa	Universidad Nacional de Lanús, National University of Lanus
UNQ	Universidad Nacional de Quilmes, National University of Quilmes
URL	Uniform Resource Locator
USB	Universal Serial Bus
USD	United States Dollar
UTC	Universal Time Coordinated
UTN-FRBB	Universidad Tecnológica Nacional – Facultad Regional Bahía Blanca, National Technological University – Bahía Blanca Regional School
UTN-FRP	Universidad Tecnológica Nacional – Facultad Regional Paraná, National Technological University Paraná Regional School
VCC	Voltage Common Collector

Index

The Arm Education Media Story

Did you know that Arm processor design is at the heart of technology that touches 70% of the world's population - from sensors to smartphones to super computers.

Given the vast reach of Arm's computer chip and software designs, our aim at Arm Education Media is to play a leading role in addressing the electronics and computing skills gap; i.e., the disconnect between what engineering students are taught and the skills they need in today's job market.

Launched in October 2016, Arm Education Media is the culmination of several years of collaboration with thousands of educational institutions, industrial partners, students, recruiters and managers worldwide. We complement other initiatives and programs at Arm, including the Arm University Program, which provides university academics worldwide with free teaching materials and technologies.

Via our subscription-based digital content hub, we offer interactive online courses and textbooks that enable academics and students to keep up with the latest Arm technologies.

We strive to serve academia and the developer community at large with low-cost, engaging educational materials, tools and platforms.

We are Arm Education Media: Unleashing Potential

Arm Education Media Online Courses

Our online courses have been developed to help students learn about state of the art technologies from the Arm partner ecosystem. Each online course contains 10-14 modules, and each module comprises lecture slides with notes, interactive quizzes, hands-on labs and lab solutions.

The courses will give your students an understanding of Arm architecture and the principles of software and hardware system design on Arm-based platforms, skills essential for today's computer engineering workplace.

For more information, visit www.arm.com/education

Available Now:

Professional Certificate in Embedded Systems Essentials with Arm (on the edX platform)

Efficient Embedded Systems Design and Programming

Rapid Embedded Systems Design and Programming

Internet of Things

Graphics and Mobile Gaming

Real-Time Operating Systems Design and Programming

Introduction to System-on-Chip Design

Advanced System-on-Chip Design

Embedded Linux

Mechatronics and Robotics

Arm Education Media Books

The Arm Education books program aims to take learners from foundational knowledge and skills covered by its textbooks to expert-level mastery of Arm-based technologies through its reference books. Textbooks are suitable for classroom adoption in Electrical Engineering, Computer Engineering and related areas. Reference books are suitable for graduate students, researchers, aspiring and practising engineers.

For more information, visit www.arm.com/education

Available now, in print and ePub formats:

Embedded Systems Fundamentals with Arm
Cortex-M based Microcontrollers:
A Practical Approach, FRDM-KL25Z EDITION
by Dr Alexander G. Dean
ISBN 978-1-911531-03-6

Embedded Systems Fundamentals with Arm
Cortex-M based Microcontrollers:
A Practical Approach, NUCLEO-F09IRC EDITION
by Dr Alexander G. Dean
ISBN 978-1-911531-26-5

Digital Signal Processing using Arm Cortex-M based
Microcontrollers: Theory and Practice
by Cem Ünsalan, M. Erkin Yücel and H. Deniz Gürhan
ISBN 978-1911531-16-6

Operating Systems Foundations with Linux
on the Raspberry Pi
by Wim Vanderbauwhede and Jeremy Singer
ISBN 978-1-911531-20-3

Fundamentals of System-on-Chip Design on Arm Cortex-M
Microcontrollers
by René Beuchat, Florian Depraz, Sahand Kashani and
Andrea Guerrieri
ISBN 978-1-911531-33-3

Modern System-on-Chip Design on Arm
by David J. Greaves
ISBN 978-1-911531-36-4

System-on-Chip with Arm Cortex-M Processors
by Joseph Yiu, Distinguished Engineer at Arm
ISBN 978-1-911531-19-7

Arm Helium Technology
M-Profile Vector Extension (MVE) for Arm
Cortex-M Processors
by Jon Marsh
ISBN: 978-1-911531-23-4

www.ingramcontent.com/pod-product-compliance
Lightning Source LLC
LaVergne TN
LVHW082125070326
832902LV00041B/2487